A.J. FOYT

A.J. FOYT

SURVIVOR CHAMPION LEGEND

VOLUME ONE

ART GARNER

Foreword by **Mario Andretti**

OCTANE
PRESS

Octane Press, Edition 1.0, October 2024
Copyright © 2024 by Art Garner

On the cover: A.J. Foyt during a break in practice at the
Indianapolis Motor Speedway in 1967. *IMS Photography Archive*

On the front endpapers: A short-sleeved Foyt after qualifying.
Revs Institute, The Bruce R. Craig Photograph Collection, photograph by Jack Fox

On the back endpapers: The first Indianapolis 500 four-time
winner in Victory Lane. *IMS Photography Archive*

Hardcover ISBN: 978-1-64234-178-2
ePub ISBN: 978-1-64234-180-5

LCCN: 2024938836

Project Edited by Faith Garcia
Layout Designed by Tom Heffron
Cover Designed by Krissy Haag
Copyedited by Faith Garcia and Dana Henricks
Proofread by Jeff Kocan

octanepress.com

Octane Press is based in Austin, Texas

Printed in China

For my wife EJ, who convinced me to write this book, then put up with me while I did.

In memory of my mom and brother, who were always there with support and encouragement.

CONTENTS

"This man is the greatest in the world at what he does. How many people ever get to say that in a lifetime?"

—Jim Murray, *Los Angeles Times*, May 30, 1977

"I love racing. You have to love this business to get into it at all. And once you're in it, you love it so much, you fight like hell to stay in it. I've neglected everything for it, my education, my wife, my kids, my home. That's bad in one way, but it's the reason I'm on top too. It's the only thing I've ever studied, the only thing I've ever really understood."

—Anthony Joseph "A.J." Foyt Jr., 1965

HEART OF GOLD

By Mario Andretti

A.J. and I battled on the track for years. It was no secret that we were rivals. But rivals aren't enemies. Neither of us had to sleep with one eye open. Rivals are just competing for the same thing, and they see each other as the main obstacle to getting what they want. He and I annoyed each other to no end because we were after the same thing. We were both obsessed with winning—and we would both go to the ends of the earth to get it done.

We had a great story together. We both had triumphs. We both had defeat. And we were both competitive to a truly absurd degree. When one of us won, it was at the expense of the other. So, I guess our rivalry was a joint accomplishment.

Anyone you compete with surely must share some similarities with you. You probably have the same passions. You've made sacrifices to try to get ahead. And it can be painful when someone else steals your glory. But ask yourself, are they not just like me? The best people to understand your desires and sacrifices are the others who made the exact same ones.

Today, A.J. and I look back on our careers and realize the reason we tangled in the first place was because we both had the same goal. We were a lot alike. We cared the same. Today we can understand and can empathize with each other. Racing is still the core of who we are and pretty much our entire existence. But now that the competition is done, we no longer have to prove a point.

Life is how you look at it. A.J. made me better. I made him better. And today we're friends. Two guys living life alike.

A.J. is a likeable curmudgeon. He tried to be tolerant when things, including me, got on his last nerve. But when things got double irritating, he could go from being minimally annoyed . . . to irritated . . . to angry . . . to losing it. But that's just the heat of the moment. And quite honestly, I can relate. There are things that drive me up a wall, too. Truth be told, A.J. Foyt is one of the really good guys. He's got a heart of gold. He's the salt of the earth behind the tirades. He's unpretentious. He's the guy you want in your corner. As solid as a rock, straight-forward, loyal, hardworking, decent, honest, truly good person you can count on. Today if I had a run-in, I'd want A.J. with me. A.J. is true-blue.

A.J. fans will love this book. And if anywhere in these pages it says A.J. hates me, I know he doesn't anymore. That was a few decades ago. Today we're BFFs.

Mario and A.J. during a friendly moment in 1972. *Steve H. Shunck Collection*

WHO IS A.J. FOYT?

Tony Stewart tells a story about going to see A.J. Foyt.[1] Stewart is the only driver to win NASCAR and Indy car national championships. He also captured American open wheel racing's Triple Crown, is a three-time NASCAR stock car champion, and is a first ballot Hall of Famer. He grew up in Indiana watching Foyt race and calls A.J. his hero. When Stewart started his own team, he took Foyt's No. 14 as his own.

Out of respect, Stewart often called on Foyt whenever they were in the same area. On this occasion he was accompanied by a young driver, and Tony introduced him to A.J., who was in his mid-eighties and about a hundred pounds over his driving weight.

Stewart and Foyt bantered, joked, and told stories as they often did. Afterward the young driver asked Stewart, "Who is that dude?" Stunned, Stewart started to explain, but was immediately interrupted.

"That dude was a race car driver?"

Not just a race car driver, Stewart said, possibly the greatest race car driver who ever lived.

In a race car Anthony Joseph Foyt Jr. had few peers. A champion's champion, his accomplishments on tracks around the world tell an incredible story and many of his records still stood thirty years after he last turned a wheel. No race is more important than the Indianapolis 500 and he was the first to win it four times, one of only four drivers to have accomplished the feat. He started a record thirty-five consecutive 500s, often while battered, bruised, and burned, and at least once barely able to walk to his car. He holds Indy car records with sixty-seven victories and seven series championships. Add victories in the Daytona 500 for stock cars and the 24 Hours of Le Mans for sports cars, and he is the only man to capture what many consider the Triple Crown of auto racing. He holds the world closed-course speed record of more than 267 miles per hour, a record he set when he was fifty-two.

"A.J. was willing to do anything to learn, to get ahead, to succeed," said Parnelli Jones, a fierce competitor and top driver from the 1960s who was one of the few sometimes mentioned in the same breath with Foyt. "He has such great desire. More determination than anybody that ever went racing. Even me."[2]

Asked once during his career who was the world's best race car driver, Foyt answered, "I think my record speaks for itself."[3]

He was right.

He is also the ultimate survivor, with a driving career spanning parts of five decades, six if you include an exhibition race when, at age five, he beat the track champion. He raced through an era when Dan Gurney, his friend and Le Mans-winning teammate, said, "You had to have a World War II mentality: sooner or later you were gonna get it." Another rival, Bobby Unser, noted "you had a fifty-fifty chance of being killed in a race car."[4]

As a twenty-three-year-old rookie at Indianapolis in 1958 Foyt was the youngest driver to qualify. He saw his mentor killed on the opening lap, teaching him one final lesson: never get close to another driver. When he ran his final 500 at fifty-seven, he became the oldest driver ever to start the race. Since retiring, he's survived heart attacks, open-heart surgery, numerous life-threatening operations, two killer bee attacks, and a near drowning when the caged bulldozer he was operating rolled down the bank of a pond and capsized.

Statistics tell only a small part of A.J. Foyt's story. A true enigma, he could be "charming beyond belief" one moment and in the next turn into the meanest, toughest, most politically incorrect son-of-a-bitch in racing—and proud of it. He likes to position himself as simple and straightforward, a what-you-see-is-what-you-get type of guy. "I ain't nothing special," he often said with a grin and a shrug. "I'm just A.J. Ain't no different than any other man."

In so many ways, nothing is further from the truth.

He is one of the most complex and intricate personalities in the history of auto racing, perhaps in all of sports. Racing from an early age with a chip the size of his beloved Texas on his shoulder, he was courageous beyond compare, yet admitted at times to being "scared shitless." He is equal parts introvert and extrovert, relishing the spotlight but often hating the things that came with it, including signing autographs and talking to reporters. He was incredibly stubborn but changed his mind often. To say he had a Jekyll and Hyde personality seems trite and cliché, but it's hard to come up with a better comparison.

In 1972 the Associated Press published a book called *Sports Immortals*, a collection of profiles on fifty athletes. Most of the stories were about stick and ball greats, including Babe Ruth, Ty Cobb, Jim Thorpe, Jimmy Brown, Johnny Unitas, Joe Namath, Arnold Palmer, Jack Dempsey, Gordie Howe, Willie Mays, and Joe DiMaggio. Foyt, who would race for another twenty years, was the only driver included. Bloys Britt, the dean of auto racing reporters at the time and longtime AP motorsports editor, wrote the profile.

"Hardnose, sometimes violent, often truculent, always intense, sometimes boisterous, many times gentle, impetuous, rough, forceful, vehement, self-made, never vengeful. He would laugh with you one minute, completely ignore you the next. He was deliberately articulate one hour, purposely unresponsive the next. He could be moody, surly, happy, smiling, taut as a banjo string under stress, a model of charm when things were going 'according to Foyt.'"[5]

More often than not he was cordial and friendly. But when he turned, look out. He was demanding of those who called him "boss" and could launch into a degrading tirade if he thought someone had screwed up or given less than 100 percent. Thirty minutes later he was often ready to go have a beer with his target. To those who stood by him he was loyal to a fault, yet unforgiving of those he felt wronged him.

He was devoted to his "Daddy," Anthony Joseph "Tony" Foyt, his constant companion and the "the only man I can trust." Yet they even clashed on occasion. When things were going wrong, Tony warned, working with A.J. was "like dancing with a buzzsaw."[6]

WRITING FOYT

Foyt is a true living legend, and writing a biography on a living legend presents unique opportunities and challenges. Obviously, the story is incomplete. Foyt celebrated his eighty-ninth birthday the year this book went to press. Although his race team is now run by Larry Foyt, his grandson and adopted son, he often goes into the race shop, attends races, and hasn't missed an Indianapolis 500 since 1955. The last chapter has yet to be written.

At the same time, it means the subject is able to answer questions about his past and many of his peers are still around. Some, including his wife, Lucy, four-time Indy winner Al Unser, and NASCAR great Cale Yarborough, have died since granting interviews for this book. He probably wasn't happy about some of the people interviewed, but he never objected. For all the controversy surrounding Foyt's life, however, it's difficult to find anyone willing to say a bad word about a living legend.

Legends, especially those built over nearly ninety years, are often based at least partially on myths and it's true in Foyt's case. Memories fade. Events are enhanced and sometimes mesh together. You don't spend more than sixty years dealing with the news media without learning to spin a story—and Foyt is nothing if not a master storyteller.

"Embellishment is the God-given right of any Texan," one of his friends pointed out.[7]

"Most sports is based on the telling of lies, especially in retrospect," says David Maraniss, the Pulitzer Prize-winning historian and author of sports biographies on Vince Lombardi, Jim Thorpe, and others. "Most recollections, especially of the athletes themselves, turn to mythology because that's not the way it really happened. The other part is in the public imagination. The heroic model is something people need."[8]

Or as golfer Lee Trevino says, "The older I get, the better I was."[9]

Foyt's 1983 biography, *A.J.: My Life as America's Greatest Race Car Driver,* written by William Neely, is a good example of what sometimes happens when a story becomes more important than the facts. Published shortly after his father's death, A.J. says he never reviewed the manuscript. Others say he was embarrassed when it was published.

It "leans so far toward hagiography that it gets rough to swallow," wrote Bones Bourcier in his excellent book, *Foyt, Andretti, Petty: America's Racing Trinity,* which helped debunk some of the Foyt myths. He recalled one reviewer of the autobiography "waiting to get to the part where Foyt actually walked on water." Donald Davidson, longtime historian at the Indianapolis Motor Speedway who knew both men well, says, "There's as much Bill Neely in that book as there is A.J. Foyt."

Still, it is one of the few sources for A.J. Foyt's early years and has been used here, especially when stories are corroborated by others and by Foyt himself. The other early biography of note, *Foyt* by Bill Libby, is much better but still has more errors than it should and was published in 1974, about halfway through Foyt's career.

To help sort fact from myth, I've relied heavily on original reporting from the day. Fortunately, there's a great deal of it. During the peak of Foyt's career many newspapers employed a dedicated motorsports reporter. Hundreds of writers and columnists from across the country attended the Indianapolis 500 every year. Now there are major cities without a printed daily newspaper and only a handful of reporters cover auto racing on a regular basis. It also was an era before cell phones and handheld tape recorders, and reporters jotted down notes longhand. Quotes from different reporters at the same press gathering seldom matched, so I've done my best to use those most reflective of an interview.

In addition, nearly one hundred personal interviews were conducted for this book with Foyt's peers, friends, news media, and team members. However, if I heard it once I heard it a hundred times: "There's a lot of stuff we did together I can't talk about."

A.J. has always been fiercely protective of his family—often at Lucy's insistence—and even now he prefers to keep his private life private. It was only at the urging of those closest to him that he agreed to crack open the door, if ever so slightly.

It's no secret for those familiar with Foyt that he swears—a lot. In mixed company it's usually followed by a "pardon my French." Some of that has been included to capture this characteristic, much more has been edited out. He often falls back on pet phrases when answering questions, starting his response with "this is quite true," or "I'll never forget . . ." Again, some of it has been left in, the vast majority deleted.

Foyt was born in the middle of the Depression and grew up in the hardscrabble Heights area of Houston. Both the city and its schools were strictly segregated. Some comments common in those days are now considered politically incorrect, yet still creep into his conversations on occasion. He proudly considers himself a "bohunk," a derogatory term for those of Bohemian decent. He certainly isn't a model citizen, nor ever wanted to be.

Yet for every story about a politically incorrect Foyt there is another about an act of kindness, of sending his plane for someone in need, arranging medical specialists to see an injured driver, and taking someone into his house to care for them. He often provided financial support, although he didn't want others to know he was the source of the funds. Even decades later he was uncomfortable talking about these acts of kindness.

"I would like people to know me as just A.J.," he said again when asked recently how he'd like to be remembered. "I had a lot of fun, I worked hard, and I never wanted to settle for nothing less than first. I never wanted to settle for second. That's about it."

AUTHOR'S NOTE

This is Volume One of the story of Anthony Joseph "A.J." Foyt Jr. It is a combination of traditional biography, narrative nonfiction, and oral history. In many ways it is also a history of auto racing in America during what *Newsweek* magazine called "The Golden Age."

We didn't initially plan to break his story into two volumes, but the depth and breadth of his career surprised even those familiar with his life. Only after five years of work, when it became apparent a complete biography and manageable book were incompatible, was the decision made.

Volume One begins with the Foyt family in Eastern Europe and runs through 1977, when A.J. wins his fourth Indianapolis 500. Volume Two will pick up in 1978, trace his driving career through retirement, and follow A.J. and his race teams in the years afterward.

The quotations in the book are drawn from hundreds of sources. When multiple paragraphs in a row have quotations drawn from the same source, I have chosen to cite that source just once, at the end of the first quotation from that source. A new endnote number is used to either signal the beginning of a quotation from a different source or to offer clarity to the reader.

CHAPTER 1

YOU DONE FAIR

May 29, 1977

The celebration had been going on for several hours when Anthony Joseph "A.J." Foyt Jr. finally made his way to the family suite on the outside of Turn Two of the Indianapolis Motor Speedway.

He'd just become the first four-time winner of the world's most prestigious auto race—the Indianapolis 500. Everyone had wanted a moment of his time and for once he obliged, answering every journalist's question, posing for every photo request, and signing nearly every autograph.

The victory hadn't come easily. After leading laps early in the race, he'd run out of fuel near the halfway point and fell behind. He'd spent the second half chasing Gordon Johncock, who'd lead a race-high 129 of the 200 laps. After both drivers made their final pit stops and with about twenty laps to go, Johncock still led by nearly ten seconds. Although Foyt was closing and getting ready for a final "banzai run," it appeared his dream of a fourth victory was slipping away, just as it had the previous three years.[1]

Johncock had been waiting for Foyt to make his move and responded, running two of his fastest laps at more than 190 miles per hour. As Johncock approached the start of lap 185, however, on the middle of the main straightaway for the entire world to see, a puff of white smoke came out of the engine of Johncock's dayglo red car.

"It just blew up! It just blew up!" he shouted over the radio to his crew, who could see with their own disbelieving eyes what was happening. Johncock pulled his car to the inside of the track, crossing the exit of Pit Lane and stopping on the grass going into the first turn. It was one of the hottest 500s on record, and he sought refuge in the stream that ran through the infield in an attempt to cool off.[2]

◄ The Ride. *Steve H. Shunck Collection*

"I thought we had it in the bag," he said. "I don't think A.J. could have got by me."

A.J. spotted the car when he went past but couldn't see the number to tell which of the three otherwise identical STP Wildcats was out. Then he noticed the crowd waving him on. Just as they had in 1961 and 1967, the fans were the first to tell A.J. he was the new leader. A moment later a crew member confirmed it over the radio and Jack Starne, who'd been with Foyt since the day after his last Indianapolis victory in 1967, displayed a "P1" sign board.

The final laps dragged on. The second-place car was forty seconds behind and Foyt slowed the last couple of laps, tears filling his eyes.

"I talked to the car, to the Good Lord, whoever would listen," Foyt said.[3]

Starting the last lap he flashed a thumbs-up to the team. He waved to fans in Turn Three and Four coming to the finish line. Flagman Pat Vidan, as always standing out in his white sport coat, added an extra flourish as he waved the checkered flag at the winner.

As A.J. slowed he spotted track owner Tony Hulman clutching two hands over his head in the same traditional victory salute Foyt first received in 1961. He could hear the crowd chanting "A.J., A.J., A.J." above the noise of the cars still racing. In the television booth, Jim McKay of ABC's *Wide World of Sports* said it was the most exciting moment in his ten years of covering the 500.

Nearly stopping across from the second-turn suites, Foyt waved to his family and friends. A photographer wearing black-and-white checkered pants ran toward the track and pulled them off, waving them as Foyt drove past. Spectators hung from the tops of fences along the backstraight and waved. Pulling on to Pit Lane, A.J. was met by a line of drivers and crew members from other teams applauding the first four-time winner. Johncock was waiting for him and the two exchanged waves.

An emotional Hulman, immaculate as ever in a light summer suit and tie despite the ninety-degree temperatures, was the first to greet Foyt when he drove up the checkered-board ramp into Victory Lane. Hulman often said he had no favorites among the drivers, but everyone knew there was a special place in his heart for Foyt.

A.J. reached out his left hand as he pulled to a stop and Hulman grasped it, affectionately touched Foyt's helmet, and then kissed the driver's hand. He bent over and hugged Foyt around the neck before pulling away, embarrassed by the show of affection and the tears in his eyes.[4]

Sponsor Jim Gilmore, who Foyt said was "like a brother," was next to congratulate him and A.J. struggled to stand in his seat and remove his helmet. His father, Tony, tried to reach him but when the crowd surged around the car he stepped back. Tony was a little more than a year removed from open-heart surgery and had given up his crew chief job to Starne. Someone thrust the traditional bottle of milk into A.J.'s hands and, still chomping on his spearmint chewing gum, he held it up for the photographers and then passed it to Starne to share with the crew.

With an interview for the tape-delayed television broadcast completed and the initial frenzy beginning to calm down, Tony was finally able to reach his son, the embrace lingering in a rare display of emotion between the two.

Arriving late to Victory Lane was A.J.'s wife, Lucy. She'd been watching the race from the suite with A.J.'s mother, Evelyn, who'd suffered several strokes and was told by doctors to avoid excitement. Following their orders had been difficult; fortunately Lucy and A.J. were friends with some of the best doctors in Houston, including several who were in the suite.

Lucy had refused to budge from her seat until her husband took the checkered flag, a superstition dating back to his first victory at the Speedway in 1961. Only then she'd been sitting nearby in the Tower behind the pits. This time, she was forced to fight her way through the crowd of people leaving the track, her son Tony at the wheel of the golf cart. She was further delayed when she directed Tony to the spot where Victory Lane had been on her last trip in 1967, only to discover it had been moved in the years since.

"I'd been to Victory Lane three times, and I thought I knew exactly where I was going," she'd say. "But nobody was there. I had to go find the new Victory Lane. Thank God I was with my son, so it didn't take long. But it was very confusing."[5]

Resplendent in a white-and-black art deco print dress and wearing large black oval sunglasses, she arrived in time for a few quick photos, when the pace car pulled up for the winner's traditional victory lap around the Speedway. As A.J. and Lucy headed for the pace car he paused, turned around, and waved again to photographers.

"See you next year."

THE RIDE

Indianapolis 500 pace cars had almost always been convertibles, with the winning driver sitting on the trunk deck, often joined by his wife, for the victory lap. The 1977 pace car, however, was an Oldsmobile Delta Royale 88, the production model available only as a hardtop coupe.

The actual pace car—driven by actor James Garner to start the race—was unique. In addition to performance enhancements, the car had a modified roof so a large part of the hardtop could be removed. Once detached, a portion of the rear roofline remained to help provide structural integrity. It looked something like a large and wide roll bar over the backseat.

While Hulman held the pace car's passenger door open, A.J. stepped on the backseat and climbed atop the roof, his legs dangling in the air. Lucy took one look at the perch and slid into the rear seat. Foyt then motioned Hulman, who typically sat in the front passenger seat if he went on the victory lap, to join him. For the first time since he took ownership of the Speedway in 1946, Hulman took a seat next to the race winner for the ride around his track.

Both men rocked back slightly as the pace car started to pull away. Foyt put his left foot on the driver seat headrest to steady himself, his right arm around the older man.

"Better hold on to me, A.J.," Hulman said. Foyt was surprised at how thin the man felt. He knew Hulman had been having health problems for the past year, but had seemed to be his vibrant, energetic self throughout the month of May.[6]

A.J. didn't have long to dwell on Hulman's health. Passing by the suites they all waved to their families, the Hulman suites being alongside and above Foyts'. The Oldsmobile slowed even more down the backstraight when spectators broke down the infield fences and ran to the car, hoping for a handshake or hand slap. Later, more than twenty-five of A.J.'s crew members piled into every square inch of one of the official GMC pickup trucks for their own victory tour of the Speedway.

Hulman, who would die before the year was out, called the day "my biggest thrill" in racing.

After meeting again with reporters, Foyt went to the team's Gasoline Alley garages, which were packed with people celebrating, spilling over into the narrow alleyway. Some of the crew members had taken refuge in the neighboring garages of other teams. It was sweltering in the narrow confines and Foyt quickly showered, changed out of his driver's suit, and headed for his suite.

The party that had begun to subside started anew when A.J. arrived. The suite was surprisingly small and simple, the narrow room no more than fifty feet long with a few kitchen appliances and a bathroom. The view was anything but simple, the glass wall overlooking the now quiet track's exit of Turn Two. A sliding glass door led to several rows of seats outside, many of which went unused during the race as Lucy and the others preferred to watch on closed-circuit television from inside. Lucy was the perfect hostess, making sure everyone had something to drink and eat.[7]

The small air conditioner was working overtime and fighting a losing battle late in the day to the constantly opening doors and a crowd well over the fire marshal's fifty-person limit.

"It was hotter than hell in there," recalled crew member Billy Woodruff, a buddy of A.J. and Lucy's son Tony, who said he was practically raised at the Foyt house. "There were so many people there that I didn't know. They should have been handing out name badges.

"You're happy. You'd made history and the whole load had been lifted off our shoulders. But it was mentally draining and you just kinda bottomed out."[8]

The crew members were easy to identify in their red-and-white checkered shirts originally designed by Gilmore's wife, Di. Starne was there, along with Cecil Taylor and Howard Gilbert, three of those who'd been with Foyt since just after this last 500 victory in 1967. Gilbert was the man most responsible for the race-winning Foyt engine and Taylor had known A.J. since 1956.

There was a constant flow of people through the suite to congratulate Foyt, including Dan Gurney, his 1967 Le Mans-winning teammate. Gurney was one of the first to tag Foyt with the "Cassius" nickname after boisterous boxer Cassius Clay, who'd since changed his name to Muhammad Ali. On this day Gurney simply called him "Super Tex." Evel Knievel, who had been in the No. 14 pit during the race and with whom Foyt often rode motorcycles, stopped by to congratulate the winner. Tony Hulman's daughter and Foyt family close friends, Mari Hulman George and her children, were in and out, their suite next door serving as an overflow destination.

During a lull in the celebration, A.J. looked across the room at his father. Tony was moving around the suite thanking crew members for a job well done. Despite the miscalculation on fuel mileage, they'd turned in the fastest pit stops of any of the leaders. When he had finished talking to the crew, A.J. caught his father's eye.

"Well Daddy, how'd *I* do?" A.J. asked. He said later he was just "cutting up."

"Did I do good?"

The room quieted as Tony contemplated the question.

"Good?" he repeated, his Texas drawl dragging out the question. "I don't know about good."

He paused again, seemingly searching for the right word.

"I'd say you done fair."[9]

The room erupted in laughter.

"That's about the nicest thing he ever said to me," A.J. would say.

Others were more effusive, including Jim Murray, the Pulitzer Prize-winning and nationally syndicated sports columnist for the *Los Angeles Times*, who was no fan of auto racing and had clashed at times with Foyt in the past. Now he had only praise.

"This man is the greatest in the world at what he does," Murray wrote. "How many people ever get to say that in a lifetime?"[10]

Even Tony eventually opened up, just not to his son.

"I'm right proud of him," he told another reporter. "About as proud as if he'd growed up and became president."[11]

————

Over the years A.J. was inconsistent when asked about his favorite or most memorable race, sometimes saying just qualifying for his first 500 in 1958 topped the list, other times it was his first victory at the Speedway in 1961, the last win for a roadster in 1964, or his first victory in his own car and with his Daddy as crew chief in 1967.

More often than not, however, it was the 1977 Indianapolis 500.

"I guess my favorite race would have to be seventy-seven," Foyt said forty-five years later. "I built my own car, had my own motor, and then Mr. Hulman drove around on the lap with me after the race."[12]

He hesitated for a moment, his eyes beginning to water.

"And I was really happy that my mother and father were still there."

CHAPTER 2

MOMMA AND DADDY

It was no surprise to anyone who knew Anthony Joseph "A.J." Foyt Jr. that he sought approval from his "Daddy" at the moment of his greatest success. From A.J.'s birth in Houston on Wednesday, January 16, 1935, until the death of Anthony Joseph "Tony" Foyt on May 21, 1983, they were constant companions, a constant thorn in each other's side—and together for virtually every important turn of their lives.

Emma Evelyn Foyt, who A.J. called "Mother" or "Momma" and most everyone else called Evelyn, played an equally important role in his life, to the point A.J.'s wife, Lucy, often referred to her husband as a "momma's boy." Evelyn fought hard to try and stop him from quitting high school and going car racing, but when that failed, she provided the support a young family needs most, helping with her grandchildren whenever asked and proving to be a solid confidant, friend, and shoulder to cry on for her daughter-in-law.[1]

When Tony and Evelyn were married in Houston on April 5, 1934, it brought together two families tracing their roots to Eastern Europe. Both families immigrated to the United States during the mid- to late 1800s. It was a time of abhorrent working conditions, religious persecution, and political unrest in an Eastern Europe that would become the epicenter of two world wars. The families suffered hardship, separation, and death. Their journeys and struggles shaped generations of hard-working people dedicated to making a better life for their families. Tony and Evelyn each lost parents at a young age to death and divorce, leaving them determined to provide the solid family foundation neither one of them experienced.

◀ The Foyt Brothers Garage. That's believed to be A.J.'s grandfather, Thomas Foyt (far left) with his hands on his hips. *Foyt Family Collection*

THE FOYTS

The Foyt family dates to the mid-1800s in what was then Austria and later became the Czech Republic. That's where Josef C. Fojt was born in 1852 and Frances Nossek in 1858. The Fojt spelling is generally considered Hungarian (and often seen as Fojtu), was a common name throughout the region, and at one time was a title given a village's mayor.[2]

Details of their life in Austria are limited, the victim of world wars and the aftermath that destroyed much of the region's governmental files. Most of what is available comes from US immigration and naturalization documents, census forms, and death certificates, but even those often vary and are incomplete. For instance, Josef's mother and father are listed as "unknown" on his death certificate. Frances knew only that her father's name was Charlie, listed his birthplace as Europe and her mother as unknown. Both Josef and Frances listed their birthday as March 19.

The couple married in 1875 and settled near Horni Lidec, a city dating to the tenth century. Located about two hundred miles east of Prague, Horni Lidec roughly means "Hungarian Ford," and the city served as a key river crossing with Hungary. It was part of the Empire of Austria until 1867 when, after coming out on the losing end of the Austro-Prussian War, it became part of the Austro-Hungarian Empire, with Hungary exerting increasing control over the region. The area included a broad cross section of religious and ethnic backgrounds, including large Jewish and German communities. While many in the area were farmers, the first industrial revolution brought great advancements in the making of iron and steel, along with increasingly difficult working conditions.

Josef and Frances immediately set about planting their own family tree with the birth of Julia in 1876, the first of ten children. About every two years another child would arrive. They were a remarkably healthy lot, unusual for the era when children often died young and mothers sometimes in childbirth. The size and health of the family indicates they were better off than most.

Josef's two sisters immigrated to America in the early 1880s and were soon singing the country's praises and sending back tales of opportunity. Antonin Frantisek Fojt—who would become Thomas Frank Foyt in the states and the future father of Tony Foyt—was born in 1888, and shortly thereafter the family began making plans to immigrate. In 1891 Josef and Frances embarked with their family on the four-hundred-mile journey to the German seaport of Bremen, the primary gateway from Eastern Europe to the United States. There they boarded the SS *Aller*, bound for America.

The *Aller* was a relatively new ship, an improved class of ocean liner. It was one of the first liners made of steel and, with a top speed of eighteen knots, among the fastest ships of the day. It was also among the nicest, with first- and second-class accommodations, although those cabins were occupied almost exclusively by American and English passengers. While no records are available, it seems likely the large Fojt family traveled in steerage, along with most other Eastern Europeans.

Among the 1,400 passengers and crew on board the *Aller* were Josef and Rosalia Gloger and their two young children, five-year-old Josef and three-month-old Marie. They'd left Paskove, Austria, located about one hundred miles north of Horni Lidec and also part of the current Czech Republic. It's unknown if the two families knew each other prior to departure, but if not, future events indicate they almost certainly became acquainted during the voyage.

The ship departed on or about July 22 (several dates are listed on various immigration and naturalization forms by the Fojts and Glogers, with July 22 the most common), arriving in Galveston, Texas, on August 8 after a relatively quick and unremarkable trip. The city was so popular with those coming from Eastern Europe it supported Czech- and German-language newspapers and schools, and it was common to hear both languages spoken on the streets.

Galveston was the largest city in Texas in 1891 and one of the busiest ports of entry into the United States. New York's immigration center was more than a year away from opening and unlike Ellis Island, which began assembling an extensive and exhaustive database of arrivals when it opened, nearly all the passenger manifests and immigration records for those entering Galveston between 1871 and 1894 no longer exist.

Disembarking in Galveston, the Fojt family, guided by Josef's sister, Katerina, traveled northwest to Bryan, in Brazos County where she lived. Bryan was a small community near Fort Worth that was seeing an influx of Eastern European immigrants. Not far away was the town of New Bremen, named after their departure port.

Cotton was king—as it had been since well before the Civil War—and with the Deep South still recovering from the war, the county had become the largest cotton producing area in the country. The Brazos River provided fertile bottomland and "probably the finest cotton land in the world," according to a government report from the era. It was the primary money crop for about 70 percent of the farms, with some corn, sugarcane, and small fruits often grown on the side. The wide-open nearby flatlands also offered ranching opportunities, with cattle, hogs, and sheep being raised in large numbers.[3]

Landowners were looking for cheap labor to work the fields and they found it in the immigrants. No strangers to hard work, Josef and the older boys were soon employed as "farm laborers" according to census reports. The workers were often referred to derisively as "bohunks," a combination of their Bohemian and Hungarian backgrounds. The *Merriam-Webster Dictionary* described them as "unskilled, uneducated, and often rough laborers." While considered a derogatory term by most, it was one A.J. would embrace and wear as a badge of honor.[4]

Three more children were born, and the family acquired land of its own and was making a go of farming. In mid-1899, however, life for the extended Fojt family and thousands of others was altered when the area was hit by back-to-back storms and record rain levels. Over a ten-day period in late June the area received nearly nine inches of rain, about what it had been averaging for the month.

"The whole country is flooded with water," reported the *Fort Worth Daily Gazette*. "It has rained almost incessantly for four days. Roads are impassible and bridges are gone."[5]

By July 4 the Brazos River was more than fifty feet above the mean level on both banks, exceeding all available flood gauges and still rising. The *Bryan Weekly*

Eagle reported the river was "eight- to ten-miles wide" at one point, though most estimates put its width at three to five miles. An estimated 12,000 square miles was flooded between Waco and where the river emptied into the Gulf of Mexico south of Galveston. More than 2,300 square miles of farmland was damaged or destroyed.[6]

"All crops on the Brazos river from Waco to the Gulf are a total loss," said the *Houston Post.*[7]

The family had dealt with flooding before, it came with working land along a major river. But this was different. The lateness of the rains not only wiped out the year's crops shortly before harvesting, it also meant it was too late in the season to replant. Government agricultural experts warned farmers it could take years for the land to recover.

In many ways the Fojts were lucky. More than 280 people lost their lives in the flooding. Thousands more were left homeless. The family was still together, but the dream of a family farm was gone. Josef and Frances were forced to look toward Houston, which was about to begin a boom of its own, driven by the railroads, automobiles, oil, and another natural disaster.

HOUSTON

The turn of the century was a time of great transition for Houston. Far from being the nation's fourth largest city it is today, Houston was barely the fourth largest city in Texas with a population of about thirty thousand. It had been a logistics center for the Confederacy, with men and goods flowing in from the west and shipping east. Prior to 1900 it remained primarily a rail hub, with nearly a dozen lines converging at the city center.

In many respects Houston was still a town of the Wild West, its dirt streets lined with saloons and brothels and the site of occasional gunfights. Hopes of making it a seaport to challenge Galveston had evaporated as the channel from the Gulf of Mexico proved too narrow and shallow for ocean-going vessels.

All that changed on September 9, 1900, when a Category 4 hurricane took Galveston by surprise and nearly wiped the city out. It remains the worst natural disaster in American history, claiming about eight thousand lives. By comparison, an estimated 1,200 people were killed by Hurricane Katrina in 2005. More than seven thousand buildings were destroyed and ten thousand people left homeless. The destruction shifted the population and economic center of Texas to Houston, fifty miles inland and protected at least partially from the full impact of a hurricane slamming on shore.[8]

The invention of the automobile and the arrival of the first car in Houston in 1901 coincided with the discovery of major oil fields in areas surrounding the city and it quickly became home base for the budding petroleum industry. Iron foundries, several of which already existed to provide material for the railroads, multiplied and grew rapidly to supply the huge oil rigs and refineries springing up seemingly everywhere. The federal government stepped in to improve the Houston channel to allow for bigger ships. Ship-building companies soon followed, requiring even more iron, steel, and petroleum.

Houston was thus on the verge of great growth when Frances arrived to pave the way for her family. By 1903 they had settled in an area known as the Houston Heights, Greater Heights, or simply the Heights, land slightly elevated from the city center but only a short streetcar ride away. The 1900 national census indicated fewer than one thousand people lived in the Heights.

At some point during and after the move to Houston, the spelling of the family name began to change. Fojt—as it appeared in the 1900 census listing their home as Brazos—became Foyt. Josef became Joseph. Census takers of the era sometimes took responses verbally and forms were written in longhand. Both were open to the interpretation of the recorder, and in a few cases members of the family were still listed as Fojt. That changed further when family members started going through the formal citizenship naturalization process. The 1910 census clearly lists the family name for Thomas as Foyt, as it appeared in subsequent editions of the Houston city directory.

Five of the older Foyt boys, including Thomas, found jobs as "iron molders." A hot, dirty, and often dangerous job, there was a large demand for those willing to do the work and they changed companies often. Thomas worked for the Hartwell Iron Works, the Marin Iron Works, and eventually R. P. Clark shipbuilders. He also was the toughest of the brothers. If there was a fight or one of the Foyt boys was in trouble, they called Thomas.

The boys, even those marrying and starting their own families, turned over most of their pay to Frances, who managed the family's finances. She distributed funds as necessary and the family set about building and acquiring housing.

With a family the size of the Foyts, the comings and goings never ceased as they settled near the intersection of West Twenty-Fifth Avenue and Railroad (now Nicholson) Street. Joseph and Frances anchored the clan in the largest house at 501 West Twenty-Fifth Avenue, with five of the youngest children. Other family members occupied row houses along the street, including those at 441, 505, and 509 West Twenty-Fifth Avenue. Zoning laws were never a big thing in Houston and the most memorable feature was a pickle factory in the middle of the block.[9,10]

At some point the Foyts and Glogers, who originally settled in the Houston area, reconnected. The two infants on the initial voyage from Europe, Thomas and Marie, were married in 1910. For a time the couple lived with Marie's mother in the Houston suburb of Brunner and their first child, Marie Francis, named for the two grandmothers, was born there in June 1911.

By the end of the year Thomas and Marie joined other Foyt family members in the Heights, settling into the house at 505 West Twenty-Fifth Avenue. That's where Anthony Joseph "Tony" Foyt, named for his two grandfathers, was born on December 15, 1913. Another daughter, Marguerite, followed three years later.

Most of the boys continued to work in area mills, although several found jobs with the railroads. By 1917 three of the boys, Thomas, Louis, and William, shifted to the Houston Car Wheel and Machine Company. The work was similar to the iron foundries but exposed them to the booming interest in automobiles and they soon caught the bug.

The roaring twenties rolled into Texas and especially Houston. Oil continued to drive the economy and the population of Houston grew six-fold from the time of the Foyts' arrival at the turn of the century to the end of the 1920s. Texas was soon the fifth most populated state in the Union.

By 1922 Thomas was ready to break out on his own. With money from Frances he teamed up with one of his US-born younger brothers, Lockey, to open the Foyt Brothers Garage. Located at 1721 Ashland, just a few blocks from the Foyt homes, it was a simple corrugated metal building with a dirt floor and a single Texaco gas pump out front.

Thomas also started motorcycle racing. The racing was for fun, and he didn't have much success, but it was something he could do with Tony and by all accounts father and son were close. It was a hard life, but no harder than most. Nearly nine years later the couple had a fourth child, Gertrude, who was born in 1925. Then tragedy struck.

Marie's breathing had become increasingly labored during her pregnancy, and she was diagnosed with an advanced stage of emphysema. Doctors recommended surgery, often a last resort when treating the disease and risky in the best of circumstances. She died shortly after the operation on August 12, 1926, with post-operative shock listed as the official cause of death.

Left with three young teenagers and an infant, Thomas remarried two years later to Lavinia Marie Guidry, ten years his junior and herself with a young boy. They took in a boarder to help make ends meet. Motorcycle racing became a thing of the past. It was close quarters in the two-bedroom home and Tony, reeling from his mother's death and upset with the new living arrangements, clashed often with his stepmother and stepbrother.

The greater Foyt family suffered another blow on August 9, 1929, when Joseph, the family's patriarch, died at seventy-seven from intestinal and heart complications. It was the first sign of the family's hereditary heart problems. Two weeks later the stock market crashed, sending the country spiraling into the Great Depression.

Through it all Frances held the family together. The Foyts were again more fortunate than most as the brothers, for the most part, were able to keep working through the Depression. Some of the women also worked to supplement the family's income.

The boys still had their share of fun. The garage became a popular gathering place for the brothers and their friends. Although Prohibition was the law of the land, drinking was a favorite pastime of the group, fueled by a family still. Things got so wild at one point, Frances moved Lockey's family across the street from the garage so his wife, Louise, could keep an eye on things.

"They were just a fun-loving people," said Marie Foyt, the wife of Joseph Foyt Sr., who was ninety-four in 2021 and the family's oldest-living direct descendant at the time, although she has since passed away. "At the drop of a hat they'd have a party."[11]

Tony spent most of his time at the garage, working as an apprentice mechanic earning ten dollars a week. He saved enough money that in 1930, at sixteen and with his father's help, he bought a race car, a 1925 Hudson Hornet, providing a desperately needed distraction. A few months later he dropped out of high school before his senior year.

"I never won no races," Tony said of his early racing efforts. "We run for nothin'. We more or less were just having a bunch of fun."[12]

Things hit bottom for Tony when his father, Thomas, passed out and was rushed to St. Joseph hospital. He was diagnosed with "coronary thrombosis and auricular fibrillation," or blood clots, most likely caused by a heart attack. The clots had spread to his brain and Thomas died at the hospital five days later, on October 19, 1933. He'd just turned forty-four.

The broken family continued to share the house for a short time, but it was a tense situation. Tony came home to find his little sister being disciplined, Gertrude forced to kneel in the corner of the room on corn kernels. Frances moved Gertrude in with Mary, one of Thomas's sisters, who adopted the young girl. Marie and Tony were considered old enough to fend for themselves. Marguerite would enter a convent and change her name to Florence, symbolic of her life's new commitment. Six months after his father's death, on April 5, 1934, Tony, twenty-one, married Emma Evelyn Monk, eighteen.

THE MONKS

The future Mrs. Tony Foyt (and A.J.'s mother), Emma Evelyn Monk, was the product of a line of strong women. Born January 23, 1916, in Harris County, she was named for two of those women, grandmothers Nora Evelyn Weller and Emma Schneider. Both branches of Evelyn's family tree were of German heritage, having immigrated to America many years apart and settling in different areas of the country.

The Monk family line can be traced back to the late 1600s to the Lower Saxony area of what would become Germany. The family lived in the village of Münkeboe and at some point adopted the Münke surname. The village was just sixty miles from Bremen, and in 1855 Harms and Annke Münke and their six children, including a three-month old newborn son, set sail for America.[13]

They undertook the trip more than thirty-five years before the Fojts and it was a more difficult and dangerous crossing. Annke died at sea, followed five days later by the infant. No causes of death are available. Eventually arriving in New Orleans, Münke was "Americanized" to Monk. The family made its way to Illinois and that's where, in 1865, one of the boys, Hiram Monk, married Rachel "Gretje" Conrad, who hailed from the same area of Lower Saxony.

The couple had seven children, including, in 1871, William Edward Monk. William listed his profession as "preacher" on future census forms and moved often, first to Nebraska, where he married Nora and had the first of five children, Arthur Wesley Monk.

Arthur inherited his father's wanderlust and at sixteen he struck out on his own, first working as a hired farmhand, then joining the Marine Corps before his seventeenth birthday. He received an honorable discharge in 1914 on the eve of World War I and a year later married Katherine "Kate" Wilson in Houston's Harris County. He was twenty-one and she was twenty-seven.

Emma Evelyn Monk was born ten months later. A boy followed in 1918, only to die when he was four. Arthur himself was ready to move on and the couple soon divorced.

Kate remained in Harris County with her daughter and went to work in a grocery store on Twenty-Sixth Street in the Heights, just around the corner from the Foyt houses. It seems likely Tony and Evelyn met during this period, although very little is known about their relationship prior to their marriage. When Tony Foyt's stepmother and stepbrother moved on, he and Evelyn returned to the home at 505 West Twenty-Fifth Avenue in the Heights and A.J. was born at nearby St. Joseph Hospital.

A second child, Barbara Jean, was born on May 16, 1937, but there was a problem. She was diagnosed with "Blue Baby Syndrome," a heart condition that affected oxygen levels and left newborns with a bluish tint. By the late 1940s, relatively minor medical procedures were developed that greatly improved the life expectancy of "blue babies," but in the late 1930s there was little that could be done. She lived just thirteen days.

Another daughter, Marlene, was born January 15, 1939. Both A.J. and Marlene say they know little of their parents' background before they were married, not even how they met.

"My dad never elaborated on his family," says Marlene. "And he was very much against putting together a family tree. My dad would say, 'Just leave my family out of it. Leave me and my kids out of it.' My mother's family I knew nothing about."[14]

Shaped by his father's strong feelings, A.J. ignored his family heritage. He speaks fondly of his Aunt Bea and Uncle Willie, his Aunt Marie and cousin Joe and their family, but he occasionally referred to other cousins as "idiots."

"I don't care to go way back in history," A.J. said. "I know I've got people that go way, way back, but why do I care? Like my Daddy said, when I won Indy, overnight, a lot of Foyts started showing up. Before that, nothing.

"I've had more people come and say I'm kin to you and I say, fine, nice meeting you. But not really. I had my own family, my own mother and Daddy. The rest of them, I never had much to do with them. I mean I was never around the family much because I was off racing and trying to make a living."[15]

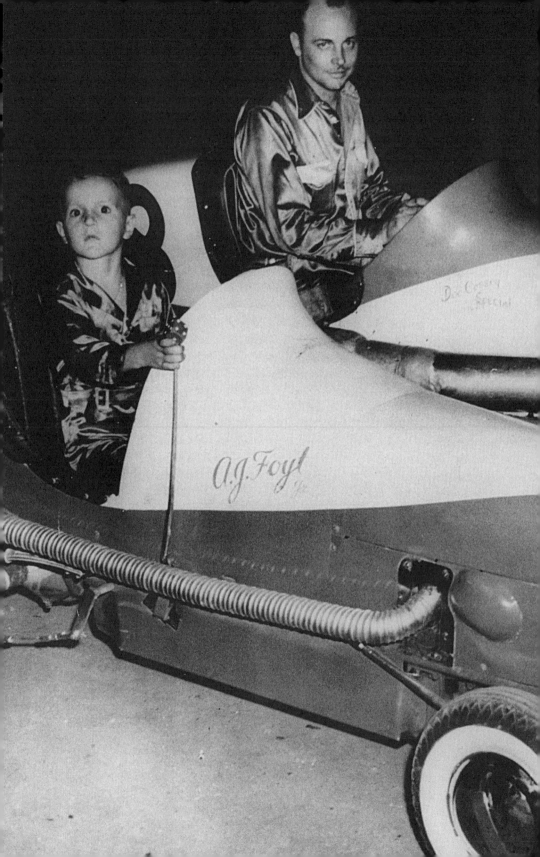

CHAPTER 3

___

YOUNG A.J.

1935–1947

There was very little of the traditional New Year optimism at the opening of 1935, the year A.J. Foyt was born. America was deep in the grip of the Depression and Europe was under the growing grip of Nazism. President Franklin D. Roosevelt was starting his third year in office and the "New Deal" was just beginning to be implemented. Lamar High School, one of several schools Foyt would pass through, was under construction thanks to federal dollars. Houston's population had surged to more than three hundred thousand and there were so many cars on its roads that city center streets were starting to be paved, although not in the outlying Heights area.

From the very beginning his parents called him A.J.

"I've had A.J. as long as I can remember," he says, but "I have no idea why." A few people called him "Little Tony," for a short time, although "junior" was never an option.[1]

Tony Foyt had begun to pull away from the extended family following the death of his father, and soon after he married he left the Foyt Brothers Garage. It wasn't long before the garage itself was gone.

"Louise finally said, 'I had enough of this shit,'" Marie Foyt remembers her aunt saying after the drinking reached new levels. Frances agreed and the garage was sold.[2]

Tony went to work maintaining the truck fleet for the Duncan Coffee Company—an offshoot of Maxwell House Coffee—and withdrew further from the family after the death of Barbara Jean. He continued to race at local tracks and acquired a small open-wheel, open-cockpit car known as a midget. He worked out of his own garage and repaired cars after hours to earn extra money. That's where A.J.'s earliest memories were formed.

◀ Five-year-old A.J. and Doc Cossey. *Foyt Family Collection*

"I can remember Daddy taking me there when I was a little bitty kid," he said. "I'd do anything, just to be with him. I was so little that he sat me up on the workbench and told me, 'Just stay up there out of the way boy.' He should have put me in the race car in the first place, because it's where I always ended up."[3]

Shortly after A.J. turned three Tony gave him a bright red race car of his own. It was powered by a small Briggs & Stratton lawn mower engine like the one used for kid's go-karts and minibikes for generations to come. Together they laid out a short racecourse around their house.

"I spent hour after hour running around the outside of the house in that race car," A.J. recalled. "I was the best three-year-old racer in Houston. I learned that if I started it into a slide just at the swing set and drove it close to the corner of the house, I could go a lot faster down my straightaway at the side of the house."[4]

Another of the Foyt families, this one headed by Tony's uncle and the oldest son, Joseph C. Foyt Jr., lived closest to A.J.'s house. Joe remained closer to Tony than anyone else in the family and he watched as A.J. ran lap after lap around the house in his go-kart.

"My daddy always joked A.J. wasn't right upstairs," said Joseph R. Foyt Jr., the son of, Joseph R. Foyt, one of the few Foyts Tony and A.J. remained friendly with. "He said A.J. would drive the go-kart around and around all day long. Tony did a lot of work on other people's cars out of his garage and A.J. would siphon gas out of those cars to keep his go-kart running. Sometimes he'd get a mouthful of gas. My dad would say, 'I think it screwed up his brain cells.'"[5]

Once the home course was mastered, A.J. ventured away from his house and out onto the street, where he attracted the attention of neighbors and, before long, the police.

"It used to make a lot of noise," Tony admitted. "Some of the neighbors would call the police. A.J. would see the police car comin' and come flyin' in the house and dive under the bed. We would pull him out, and the officer would make him promise not to speed anymore. But the urge would come back, and he would be out there again as fast as he could with that little engine poppin' away."[6]

Life stabilized at the Foyt household, although it was tight quarters after Marlene was born on the day before A.J.'s fourth birthday. Tony and Evelyn were committed to providing the family atmosphere they'd never experienced. Money was tight for nearly everyone and neighborhood kids would pool their pennies to buy an ice cream cone they could share. Occasionally on weekends Evelyn packed a picnic lunch and the family drove to the town of Kemah on Galveston Bay.

At times Foyt painted the Heights as a tough neighborhood. "You either learned to take care of yourself or you got the shit beat out of you," he said in his autobiography. At other times he described it as a very normal place to grow up.[7]

"The Heights was made up of small, mostly neat homes like ours, where middle-class people lived," he said. "We had a two-bedroom frame bungalow and plenty of food and clean clothes to wear that were mostly new. It was a good childhood. Very American."

Robert "Bobby" Waltrip was five years old when he moved to the Heights the same year A.J. was born. He grew up about a half mile away from the Foyts on Heights Boulevard and they later became close friends. He remembered the Heights as an "upscale and highly respectable place to live. Heights Boulevard was a wide street, lined picturesquely with trees and broad spans of grass."[8]

Christmas was the biggest day of the year in the Foyt household, and the family went all out on decorations.

"That was *the* day in the family," A.J. said, a tradition he'd carry over to his own family. "My Momma and Daddy, that's what they lived for. They decorated everything. On Christmas Eve my Daddy would sing Bohemian carols."

For entertainment Tony and Evelyn played Texas 42 with Marie and Joseph, a dominos game once called the "national game of Texas." Evelyn also was part of a regular Friday night penny-ante poker game with the neighborhood ladies.

By the time A.J. was five, Tony built his son a replica midget, painted blue and white and carrying No. 8, just like the car known as the "Silver Bullet" that was driven by A.J.'s favorite driver, Doc Cossey. "Daring Doc" was the track champion at the Houston Speed Bowl where Tony often raced his yellow No. 20 midget. While most of the midgets used Ford or Offenhauser engines, the one in A.J.'s car put out just three horsepower.

"But it would go fifty miles an hour," Tony said of his son's car, "and he would go fifty in it."

Often when Tony was at a track, A.J. made exhibition runs in his car between races, helping to keep fans entertained. Billed as "the world's youngest race car driver," he became a fan favorite, used to hearing the cheers of the crowd.

It was at this early age that Foyt picked up a chip on his shoulder, where it would remain for the rest of his life. Despite the exhibition runs—or perhaps because of them—he said he was constantly teased about his Daddy's cars, which were often ragged in appearance and seldom ran up front. Tony had neither the money nor time to build a first-class racer, nor the driving talent to carry a car.

Many successful people, not just athletes, have a chip on their shoulder motivating them to greatness. Foyt made it clear in the first paragraph of his autobiography what drove him.

"If I heard, 'Whatsamatter, kid, can't your Daddy build race cars?' once, I heard it a thousand times. If I had to pick one thing that made me a winner, that would be it."[9]

MATCH RACE

One night in 1940 at Buff Stadium, a quarter-mile dirt track in Houston where A.J. often made demonstration runs, he challenged Cossey to a race. Here's how he recalled the conversation in his autobiography.[10]

I walked up to him in the pits and said, "Doc, I can outrun that midget of yours."

"Sure kid," Doc said and went right back to the story he was telling a couple of other race drivers.

"I mean it, Doc. I can beat you." I wasn't going to give up.

"Are you serious, kid?" he said, knowing damn well I was. "Just hold on." He finished his story and went over to Daddy. "Tony, is this kid serious? Do you want to let him race me?"

Racers can't stand to be challenged, not even by a kid.

Daddy didn't know a thing about it, but I can remember him laughing like hell. "What'd he say?" he asked Doc.

"He said he could outrun me," Doc said.

"Well, he probably can," Daddy said. That's all it took.

Tony backed up his son. When the track manager got wind of the challenge, he realized the promotional value of a match race and hyped the event. The good-looking Cossey, with a thin Clark Gable mustache, was also a fan favorite. While most drivers competed in a grimy T-shirt and pants, Cossey adopted a style worn by drivers in Southern California—flashy silk shirts and crisp white pants, a flair A.J. would later emulate.

A photo of the pair before the race shows Cossey with an uneasy smile, not sure what to make of the situation. Foyt called it an "I'll take it easy on you, kid," grin. A.J. has his game face on, a look of determination other racers would see for decades to come.

"Doc was still grinning when the man dropped the flag," is how Foyt remembers it. "Goodbye Doc. I got the jump on him and beat him into the first corner. I threw the midget sideways and I could hear the crowd cheering."[11]

His first race may also have been the start of the mythology and legend that is A.J. Foyt. Cossey said years later he didn't recall much about the race and if Foyt won, implied he must have let the kid finish first.

"I don't remember if he beat me or not," he said. "I can remember that I had a lot of trouble slowing down and letting him catch up to me. You couldn't run those (midgets) at slow speeds, and I had to keep slowing down and speeding up for him. It was just one of those exhibition races between races."[12]

Not surprisingly, Foyt felt differently.

"Doc and I knew damn well that he didn't let me win." Even more importantly, "Daddy knew it."[13]

It can be debated whether Cossey, who'd go on to win the Texas/Oklahoma midget championship in 1941 and remain one of the region's top drivers well into the 1950s, let A.J. win. One thing is not debatable: it's when Foyt decided he wanted to be a race car driver.

"If ever a kid knew that he had chosen the right profession for himself, I knew it at that moment. The feeling of that car sliding—the sort of bubble-in-your-stomach feeling—was one I'll never forget. That and knowing that I could stop the slide anytime I wanted—the power that I had to control the car—beat anything I had ever felt."[14]

Tony said nothing afterward, no words of encouragement or congratulation. It was an era of tough love, long before participation trophies were handed out like candy on Halloween. His daddy's reaction was A.J.'s first indication that victory was expected, excellence assumed. At the same time, they were now a team, A.J. seldom leaving Tony's side.

With success at the racetrack came problems at school. The potential was there but not the interest. He was going to be a race car driver and didn't see anything in class that would help him reach that goal.

He'd do anything to avoid going to school. On one trip to Helms Elementary he broke free from his mother and jumped in a mud puddle, forcing her to take him home. Tony wasn't having any of that, cleaning him up and putting a girl's dress on him and taking him back to school. That didn't always work either.

"My father said Tony would take A.J. to school and before Tony got home, A.J. would be in the front yard playing," says cousin Joe Foyt. "He said Tony would beat that boy, trying to keep him in class, but he just wouldn't stay in school."

Helms was a tough school. It was located across the street from the Oriental Textile Mills factory, which employed mainly low-wage workers, whose children often attended Helms.

"I found many of them to be tough kids, used to fights on the playground," Waltrip remembered, saying he and A.J. both learned an important lesson at the school. "Sometimes you have to fight to protect your turf. You can't let bullies get the best of you."[15]

In early 1941 Tony joined with another area midget racer, Dale Burt, to open an automotive repair shop, the B & F Garage at 527 Colquitt near Houston's mid-town area. The two men shared much in common. Burt, originally from Austin, lost his father before he was two years old and lived for a time in an orphanage with his three sisters as his mother refused to split up the family. They were eventually returned to their mother, and Burt turned to motorcycles as an escape. He was kicked out of high school for racing a motorcycle up and down a hallway and never went back, taking a job in a local body shop where he drove the wrecker while learning to work with metal. Many of the local racers visited the shop, and when Burt turned twenty-one he talked one of the men into letting him drive their car at a local track. He proved to be a good driver, good enough to have car owners pay him to drive their racer.

Both men were the strong, silent type, slow to warm up to people and typically opening up only when surrounded by other racers. Burt also had a sharp tongue and was a master needler, his primary targets being the other competitors.

The B & F Garage quickly earned a good reputation. Tony focused on engine and mechanical repairs while Burt handled bodywork and fabrication. Both men continued to race. The economy was beginning to show signs of improvement, and for the first time in ten years there seemed to be a light at the end of the tunnel.

Then came December 7, 1941.

Like so many families across America, the Foyts huddled around the radio in their living room listening to President Roosevelt refer to the Japanese bombing of Pearl Harbor as "a date which will live in infamy" and call for war on Japan, warning, "There is no blinking at the fact that our people, our territory, and our interests are in grave danger."

The next day Tony joined Burt and tens of thousands of others volunteering for the armed forces. But at nearly thirty years of age and with three dependents at home, Tony didn't fit the profile of those being immediately called up for ninety days of basic training before shipping overseas. He joined the Texas National Guard instead and spent time at Ellington Field, located southeast of Houston. The base became a key training site for pilots, navigators, and bombardiers and Tony helped keep the planes in the air. It was nearly a year before he was called to active duty, with the notation he'd proven himself to be a skilled mechanic. He was assigned to the Army Air Corps where he became a sergeant and was sent to California, where he worked on planes headed for the Pacific Theater.

At twenty-three and single, Burt, who listed the Foyt household as his home address, was quickly called up. For a time he was also stationed at Ellington Field, where he and Tony joked the sooner they went into action, "the sooner we'll get this thing over with."[16]

With both men in the service the garage closed and Evelyn took a job at the Deleon hardware store in nearby Bellaire. A.J. and Marlene spent most of their time with Evelyn's mother, Kate, and some with their great-grandmother, Frances, until she passed away in 1943.

Even during the war, with no races being run, A.J. thought about little else and his schoolwork continued to suffer. He remembered, "My fifth-grade teacher sent home a note from school that said, 'I don't know what to do with A.J. Every paper I pick up has a picture of a race car on it—no answers, just a race car.'"[17]

The war ended with Japan's surrender in August 1945 and by October Tony was back in Houston. Burt was discharged in January of 1946. Almost immediately racing started again throughout the country and both men were soon back at the track.

The B & F Garage reopened soon thereafter, and business was good, taking up an increasing amount of both men's time. Racing was becoming more complicated.

"Before [the war] it was the man who drove the hardest that won," Burt said. After the war, "You had to invest more money in your rig and work the whole night sorting out gear ratios and tire sizes. You had to be an engineer to compete."[18]

Tony soon made a series of life-changing decisions. He made Evelyn happy and retired from driving race cars. Burt was seven years younger and, most importantly, the better driver. Tony would run the garage and serve as the team's chief mechanic. Burt would help with fabrication at the shop and drive the team's cars. In August Burt also made a significant move of his own and proposed to Gwen McCoy. Tony and Evelyn stood up for the couple at the wedding and A.J. and Marlene had roles as well.

The B & F team raced three to five times a week at area tracks during the summer, with A.J. often tagging along. On one trip for a race in Dallas, however, Tony and Evelyn decided to leave their children at home because it would be early morning before they returned. A.J. was put in charge. That's when the trouble started.

Tony had left one of the team's two midgets sitting on a trailer in the home garage and the temptation was too great. A.J. and some friends rolled it off the trailer and push-started the car. A.J. soon began running laps around the house, just as he had done with the toy car when he was three years old. Only the midget was more powerful, and the knobby tires began ripping up the grass. He bounced off the swing set that served as a course marker on those early runs and sent it flying. He clipped the apex of one turn a couple of times, which also happened to be the corner of the house. Things went from bad to worse when the engine backfired and the car caught fire. By the time A.J. got it stopped and put the fire out with the help of his buddies, the body panels were badly charred. He cleaned it up the best he could, rolled it into the garage, and headed for what he hoped would be the security of the bedroom.

"I thought bed was the safest place," he said. "I figured Daddy wouldn't beat me too bad if we were both asleep in that room."

As expected, it was late when Tony and Evelyn returned home—about 5:30 in the morning according to Tony, while A.J. believed it was closer to 2 a.m.—but the darkness couldn't hide the trashed yard.

"The grass was chewed to pieces and there were tire gouges all around," Tony said. "Then I went into the garage and saw the midget. It was sitting there with the paint all scorched."[19]

Tony headed straight for A.J.'s room with Evelyn in hot pursuit.

"He played like he was asleep, but he wasn't, I could tell. My wife said, 'Don't say anything to him right now when you're so mad,' so I didn't wake him up.

"But I knew right then, standing there in that kid's bedroom, that he would have to race. There just wasn't going to be any other way."

A.J. told several versions of the story over the years. In his autobiography he said, "There was the sound of breathing. The kind of breathing somebody does when he's madder than hell. He didn't say a word. I knew he was standing there in the doorway with his arms folded. Then he went away."[20]

In a more dramatic version he'd tell *Sports Illustrated* years later, he recalled his mother pleading, "Please don't whip him, please don't whip him," and his father yelling at him, "You do something like that again, I'll beat you to death."[21]

While A.J. avoided physical discipline in this instance, Tony Foyt was no doubt a strict disciplinarian and a believer in the "spare the rod, spoil the child" proverb. A.J. wasn't spoiled but would say "whippings," as he called them, were for special occasions, lying being the worst offense in Tony's book.

"I never got that many whippings," A.J. said, "but, whew, when I did, my Daddy tore my ass up."

Despite their early-morning return from Dallas, Tony was up and waiting for A.J. when he came out of his room for breakfast. Expecting the worst, A.J. said he was sorry and was surprised by his father's reaction.

"I guess you're gonna be a race driver," A.J. recalls his daddy saying. Tony went on, reflecting on his own career. "You gotta promise me one thing, always drive good equipment. If you're not gonna drive the best race cars in the best shape, then don't even bother."

From that point forward, at eleven years old, A.J. Foyt's destiny was closely tied to racing. He spent even more time in father's garage, pushing a broom, listening, and watching. A motorcycle replaced the go-kart and midget, and he started riding it around the shop.

In 1947, driving the B & F midgets, Burt emerged as one of the top drivers in the area. He was especially strong at the new Central Texas Speedway in Waco. The one-fifth-mile oval was attracting some of the area's top competitors, including Harry Ross, Cecil Green, Mel Wainwright, Jud Larson, and Buddy Rackley.

While the team's Ford engine was at a horsepower disadvantage compared to the Offenhauser engine only a handful of the competitors could afford, they had an ace in the hole. At the time most midgets were equipped with a hand brake mounted on the outside of the driver's cockpit. When Burt and Tony Foyt found a way to move the brake to a pedal inside the cockpit, similar to a passenger car, they decided to leave the brake handle mounted to the outside. Sometimes Burt would decoy the others into thinking he was braking his car, and the drivers would slow prematurely. At other times he wouldn't use the hand brake at all, watching as cars sailed past before the driver realized he was going too fast.

By Labor Day, Burt was among the favorites for a special 500-lap, 250-mile race at Storywood Park Speedway in San Antonio, a track where the team sometimes raced. With a field of thirty-three cars—just like the Indianapolis 500—it was the longest midget race in the country, with the biggest field and with the winner guaranteed $1,700, it was among the richest.

San Antonio temperatures average in the mid-nineties during September and the area was suffering through a record drought that year. Even with a 10 a.m. start, A.J. said, "It must have been one hundred ten degrees in the shade, and there was no shade." Not long after the start of the race drivers began pitting, not for fuel, but for water.

Burt was one of only a couple of drivers able to keep up in the early going with Cossey, the eventual winner. Stories vary on how and at what point in the race Burt lost control of his car. One has him pitting for water at lap sixty-four and losing control when he went to toss his cup away. A.J.'s more dramatic account has a fellow driver trying to toss a wet towel to Burt about halfway through the race. Unsure what was happening Burt ducked, jerking his steering wheel and losing control.

Regardless of when and how Burt lost control, his car broke through the wooden fence surrounding the track and went down an embankment, rolling several times. "Dale had come partway out of the car, and each time it rolled it crushed his legs under the driveshaft," Foyt said.

Burt's legs were badly broken, and he also suffered extensive internal injuries. He spent several months in the hospital and A.J. visited him often, even painting the driver's toenails.

For some starstruck boys, Burt's crash and serious injuries may have served as a wake-up call, an alarming lesson on how tough the sport was, causing them to rethink their dreams. Not Foyt. He'd already developed the "can't happen to me" attitude shared by so many racers.

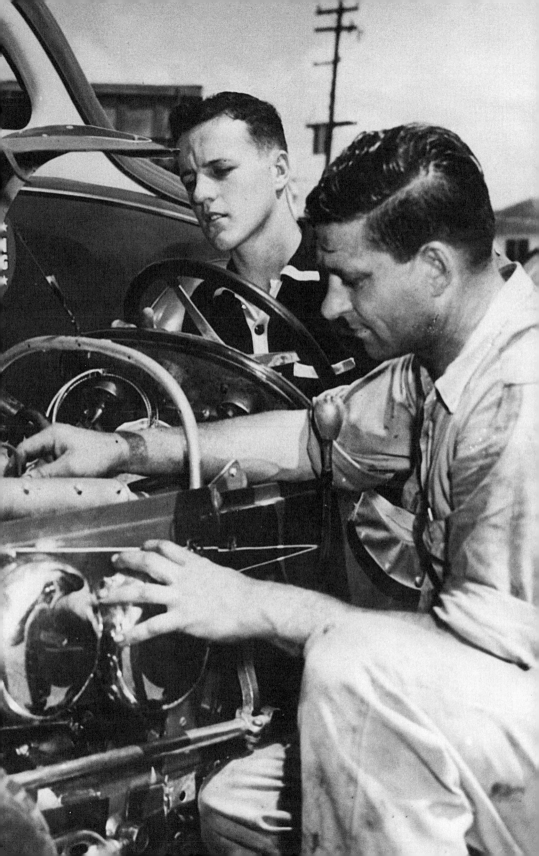

CHAPTER 4

BASIC TRAINING

1948–1952

By May 1948 Dale Burt was finally able to race again and was soon running among the leaders at Waco's Central Texas Speedway. By midsummer he was ready to test his skills at a higher level. It was now or never. His wife, Gwen, was talking about starting a family and he figured when that happened his driving days were numbered.

The Midwest Midget Auto Racing Association staged races almost nightly on warm summer evenings, with good purses attracting top competitors from around the country. Drivers earned one hundred dollars just for showing up and could make between $1,000 and $1,500 a week with a little luck. Burt held his own against many of the same drivers when they came to race in Houston during the winter; now it was time to challenge them on their home turf.

As he and Tony Foyt prepped their midget for the trip, they agreed Tony would stay back and run the business. They talked about the challenges Burt would face without any mechanical support, although Dale had someone in mind. He'd watched young A.J. around the shop and was impressed with his knowledge, skill, and willingness to learn. With the car loaded on a trailer and ready to go, Burt turned to his partner. Here's the way A.J. remembered the conversation.[1]

"Can he go Tony?" He cocked his head in my direction.
"Aw, he wouldn't want to go all the way up there, would you A.J.?"
I wasn't there to answer. I was on my way to pack.

It was A.J.'s first road trip, his first venture outside of Texas. Occasionally they'd sleep in the car, but mostly they and several of the other racers used the twenty-five-dollars-a-week Pine Lodge Motel in Decatur, Illinois, as a base of

◀ "What I didn't inherit, I learned." *Foyt Family Collection*

operations. A.J. says Burt treated him like a son and made him eat vegetables and drink milk.

It marked Foyt's first exposure to the traveling racing community he'd become part of. They moved from track to track like a nomad tribe wandering from water hole to water hole. They'd help each other repair their cars, then do everything possible to beat them in the next race. As much as the racing and competition, it was this relationship of closely tied drivers that A.J. enjoyed. Like Burt, many of the men were veterans, and the traveling group represented as close as they could come to the band of brothers' camaraderie they'd experienced during the war.

The constant kidding and banter reminded A.J. of evenings at the garage. The language was rough, but he'd heard it all before. There were practical jokes and before long he joined in, egged on by the men. Firecrackers were often at the center of the pranks and in one memorable moment, he endeared himself to the group.

"You could buy fireworks almost anywhere in those days," Foyt said. "I bought the biggest firecracker anybody had ever seen. The guys called it A.J.'s bomb. The man I bought it from said it was as powerful as a quarter stick of dynamite."

The time to use the bomb came when several of the race teams stopped at a gas station and Burt went to use the bathroom. A.J. had been waiting for just such a moment.

"I tossed it inside and it landed about five feet from where he was sitting. I can still see him getting up and trying to get to it before it exploded, but his pants were down around his ankles, and he fell flat on his face. He just covered his head with his arms. When it went off, it sounded like an atomic bomb."

Naturally there'd be the occasional on-the-track incidents and disagreements between drivers that at times were settled with their fists, combatants often emerging with a new respect for their rival.

"The drivers were good guys, and we became sort of a family," Foyt said. "What I liked most was that they didn't treat me like a kid. I was one of them. It was the basic training of a racer. It was maybe the best summer of my life."

Forty to sixty cars showed up most nights for a race, meaning many drivers didn't qualify for the main event, which typically started eighteen cars. Non-qualifiers collected their one hundred dollars and moved on to the next race. Burt proved himself competitive and at one point was driving for several different owners who offered to pay him to drive their cars. Records are sketchy, but on several occasions he was the fastest qualifier, setting at least one track record and winning a number of heat races. Yet it does not appear he ever broke through to capture a main event during the trip, something that wasn't lost on young Foyt.

"He had nearly everything it took to be a winner," A.J. said of Burt. "He was smart enough and brave enough, and he didn't mind being greasy and hot and tired and a little hungry most of the time. Those actually were the things it took to be a *racer*. What it took to be a winner was a hunger for the checkered flag that was stronger than anything else. *Anything*. And he didn't have that. It seemed to me that Daddy and Dale didn't care if they won or not."

DALE BURT

Burt began to dial back his racing in 1949, running only occasional local events. He and Gwen started their own family in 1950 with the birth of a daughter, Donna Dale Burt. When his wife soon became pregnant again and daughter Linda arrived, Burt decided it was time to find full-time employment other than driving a race car.

"My mother was convinced being a race car driver was not something she thought he should be doing," Donna Burt says. "The first sentence she tried to teach us girls was 'Daddy, please stop racing.' He cut back his schedule, although in 1951 he bought an insurance policy and still listed his occupation as race car driver. But he decided he needed an occupation that paid a little more regularly."[2]

While the B & F Garage was doing well, there wasn't enough business to support two full-time mechanics and Burt joined Sports Cars Incorporated, a company specializing in import cars, including Houston's first Jaguar dealership. It was run by "Big Jim" Hall, a former racer who often helped Houston-area drivers in need of work, eventually including A.J. (Big Jim is not to be confused with another Texas racer, Jim Hall of Chaparral fame.)

Tony moved the garage to 2212 Milford Street soon after, while retaining the B & F name. Burt would eventually strike out on his own, opening Dale Burt Automotive in 1956 at 2506 Bartlett Street, less than a mile away. They catered to different clientele, Burt earning a reputation as the best import car mechanic in the city.

Through it all, the families remained close. When the Burts moved in September 1951 to the Braeburn Terrace area of southwest Houston, a new neighborhood of about fifty homes, the Foyts soon followed, moving a block away, at 5902 Cypress Street.[3]

"It was a wonderful neighborhood," Donna Burt recalled. "Everybody knew everybody. Everybody's parents knew everybody's kids. We grew up in each other's pockets. I probably spent more time with Aunt Evelyn and Uncle Tony than at my own home."

The two families often had Sunday dinner together. The friendship between Tony Foyt and their father and the similarities of the two men was not lost on the Burt sisters.

"I never heard either of them say a bad thing about the other," Donna Burt said. "Uncle Tony was the same as my dad: smart, figure it out, work hard, get it done. Provide for your family, take care of your business, take care of your neighbors. Whatever either of them needed, the other was right there to help."

With two girls less than two years apart in age, Tony would join Dale for father/daughter events at school. Birthday parties were often held at the Foyt home. A.J. would get into the act, calling the girls on Christmas Eve and posing as Santa Claus.

"Linda and I never did recognize his voice," Donna says.

Burt continued to run the occasional race and picked up his last trophy in 1957. When A.J. started racing at Indianapolis he would attend whenever possible, and the entire family was there for Foyt's first victory at the Speedway in 1961. Burt became Houston's Goodyear racing tire distributor in the mid-1960s and kept both his shops open until the early 1990s, continuing to work on race cars throughout.

"Dale Burt has probably worked on as many Kurtis race cars as I have," said Frank Kurtis, the famous builder of midgets and sprint and Indy cars.

Though racing kept A.J. on the road more than he was at home, he would stop by Burt's shop when he was in town. Even after winning a couple of Indy 500s, he remained a primary target of Burt's needling. When Burt passed away in 2010, A.J. and son Tony served as honorary pallbearers.

Given the closeness of the two families and Foyt's obvious affection for the Burts, his assessment that "It seemed to me that Daddy and Dale didn't care if they won or not" might seem harsh. Yet when Donna Burt asked her father specifically about the quote, Dale Burt responded he'd been treated "fairly." More likely it was an indication of A.J.'s drive to be the best that would continue to separate him from other racers.

DROP OUT

Back at home following the road trip with Burt, Foyt returned to school, although there was no improvement in his studies. He attended Hamilton Middle School in the Heights and then Pershing after the family moved to Braeburn Terrace.

By state law, all Houston schools were strictly segregated. The landmark *Brown v. Board of Education* Supreme Court decision outlawing segregated public schools wasn't handed down until 1954, and even then Texas continued to fight the ruling.

Foyt bounced between Lamar and San Jacinto high schools. Both were considered among the better high schools in the Houston area, Walter Cronkite having graduated from San Jacinto a few years earlier. Both also taught courses in hard knocks and A.J.'s claims to being kicked out numerous times for fighting are probably not an exaggeration.

"I was in hundreds of fights while in high school," says his friend Bobby Waltrip.

A good athlete, strong and fleet of foot, A.J. played football early in high school before a knee injury ended his involvement. Not that it mattered. Foyt's real education started shortly after the last bell of the school day rang, when he arrived at his Daddy's garage. By 1950 not only was he learning to work on cars, he also started driving the shop truck to pick up parts and run other errands.

"By the time I was fifteen, there wasn't much I didn't know about building and tuning race cars," he said. "I was a mechanic the day I was born. What I didn't inherit, I learned."[4]

When he wasn't at the shop he was nearby, splitting time between a couple hamburger joints located within a block of each other on Houston's South Main Street—Stuart's Club Grill and Prince's Drive-In, which advertised its burgers as "Fit For a King." Both featured scantily clad car hops. In a scene repeated at drive-ins all over America in the early 1950s, teenagers would meet, hang out, and cruise from one to the other, showing off their cars. Eventually some of the guys would want to do more than show off their cars, and the nearby Old Spanish Trail Highway—or OST as it's known in Houston—provided the perfect location.

The OST was one of the first paved roads in Houston and part of the southern transcontinental highway stretching from coast to coast and completed in 1929. By 1950 it was largely supplanted in the Houston area by more modern roads, but it offered the perfect outlet for teenagers looking to race their cars. Veering off Main Street, it provided several miles of mostly straight, mostly flat, and lightly traveled highway. Foyt didn't have a driver's license or a car but says it didn't slow him down.

"I could outrun almost everybody at the drive-in," he said. "I learned that within the first week by driving other guys' cars. We ran top end, which meant it was a standing start, run wide open—which was over one hundred miles an hour—to a certain point and then shut down."

Foyt turned sixteen in early 1951 and got his license shortly thereafter, followed by his first car. He bought a Ford with the money he'd earned working at his Daddy's shop, bucking the trend among his friends who were buying Oldsmobiles. He rebuilt the car and not only claims it was the fastest of the group, but also the best looking, the result of "a hundred coats of hand-rubbed lacquer."

The police eventually caught on to the nightly OST outings and the group was forced to move a few miles further west to Stella Link Road, trying to stay ahead of the rapidly sprawling Houston landscape. The road would eventually become part of the Eisenhower Interstate Highway System, which required one mile in every five to be straight so it could be used as an airstrip in time of war. In peacetime it made for a perfect dragstrip.

When Marlene Foyt heard about her brother's racing prowess, she used it against him. She enjoyed dancing, a profession she would successfully pursue, and found an able—if reluctant—partner in A.J. They'd often practice her routines at the local Gateway Roller Rink, where A.J. sometimes played roller hockey.

"A.J. was a fabulous roller skater," Marlene says. "He would help me do my dance moves. I wouldn't trust anyone else. Every time I had a new trick, I'd make A.J. help me. He used to catch all the girls in the class."[5]

A good-looking kid with a great smile, he'd also show off for the other girls.

"He'd do cartwheels and push-ups on his fingertips. He'd stand on his head and walk on his hands."

Eventually the police caught on to the racing on Stella Link and A.J. was picked up by the police after trying to outrun them. The cops said they were going to call his father.

"I said just put me in a reformatory school. I didn't want to go home because I knew what was going to happen. I just knew he was going to beat the shit out of me. When I did something wrong, he tore my ass up.

"The cops said, 'Mr. Foyt, we think you've got a good boy' and made him promise not to beat me. Instead, he said I had to be at the shop every day for a year at three-thirty to work. On Christmas Eve I still had about a month to do and my grandma, my momma's mother, she said, 'Let him go out.' He said, 'I said one year.' And that was it."[6]

As a last resort, A.J. was enrolled in St. Thomas, an all-boys Catholic prep school where classes were taught by priests from the Basilian order. The school's motto was "Teaching Goodness, Discipline, and Knowledge," the emphasis on discipline when it came to A.J. He was in a fight the first day of classes, but rather than expel him—which would have been fine with him—they gave him detention.

"What little bit I learned in school, I learned there," Foyt says of his time at St. Thomas. "I still got in fights all the time, but the fathers would beat the shit out of me. Nowadays in school you can't do nothing like that. But I respected them for it. My damn music teacher, if you didn't listen, he had that music stick and he'd tell you to hold your hand out and he'd crack it, and I mean it wasn't an easy crack. It hurt. You didn't dare move it, cause if you did, you're gonna get another one."

At their new home the family fell into a routine. Chores were expected to be done properly and on time.

"As long as I can remember, we had chores to do," Marlene recalled. "My brother did the manly chores with my dad, and I did the female chores with my mom. A.J. and I had our friends but [our parents] were our best friends. Mother was very firm with what she wanted, but I never heard my mother and Daddy argue. If they had a disagreement, I never heard it. Family works for family. When you leave the shop and go home, you don't talk business. You don't carry the business home."

B & F GARAGE

Moving the garage turned out to be a smart and fortunate business decision. The new location was in the shadow of Rice Institute, the city's first center for higher learning and later known as Rice University. Nearby was Memorial Herman Hospital, soon to become the centerpiece of the Texas Medical Center (TMC). The center would grow to be the world's largest, covering more than two square miles and employing more than one hundred thousand people. More heart surgeries would be conducted at TMC than anywhere else in the world and it became home to the renowned MD Anderson Cancer Center.

The B & F Garage quickly built a reputation for quality workmanship and attracted many young professionals employed at the university and hospital. Among those was Dr. Michael DeBakey, who pioneered the mobile army surgical hospital (MASH) unit during World War II. He was the new head of surgery at the Baylor College of Medicine, which itself was relocating from Waco to become part of the TMC.

DeBakey brought along his young protégé, Denton Cooley, who enjoyed hearing the men in the garage talk about racing. Cooley later attended several Indy 500s with Tony and A.J. The doctors also became two of the world's most famous heart surgeons; DeBakey performed the first successful heart bypass and Cooley the first artificial human heart transplant. Both earned the Presidential Medal of Freedom for their work. In the early 1950s, however, they were just two young doctors looking for a good place to have their cars worked on.

The garage was in the center of Houston's auto racing community, near such tracks as Meyer, Belair, Arrowhead, and a relatively new one, Playland. At night the garage became a gathering place for local racers and visitors in town to compete at one of the tracks. It was a place to work on your car and talk racing. During these times A.J. saw a different side of his father, relaxed and bantering with the others. It was an atmosphere he enjoyed.

Among those drawn to the garage was James "Jimmy" Greer. Nine years older than A.J., he was closer in age to the son than the father, but his life experiences were closer to the elder Foyt. He'd joined the crew of an armed merchant marine ship at the start of the war when he seventeen and sailed around the world twice, spending most of his time in the "CBI," or China, Burma, India area of operations.

Back in Houston after the war, Greer worked odd jobs during the day while attending the University of Houston at night in pursuit of an engineering degree. For fun he raced boats, really nothing more than runabouts. You make a boat go faster just like you make a car go faster, with a better engine.

"Money was tight, and of course everything I had was used—engines, cylinder heads, everything," Greer said. "One thing you could do was port the cylinder heads, to modify the intake and exhaust to improve air flow. Back in those days porting the cylinder heads stripped the chrome away and you had to re-chrome them. That cost thirty bucks. Thirty bucks I didn't have. Then I heard about this guy who could do it without stripping the chrome away."[7]

Outboard engines also were popular with top midget drivers, including Cossey and Buddy Rackley. "This guy" turned out to be Tony Foyt, whose rapidly growing reputation was well-earned.

"He was just an excellent, excellent, mechanic. No bullshit about him. Helluva guy."

Greer played an interesting and increasingly important role between father and son. He had the maturity of Tony that came from his wartime experiences, but being closer in age to A.J., was more in touch with what was going on with teenagers. When he heard A.J. and some of his friends were sneaking into the nearby Arrowhead track and running laps at night he warned the boy against it but didn't tell Tony.

However, when Greer arrived at the shop one afternoon to see A.J.'s 1950 Ford with a flattened roof and heard a story about falling asleep at the wheel on Stella Link Highway and driving into a ditch, he'd heard enough.

"A.J. was a crazy kid," Greer said. "But there's no way you could turn a car over in a ditch on Stella Link, no way. I told him his daddy might not know Stella Link, but it was my backyard, and I knew there was no way to turn a car over there.

"He admitted he was racing backward on a closed racetrack [Arrowhead] with the lights on and two guys were racing forward. He said 'I lost it and turned it upside down. We rolled it back over and I got in it and drove it back to the shop.'"

That's when Greer confronted father and son. A.J. recalled it in his autobiography:

"Tony, you might as well let the kid race. He's doin' it on his own anyway and he's gonna get hurt," Jimmy said.

"Whattaya mean he's doin' it on his own?" Daddy asked.

"Well if you buy that 'Stella Link in the ditch' bullshit, you're not as smart as I think you are. Let him race where he'll learn it right."

I figured the best thing to do at this point was to keep quiet.

Daddy thought about it. For a long time.

"Okay, goddammit, A.J. I knew this day would come sooner or later. I'm gonna let you race, but you gotta stop racing on the street. I'll tell you right now, if I catch you racin' on the streets again, I'm gonna whip your butt. Right in front of your buddies."

He meant it. And he would have done it. So I never raced on the streets again. That is if you don't count rental cars.

Unable to get kicked out of school, A.J. finally decided to quit. Racing season was fast approaching, and he needed to work on his car. After all, his father had never graduated.

"I thought I knew more than they did," Foyt said of his decision to drop out. "When I started racing, I felt like I could learn a lot more racing than I could going to school."

It was one of the few decisions—perhaps the only one—Foyt would later admit to regretting.

Because he was underage, A.J. needed one last thing before he could race: his mother's signature alongside his father's on a release form. That was proving difficult to come by, and Tony Foyt eventually recruited Greer to help.

"The scariest thing I ever did was going with Tony to see Evelyn," Greer says. "I knew A.J. was a momma's boy and there was going to be hell to pay. There was a knife laying on the drain board in the kitchen and she drew back on Tony. He ran out the door and left my ass in there with that knife and that crazy woman. She had curse words I hadn't even heard."

Already upset over A.J. quitting school, Evelyn at first refused to sign the consent form. Greer says they eventually wore her down and she signed the release. Other accounts indicate Tony forged his wife's signature. Regardless, the tracks deemed A.J. eligible to race.

"I remember the first night like it was yesterday," Greer said. "Evelyn was at the back door crying about her baby going racing. She said she'd kill us if he got hurt. He had on white pants, a red silk shirt, and a red helmet."

Greer would graduate with an engineering degree and become one of Houston's leading businessmen, providing most of the windows for the gleaming skyscrapers that were about to sprout up all over the city. He also continued to play an important role in Foyt's life, serving as everything from a business advisor to a sponsor and entrant of A.J.'s race cars.

"Jimmy is a damn good man and the best angel A.J. ever had," says John Mecom Jr., another Houston business mogul and Foyt benefactor. "A.J. should probably give him more credit for what he did, from racing to everyday life."[8]

Next stop, Playland.

CHAPTER 5

PLAYLAND AND BEYOND

1952–1955

Playland was first and foremost an amusement park. Located at 9200 South Main Street in south Houston, it was just down the road from the burger joints, the Old Spanish Trail, and the B & F Garage. Its main feature was the Skyrocket, a wooden rollercoaster billed as the world's longest at a mile and a quarter when it was completed in 1924. Reaching heights of 110 feet, followed by drops of ninety feet, it had been moved to Playland from a park in the Heights area in 1941 and rebuilt by John Miller, the father of the modern rollercoaster.

Playland Speedway was added in 1948 to take advantage of the booming post-war Houston racing scene. The quarter-mile dirt track hosted races for several different types of cars, along with the ever-popular demolition derby and figure-eight events.

"The roller coaster was behind the track, and you could see the Ferris wheel," says Marlene Foyt, who often attended the races at Playland. "You knew everybody, all the drivers and the families. A couple of times I was the trophy girl. Everybody called [cheered] for this person or that person. It was just your typical little town racetrack."[1]

The first step on the local racing ladder was stock cars, or as most called them, jalopies. With a green light to start racing, A.J. Foyt bought a 1939 Ford coupe for one hundred dollars and went to work. He remembered being teased about the way his daddy's cars looked and vowed it wouldn't happen to him. By the time he was done it was one of the best-looking cars around.

"It ran like a million bucks and looked like two million," Foyt said of the finished product, which was part of the problem. While the gleaming black coupe with gold numbers—No. 1 of course—won the best-looking car award

◄ Foyt and Billy Wade (center, in helmet). *Revs Institute, The Bruce R. Craig Photograph Collection*

four weeks in a row, Foyt had nothing to show for his on-track action. He was reluctant to mix it up during a race for fear of damaging his car. Finally, his father stepped in. Tony was preoccupied fielding cars for Houston millionaire Ebb Rose but saw enough of A.J.'s racing to spot the problem.[2]

"If you wanted to build a show car, you should have built a show car and showed it down at the Coliseum," father told son. He suggested letting M.J. Burton drive the car. Burton was a tough, no-nonsense competitor, one of the area's top modified drivers and a regular winner at Playland. He no longer competed in the jalopy races but agreed to drive the Foyt car as a favor to Tony. A.J.'s car was battered by the end of the night, but Burton had won both his heat races and the main event.

"It taught me a good lesson," A.J. said. "If you're gonna build race cars, race them. From that day on, I always had good-looking race cars, but I also ran the ass off of them."

Despite Evelyn Foyt's resistance to her son driving, she seldom missed a race. She shared the superstitions of many racers, superstitions she passed on. And while proud of her son, she also worried about him.

"My mother was very superstitious," Marlene said. "She didn't like it if you were eating peanuts. And don't you dare wear green at a racetrack where A.J. was racing. She'd tell you to go change clothes. If you were wearing green, she was very frank to tell you, 'Do not call for my son and do not sit by me.'

"I don't think there was a race he was in that she didn't just sit on pins and needles worried that something would happen. She was so proud of her son, but she was worried too. She would admit she was scared."

One driver Foyt hoped to emulate was Cecil Green. Of all the drivers who worked their way up through the various series in Texas in the years immediately following World War II, none was more successful than Green. Four years younger than Tony Foyt, he'd developed a reputation before the war as a "wild and fearless" driver who liked to run the high side of the track next to the outside retaining wall, or "rim-ride" as it was sometimes called. He'd also developed a reputation for crashing.[3]

After serving in the army and seeing action in the South Pacific, Green seemed more under control when racing resumed. He won more than thirty midget feature events in 1948 along with the Southwest Championship, retaining the title in 1949 and 1950. He was spotted by Indy car owner John Zink, who agreed to sponsor him in the 1950 Indianapolis 500. After turning in the second-fastest qualifying time, he was running with the leaders when rain stopped the race at 345 miles, relegating him to a fourth-place finish. The following year he was leading the 500 when he dropped out after two hundred miles with a mechanical problem. If ever there was proof a local boy could make good, Green was it.

Two months later he was dead, his neck broken in a crash while trying to qualify for a sprint car race at the high-banked Funk Speedway in Winchester, Indiana. He apparently hit an oil slick and crashed through a short guardrail before tumbling down a twenty-five-foot embankment. A second driver, Bill Mackey, died minutes later from skull fractures in nearly the same manner. In what became known in the racing world as "Black Sunday," a third driver, Walter Brown, was killed about the same time while attempting to qualify for the Indy car race at Williams Grove Speedway in Pennsylvania. All three had driven in the Indianapolis 500.[4]

If the deaths of Green and the others had any impact on Foyt he gave no indication, and by mid-1952 he was winning races in his stock car, to the point he started eyeing the midget in his daddy's garage. Dale Burt was still driving the car on occasion and winning races in the "B" class for cars with the less powerful Ford engine. Before long A.J. was up to his old tricks, sneaking out and running laps at nearby Arrowhead Speedway in the midget, just as he'd done several years earlier with the Ford. This time it was Burt who realized what was going on and told Tony he was ready to step aside and let A.J. race their midget. When Tony said he didn't think his son was ready, A.J. exploded.[5]

"Well, to hell with it, I'll get my own ride."[6]

"Go ahead," Tony countered. "Get your own ride. Just make sure it's not a piece of junk. If junk's all you can find, you better stay with stock cars."

He didn't exactly ignore his father's advice, turning to Red Fondren, an owner whose midget wasn't junk but wasn't a winner either. Not yet having the experience and knowledge to make the improvements needed to the make the car faster, A.J. struggled and by the end of the year there were no real signs of improvement.

DEATH ON THE WATER

Just a few days before his eighteenth birthday in 1953, A.J. received another stark reminder of how short life can be.

One of his friends, Robert William (Billy) Luer, who lived around the corner from the B & F Garage and was a freshman at the University of Houston, had enlisted in the US Air Force. He was due to report on Friday, January 9, and with the weather unseasonably warm, A.J. and another friend, William (Billy) Long, decided to take Luer for one last boat ride on Galveston Bay, where the boys sometimes went fishing.[7,8]

It wasn't long after they took the twelve-foot fishing boat with a small outboard motor from the calm waters of Kemah Harbor into the bay that the weather began to change. The temperature dropped and the water picked up a chop, although at first it was nothing the boys couldn't handle. Foyt, who hadn't learned to swim, put on one of the three life jackets, more for warmth than anything else.

As the swells increased the boys decided to turn for home, but it was too late. Several waves washed over the boat, capsizing it and tossing all three into the water. Luer and Long swam to the boat and, after they were unable to right it, clung to the side. Foyt was caught in the waves and pulled away from the other two, kept afloat by the life jacket. The current carried him about a half mile before he spotted a light beacon and half bobbed, half dog-paddled to the buoy, where he grabbed on to the side.

A boat bringing offshore oil workers back from their shift eventually spotted Foyt and pulled him from the water. Numbed from the cold, he remembers crew members slapping his face. Foyt told them about his friends and the capsized boat was soon found, Long still holding on to its side. It was too late for Luer, however, who'd slipped away into the rough and cold water and drowned.

"If I hadn't put on that life jacket, I wouldn't be talking to you today," said Foyt, who eventually learned to swim. "I've had boats and raced boats, but I've respected the water ever since."[9]

GREER GETS AN ENGINE

When the 1953 racing season started, A.J. still couldn't win with the Fondren car, but he was getting more competitive. Others were taking notice, including Jimmy Greer, who went to Tony with an idea. First, he convinced his friend it was time to let A.J. drive the family midget. Then Greer said he knew where they could get an all-important Offenhauser engine.

Greer was aware Joyce Green, Cecil's widow, still had the Offenhauser-powered midget he'd been driving before he was killed. Greer figured the engine would cost about eight hundred dollars. His first step was to convince his wife to withdraw the four hundred dollars in their savings account and put it toward the engine. Tony and Dale Burt also contributed to the fund.

Convincing Joyce Green to sell was a little more challenging. She'd remarried to another race driver, who'd been killed in a crash shortly afterward. Now she was hesitant to sell the engine, not wanting to put another life at risk. It was only when Greer convinced her that A.J. was more at risk if he continued to drive Fondren's car that she relented.

A.J. went to work installing the Offy. The body of Tony's car was never going to be an award winner, but when the red and blue No. 2 midget rolled onto the track with A.J. behind the wheel it was fast. Very fast.

"I don't think there ever has been a happier time for me than when I was building that midget," A.J. said. "I knew what a big step it was—right in the direction of Indianapolis."[10]

He broke the track record at Playland Speedway the first time he ran the car, topping a mark set by 1950 Indy 500 winner Johnnie Parsons. The next night he won the trophy dash for the fastest qualifiers, his heat race, and semifinal, setting up a showdown in the feature with Buddy Rackley, who'd swept his preliminary events. With an inverted start, often used in short track racing to add excitement, he lined up next to Rackley in the last row. Rackley led early as the two worked their way through the field, A.J. never more than a half-car length behind.

"Buddy was the track champion, a good driver, and a good friend," Greer recalled. "Still, this was racing, and no quarter was being given. Protecting his lead, Rackley kept one wheel inside Foyt's, blocking him from moving forward. On the last lap A.J. stood on it, drove over the wheel, and beat him to the line by three or four feet. The crowd went crazy."[11]

Watching from the pits, Tony Foyt turned to Greer.

"I believe we have a race car driver," Tony said.

"No shit!" Greer said.

In what would become a semi-regular experience, A.J. said he nearly came to blows with Rackley afterward.

"Buddy said I chopped him off and I said he tried to drive me into the wall. You could usually count on a fight a week, but they were clean fights—no guns or knives or any of that bullshit."[12]

Along with his mechanical skills, Tony had taught A.J. never to back down. While growing up in the Heights, A.J. learned not to come home looking for sympathy after a fight as his father simply turned him around and sent him back into the fray. A.J. inherited his father's temper and stubbornness and it was this give-no-quarter, ask-no-quarter attitude that helped endear Foyt to fans wherever he went—and often alienated him from other drivers. And at the track, Tony was always there to back him up.

"One night in San Antonio, some guy came up and hit me while I was still strapped in the car," A.J. recalled. "I couldn't get to him, so Daddy beat the hell out of him."

LUCY

For all his toughness, early on A.J. displayed a sense of flair and style. He typically wore the red silk shirt and crisp white pants in the manner of Johnnie Parsons and Doc Cossey and the style popular on the West Coast. He added red golf gloves and considered them lucky. Some called him "fancy pants," but never to his face.

Foyt was incredibly warm and charming when he wanted to be. Handsome, even with a receding hairline at an early age, he had a rock-solid build at just under six foot and 185 pounds. A bright and natural smile came easily when things were going well.

One of those charmed was Lucy Ann Zarr, a student at Lamar High School that he'd been dating for a little more than a year. Lucy was three and a half years younger, having been born on September 24, 1938, to Luther and Elizabeth Zarr in Temple, Texas, about 275 miles northwest of Houston.

Luther Zarr, a doctor, moved the family to Houston shortly after Lucy's birth, where his father was co-owner of the small Heights Hospital. Initially the Zarrs lived within a couple of miles of both the hospital and the Foyts, although the families didn't know each other. It wasn't long before the Zarrs moved again, this time to a home on Del Monte Drive in the River Oaks area, well on its way to being one of the swankiest neighborhoods not only in Houston, but in the entire country. Their travel was sometimes reported in newspaper society pages.

It was just a short walk for Lucy to Lamar High School, called Houston's "society school" and considered on a par with the better college prep schools. Foyt had briefly attended Lamar before being thrown out for fighting and transferring to St. Thomas. While they never attended high school at the same time, a friend who knew them both thought they'd be a good match. A.J. believes it was one of his old girlfriends who tried to set them up; Lucy says it was one of her friends. One thing for certain, it didn't happen immediately, and it didn't go smoothly.[13]

"I was supposed to go out with her, but I was working on my race car, and I put her off two or three times," Foyt said.[14]

Lucy, a stunning blonde, wasn't used to being stood up or put off.

"We didn't take to each other for a while. He wasn't my favorite person at the time. I think he broke a date, so then I broke a date. Neither of us was sure if we even wanted to go out. But there must have been something there. We finally got together and pretty much stayed together ever since."

It wasn't long after Lucy and A.J. started dating that her father died after suffering a heart attack in June 1954. He was just forty-three. He'd been diagnosed with heart disease and suffered several heart attacks prior to his death yet had ignored doctors' recommendations to give up strenuous activities. His reasoning left a lasting impression on Lucy and went a long way toward shaping her views on A.J. and life in general.

"His favorite thing to do was deep-sea fishing," she said. "After his heart attacks his doctor told him he shouldn't go out anymore, that it was too dangerous. I asked him why he kept doing it. He said, 'If I die doing that, I die happy.' So that's the way I always looked at it. That's the way I would look at it with A.J. If he died during a race, he died doing what he wanted to do. That would be my outlook."[15]

Before long Lucy was attending races at Playland. She'd ride with Tony and Evelyn to events as far away as San Antonio and Corpus Christi, an indication the relationship was more serious than his previous girlfriends.

"I didn't know anything about auto racing," Lucy said. "I'd never even *heard* of auto racing. It wasn't part of my family's life. I knew he was interested in it and his father had race cars. I knew he was working his way up. But that's when I first started learning about racing."

Just about a year after their first date the couple decided to get married, only they'd have to do it secretly. Lucy wanted to graduate from high school and knew she could be suspended for being married if anybody found out. Not sure how their parents would react, they decided to live apart until they were ready to tell people.

"She wasn't wild about racing, and it was life itself to me," Foyt said. "We fought like cats and dogs. We didn't have a thing in common. So we did the only sensible thing. We got married."[16]

First things first, Foyt went to Indianapolis to see the 500 for the first time. He was sitting in the second-turn grandstands with friends when Bill Vukovich, who'd won the race in 1953 and '54, was involved in an accident, his car flipping over the wall and bursting into flames. Vukovich was killed instantly.

There was no discussion of Vukovich's death when he returned to Houston, only the Speedway. A.J. and Lucy were married little more than a week later, on Wednesday, June 8, 1955, by the justice of the peace in Richmond, Texas, a small town about thirty-five miles from Houston, where they figured no one would find out. She was three months short of turning seventeen and he was twenty. Legend has it he raced that night and knocked two other cars on their roof, although there are no records of an event and Foyt says he doesn't remember it.[17]

He does remember, "It cost me ten bucks for a marriage license, ten bucks I didn't have. We'd always say happy anniversary, but we never really celebrated it."

Secrets like that are hard to keep and it wasn't long before A.J.'s sister Marlene heard other girls whispering about the marriage. Evelyn heard the same rumors and began grilling Lucy at the races. Marie Foyt remembers sitting with the group one night at Playland.

"A.J.'s, momma kept saying, 'Lucy, are you and A.J. married?' Lucy kept saying, 'No, I told you we weren't married.'" When the rumors continued, Lucy realized the first person she'd better tell was her mother.[18]

"My mom kind of had a clue," Lucy recalled. "She wasn't happy about it. At the time my mom didn't think too much of him. I was young and he was young, and she wasn't really in favor of that situation. But she eventually consented and came to really love him."

"Finally, she told her momma we got married," A.J. says. "Then her momma came over to tell my momma and the shit hit the fan."

It doesn't seem to have been nearly as bad as Foyt implies, and when the dust settled the couple moved into a small apartment. Within a month Lucy was pregnant.

RACING ON THE BRINK

Three days after A.J. and Lucy secretly married, the auto racing world was rocked by the deadliest day in the sport's history. Eighty-three spectators and a driver were killed in France during the running of the 24 Hours of Le Mans when a car traveling at racing speeds sliced into a crowded grandstand along the main straightaway.

This came on the heels of the deaths of two of the sport's biggest names, Vukovich at Indianapolis and two-time Formula One champion Alberto Ascari, who was killed testing a Ferrari at Monza.

France, Germany, Spain, and Switzerland ordered an immediate pause to all racing. Although there were no cancellations in the United States, the danger of auto racing hit the front pages again when Indianapolis pole winner Jerry Hoyt was killed in an Oklahoma City sprint car race on July 11. The next day Senator Richard Neuberger called on his colleagues to ban the sport.

"I think the time has come to forbid automobile racing and similar carnages in the United States," said the Oregon Democrat. "I doubt if there is as much bloodshed in Spanish bullrings as there is today occurring on automobile racetracks in this country. I believe the time has come for the United States to be a civilized nation and stop carnage on racetracks. The deaths on our highways are sad and tragic, but at least they are not purposely staged for profit and for the delight of thousands of screeching spectators."[19]

Although Congress took no action, pressure on the American Automobile Association, racing's governing body in the country since the turn of the century, became so intense it announced it would wash its hands of the role at the end of the year and "disassociate itself completely from all types of automobile racing in the United States."

Foyt said he didn't remember the political turmoil around racing in mid-1955. After finding success at Playland, he'd begun fighting his way to the top of one of the toughest circuits in the country while making the rounds of tracks in Texas, Oklahoma, and Louisiana.

He also added a new car to his stable, a modified 1932 Ford, as stock cars, jalopies, and modified racers began to challenge midgets in popularity. Sponsors were more interested in the larger cars and not only did Foyt talk L.S. Garner, owner of Garner Truck Lines, into sponsoring his car, he also went to work at his company. He painted the car bright yellow, with the No. 2 styled after a two-dollar bill. As always, A.J. took a special interest in the appearance of his car and insisted on racing with a hood and grille in place, even though both were often quickly damaged in a race and most teams elected not to use them.[20]

He started running against tougher competition and occasionally for different car owners. The Oklahoma Fairgrounds often attracted top talent, and he raced his midget there against Parsons and future Indy 500 competitors George Amick, Rodger Ward, Lloyd Ruby, and Johnny Boyd, with Amick winning while Foyt spun early. He raced his stock car there against Jim Rathman and Marshall Teague, who would go on to win the national championship that year in his Hudson Hornet. He even tried drag racing, topping one hundred miles per hour and posting one of the top three times in a Fourth of July meet.

In an August midget race at Corpus Christi Speedway won by Rackley, it was Cecil Elliott who made a lasting impression on Foyt. Elliott flipped his car in a heat race and was trapped underneath and briefly knocked out. Pulled from his car and revived, Elliott helped roll it back over and ran the feature to the cheers of the crowd. He didn't win, but the effort and fan response did not go unnoticed by Foyt.[21]

Things didn't always go smoothly. At a race in San Antonio, Tony ordered their midget put on the trailer, saying A.J. was driving recklessly and going to kill himself. A.J. went to drive for another car owner, winning the feature event. That didn't make the ride home any easier.

"I told Daddy—I was cocky—'See I won the race anyway,'" A.J. recalled. "He said, 'Boy, shut your damn mouth before I slap the shit out of you.'"[22]

UNCLE SAM WANTS YOU!

Like all American males reaching the age of seventeen and a half, A.J. had registered for the draft in 1952. The induction age was eighteen and a half, and at the time several of Foyt's future competitors who were a few years older were already serving in Korea, including Dan Gurney and Lloyd Ruby. Foyt caught a break when two weeks after he became eligible for induction the Korean War Armistice was signed on July 27, 1953, and the military began a rapid drawdown.

A little more than two years after the end of the Korean War, however, a new so-called Cold War was starting to heat up, and an induction notice to report for a physical arrived in the Foyt mailbox. A.J. wasn't home—he was off racing and didn't have enough money to make a special trip home for his appointed physical. He asked Lucy to visit the induction board and plead his case.

Although the paternity draft deferment for married men had recently been lifted, it didn't hurt to have the young, pretty, and obviously pregnant Lucy visit the board office. Officials agreed to give her husband an extension, not an uncommon occurrence. About six months later he received another notice that he was no longer up for induction and did not have to report. By the early 1960s, as America became more involved in Vietnam and the draft ramped up again, Foyt had just moved beyond the induction cutoff age of twenty-six.

At the end of the 1955 racing season Foyt was on a tear, winning the last five modified races of the year at Playland, often battling with Billy Wade who drove a car built by Tony Foyt. A.J. already had bigger things in mind and started working on a plan with a new goal in mind: Indianapolis.

————

Racing continued at Playland Speedway through the 1950s and the track was eventually paved. Foyt made occasional appearances, typically to present a trophy to a race winner or track champion. That ended in 1959 when three people, including Playland co-owner Sam Slusky, were killed when a car crashed through a guardrail. The track closed soon afterward. By the early 1960s the Skyrocket was no longer functional. The Astrodome opened nearby in 1965, and by 1968 Playland had been replaced by AstroWorld, another amusement park.

CHAPTER 6

FAIRGROUNDS

1956–1957

Despite his growing success on the racetrack, money continued to be an issue for A.J. and Lucy Foyt, and with a baby on the way he took a job as a mechanic at Sports Cars International, the same group of import car dealerships and repair shops Dale Burt worked for. The newlyweds rented a small apartment off Westheimer Road in Houston and learned to ignore the trains that rumbled regularly along the tracks just across the street.[1]

The couple's first child, Anthony Joseph Foyt III, arrived on March 7, 1956, and they decided to call him "Tony" after his grandfather. The couple were determined to make it on their own and turned down offers of assistance from Lucy's mother, who had started dating a prominent Houston lawyer.

"She was wealthy when she married A.J.," Marlene Foyt said of Lucy. "She gave up everything. I saw the girl who was very wealthy save for a whole year just to buy a dress. All she had to do was ask her mother, but she never did."[2]

There was one exception. With the racing season approaching, A.J. needed a new race car and Elizabeth Zarr agreed to co-sign a bank note toward the purchase of a midget.

"I'll never forget, it was Citizen's State Bank and the man's name was Mr. Thomas," Foyt said. "I needed fifteen hundred dollars to buy this midget. My mother-in-law signed the note, which she guaranteed for me to pay back."[3]

"I paid it all off," he said of the loan. "But I'd tease her that was the most expensive signature I ever made. She was nearly ninety-four when she died, and I was still doing things for her, which I was glad I was able to do. But I'd always tell her that was a very expensive signature."

◀ Ready for the fairgrounds. *Revs Institute, The Bruce R. Craig Photograph Collection, photograph by Dave Knox*

The 1956 season got off to a good start, with Foyt setting another track record at Playland and taking an early lead for the track championship. By May he was ready to make a bold move, setting his sights on Indianapolis and hauling his new race car behind him. His target wasn't the Indianapolis 500, but the "Night Before the 500," a midget race held at the West Sixteenth Street Speedway, a quarter-mile paved oval across the street from the big track. Even that modest goal could be considered brash for the twenty-one-year-old driver looking for his first feature victory on a national stage.

The "Night Before" was a full day of racing with three feature events, one each in the afternoon, evening, and late night, each feature supported by qualifying and heat races. The event always attracted a large field of competitors, many like Foyt hoping to get noticed. He failed to qualify for the first two features and was working on his car prior to the third series of preliminaries when he was spotted by several drivers competing in the 500 the next day. Among the drivers was Jimmy Reece, who'd been to the B & F Garage in Houston several times. An accomplished midget, stock, and Indy car driver, Reece was making his third start in the 500. He stopped and asked Tony Foyt's kid what he was doing.

"I told him I was jacking around a little weight," A.J. said, a common move to adjust the pressure on the wheels and tires in an attempt to improve a car's handling. Reece shook his head no.[4]

"The only place you need to jack some weight is up front on the right," he said. Now it was Foyt's turn to wonder aloud what Reece was talking about.

"The throttle foot," Reece said. "Put a little more weight there." It was a lesson Foyt says he'd never forget. For years to come, when asked what made A.J. Foyt a great race car driver, he pointed at his right foot.

He qualified sixth for the final feature event—more the result of attrition among the other cars than the increased speed of his. He finished fourth in his heat race and sixteenth in the finale, earning sixty-eight dollars for the day's work. Shorty Templeman, who'd failed to qualify for the big 500, won all three features. The next morning Foyt tried to enter the Speedway's famous Gasoline Alley where the teams worked on their cars, telling the guard he'd driven the night before across the street.

"Come back when you've got a ride here instead of across the street," the guard laughed.

"That might be a lot sooner than you think," Foyt shot back, heading for Turn One and a seat in the grandstands.

Although the Speedway's front straightaway remained paved in bricks, much of the track had been resurfaced prior to the 1956 race, resulting in record speeds in practice and qualifying. In the race, however, the combination of higher speeds and a tire manufacturing problem led to a record eleven yellow flag periods. Foyt's Turn-One seat provided a good vantage point for many of the incidents, beginning when the leading Novi of Paul Russo blew a tire and spun into the wall on lap twenty-one.

"It sounded like a cannon," Foyt said. "I thought the car was coming right into my lap."[5]

A few laps later five cars tangled in front of him. Then Jimmy Daywalt blew a tire and slammed the Turn Two wall, and Foyt watched as the unconscious driver was pulled from the car.

Pat Flaherty, wearing a dirty T-shirt with the sleeves cut off, drove to victory. Second-place finisher Sam Hanks, who'd promised his wife he'd retire after the race, changed his mind after coming so close to winning. Reese finished ninth. Daywalt would recover from his broken bones and burns, but Foyt left the Speedway wondering if a return to Indianapolis was in his future.

"I didn't know if I wanted to do this crap," Foyt thought as he headed back for Texas. "I was used to running local short tracks. I said this is a little too rough for old A.J. Foyt."

The doubts didn't last long. When Foyt returned from Indianapolis, he was a force to reckon with on the Texas tracks. In late June he won a big event at Pan America Speedway in San Antonio, beating the local favorites and a field that included top regional drivers Buddy Rackley and Harry Ross, a feat he repeated on July 21. Before long he was thinking about the next level of competition and itching to try his hand in a sprint car. He also wanted to test his skills on the traveling circuit, just as Dale Burt had done nearly ten years earlier.

Ross was another Houston-area driver having a good summer. Sometimes Foyt won and sometimes Ross won, as he did in a Fourth of July weekend race at Corpus Christi Speedway. He was a few years older than Foyt and also looking to try something bigger and better when he landed a sprint car ride on the so-called "Fairground Circuit." Not only that, he also had a backup car and offered it to Foyt. Burt urged him to make the trip, and A.J. jumped at the chance.

A sprint car was a big step up from the midgets Foyt and Ross were used to driving. Although similar in appearance, sprint cars were bigger and more powerful and just a notch below the "big cars" or "champ cars" running at Indianapolis.

While Ross was driving an Offenhauser-powered car, Foyt's came with an old GMC truck engine. It was sometimes called a "Jimmy," the nickname soldiers in World War II gave "G-M" products. It was "not much better than something you'd find on the street," Foyt said.[6]

The Fairground Circuit was a series of races held to help sell tickets to the state, regional, and local fairs staged across the country each summer. Sprint cars, midgets, stock cars, and motorcycles often shared the limelight, each group featured on a different night during fair week.

The largest state fairs—including those in Indiana, Illinois, and New York—were aligned with the United States Auto Club (USAC)—which had replaced the AAA as the organization overseeing the Indianapolis 500—and featured many of the country's well-known drivers. Races at the smaller fairs—like those in the Dakotas, Kansas, Iowa, and Oklahoma—were managed by the International Motor Contest Association (IMCA) and featured a group of traveling racers taking on local competitors. It was the IMCA series that Ross and Foyt entered.

The smaller fairground tracks usually featured the only grandstand on the grounds and were typically multi-purpose, used for horse and car races, animal competitions, and band concerts—just about anything that involved seating for a crowd. There was often little or no track preparation. The track might be muddy after one of the Midwestern thunderstorms that sometimes kicked up in late summer afternoons, but more often than not it was dry, the cars churning up huge dust clouds. Races were kept short in an effort to hold the dust down, even feature events typically being ten miles or less.

Following his first airplane trip, an exhausting and scary ride of more than eight hours in a four-seat, single-engine Cessna 182, Foyt and Ross arrived at Nodak Speedway, a half-mile dirt track at the North Dakota Fairgrounds in Minot, for a race on August 4, 1956. After a practice session indicated the Jimmy would be uncompetitive, A.J. went looking for a better ride. He talked Ennis "Dizz" Wilson, one of the top sprint car owners on the circuit, into letting him test one of the cars. Although Foyt was fast, Wilson said he was reckless and wouldn't allow him to drive the car in the race.

"They didn't think I'd live to be twenty-two," Foyt recalled.

More impressed was Les Vaughn, who ran a moving van and storage business based in Omaha. He also owned an auto repair shop and had a stable of eight race cars. He was familiar with Foyt, his company's tow trucks having provided wrecker services at tracks throughout the Southwest, including Playland. But the young driver's performance in a sprint car was something new. Although Vaughn already had a driver for Minot, he offered Foyt an opportunity to drive at the end of the month, when the series moved to the Minnesota State Fairgrounds in St. Paul.

In between were stops for Ross and Foyt in Oskaloosa and Denison, Iowa, and Springfield and Sedalia, Missouri. Nights were sometimes spent sleeping in or under a car. When the teams and drivers finally arrived in St. Paul, Foyt had done little to distinguish himself while driving the Jimmy.

One of IMCA's showcase events was the Minnesota State Fair, having attracted more than a million visitors in 1955. A race was scheduled for each day of the fair with the sprint cars—or "speedway-type cars" as the *Minneapolis Star* called them—where they were the main attraction.[7]

A record fifty-four cars were entered, and to help create excitement a special qualifying day was held on Friday before the fair opened. Only the thirty-two quickest cars would advance for the week of racing, the fastest qualifier earning the pole position for all subsequent events.

Nowhere in the *Star's* preview article was Foyt's name mentioned. He was a novelty, a Texan who at twenty-one was the youngest driver entered and drove Vaughn's trademark pink-and-black car. When he turned in the fastest time early in qualifying the fans politely applauded. They watched as driver after driver attempted to better Foyt's mark without success. Then it was time for Tommy Smith, the local favorite, winner of the previous year's event, and the defending state champion.

He hadn't completed a lap when the steering arm on the car snapped, sending it into a series of rolls and Smith to the hospital in critical condition. He'd eventually recover and race again, but any thoughts of a career as a driver on a higher level ended that day. Foyt was on the pole.[8]

After qualifying, Foyt and Ross made a five-hour trip to Red River Speedway in West Fargo, North Dakota, for a Saturday race, one of the smaller events on the IMCA schedule. He was back in the Jimmy, but it didn't matter, as he surprised the other drivers and spectators by capturing his first sprint car victory. Jack Jordan, who'd been on a hot streak, winning two of the three previous IMCA events, finished second, with Ross relegated to fourth.

Back in St. Paul for the Sunday afternoon kickoff to the week of racing, Foyt came down to earth. He may have been the fastest qualifier, but series regulars Bill Chennault and Leland "Bud" Randall were the class of the field. Both soon passed Foyt, who was out of the race by the halfway mark in the twenty-lap, ten-mile feature with a faulty magneto.

Dirt tracks typically feature three types of drivers. Railbirds are those hugging the inside of the track where the surface often becomes slick and hard, almost like pavement. Then there are the rim riders who like to run on the "cushion" of dirt that builds on the outside of the track.

Finally, there are those who would run high along the outside of the track on the straightaway, dive low into a turn, and slide to the high side of the track again on exit, destined to repeat the move—or try to—turn after turn, lap after lap. Dubbed a "slide job," the move was the most dramatic and often brought the crowd to its feet. It was also the most disconcerting to those drivers running high or low on the track.

Foyt would become a master of all three, but at the Minnesota Fairgrounds he ran high down the straight before diving into the turns. The fans loved it; the other drivers did not. In the series opener he raced briefly with Jordan before dropping out. Afterward Jordan approached him in the pits, warning him not to "chop" him in the corners again.

In the second race of the week Chennault and Randall again passed Foyt at the start, Randall going on to victory. Foyt found himself matched once more with Jordan. Sometimes a driver/car combination is evenly matched with another driver/car. They find each other on the track, and that was the case for Jordan and Foyt in Minnesota.

Each time Jordan closed in on the bottom of the track A.J. would dive into the turn, and each time Jordan backed off. Foyt eventually finished third and Jordan fourth. Afterward Jordan, who was thirteen years Foyt's senior, went after the younger driver. A.J. recalled the confrontation in his autobiography.[9]

"If you chop me off again, punk, I'll put you right into the fence," Jordan said.

"You drove under me," Foyt said, "I don't know how you can figure I chopped you."

Foyt says he walked away at that point. He had considered Jordan a friend, but things were changing. He was now beating Jordan consistently on the racetrack. The more he thought about being called a punk, the madder he got. He sent Lucy back to the motel with Vaughn and returned to confront Jordan, who Foyt said was backed by four crewmen. From the autobiography:

"I walked up and put my nose about two inches from Jack's and I said, 'What did you call me.'"

"Listen, punk," Jordan repeated, "I meant just what I said, and if you got any swingin' to do, you better get started."

Foyt says he punched Jordan in the mouth, and the battle was on.

"One of his crew grabbed me and I decked him. Another got me from behind and held my arms and Jack hit me so hard that blood ran down into my eye. But I got loose and I beat the hell out of Jack and two of his crew members. The others quit."

"I can't have people thinkin' I'm a punk, can I?"

There is every reason to believe Foyt and Jordan tangled. Did Foyt best all five by himself? Who knows. There were no reports of trouble in any of the Minneapolis and St. Paul newspapers covering the event. Jordan would load up his car and leave soon afterward, electing to skip the Sunday finale in Minnesota for a smaller event in Kansas. He wasn't the only one making the haul to the Belleville High Banks as several other drivers, including Ross, figured Chennault and Randall had the field covered and also left.

Maybe Foyt should have joined them. He suffered transmission problems early in practice and Vaughn's car couldn't be repaired in time for the feature. As they had all week, Chennault and Randall battled early before a record crowd of more than thirty-two thousand, but this time California driver Johnnie Pouelsen snuck by for the victory.

"Pouelsen Wins Feature, Foyt Blanked," read the headline in the *Minneapolis Star*. While the article noted Foyt "didn't win a nickel," it pointed out that his youth, aggressiveness, and pink car clearly made him "the crowd favorite."[10]

The next race on Foyt's IMCA schedule was slated for September 18 at the fairgrounds in Hutchinson, Kansas. Included in the field was Pouelsen, who was riding a hot streak, Lloyd Ruby, and Don Hutchinson.

Hutchinson, twenty-four, was "one of the most promising young drivers licensed by IMCA." He'd been a successful motorcycle racer before joining the series in 1955, earning rookie of the year honors. He was fourth in the national point standings and coming off two victories where he bested the likes of Randall, Chennault, and Pouelsen.

Foyt and Hutchinson were both in an early heat race. Hutchinson was leading and on the outside with Foyt moving under him in every turn but unable to complete the pass. On lap six the cars touched, Hutchinson's darting to the right and breaking through a wire fence designed to keep horses on the track, not race cars. The car rolled over several times, coming to rest upside down with Hutchinson unconscious and pinned underneath. Foyt was dazed after being thrown clear of his car.[11]

With only a single ambulance at the track, both drivers were loaded in the back for the trip to the hospital. "I remember them saying 'This guy is gone' and hoping they weren't talking about me," Foyt recalled.[12]

Hutchinson was pronounced dead of head injuries shortly after they arrived at the hospital. Foyt stayed overnight for observation but was released the next day with what was described as "minor head injuries." He was back in action the following week, this time at the Oklahoma State Fair. Running against a second-tier group of drivers he won his heat race before coming home fourth in the feature.[13]

CROSSROADS

Even with the occasional good finish, money was tight. A.J., Lucy, and Tony continued to travel together, towing the midget behind their station wagon, with A.J. landing occasional sprint car rides.

"It was hard at first, but everybody's life is hard," Lucy recalled. "Nobody comes out a winner in the beginning. A.J. was working on the cars himself. He was doing okay, winning some races. It wasn't tremendous amounts, but he was winning enough for us to get by."[14]

It was at a midget race in Michigan that A.J. and Lucy reached a crossroads and decided on a course of action that would guide them for the rest of their lives. They were staying in a cheap motel and with weather bad, A.J. went to the track while Lucy stayed in the room with the baby.

"I had a Peeping Tom or somebody who started banging on my door," Lucy said. "I called the manager, and he called the police. They wouldn't let me stay there any longer, so the police drove me out to the racetrack, which scared A.J. to death. He'd thought I'd gone out in the car and had a wreck or something."

Adding to their problems, Foyt failed to qualify for the race. With only enough money for gas and a little food for the baby, they decided to drive nonstop back to Houston. Along the way they discussed their future and their desire for more children and reached a decision. Traveling the racing circuit was difficult under the best of circumstances. Traveling with a young child was nearly impossible. Lucy would stay in Houston and raise their children while A.J. went racing.

"That was a bad time, but we survived," Lucy said. "The baby survived. But that's when we decided traveling wasn't so much for me, it was just too hard to travel with babies. At that time drivers didn't have fancy motor homes. You made up a bed in the backseat of the car. It was a long drive home to Houston, but it was worth it."

One topic that wasn't discussed was whether A.J. would continue racing.

"I never questioned his future in racing. I never did. I knew that's what he wanted to do. There were times when I thought about it, but I never brought it up."

Thus, it was A.J. who departed alone in early 1957 for Florida and a new series of midget races USAC was staging called the Tangerine Tournament. Comprised of eleven races over a one-month period with guaranteed purses of two thousand dollars, the tournament attracted the nation's top midget drivers, including 1956 national champion Shorty Templeman, Don Branson, Andy Linden, and Rex Easton. Sonny McDaniel led a contingent of Texas drivers, including Ruby and Foyt, who sometimes roomed together on the road.

"We spent many nights sleeping in our cars or motels, living on what we earned the night before," Ruby said. "If I needed a few dollars to get by, Foyt would help me. If I was going good and he needed help, I'd help him. We got to know each other pretty well during [that time] in Florida."[15]

The series was a major success for USAC, with a large number of cars entered for most of the races and good crowds turning out. The same couldn't be said of Foyt, who qualified for less than half the races. He won an occasional pre-liminary or heat race but lacked consistency. Ruby finished sixth in the final point standings and McDaniel won one of the feature events to lead the Texas drivers, as Linden won the overall title. Foyt failed to crack the top fifteen in the final point standings, and when the tournament ended he found himself without enough money to get back to Houston. He telephoned home and his mom raided the piggy bank she kept for her weekly penny-ante poker games.

"I just didn't make no races," Foyt said. "I was out of money. My mother rolled twenty-two dollars' worth of pennies, took it to Western Union, and sent it to me so I could buy enough gas to get home."

In Houston, Foyt went back to work, making only an occasional race start. One of the few races he did make was a midget event at Phoenix. He never challenged for the lead, finished tenth overall, and was stunned along with everyone else when Jordan, the driver he'd tangled with the year before, spun wildly into the wooden fence and launched into a series of flips, taking out more than one hundred feet of planking. He suffered a fractured skull and never regained consciousness as he hung on for two days before succumbing to his injuries.[16]

It wasn't until May that Foyt caught a break. Branson had been driving a midget for Elbert Willey and enjoying a fair amount of success, including second place overall in the Tangerine Tournament. He hadn't won yet, but his perfor-mance earned him a shot at the Indianapolis 500. With Branson taking his rookie test at the Speedway and a race coming up, Willey offered the car to Foyt. Built by Frank Kurtis, one of the best in the business, it was called a "roadster midget" because it featured an offset engine like most of the cars running at Indianapolis.

Ruby landed an even sweeter deal. Templeman was also busy at Indianapolis and the car he'd driven to the title the previous year—the same one he'd used to sweep the "Night Before the 500" races—was available.

The first stop for the two Texans was a place both were familiar with, Taft Stadium in Oklahoma City. The Stadium typically hosted high school football games and track meets, along with an occasional auto race. Racing on a Tuesday night, Ruby passed Easton on the last lap of the one-hundred-lap feature to win by a few feet for his first major USAC victory. Foyt finished fourth, although the local newspaper referred to him as "A.J. Floyd."[17]

Five days later they were in Kansas City at Olympic Stadium, another quarter-mile dirt track, where it was Foyt's turn to score a breakthrough. He took advan-tage of several breaks, including prerace favorite Johnnie Parsons arriving too late to qualify. After winning two of the preliminary races, Foyt spent the first eighty-six laps of the one hundred lap feature chasing Easton until the differential broke in the other driver's car. A.J. then held off Ruby, who'd been the fastest qualifier, for the victory.[18]

From Kansas City Foyt went to Indianapolis, where he was again relegated to watching the 500 from a seat in Turn One. Hanks, who'd returned to the Speedway against his wife's wishes, emerged victorious, driving a new type of "laydown" car. Run at record speed, it was a relatively safe and uneventful race. Afterward Hanks announced his retirement.

"That's it, I'm all done," he said in Victory Lane. "The next time I see this track, it will be from the grandstand. I've had it."[19]

None of the two hundred thousand people at the Speedway realized Hanks's retirement set in motion a game of musical chairs that would elevate Foyt to the ranks of Indy 500 starters faster than he could have dreamed.

THE HILLS

Two weeks later Foyt was back in Vaughn's sprint car for the start of the IMCA racing season. After two years of an uneasy truce between the IMCA and USAC sanctioning bodies, open warfare broke out shortly after the 500. Salem Speedway and several other high-banked, half-mile Midwest tracks were at the center of the battle, and money was at the root of the argument. USAC car owners and drivers were demanding larger purses from the tracks that included Salem, Winchester, and Fort Wayne in Indiana, along with Dayton Speedway in Ohio. Combined, the high-banked tracks were known as the Hills.

When Salem's owners said prior to its June race they couldn't meet USAC's financial demands, the organization countered by saying it couldn't guarantee how many cars would enter the event. The track then broke with USAC and signed with IMCA to stage the race, the first time IMCA would run at Salem since 1954. USAC responded by scheduling a sprint car race the same day in Terre Haute.

That's how Foyt found himself about one hundred miles south of Indianapolis on June 16 in the infield of Salem Speedway. The thirty-three-degree, high-banked, paved track was unlike anything he'd driven before. Most of the tracks he'd raced on were dirt and came with little or no banking. Even the turns at the Indianapolis Motor Speedway had just nine degrees of banking.

The Salem banking made it one of the most daunting and physically demanding short tracks in the country, putting a premium on skill, stamina, and courage. Built in 1947, two drivers had been killed on the first lap of the first race ever held there. Among the drivers who'd died on the high banks was Bob Sweikert, the 1955 Indianapolis 500 champion who'd won six sprint car races at the track and was called "the greatest driver I ever saw" by Chris Economaki, a leading motorsports journalist.[20]

For some of the USAC regulars it didn't matter what the Hills paid, they weren't going to race on them. Reese called the series of races "the idiot circuit." Three-time national champion Jimmy Bryan said he wouldn't race on the tracks, even if it cost him another title.

Not everyone agreed.

"If you wanted to be a racer, that's what you had to do," said Jim Rathmann, the 1960 Indy 500 winner. "The guys who didn't run there, they were flat-ass chicken."[21]

Foyt adapted quickly to the high banks.

"Sure I like them, they're great," he said before the race. "It's not at all like driving other tracks. Man, you stay on it all the time at Salem."

Years later he admitted, "I wasn't smart enough to be scared. It was very fast. I knew I had to try driving on high-banked turns to make up my mind about racing."[22]

Also entering the race were several drivers making a late switch from USAC to IMCA, including Bob Cleberg, a Salem veteran who turned in the fastest qualifying time, with Foyt second. Cleberg's car was powered by a 220-cubic-inch Offenhauser engine, the maximum size allowed under USAC regulations. Foyt's was equipped with a 270-cubic-inch Offy, IMCA rules allowing unlimited displacement.

Foyt took the lead on the first lap of the thirty-lap feature, Cleberg moving in front on lap ten. Foyt regained the lead four laps from the finish and held on for his second win on a national stage. The victory didn't go unnoticed.

"An old axiom in auto racing says future champions 'cut their teeth' on the high banks of Salem's half mile asphalt oval," wrote Bob Owens, who regularly covered Salem races for the *Louisville Courier-Journal*. "If that holds true for 22-year-old A.J. Foyt . . .[he] may realize his No. 1 ambition to someday win the Indianapolis 500-mile race."[23]

Owens wasn't the only one thinking that way. Although Cleberg went on a hot streak, winning four of the next five races, they were all on dirt, and it was Foyt's victory on the paved and high-banked Salem track that caught the eye of Indy car owners.

While Foyt won the battle of Salem, USAC won the war as its sprint car race the same day at Terre Haute drew nearly twice the crowd. By July, Salem was back in the USAC fold, agreeing to increase the purse while Mari Hulman George, the daughter of Indianapolis Motor Speedway owner Tony Hulman and a race car owner, personally guaranteed a full field of cars for the next race.

"Let's face it," she said, "we need you and you need us."

With USAC reasserting its dominance, Foyt decided it was a good time to switch from IMCA and applied for membership. As a result, he was back at Salem less than a month later, this time facing a full contingent of USAC drivers. Among them was Pat O'Connor, the national champion, who qualified on the pole and led every lap. Foyt won a heat race and finished sixth in the feature, his performance continuing to impress other drivers and car owners.

"People saw me run some pretty good races on the high banks," Foyt said. "I really liked the high-speed banks, and I ran awful good. Dayton and Winchester, too. They figured if you run well there, you might not last long, but you could win some races."[24]

Another driver impressed by Foyt was Elmer George, who'd won the three previous USAC sprint car events at Salem before O'Connor broke the string. George was on the rough side, a former cowboy and rodeo bronc rider who'd turned to auto racing for new thrills. That's where he met the then Mari Hulman. She had her own wild side, and before she was twenty she'd bought herself midget and sprint cars and towed them from race to race, hiring different drivers along the way for her H.O.W. (Hell On Wheels) Special. George started driving for her at the end of 1955 and they'd been together ever since, marrying a month before the 1957 Indianapolis 500, where he'd crashed on the pace lap and failed to complete a lap.

Mari was only three weeks older than A.J. and, "We got to be close friends," Foyt said. "Mari would be towing her car and I'd be towing mine and sometimes we traveled together."

The Georges introduced A.J. to Tony Hulman and there'd been an immediate connection. Hulman was always accessible and supportive of drivers in need, but there was something special about Foyt. Maybe it was his youth, his passion for the sport, or the respect for elders instilled in A.J. by his parents. He would always be "Mr. Hulman" to A.J. Whatever it was, the bond only grew stronger in the years ahead.

"I was nobody," Foyt said. "They gave me a place to live and food to eat when I had nothing." The Hulmans became "like a second family to me."[25]

TONY HULMAN

Born in 1901 in Terre Haute, Indiana, Tony Hulman attended his first Indianapolis 500 in 1914 and seldom missed a race thereafter. Although outwardly quiet and reserved, he was competitive by nature and an outstanding athlete in prep school and college. He played end on the undefeated 1923 Yale football team and received some All-American recognition. He also won the college high hurdles championship, along with nearly a hundred other track medals.[26]

After graduation he joined the family business, Hulman and Company, a general wholesale firm best known for Clabber Girl Baking Powder. He diversified the business, investing in oil and gas companies and real estate, rapidly increasing the firm's value. He took Mary Fendrich to the Speedway on their first date, and they were married in 1926.

In the days following the end of World War II, Hulman was part of a consortium of Indiana businessmen bidding on the Indianapolis Motor Speedway. With racing suspended during the war, the track had become overgrown with grass and weeds and the mostly wooden grandstands were rickety and unsafe. Owner Eddie Rickenbacker was now in charge of Eastern Airlines and had no interest in the daunting task of restoring the Speedway. He wanted to sell, and most of the potential buyers wanted it for the land, not the racetrack.

The Indiana group fell apart as the bidding rose, and a group from Texas emerged as the most likely to get the track. That's when three-time 500 winner Wilbur Shaw stepped in and convinced Hulman to purchase the track on his own. After some hesitation he bought it for $750,000, just $50,000 more than Rickenbacker paid for it in 1926. Shaw became president and general manager as Hulman stayed in the background.

In seven months, the track was rebuilt sufficiently to stage the Memorial Day race in 1946 and it proved to be an enormous success. Each year thereafter Hulman poured the proceeds from the event back into the facility. When Shaw was killed in a plane crash in 1954, Hulman emerged from the shadows and took over running the Speedway. His other businesses continued to flourish, and by 1958 he was worth an estimated one hundred million dollars, which would have made him a billionaire in 2024 dollars. Despite his wealth he continued to be unassuming and lived modestly for the most part, although he did maintain homes in Terre Haute and Indianapolis and a 750-acre estate east of Terre Haute known as the Lodge.

"He was a regular, hardworking guy," said his grandson, Tony George, who called him Papa. "He wore a suit almost every day of his life. Rarely did you see him not in a suit. He was modest and humble. He'd wear a suit, get it all sweaty, pull the sleeves out and hang it up, then wear it again the next day. He was just a regular guy. He was always very supportive, came to all my games. Sitting up in the stands in a suit. When I was twelve or thirteen he started taking me to races."[27]

"Whenever my grandfather was asked who his favorite driver was, he'd always be like Switzerland, very neutral, and not pick anyone. Then he'd see A.J. and say, 'You know you're my favorite, right?'"

They were an odd combination from the start, the multi-millionaire Yale graduate who always wore a suit, and the high school dropout who would qualify for his first 500 in a T-shirt.

"He is one of the greatest men in the world," Foyt would say about Hulman. "He is a great personal friend. When I didn't have a nickel I stayed at his home. The man has been fantastic. He's just super to everybody who walks down the street."[28]

FIRST INDY CAR RIDE

Several Indy car owners approached Foyt with offers of a ride for the August 17 race at the Illinois State Fairgrounds in Springfield. Unsure what to do, he went to Rodger Ward for advice.

Ward was a member of a hard-driving and hard-living group of Indy car drivers. He had not yet teamed with A.J. Watson, for whom he would win two Indy 500s and national championships. Ward also had a reputation as a master of mind games who sometimes pointed a competitor in the wrong direction. So when he recommended Foyt drive the car of Chapman Root rather than that of John Wills, Foyt picked the Wills car. When Foyt qualified for the race and O'Connor failed to make the field in the Root car, he went to Ward and gloated that he'd outfoxed the veteran driver.

The race was a flag-to-flag victory for Ward, who waited until the main straight before lapping Foyt, giving A.J. the finger as he went by. For once he'd been telling the truth. O'Connor did well the rest of the year, while Foyt failed to qualify in three of the next four races.

"A.J. never forgave or forgot," Joe Scalzo, a leading auto racing historian of the era, wrote of the incident. "For the rest of both men's careers, A.J. raced against Rodger as if he were on some special mission to beat him, to really stick him. In turn, Rodger, whenever he could, responded by making A.J. work the hardest for what he got."[29]

With his USAC license in hand, Foyt wanted to race everything, and owners began lining up to give him an opportunity. He entered eighteen races over the next five weeks and was soon running in three different USAC series for three different owners: Wills's Indy car, a midget for Robert Higman, and a sprint car for Bill Cheesman. The Cheesman car was handled by Wally Meskowski, one of the top mechanics in the sport. Meskowski had tabbed A.J. to replace Eddie Sachs, the team's regular driver, who'd been injured.

Foyt was having the most success in the midget, with a third at Raceway Park in Indianapolis and a second at Chicago's O'Hare Stadium before scoring another feature victory in September at Kil-Kare Speedway in Xenia, Ohio. He also made an impact on Higman away from the track.

"He was already a fierce driver, but you wouldn't have believed his table manners," Higman said. "He was so polite, a real gentleman."[30]

Reporters began comparing Foyt to Troy Ruttman, who at twenty-one won the 1952 Indianapolis 500. Nearly every article referred to him as some variation of the "handsome Texas lad." One noted, "At only twenty-two years old, A.J. is the most talked of, and potentially has the brightest future, of any of the drivers coming up in the racing world."[31]

After failing to qualify in the Wills Indy car for several races, Meskowski came on board to help, and Foyt managed to make the last three events of the year. While often one of the slowest qualifiers, he raced well and finished the year with back-to-back top-ten finishes.

At the end of the season Wills wanted to hire him for the coming year and other owners also approached him. At first Foyt seemed headed for Federal Engineering, a Detroit-based longtime Indy car competitor. It was a step up from Wills's car but only marginally, the team having failed to qualify any of its three cars for the 1957 Indianapolis 500.

Then Jimmy Bryan dropped his bombshell.

After winning the last race of the season in the Dean Van Lines Special and clinching his third national championship in four years, Bryan announced he was splitting with car owner Al Dean and chief mechanic Clint Brawner. Despite his overall success, the best Bryan could show for the Indy 500 was a second and a third, and he'd come to believe he'd never win the race with the team. When Hanks retired after winning the 500 earlier in the year, Bryan set his sights on the victorious car, the unique "laydown" design. At the end of the season Bryan approached car owner and mechanic George Salih, and the pair quickly reached a deal.

"I feel sorry about splitting up with Dean and Brawner, but sometimes business has to come before sentiment," Bryan said, noting he'd turned down other offers "but this one was too good to pass up."[32]

Publicly, Brawner said, "I don't know who I'll get to drive the car. I don't have anyone in mind."[33]

Privately, he told Dean they should consider Foyt. He'd met the young driver earlier at the Speedway and found him to be "a shy, modest, extremely polite kid" who "asked a lot questions. Damn intelligent questions for a rookie. A.J. obviously knew a lot about race cars."[34]

"Foyt was the very first replacement driver I thought of," Brawner said in his autobiography, *Indy 500 Mechanic.* "It seemed to me the older veterans were slowing down, while a whole wave of new young drivers was coming up. A.J. looked ripe. All I heard were stories about how sensationally Foyt drove a sprint car [at] Salem . . . and anyone who goes fast there has to have ice water in his veins."

Despite the potential, Brawner knew, "What I was doing was a big gamble. Here I was switching from one of the great champions, Jim Bryan, to an as-yet unproven rookie. No matter how much natural talent Foyt possessed, and he possessed plenty, there was no way he was going to win immediately. I was going to have to invest a couple of years of my time in A.J.'s racing education. Yet I was sure it was a gamble worth taking."

Dean called Foyt and asked him to come for an interview to Los Angeles, where his moving company, one of the largest in the country, was based. He pointed out that the Dean Van Lines Special had been driven by some of the very best in the business and that it was a great responsibility for a newcomer to the big car ranks to try and fill those shoes.

"I know Bryan is a great driver, but I'm not over-awed," Dean said Foyt told him. "That statement was the clincher. I handed him the pen right then and said, said, 'Sign!'"[35]

The announcement was made on December 21, an early Christmas present for the Foyt family.

"I mean, this is the car that Jimmy Bryan had just won the national championship in," Foyt recalled. "I was speechless, to be quite truthful. Clint said a couple of guys he really trusted had watched me at Salem and they were impressed. I guess he liked how I handled my first few Champ Car races, because he was at all of them. Back then, if you were crazy enough to run Salem and Winchester, they figured you might be good at Indianapolis. I never dreamed I'd be good enough to qualify at Indianapolis, but Al Dean gave me a chance."[36]

––––––––––

It was an incredible turnaround for a year that started in Florida with Foyt out of cash and waiting on his mother to wire him money so he could get home. He'd run thirty-five midget races and finished with two victories, seven second-place finishes, and was fifth in the final standings. He'd run a handful of sprint car events—including the win at Salem—and five "big car" races, finishing twenty-sixth in the standings.

While Foyt's year ended on a high note, the same couldn't be said for Andy Linden, who'd started the season by winning four of eleven Tangerine Tournament races and the series championship. He'd gone on to win three sprint car races and a pair of midget events, finishing fifth in the Indianapolis 500 and sixth in the final big car standings. A fan favorite, he seemed on the verge of joining the sport's elite.

Linden was racing in one of the final events of the season, a November midget race at Clovis Speedway, a half-mile dirt track near Fresno, California. His car caught a rut in the track, darted into the outside wooden fence, and somersaulted out of the track, eventually coming to a rest on top of him. He was unconscious when pulled from the car, his cracked helmet falling away.[37]

Listed in critical condition and given a "fifty-fifty chance" to live by doctors, he remained in a coma for nearly three weeks and spent several months in a semi-conscious state and more than a year in the hospital. Confined to a wheelchair for several years, he eventually taught himself to walk again, but he never returned to the racetrack.

CHAPTER 7

DEAN VAN LINES

1958

A.J. Foyt may have been the hotshot new driver of the Dean Van Lines car, but he still couldn't get into Gasoline Alley at the Indianapolis Motor Speedway on May 1, 1958.

Clint Brawner was completing the overhaul of the team's four-year-old Kuzma race car, and neither was at the track for the first day of practice. To the notoriously obstinate Speedway security staff, no car meant there was no reason for a driver to be wandering around. "Come back when you've got a car," the guard said.[1]

"Same old bullshit," Foyt said.

He'd already missed the opening race of the 1958 Indy car season at Trenton while his car was being rebuilt. Bumped from the Bill Cheesman/Wally Meskowski sprint car when Eddie Sachs returned from injuries, Foyt had moved to a sprinter owned by Ray Erickson, another perennial top contender. After three early-season races, including second- and third-place finishes, A.J. arrived at the Speedway tied with Ed Elisian atop the Midwest sprint car standings.

Despite not having a race car, much of the early attention at the Speedway was on Foyt, who was "twenty-three, but looks seventeen."[2]

"A fast-rising star" said the Speedway's press guide. "Though his career in racing has been short by way of comparison to other rookies, Foyt has showed unusual promise which has earned him a driver's test. Practically unheard of insofar as national competition was concerned two years ago, he moved into the headlines during the 1957 season as a steady midget campaigner. His smooth, easy driving style soon caught attention of big car owners and earned him a chance in both Midwest sprints and national championship competition. He gave a good account of himself in both divisions."[3]

◀ A.J. and Clint Brawner at Indianapolis. *Foyt Family Collection*

Other drivers were beginning to accept him, and he fit easily into the banter they shared. One report said he was a "good talker" and "personable. He likes to kid with his fellow drivers and because of his Texas birth, naturally bears the brunt of many puns and jokes directed at the Lone Star State. Usually, however, A.J. is the one who does the needling."[4]

One of his favorite foils was Sachs, a notorious jokester himself, who could take it as well as give it out. "He told me no one passes him on the banks," Foyt said of Sachs. "I told him he had better not qualify in front of me at Dayton because if he did, he was going to be passed." Sachs had the last laugh, qualifying and finishing ahead of the newcomer.

Pat O'Connor and Tony Bettenhausen were two veteran drivers with whom Foyt became friendly, Bettenhausen having encouraged him early on to pursue the dream of driving in the 500. A new friend was rookie Jerry Unser, twenty-five. Along with the twenty-nine-year-old O'Connor, they were closer in age to Foyt than most of the other drivers at the Speedway. All three had young boys about the same age.

Thanks to the contract with Dean and his on-track winnings, A.J. and Lucy had bought a home in Houston during the off-season. His friendship with Elmer and Mari George continued to grow, and he was invited to stay at their house near the track while in Indianapolis. When Lucy arrived, she and Mari hit it off and they became good friends, the couples sometimes traveling and vacationing together in the future. In years to come Elmer, Mari, and their children would often visit Houston during the Christmas holidays, arriving on December 26 to celebrate Mari's birthday.

No one was more helpful at the track than O'Connor. A favorite of drivers and fans alike, he'd been impressed by Foyt's sprint car performance at Salem and took a liking to the kid from Texas.

"That track out there does strange things to a car," O'Connor told him. "The brick pavement sets up a sort of vibration pattern that can drive you crazy if you listen to it. But you have to be aware of it and if it changes, you know something is happening to the car."[5]

When Foyt's car finally arrived, rain and a blown engine played havoc with the practice schedule, and an increasingly frustrated Foyt was still looking to finish his rookie driver's test a week after the track opened. The test, run in ten-lap increments of gradually increasing speeds, was observed by officials and other competitors and was required of all first-year drivers.

When the rain finally stopped after four days of little action, O'Connor suggested Foyt follow him around the track for a few laps. As Firestone's lead test driver with nearly five thousand miles at the Speedway, *Sports Illustrated* said, "O'Connor knows the track better than any man."[6]

As a rookie who'd yet to pass his test, Foyt was limited to 120 miles per hour, and while the veteran O'Connor could run as fast as he wanted, easily above 140 mph, he held his speed to the rookie limit. After a couple of slow warm-up laps, the duo began to lap the track in tandem.

"I saw a puff of smoke from O'Connor's exhaust, and I knew we were on our way," Foyt said. "We went high in Turn One, down across the turn and into the short chute, down low through Two, and out toward the concrete wall coming into the back straightaway. We turned two or three laps at this speed and then O'Connor waved. I knew he was moving out. He had shown me his way around the Speedway and now he had a job of his own to do."[7]

Foyt finally passed his rookie test on Friday, May 9. The Speedway's chief steward, Harlan Fengler, praised his smooth driving style, saying Foyt "acts like he was sitting there looking at TV."[8]

No longer restricted by rookie speed limits, Foyt turned in the fourth-fastest practice lap at more than 145 mph. His speed was considered "unofficial" however, as only timed laps in qualifying and the race went into the record books.

With temperatures in the mid-seventies on the first day of qualifying, most drivers, including Foyt, wore only a T-shirt and slacks. A.J.'s shirt was emblazoned with the seal of his Dean Van Lines sponsor and a reference to the team's three national championships. He also wore a new helmet meeting the Speedway's recently upgraded safety specifications.

While qualifying for most races is based on the speed posted by driver and machine for one lap, Indianapolis is unique, as it is in so many ways. Starting position is based on the average speed of four laps. Qualifying was spread over four days and two weekends, with the starting lineup further separated by what day you qualified on. First-day qualifiers started up front, followed by second-day qualifiers, third-day, and fourth. Once thirty-three drivers were qualified "bumping" started, the car with the slowest qualifying speed being knocked out of the race if someone went faster.

Although he failed to match his practice speeds, Foyt set a rookie record in qualifying, averaging more than 143 mph, good for twelfth on the starting grid. Dick Rathmann and Elisian, who'd battled all month to see who was fastest, grabbed the top two spots. Rathmann earned the pole with the fastest four-lap average, while Elisian set a single-lap record. Jimmy Reece was third fastest and would start on the outside of the front row. O'Connor qualified fifth, with Bryan in seventh. Bettenhausen was ninth and would start directly in front of Foyt.

Elisian's month-long performance was a surprise, having never finished higher than eighteenth in four previous starts. Supporters pointed out that he was in a competitive car for the first time, the one in which Troy Ruttman qualified third the year before. Detractors, and there were many, said he was driving over his head. *Sports Illustrated* described him a few days before the race as "An inarticulate, fleshy and powerful Californian [and] until now, a singularly erratic and unsuccessful driver." An admitted gambler and not a very good one, Elisian said before the race he owed about thirty thousand dollars in gambling debts.[9]

As the race approached, Brawner and Dean tried to manage expectations.

"This guy can go," Brawner said. "It may take a little time. You don't become Bryan overnight. But Foyt can become one of the best." Dean had a harder time containing his excitement. "Bryan's boots are big ones to fill, but Foyt may bring me my first 500 victory one of these years soon. The kid can cut it. I really believe he can run with the veterans right off."

In the years to come, whenever Foyt was asked about his career highlights, he sometimes said—even after winning a fourth Indy 500—that qualifying for his first Indianapolis race ranked at the very top.

"You know what I'm most proud of?" he'd say, "I used to listen to the race in my daddy's shop on the radio. To be good enough to make my first [500] was something I'll never forget."[10]

A further sign he'd made the club: several of the drivers took Foyt to their favorite watering hole. Mates' White Front Tavern, opened shortly after the repeal of prohibition, was a "sort of Mason's lodge for racing people." Located at 3535 West Sixteenth Street, it was less than a mile east of the Speedway's entrance. The most expensive item on the menu was a three-dollar T-bone steak, and it was a gathering place for drivers, crew members, and hangers-on.[11]

"Everybody used to meet at the White Front," Foyt recalled. "When I first qualified, I went there with Jimmy Reece and Bettenhausen and Don Freeland. I said I wanted a Coke and they said why don't you have a screwdriver? I asked what the hell that was and they said it's orange juice. I said I ain't got no money to buy that, but they said they'd buy me one. I think I had two or three. I got up to go pee and the room spun. I sat down and said, 'Shit, what is it?'

"Man, I was dizzy. I went home and hugged the toilet all night. The next day they all said, 'We understand A.J. is sick.' They knew what they did to me. I wanted to tell them, 'I'm not sick, I'm dying.' I haven't had a screwdriver since 1958. It was my first one and last one."[12]

THE FIRST 500

There are few sporting events with the pomp and pageantry of the Indianapolis 500. The Kentucky Derby and Super Bowl are two that come to mind. The day's activities and buildup to the start are as carefully choreographed as a military operation and managed on a minute-by-minute basis.

A.J. and Lucy moved to the Holiday Inn across from the track before the race. He was awake by 4 a.m. but waited until it was closer to six before heading to the track. Lucy, pregnant with their second child, would wait until later. No women were allowed in Gasoline Alley or the pits, and she would be sitting in the grandstands with the other wives and families. A.J.'s father was there, working with the pit crew and assigned to change the right-rear tire if necessary, a role he often filled in the years ahead.

Despite being a focus of the prerace hype, Foyt darted unrecognized between cars in the never-ending line of traffic inching toward the Speedway's gates. He mingled easily with the throng of spectators, some of the more than 185,000 expected to attend the race. The gates to the Speedway were already open, marked by the explosion of a military bomb, the concussion of which was felt seven miles away in downtown Indianapolis. The bomb set off an Oklahoma-style land rush of fans vying for their favorite spot to watch the race from the infield, the inside of Turn One being the choice of many. Some were already busy building elaborate scaffolding from which they could tower over the track and watch the race. A marching band slowly circled the track, serenading early arrivals.

Once he arrived at the gate to Gasoline Alley there was none of the drama of previous years or even earlier in the month. The guards knew him by now, but he still made sure his credentials were visible as he entered. He began to work his way back to garage number forty-eight, where the Dean Van Lines Special was housed, and was surprised by the large number of people who'd somehow gained entry and were already milling about.

Once in the garage there was little for him to do, and he'd learn not to arrive at the track so early. The car had been gone over numerous times since the final practice session and a couple of crewmen mindlessly wiped it down for the umpteenth time.

"I wasn't exactly scared," he said. "I was nervous. It was a big thing, something I'd been looking ahead to for a long time, and it put your nerves on edge with all the waiting. Being there ready to go, wondering if you'd ever go, and wondering what would happen when you did go. Damn it, it's a worry waiting and it's something you've got to get used to."[13]

He glanced at a newspaper and was surprised to read that O'Connor, who'd been featured on the cover of *Sports Illustrated* earlier in the week and considered the race favorite along with Bryan, was telling reporters he'd retire if he won the 500, just as Sam Hanks did the previous year.

"I don't want to be a race driver all my life," O'Connor said. "I'll retire from racing if I win the 500. If I don't win this year, I'll keep trying for three or four years. But that'll be all. Then I'll devote full-time to my businesses."[14]

The Dean Van Lines crew began rolling the car out to Pit Lane a little after 8 a.m. and Foyt went out shortly thereafter, wearing a crisp new all-white uniform. There was some applause and shouts of encouragement as he walked out through the crowd, but nothing like the cheers that erupted when Bryan, O'Connor, and Sachs came out later.

The pits were a confused mix of race cars, crew members, and spectators. For the second straight year the cars were in their pit stalls and would enter the track in single file, rather than being staged in eleven rows of three on the track behind the pace car, as had been done prior to 1957. It hadn't worked very well the year before, with two cars eliminated before the start of the race as they tried to move into position. Speedway officials were confident the system would work better the second time around.

While this was going on, the Purdue University marching band came strutting down the front straight led by its famous "Golden Girl" majorette and the "world's largest drum," standing more than ten feet high. The band paused at the start/finish line and played Indiana's state song, "On the Banks of the Wabash, Far Away," marking the official start of prerace ceremonies.

As the final notes of "Wabash" faded, they were replaced by the sound of thirty-four Indy car engines as the starters and first alternate were allowed to warm up the engines. Most of the drivers were by now on Pit Lane, and Foyt mingled and joked with them, belying his rookie status. The crowd and noise continued to grow, and it wasn't until a single trumpeter played "Taps" at exactly 10:40 a.m. that they quieted. The Purdue band played the national anthem and rolled into "Back Home

Again," sung by Brian Sullivan, a tenor with the Metropolitan Opera. At the end of the song hundreds of balloons were released, which also served as the signal for drivers to get into their cars. A.J. didn't have to be told twice.

"I don't care who it is, if you run here one time or fifty times, when "Indiana" plays, your stomach tightens up," Foyt would say. "And if they say it don't, they're just lying to themselves. Every time I started a race here, you get nervous. When people say they don't, they're just kidding themselves."[15]

Foyt settled into place and fastened his safety belts. Only the traditional lap belt was required in 1958, but the Dean Van Lines Special was fitted with a shoulder harness and Brawner checked to make sure all were tight. The car featured a newly installed roll bar behind the driver's head, "recommended" but not required by USAC regulations.

Foyt had fitted a small visor to the helmet and moved his goggles into place. He'd decided against the red bandanna he often wore on dirt tracks, the windscreen having provided plenty of protection during practice. Then he settled back and waited.

"A few people came up and I saw their mouths moving and they smiled and tapped me on the helmet," he said. "It's the nice part about having earplugs in and a helmet on, you don't have to answer a lot of bullshit questions."

He thought of the drivers' meeting the day before when Fengler covered the same ground he'd heard repeated all month: "The race is not won on the first lap—your reputation does not depend on one race," although Foyt wondered about the second half of the statement. He also remembered Hanks, now the Speedway's director of racing, warning him and the other rookies to watch the draft off the lead cars at the start, saying it could pull them into the turns faster than they realized. There would be two warm-up laps behind the pace car before the start of the race, a parade or formation lap to get the cars into the eleven rows of three, and a pace lap to bring the cars up to speed.[16]

It wasn't until Tony Hulman grabbed a microphone that Foyt says he heard anything after getting into his car, and it was the words he'd been waiting for: "Gentlemen, start your engines!"

With his car started and idling smoothly, Foyt looked ahead and immediately thought something was wrong. The first three cars were already out on the track, ahead of the pace car and disappearing around Turn One, while the rest of the line crept down Pit Lane.

"I could see Dick Rathmann and Elisian. They were pulling away from the field. Jimmy Reece moved up with them, and there was a big gap between the first row and the rest of the field. I thought, 'Those two bastards are going to ruin everything.' As we came out of Turn Four, we got the sign for one more lap."

Driving the pace car for the first time was Hanks, who at first floored the mammoth Pontiac Bonneville convertible in a failed attempt to catch the three cars out front. He then slowed the remaining thirty racers to a crawl, hoping the three breakaway cars would circle the track and move through the field to take their front-row positions. Coming out of Turn Four on the second lap he looked over his left shoulder hoping to see the front row in place but saw only O'Connor, who should have been in the middle of the second row. With no radio communication and unsure of what to do, Hanks pulled down Pit Lane as planned.

Standing at the start/finish line and watching as the cars began to accelerate was Fengler, a former driver and car builder who was working his first race as chief steward. He ordered the flagman to wave a yellow flag and called for the yellow caution lights to be turned on, voiding the start. It wasn't until nearly a lap later that Foyt saw Rathmann flash by on the inside of the track, as Elisian and Reece went by him on the outside at high speed. Seeing the front row weaving into position, Fengler elected to start the race and the first three, carrying more speed than the rest, leaped ahead into Turn One.

Rathmann led through Turn One and Turn Two and down the backstraight. In a desperate attempt to take the lead, Elisian went into Turn Three too fast and too low, his car skidding up the track as he lost control. Rathmann tried to go higher, but Elisian slid up into him and both cars hit the outside wall.

Reece went low to avoid the two crashing cars, slowed, and was rammed from behind, the impact sending his car into a 180-degree spin. Next on the scene was O'Connor, who went even lower, onto the edge of the grass, before losing control and shooting up the track, going up and over the front of Reece's backward car. O'Connor's airborne machine did half a barrel roll, landed upside down, and then bounced again, landing on its wheels. It backed into the outside wall before sliding down into the middle of the track and stopping. O'Connor's car was not fitted with a roll bar, and doctors said later he most likely was already dead when the car stopped and a fire started, his neck fractured when the car landed upside down.

At the time it was the worst accident in Speedway history, with fifteen cars involved, and Foyt was right in the middle of it.

"I thought, 'Oh shit, I've come this far and it's all over.' I didn't even make a lap. I looked for a place to go. There were cars sideways in front of me, so I spun my car to keep from hitting them . . . While I was sideways, I saw a car go up and over another car and flip right out of the Speedway."

It was Unser, who escaped with only a dislocated shoulder, whose car Foyt spotted. A.J. somehow made it through the melee, spinning through the grass without hitting anything. He kept the engine running, which allowed him to pull away from the accident scene and join the line of remaining cars slowly following the pace car.

The accident site was still chaos as he approached it a second time. Safety officials, ambulances, and race cars were scattered everywhere. He could see O'Connor's car burning. Another slow lap and the fire was out.

"Don't look," Foyt told himself as he approached O'Connor's smoldering car. "Don't look."

He looked. O'Connor was still in the car. The next lap O'Connor was gone, but the vision haunted Foyt. Pitting for new tires and to have his car looked over, he wasn't sure he could continue.

"Going around under yellow after that accident and seeing him still in the car was hard to take," Foyt said. "It really bothered me because Pat had helped me and given me advice and was such a good guy."[17]

Foyt, who would say he was "petrified" at one point, wasn't the only one having difficulty with the situation. Bryan said he was "shocked" by the Turn Three carnage.

"It was awful," he said afterward. "I never saw anything like it in my life. I was sick the whole race. It was a nightmare I lived with for 200 laps."[18]

Despite the concerns, after fifteen slow laps and more than twenty minutes, Foyt and all the other remaining drivers were still in their cars when the green flag waved again. Foyt ran well at times but was never in contention to win. There were seventeen lead changes, with Bryan turning back challenges from Bettenhausen, Johnny Boyd, and rookie George Amick.

Foyt lost control of his car in Turn One on lap 148, spinning and nearly hitting the outside wall before coming to a stop in the middle of the track. Race-day news reports said he may have hit an oil slick, but Foyt later said a broken water hose doused his tires and caused them to lose traction.

"My crash scared me some, but when I walked away from it, I felt better about it," he said. "Any time you can walk away from one it wasn't a bad one and you laugh about it later."[19]

"But that [his first 500] was some experience. It gets a hold of you and won't let go. It's more people and more money than a man could dream of, the fastest cars and the best drivers anywhere, dangerous as it could be, and so damned nervy and exciting it sort of sends a shiver through you. Nothing can compare to it. You race wherever you can, whenever you can, but May at Indianapolis is what matters the most."

Bryan went on to win the race, justifying his decision to leave the Dean team. He was followed closely by Amick, who was named rookie of the year and may have won if not slowed by a long pit stop. Foyt's sixteenth-place finish was good for $2,849, of which he received 40 percent.

Afterward the focus was on the opening-lap crash. Rathmann said Elisian was "going fifty miles per hour faster than he ever could go through that corner. I'll never forgive Elisian for what he did. Pat O'Connor was the most honorable guy in racing."[20]

At first Elisian said, "I just went into the corner too fast and lost it. In fact, we both went in too fast." He later amended his story, saying "I don't know why I lost it. I had driven through that corner faster. I have had these hot dogs [other drivers] spin in front of me and run me through the wall on the other tracks. It sure wasn't intentional. I liked O'Connor as well as anybody."[21]

The next day USAC's racing director, Duane Carter, suspended Elisian "for the safety and well-being of himself and his fellow competitors," citing "a series of errors in judgment."

Even Elisian's car owner, John Zink, seemed to point the finger at his driver, adding, "Maybe it was my fault as well. If Elisian hadn't driven, we'd probably have won the race with Reece."[22]

While many in the racing world were quick to blame Elisian, Foyt wasn't one of them. Elmer George and Elisian were friends, and Foyt had gotten to know Elisian as a result. He tried to explain his thoughts on what happened years later in his autobiography.

When I came by the pits, I could see Ed Elisian sitting on the pit wall. His helmet was off and his head was in his hands. I wondered how it could have happened. But I knew the answer just as well as any of the drivers. You race all month with a guy and you build up this rivalry. It almost becomes a hate. But it isn't. Only race drivers feel it. Maybe some people feel it on the highway. There are just some people who don't like to be passed. But in racing it builds up so much stronger. It becomes an obsession. I guess that's what happened to Elisian and Dick Rathmann. They just got overcome with the obsession to beat each other.

The loss of O'Connor was felt throughout the sport.

"People who follow racing know they shouldn't get too close to drivers; they know that it might bring on heartache," wrote sports editor Wayne Fuson in the *Indianapolis News*. "But O'Connor was a fellow you couldn't help but like and get to know well. Pat was one of the finest men I ever knew, in or out of racing. I never heard anyone say even one critical word of him."[23]

Foyt often said he learned one last thing from O'Connor.

"The O'Connor lesson was, don't get close friends," he repeated years later. "I didn't have a lot friends. Well, I had a lot of friends, don't get me wrong. But not ones I was close to. I'd say I'd rather be your friend—close but not *that* close—so if you got killed it didn't bother me that much. I know a lot of people got upset by that."[24]

RACE OF TWO WORLDS

No sooner was the 500 over than Foyt started lobbying Dean to take him to Italy for the 500 Miglia Di Monza as it was officially known, although it was commonly called the "Race of Two Worlds" in the US, or "Monzanapolis" in Europe.

Run for the first time in 1957, the race was supposed to pit the top teams from Formula One and Indianapolis against each other at the Autodromo Nazionale Monza in Italy, the oldest continuous F1 racetrack. Known for the steeply banked oval portion of the track, Monza had only recently been rebuilt after falling into decay during World War II.

The first event was less than successful as most of the F1 teams skipped it, saying the rules were stacked against the Europeans. Rather than race on the combined oval and road course grand prix track, it was run only on the oval. The race also had a rolling start versus the standing start Europeans were used to, and it was run counterclockwise like at Indianapolis, rather than the clockwise direction typically used in Europe. The distance was set at five hundred miles, while F1 cars were designed for shorter sprint races.

Even though the race was broken into three heats—partly as a concession to the Europeans and partly because the rough track had everyone concerned—only a handful of European sports cars participated. Bryan drove the Dean car to victory, the team winning forty thousand dollars, making it second only to Indianapolis when it came to prize money.

Despite the inaugural year problems, the race was being run again in 1958. Several of the European teams built special cars for the event and ten American Indy car drivers were invited. Dean had promised his car—the one Bryan drove to victory a year earlier and Foyt drove at Indianapolis—to F1 champion Juan Manuel Fangio. Another Indy car was promised to Maurice Trintignant, who'd just won his second Monaco Grand Prix a few weeks earlier and had won the 24 Hours of Le Mans. Several American drivers were entered in European cars, including Phil Hill in a Ferrari and Maston Gregory in a Jaguar. Another American, Carroll Shelby, was named the relief driver for the Europeans.

Foyt argued that the American team also needed a relief driver. Brawner went to bat for him, and they finally convinced Dean to cover A.J.'s expenses. During practice Foyt helped set up the Dean car and ran laps faster than Fangio. When it came time to qualify, however, the five-time world champion delivered, turning in the car's fastest lap and third-fastest time overall. Luigi Musso put a Ferrari on the pole.

Race day was hot and humid, and Foyt figured Fangio would need relief. Those hopes were dashed when a burned piston was discovered after morning warm-ups. The team went to work changing the engine and Fangio would eventually start the third heat but last only two laps before the fuel pump broke.

The first heat was the best race yet between the American and European teams, with Musso leading initially in the Ferrari before being passed by Jim Rathmann and Bryan. Stirling Moss ended up the top European finisher, in fifth place.

Word came after the heat that Trintignant wanted out of his car following a tenth-place finish. To be fair it wasn't a very good car, a four-year-old Kurtis chassis that failed to qualify at Indianapolis with a small and tired Offy engine. Trintignant had qualified it fifteenth out of nineteen starters, the slowest of the American cars. But it was a car in need of a driver, and Foyt was a driver in need of a car.

He moved up a couple places at the start of the second heat and soon found himself in heady company, chasing Moss in the Maserati while trying to fend off Hill's Ferrari. Moss would finish sixth with Foyt seventh, while Hill was forced to pit for tires. In the third heat it was Moss's turn to chase Foyt until the steering of the Maserati suddenly sheered away, throwing his car into the outside wall.[25]

The strain on the engine eventually proved too much for Foyt's car and it broke a crankshaft, although the car was credited with a sixth-place finish overall. A.J. clearly enjoyed the experience.

"It was like driving on a washboard," he said of Monza. "That's really a race. I'm really going to try to get back next year and run a little bit. Those Europeans are really going to be out to get us. They've been watching us now to see what we do, and this year they built a car or two for that race. Next year, they're going to have some more special cars in there, you can count on it." Foyt was wrong. There would be no third Race of Two Worlds.[26]

"I'VE GOT EVERYTHING TO LOSE."

From Europe, Foyt went to Atlanta for the Fourth of July, where a one-hundred-mile race was held on the dirt track at Lakewood Speedway. Qualifying fifth,

Foyt finished eleventh after narrowly missing the spinning car of Art Bisch, who'd been part of the Indianapolis rookie class and already won his first champ car event.

"I was coming into the turn and there was Bisch's car, right in the middle of the track," Foyt said. "Their caution light wasn't working right that day, and I went into that turn full bore. When I saw that car, I had the choice of either hitting [it] or hitting the wall. I went for the wall. I knew if I hit that car and Bisch died, I'd always feel that if I hadn't hit the car he might have lived."[27]

Although Foyt avoided the stalled car, Jack Turner could not and hit it broadside. Bisch died two days later from his injuries. Tragedy struck again in September at Trenton when Reece was killed in a last-lap accident. In a race where Foyt started and finished eleventh, the throttle on Reece's car apparently stuck open, sending him into and over the wall. He was thrown from the car as it tumbled down the hill outside the track and was pronounced dead of multiple injuries.

Through it all Foyt maintained a heavy schedule, typically running at least two races a week. He made an increasingly rare start in a midget race on August 13 at the Cincinnati Race Bowl, where he spun and was hit by another car, sending him to the hospital overnight with back pain, although he missed only one race.

While there was some improvement by the end of the year with second-, third-, and fourth-place Indy car finishes, he ran the entire season without a feature event victory. It was the first time since he'd left home three years earlier that he'd gone winless.

At the same time, two of the sport's biggest names and a promising rookie had been killed. When Foyt was asked why he raced, he seemed to make a pretty good argument why he shouldn't, and that perhaps he wouldn't be doing it too much longer.

"I've got everything to lose in racing," he admitted. "We have a nice big home in Houston, even have a maid. I figure it's just like any other sport, you only have so many years in which you can be at the top, and when you are there, you might as well save your money. I turn my checks right over into AT&T stock. That's like a savings account."[28]

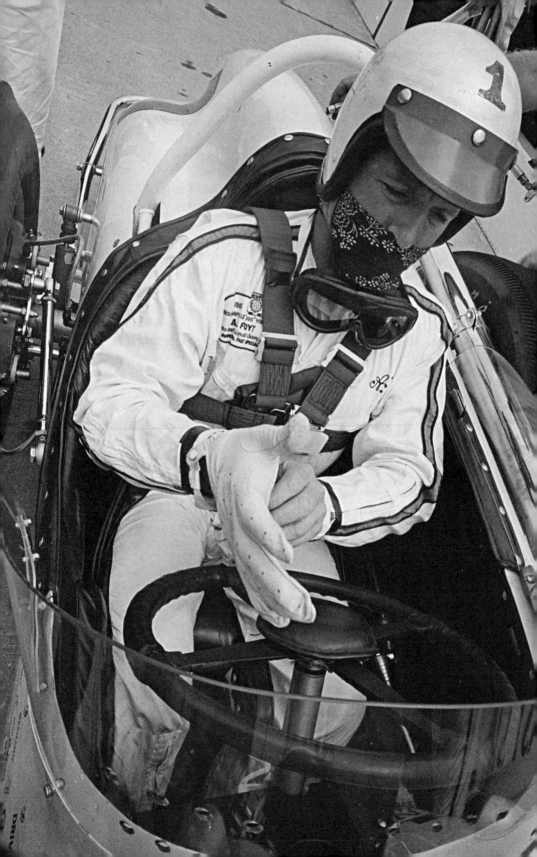

CHAPTER 8

A DEADLY PROFESSION

1959

The deaths of Pat O'Connor and others didn't go unnoticed. In a stunning cover story in the January 1959 edition of *Mechanix Illustrated* magazine headlined "Auto Racing Is Murder, It Must Be Outlawed," Oregon Senator Richard Neuberger called for legislation banning the sport. It wasn't the first time a politician tried to regulate racing, with a California ballot proposition having failed in 1932.[1]

"Some people call this sport," wrote Neuberger, who'd been critical of racing following the deaths at Le Mans in 1955. "I call it wanton, tragically unnecessary bloodshed. Some call it healthy, exhilarating competition. I call it shameful and uncivilized . . . It is a lowering of the essential dignity of man. It approaches dangerously close to the raw crowd lust of the Roman 'circuses' where the populace jammed the arenas to watch gladiators battle to the death.

"Every step of the way, car racing has been accompanied by massacre. Tracks all over the country have counted—are still counting!—their dead. I believe the time has come for the United States to become a civilized nation and to stop this carnage which has persisted too long."

A.J. Foyt was more concerned about winning a race than what the senator from Oregon was saying, and he almost got one in the opening event of the year. Ray Erickson had bought a new sprint car from master builder A.J. Watson, and Foyt finished second to Don Branson in Birmingham, Alabama. Then he was on his way to Florida, where USAC was planning its first race at the sport's newest coliseum, Daytona International Speedway.

◀ Foyt was an early adapter of safety features such as flame-retardant uniforms and shoulder harnesses but preferred the feel of golf gloves over the thicker safety gloves. *Revs Institute, The Tom Burnside Photograph Collection*

They'd been racing cars on the wide beaches of Daytona since the late 1920s when a world land speed record was set there. By the mid-1930s, stock car events were regularly held on sandy ovals of various configurations, although the races were often poorly run and dangerous. After World War II, Bill France, who'd moved to Daytona during the Depression and had been involved in promoting events prior to the war, started the National Association of Stock Car Auto Racing (NASCAR) to try and organize the sport. NASCAR was soon staging races on the beach and other tracks throughout the South. In 1955 it held a race for eighty-some cars on a 4.5-mile track, using both the beach and Highway A1A near Daytona.

France realized the days of racing on the beach were numbered. Rising speeds created safety hazards and the wide-open spaces made crowd control and collecting entry fees from spectators next to impossible. At the same time, the races attracted crowds to the seashore and were an economic boom for the area. So when France approached the city council for land on which to build a closed-course racetrack, it quickly agreed to a fifty-year lease at ten thousand dollars a year.

Five years in the planning and making, the track was France's brainchild. The 2.5-mile, D-shaped tri-oval matched Indianapolis in length and its thirty-one-degree high banked turns dwarfed those of the Speedway. The configuration not only allowed for higher speeds, it provided an opportunity for fans to see the entire track, an impossibility at Indianapolis. France promoted the track as a Super Speedway and Daytona Beach as the "World Center of Racing," a clear shot at Indianapolis's claim to be the "Racing Capital of the World."

There was only one problem as the opening of the new speedway approached. France was nearly broke. Paving the high banks required new equipment and techniques. Construction had dragged on. Desperate for additional funding, France approached USAC about holding an Indy car race at the facility.

Despite concerns about France's ambition and ultimate goals, USAC was eager to expand its road racing operations and agreed to kick off its 1959 season at Daytona. A one-thousand-kilometer USAC sports car race on Sunday, April 5, would be the feature event and hopefully become the centerpiece of its road racing series. A support event featuring Indy cars would be held on Saturday on the oval track, followed the same day by a "Formula Libre" race on the oval, open to cars of any configuration. USAC and France hoped to attract the Ferrari, Maserati, and other Formula One teams to the Libre event. The two groups also agreed to stage a July Fourth doubleheader at Daytona for Indy cars and NASCAR's stock cars.

The first sign of trouble came in early February, when the track scheduled several days of open testing shortly after paving was completed and in advance of the first Daytona 500 stock car race, set for February 22. As part of the test, Marshall Teague, who'd competed in both NASCAR and the Indianapolis 500, would attempt to set a world closed-course speed record in an Indy car. His target was Tony Bettenhausen's lap of more than 178 miles per hour at Monza.

Teague, from Daytona Beach, had been a big part of NASCAR's success in the late 1940s and early 1950s. Known as the "King of the Beach," he'd recruited Smokey Yunick to be his mechanic and the Hudson Motor Company in Detroit to provide a car and sponsorship, the first manufacturer involvement in NASCAR. They'd dominated at times, Teague and the "Fabulous Hudson Hornet" at one point winning twenty-seven of thirty-four feature events.

After a falling-out with France in 1953, he'd raced in stock car events run by the rival AAA and at Indianapolis where, in a rare recognition of his prior accomplishments, he was allowed to compete despite having no Indy car experience. He'd run as high as second in the 500 and had a best finish of seventh in 1957.

Teague was using the same Sumar Special, based on a Kurtis Kraft chassis he'd driven at Indianapolis, although highly modified for the Formula Libre event. Aerodynamics was a black art and the car's full fender flares and enclosed cockpit were based on what "looked good" rather than on science. It was considered the ultimate "slip streamer" in the vernacular of the day, although it had been tried at Indianapolis without success and abandoned. Power came from a 270-cubic-inch Offenhauser engine, larger than those allowed at Indy.

Two days of testing left Teague short of the record and he was still working up to speed on Wednesday, February 11, when the car appeared to dip entering Turn One, did a half spin, and then flipped five times, ejecting Teague. He was found still strapped in his seat, about 150 yards farther down the track from the crumpled race car. Teague, thirty-seven, died instantly, becoming Daytona's first racing casualty.

Eleven days later the first Daytona 500 was held, and it proved to be a success beyond France's wildest dream. Fifty-nine cars started the race, with more than forty thousand spectators packing the grandstands. The lead officially changed hands thirty-four times at the start/finish line and countless other times around the track, the event somehow being run without a caution flag. With cars three wide at the checkered flag, France declared a photo finish, milking it for promotional value during the next three days before declaring what the photo clearly showed: Lee Petty was the winner.

So it was with a mixture of anticipation and concern that the Indy cars began arriving in Daytona at the end of March. Missing was Jimmy Bryan, the Indy 500 champion, who decided to skip the race.

"You can't make [one] mistake on these high-speed tracks," Bryan said. "I don't like them, and I never even considered entering the race at Daytona."[2]

Qualifying was stretched out over three days and Dick Rathmann, driving another Sumar Special, set a US closed-course speed record on day one to capture the pole. His speed was surpassed the next day by George Amick, the Indy 500 rookie of the year, who'd been hired by George Bignotti to replace Jimmy Reece. Amick's speed of 176.88 mph came on the second day, however, and he would start ninth. Foyt led the third-day qualifiers, although he was nearly eight miles an hour slower than Amick.

Jim Rathmann, the Monza winner, jumped off to an early lead in the race, passing his brother and Rodger Ward at the start. Ward took the lead for several laps before Jim Rathmann moved back out front and led the remainder of the race.

On the last lap, Amick and Bob Christie, fighting for third place and nearly half a lap behind, came together between Turn One and Turn Two as the leaders exited Turn Four. All eyes were on the front-runners, and few saw the accident. Christie said a gust of wind, measured at upward of twenty-five mph at times during the race, hit the cars and sent Amick's sliding.

The car skated through Turn Two and up the track, hitting the fence at the start of the backstraight and tearing out "fifty feet of the guard rail and shearing off eight 7x7-foot posts supporting the rail," according to the *Indianapolis Star*. "Then it got airborne, sailed seventy-five feet through the air, hit and took another flip of about sixty feet, landing upside down. Skid marks indicated the car probably flipped ten times."[3]

Another report said the car "was crumpled like a paper wad."[4]

Race winner Rathmann passed by the still-sliding Amick, dodging flying debris as he went. Bill Cheesbourg stopped and ran to Amick's car, turning away when he realized there was nothing he could do. Amick was already dead.

"I've never seen one that bad before," said Rathmann, who averaged 170.260 mph, well above the record he'd set at Monza, making it the fastest automobile race ever run at that point.

Despite the fatality and damage to the guardrail, the teams began preparing for the Formula Libre event. It was little more than a second race for the Indy cars as it had failed to attract any outside interest. None of the F1 teams made the trip to Daytona and all the sports cars on hand for the next day's endurance race decided to skip it as well.

Citing winds and possible driver fatigue, race officials cut the length of the event in half to fifty miles. Several teams, including Dean Van Lines, opted out. Ward took an early lead and was out front when he went for a wild ride at nearly the same place where Amick crashed, spinning four times before he was hit by another car. With Ward out, Jim Rathmann went on to an easy victory over his brother Dick.

"For the first time in my life I thought, 'This is it,'" Ward said. "I don't feel a race car can be built that will be safe at those speeds. The race driver only has a certain few opportunities to escape trouble. It's always a big gamble and it doesn't make sense to throw away any of your chances for survival."[5]

Foyt would compare driving an Indy car at Daytona to "sitting on the wing of an airplane. I always liked the high banks of Salem and Winchester in a sprint car. But Daytona was scary. It was no place for an Indy car."[6]

Despite his concerns, Foyt was one of a handful of drivers from the Indy car ranks who stayed for Sunday's sports car event. The 3.81-mile Daytona road course used nearly the entire banked track with a 1.5-mile infield course. The race was run clockwise or European style, and with no chicane to slow the cars on the backstraight, the sports cars ran flat out for most of the NASCAR oval.

Driving a Lister sports car with a Corvette engine and making one of his first starts on a road course, Foyt worked his way up to second and was challenging race leader Carroll Shelby before both drivers suffered car problems. The scheduled one-thousand-kilometer race droned on endlessly and as darkness approached was eventually shortened to six hours. A pair of South American drivers took the checkered flag in a Porsche, covering about nine hundred kilometers.

Attendance for the USAC events was disappointing, estimates ranging from four thousand to fourteen thousand for Saturday's races and six thousand on Sunday. After the disastrous weekend and poor attendance, USAC canceled its portion of the July Fourth doubleheader and would never return to Daytona.

Foyt, however, would be back.

THE LAYDOWN CAR

The opening of the regular 1959 Indy car season came two weeks later in Trenton, New Jersey, only not for Foyt. He failed to qualify for the twenty-two-car field.

The race was marked by the death of Dick Linder, a thirty-six-year-old driver trying to make the move into Indy cars. He'd had some success driving stock and sprint cars at Trenton but was making only his fifth "big car" start. Linder was running near the front of the pack when Branson lost control of his car. Linder's car hit the front of Branson's, catapulting him over the outside guardrail and into a series of flips.[7]

The failure to qualify at Trenton was an indication of deeper troubles to come for the Dean Van Lines team as it assembled in Indianapolis in early May. Although only Foyt's second time at the Speedway, he was becoming increasingly vocal and expressing his opinions with growing forcefulness. At the root of the problem was the new "laydown" car Al Dean had bought from Eddie Kuzma to replace the 1955 roadster that had served the team so well.

Introduced in 1957, and as the name implied, the car's engine was laid on its left side, creating a lower center of gravity and shifting weight to the left, important for a car making two thousand left-hand turns during a five-hundred-mile race. In theory it provided for a better-handling car and allowed for more aerodynamic bodywork with reduced wind resistance. Laydown cars had finished first and second in two consecutive Indy 500s.

There'd been a stampede of owners looking to buy laydown-type cars for 1959 and nearly as many people willing to build them. Of the four major car builders—Kuzma, Frank Kurtis, Quincy Epperly, and Watson—only Watson elected to stick with the so-called "upright" design.

Kuzma had built several of what he called "flat-engine" cars for the 1958 race, with disappointing results as none were able to qualify. He was certain he'd fixed the problems for 1959 by stiffening the chassis, and in addition to Foyt's there were a number of new Kuzmas spread throughout Gasoline Alley, including one for Eddie Sachs.

Initially excited about Dean's decision to spend twenty thousand dollars for the new car, Foyt had been unhappy with it at Daytona, although he thought it had more to do with the track than the machine. His unhappiness shifted to concern after failing to qualify at Trenton. Despite the early-season problems, he remained extremely confident in his own ability, even though he'd yet to win a big car race and hadn't even finished in the top five in an Indy car on a paved track.

"I always felt that it was a lot more the driver than it was the car—maybe 75 percent to 25 percent—so with a top car, I really thought I could win," Foyt said. "I knew I had the ability."[8]

Brawner went back to work on the car after Trenton and was late getting it to the Speedway, Foyt not turning laps until May 11. Several other teams using new laydown cars already were complaining about handling problems and there was more than a little concern as Foyt turned his first laps. In his autobiography he recounted the conversation with Brawner after returning to the pits.

Clint rushed over to the car, about as excited as I had been.

"How's it feel?" he asked.

I didn't know how to tell him. I figured the plain truth was best.

"It doesn't handle worth a shit," I said.

Clint and Al and everybody on the crew said it in unison: "It doesn't handle worth a shit?"

"Whattaya mean it doesn't handle worth a shit?" Clint said.

"I mean, it doesn't handle worth a shit," I said. "You know, like crap." I never was much on mincing words.

"Wait a minute," Clint said "You mean to tell me that car doesn't handle. How do you explain the fact that laydown roadsters won the last two races here?"

"Well they didn't win them in this car," I said. "And I'll tell you one more thing, I don't see how they won at all. I mean, I don't think they're as good as the old-type roadsters."

"Listen to the expert," Clint said. "One race and he's an expert."

"Screw you," I said. "I'm out here drivin' it and I know how it feels."

Eddie Sachs came over and joined in our friendly little conversation. "That sled handle any better than my laydown?" he asked. "I mean, mine doesn't handle worth a shit."

Eddie Sachs knew what he was talking about. Here's a guy who had been at the Speedway six times. You can't tell a goddamn mechanic a thing. You really can't.

Even allowing for a heavy dose of hyperbole A.J. acknowledges was added throughout the autobiography, it doesn't paint a pretty picture of the team's situation early in the month. The excerpt also provides an early look at Foyt's views on crew chiefs and mechanics.

Brawner, on the other hand, could be excused for questioning Foyt. With Bryan as his driver, the team won seventeen champ car races from 1954–1957 and three national championships, finishing second in the other. Brawner didn't expect to start winning races immediately with the inexperienced Foyt, but he wasn't expecting to get lip from the kid either. Dean, having dug deep into his pockets for the twenty grand to buy the new car, was frustrated with both. Part of the problem was both men were alike in many ways.

"He was rough and gruff" is how Jim McGee, a future 500-winning crew chief, described Brawner, his mentor. "His work ethic was incredible, and he was just so clever at building things. He knew how to make things work. He could repair or build anything. Clint's famous saying was 'A man made it, a man can fix it.'"[9]

Brawner went back to work on the laydown car alongside A.J. and Tony Foyt, although they often found themselves at odds on what to do. Things weren't helped when Elmer George, driving the team's four-year-old upright Kuzma, began turning laps faster than Foyt.

In addition to challenges being presented by the laydown cars, there was another problem at the Speedway: a lack of experienced drivers. On the second day of practice, Foyt's friend Jerry Unser went into a slide in Turn Four while warming up. The car shot up the track, hit the wall broadside, and exploded. Unser, who was wearing only a short-sleeve shirt and slacks as was allowed by the rules, was hospitalized with third-degree burns over 35 percent of his body.

While Unser's team set about repairing the car, the search for another driver highlighted the lack of qualified replacements. Several other car owners were having a hard time finding a driver. Only thirty-four of the entered drivers had made a previous start in the 500. Johnnie Parsons added to the problem when the 1950 winner announced his retirement.[10]

"To drive a race car, it has to come from the heart, and I don't seem to have it anymore," Parsons said. "When you get down to the end of those straightaways and can't hold your foot down anymore, it's time to quit. I like to drive, but not this fast."[11] Things were so bad Kelly Petillo, who won the 500 the year Foyt was born, tried to file an entry. Petillo had one of the most unusual histories of any 500 winner. He'd been in numerous run-ins with the law and spent the last ten years in prison for attempted murder. Released in early 1959, he tried to file an entry for the race but was refused, the Speedway citing his age, fifty-five, which would have made him the oldest driver ever to start the 500. Ironically, Foyt would eventually become the oldest driver ever to compete in the race—at age fifty-seven.

While the Dean Van Lines team continued to struggle with Foyt's car, several others began to make progress. Johnny Thomson qualified his shocking-pink laydown, built by Lujie Lesovsky, on the pole. Sachs was the best of the Kuzma machines in second, while Jim Rathmann was on the outside of the front row in the new Watson upright.

Missing from the first day's qualifiers was Bettenhausen, who'd been among the fastest drivers all month thanks to an experimental Offenhauser engine, rumored to have fifty to sixty more horsepower than the typical powerplant. The defending national champion—who earlier in the week bragged about being upside down in a race car twenty-seven times—made it twenty-eight, hitting the outside wall and destroying the car and eighteen feet of the guardrail. Bettenhausen then moved into his backup machine and led second-day qualifiers.[12]

Bettenhausen's misfortune ended up benefiting Foyt when A.J.'s engine seized during his first attempt to qualify. When the parts needed to repair the engine failed to arrive the next morning on a plane from Los Angeles, Dean pulled out his checkbook again, coming up with eight thousand dollars to buy the special engine out of Bettenhausen's destroyed car.

Brawner and Tony Foyt managed to change the engine and have the car in line to qualify by the end of day two, only to have it start raining. Foyt would have to wait another week. Word came later that Unser had died. Foyt had visited him several times during the two weeks since the accident and thought he was recovering. When Unser's kidneys started to fail, however, the end came quickly.

Two days later, Bob Cortner, who'd passed his rookie test the day before, lost control in high winds and hit the outside wall in Turn Three, dying later that night of massive head injuries. Cortner was wearing a seat belt but not a shoulder harness, which was still optional equipment. Speedway and USAC management came under immediate attack for allowing unqualified drivers on the racetrack.

"There is no pattern, I have no explanation," said Henry Banks, USAC's director of competition. "Since taking over this job I have done everything I know how to prevent the tragic accidents. I feel a deep responsibility. We screen all drivers and inspect the equipment. I believe we take all the necessary precautions we can possibly take. USAC drivers are the cream of the crop."[13]

Even with the special engine, qualifying the Dean Van Lines car wasn't easy. The first attempt was judged too slow. A.J. said he waved it off, Brawner said he made the decision. Eventually Foyt qualified seventeenth, at a speed slower than he'd posted his rookie year. With the field finally set, eleven drivers had not competed in the previous year's race. Five were rookies, although Foyt, at twenty-four, was again the youngest driver, and by a wide margin—no one else was under thirty.

The struggles continued right up until race day. A.J. clashed with Brawner when he wanted to take advantage of the final practice session. Known as Carb Day, the session was originally designed to allow teams to set an engine's carburetor based on weather conditions closer to the race. Almost all the race engines now used electronic fuel injection and didn't require adjustment based on the weather, but both the practice and its name had become Indy traditions. Brawner, however, worried about the dependability of the engine, overruled his driver and the car stayed parked.

For the most part the disagreements within the team stayed behind the closed doors of Garage 48, over which a sign proclaimed, "The Eyes of Texas Are Upon You." One of the few references to Foyt during the month mentioned how the "soft-spoken Texan" was becoming a fan favorite, thanks in part to his youth, a great smile, and a natural charisma.

"Good looking race driver A.J. Foyt and his pretty blonde wife, Lucy, stopped for a brief visit," wrote one reporter. "Foyt is a well-mannered, easy speaking young man. He doesn't stutter and stammer for words."[14]

Despite the growing popularity, the *Indianapolis News* rated Foyt no better than a twenty-five-to-one long shot to win the race, worse odds than twenty other starters. Jim Rathmann was the seven-to-one favorite.

USAC issued revised regulations for the race, requiring drivers to wear long-sleeved uniforms treated with an "anti-combustion-proofing solution and re-treated after each laundering." Foyt's uniform was accented by two wide vertical red stripes, and he had his helmet painted red for the race, although he again decided against wearing a bandanna. Despite all that had happened during the month, Foyt remained confident and was looking forward to his second start.[15]

"The tense feeling before the race is terrific," he said. "As time draws closer it's pretty tough. But once the race is underway, everything is a whole lot better. I'm in good physical condition and that helps a lot."[16]

Given everything that transpired during the month, Foyt's race itself was relatively uneventful. He slowly worked his way into the top ten, taking evasive action to avoid an early accident that eliminated four cars. After rising as high as fifth during a series of pit stops, he overshot his pit and faded late in the race, finishing tenth. He covered the full five hundred miles for the first time, but Brawner and Foyt were both disappointed. Foyt blamed the car while Brawner thought his driver tired. The new Watson uprights finished first and second, Ward leading Rathmann across the finish line.

The next week the 500 found itself under attack again, in a story headlined "BEWARE! The Indianapolis 500 again proves deadly and the case against it grows with the toll."[17]

This time it wasn't some obscure screwdriver book and liberal senator calling for an end to the Indianapolis 500. It was *Life* magazine, read by more than 1.5 million people each week and one of the country's most popular publications. The article was accompanied by a "Death Map," showing the location where the twenty-seven drivers, twelve mechanics, and five spectators had been killed at the Speedway, along with a photo of each driver.

"Every year on Memorial Day the huge crowd comes to the track to see a contest—but keeps in mind the exciting probability that it will see violence, smashed cars and death itself," read the story, which did not include a byline.

In an accompanying article headlined "Last Year's Widow Tells Her Story," under the byline of Mrs. Pat O'Connor, she tried to explain how she'd been able to support her husband despite his deadly profession.

"Even when I was half-sick with fear inside, the most important thing was never to let Pat know it," Analice O'Connor wrote. "He was a race driver when I married him, and I never tried to change him. He was doing the thing he loved."[18]

The stories appeared five pages after a thirty-five-thousand-dollar Firestone ad featuring its research program at the Speedway. Company officials were furious and immediately put its five-hundred-thousand-dollar advertising contract with the magazine under review, although nothing more came of it.[19]

ED ELISIAN

Foyt followed with a third at Milwaukee, his best result yet in a big car on a paved track. It was the high-water mark for Foyt's Indy car season, however, as a series of mediocre finishes followed.

He continued to perform well in Erickson's new sprint car, finishing in the top five in seven of eight races over a two-month period, although failing to post a victory. That came to an end when USAC lifted its suspension of Ed Elisian. Erickson sold the car back to Watson, who wanted to reunite with his former driver. Without a sprint car ride, Foyt went back to his midget, nearly winning at Terre Haute before running out of fuel.

Foyt's midget and sprint car racing was a sore point with Dean and Brawner. They didn't like their young driver taking chances in what they considered minor events. For his part, Foyt thought the car owner and chief mechanic had agreed to provide parts and assistance for his other cars. The help had been slow in coming.

While the Dean team was better funded than most, it didn't mean there was unlimited money available. Expenses at Indianapolis were higher than expected and Brawner, who'd grown up during the Depression, wasn't one to spend freely.

Adding to his problems, Foyt found himself caught up in an argument between Elmer George and USAC officials after a race at Langhorne. George was leading on lap seventy-one of the one-hundred-lap event when his crew thought one of the car's tires was coming apart and signaled him to pit. Despite losing the lead he refused to stop, even ignoring a black flag from officials.

USAC official Tommy Nicholson, who was the race's chief steward and the eastern supervisor for the organization, suspended George for thirty days for ignoring the black flag. When Nicholson refused to pay the driver, George attacked him, grabbing his glasses and ripping his clothes. At first USAC tried to cover up the fight involving Tony Hulman's son-in-law, but by the next day the story was out, and George was suspended pending a further investigation.

Saying it was "98 percent personal" between the two, George claimed, "He did it just to try to agitate me. I was in a rage of temper and I played into his hands."[20]

The USAC board held a hearing and although Hulman recused himself, Foyt and Elisian spoke on behalf of their friend. Both said it was hard to see signs from the pits and flagman, both located on the inside of the track. They added that a driver was the best judge of when to change tires and said they were surprised USAC was "throwing the book at him."[21]

Despite the testimonies, George was suspended for a year and fined five hundred dollars. It could have been worse, one USAC official saying a lifetime ban was considered.

Foyt and Elisian had an unusual relationship. After being blamed by many for O'Connor's death, Elisian had struggled finding quality Indy car rides. He approached Brawner and Dean about driving for them, promising the pole at Indianapolis in 1960 if they bought him a new car. The pair agreed saying they'd field a two-car team for him and Foyt in the coming year.

When Foyt found out he was livid and confronted Elisian in the Dean garage, the pair going "toe to toe, throwing wild haymakers at one another," according to Brawner. Foyt said Brawner jumped on his back and eventually separated the two drivers, after which an uneasy truce existed.[22]

By late summer frustrations were running high on the Dean team. Engine problems knocked Foyt out of a dirt race at Springfield on August 22 and again a week later at Milwaukee, this time with wider consequences.

After qualifying eleventh for the Labor Day event, the engine in Foyt's car started leaking oil shortly after the start and just twenty-five miles into the two-hundred-mile race blew up completely. Two laps later Elisian skidded on the fluids from Foyt's engine and hit the wall, sliding for more than two hundred feet before flipping upside down, directly in front of the crowded stands.

The roll bar collapsed, trapping Elisian in the car. Unlike the accidents of O'Connor and others, who died on first impact, fans watched in horror as he struggled to get out of his machine while yelling for help. A moment later it was on fire and with race cars still circling the track, it took safety workers more than five minutes to extinguish the blaze. By then Elisian was dead.[23]

Foyt was in the pits when the crash occurred. The race was eventually stopped for about twenty minutes while the track was cleared, and when the drivers were asked to return to their cars Jim Rathmann balked. He'd seen enough. Foyt volunteered to take over, driving to a fourth-place finish.

————

With the death of Elisian, Watson was in need of a driver for his sprint car and offered it to Foyt. The move soon paid off for both. In a dominating performance two weeks later at Salem Speedway, Foyt posted his first victory in more than two years, qualifying on the pole and leading all one hundred laps.

The race was not without incident, as Foyt slid wide in a corner with five laps remaining, allowing Branson to close the gap. Coming out of the last turn, Branson went low to try and pass Foyt, who also came down the track. The right front of Branson's car touched the left rear of Foyt's and Branson backed off, the second-place finish securing him the Midwest sprint car championship. Afterward, Branson said he felt Foyt "squeezed" him at the finish line.[24]

Whether A.J. squeezed Branson or not didn't matter to Watson, who let Foyt drive the car again on October 11 in the inaugural sprint car race at Meyer Speedway, a new half-mile paved track in Houston. In addition to Branson and Bettenhausen, Foyt was facing a trio of relative newcomers—Parnelli Jones, Jim Hurtubise, and Roger McCluskey.

All three were making one of their first USAC starts, having dominated West Coast events. Jones had been all but unbeatable on his home track of Ascot Park in Los Angeles, before venturing out on IMCA's fairground circuit with similar results. McCluskey often finished second to Jones, and on the rare occasion when Parnelli wasn't in Victory Lane, he usually was. While most USAC sprint cars were powered by Offenhauser engines, both Jones and McCluskey drove Chevrolet-powered sprinters, fast becoming the hot West Coast setup.

Jones qualified on the pole with Foyt second. As Jones led the field down for the start his throttle jammed open. He pulled to the side, quickly freed it, and rejoined the race, but at the rear of the sixteen-car field. While Foyt led all fifty laps, the crowd cheered Jones as he fought his way through the field to finish third.[25]

The Indy car season ended for Foyt much the way it started as he spun and failed to qualify for the Golden State 100 in Sacramento on October 25. The track was heavily rutted and in poor condition and he stayed for the race, hopeful of being needed as a relief driver. He eventually replaced a driver named Bill Homeier and despite the pit stop to change drivers, Foyt came back to finish fifth.

Hurtubise, in just his third USAC big car start, won the race, and if anybody needed a victory more than Foyt it was the driver fans called "Herk," short for Hercules. His wife, Jane, had run out of gas on the way to the track and sat in the stands wondering how she would pay the babysitter of their two infant children with only one dollar in her purse.[26]

Despite finishing the year on a high note, winning a midget race at Corpus Christi Speedway in Texas, it could only be considered a disappointing season for Foyt and the Dean Van Lines team. He'd finished tenth at Indianapolis and fifth in the season's final point standings but failed to win a champ car race for the third straight year, despite driving for a team that won regularly before his arrival. At the same time several other drivers, including Hurtubise, had posted their first big car wins. By the end of the year the relationship between Brawner and Foyt had grown increasingly contentious.

"You win or you lose," Foyt said at one point. "I can win, but I don't think the car can."

"My cars have won plenty," Brawner shot back.

"The rift that started with the Dean Van Lines team and me didn't get any better, despite the fact I came close to winning a couple of races," Foyt said in his autobiography. "I thought it was the car. They thought it was me."[27]

Despite the problems, Dean and Brawner assured their driver, who'd signed a three-year contract running through 1960, they were committed to the relationship. Foyt, still smarting from the team's plan to add Elisian and the failure to support his other racing efforts, put out the word he was looking to make a change.

He soon received an unexpected phone call.

CHAPTER 9

BREAKTHROUGH

1960

It had been a tough couple of years for George Bignotti. Both Jimmy Reece and George Amick were driving for Bignotti when they died in crashes. Johnny Boyd, badly burned at Langhorne in the middle of the 1958 season, had raced only three times for the team in 1959. And the team's dirt track ace, Jud Larson, was diagnosed with a heart attack and sidelined, although Bignotti thought he'd simply had too much to drink the night before.

In their place Bignotti tried several drivers during the second half of 1959, including Don Freeland and Bobby Grim. Both performed well and he was considering one of them for 1960 when he heard A.J. Foyt might be looking for a ride. Foyt was ten years younger than the other drivers.

Like Clint Brawner, Bignotti saw something special in Foyt. For all his aggressiveness and inexperience, the young driver seldom made a mistake on the track. He had a rare talent for taking a car to its limit and keeping it there without crossing the line. "The hairline limit between the quick and the dead" is how Ken Purdy, perhaps the most acclaimed American motorsports writer of the 1950s and '60s, phrased it.[1]

Growing up in the San Francisco area, Bignotti had followed his two older brothers into auto racing. He did some driving in their jalopy and midget entries, winning fourteen of eighteen races one year. His real skill, however, was turning wrenches rather than a steering wheel. With Freddy Agabashian doing the driving, Bignotti's midgets won three consecutive Bay Cities Racing Association championships from 1946–1948. Agabashian went off to Indianapolis and Boyd added a fourth BCRA title to Bignotti's collection in 1951.

Thinking a career as a racing mechanic probably wasn't the best thing for raising a family, he opened a flower shop in Oakland but was soon drawn back to

◀ Foyt's first Indy car victory was at Du Quoin Fairgrounds on September 5, 1960. *Revs Institute, The Bruce R. Craig Photograph Collection*

the sport. He made his first trip to Indianapolis in 1954, working on Agabashian's sixth-place car, and went to work for roadster king Frank Kurtis in 1955.

In 1956 Bignotti partnered with Bob Bowes, owner of Bowes Seal Fast, a successful automotive aftermarket company that specialized in tire repair products. The Bowes family had sponsored Indy cars since the early 1930s, including the 500 winner in 1931. Over the years such drivers as Rex Mays and Louis Meyer drove for the team, but it had been a long dry spell since its 500 victory.

Bignotti and Boyd had reunited and finished in the top ten at Indy and the final USAC point standings for three consecutive years before the 1958 crash at Langhorne. With Boyd now running a limited schedule and still looking for his first win, Bignotti decided a more aggressive driver was needed to take the team to Victory Lane.

When he approached Foyt about driving in 1960, it was a better offer than the driver could have hoped for. There were few Indy car teams better than Dean Van Lines, and Bowes was one of them. Bignotti offered Foyt $6,500 (about $68,000 in 2024 dollars) and the standard 40 percent of earnings to sign. He sealed the deal by telling Foyt he'd make sure there was a sprint car to drive and A.J. could also drive in midget races. Foyt said he needed to talk with Dean, and according to his autobiography, the call was short, but not sweet.

"I called Al Dean and said, 'I know I signed a contract for 1960, but you all backed out of your deal with me on parts for the sprint car, so I quit.' End of conversation. End of me and the Dean Van Lines Special."[2]

Dean didn't take the call well. When Bryan left he could have picked just about any driver, but he selected the virtually unknown Foyt, seeing him as someone he could build his team around. He'd spent accordingly, paying Foyt's way to Europe for the Race of Two Worlds in 1958 and buying a new race car and engine for 1959. Feeling burned, he went out and hired veteran Eddie Sachs.

"I'm getting tired of giving guys breaks and having them get away from me," Dean said. "I hope Sachs will be more loyal than Foyt or Bryan were."[3]

"A.J. is an impatient son of a bitch," Sachs said, excited about his good fortune. "He won't wait for anyone or anything."

Brawner seemed to understand, but that didn't make it any easier. "I was surprised Foyt left," he said. "My cars have won plenty. It takes a while to get together, and we were just getting things right. But he was in a hurry."[4]

As usual, Foyt got the last word. "You have to go where the dough is going to be."

It was the first sign of a trait Foyt would display often during his career, a willingness to jump from one top car and team to another when he thought the move might give him a better chance at winning. It didn't always work, but it did more often than not.

Despite the bitter breakup, Foyt often thanked and praised Dean and Brawner for giving him his first big break.

"Clint was great to me, taught me so much, was very patient, and we never had a cross word," Foyt would say, time perhaps dimming the conversations recounted in his autobiography. "I was running my own sprint car, and I was trying to buy some parts but I didn't have any money. Clint was kinda tight with money. George Bignotti offered me a contract that included a sprinter. That's why I changed teams."[5]

Brawner also softened his tone, writing off their disagreements as the normal back-and-forth between driver and crew chief. "Foyt was not then as temperamental as he became later. He didn't give me any trouble. These guys always blame the cars and not themselves when they don't do well. You could see he was going to do well. It was just a question of how well. He was just a young guy who wanted to go fast and he wasn't happy when he didn't."[6]

Sachs went on to win three races, capture two pole positions at Indianapolis, and stay for the full length of his three-year contract, leaving the team at the end of 1963 only when Dean refused to buy a new car.

Brawner and Dean eventually did give another unknown young driver a chance—Mario Andretti in 1965. Together Brawner and Andretti won seventeen races, three national championships, and the 1969 Indianapolis 500—although Dean died of cancer in 1967 without realizing his dream of winning at the Speedway. Brawner's cars would win fifty-one champ car races and he'd be inducted into the Indianapolis Motor Speedway Hall of Fame in 1984 as one of the sport's most successful crew chiefs.

BIG GEORGE NOTTI

In January, Foyt joined Bignotti in Indianapolis to visit car builder Quin Epperly's shop. A.J. had a nickname for seemingly everyone and quickly tagged his new crew chief "Big George Notti." Proud of his Italian heritage, Bignotti never liked the moniker's mafioso connotations and let Foyt know it. As a result, A.J. seldom used it when "Big George" was within earshot.

The Bowes team had run two "laydown" cars at the Speedway in 1959, one built by Epperly and driven by Boyd, and a copy built by Frank Kurtis and driven by Larson. Even though the traditional "upright" roadsters had finished one-two, laydown cars were fourth, fifth, and sixth, and Bignotti wasn't ready to give up on the design, asking Epperly to overhaul both cars. Bowes also ordered a new dirt track champ car for Foyt from Wally Meskowski, although it wouldn't be ready for the start of the season.

Foyt's sprint car plans solidified when A.J. Watson signed him for a full season. The car now sported the No. 2 Foyt earned by finishing second in the Midwest series, a dark blue paint job, and sponsorship from the Dart Kart, a popular go-kart company owned by Watson's brother-in-law and future Indy 500 driver Mickey Rupp. Just in case there were any open dates, midget owners lined up to offer A.J. a ride.

The expanded schedule paid immediate dividends at the first race of the season on February 7 at Ascot Park. Driving the midget of West Coast owner Jack London, he traded the lead with teammate Davie Moses, before edging ahead on the last lap.

On March 20 at Meyer Speedway in Houston, he faced off again with Parnelli Jones, who was planning to run a full season of USAC sprint car races. Promoters quickly set up a one-hundred-dollar match race for Foyt and Jones. While Don

Branson was still the driver to beat on dirt, Foyt and Jones were fast becoming fan favorites and emerging as drivers of the future.

The two went at each other hard in the match race, more like there was a thousand dollars at stake, Jones emerging the victor. Anticlimactic but true to form, Branson won the feature, ahead of Hurtubise. Although Foyt led early, both he and Jones faded late.

After the Houston race, Foyt and Watson ran primarily in USAC's Eastern Championship series at the behest of their sponsor, while Jones concentrated on the Midwest Championship, the fans benefiting whenever their paths crossed.

Foyt was back in Los Angeles in early April to run a USAC-sanctioned event at Riverside International Raceway. The organization was still trying to develop its road racing series and urging its Indy drivers to participate, with Rodger Ward and Lloyd Ruby also entered.

The trio decided to run the midget race at Ascot the night before and this time it was Moses who triumphed over his teammate, winning for the third time in four starts. Three years older than Foyt and considered an up-and-comer in midget circles, Moses then left for a race in Sacramento, while Foyt and the others headed for Riverside.

The sports car event attracted some of the top road racers including Carroll Shelby, Dan Gurney, and Jack Brabham. Dale Burt entered a C-type Jaguar powered by a Chevrolet engine for Foyt, but he went off the track in practice and the car was too badly damaged to qualify. Shelby won the race, which was marred by the death of driver Pedro von Dory, whose car slid off the track and rolled down the embankment in the esses. Afterward Foyt was stunned to learn Moses had died earlier in the day after losing control of his car and rolling it four times at Sacramento.

At Trenton on April 10 for the first race with Bignotti and Bowes and the start of the Indy car season, Foyt started fourth and finished fifth in the team's old dirt track car, the updated laydown not ready yet. Ward began the defense of his 1959 title by leading all one hundred laps.

Three races in the Watson sprinter followed, Foyt winning at Reading and the first of two at Langhorne. In the second race of the doubleheader he led the first forty-seven laps before shredding a tire with three to go, Hurtubise inheriting the win.

Despite missing out on the hat trick, Foyt was in good spirits when he arrived in Indianapolis for the first day of practice. The dangers of competing in other series became apparent that night in New Bremen, Ohio, when he rolled the midget he was driving. He walked away and tried unsuccessfully to qualify the battered car but decided not to run any more events until after the 500.

Back at the Speedway he didn't find the Kurtis laydown any more to his liking than the Kuzma version. The relationship between Foyt and Bignotti began showing signs of volatility almost immediately and they argued over chassis setup. Making matters worse, not only was teammate Boyd running faster, so was Sachs. The Dean Van Lines team had bought a new "upright" car for Sachs to drive and he put it on the pole, setting a track record in the process. Foyt wanted to make changes to his car before qualifying, but Bignotti overruled him. A.J. qualified sixteenth with the first day's slowest speed, three places behind Boyd.

"I didn't want to settle for that, but the crew has been so patient," Foyt said, trying to control his frustration at qualifying slower than he'd been running earlier in the month. "We've changed a lot of things. One lap in practice I got 144 and the next one I was down to 136. Maybe it was just me."[7]

Away from the track things were better as A.J. and Lucy were again staying at the home of Elmer and Mari George. Young Tony was with them, and it was a relatively quiet time compared to some of the other drivers, a night out at the Foyts' favorite Mexican restaurant or a drive-in movie with Tony among the month's highlights.

"I won't even touch a beer the week before the race," Foyt said of his prerace routine. The night before, "I'll go to bed about 10 p.m. and get up at 7 a.m." He said he expected to have a big breakfast including "one of those Texas-sized steaks with french fries," a switch from his typical morning favorites, a cheeseburger, chili, and a Coke.[8]

New daughter Terry was at home in Houston, the grandmothers doing tag-team duty caring for her. Evelyn took the early part of the month before driving to Indianapolis with friends, stopping along the way to see different parts of the country. Lucy's mom, Elizabeth, took the second half of the month.

A.J.'s father also joined the team, helping with the engines. Stronger and more agile than men half his age, Tony continued to handle the right-rear tire on pit stops, the most dangerous position on the crew as it was exposed to other incoming cars.

Hopes that the car would race better than it qualified seemed justified at first as Foyt moved up quickly, only to drop out of the race before the halfway point with a burned-out clutch, finishing twenty-fifth. Boyd fared even worse, burning a piston and finishing twenty-seventh. Jim Rathmann won an exciting race with Ward in an event featuring a then-record twenty-nine lead changes.

Afterward Bowes blamed the laydown design and hinted at a one-car operation for 1961. "I had two laydowns this time," he said. "Next year I'm coming back with just one straight-up."[9]

That night Foyt had a meltdown. Hurtubise had broken the track record in qualifying and was Rookie of the Year. Another rookie and old running mate, Lloyd Ruby, finished seventh. Foyt unloaded to Lucy, questioning whether he had what it took to compete at Indianapolis.

"That's disgusting," he recalled saying of the finish in his autobiography. "I've been trying so long and so hard to win and what have I got to show for it? This is it. I've had it. I'm through."[10]

"I'm no better off than I was with Clint Brawner. I'm sick of this."[11]

Lucy, who many years later said she vaguely remembered the incident, let her husband blow off steam. Eventually he quieted down. She'd been through it before, and while she was no fan of racing she knew he wouldn't be happy doing anything else.

"If he didn't win, he'd always think of a thousand things he should have done," Lucy would say. "He was hard on himself. He'd throw temper tantrums, but he learned that didn't help. He finally learned you can't win them all. You have to take the good with the bad."[12]

"I think he had a little self-confidence problem," she said, although others found it hard to believe. "I think it took a long time to build up his confidence. I was the one he talked to, and I could see that. Maybe he pushed himself a little too hard sometimes and pushed the people who worked for him a little too hard. He just wanted them to be the best."

A.J. would often challenge his wife's assessment. "One thing: I'm not insecure, as Lucy says I am. Let's set that straight right now," he said on page two of the prologue to his autobiography.[13]

Lucy convinced him to run the next race at Milwaukee, just a week away. He'd run well there in the past. Foyt agreed, but with a caveat.

"I said I'd try it just to please her. But I also said if I didn't do well, I was gonna pack it in."[14]

The laydown design that was such a handful at Indianapolis proved to be much better on the flat Milwaukee oval. He qualified fourth while 500 winners Rathmann, Troy Ruttman, and Jimmy Bryan all failed to make the field. He led his first laps in an Indy car before finishing second to Ward. There was no further talk of quitting.

He followed Milwaukee with a midget victory June 10 at Anderson (Indiana) Speedway, coming from seventh at the start to take the lead midway through the one-hundred-lap event.

That set up a return to Langhorne for the champ cars. Foyt was one of the few drivers looking forward to the race. His best finish in an Indy car, second, had come at Langhorne, and he'd dominated the sprint car races at the track earlier in the year. And the new Meskowski dirt car was finally ready to debut.

PUKE HOLLOW

Langhorne Speedway was the most feared racetrack in America. Opened in 1926 just outside of Philadelphia, it was the first dirt track built exclusively for auto racing. A unique circular design differentiated it from the dual-purpose oval tracks hosting both horse and car races.

Most oval tracks have two straights and four corners. Sometimes the corners are banked. Drivers accelerate on the straights and brake for the corners. Langhorne, nicknamed "The Horne," was one mile of constant turning with no banking. The trick for a driver was to stay off the brake and on the gas, the cars sliding and dancing on the edge of control the entire lap—lap after lap. The track also ran downhill and uphill, one end being thirty feet below the other. Because it was round and flat, drivers weren't able to see very far ahead, and when dust began to build as the track dried out, visibility was often limited to just a few car lengths. Despite all the challenges, the track was incredibly fast, faster than the one-mile paved oval at Milwaukee.

Then there was "Puke Hollow." No matter how well the track's fine-grained dirt-and-oil surface was groomed before an event, it inevitably became filled with potholes and deeply rutted during practice and qualifying. Located just past the start/finish line at the low end of the track, legend said Puke Hollow's constantly changing surface became so rough drivers would get ill from the jostling. Others said they threw up just thinking about the track.

"That was the most dangerous track on earth," said Bobby Unser. Andretti agreed: "I can't imagine another track being that dangerous. I never lost sleep over debuting anywhere in the world, even with Formula 1. The night before Langhorne, I was actually really concerned."[15]

Several drivers simply refused to race there, including the top two finishers from the Indy 500, Rathmann and Ward. While Rathmann wasn't running for the season-long championship, Ward knew his decision would cost him points in the defense of his title.

"I don't need this bullshit," said Ward, who last raced at Langhorne in 1958. "There's no reason to go to a racetrack that you're not comfortable on. It makes no sense to me."[16]

One surprise entry was Bryan, the three-time national champion who'd won at the track in 1954 and 1955. "If I could drive a sprint car every weekend at Langhorne, I mean, no place else—I'd do it in a minute," Foyt recalled Bryan telling him.

But Bryan hadn't raced there since 1957 and had been running a limited schedule since winning at Indianapolis in 1958. When offered a ride by Watson in Ward's car, Bryan said he first wanted to make sure it was okay with the regular driver.

"I wish you wouldn't ask," Ward says he told Bryan. "That joint scares the shit out of me."

Bryan, tall and stocky, sporting a crew cut and an ever-present unlit cigar, was popular with both the fans and drivers and a master racetrack prankster and needler. He was also extremely confident.

"Nobody ever drove an automobile with more authority than Jimmy Bryan," wrote one reporter hyping his return." Bryan characteristically laughed off Ward's warning.[17]

"Ward says I'm crazy, that I'll kill myself. Hell, I'm only thirty-three, and I'm in good shape. Surely I can get around a track that I know as well as that one. Besides, I'll be careful."[18]

Having earned the tag "Earth Mover" early in his career for his skill on dirt, Bryan proved he could still hustle a car around the track, qualifying second to Branson.

Foyt struggled with the new car, qualifying ninth. Most dirt cars used a spring front suspension with torsion bars in the rear. The new car featured torsion bars front and rear and the team was having trouble tuning it for the challenging Langhorne surface.

As the drivers gathered for their prerace meeting, word spread that Al Herman, whom most of them raced against in the 500, had been killed the night before in a first-lap accident in a midget race in West Haven, Connecticut. Someone mentioned that two other drivers had been killed in Europe and that Stirling Moss, generally considered the best foreign driver, had been badly injured in yet another crash, breaking both his legs. At the drivers' meeting officials asked everyone to take it easy at the start. Trying to lighten the mood, Bryan wondered aloud if it was still okay to race into Turn One.

Starting alongside Branson on the outside of the front row, Bryan did just that, driving hard into Puke Hollow and sliding high on the track, his car bouncing fore and aft. He still seemed to be in control when the car lurched skyward, rolled several times, and started cartwheeling end over end, and as high as fifteen feet in the air. Bryan's lifeless body, restrained by a seatbelt, flapped about like a bronc rider. Both his neck and back were broken, and he was pronounced dead at a nearby hospital. Like Pat O'Connor's death, it had a lasting impact on Foyt.

"It was a terrible accident," he recalled. "He'd retired and wasn't racing no more. Then he came out of retirement. That's the reason I always said that I'd never come out of retirement. I always said when I'm through, I'm through."[19]

Foyt would go on to dominate at Langhorne in coming years, winning a record eight times between 1960 and 1964. "It was a helluva racetrack," he said. "You had to be in good shape to race it. That was the biggest thing. It was fast. I kind of enjoyed it, but it was a very dangerous track."

Following Langhorne came a string of seven sprint car events in which Foyt found it increasingly difficult to beat not only Branson, but also Jones and Hurtubise and their Chevrolet engines. Jones won three straight at one point, and following a dominating victory at New Bremen with Foyt second, the headline in the local paper read "It's That Jones Boy Again."

Foyt lobbied Watson to switch to a Chevrolet engine, but the car owner was loyal to Offenhauser and refused. Even on the high banks of Salem for the annual Labor Day weekend race, where Foyt had been hard to beat, it was Jones's turn to impress. He led from start to finish, lapping the field and setting a world speed record for a half-mile track.

The next day, when Foyt needed it most, he got a break that turned his season around—and perhaps his career.

Thirty-four cars showed up on Monday, September 5 for the traditional Labor Day Indy car race at the fairgrounds in Du Quoin, Illinois, known as the Magic Mile, with only eighteen supposed to make the field. Foyt considered himself jinxed at the track, having failed to qualify for the previous year's race.

Branson qualified on the pole with Ruby in second, Hurtubise was third, and Foyt fourth. With track temperatures topping one hundred degrees, Branson led early but was soon passed by Jim Packard, who came charging up from sixth in an eight-year-old car to take the lead. Foyt then passed Branson and set off after the leader.

Although Packard was a couple years older than Foyt, they'd been on similar paths, competing against each other since both had started their careers in IMCA in 1955 before eventually moving to USAC. Packard had finished third at Milwaukee and second at Langhorne earlier in the year, before breaking through for his first champ car win two weeks earlier at the Illinois State Fairgrounds. Handsome, with a jet-black Elvis-style haircut, Packard was a fan favorite for his hard driving style as much as his good looks.

Packard stretched his lead to more than twenty seconds over Foyt while lapping every other car. The pace eventually took its toll, however, the right-rear tire on Packard's car shredding on lap seventy-five of one hundred. Foyt inherited the lead and cruised to his first "big car" victory, finishing nearly a lap ahead of Tony Bettenhausen. Wearing a ten-gallon cowboy hat, his uniform soaked in oil, Foyt displayed a pair of blistered and bloody hands in Victory Circle, having elected to go without power steering because of its slight drain on horsepower. The crowd cheered for Foyt and roared for Packard, with A.J. adding to the praise.

"That boy Packard was outrunning me, but we just outlasted him. That boy was really going. It's too bad it had to happen to him, but that's racing luck."[20]

Foyt pocketed more than five thousand dollars for the win and noted he'd won back the twenty dollars he'd lost to J.C. Agajanian the night before playing gin rummy. The victory jumped Foyt into third place in championship points, with Packard close behind in fourth. Rathmann, still in second thanks to his points from the Indianapolis 500, was not running the dirt track races and as a result would not be a challenger in the final standings. After skipping Langhorne, Ward, clinging to first place, had run into a string of bad luck, failing to score points.

Foyt, "the exuberant young Texan with the smile from Texarkana to El Paso," was suddenly the hot story. Two weeks later he again benefited from the misfortune of other drivers in the biggest dirt track race of the year, the Hoosier Hundred at the Indiana State Fairgrounds. Ward qualified on the pole and immediately took the lead, with Alvin "Cotton" Farmer second and Foyt third. It was a wild race with multiple spins and cars flipping, but no serious injuries.[21]

After a rock cracked the front of the car's exterior tank, Foyt realized the oil sprayed out only when he slowed and the oil surged forward. He adjusted his driving to maintain a constant speed and avoid braking. It wasn't the fastest way around the track, and he wouldn't be able to challenge the leaders, but car owner Bob Bowes credited the move with keeping him in the race, with the goal of picking up valuable championship points.

If Foyt hadn't modified his style, "he might have gone ten to fifteen laps more," Bowes would say. "After he caught that rock we were just hoping he could finish."[22]

Those hopes changed drastically on lap sixty-eight when Ward abruptly slowed, his car dead. At nearly the same moment Farmer pulled in the pits, having been badly cut by a rock thrown up by one of the cars. Foyt suddenly found himself in the lead, which he held to the finish.

Admitting it "looked kind of bad" in the early going, he said the end result was "too good to be true."[23]

"I didn't believe it," Foyt said as a pool of oil formed under his stationary car. "My crew gave me the board that I was third one lap and the next time they told me I was leading."[24]

Looking to keep the momentum going, Foyt and most of the other Indy car regulars entered a sprint car race at Allentown, Pennsylvania, on September 24. The track was in poor condition, as often happened late in the season, badly rutted and dusty. He spun before the field received the green flag, forcing a restart. On the second attempt the race was only a half lap old when Johnny Thomson lost control, caught a rut, and began to flip, crashing through the inside wooden fencing, the driver thrown free from the car. The crash was eerily similar to one two months earlier that Thomson had walked away from. He'd briefly retired after that accident, returning a week later saying, "I have two or three good years ahead, then I'll quit." This time the car landed on him, and he was taken from the track in an ambulance.[25]

Once the race was finally underway there was no stopping Packard, as he led all twenty-five laps with Hurtubise second and Foyt third. The victory celebration, already muted, ended when word arrived that Thomson had died from his injuries.

Known as the "Flying Scot," the popular Thomson, thirty-eight, was the antithesis of the stereotypical race car driver. He was five foot six and 150 pounds, quiet, polite, and unassuming. Few were aware he'd been a highly decorated World War II B-25 bomber crew chief. He spent his spare time on a farm not far from the Allentown track with his wife and four children, all under age ten. He seemed not to mind when other drivers joked about his quiet lifestyle.

"On the track there'd been no questioning his skill," wrote Wayne Fuson in the *Indianapolis News.* "He was kidded occasionally about this devotion to home and family, but the kidders secretly admired him for it. He was a race driver's race driver. It was a job to him, a job that he both respected and feared. He was not the bragging kind, but he was one of the most respected in the business."[26]

Tommy Hinnershitz, a seven-time sprint car champion and Thomson's close friend, immediately announced his retirement. The rest of the drivers headed for Trenton, less than a two-hour drive, where there was an Indy car race the next day.

Branson and Foyt qualified one-two and Foyt was leading with just ten laps left when he was forced to pit for fuel, eventually finishing third. Sachs, an Allentown native and another friend of Thomson's, earned the victory with Ward second.

With only a pair of short midget races scheduled for the first weekend in October, Foyt headed home for Houston, his first off weekend since early July. That's where he learned that Packard had been killed in the race at Fairfield, Illinois.

After hitching a ride with Jones to the track, Packard was driving Jones's old midget when something apparently broke in the steering. The car went into a series of flips, killing Packard immediately. It fell to Jones to return Packard's suitcase to his wife, who had one small child at home and was pregnant with another. Jones called Packard's death "one of the hardest things I've ever had to deal with."[27]

Packard was the fourth Indy car driver to be killed in the four months since the 500, a fact not lost on *Sacramento Bee* columnist Wilbur Adams.

"The big cars are supposed to race on the state fair ground track on the last Sunday of the month," Adams wrote in a preview of the upcoming event. "We say supposed to because the casualty rate among the drivers has been so high there may be none alive by October 30."[28]

Years later Foyt said, "I didn't really know Jim Packard. I knew him as a hard race driver. But he got killed in a little dirt race."[29]

"Whenever anybody was hurt or killed it was a bad time," Lucy said. "For a while it happened a lot. You didn't know who would be there from race to race."

NEW CHAMPION

Foyt returned to Indianapolis early the following week and was at the Speedway when Jack Brabham, fresh from winning the F1 world championship, tested his rear-engine F1 Cooper at the track. "Black Jack" was considering the possibility of racing it in the 500.

Encouraging Brabham was Ward, who picked him up at the airport and then gave him a tour of the track in a station wagon. Brabham passed all the stages of an unofficial driver's test before lunch and was soon running laps at nearly 145 mph, good enough to qualify for the previous 500 despite giving away a hundred cubic inches of engine displacement.

"He had this little Cooper, but I didn't pay no attention to it," Foyt said of Brabham's test. "At that time I wasn't worried about nobody except our own team."[30]

Foyt spent most of his time grilling Watson about his new roadster design. Bowes and Bignotti had agreed to purchase a new roadster for Foyt to drive in 1961, replacing the dreaded laydown car. Floyd Trevis was building the car based on Watson's design, Watson himself being too busy with projects for his own team.

On the track after a two-week break, Foyt clinched the Eastern sprint car championship with a win at Williams Grove Speedway, edging Hurtubise. Then it was Jones's turn, taking the Midwest sprint car title with another win at Meyer Speedway. It wasn't easy, Foyt and Jones trading the lead five times over fifty laps.

Even though Ward remained in first place in the season-long points standings as the teams arrived in Sacramento for the penultimate race of the Indy car season, the combination of Foyt, Bignotti, the Meskowski dirt track car, and a little bit of luck was considered the favorite. The track surface was in poor condition, and after qualifying seventh Foyt gave Bignotti an earful about what he wanted done to the car.

"We had to make many changes which we felt would adapt the car more to the track and also give A.J. a better feel for the car," Bignotti said. "We changed the tires, readjusted the chassis by raising it slightly to make it ride better and redistributed the weight on each wheel. We got the job done just in time."[31]

Foyt got a break before the race even started, the new cars of Ruby and Sachs slamming together in practice, sending Sachs's car into a series of flips. The crash knocked both cars out of the race and put Sachs in the hospital. In the race Ward lasted only one lap before burning a piston in his engine. Branson and Hurtubise led early while Foyt searched for the fast way around the track. He eventually found it and moved to the front, stretching his lead to twenty seconds over Jones at the finish. Foyt again had shown his ability to set up a car and adapt his driving style to the track.

"I drove my race on what I call a diamond pattern. I found my car was performing alright going against the grooves, so I adjusted myself accordingly. I would ride high on the straightaway and start broad sliding into the turns."

The victory, combined with Ward's poor finish, gave Foyt a 120-point lead heading into the final champ car race of the year, November 20 at the Phoenix Fairgrounds. Even if Ward won the race, Foyt only needed to finish fifth or better to win the championship and he received plenty of advice on how to approach the event.

"Everybody I talked to said the same thing, 'You've got the championship all won, so take it easy,'" Foyt said in his autobiography. "Just get out there and stroke it. Bignotti said, 'Take it easy,' Bowes said, 'Take it easy.'"[32]

Foyt seemed to be taking their advice after qualifying ninth, his worst start of the year in the Meskowski car. Ward was even worse, back in thirteenth. Once the race started, however, both drivers moved toward the front. Rather than let Ward set the pace and simply keep him in sight, Foyt ran hard, passing Hurtubise and moving into the lead after twenty-four of the one hundred laps. Ward pitted and dropped a lap behind and both he and Hurtubise spun out trying to catch the leader. Once again Foyt wore a cowboy hat into Victory Lane, where he was backed by his father, Bowes, and Bignotti.

In his autobiography Foyt is quoted as saying he ran the entire race "wide open, I was on the verge of losing it all day." In his comments immediately afterward, however, he said, "After Hurtubise spun out, I slowed down. I was running so slow the engine almost stopped. I never even stood on it—a more likely scenario."[33]

By year end there was no denying that at twenty-five Foyt was the sport's brightest rising star. He was the youngest USAC champion ever and the first driver since Bryan in 1956 to win the championship without scoring a point in the Indianapolis 500.

He celebrated four nights later by competing in his first Turkey Night Grand Prix midget race, which after twenty years was moving to Ascot Park. Of course Foyt won. Despite starting eighteenth, he drove London's midget into the lead after sixty-nine laps and that's where he was when the race was stopped because of fog after 122 of the scheduled 150 circuits. Hurtubise was second and Jones third.

"I thought my goggles were fogging over," Foyt recalled. "You were coming off [turn] four and you were just blind for maybe half a second, but you were running real fast up against the fence. They must have let it run like that for ten to fifteen laps—it was dangerous. Finally the fog just came down real thick and you couldn't see nothing. That was a spooky night."[34]

It had been a remarkable year. After questioning whether he should continue racing following the disappointing 500, he'd qualified for every Indy car race, a feat accomplished by only Branson and Hurtubise. He'd won four of the final six champ car races and the national title, twenty sprint car races and the Eastern championship, and made sixty thousand dollars, easily the most he'd ever banked in a season.

"I know I'd never have [won the Indy car championship] if I hadn't been very lucky," he acknowledged. "Lucky on the track and lucky to always be driving running machinery."[35]

"I never in my wildest dreams expected to make that much money in auto racing. I told Lucy, this is the most money I'll ever make. The only thing that could be better than this would be if I won Indy."[36]

He had a point. His winnings were only about half of what Rathmann earned while running only five races, thanks to his victory in the 500.

A.J. meant to change that, telling a friend, "Indianapolis, here I come."[37]

CHAPTER 10

NUMBER ONE

1961

Although he'd yet to win a big car race on pavement, part of A.J. Foyt's excitement about the coming year was the decision by George Bignotti and Bob Bowes to order a new speedway car, a copy of the 1960 race-winning Watson upright to be built by Floyd Trevis.

Foyt also was happy with Bowes's decision to run only one car during the season, which meant Johnny Boyd, who'd driven for the team for the past five years, was without a ride. It didn't take long for Boyd to land, catching on as Rodger Ward's teammate on A.J. Watson's powerful Leader Cards team.

In addition to the No.1 on his car, Foyt had the number painted on his helmet, although he acknowledged it meant little once the season started.

"The national championship means nothing when that green flag falls. Then nobody's a champ until he gets the checkered first."[1]

Despite his success teaming with Watson on the sprint car circuit in 1960, the car owner's refusal to switch to Chevrolet power led Foyt to run his own operation for 1961, with Bowes agreeing to provide sponsorship. USAC was combining the Midwest and Eastern tours into a single championship and as a result there would be two No. 1 cars running during the year, Foyt and Parnelli Jones each having earned the right to wear the number assigned to the previous year's champion.

For good measure, Foyt started 1961 on February 5 by competing in his first stock car race since the Playland days, a USAC event in Arizona. The organization was trying to prop up its stock car series in the face of NASCAR's rapid growth, and a handful of Indy car regulars turned out, although Foyt was headed home before the race was half over.

He opened the midget season March 19 with a victory in Jack London's car at Orange Show Speedway in San Bernardino, California, and followed it a week

◄ Indianapolis Victory Lane with Lucy. *IMS Photography Archive* later on the other side of the country by winning the sprint car race at Reading, Pennsylvania. Despite the victory, Foyt quickly discovered car ownership wasn't easy.

"They tell me you can make a lot more money if you own your car, but I don't know about that," he said. "It's a lot of trouble. I've been working on it for the past three days and I'm still not satisfied. I'll have to work on it more when I get back."[2]

First he went to Trenton for the April 9 opener of the Indy car series. The new car wasn't ready, and he was forced to start the old laydown model. Further slowed by a balky engine, he qualified and finished fifth. Eddie Sachs was impressive while driving the Dean Van Lines car to victory and afterward only wanted to talk about Indianapolis, a race he'd never finished.

"I know I'm going to win it," he said. "I've got it all figured out. Just like I had today's race figured out. I told everybody I was going to win today and they laughed because they thought I was kidding. I wasn't. It worked out like I had it planned, and now it's my time to laugh.

"I'll win it because I want to win it so much. And when I win it, I'll quit. Retire. Get me a steady job and enjoy my investments. I won't even go on the track to drive the pace car. Racing has been good to me, and I enjoy it. But the laughs are not as funny as they used to be."[3]

Adding insult to injury, hauling his sprinter back to Indianapolis Foyt picked up a speeding ticket in Springfield, Ohio, for going seventy miles per hour, the sixty-dollar fine drawing national attention.

There were a midget race and two sprint car events remaining before action shifted to Indianapolis, and Foyt won two of three. The combined sprint car series was proving extremely competitive, with newcomer Roger McCluskey winning at Williams Grove Speedway. Jones, looking for this third straight victory at Salem, qualified on the pole and led the first twenty-three laps before being black-flagged for an oil leak. Foyt, who'd been running second and waving at officials, pointing to Jones's car for several laps, took over to win. Afterward Foyt heard something he hadn't heard in the past—booing. Although the fans' target was the officials who decided to black-flag Jones, it startled Foyt. For his part, Jones handled it gracefully.[4]

"Someone was throwing oil," Jones said. "It might have been my car. I don't think so, but we have to have officials. They did what they thought was right. There'll be another race."[5]

DEATH OF A CHAMPION

It was a cocky Foyt, winner of four of the year's first seven races, who arrived in Indianapolis for the start of practice. He was becoming increasingly close to Tony Hulman through his relationship with Elmer and Mari George, even promising the track owner over dinner he was going to win the Golden Anniversary running of the race.

He was in demand on the local personal appearance circuit many drivers used to supplement their income, touring eight Kroger grocery stores shortly after his arrival, spending about thirty minutes meeting fans and signing autographs at each market. It wasn't his favorite thing to do, but the money was good and besides, his car wasn't finished.

When it finally arrived the new Trevis was a stunner—gleaming snow white with a red nose, trimmed in the traditional black and white highlights, with a big red No. 1 on each of the car's rear flanks. The finishing touches were applied by Dean Jeffries, who was becoming well known in Gasoline Alley for his artistry, and the car eventually would win an award at a Los Angeles hot rod show for its paint job. Only nine of the sixty-nine cars entered were new, including the new Watsons for Boyd and Ward and the cars of Tony Bettenhausen and Lloyd Ruby that were entered in 1960 but not raced.

The car attracting most of the attention was the rear-engine Cooper of Formula One champion Jack Brabham, who returned after his successful test the previous year. The car featured a longer wheelbase and a beefed-up suspension, slightly offset to the left to better handle Indy's sweeping turns. The Coventry Climax engine was bigger and converted to run on methanol like the Offenhauser. Still, the car was tiny, Clint Brawner saying it made the roadsters "resemble Mack trucks."

Causing the biggest ruckus was its color, a dark "forest" green also known as British Racing Green. Ever since Gaston Chevrolet won the 1920 Indy 500 and national championship in a green car, only to be killed late in the year, the color was considered unlucky in American racing. Foyt, among others, avoided the color at all costs, even refusing to ride in a green passenger car.

It soon became apparent it could finally be Bettenhausen's year. Twice a national champion and winner of twenty-one Indy car races, top among active drivers, he'd started every 500 since World War II but was still looking for his first victory. As Indy qualifying approached, he set an unofficial track record and predicted he'd officially break through the 150 mph barrier. Also looking for his first 500 victory was his car owner, Lindsey Hopkins, the millionaire Coca-Cola distributor from Atlanta who'd been entering cars in the race for ten years with a couple of second-place finishes to show for his efforts.

So confident was the team that they left Bettenhausen's car in Gasoline Alley early Friday before qualifying, planning to run a few laps late in the day when the track was cool, a period becoming known as "happy hour." Bignotti decided to wait, too, and Foyt was sitting on the pit wall alongside Sachs, trading barbs with other drivers and crewmen.

Bettenhausen, forty-four, was talking with Paul Russo, forty-seven. They were two of the oldest drivers on the circuit and more than just good friends. They started their careers in the 1930s driving midgets as part of the prewar "Chicago Gang," a marauding group of drivers who competed throughout the Midwest and South, sometimes using Tony Foyt's garage as their base in Houston.

Both were preparing for their fifteenth 500. They'd shared their best Indianapolis finish, a second in 1955. After Russo failed to qualify, Bettenhausen suggested they share his car, which would start second. Two pit stops for fuel and tires would be needed and as the lack of seat belts made driver changes easy, Bettenhausen theorized two drivers would be better than one. He drove the first and last segments and Russo the middle portion of the race. Even though Bettenhausen drove forty-six more laps, he insisted Russo be listed as a co-driver rather than a relief driver, and that they evenly split the second-place purse and points.

While Bettenhausen was the odds-on favorite to capture the pole position, Russo was struggling to get up to speed. On paper he was in a good car, the 1959 Watson roadster Ward drove to victory and that performed well in the 1960 race. But the car arrived at the Speedway late and after a day of practice he asked Bettenhausen to drive it for a few laps.[6]

Often called "test hopping," having another driver run a few laps in your car to get a second opinion on its performance was common practice at the Speedway. Sometimes the test hopper might spot something wrong or make a suggestion, other times he simply reinforced what the primary driver was already saying. As speeds and the race purse rose in later years, few drivers and even fewer car owners would be agreeable to test hopping.

Bettenhausen was never reluctant to test another car, especially for a friend. Before climbing in Russo's machine, he checked with Hopkins to make sure it was okay. Knowing the relationship between the two drivers Hopkins reluctantly agreed, asking Bettenhausen "not to run fast," and realizing it was a futile request.

Bettenhausen ran four laps—a mock qualifying run—at more than 145 mph, easily fast enough to make the race. As he passed the start/finish line his regular crew chief, Jack Beckley, waved him into the pits. He'd proved his point.

Coming out of Turn Four, Bettenhausen seemed to be headed for Pit Lane. Some observers said he was working with the weight jacker, attempting to change the balance of the suspension. Others said he held up a hand and extended a finger, indicating one more lap. Still others said he appeared to be braking.

As the car approached the pit entrance it swerved back toward the track, and then made a hard right turn, directly into the three-foot high outside concrete wall. The car jumped into the air at impact, landing on top of the wall, ripping into the steel cable fencing designed to protect spectators. The car launched into a series of barrel rolls against the barrier, tearing out more than 250 feet of fencing and support posts, before coming to a rest on the wall near the start/finish line, upside down, with the driver's cockpit in the grandstands and the rear of the car perched high in the air, the tires still spinning.

Several drivers standing nearby ran to the car but were driven back when it caught fire. Sachs put his hands on his head and started to cry. Foyt grabbed his helmet and headed to the team's garage. Both knew what doctors later confirmed, Bettenhausen was already dead.

Foyt was alone when he entered garage No. 83, the team and car still on Pit Lane. He pitched his helmet against the wall and watched as it ricocheted across the floor. He thought about how Bettenhausen had been one of the few drivers willing to share information about the Speedway. How Tony talked him into drinking too many screwdrivers. How he joked about being upside down in a car twenty-eight times. "I never worry about crashes as long as I can count them," he'd said. Foyt, who freely admitted he often scared himself in a race car, could never understand when Bettenhausen said "I absolutely have no fear in a race car. It may seem tremendously dangerous to you, but it doesn't seem so to me."[7]

"It is something I'll never forget," Foyt would say. "Tony was special, a great driver and a great guy. He helped other guys. Which most won't. You got to go on, but when a guy like Tony goes, it gets harder."[8]

When the team didn't return, Foyt retrieved his helmet and headed back to the pits, thinking they wanted to run a few more practice laps. They were starting to pack up when he reached Pit Lane, the announcement being made the fence would take too long to repair. The track was closed for the day.

It was left to crew chief Beckley to call the Bettenhausen family farm in Tinley Park, Illinois, where Tony's wife, Valerie, was getting the four children, ages nine through nineteen, ready to attend qualifying. Two of the boys, Gary and Tony Jr., would eventually drive in multiple 500s, while the third, Merle, would lose an arm in a racing crash.

"There's been an accident," Beckley said.

"Tony?" Valerie asked.

"Tony."

"All the way?" she asked.

"All the way."

Bettenhausen's death loomed over the first weekend of qualifying. Sachs was the fastest, capturing his second consecutive pole position and immediately becoming the new race favorite. Hurtubise was second and newcomer Jones fifth. Foyt was seventh, his best starting position yet. Brabham, shuttling back and forth to Europe where he was competing in the Monaco Grand Prix, qualified thirteenth.

A few days later Foyt joined Hulman, Hurtubise, and several other drivers in Tinley Park for the Bettenhausen funeral. At the track Russo took Bettenhausen's car out for several laps but was unable to reach qualifying speeds. Lloyd Ruby eventually qualified the car, setting the second-fastest official time of the month, although it would come during the second weekend.

On hand to mark the special festivities surrounding the fiftieth anniversary of the first 500 in 1911 was race winner Ray Harroun, eighty-two, driving his bumblebee yellow Marmon Wasp slowly around the Speedway. More than 250,000 people were estimated to be in attendance and Foyt's car was ready before he was, the Trevis being the first car pushed out to Pit Lane. The increased speeds during practice had led to increased buffeting, especially in traffic, and A.J. decided to wear his red bandanna for the first time in the race.

While Sachs was the favorite of both the oddsmakers and fans, it was Hurtubise who took the lead at the start and led the first thirty-five laps before pitting. Jones took over to lead his first laps in the 500 and was still up front when a five-car accident on the front straight slowed the field. No one was hurt but debris was scattered everywhere, and a small piece of metal was tossed up and hit Jones above the eye, blood beginning to flow down and fill his goggles.

Knowing it wasn't time to make a pit stop, Jones raised the bottom of the goggles on the straights to let the blood flow out. For twenty laps he held on to the lead during the caution, draining the blood on the straights. It wasn't until his engine started to go bad that he began to fall back. The engine eventually lost a cylinder, but he'd soldiered on and finished twelfth.

On lap seventy-six, it was Foyt's turn to take the lead for the first time at the Speedway.

"I thought about the radio broadcast of the race," he said in his autobiography. "I knew exactly what Sid Collins was saying on the radio, because I had heard his broadcast of the race almost all my life. I knew he was talking about me."[9]

In fact it was Collins's sidekick, former driver Freddie Agabashian, who broke in on the announcer, shouting "Foyt's going for the lead!" as the front-runners entered the first turn.[10]

At first Collins sounded perturbed by the interruption, but when Agabashian excitedly repeated it, he asked the broadcast team's corner announcers to describe the action. In each case they were too late—"the leaders just went by me"—as Foyt passed Jones going into Turn Three. By the time he crossed the start/finish line for the first time as the leader, Foyt was "fifty, fifty-five car lengths ahead" and Collins was ready for him.

"He, of course, is a rather quiet fellow and very, very modest and in fact, it's hard to get him to ever say anything," the voice of the 500 said. "Everybody feels the Texan has a destiny and date with greatness and perhaps today he's going to do it."

The lead was short-lived as Troy Ruttman took over the front spot, but when he dropped out just past the halfway point, the race turned into a battle between Foyt and Sachs. Seven times they traded the lead, as each prepared for their final planned pit stops.

Sachs pitted first and made a clean stop, refueling and changing tires in a quick twenty seconds. Foyt was next and it was immediately apparent that Frank Catania, the crew's assistant chief mechanic who was manning the fuel hose, was having a problem. The team was using a new aircraft type fuel nozzle that cut off the flow of fuel when disengaged. It worked fine in practice and during the first two stops, but now Catania couldn't get it to engage. As the tire changers finished their duties, they crowded around the fueler. Bignotti, who handed Foyt water and new goggles, joined the group, but nothing worked. Foyt kept looking over his shoulder, aware something was wrong, but unsure what. Bignotti finally slammed the cap to the tank's vent closed, tapped his driver on the helmet, and pointed for him to go back on the track. The stop lasted twenty-nine seconds and Foyt found himself in second place.

Bignotti turned to his fueler and asked how much methanol he'd been able to get into the car. "Not a drop," Catania said, tossing the hose aside in disgust. They did some quick calculations and figured Foyt would have to slow to a crawl and average better than two miles per gallon in order to finish the race, costing him not only first place, but several other spots. They decided not to tell their driver and to let him run hard in pursuit of Sachs.

It took Foyt only four laps to run down and pass Sachs, and A.J. wondered if something was wrong with the other driver's car. His own tachometer was indicating 7,000 rpm at the end of the straight, 200 rpm higher than at any point earlier in the race. He knew he was turning fast laps and in fact, he was running faster than his qualifying speed.

Then Foyt saw the sign from his pits, "Late Stop," and guessed what happened. He was running light and would have to pit again. If there was any doubt the next sign removed it: "Fuel Low." Another lap and the board read "Keep Going." It wasn't long, however, before the engine began to stumble on the straights, what little fuel remaining sloshing to the back of the tank and away from the fuel pickup point.

Sachs was trying to keep pace and driving harder than ever. He could see Foyt's pit signs but wasn't sure to believe them. His only hope was to keep pressure on the younger driver.

In the pits Bignotti gave up trying to fix the team's high-tech nozzle and began looking for another he could borrow. He was in luck as Len Sutton, the driver pitted next to Foyt, was already out of the race and the team agreed to loan its tank to Bignotti, who moved it as close to the Foyt pit as possible. The word went out on lap 183: "Come In."

"My heart sank," Foyt would say. "I said, man, here we've raced all day, and it looked like we had it won. And now I've lost it."[11]

The crowd roared as Foyt headed down Pit Lane and Sachs waved as he went into the lead. Unaware of the new refueling tank, Foyt slid past Catania holding the hose and into his original pit box, forcing his team to roll the car back. Unfamiliar with the new hose, Catania again struggled as the team went to change the right-side tires, already badly worn from the battle with Sachs. It took twenty-eight seconds before Catania could get fifteen gallons into the car and Foyt headed back on the track, hopelessly behind.

It wasn't long until Sachs realized it was his turn to worry. Both of his right-side tires were beginning to show white warning cords, indicating a tire needed to be changed. The right-rear was particularly worrisome. With less than ten laps remaining he thought he could finish but with five left the vibration became more than Sachs was willing to risk and the crowd roared again as he headed for his pit.

Sachs was more than ten seconds behind when he returned to the track. He closed on Foyt but it was too late, the eight-second difference at the finish the second-smallest margin in race history at the time. Bignotti, perched atop the team's original fuel tank, waved a fifty-cent souvenir checkered flag as Foyt went past and then ran with the rest of the team toward Victory Lane. Standing at the end of Pit Lane, Hulman clutched both hands above his head in his traditional salute to the winner.

"I was ready to settle for second," Foyt admitted in Victory Lane. "You gotta get the breaks."[12]

All was seemingly forgotten about the botched pit stop, although Foyt later admitted when he was called back to his pit, "I wanted to run right over those guys."[13]

Foyt was surprisingly subdued at first, "about as composed as any man who ever drove into Victory Lane," according to the *Indianapolis Star*. Spotting Hulman he perked up, reminding the track owner of their dinner discussion the previous summer.

"You told me to win the anniversary, Tony, remember?" he shouted, Hulman smiling and nodding his head yes. Unlike Sachs, who'd promised to retire if he won, Foyt said he'd drive for at least another ten years.

"I'll run in all the races I can get in," he said. "I'm gonna race until I'm thirty-five or thirty-six, then *maybe* I'll retire."[14]

Arriving late to the ceremony was Lucy Foyt, who had refused to leave her seat in the tower alongside Mari Hulman George until the race was over. She could have passed for a Hollywood starlet in white bejeweled sunglasses and an elegant summery dress, her shiny blonde hair hanging to her shoulders and a single string of pearls around her neck.

"I wouldn't believe it," she said of her late arrival. "I was determined to just sit where I was in the Tower until the race was over. I was anxious. I was sorta numb I guess."[15]

"This is the greatest thing that ever happened to us," Lucy said, adding, "It is the biggest moment in our *racing* lives. I feel wonderful."[16]

Just twenty-two years old and suddenly thrust into the spotlight, Lucy had a reason to be numb. Someone asked her what they planned to do with the money and where they would go on vacation.

"What vacation?" she said. "I'm going home and A.J.'s going to Milwaukee. Race drivers race, so their wives don't get vacations. We've talked about winning the race a lot but we never got around to thinking about what we'd do with the money."[17,18]

She was already planning a quick shopping trip. Having sent most of her clothes back to Houston, she needed to a get a dress for the Victory Banquet.

Missing the drama of the final laps and Victory Lane entirely was the rest of the Foyt clan, including Evelyn and Marlene Foyt and Dale Burt and his family. They'd been watching the race from seats in Turn One on the outside of the track. When A.J. was forced back to the pits for more fuel, Burt suggested they make their way back through the tunnel to Gasoline Alley, otherwise they'd never be able to buck the surge of the crowd leaving the track.

"Mother didn't want to go," Marlene recalled. "She never left before a checkered flag. But I said we had to leave, or we would never get to the garage. I said A.J. had a sure second place, so we should go."[19]

They were in the tunnel under the track when the roar of the crowd and then the announcer informed them that Sachs was pitting, followed by another roar when A.J. retook the lead. Now Marlene wanted to run back to their seats, but the superstitious Evelyn refused, insisting they stay put until the race was over.

Pulling into the pits after the race, a despondent Sachs threw up his hands in surrender, then dropped his head to the steering wheel. The pit stop cost him at least sixty thousand dollars and much more: his lifelong dream. He faced repeated questioning about the decision to stop, even wife Nance asking if he really had to pit.

"Yes honey, I'm sorry, I did," he said. "I was driving around and I was thinking, 'This is it. Now you've won.' I had tears in my eyes. I began to sob. I was thinking about what I'd say in Victory Lane. Then the tire started to go and I had to quit. Better second than dead."[20]

"Boy that guy was really going," he said of Foyt. "You gotta give him credit. You have to say Foyt had some bad luck and I inherited the lead. I really didn't earn it. Then I had to stop and he got it back."[21]

A Firestone engineer checked the blistered tire and agreed with Sachs, saying it would not have lasted until the end of the race.

Others, led by Brawner, weren't so sure. "He should have chanced it, kept going," said the crew chief still looking for his first 500 win. "Ran the tire clear around on the rim if he had to. Foyt couldn't have caught him. Eddie should have known that the tire would have lasted."

Car owner Dean admitted being torn over Sachs's decision. "I don't know what Eddie should have done. I wanted him to keep going, but then I wasn't in his place. If he'd blown the tire and been killed, I would have felt a helluva lot worse than I do now."[22]

In the Bowes Seal Fast team garage, just a few doors down from where Sachs faced the media, a raucous celebration broke out. It was the first 500 victory for the team since 1931 and the first ever for Bignotti and Bob Bowes Jr. A.J. was finally joined by the rest of the family and the Burts, who took part in the fun. When the celebration began to wane, A.J. and Lucy put the Burt girls in the back seat of the Thunderbird pace car and gave them a ride around the track.

Foyt led a race high seventy-one laps, set a speed mark for the 500, and picked up a record first-place purse of $118,000, supplemented by another $10,650 paid to the winner by companies whose products were used on the victorious car.

Overlooked by most in the wild finish and victory celebration was Brabham's ninth place in the rear-engine car. Foyt noticed, however, saying, "That guy's a real professional."

The debate over Sachs's decision to stop carried into the next day, although Sachs never wavered on his decision. "I knew at lap 194 the right-rear was going to go. I'm not sorry. I finished the race for the first time. And I'm here."[23]

Asked again if he would have pitted, Foyt paused for a long time before mimicking Brawner. "I don't think so. I think I'd have run her right to the rim. But it's hard to say." Years later in his autobiography he said, "I would have stayed out there."[24]

In many ways Foyt's victory at Indianapolis marked a changing of the guard. "A New Era Opens at Indy's Golden Jubilee" is how *Sports Illustrated* put it. Gone were most of the drivers from the 1950s—Pat O'Connor, Jimmy Reece, Tony Bettenhausen, Bill Vukovich, and too many others. Replacing them were Foyt, Hurtubise, and rookie of the year co-winners Bobby Marshman and Jones. Brabham's performance in the underpowered rear-engine car provided a glimpse of the new cars and foreign drivers on the horizon. One thing, however, would remain a constant through it all—A.J. Foyt.[25]

At the awards dinner Foyt recognized Brawner for giving him his big break. He also said he was having a special victory ring made for Lucy. "I was just about ready to quit and go home," Foyt said, harkening back to the previous year's disappointment. "But Lucy talked me into going to Milwaukee. My luck changed and I won the national championship."[26,27]

When the total purse came up just short of four hundred thousand dollars, Hulman told Foyt to come by his office the next day and he'd give A.J. a personal check for six thousand dollars.

After the awards dinner and at the behest of Hulman, Foyt went on a promotional tour to New York City. It included an appearance with Harroun on the popular television show *What's My Line?* The two race car drivers barely spoke, and the celebrity panel failed to guess their profession, but Foyt took advantage of the opportunity afterward to ask the winner of the first 500 when he knew it was time to retire.

"He told me, 'You'll know A.J. It'll come to you all of a sudden, and deep down, you'll know.' I never forgot that."[28]

Returning to Houston, Foyt asked his father how much he owed on the house, Tony telling him "It's none of your business." A.J. then went to the bank and paid off the loan, although he was confronted afterward by his angry father.

"Daddy got mad at me. He said, 'Why did you do that. I don't need you to do it.' I said, 'Daddy, you and Momma worked hard all your life, you gave me everything you possibly could. If something happened to me tomorrow, I would know that you have a place that is paid for, and you do not have to worry about it. That is just thanking you and Momma for what you did for me through the years.'"[29]

While in Houston, Foyt continued to spend time at his father's garage, helping out where he could. He also experienced a rare moment of praise from his father, if indirectly.

"I was working under the dashboard of this car when a lady customer came in and said, 'Tony, your boy had a great, great weekend. Aren't you very proud of him?' He said, 'Yes.' She said, 'Well, what is he doing now?' He said, 'He is over there working on that car.' And the lady came over and said, 'I cannot believe you are doing this.' I got out from under the dashboard and the lady, I wish I could remember her name—she looked at me like you've got to be crazy to still be working! I will never forget that. That has been my whole life. I enjoy working."

JONES AND HURTUBISE

Foyt posted another Indy car victory a couple of weeks later, on the dirt at Langhorne, beating Jones and benefiting when leader Hurtubise spun. One month to the day after winning the Indianapolis 500, Foyt won a twelve-and-a-half-mile midget feature on the dangerous high banks of Anderson Speedway.

Foyt, Jones, and Hurtubise squared off throughout the summer, generating excitement and big crowds wherever they went. Just when Foyt seemed unbeatable, Jones went on a tear, winning three straight sprint car races heading to a July 23 race on the high banks of Dayton (Ohio) Speedway.

Jones qualified on the pole with Foyt in second. They went at each other for thirty laps, Jones leading at the start/finish line, but Foyt was often alongside and never more than a car length behind, where he was at the finish.

"I was scared today," Jones said. "I wanted this one because it meant the first time in my life I'd ever won four straight features. Sure I want to keep winning, but I want to run so I feel safe."[30]

Jones added a fifth straight win a week later at Indianapolis Raceway Park, before Foyt put an end to the streak, leading from start to finish at Salem, with Jones third. The win put Foyt back in front in the battle for the national sprint car championship, a slim four points ahead of Jones, setting the stage for an important doubleheader, two fifty-lap features at Langhorne.

Hurtubise proved too strong for either driver, winning both events. Foyt took a rock to the face midway through the first race, shattering his goggles and cutting his eye. Although he managed to finish second, he was sent to the hospital before the second race and failed to score any points. As a result, Jones's runner-up finish was enough to move him back into first for the national championship and the two victories put Hurtubise in second.

The injury didn't slow Foyt the following weekend as he ran three races over the Labor Day holiday, capping it with an Indy car dirt victory at Du Quoin. He'd win two more sprint car races and two Indy car events during the month, closing in on the big car championship but unable to gain on Jones in the sprinters.

One of the victories came in the Hoosier 100, the top dirt track race on the Indy car schedule and the second-richest payday of the series following the 500. The victory virtually clinched a second straight national championship, but afterward Foyt was in a hurry to get his portion of the $12,615 purse and hit the road. He was towing his sprint car six hundred miles to Reading, Pennsylvania, where he was entered in a thirty-lap feature the next day.

Bignotti gave him a hard time, asking, "Didn't you make enough money today?" The trip to Reading paid off when, facing a mixture of local drivers and a handful of Indy car regulars, including Jones and Hurtubise, Foyt qualified on the pole and led all thirty laps, setting a track record in the process.[31]

After the weekend sweep the accolades began to roll in. Of the last ten USAC national championship events on dirt, Foyt had won seven, finished second once and third once.

"Foyt now clearly has won ranking as the hottest dirt-track driver to hit the racing scene since the late Jimmy Bryan," wrote Jep Cadou Jr. in the *Indianapolis Star*.[32]

Crosstown writer Wayne Fuson of the *Indianapolis News* added that Foyt's schedule made him the "racingest USAC champion of all time."[33]

Incredibly, perhaps Foyt's best performance of the year—both on and off the track—was yet to come. The October 1 Hut Hundred at Terre Haute was the biggest and richest midget race of the year. More than thirty-six cars were entered, including those for Hurtubise (winner of three straight sprint car races at the track), Jones, Marshman, and most of the country's top USAC drivers. Promoter Don Smith called it "the best field we've ever had for this race."[34]

Heavy overnight rains and forty-five-degree temperatures left the track "looking like a plowed-up rice paddy just after a monsoon." A preliminary race was cancelled, and the start of qualifying was delayed for more than three hours while work crews attempted to "pound the water-logged oval into something resembling a racing surface."[35]

With the fall days growing shorter and promoters loath to provide refunds to the 3,500 spectators, the track was opened for a short practice session. Although three cars became stuck in the mud, it was deemed ready for qualifying, officials hoping by the time it was over the track surface would be ready for a race. Foyt drew the first qualifying spot, when the track would be at its worst.

He posted a time far slower than he'd run in the past and then watched as the track and cars got faster and faster. He ended up twenty-fifth in the twenty-four-car field. Anticipating he might be bumped, Foyt arranged to rent another car and was putting new tires on it to make another run when USAC officials ruled qualifying was over. It was not a popular decision with either the driver or the remaining wet and cold fans, many of whom had turned out to see the Indy 500 winner.

His next move was to approach the twenty-fourth and last qualifier, Dick Northam, and offer him two hundred dollars—double the guaranteed minimum payout—to withdraw from the race. With little chance of winning that much money, Northam jumped at the offer, putting Foyt back in the field in his original car. He'd be starting last, but at least he was starting.[36]

The surface was still muddy and dangerous when the green flag dropped, and all the drivers moved to the inside of the track, falling in line behind pole sitter Bob Wente. Except Foyt, who moved to the high side. Rim riding was dangerous but faster, and he started running two seconds a lap quicker than anyone else. He passed ten cars in the first three laps, moved past Jones and Hurtubise and into third by lap thirty-two, and past Wente on lap thirty-nine.

The incredible pace was doing a number on Foyt's tires and gas mileage, however, and he was preparing to make a pit stop when his luck changed. The track surface had continued to deteriorate and become deeply rutted. Several cars crashed and Wente spun when the mud buildup caused his throttle to stick wide-open. Officials decided the track would soon be too dangerous to continue, and with not enough daylight remaining to repair the surface and finish the race, it was decided to end it after seventy-five of the scheduled one hundred laps. That allowed Foyt to slow his pace and take the victory. For his efforts, A.J. pocketed about six hundred dollars, minus the money he paid Northam.

Despite the early finish ensuring a Foyt victory, he was one of the few drivers who objected to the race being cut short. "I never heard of canceling a race when the sun was shining," he said over the PA, endearing him to the crowd, if not to the promoters.[37]

He finished the year with a couple more midget victories, although one at Ascot Park was not without incident. Coming from tenth starting position, he closed on leader Jones midway through the forty-lap event. He bumped Parnelli from behind, knocking him up the track and out of contention, Foyt going on to win.

Jones was hot afterward, and some expected fireworks two weeks later when they squared off again at nearby Orange Show Speedway. But by then Jones had cooled off.

"There's no bitterness," Jones said. "Naturally I'll be out to beat A.J. this time. I know A.J. definitely didn't hit me intentionally. After all, we've run together 50 times this year and only touched in one other race.

"I was leading at Ascot by quite a bit when A.J. started to gain on me. I knew it was only a matter of time because I wasn't getting the same throttle response from the car as I did earlier in the race. I had been taking the corners high and when he caught me, I came in low, trying to hold the lead. Well, A.J. anticipated I'd go high again and tried to shoot under me. He couldn't avoid striking my car. I went into a spin and that was that."[38]

The showdown never materialized. Jones's car broke in practice and Foyt went on to win his third consecutive race at the track.

Jones's day was coming, as he scored his first big car victory in the final Indy car race of the year at the Arizona Fairgrounds. Foyt was never in contention and dropped out early with engine problems. It was a continuation of late-season problems that saw him drop out of four of the last five Indy car races, all due to engine problems of some sort.

He bounced back to win his second straight Turkey Night Grand Prix at Ascot Park. More than 7,200 fans turned out for a race billed as a matchup of champions with Foyt, sprint car champ Jones, and midget champion Jimmy Davies entered.

The victory was his ninth in thirteen midget races (good for sixth in the point standings). He added six sprint car victories for third in the point standings, and his four champ car victories paved the way for his second consecutive national championship.

Foyt estimated his winnings at about $170,000, more than any race car driver had ever earned before, making him one of the highest earning athletes for the year. By comparison, Willie Mays, baseball's highest paid player, earned eighty-five thousand dollars. A.J. said he was investing more than half his earnings in oil, real estate—including property on Lake Travis near Austin—and, in typical Texas style, livestock.

"It's been a pretty good year," he said, "and I want to have something left when I'm through racing."[39]

There was no indication, however, that he was considering retirement.

"If there's a race anywhere, I'll probably be in it," he said. "I enjoy it. And I'm real proud of my record."[40]

What did his wife think about his busy racing schedule?

"She doesn't care much for it. It makes her nervous.

"I believe what will be, will be. Of course, I believe you can rush it, but if you use your head, you're going to be fairly safe, unless something freaky happens. In that case it might even happen on the highway. None of us are going to get out of this world alive and I'm having fun. The sport has been good to me. I owe it something."

The year all but over, the awards flowed in. An "A.J. Foyt Day" was staged at a Houston shopping mall. Among those turning out to honor the local hero was Doc Cossey, from the match race with the five-year-old Foyt at Playland Park.

A.J. and Lucy spent New Year's week in LA, where he was named Automobile Racer of the Year by the *Los Angeles Times*. In a close vote he edged local boy Phil Hill, who'd become the first American to win the Formula One world championship. Foyt was honored alongside Roger Maris, who'd hit a record sixty-one home runs, football's Woody Hayes and Jim Brown, and others.

There was no New Year's Eve night on the town, however. There was a midget race to run at Ascot that night, where he finished second to Jones.

At some point near the end of the year Lucy asked her husband what was left for him to accomplish in racing. "You've won everything," she said, "what else can you win?" She'd say later she wasn't asking him to retire, but that's the way he took it.

"I love you and I love the children, but I'm not gonna give up racing," A.J. said. "If you want a divorce, I guess we'll have to get a divorce. I don't want a divorce, but I'm not gonna change my occupation because I love doing it."[41]

Lucy never asked again about his future racing plans.

CHAPTER 11

A RACING CHAMPION

1962

The vacation photos from Hawaii belied the problems within the Bowes Seal Fast team. A.J. and Lucy Foyt were stretched out on the beach at Waikiki, Diamond Head looming in the background.

Bob Bowes had arranged the trip, partly to reward the leaders of his race team after they'd won the Indianapolis 500 and a second straight national championship, and partly hoping the idyllic setting would heal the wounds between them. He'd become worried as the bickering between Foyt and Bignotti increased in frequency and intensity late in the year as the team failed to finish four of the last five races.

Foyt also was recovering from surgery for internal hemorrhoids that had bothered him toward the end of the year, and doctors ordered him to rest, an unlikely possibility if he stayed home. Lucy convinced him to join the others on a five-day cruise from Los Angeles to O'ahu aboard the luxury ocean liner *Lurline*. The group checked into the Halekulani Hotel upon arrival, at the time the island's most famous and lavish resort.[1]

It was a rare vacation for the Foyts. Lucy fell in love with the islands during the couple's two-week stay and returned regularly in the years ahead, often with her mother, children, and Mari Hulman George and her children, who'd become an increasingly close friend. A.J. was antsy after a couple of days, and it was apparent to Lucy that he wasn't the vacationing type.

"Nooo!" she'd say when asked if her husband liked to vacation. "That's the last thing he wants to do. He's not a good sightseer and he isn't interested in shopping and doing all that. No. No. No. He'd rather be busy. That's how he relaxes."[2]

Foyt nixed plans for a return cruise to the mainland.

"I said one week out on the ocean was enough for A.J." he recalled. "I said I ain't taking no more boat trips and that's been my last boat ride."[3]

◀ The Champ. *IMS Photography Archive*

The downtime did give Foyt an opportunity to work on his schedule for the coming year. As the biggest name in American racing, promoters across the country were calling and offering him appearance money if he would race in their event. Bowes made it more challenging, asking him not to compete in any sprint car races before the 500. Too many drivers had been hurt in those cars in the days before the 500, Bowes said, to risk injury by competing in one.

Foyt reluctantly agreed, scheduling more stock car and sports car races instead. He signed on to run Pontiacs in USAC stock car races with Ray Nichels, whose cars had been victorious in both USAC and NASCAR. He also committed to competing in the Daytona Continental, a new three-hour sports car race at Bill France's Daytona International Speedway.

While a number of sports car races had been run at the track since the first ill-fated USAC sponsored weekend in 1959, this was the first event at Daytona to be sanctioned by the Fédération Internationale de l'Automobile (FIA), auto racing's international governing body. As a result, it attracted many of the world's top road racers including Dan Gurney, Phil Hill, Jim Clark, Stirling Moss, Rodger Ward, Roger Penske, and Jim Hall, along with stock car drivers Fireball Roberts, Marvin Panch, and Joe Weatherly.

Foyt was driving one of four Pontiac Tempest LeMans (unlike the race, the car name was one word) entries along with Ward, Paul Goldsmith, and road racer Harry Heuer. The Tempest was a new compact sedan introduced at the 1960 Paris Auto Show by Pontiac to target the small European cars beginning to make inroads with American buyers. The sporty LeMans coupe was new for the 1962 model year and the company was looking to live up to its boastful name at Daytona.

France worked hard to attract a cross section of the world's best drivers and Foyt was paired with NASCAR driver David Pearson, who was coming off a big year with victories in the Charlotte World 600, Daytona Firecracker 250, and Atlanta 400. Goldsmith was teamed with Junior Johnson and Ward with Cotton Owens, although none of the NASCAR co-drivers would actually drive in the race.

While previous races on the Daytona road course were run "European style," or clockwise, the Continental was run in the style of American oval track races, counterclockwise, making it in effect an all-new track for the drivers. The Pontiac team surprised the road racers with their purpose-built Ferrari, Porsche, Lotus, and Chaparral race cars, Foyt qualifying on the pole with Ward alongside. Records are sketchy, but it appears Foyt's car was fitted with a special 421-cubic-inch engine, the other Pontiacs with a smaller 389 engine. Powerful but unproven, Foyt knew there was very little chance of his engine lasting the entire race. So, he did the next best thing. He bet Ward ten dollars he'd lead the first lap.[4]

The race used a "Le Mans start," with drivers lined up across from their cars. They'd run to their car at the drop of the green flag, jump in, start up, and roar away.

Leaving nothing to chance, Foyt edged toward his car as the start approached. He was shooed back several times by an official who eventually gave up, allowing Foyt a head start as he sprinted across Pit Road when the green flag flew. Because the start was taking place in the pits, the first lap skipped the infield portion of the course and used only the NASCAR oval. First away, he led the entire lap to win his bet with Ward, before being passed by Penske going into the first turn of the infield course. On lap two Foyt was in the pits, the engine destroyed.

"A.J. was very determined to lead that first lap," recalled Penske, who was racing against Foyt for the first time. "I was certainly aware of A.J. and his success. He had a reputation as a very tough and hard-nosed racer and that was certainly my experience. He may not have had the road racing background in the early 1960s, but A.J. adapted quickly to any discipline. He was always up for a challenge."[5]

Gurney won the race in dramatic fashion. With a big lead as the race approached its three-hour conclusion, he noticed a problem with his car's engine. Not expecting to finish another lap, he parked high on the track and just short of the start/finish line, rolling across the line and down the track after the checkered flag flew.

While in Daytona and at the urging of France, Foyt, along with Goldsmith, Ward, and Gurney, approached FIA officials seeking clarification on their eligibility to compete in the upcoming Daytona 500 stock car race. Although recently certified by the FIA, USAC was telling its drivers that anyone who competed in the event would be banned from the Indianapolis 500. The FIA promised to look into the matter, but it would be too late for the 1962 Daytona 500.[6]

That's why Foyt found himself on the other side of the country a few weeks later, running USAC stock car races at Ascot and Clovis speedways—a couple of half-mile dirt tracks—and winning his first stock car race. Both races were promoted by J.C. Agajanian. Like France, "Aggie" was a master promoter and well aware of Foyt's drawing power, willing to pay the driver's "appearance fee" or "expenses" as A.J. sometimes referred to the payments.

"They're pretty easy, but a lot of fun," he said of the stock car events. "Besides, the money's just as green."[7]

He finished the West Coast swing by competing in twin USAC stock car races at Riverside on March 18. He qualified on the pole for the first race but was knocked out early by a faulty fuel pump. Forced to start the second heat in twenty-fifth position, he raced to the front, passing leader Gurney after just ten laps, before the transmission broke two laps later.

In addition to banking appearance fees, Foyt said he felt a responsibility to run in as many events as possible.

"I'm going to be a racing champion," he said. "I love this game. I owe racing and racing fans everything."[8]

That took on a whole new meaning when the FIA brokered a deal between USAC, NASCAR, and the Sports Car Club of America (SCCA) allowing drivers to compete in races sanctioned by other groups when the event carried a full international sanction. It meant NASCAR drivers, including Richard Petty, Roberts, and Weatherly, were eligible to compete in the Indianapolis 500, while USAC drivers, including Foyt, Ward, and Goldsmith, could compete in the two NASCAR events on the FIA schedule, the 500-mile races at Daytona and Atlanta. Foyt scrapped plans to drive the LeMans in the 12 Hours of Sebring and instead entered a Nichels's Pontiac in the Atlanta 500 scheduled for March 22.[9]

The 1.5-mile Atlanta track completed in 1960 was new to Foyt, but it fit his style. Although a mile shorter than Daytona, its turns were banked nearly as steeply and as a result it was extremely fast. He was confident it wouldn't take long before he was running up front with the NASCAR regulars.

"I think I'll adapt pretty quickly," he said of the car and the track. "They're going real fast now, almost as fast as an Indianapolis car, and it's a lot of fun to drive them."[10]

Pontiacs were the car of choice and Pearson put one on the pole. Foyt qualified ninth, sixth among the Pontiacs but ahead of teammate Goldsmith and NASCAR regulars Weatherly, Johnson, and Owens.

Then the rains came. With the first date rained out, NASCAR officials rescheduled for the following Saturday, March 31, so as not to conflict with Sunday's USAC Indy car race at Trenton. They also promised to have a helicopter standing by to shuttle Foyt to the Atlanta airport so he could make a flight to New Jersey.

Not everyone in NASCAR was happy to have Foyt participating. Some, like Banjo Matthews, who qualified fourth at Atlanta and would one day build stock cars for Foyt to drive, enjoyed A.J.'s constant banter. Others, while realizing Foyt helped promoters sell more tickets and gave their sport increased visibility, were rubbed the wrong way by the perceived special treatment he received and the new level of gamesmanship he'd brought to the garage area.

"He would go around doing crazy things and saying wild things," one driver, who didn't want to be named, told a reporter. "It got on a lot of people's nerves. Then some of us realized what Foyt was doing. He was deliberately trying to get us emotionally upset. It's the same thing Joe Weatherly's been doing for years. Joe clowns around, but he's dead serious when the race starts. Foyt just carries the clowning to a higher degree."[11]

When both races were rained out the following weekend, NASCAR was forced to reschedule Atlanta for June 10, in direct conflict with the Indy car race at Milwaukee. Foyt's NASCAR debut would have to wait.

TROUBLE WITH SACHS, BIGNOTTI

The 1962 Indy car opener at Trenton, reset for April 8, was one of the first races shown on a same-day, taped-delayed broadcast on ABC's popular *Wide World of Sports* program. Foyt took the lead from Parnelli Jones and cruised to a seven-second victory, saying later he "never really opened up."[12]

Jones agreed. "Nobody was going to catch that boy today."

The season was barely underway, and the Speedway wouldn't open for another two weeks, when suddenly there was more action off the track than on. On a Detroit promotional tour for sponsors Dean Van Lines and the Autolite spark plug division of Ford Motor Company, crew chief Clint Brawner mentioned that his team planned to use an innovative two-way radio hookup to improve communications between the pits and driver Eddie Sachs. Sachs said he was hopeful the radio would keep him focused and his speed up. He added if he had the radio a year earlier, he would have been able to alert his pit crew when he needed to change a tire late in the race.

Although he never mentioned Foyt directly, Sachs blamed his second-place finish on poor coordination between driver and pits. "Even with all the confusion last year," he said he could have won by twenty seconds.[13]

When the United Press International news service recapped the interview and distributed an article to newspapers across the country, writers on the racing beat telephoned Foyt, asking variations of the question: "Eddie says he could have beat you by twenty seconds except for the confusion in the pits. What do you think?"

Reporters couldn't have reached Foyt at a worse time. Doctors had ordered him home for bed rest with flu-like symptoms, including nausea and headaches. Foyt said doctors described it as "virus Polio," although "not the paralytic kind." When Foyt heard what Sachs reportedly said, he exploded. He was already upset with Eddie, who'd tested an Indy car at the Atlanta track and convinced USAC it was too fast and dangerous to hold a race there. Foyt saw it as a missed opportunity for a reported one-hundred-thousand-dollar payday.[14]

"The newspaper guys here called me last night and told me about Sachs' speech," Foyt told the *Indianapolis News.* In an article headlined "Foyt Calls Sachs 'Dumb, Cry Baby'" A.J. was quoted saying "If he wants to throw words around, I can too. And I can back up what I say.

"He was lucky to finish in second place. Sachs is a dumb race driver. He's a real cry-baby if you ask me. I just played with Eddie. If he hadn't been so dumb, he would have stopped for a new tire at the same time I made my fourth pit stop. He's one I don't worry about. Everybody knows the kind of driver Eddie is and nobody pays any attention to his excuses. He always has a lot of excuses."[15]

Sachs, in New York for another promotional event, was surprised when told of Foyt's remarks.

"Isn't that fantastic. I gave Foyt tremendous credit as a driver. When I lost I was a gentleman. He spent all year as a champion. He should have been me and tried to live with second place. I wish him a lot of luck this year, but I'm going to try very, very hard to change just one spot."[16]

The subsequent articles touched off another round of barbs between the two. Brawner eventually stepped in, hoping to quiet the argument between his former and current drivers.

"It's just a ridiculous, childish thing," Brawner said. "The way they're carrying on isn't going to help auto racing a bit. All it will do is make some newspaper headlines." He also came to the defense of Sachs. "Eddie has a lot of friends at the Speedway. And for that cry-baby stuff, Foyt is something of a cry-baby himself."[17]

The feud caught the attention of Bob Talbert, a young journalist for *The State* newspaper in Columbia, South Carolina. In 1962 he covered the auto racing beat, but he would eventually become one of the top general-interest journalists in the country, writing a daily *Detroit Free Press* column for more than thirty years. He tried to explain what was behind the feud.

"When you live on the hairy edge of death, you are apt to catch yourself running off at the mouth a bit too much," he wrote. "But it's good for your system to spit out the venom, so the psychologists tell us."[18]

"So, you see race drivers popping off all the time. Some of the time the words the drivers say are planted by $-hungry promoters, intent on luring an extra fan with a 'feud' bally-hoo."

Talbert quoted Russ Catlin, a NASCAR press agent who didn't have much good to say about the drivers from the rival USAC organization.

"The great auto race drivers of the world have all had supercharged egos and heavy-duty tempers. Some of the meanest men in the world have raced, and are still racing, at Indianapolis. Don't cross 'em. Indianapolis is a disease of mind and heart. I guess you could say the big-car drivers begin to act like the sensitive thoroughbred horses that race in the Kentucky Derby. The drivers are high strung, living at a taut and ever-rising pitch."

Talbert was right about one thing: The only people happy with the long-distance feud between Foyt and Sachs were the promoters of two upcoming events where both would be competing: stock car races at Indianapolis Raceway Park and Langhorne. Both participated in a prerace media blitz before the race at IRP, with Sachs reverting to his happy-go-lucky self and patching things up with Foyt, the pair pictured laughing together at the track.

"We are much better friends the last four days than we've ever been," Sachs said. "The trouble is, Foyt can't get publicity unless he uses my name. He's gotta run me down. Just the other day he said to me, 'Eddie, I can't go anywhere without someone asking me about you.'"[19]

The two found themselves racing each other hard but clean for the first half of the IRP race, but neither was around at the finish, Sachs blowing an engine and Foyt blowing a tire and hitting the wall.

"Foyt wore out his car and mine," Sachs said, then emphasized he was joking.

Any doubt the feud was over came at the annual USAC awards dinner held a couple of weeks before the 500. Lucy, pregnant with their third child due in August, went to Indianapolis in late April, ahead of her normal early May date. Along with Sachs's wife, Nance, she arranged for the couples to arrive together at the Indianapolis Athletic Club and sit together while photographers snapped away.

The "feud" would have long-lasting effects, however. It went a long way toward souring Foyt's relationship with the news media. Never great to begin with, it became increasingly tenuous in the years ahead. Gone for good was the "quiet," "shy," and "soft-spoken" young driver referenced in earlier news media reports.

"I guess I'm going to have to keep my mouth shut from now on," Foyt said. "People quoted me as saying all kinds of things."[20]

———

Publicly, Foyt continued to praise Bignotti and the team before arriving at the Speedway.

"I think we've got a good chance to win it. First of all, you've got to have a good car, good mechanics and good luck. The combination is no good without all three. I had a good car and good mechanics with Dean Van Lines, but not good luck and I couldn't win a thing. Now with Bowes Seal Fast, the combo is going for us."[21]

He went a little overboard when talking to a reporter from the *San Francisco Examiner*, his crew chief's hometown newspaper, calling Bignotti "a mechanical genius" and comparing him to a "skilled surgeon."[22]

It didn't take long for the bickering between Foyt and Bignotti to start anew. After nine laps of practice at the Speedway Foyt was back in the pits. The "Aloha Spirit" developed in Hawaii and carried over through the Trenton victory was gone.

"It darts," Foyt said of the race-winning car from the year before. "It runs like a snake, and when I turn it loose, we head for the infield." He also complained the tachometer didn't work, and he didn't like the seating position or the footwell, finally asking Bignotti, "What did you do to it?"[23]

Bignotti tried to assure Foyt the settings were unchanged from the year before, but the driver wasn't hearing it, ordering the car back to the garage so it could be "fixed." When Bignotti went to work on the front end to address the "darting" issue, Foyt attacked the seat, wrestling it from the car. When he grabbed a hammer and began pounding away, Bignotti walked out.

"I can't stand it when he gets the hammer," Bignotti said as he went to check on another car. Which was part of the problem. Bignotti was helping two other teams at the track, and he'd spent much of the off-season working on those machines. One was the car Foyt drove in the 500 in 1960. It had been sold to a new team from Bignotti's hometown and he had agreed to help them out.[24]

The other was the Epperly laydown car Johnny Boyd had driven in 1960 but several drivers had failed to qualify in 1961. Bignotti had updated it and hired Goldsmith to drive it. He attempted to placate Foyt by having Nichels serve as the car's crew chief while at the Speedway. While A.J. got along well with both Nichels and Goldsmith, a talented driver, this was different. He wondered why the team wanted to switch from the one-car effort that worked so well the year before.

With the seat finally battered into an acceptable shape, Foyt asked where Bignotti was. Told he'd gone to check on another car, he sent a crew member chasing after him.

"You [ask] George, 'Is he working on this car or that one?' That's an order from Foyt."

Bignotti returned a short time later and the pair put the seat back in the car. The crew chief also said he'd discovered the footbox had been changed from the previous year without his knowledge and the original would be put back in the car overnight. Happy with the outcome, Foyt turned to Bignotti.

"The trouble with us is we're too softhearted."

Bignotti wasn't the only one spread thin. Foyt was the sport's new darling, and with the added attention came added expectations, scrutiny, and pressure. There was no avoiding the crunch of people wanting a moment—or more—of his time.

"Young, handsome, and with the savvy of a man who takes life and shakes it until it rattles," one reporter wrote of Foyt. "He epitomizes the wish of every man who has run in the Circus Maximus of auto racing."[25]

Bignotti could see its impact.

"These drivers are all high-strung, nervous and temperamental. This guy has a thousand things on his mind. Everybody wants him to do something for them. Talk, go someplace. He gets flustered. They all do."[26]

CRACKING 150

Much of the early interest at the Speedway centered around who would be the first to break the 150-miles-per-hour barrier. The front straightaway had been paved during the off-season, only a yard of bricks remaining at the start/finish line. Jones and Sachs each predicted he'd top 150 in qualifying. Although Foyt let his crew know he expected to be the first to hit 150, he avoided making public projections, saying only he was happy the bricks were gone.

"Last year when I won, it was so rough driving over those bricks I thought my kidneys would fall out."[27]

Jones, the fastest driver all month, was the only one to run laps of more than 150 mph in qualifying, taking the pole position. Sachs lost a wheel and brushed the wall trying to reach the mark. Foyt barely topped 149, qualifying fifth.

Despite the success of Jack Brabham and the rear-engine car the year before, he'd decided to focus on the grand prix circuit in 1962. Only one of the "funny cars" managed to qualify, a machine built by land speed record holder Mickey Thompson and driven by Gurney, a winner in Formula One but a rookie at Indianapolis. After driving a roadster to pass his rookie test, he qualified a solid eighth.

Foyt was dismissive of Gurney and reports that other Grand Prix drivers wanted to try their hand at Indy. "I think he'll be just another driver," he said of Gurney. "I don't think Stirling Moss could make it. Of course, we'd have a hard time adjusting to Grand Prix racing in Europe."[28]

Safely qualified for the race, Foyt agreed to test hop Sachs's Dean Van Lines car, a practice he'd avoided following the death of Tony Bettenhausen. After his qualifying accident, Sachs had watched his teammate crash and end up in the hospital with back and leg injuries and a possible skull fracture. Sachs had been having trouble getting his car up to speed ever since.

"We're trying to get him over his disbelief in his car," Al Dean told Foyt while making the request.[29]

After a few laps above 145 mph, Foyt returned to the pits and told Sachs and Brawner the car was fine, although he suggested a few changes to the front suspension. He also couldn't avoid a little gamesmanship.

"It's as good as my car," he said loud enough for reporters to hear. "It's better than mine."

Foyt also hopped in Goldsmith's car. He still didn't like having a teammate and he didn't like driving the laydown car any more than before. But he liked Goldsmith, a former motorcycle racing champion and teammate on the Nichels stock car team.

Sachs and Goldsmith each qualified easily on the second weekend. Shortly afterward news leaked out the Goldsmith car had been sold and there was talk the No. 1 car was next. An upset Foyt confronted Bowes and Bignotti. He was only partially placated when told, "We are not interested in any kind of sale until after the 500."[30]

A few nights later Foyt decided to ignore Bowes's request and run his first sprint car race of the year, a fifty-lapper at Indianapolis Raceway Park. It was his first time driving a Chevrolet-powered sprinter and he qualified on the pole with

Jones, who'd won three straight sprint car races at the track, alongside. Jones led from the start and the pair set a frantic pace, lapping every other car in a race filled with Indy 500 starters. Foyt was finally able to get the lead with fourteen laps remaining and held on for the victory.[31]

"The sprint car race helps settle you down and ease the tension," he said of the decision to race. He sounded less confident when asked if he could repeat his performance in the 500, saying he was unhappy with the final Carb Day test. "The way it's acting, I don't know if I can go fast enough to even stay up with the pack. If my car will handle, I'm real confident I can win again. I have had considerable success on the championship trail and this has given me increased confidence in my own ability."[32]

To no one's surprise, Jones jumped into the lead of the 500 from the start. While others seemed content to let him go, hopeful his pace would be too hard on the car, Foyt moved from fifth to second in two laps and took up the chase. He moved in front on lap sixty when Jones pitted for fuel and tires, giving the lead back two laps later when he headed toward his pit.

A loose bolt in the right-front wheel somehow kept the brakes from fully engaging and Foyt slid through his pit, forcing him to go around another lap. The second stop was a Keystone Cops affair, crew members fumbling about to try and find the problem. Foyt eventually got out of the car to take charge himself. Discovering the broken bolt he sent a crewman back to the garage to find another, yelling at him to run when he didn't move fast enough. Finally repaired but hopelessly behind Jones, he rejoined the race. He didn't make it far. Before he could complete a lap he found himself going backward, a tire bounding past. During the confusion of the pit stop the nut on the left-rear tire had been loosened but not tightened. There was nothing Foyt could do except three-wheel the car harmlessly to the inside of the track.

Coming up to lap Foyt at the time was Jones, who slammed on his brakes only to have the pedal go to the floor. He was out of brakes. He swerved, avoided Foyt, and was able to continue, but his chance at victory was over.

Rodger Ward went on to win, his second time in three years, and he took a commanding lead in the national championship. Gurney ran with the leaders early but was out before the halfway point, although it was enough to convince himself and his guest, Lotus guru Colin Chapman, that rear-engine cars were the wave of the future. Sachs turned in the drive of the race, coming from a twenty-seventh starting position to finish third.

"When I won in '62," Ward would say, "I've got everybody in the field beat—except Jones. And there ain't any way in the world I can beat him. I can race Foyt on his own terms and beat him. He had gotten angry at Bignotti and decided to set up his own chassis for the race. He was having some handling problems.

"Foyt would outrun me on the straightaway—and then I would just drive all over him in the corners. Foyt is such a great driver that even when he adjusted himself out of business, he was still overcoming it with his driving ability. This is what makes him so great. He has such fabulous determination. When it ain't working, old A.J. just grits his teeth and drives it a little harder."[33]

Afterward Foyt was furious with Bignotti, complaining that the crew "were all thumbs. The only one I can trust is my dad," a refrain he would repeat in the years ahead.[34]

In 2021, Bobby Dorn visited Foyt's team garages on the fiftieth anniversary of A.J.'s first 500 victory. To celebrate the anniversary, the A.J. Foyt Enterprises entry of J.R. Hildebrand carried the No. 1 and a paint scheme similar to the 1961 winning Bowes Seal Fast car. Dorn, the last living member of the winning pit crew, wore a replica of the uniform worn by the team on race day, all white with a black shirt pocket. Foyt and Dorn, who split with Foyt after 1962 but went on to have a long career with a number of race teams, posed for photos with the new car. They spent only a few minutes together after the photos, however, and later A.J. was asked why.

"Son of a bitch was the one who didn't get my wheel tight in '62," he said.

BOOS

The last place Foyt wanted to be on June 10 was Milwaukee.

Unsure if his Bowes/Bignotti car was going to be sold, Foyt went out after the 500 and purchased Smokey Yunick's Watson roadster. It was a good car, the one Jim Rathmann had driven to victory in 1960, challenged Foyt with in 1961, and just drove to a ninth-place finish. If he had to, Foyt figured, he'd start his own team.

He was still upset about the way his race ended, certain he would have won if not for the foul-up in the pits. He wanted to be in Atlanta for the rescheduled NASCAR race. Atlanta paid more than fifteen thousand dollars to the winner, twice what the Milwaukee winner would take home. But Henry Banks and other USAC officials, he said, were pressuring him to race at Milwaukee.

"I wanted to run there [Atlanta] because there's more money," he said. "I'm afraid to run though. They [USAC] could make it mighty tough for me."[35]

He talked about switching permanently to NASCAR, running only the Indianapolis 500 on a FIA license and spending the rest of his time in the South, where they raced two or three times a week.

"I'm thinking about driving the NASCAR circuit," he said. "I've talked with Bill France about it. I may drive there next year."[36]

Despite the obvious distractions, Foyt didn't allow the controversy to affect his performance on the track, as he qualified on the Milwaukee pole. He took the lead at the start, but the real show was put on by an up-and-coming driver named Don Davis, who'd finished a surprising fourth at Indianapolis.

While most of the drivers, including Foyt, were in the same cars they raced at Indianapolis, Davis only had a dirt track car available, one of three in the race. It was the only one powered by a Chevrolet engine, however, built by up-and-coming engine man Herb Porter. After qualifying seventh, Davis immediately began working his way to the front, leaving Parnelli Jones and Jim Hurtubise in his wake and passing Foyt to take the lead after just thirty-five laps.

Foyt chased him until lap seventy-seven of one hundred when, "almost simultaneously" according to the *Indianapolis Star,* the right-front tire on Davis's car blew and he was bumped from behind by Foyt, sending the leader into a spin.

Davis was forced to pit for a new tire, while Foyt moved out to nearly a five-second lead over Hurtubise and Jones.[37]

During a late caution flag, Hurtubise and Jones pulled up behind Foyt, a violation of rules often loosely enforced. It provided the fans with an exciting finish, as both drivers attempted to pass Foyt on the last lap without success.

Davis's flat tire and the contact with Foyt may have appeared simultaneous to the *Star* reporter, but the crowd of thirty thousand thought differently. They cheered Davis, who finished eighth, while booing Foyt when he pulled into Victory Lane.[38]

It was a new experience for the Texan and, upset by the fan response, he barged into the officials' building complaining about how they handled the late yellow flag.

The complaint quickly turned to money when he confronted race organizer Tom Marchese. Foyt felt he should receive more than the $7,625 first prize as the reigning USAC champion. When Marchese explained the car had been entered by Bignotti, not Foyt, A.J. demanded five hundred dollars in appearance money. Rebuked again, he unleashed a diatribe of invectives against Marchese and challenged the sixty-five-year-old to a fight, forcing police officers to intervene. While Marchese did not press charges, he did file a report with USAC and it was a contrite Foyt who talked with reporters the next day.[39]

"I was angry and said a lot of things—most of which I can't even remember now—and I am sorry," he said. "I have apologized to both Tom Marchese and the officials of the United States Auto Club. It was a misunderstanding on my part."[40]

The apology came too late for USAC. Foyt was already in the organization's doghouse for his comments about switching to NASCAR and being forced to race at Milwaukee. Calling the incident a "disgraceful assault," Banks leveled a one thousand dollar fine on Foyt, the largest in series history at the time, and warned, "Any recurrence will result in complete suspension from USAC for an indefinite period of time."[41]

USAC also addressed Foyt's complaint, fining eleven drivers small amounts for moving up under the yellow and promising to control the situation in the future. Foyt agreed to participate in a press conference where the fine was announced.

"They gave me a real good shake," he said. "I feel ashamed and I'm sure it won't happen again. It looked bad on racing, USAC and myself. They did a nice job of surveying it."[42]

Three weeks later the track and surface changed—Langhorne on dirt—but the results were the same. Foyt started on the pole and led all one hundred laps, with Jones second and Hurtubise third.

The race was marred, however, by the death of Hugh Randall, who was driving in his first Indy car event. After failing to qualify, he'd volunteered to serve as a relief driver on the rugged and dangerous track.

"I'd give anything to have a car in this race," he said before the start. "I've got to make some money and you can't make any standing around. You don't expect to get a good car right off. But if you take a clunker and make it go, then the big owners notice you and maybe give you a ride. You just need one break and you've got it made."[43]

He got his chance, serving as the second relief driver in a nine-year-old, ill-handling clunker. He completed only one lap before losing control in Puke Hollow. The car rolled twice, coming to rest on top of Randall, his neck broken. It would come to light later that he was the third driver to die in the car. Foyt remembered exchanging good-natured jabs with the driver before the race.

"It's a shame," he said. "He was a good driver, but he never got a break."[44]

The series returned to Trenton next, where Foyt had won the first race of the year. From the start nothing seemed to go right. He argued with Bignotti over which car to run, the crew chief insisting the team's dirt track car was better suited for the summer race than the speedway car Foyt drove to victory in the spring. It was not an unusual choice, as more than half the teams decided to use their dirt cars on the slick surface.

Although he was the fastest qualifier, Foyt clashed again with Bignotti on chassis setup. As if to prove a point he ran the car hard and twice stopped for new tires. He was the only car among the leaders to pit, dropping him from first at the start to seventh at the finish. Ward drove to an easy victory in his speedway car, all but clinching the national championship in the process.

"I could see that Foyt was having tire trouble, so I didn't go all-out," Ward said. "I'd much rather have the tires take care of him. He's just too tough for one man to handle without some help."[45]

Foyt and Bignotti traded barbs verbally afterward, Foyt finally storming out of the garage. Even though they'd won eleven of twenty-nine races together, he'd had enough, submitting his resignation to Bowes a few days later.

Publicly Foyt denied there was friction with Bignotti, using the classic "it's me, not you" reason for the breakup.

"I simply decided it was time to call it quits because I just wasn't getting everything out of the car I should and wasn't giving it justice. Sure we had our differences, but so does everybody else. There were no major problems, just little ones."[46]

Everyone within earshot of the team in the garage area knew differently.

"We were always arguing because we both thought we were smarter than the other one," Foyt would say. "George was damn good, but I knew what I wanted with my car. We both wanted to win more than anything. He wasn't wrong; he just wanted to do things differently, and we argued so much I decided to call it quits.

"We finally agreed on one thing. It was best that we part company."[47]

Foyt briefly considered running the car he'd purchased from Yunick until he received a call from Lindsey Hopkins, the millionaire Atlanta car owner. He had a good team, a good car, and a good crew chief in Jack Beckley. He was in need of a driver, and Foyt accepted the offer.

After telling reporters "It was a friendly separation, probably for the best," a disgusted Bowes sold his interest in the team before the week was out. He would sponsor cars again in the future but was through as a car owner.[48]

The new team owners were Shirley "S.D." Murphy, an executive at Sheraton Hotels, and William "Bill" Ansted Jr., owner of Thompson Industries in Indianapolis. Both had previously owned multiple cars in the 500. Ansted, who first went to the 500 with his father in 1919, had participated in fourteen 500s, while

Thompson had entered cars for fifteen straight years. Each was looking for their first victory. The new driver of the Ansted-Thompson Special was Bobby Marshman, who'd been released by Hopkins. Bignotti would continue as crew chief.[49]

While waiting for his first race with his new team, Foyt decided to run a sprint car event for A.J. Watson on August 12 at New Bremen Speedway in Ohio. He finished third in what would have been a forgettable race except for a freak accident that took place after it was over.

Davis, the driver who'd been so impressive early in the year at Indianapolis and Milwaukee, took evasive action after getting the checkered flag when the car directly in front of him blew a tire. Davis lost control of his own machine, skidding into the wall and rolling twice. The impacts flattened the roll bar, although the car landed upright. At first Davis answered questions and seemed okay, before he lapsed into semi-consciousness. He was taken eighty miles by ambulance to a hospital in Dayton, where he died three days later.[50]

GRASS IS NOT ALWAYS GREENER

Foyt had an inauspicious start with the Hopkins team on August 18, running out of fuel three laps from the finish while battling Jim Hurtubise for the victory on the dirt track at Springfield, Illinois. Foyt had taken the No. 1 car with him, and the next day the teams were back in Milwaukee, where Foyt's summer spiral had started.

It was the Tony Bettenhausen 200, the second-longest and most important race of the year (next to Indianapolis) in terms of points. It was the last chance to catch Ward, and if ever Foyt wanted to win a race that summer, this was it.

Things started slowly as he qualified a disappointing seventh, Marshman putting the Bignotti car on the pole. Ward took an early lead once the race started while Foyt moved toward the front, passing Jones for second before the halfway point. Foyt closed to the rear of Ward's car and got alongside several times but was never able to lead a lap. By the finish Ward and Foyt had lapped the entire field, with Marshman in third.

As disappointing as second was, it would be the team's high-water mark. The Hopkins cars were fast, but fragile. Foyt hadn't won a race of any kind, his sprint and stock car efforts struggling as well.

Back in Trenton after two months, where Foyt first decided to leave Bignotti, he again qualified on the pole, only to fade to a fourth-place finish. After six races with Hopkins, he had only a pair of second places to show for his efforts. Bignotti and Marshman hadn't done any better: a pair of third places.

"The biggest problem I had at that stage was with the car," Foyt would say. "It wasn't as good as Bignotti's car. It's not that Jack Beckley wasn't a good mechanic, he was. It's that he and I didn't get as much accomplished as George and I did."[51]

Foyt said he realized, "Even with the fighting, I was better off with George. Now I don't admit to a whole lot of mistakes, but leaving Bignotti was one of them. I figured I might as well swallow my pride and patch things up."

Foyt went to Bignotti, admitted he'd made a mistake, and asked to reunite with the chief mechanic, a major concession on his part. He discovered Big George didn't like losing either. For his part, Bignotti said, "A.J. is not . . . uhhh . . . the easiest guy in the world to get along with, but I guess we work better together than we do apart. A.J. is one of the few drivers in the business who understands everything about cars. He doesn't have to do his own work anymore, but if he had to, he could build his own cars. When some little thing goes wrong, he can tell you exactly what it is and when he says he can fix it himself, he is telling the truth."[52]

To jump start his sprint car effort, and because he was tired of trying to convince A.J. Watson to put a Chevrolet in their car, Foyt bought one, rebuilding and installing the engine himself. It took three races, but he managed to return to Victory Circle at Salem. It was his first start on the high banks after swearing off such tracks more than a year before. After qualifying second, he took the lead from pole sitter Jones when the other driver stopped with engine problems. He was never headed, although a disintegrating right-front tire kept things interesting.

"I saw my tire blistering about lap sixty [of one hundred]," he said. "I asked myself, 'Should I go in?' I said, 'No.'

"I went high so if it popped, I'd just brush against the rail. I just gambled and I won. But I'll tell you, I could hear my heart pounding the last fifteen or twenty laps."[53]

He followed with stock car and midget victories in the following weeks, finishing the hot streak with a win in his first Indy car race back with Bignotti. Rather than switch numbers again, Foyt was in the No. 14, a number Bignotti had used in the past. He qualified on the pole and ran away with the race at the California Fairgrounds in Sacramento. Afterward he again stated the obvious.

"Bignotti is the best mechanic in the business, and I sure made a mistake breaking up with him this year."[54]

It only seemed fitting that Marshman, who moved back to the Hopkins team when Foyt returned to Bignotti, won the last big car race of the year at the Arizona State Fairgrounds. Foyt was running second and closing in when Elmer George's car vaulted into the grandstands, injuring twenty-one spectators and ending the event early.

With the champ car season over, Hurtubise convinced Jones and Foyt to join him for the Salton City 500, an endurance boat race held on a thirty-five-mile triangular course on the Salton Sea, located in the desert south of Palm Springs and east of San Diego. Billed as the Indy 500 of boat racing, the winner's guarantee of $6,600 was supplemented by a lifetime supply of beer.

More than seventy boats started, with Foyt piloting one entered by Rudy Ramos, the event's defending champion. Thanks in part to the entries from Foyt, Hurtubise, Jones, and Mickey Thompson, more than fifty thousand spectators watched from the water's edge. Hurtubise disappeared at the start and lapped the field before his boat caught fire during a refueling stop. Foyt ran second until dropping out with engine problems, and Jones discovered hitting a boulder in the water can be just as bad as hitting a wall at Indy.[55]

During the year Foyt had become increasingly friendly with Jones and Hurtubise. Nothing earns respect more than winning, and each of the three showed the other two that on any given day they were tough to beat. Jones won both the midget and sprint car titles and he and Hurtubise both scored Indy car wins. Foyt matched Ward's four champ car victories while finishing second to the Indy 500 winner in the national championship.

Knowing his aversion to being second, Foyt was asked if he would stick with No. 14 rather than the traditional No. 2 during the coming season. He said no, he wanted No. 2 to serve as a reminder and inspiration for himself and the team. He especially wanted to beat Ward, something the newly crowned champion said he understood.

"I was champion when Foyt was breaking in, so he set his sights on me," Ward said. "He won the title from me, and now that he's lost it back to me, it's really hurt him. Pride is very important to a race driver and Foyt is very proud. He's also young and impetuous. He's also hot tempered. He's a tremendous race driver, but he often takes his anger out on equipment, and doesn't use the best judgement all the time. You have to know when to run hard and when not. But he's gaining experience. If he seems to want to beat me more than anybody else, I can understand, because that's the way I feel about him."[56]

CHAPTER 12

FUNNY CARS AND FURRINERS

1963

The 1963 season started with a rare moment of agreement between three of the major motorsports organizations overseeing auto racing in the United States: USAC, NASCAR, and SCCA. Thanks to the peace treaty brokered by the international FIA governing body, the three groups committed to allow drivers belonging to their organization to compete in FIA-certified events staged by the other groups.

The first race to be held under the agreement was a new one, NASCAR's Riverside 500 scheduled for January 17. It boasted the sixth largest purse in American racing at more than sixty-six thousand dollars, making it the highest-paying race in the western United States.

The event also marked the official return of Detroit's auto companies. After being forced from the sport by the Automobile Association of America's withdrawal from racing in 1957, the Big Three had almost immediately started to return through backdoor support of race teams and drivers. The money often came from advertising and marketing budgets, with top executives turning a blind eye to the participation.[1]

Pontiac and Chevrolet were the first and most aggressive, although Chrysler had returned in earnest in 1962. Henry Ford II ended the charade, noting his company was "selling safety, while Chevrolet was selling cars" and announcing that the Blue Oval would officially return to racing "with both feet" in 1963.[2]

The return of the factories, a large purse, and the FIA sanction attracted a huge field of cars and drivers to Riverside. In addition to the NASCAR regulars, many top USAC drivers entered, including A.J. Foyt, Paul Goldsmith, and Len Sutton in Pontiacs and Parnelli Jones and Troy Ruttman in a pair of Mercurys.

◀ Foyt leads a group of roadsters and the rear engine "funny cars" of Dan Gurney (93) and Jimmy Clark (92). *Revs Institute, The Tom Burnside Photograph Collection*

Not everyone was happy with the interlopers, especially Fireball Roberts, the biggest name in NASCAR and the defending champion of the Daytona 500.

"I was all for it at first," Roberts said. "I thought a fair driver exchange would upgrade the sport. But I thought it would be a reciprocal deal and that we'd get a shot at winning back some of the money in USAC events. But USAC has placed roadblocks in the way of NASCAR drivers trying to enter the Indianapolis 500. It isn't a fair situation. We're opening up our big money races to them and getting nothing in return."[3,4]

Pontiacs swept the first four spots in qualifying with Foyt second to Goldsmith, although the results were misleading. Everybody's favorite, Dan Gurney in a Ford, was late getting to the track and missed pole qualifying. He set a track record when he finally arrived but started eleventh because of his tardiness.

Foyt led the first two laps, before being passed by Goldsmith and then Jones. It was just a matter of time before Gurney moved to the front, where he stayed for the rest of the race. Only Foyt kept Gurney in sight as they lapped the rest of the field during the six-hour grind. Ruttman finished third, giving non-NASCAR drivers the top three spots and nearly half the purse.[5]

Foyt and Roberts took advantage of FIA sanctioning for their next race, a 250-mile SCCA sports car event on February 16 at Daytona. For the first time the sports cars would run on the oval rather than the combined oval and road course. Chevrolet built more than a dozen special Corvettes for the event to take on a collection of Ferraris, Porches, and a lone Pontiac Tempest.

NASCAR regulars Junior Johnson and Rex White qualified on the front row, both driving Corvettes entered by Mickey Thompson. Roberts was third in a Ferrari with Goldsmith fourth in the Tempest. Foyt was sixth in a Corvette entered by John Mecom Jr. and sponsored by Nicky Chevrolet, a Chicago-based dealership known for high-performance parts and the world's highest-volume GM dealership. A.J. nicknamed the car "Nicky Nouse."

Several Formula One drivers were entered, including Innes Ireland, whose biggest victory to date was the 1961 United States Grand Prix at Watkins Glen, New York. At Daytona he was driving a Ferrari for a team based in Victoria, Texas, and pitted next to the Corvette. At one point he confronted Foyt.

"A.J. was still sitting in the car and Innes leaned down and started screaming at A.J. for something he'd done," recalled Mecom, another Houstonian and Foyt backer. "That was a big mistake. You don't scream at A.J. He grabbed Innes and pulled him through the car window. Now there was hardly room for one person in the car, let alone two. A.J. explained the facts of life to him real quick. They never had another problem—in fact they became friends. But it was an indication A.J. wasn't going to take any lip, even if the guy was a Grand Prix winner."[6]

Race day dawned misty, and as the start approached the track was made "slippery and dangerous by a steady drizzle." While an event had never been run on a wet high-banked oval, it was common practice for sports cars to race in the rain and the decision was made to go ahead as scheduled. Johnson, Joe Weatherly, and a number of others pulled out. Only fourteen cars started.[7]

Goldsmith dominated, winning by more than two laps over Foyt. Surprisingly, there wasn't a single yellow flag as caution took precedence over speed. The race would be held again the following year but on the road course.

Next up was the Daytona 500 stock car race, and eight USAC drivers entered, including Indy 500 winners Foyt, Ruttman, and Rodger Ward, along with Jones, Gurney, Goldsmith, Len Sutton, and Jim Hurtubise.

Foyt's first Daytona "taxicab" start—as he called the stock cars—reunited him with Billy Wade. The pair had often battled at Playland and other Houston tracks in jalopies and modifieds in the mid-1950s, Wade sometimes driving a car for Tony Foyt. They'd gone in different directions since the Houston days, with Wade now driving for one of the top NASCAR teams.

Despite the long list of NASCAR and USAC stars entered, it was car builder Smokey Yunick and an unknown driver who captured everyone's attention. Yunick's Pontiacs with Roberts driving had been nearly unbeatable the past two years. But Chevrolet decided it wanted to build a performance image to match its sister division at General Motors and lured him away. To replace Roberts, who was still under contract to Pontiac, Yunick said he wanted someone "no one has ever heard of before."

"What I would like to do is find a new young guy to drive both stocks and Indianapolis for me," Yunick said. "It wouldn't matter so much how good he might be right now, if he had ability and was willing to listen."

True to his word, Yunick signed a driver from the USAC ranks, Johnny Rutherford. Even among the USAC regulars Rutherford was a virtual unknown, having spent only a year on the sprint car circuit while competing in four Indy car events. He was still looking for his first major victory in any kind of car and had never driven on a track more than a mile long—and that had been a dirt track.

Three years younger than Foyt, Rutherford had followed a similar racing path, driving jalopies and modifieds on Texas short tracks. He graduated to the IMCA series and, after having some success, made the jump to USAC in 1962. The rookie surprised everyone at Daytona, setting a closed-course speed record in practice and winning one of two qualifying races used to set the field for the 500.

After finishing third in his qualifying race, Foyt ran up front in the 500 and even led a few laps before blowing a tire as he neared the start/finish line on lap 142. He managed to maintain control of his car and turned back onto Pit Road but was disqualified for entering the pits from the wrong end.

Rutherford finished ninth after making a "rookie mistake," getting caught in the crosswinds coming out of Turn Two, spinning, and brushing the guardrail, requiring a lengthy pit stop for repairs.[8]

Two weeks later it was an excited Foyt who waited in the lobby of the Atlanta airport Holiday Inn for Jones and Hurtubise. The three drivers had flown in the night before to participate in media day activities for NASCAR's Atlanta 500 and were headed out to the track.

It was announced a few days earlier that Foyt would be driving Yunick's Chevrolet at Atlanta. That surprised Nichels, who'd provided the Pontiac stock cars he'd driven for the past several years and had entered one for him at Atlanta.

Instead, Foyt switched to the car in which Rutherford set the track record at Daytona. If there was one thing A.J. liked, it was a fast race car.

There was one problem as the three drivers gathered. No one had a rented a car or arranged for a ride to the track. Team members already were gone. Cell phones and ride share services were decades off. So A.J. convinced the others to hitchhike to the track, some twenty miles south of the hotel.

"Ray Nichels came by, but he didn't stop," Foyt joked later. It wasn't long, however, before a Corvette pulled up and the three of them somehow squeezed in the car. Once they got to the track, Foyt's upbeat mood continued.[9]

"It's the fastest car out there," he said of his new ride. "I am not making any predictions, but there's going to be only one winner of the race and you're looking at him."

The switch meant the normally superstitious Foyt would be driving car No. 13. At Daytona he'd taken great delight in touching the car and then Weatherly, rubbing the bad luck off on the other driver. But superstitions went only so far.

"If I win, No. 13 is great," he said. "If I get upside down, it's no good and I'm superstitious again."[10]

The NASCAR regulars were more receptive to Foyt's verbal jousting and ribbing the second time around, and he met his match in "Little Joe" Weatherly, the two-time defending series champion. Weatherly was NASCAR's version of Eddie Sachs, a clown off the track who enjoyed the banter with other drivers as much as Foyt. Weatherly also learned early on what others would discover: While Foyt relished the psychological games played off the track to try and intimidate competitors, he respected and accepted those who gave it back.

At Atlanta the attention was on Chevrolet's "Mystery Engine," with some competitors challenging its legality. NASCAR regulations required an engine be available for purchase at dealerships and reporters found it impossible to locate one. After Foyt qualified fourth, Weatherly accused him of sandbagging, calling him "Ol' Balloon Foot." Foyt questioned Weatherly about pulling out of the Daytona sports car race because it "rained a little" and invited him to try on an Indianapolis-style car.[11]

"Imagine me, driving one of those cucumbers with hay-raker wheels on that rock pile," Weatherly responded. Yunick declared the verbal exchange a standoff, saying, "A.J. has dished out as much as he's received."

At the start Foyt followed the Chevy of pole sitter Johnson and then moved to the front when the leader's engine blew. He led for the next fifty-six laps before being sidelined by a transmission problem.

It was an abnormally hot and humid day for Atlanta in March and an unusual inversion layer had many drivers complaining about the effects of carbon monoxide poisoning. Richard Petty, for one, was looking for a relief driver for his Plymouth. Most drivers were under contract to an automotive brand and the Petty crew was having a hard time finding a replacement. Foyt, who considered himself a free agent, barely paused before running to the Petty pit. The team lost several laps making the driver change but Foyt soldiered on for another three hundred miles, bringing the Plymouth home in eighth, while Petty was one of six drivers sent to the hospital.[12]

"I got gassed up real bad," Petty recalled. "I was out of it. Got that carbon monoxide poisoning. Took me a week to find out where I was at."[13]

Petty was one of those who accepted Foyt early on.

"Here's the deal, there's all this hearsay about different people before you meet them," Petty said. "Foyt, the way I understood it, was the top dog at the Indy deal, and he let everybody know about it. He wasn't cocky, but everybody understood he was the guy to beat.

"But when he came to NASCAR and ran with us, he was just a regular ol' guy. He didn't think he was anything special. He came in and got along with everybody and everybody got along with him. Just because he was A.J. Foyt and had won some Indy races and stuff like that, he didn't try to impress our crowd that he was better or worse or different than what we were.

"There might have been some [resentment], but there was nothing out in the open. I think everybody welcomed him because it gave us that much more publicity. You have an Indy winner, somebody who has won championships and such, coming in here and it put a check mark by NASCAR. At that time NASCAR wasn't nearly as big as Indy car. Indy car was really the predominate racing organization in the United States."

MR. FOYT

Hurtubise was now a constant companion of Foyt, the duo often traveling from one race to another and sharing a room on the road. From Atlanta they went to Florida, where the Corvette A.J. drove at Daytona was entered in the 12 Hours of Sebring, then America's premier road race. Hurtubise was to be his codriver.

Carroll Shelby rolled out a fleet of his recently introduced Ford-powered Cobras for the race. Ferrari would become the ultimate target of Shelby and Ford, but in 1963 the goal was simply to topple the 'Vette from its perch as America's top sports car. Shelby put together an impressive list of drivers including Gurney, Roberts, Phil Hill, and Ken Miles.

Both teams suffered extensive car troubles and while a Cobra won the class battle, Ferraris swept the first six places. The Foyt/Hurtubise car was well behind at the halfway mark and soon dropped out with engine problems. Although Foyt denied it, part of the lore is that Foyt blew the engine on purpose so he and Hurtubise could get an early start for the airport and a flight to Reading, Pennsylvania, where the USAC sprint car season opened the next day.

Back in Wally Meskowski's sprint car at Reading, Foyt started the year in grand style, turning in the fastest qualifying time, winning his heat race, and leading all thirty laps to capture the main event. The race was not without incident, however, as a water hose broke loose after the finish and sprayed Foyt, burning his hands and legs badly enough to require treatment at the track.

A week later at Williams Grove Speedway he wasn't as lucky, tangling with Rutherford in a heat race.

"Rutherford was tooling around in the groove and Foyt figured that wasn't the place for a rookie to be, that the groove should be reserved for the champ," read one report. "So he tried to instill the Fear of Foyt in Johnny by zooming around him and snapping him off tight. But Rutherford didn't give an inch and Foyt had no place to go but into a spin. Foyt was fuming and Rutherford didn't blink an eye."[14]

"Now Mr. Foyt knows I don't scare so easy," Rutherford said.

A few laps later Foyt spun in the same spot, his car catching a rut and rolling several times. Crawling out unhurt, he helped right the car and went to work pounding it back into shape. He repaired it in time to start the main event but failed to finish.[15]

After spending the week rebuilding the car, Foyt won the first of two fifty-lap features at Langhorne, but only after Hurtubise ran out of fuel with two laps left. A.J. then dropped out of round two with a busted transmission after leading the first ten laps.

The second race was stopped ten laps from the finish and Roger McCluskey was declared the winner when the car of Bobby Marvin, twenty-three, skipped across the ruts in Turn Two and hit the outside guardrail, destroying a large part of the fence. The car flipped twice and caught fire before landing on its wheels and rolling back into traffic, where it was T-boned by the car driven by Bud Tinglestad and exploded. With no firefighters in sight, Tinglestad ran to Marvin's car and tried unsuccessfully to pull him out, before being dragged away from the inferno. He was taken to the hospital with burns on his hands and legs, while Marvin died that evening of his burns.[16]

Standing along the inside guardrail that day was another twenty-three-year-old, Mario Andretti, a local hot shot from nearby Nazareth, who was waiting for a crack at the big time. He'd get it a week later when the owner of Marvin's rebuilt car allowed Andretti to drive it in a local race at Allentown Fairgrounds. Andretti would make several additional USAC starts later in the year.

"It was such an eerie feeling for me," Andretti would say. "I watched him burn. It was so horrible."[17]

FUNNY CARS

As the teams gathered for the start of the champ car season on April 21 at Trenton, all the talk centered around the new rear-engine cars expected at Indianapolis in May. They'd been impressive during March trials at the Speedway, with Gurney reportedly turning a lap at better than 150 miles per hour.

While the factory Lotuses tested at Indy by Gurney and Jim Clark were nowhere to be seen at Trenton, the USAC regulars received an early wake-up call in the form of a three-year-old Lotus in the hands of Lloyd Ruby.

Ruby had driven the car in the 1961 United States Grand Prix at Watkins Glen and updated it to meet USAC specifications. Powered by the same 2.7-liter Climax engine used in the grand prix, it gave away an estimated 100 horsepower to the bigger 4.2-liter Offenhauser engines. The horsepower deficit was balanced by an estimated 500-pound weight savings.[18]

Foyt and Bignotti countered with the ultimate in old tech, their 1960 dirt track car. Ruby set a track record to capture the pole and led thirty of the first forty laps, the superior handling of the Lotus more than equal to the Offy's horsepower edge. A seized gearbox ended Ruby's day and, with the Lotus out, Foyt led the final seventy circuits. Despite Foyt's win, Ward, the reigning USAC national champion and Indy 500 winner, was one of those saying he'd seen the future of their sport.[19]

"I feel there is great potential in the rear-engine cars," he said. "The Lotus-Fords already have proved they could be competitive. On the other hand, some of the drivers of these cars are relatively inexperienced at the Speedway and so are their crews. Whether one will be able to win this year is problematical. If not this year, certainly the trend toward this type of car will be great next year."[20]

Foyt wasn't so sure. "If one of them ever hits the wall, man, I'd sure hate to be in that one. That driver would be cooked right now. You run a risk any time you get into a race car. But it looks to me like you run a greater risk riding in one of those funny cars."[21,22]

Emerging as an issue at Trenton were the smaller and softer compound tires Firestone provided to Ruby for the race. Firestone said the lightweight Lotus allowed for a tire design that provided improved traction. Gurney's fast lap at the Speedway was reportedly run during Dunlop tests with a similar soft tire. There were reports Firestone was providing even smaller tires for the twelve-inch wheels of Mickey Thompson's new rear-engine cars.

Foyt, for one, wasn't happy about the special tires and didn't see the rush to rear-engine cars as a good thing, especially after his car owners dropped thirty-five thousand dollars on a new Watson roadster. He used the winner's soapbox at Trenton to speak out.

"If they let us use those soft tires to qualify the Offys, we'd really show 'em some new track records," he said.

While the teams began converging on Indianapolis, the first stop was Raceway Park, where the inaugural Yankee 300 USAC stock car race was being held. The race on the facility's road course was added to the schedule partly to placate NASCAR, although only Roberts entered.

The split with Nichels had left Foyt without a ride for the USAC stock car season, but he quickly remedied that, signing on with Norm Nelson. The 1960 stock car champion, Nelson's two-car team was shifting from Ford to Plymouth and was ecstatic about landing Foyt.

The race attracted an impressive entry list, including four of Nichels's Pontiacs. Foyt's old car was being driven by the national road racing champion Roger Penske, with others for Ruby, Sutton, and Goldsmith. Holman Moody Fords were entered for Curtis Turner and Roberts, and there was a quartet of Mercurys for Jones, Ruttman, Ward, and Gurney.

Jones qualified on the pole and led the first twenty-seven laps before dropping out with rear-end trouble. Penske, Roberts, Turner, and Gurney all took turns out front in a race that featured eleven lead changes. Foyt spent most of the first half of the event fighting back from several problems with his car, including a flat tire. The others eventually slowed or dropped out, giving Foyt the win and Plymouth its first USAC victory.[23]

"That performance showed his determination and toughness as a driver," Penske recalled. "He kept moving forward throughout the race and at the end he was the one in Victory Lane."[24]

A grinning Foyt said, "The breaks eventually even out. I'd gain a lap, then right away I'd lose it back. I was going as fast as everybody else, but all the breaks went against me until late in the race. I'm going to stay with Norm the rest of the season, that is unless he fires me."[25]

Especially happy with the results was Langhorne promoter Irv Fried, who'd made a special trip to Indianapolis to secure Foyt for the upcoming stock car race at his track.

"A.J. Foyt is the greatest driver I've ever seen," Fried said, already hyping his event. "Probably the greatest driver who ever lived. A lesser man would have given up in disgust. But A.J.—that boy don't know how to quit. He showed them all how a car was supposed to be driven."[26]

TIRE PROBLEMS

No sooner had the opening ceremonies been completed and the Indianapolis Motor Speedway opened for practice on May 1, 1963, than a group of unhappy team owners, drivers, and mechanics gathered in Gasoline Alley. Their target wasn't the new rear-engine "funny cars" or engine supplier Ford Motor Company, even though those new challengers threatened to make millions of dollars of the owners' investments obsolete.

They converged on the Firestone office complaining about smaller, wider, and softer tires being supplied to the rear-engine teams. Even though a Lotus had yet to take the track in May, the others knew about the speeds turned during testing and said the new tires provided a distinct advantage over the narrow and harder eighteen-inch tires the roadsters had been using for years. A petition circulated saying the undersigned would not compete in the race unless the tires were shared with everyone or withdrawn.

In an attempt to deflect the complaints, Firestone said it developed different types of tires for different types of cars, just as it did for passenger vehicles, and smaller tires were made for lighter-weight cars. The company had a point: The Lotus-Fords were at least three hundred pounds lighter than the average roadster. Adding insult to injury, Firestone agreed to provide the tires to Smokey Yunick, who had developed a new "lightweight" roadster.[27]

"We have no intention of withdrawing the fifteen-inch tire," the company said in a statement. "It was our obligation to meet the requirements of these smaller cars who had requested small tires. Firestone feels that all tires in this year's race will be the best ever in performance in any of our experience in thirty-five years."[28]

As soon as the Lotus-Fords took the track and the faster they went, the louder the complaints. Fans turned out in record numbers to see the new cars and high speeds. In addition, the Fords were running on gasoline rather than the traditional methanol and would need to make only two pits stops, compared to a minimum of three for the roadsters.

Frustrated by all the talk and no action, Foyt flew to Langhorne for the 150-mile stock car race. He set a track record in qualifying and won by more than two laps, breaking a record set by Roberts in 1957. Even though the event took four hours to run, a cocky Foyt nodded when asked if it was as easy as it looked.[29]

"Probably the easiest race I've ever won," he said. "I was running at half to three-quarters throttle all day."[30]

It was already his fifth victory of the year driving three different types of cars on four different types of tracks—paved, dirt, road courses, and ovals. Despite the length of the race and plans to fly back to Indianapolis as soon as it was over, he lingered after, talking to reporters, signing autographs for all comers, and surprising those who'd heard Foyt could be brusque and his signature hard to come by.

"He had to be tired," noted one reporter, "but he took time to autograph every piece of paper thrust at him by admiring fans."[31]

Back in Indianapolis, Foyt went to the recently opened ninety-six-room Speedway Motel, where he and Lucy were staying. Lucy and Mari Hulman George would go horseback riding nearly every morning before going to the track. The three children were at home with the grandparents—Tony now seven, Terry, four, and Jerry, eight months.[32]

The next day at the Speedway, Foyt decided to take matters into his own hands, saying Firestone was favoring the "little shitboxes" and "kowtowing to a bunch of foreigners," or "furriners" as he called them. He believed the Firestone moves were personal, in retaliation for his running Goodyear tires in NASCAR. He called Goodyear's offices in Akron, Ohio.[33]

"When it comes down to it, I'm as loyal as the next guy," Foyt would say. "When it's deserved. Firestone hadn't really done anything for me, personally. I mean, nothing they hadn't done for Indy racers in general. So when they turned around and gave them other guys special tires, that was too much. It was time for me to switch to Brand X."

The next day a Goodyear truck rolled into Gasoline Alley for the first time since Tommy Milton won the race on its tires in 1921. The truck was loaded with the same tires used in the stock car races at Daytona and Atlanta and accompanied by a phalanx of Goodyear engineers. Foyt made a big show for photographers of helping mount tires on his car and insisted on running practice laps, despite gusting winds keeping most cars parked for the day.[34]

"It felt like a tornado, it picks the whole car up and moves it over," he said, although he still turned his fastest laps of the month. "So far, so good. The tire wear looks real good now. We'll have to run them at higher speeds to learn more."[35]

With the appearance of the Goodyear tires and threats of legal action, it wasn't long before the fifteen-inch Firestones magically appeared in the garages of other teams. Jones took to the track and turned an unofficial lap of more than 152 mph, the fastest ever run at the Speedway.

Eleven of the sixty-six entries were rear-engine, including three Lotus-Fords. In a somewhat surprising move, the Ruby team elected not to enter the Lotus that ran so well at Trenton, sticking with a proven roadster instead. Novi-powered cars also were back at the Speedway for the first time in four years, revitalized by Andy Granatelli and with Hurtubise signed as the driver. Eight new Watson roadsters were spread throughout Gasoline Alley.

Foyt had a pair of cars to choose from, the new Watson and the three-year old Trevis, both with stunning new Dean Jefferies paint jobs and wearing No. 2. To avoid the conflicts of the year before, George Bignotti agreed to work solely on the team cars and A.J. was the only listed driver. The cars were called Sheraton-Thompson Specials, a nod to the hotel chain being a more consumer-friendly connection.

Several NASCAR drivers were on hand to take their driver tests, including Johnson, White, Tiny Lund, and Curtis Turner. Johnson, whose car was fitted with a roll cage similar to his stock car, left after running the 120 mph first stage of his rookie test. "These cars go too fast for me," he said. "There is too much wind in your face here."[36]

"I wasn't exactly what you'd call afraid," said Johnson, one of NASCAR's toughest drivers, after qualifying on the pole later in the week for the Charlotte World 600. "But I'll tell you one thing, if I get in something I'm scared of—I get away from it. Those Indy drivers—Jones, A.J. Foyt, and them—they're a nice bunch of guys. I don't think they're crazy because they drive there. It's their type [of] racing. That's what they started on and to them it's no more [dangerous] than stock car racing is to us. But I wouldn't drive there under any circumstances. It's definitely real dangerous."[37]

It didn't take long for Foyt and the Goodyear engineers to realize the stock car tires weren't right for the Speedway and announce development work would begin immediately on a tire for 1964. Foyt went back to using Firestones but wore his Goodyear hat for the rest of the month. He also settled on qualifying the Trevis, based on "pure sentiment."

For the second straight year no one was able to challenge Jones for the pole position. Hurtubise was second in the Novi and Clark fifth in a Lotus. Wind and rain played havoc with the first day's action and Foyt waited until day two, turning in the second-fastest overall time, good for an eighth-place starting position. Gurney, after a crash in his primary car, qualified the backup Lotus in twelfth.

Safely in the field, Foyt brokered a deal to put Ebb Rose into the team's second entry and tested the car to make sure it was ready. The millionaire son of a Houston trucking magnate, Rose qualified the second weekend, acknowledging, "I would never have been able to do it if A.J. hadn't set up the chassis."

Through it all, the relationship between Foyt and Bignotti seemed greatly improved from the previous year. They still argued, mostly over chassis setup, but there was a civil tone to their disagreements. As always Bignotti ran a tight ship, the crew dressed in matching white uniforms, the garage and cars spotless. As the race approached, Big George handled the final engine rebuild himself.[38]

Foyt put himself in the middle of a hornet's nest a few days before the race when he instigated a verbal battle between Sachs and Jones. They were all sitting together at an awards luncheon and Sachs, who never needed much instigating, kept predicting Hurtubise would lead the first lap of the race. A riled-up Jones bet Sachs five hundred dollars he'd not only lead the first lap, he'd lead the first ten. Amused by it all, Foyt kept jabbing Sachs in the ribs, saying, "I didn't know he could get so mad." It's unclear, however, if the bet was ever made.[39]

While Jones was once again the odds-on favorite to win the race, many in Gasoline Alley doubted his car would withstand his hard-charging style. So confident was Foyt, when everyone was asked during the drivers' meeting to commit to appearing live on Sunday night's *Ed Sullivan Show* if they won, only he hesitated. He had a stock car race to run that day and wanted to make sure there wouldn't be a conflict.

Although Hurtubise led the first lap, Jones quickly took over, building a straightaway lead during the first sixty laps. When Jones pitted, Clark and Gurney ran one-two before their stops. Foyt, Sachs, Ward, and McCluskey were having a good race amongst themselves, but they were no match for Jones or Clark.

The race ended in controversy when Jones's car began trailing blue smoke, a sign of an oil leak. Chief steward Harlan Fengler had promised to black-flag any car leaking fluids and earlier in the race he'd done just that, parking Hurtubise's Novi. Now he hesitated, reluctant to black-flag the leader. Chapman and Agajanian approached Fengler and began to argue and while they did, the leak dissipated. Fengler decided to let Jones continue, and he went on to top Clark by about ten seconds.

Sachs and McCluskey crashed, blaming oil from Jones's car, with Foyt moving up to finish third. The arguments carried on after the race, Jones and Sachs coming to blows at one point. Clark refused to criticize Jones and USAC, even posing for photos with the winner the next morning. "I wish to congratulate Parnelli Jones for his great victory," Clark said. "I think Parnelli deserved to win the race and I hope all this business dies down."[40]

Clark said he learned a lesson from Foyt.

"I was told emphatically that you would be penalized a lap if you passed anyone under the yellow. I absolutely did not pass a single car under the yellow until very late in the race when I saw Foyt pass a bloke and finally decided I better do it too."[41]

Foyt also disagreed with those questioning Jones's victory, saying, "You win any way you can. He had the fastest car and deserved to win." He also said Clark "handled it well," both on and off the track.

"I have always thought it was more Clark than it was the car," he'd say. "There are a few drivers—damn few—who can really handle a car right. There are a lot who can drive a good car and drive it fast, but I can count on one hand the ones who can take a poor-handling car and do well with it. Clark appeared to be of those select few. I was glad to see Clark stand up there and say, 'Okay, boys, I'll play it your way from here on in.' That's what he said, in effect. And that was ballsy."[42]

High praise indeed.

At the end of the day a roadster powered by an Offenhauser engine had triumphed. There was little doubt, however, what the future course of racing held. Three of the four rear-engine cars finished in the top ten and teams were already scrambling to line up new cars for the coming year.

Anyone who didn't recognize the changes ahead was likely to experience the same fate as the dinosaurs.

CHAPTER 13

A SUMMER ON THE RUN

1963

It wasn't until three weeks after the 1963 Indianapolis 500, in a race at Langhorne, that A.J. Foyt's season really took off. He was a heavy favorite at the track, having won five races over the past three years in three different types of cars. Even Parnelli Jones sounded like he was racing for second.

"Foyt definitely is the man to beat," Jones said. "He fits [Langhorne] like a glove. It's a track that you must attack, take by its throat and shake it and show it who's boss."[1]

"Very few drivers will win at Langhorne playing it safe. You can stomp down on the gas almost the entire trip if you've got the guts to do it. And A.J. has the guts. He's the toughest driver I know. Foyt fights the track."

It was Bobby Marshman, who'd succeeded Foyt as the circuit's hot young driver, who took the early lead. "I'd never have caught him if he kept going like that," Foyt admitted. "I was resigned to second place." But as so often happened at Langhorne, the track reigned. An exhausted Marshman was forced into the pits on lap sixty-three of one hundred for a relief driver.

"The track and centrifugal force beat my neck to a pulp," Marshman said. "I just couldn't take it any longer."[2]

With Marshman out, Foyt cruised to the victory and pulled within ten points of Jones in the championship race. It was Foyt's third straight win at The 'Horne.

"If they ever close this place," he said, "I guess I'll just have to retire."[3]

From Langhorne Foyt went to Daytona Beach where he practiced Smokey Yunick's Chevrolet for the July fourth Firecracker 400. After setting one of the fastest times in practice he flew back to Indianapolis for a sprint car race at IRP. He was becoming increasingly frustrated with A.J. Watson's loyalty to

◀ Foyt (No. 2) races with Roger McCluskey (No. 12) and Don Branson (No. 1) at Salem Speedway. *Revs Institute, The Bruce R. Craig Photograph Collection*

Offenhauser. Despite rule changes allowing for larger Offy engines, Chevys were on a ten-race winning streak. He qualified sixth and fought past all but one of the Chevrolets, finishing second to Roger McCluskey.

Back at Daytona, Foyt walked into the middle of a seemingly never-ending battle between Yunick and NASCAR's Bill France, the car owner complaining that the organization's rules favored Ford. At the time NASCAR staged qualifying races to set the Firecracker field, and after starting second, Yunick ordered Foyt into the pits after two laps in protest. It meant Foyt would start the main event in thirty-first.

He raced his way to the lead pack and chased Johnson in a sister Chevrolet, both cars eventually succumbing to engine problems. Afterward Yunick said he was parking the Chevy and retiring from NASCAR. His retirement would be short-lived as he continued to field cars in NASCAR and at Indianapolis, but Foyt never drove for him again. Their short relationship, however, left a lasting impression on both men, who became lifelong friends.[4]

"I remember the day A.J. started at Indianapolis, 1958, the same year I started," Yunick said years later. "He was cocky, with talent running out both ears. He went on to become, arguably, the best driver this country ever had. There was a time, and quite a lengthy time, we absolutely couldn't beat that son-of-a-bitch, no matter what we tried. It didn't make any difference if it was a midget or a sprint car, an Indy car, sports car, stock car, whatever it was, he just went like a bat out of hell. When he was really good, like at Indy, he'd kill himself three times a lap and never put a scratch on the car. It was amazing what the guy could do."[5]

"I LOVE MY SPRINTER."

Three days later and back in Norm Nelson's Plymouth, Foyt hounded pole sitter Paul Goldsmith at IRP until the race's halfway point, the pair putting two laps on the rest of the field. Foyt caught a break when Goldsmith made his pit stop only to have the caution flag displayed, allowing Foyt to maintain a lap lead when he stopped. Goldsmith eventually crashed trying to catch up.[6]

The victory moved Foyt 500 points ahead of his car owner Nelson in USAC's stock car division. Midway through the racing season he was second in two other USAC series, to Jones in champ cars and to McCluskey in sprinters. While the champ car title was clearly most important, Foyt decided to pursue something never previously accomplished: winning all three championships in one year.

The sprint car title was the most challenging and seemingly out of reach. While Foyt was winning the stock car race at IRP, McCluskey was winning the sprint car race at Williams Grove Speedway and held a commanding lead in the points. It would be hard to make up points in races Foyt couldn't enter.

From Tucson, Arizona, McCluskey was five years older than Foyt. He'd come up through the tough California Racing Association's sprint car series with Jones and Hurtubise. He was friendly with Mari and Elmer George, sometimes driving the couple's car in the early 1960s. As a result, he'd become part of Foyt's loose circle of friends.

Midway through the 1962 season McCluskey hooked up with car owner Bruce Homeyer, whose Konstant Hot Special had been driven by several drivers, including Foyt. In McCluskey's first race in the car he captured the pole, won his heat race, and led every lap of the feature. The combination had been hard to beat ever since, with Homeyer winning the owner's championship in 1962. Now McCluskey was running the entire series, had already won five races, and held a commanding lead in driver points.

After winning two of the year's first three sprint car races, but landing on his head in the other, Foyt had shifted his focus to stock cars prior to the 500, which were safer and paid more. He'd also discovered they weren't as much fun. The sprint car title might be a long shot, but he was going to try, despite the objections of others.

"I love my sprinter," he said. "I can't give it up. I love it."[7]

He drove two races in Watson's new Offy-powered sprint car, getting blown off by McCluskey in both. Feeling he needed a Chevrolet engine to have a chance, Foyt left Watson and once again started fielding his own sprinter. He purchased a three-year-old Chevy-powered car from Elmer George, who'd decided to retire from racing and move out west to run a dude ranch. He also bought a new plane to help him jump from race to race. And to keep the peace in Houston, he had a swimming pool installed at home.

His plans were immediately dealt a blow when the Trenton 150 Indy car race set for July 21 was postponed a week by rain, setting up conflicts with both a sprint car and stock car race set for the same day. There wasn't a plane on the planet that could have him three places at the same time, but he was going to try, and it kicked off an incredible string of events for Foyt.

- Friday, July 26, Hatfield (Pennsylvania) Speedway: An incredible field of Indy drivers, in the area for the rescheduled Trenton champ car race, turned up for the ten-mile feature on a one-third-mile dirt track. Jones led all thirty laps to win, followed by Marshman, who'd moved into the Meskowski sprinter Foyt drove at the start of the season. McCluskey was third, Foyt fourth.
- Sunday, July 28, Trenton (New Jersey) International Speedway: Predicting he would "take the lead for the national championship at Trenton" before the start of practice, Foyt did just that, setting a track record while qualifying on the pole and leading all 150 laps. Ward moved into second as Jones dropped out early with car problems.[8]
- Week of July 29: From Trenton he flew to Indianapolis for the start of Goodyear tests at the Speedway. Using the car Ebb Rose drove in the 500, he averaged more than 151 miles per hour over ten laps, faster than his previous qualifying speed.
- Sunday, August 4, Salem (Indiana) Speedway: In a major blow to his sprint car title hopes, Foyt didn't make it through his heat race, dropping out with clutch problems. Ironically, Don Branson, now driving the Watson Offy, won and broke the string of Chevrolet victories.
- Sunday, August 11, Milwaukee: The engine in his Plymouth stock car blew after just nine laps and he finished thirty-fifth. Don White, second in points, finished second to Jones.

- Thursday, August 15, Milwaukee: Jones and White again finished one-two in their stock cars. Foyt finished fourth as his points lead, five hundred points only two races earlier, dropped to just fifty.
- Saturday, August 17, Illinois (Springfield) State Fairgrounds: He qualified on the pole for the one-hundred-mile Indy car dirt race but finished second to Ward, who became Foyt's closest championship contender.
- Sunday, August 18, Milwaukee: A sold-out crowd saw the clearest picture yet of the future of Indy car racing as the rear-engine cars of Jimmy Clark and Dan Gurney made their first appearance since the 500. Clark, with the Formula One championship all but wrapped up, qualified on the pole with Gurney alongside. Clark led all two hundred laps, while Foyt forced his way past Gurney halfway through the race. Near the end, Clark closed on Foyt with the possibility of putting a lap on the field but thought better of it. "I tried everything I could think of to catch up," Foyt said, but added, "I don't think they proved anything. We had only 20 minutes to get our car ready and they had two days." Watson, however, acknowledged for the first time he was building a rear-engine car.[9]
- Sunday, August 25, Illinois State Fairgrounds: In a stock car race, Foyt led the first ninety-six laps, then ran out of gas and had to pit for a splash of fuel. He finished second then had words with car owner Nelson.
- Saturday, August 31, Du Quoin (Illinois) State Fairgrounds: He led all twenty-five laps in his sprint car, pulling within 205 points of McCluskey, who finished sixth.
- Sunday, September 1, Du Quoin (Illinois) State Fairgrounds: Mad at Nelson, Foyt signed on to drive for Ford, bumping Hurtubise from the ride. "I was naturally disappointed because he had promised he would drive for me the rest of the year," Nelson said. "However, I told him that if he thought he was bettering himself, then he should make the move. If he didn't want to drive for me anymore, then he wouldn't be doing his best job anyhow." To replace Foyt, Nelson hired Goldsmith, USAC's defending stock car champion, who'd been left without a ride since the demise of Nichels's Pontiac program. Nelson and Goldsmith finished one-two, as Foyt dropped out early and failed to score a point.[10]
- Sunday, September 1, Lakeside (Kansas) Speedway: Immediately after finishing the Du Quoin stock car race, Foyt flew to Kansas City for a fifteen-mile sprint car event. Driving Watson's sprinter, he finished second to Branson and flew back to Du Quoin.
- Monday, September 2, Du Quoin State Fairgrounds: Ward led the Indy car race from the pole. Foyt passed him before the halfway point, leading the final fifty-eight laps for the win.
- Wednesday, September 4, Indiana (Indianapolis) State Fairgrounds: He qualified on the pole for the stock car race but White, his new Ford teammate, dominated. Foyt was ready to settle for second when White was forced to the pits with a busted suspension with five laps remaining. "Don deserved to win this," he said. "I don't think I could have gotten by him."

- Sunday September 8, Langhorne Speedway: Goldsmith, driving the same car Foyt used for a record-setting victory at the track in May, led 248 of 250 laps to win, eclipsing Foyt's mark in the process. A.J. crashed out when he hit the wall avoiding a spinning car. Climbing in the passenger window of White's car for a ride back to the pits, he spotted the Dodge of rookie John Kilborn, who'd hit the fence and was getting the fender pulled away from the tire.

"Foyt yelled and asked if I needed relief," Kilborn said. "I yelled back that I was fine. Then he said he sure did need the points and would like to take over. It occurred to me that it was a poor way to lose a championship, standing on the sidelines because of a wreck which wasn't his fault. So I just unbuckled, climbed out and told him to take off. That was the fastest ride my car has had this year."[11]

Returning in fourteenth place, Foyt turned the fastest laps of the race and drove to a third-place finish, although six laps behind Goldsmith, with Nelson second. Both Nelson and White moved past him in points and Foyt bristled at the suggestion that his decision to take a big paycheck from Ford would cost him the championship.

"If I had it do over again, I'd do the same thing. But it wasn't just money. I'd rather win a race than have money. And the big race I want to win is in Indianapolis. That's all I can say right now."

The implication was clear: Foyt made the move in hopes of securing a Ford engine and perhaps a Lotus for Indianapolis. "Yeah, I've heard the same thing, and maybe it's true," Nelson said. "A.J. just told me that Ford had offered him a deal he couldn't turn down and he was taking it. So I got in touch with Goldsmith and I'm tickled pink we beat Foyt today."[12]

- Saturday, September 14, Indiana State Fairgrounds: Ward led from start to finish in the Hoosier 100 and gained in the Indy car championship. Foyt battled with Rutherford throughout, finally getting past for third place with three laps remaining.[13]
- Sunday September 15, Milwaukee: In a stock car race won by Jones, all three championship contenders were involved in a five-car crash on lap fifteen as they tried to avoid a car stalled on the backstraight. The Fords of White and Foyt were knocked out while Nelson was able to continue, although at a greatly reduced rate. White returned in a relief role, but Foyt was sent to the hospital with facial cuts and observation for a possible concussion, although he left as soon as the cuts were treated. White scored enough points to take the overall lead.[14]
- Saturday, September 21, Allentown (Pennsylvania) Fairgrounds: Foyt finished second in the sprint car race to Johnny White, who was making the jump to USAC after winning the IMCA title. Also making his first USAC sprint car start was Mario Andretti.
- Sunday, September 22, Trenton: Foyt wasn't the only one rolling up the frequent flyer miles. After competing in a saloon car race in Oulton Park, England, on Saturday, Clark, Gurney, and Colin Chapman combined

chartered flights with a commercial flight between London and Montreal, arriving in Trenton about 2 a.m. for a few hours of sleep before heading to the track.[15]

In a repeat of Milwaukee, Clark and Gurney again qualified one-two, Clark breaking Foyt's track record by more than six miles an hour. Foyt qualified seventh. Clark led the first forty-nine laps before dropping out with an oil leak. Gurney took over, leading the next ninety-seven before dropping out with a similar problem. Foyt led the final fifty-four laps, giving Goodyear its first Indy car victory in recent history. Goodyear provided free tires to the teams and twenty of the twenty-six starters used them, while the two Lotuses were on Dunlops.[16]

The victory, coupled with Ward's failure to complete ten laps, clinched the Indy car title for Foyt, his third in four years. Despite the early dominance of the rear-engine cars in the race, he still wasn't ready to join the revolution just yet, although he was clearly hedging his bets.

"It doesn't look good for our cars," he said. "We can only improve them a little each year, while the new cars are just starting and can be improved a lot. I think they're too damned dangerous, but if they turn out to be the fastest cars, I suppose I'll have to get me one. We're talking with the Lotus-Ford people about building us a car. We hope to buy one from them in time for next season. Let's face it, they're the cars of the future. But not the present."[17]

The Trenton victory capped an incredible run of eighteen races in forty days, including eight in twenty days surrounding Labor Day. He'd wrapped up the all-important champ car title, lost the stock car championship, and had only a mathematical chance of overcoming McCluskey's sprint car lead. Ward was gracious as always in acknowledging the new Indy car champ.

"Naturally I would like to have won the title again this year," he said, "but I can't see being blue about not winning. After all, I was beaten by A.J. Foyt, a man I consider the greatest race driver in America today. There is nothing disgraceful about being beaten by the best there is."[18]

The end of the string of weekly races didn't mean Foyt was slowing down. He was already looking ahead to 1964, and as soon as Trenton's post-race requirements were finished, he headed for the airport, where one of Goodyear's corporate planes was waiting. With IMS unavailable—the Speedway's short straight between Turn Three and Turn Four was torn up while a new tunnel was put under the track—the next test was set for Goodyear's desert proving grounds in San Angelo, Texas, more than 250 miles southwest of Fort Worth. The massive facility included a five-mile oval with eighteen-degree banked turns.

For one young Goodyear engineer, Leo Mehl, it was his first real exposure to Foyt. Mehl would go on to become Goodyear's worldwide director of racing in a little more than ten years, thanks in a large part to Foyt's success on Goodyear tires.

"Somebody appointed Foyt, probably himself, the training officer for young Goodyear engineers and unfortunately, I was one of his first students," Mehl would say. "I remember going to the race in Trenton. It was very cold and the tires were terrible because they wouldn't warm up. Goodyear had a company plane, a Lockheed Lodestar, which was very reliable, but it only flew about 150 miles per hour. A.J. and I got on the plane and I got eleven hours of continuous instruction. I never asked to use the company plane again."[19]

While Jones was Firestone's lead test driver and others, including Marshman and McCluskey, ran tests for both companies, Foyt was the clear favorite of the Goodyear engineers. He had a unique ability to consistently run flat-out laps and then clearly explain the handling characteristics of the tires. Many drivers disliked the boredom of tire testing, where consistency and endurance were as important as sheer speed, but Foyt embraced it.

"The thousands of miles I put in at Indy in tire tests didn't hurt me," he'd say. "I developed a style that was going to be hard to beat. No longer did I have to worry about some of the older guys and all their experience. I had crammed a lifetime of experience into a very short period. And the nice thing was, I had it my own way. I learned it exactly the way I learned to win in every phase of racing on the way to Indy. Nobody told me how. I did it and then I improved on it until it was perfect."[20]

Any miracle hopes Foyt had of a sprint car title came undone along with his right-rear tire September 29 at Salem Speedway. After setting a track record in qualifying and leading the first sixty-eight laps, he was forced to pit for a new tire, losing three laps in the process. He made up one of the laps, but McCluskey was too far ahead, winning the race and clinching the championship.

His luck seemed to take a 180-degree turn the following week at Williams Grove Speedway when he failed to lead a lap but was named the winner when the apparent victor was disqualified for using an oversized engine. Foyt seemed not to care as his day had been marred by a confrontation with newcomer White.

In an incident similar to his run-in with Rutherford earlier in the year on the same track, Foyt was upset with the line White took during a heat race. Saying he'd been repeatedly cut off, he confronted the other driver while White was still in his car, then exchanged words with White's pit crew.

While the incident went unnoticed by most and generated no immediate media coverage, on Monday Tommy Nicholson, USAC's eastern zone supervisor who was at the race, filed a report saying Foyt, who'd only recently gotten off his year probation for the incident with the Milwaukee promoter, hit White. Nicholson wrote Foyt's conduct "was most reprehensible" and that he'd been loudly booed by the fans afterward.

On Tuesday, USAC's director of competition, Henry Banks, announced he was suspending Foyt, sending telegrams to his Houston home and to Goodyear's San Angelo track, where he'd gone for more tire testing.

"You are charged with misconduct considered detrimental to USAC and organized racing," the telegram read. "Based on evidence on hand, you are hereby suspended from participating in further USAC events until my recommendations can be reviewed by the USAC executive committee, which will be assembled within seven to ten days."[21]

Foyt didn't learn about the suspension until Wednesday at the Goodyear facility when someone showed him a newspaper article. A reporter soon tracked him down and Foyt denied the allegations.

"I never even swung at the guy," he said. "He had been cutting me off at the corners for four or more races and several times locked wheels with me. I want to race fair and square, so after Saturday's incident I went over to his pit to tell him about it. I wasn't angry, I just wanted to tell him to lay off. I never even raised my hand against him."[22]

He doubted White had complained, guessing it might have been one of the driver's crew members or a spectator. "White's not that type of guy."

Foyt cut the interview short, saying he had to get back to work. The tests were going well, with several laps around the big track of more than 190 mph. He and Bignotti were using tin snips to trim the car's plexiglass windscreen and reduce wind resistance. The effort worked and he clocked a lap at 200.4 mph, the first known lap on a closed course of more than 200 mph. It topped a previous mark of more than 186 mph set a few weeks earlier by Jim McElreath during tire tests at Firestone's similar facility in Fort Stockton, Texas.[23]

That evening Foyt telephoned Banks to plead his case. He was facing a one thousand dollar fine and a possible yearlong suspension, but he was more worried about missing the Riverside Grand Prix sports car race he planned to run that weekend. While denying he'd hit White, he did admit, "I had him around the neck and was holding him because I thought he was going to hit me, but I didn't punch him. I had his mechanic around the neck at the same time because I thought he was going to hit me, too." He offered to take a lie-detector test and asked for a public hearing, agreeing to post a hundred-dollar bond to hold the event.[24]

Thursday morning Banks reversed himself, "temporarily" lifting the suspension, noting he had received "conflicting reports" about what happened. He also warned Foyt was "by no means off the hook."[25]

In Houston when word came on the reversal of his suspension, Foyt headed to the airport. Practice was already underway at Riverside, a race that attracted many of the world's top road racers. The F1 stars who made an appearance included Clark, Gurney, Graham Hill, John Surtees, and Richie Ginther, while the American road race contingent was headed by Penske, Bob Bondurant, Ken Miles, Walt Hansgen, and newcomer Dave MacDonald. There was even a handful of other Indy car drivers entered, including Ruby, Ward, and Jones.

Foyt was anxious to test his skills against the world's best road racers and get behind the wheel of a rear-engine car. His road racing experience to date was almost exclusively in front-engine production cars, like the Tempest and Corvette at Daytona and Sebring and stock cars at IRP and Riverside.

Foyt was set to drive a car purchased for him by John Mecom Jr., the twenty-three-year-old son of a Texas oil tycoon. Mecom's parents were friends of Tony Hulman, and he'd been attending the Indianapolis 500 since a young age. He'd tried racing himself but succumbed to family pressure not to drive and formed a race team instead. Penske and Augie Pabst, scion of the Milwaukee brewing family, were among the team's drivers, and Mecom's fleet of cars included a Cooper Climax for Penske and a Lotus 19 for Pabst. Word was Mecom spent more than a million dollars on the team, and someone asked his father if he was concerned about his son's spending.

"At that rate," the elder Mecom responded, "he'll be broke in about two hundred years."[26]

The Mecom-Foyt relationship had started at the B & F Garage in the early 1950s.

"Tony's shop was a place you'd drop in to from time to time and check out whatever race cars were there," Mecom said. "A.J. was already building his reputation at Playland Park. He was the local hero. I got to know him then and became friendly with Jimmy Greer too."[27]

Mecom purchased a Scarab for twenty-seven thousand dollars for Foyt to drive. It was originally built by another millionaire heir, Lance Reventlow of the Woolworth department store fortune, and son of socialite Barbara Hutton. Reventlow had bankrolled the Scarab team, building eight different race cars, including the first American-made machines to compete in F1. Dean Jeffries worked on the design of the cars and Phil Remington served as the team's chief engineer, two names that would continue to play important roles in Foyt's career.

The racer purchased by Mecom was a one-of-a-kind rear-engine sports car and the last Scarab built. Reventlow set a track record at Riverside in the machine in 1962 before damaging it in practice, parking it, and walking away, tired of auto racing. Despite the expense and rarity of the car, Foyt's minimal road racing experience didn't concern Mecom.[28]

"Back in those days you didn't classify drivers to a type of car," Mecom said. "They were just drivers and A.J. was one of the ones who could drive and do anything with the car. There wasn't any special design; it was kind of like we're both from Houston and we're friends. You just tried to get the best."[29]

Despite spotting most of the competition a couple days of practice, Foyt qualified the Scarab seventh in a field of more than thirty cars. He quickly learned sports cars were more fragile than what he was used to, the gearshift lever breaking off in his hands after just five laps. The relatively unknown MacDonald, driving one of Carroll Shelby's King Cobras, lapped the field to win in front of an enormous crowd of eighty-two thousand.

Foyt and many of the same drivers made the trip up the California coast the following week to Laguna Seca Raceway, a tight and demanding 1.9-mile track with significant elevation changes and set in the idyllic Monterey Peninsula. It was Foyt's first visit to the track many drivers considered the most challenging road course in America, and he again qualified seventh.

Another large crowd turned out, estimated at more than sixty-five thousand, with MacDonald giving the King Cobra its second straight victory. Foyt never challenged for the lead but benefited from the high failure rate among the other cars to finish second, the only car on the same lap as the winner and ahead of third-place Jim Hall in his Chaparral. If nothing else, Foyt discovered he could be competitive against the world's best racers.

A week later he was on more familiar footing, the mile-long dirt track at the California State Fairgrounds in Sacramento. With an eye toward the coming year, the team debuted its new dirt car, rumored to have cost a stunning sixty thousand dollars. It was another Wally Meskowski–built machine, replacing the team's three-year-old model. Rutherford led early before crashing out. Ward won easily as Foyt brought the new car home in second.[30]

The next day Foyt was back in Indianapolis at the Speedway, where he'd invited the Lotus team to join him for a Goodyear tire test. Foyt and Bignotti continued to lobby Chapman and Ford for a car and the company's new double-overhead cam engine. Both were noncommittal, especially with a possible suspension hanging over Foyt's head. A.J. was an interested spectator, watching intently from the grandstands outside of Turn One when Gurney took to the track for a few slow laps with the new engine.[31]

In case a deal with Lotus failed to materialize, Bignotti was working with Joe Huffaker, another San Francisco area car builder, who'd built a promising rear-engine car. Using a heavy and underpowered Aston Martin engine, rookie Pedro Rodriguez had been unable to qualify earlier in the year, but the car showed promise. Bignotti was working to reduce the weight of the Offy and agreed to share the engine with Huffaker, who would provide a car in return.[32]

One obstacle to the Ford engine was cleared up on Halloween, when the USAC board met. Wearing a suit and tie, Foyt said he went to White after the heat race because the other driver was "chopping me off" in the turns, something Foyt had warned him about in the past.

Although invited to participate, White was a no-show, perhaps believing there was nothing to gain from confronting USAC's national champion. Foyt and four witnesses testified, including USAC's Nicholson, McCluskey, Foyt mechanic Barney Wimmer, and White mechanic Joe Pittman. All of them admitted not personally witnessing Foyt taking a swing at White or making unsportsmanlike gestures toward the fans.

"Foyt called me a bad name and pushed me to the ground," Pittman testified.[33]

"I had no intention of fighting," Foyt said, claiming he didn't throw a punch and noting White never took off his helmet. "I'd never hit anybody's helmet with my bare fists. It would be like hitting a brick wall."[34]

He acknowledged bear-hugging White after the other driver had climbed from his car and appeared ready to hit him. He also denied making an obscene gesture toward the crowd, saying, "All I did was bow."[35]

McCluskey backed Foyt up. "A.J. didn't hit White. If he had, he would have torn his head off."

Putting in a good word for Foyt was Harry McQuinn, chief USAC championship race steward. Since the Milwaukee incident, he said Foyt had "conducted himself like a gentleman, has adhered to all the rules and regulations and has been an excellent example of USAC in the past year."

The full nineteen-member USAC board deliberated for only thirty minutes before returning with a unanimous decision. President Thomas Binford announced the ruling, saying the evidence, "as originally presented to us, was different than that which was presented today. The decision of the board is that there is not sufficient evidence to substantiate the charge." Foyt was put back on a one-year probation and Binford said the board "asked me to caution you that as a champion and a gentleman, you have more responsibility than other drivers."[36]

His named cleared, Foyt began to shuttle between Indianapolis and Los Angeles, testing at the Speedway during the week and racing at Ascot Park on the weekends. With snow possible at any time in the Midwest, and Goodyear's deadline for deciding on a final compound for the 500 fast approaching, it was imperative he continue the testing at the Speedway. But no one understood Foyt's drawing power better than Ascot's J.C. Agajanian, who covered the cost of shipping Foyt's sprint car to the West Coast and the driver's expenses, along with a substantial appearance fee. In the first of three year-end appearances, Foyt led all thirty laps to beat Jones and McCluskey. The next week it was Jones's turn, followed by Foyt and McCluskey.

Between the two Ascot events and using the team's backup car, Foyt set an unofficial speed record at Indy of 154.5 mph during the final Goodyear test at IMS. Jones, in his race-winning car, had turned an unofficial lap of 153.5 mph during an earlier Firestone test.

"These old cars are still running pretty good," Foyt said. "It felt really good."[37]

BAHAMAS SPEED WEEK

Even with the conclusion of the NASCAR and USAC schedules and the end of tire tests at the Speedway, Foyt's season wasn't done. Mecom entered his fleet of sports cars in the Bahamas Speed Week, a series of races held on a road course laid out at Nassau's Oakes Field, an abandoned World War II British air base. Sponsored by the Bahamian government to promote tourism, it was viewed as a year-end holiday by many in the road racing community.

Not Foyt. The Scarab he'd driven earlier at Riverside and Laguna Seca was equipped with a new lightweight Chevrolet engine, and while others spent time poolside, he worked on fine-tuning the car. He borrowed a friend's Volkswagen Beetle and drove the course to become more familiar with the layout. Some joked about the intensity Foyt brought to the event and implied he'd been lucky in the West Coast races. No one questioned his courage or determination, only his skill. His constant banter bothered some, and one joke making the rounds was A.J. stood for "All Jaw."[38]

Foyt had the last laugh, winning the week's two biggest races, the Nassau Trophy and Governor's Trophy events, each time defeating Rodriguez in a quasi-factory team Ferrari. Penske, in another Mecom team car, was clearly the fastest combination but suffered problems in both main events. Ironically, the only race Foyt entered and didn't win was the Texas Classic, a five-lap trophy dash in which Penske came home first.

"I learned a lot by following them through the corners in the preliminary races," Foyt said. "I would hang on their tail and see what line they took—when they shut off, when they hit the brakes, when they shifted gears. When I thought I had it, I'd pull by and hit the pedal. I had my spins and went off course, but I learned."[39]

One of those he followed early on was MacDonald, the hottest thing in sports car racing and winner of the races at Riverside and Laguna Seca. Foyt tried to pass MacDonald going into the track's hairpin turn, but he was going too fast and headed down the escape road.

"Foyt got in too hot and couldn't turn," MacDonald said. "But he kept standing on it and disappeared into the jungle. I could hear his engine revving like crazy and out of the side of my eye saw bushes being torn out of the ground, palm trees getting knocked flat. That was Foyt. Finally he came shooting back onto the track ahead of me. He'd passed me while he was still in the jungle. He was like an earthquake."[40]

A large media contingent, guests of the tourist board, heaped praise on Foyt. "The win gives Foyt a victory in every major type of race car," read one report, "and over the high-speed brutes of the international circuits—a feat no other driver in the world has ever accomplished."[41]

Not everyone on hand was ready to crown Foyt the world's best racer. Stirling Moss, considered the best in F1 when he retired earlier in the year after a crash that nearly killed him, was on hand to provide commentary for ABC's *Wide World of Sports*. He noted "this is a fairly easy course, and Foyt is just learning. I think he will have to meet some of the top drivers that travel Europe before he can make any statement. However, I like the idea of the American drivers taking interest in the sport. I have never liked the oval driving. Tried it once, but I prefer the twisting chases a bit more."[42]

Foyt said, "I would like to try some of the European races," noting he was under contract to race almost every weekend in the United States. And besides, the European events didn't pay enough.

"Them sporty cars is all right," he said, "but remember, I'm just a poor working boy who can't afford to race for fun."

It was an incredible end to an incredible season. True to his promise to be a "racing champion," he'd started more than fifty features and countless heat and qualifying events. In Indy cars he'd won his third national championship in four years, completing all twelve races, winning seven, and finishing in the top four in the first eleven, a flat tire at the Phoenix finale the only thing keeping it from it being twelve straight. He finished second in both the stock car and sprint car championships despite running partial schedules. He'd competed in his first three NASCAR events, leading laps in each, before closing out the year winning two big sports car races.

Along the way he'd driven a stock car for all three Detroit automakers and four different brands. By reaching out to Goodyear he'd set in motion steps that would forever change the face of auto racing, not only at Indianapolis, but at tracks around the world. He'd also clashed with other drivers, team owners, manufacturers, sponsors, and sanctioning bodies.

He'd become the sport's biggest name.

And he was just getting warmed up.

CHAPTER 14

THE DINOSAURS

1964

The reason for A.J. Foyt's switch to a Ford stock car in USAC midway through the 1963 season became clear in early January 1964 when it was announced he would drive for a new Ford team formed by Banjo Matthews in FIA-sanctioned NASCAR events. Matthews, recently retired after a NASCAR career focused on the circuit's big tracks—primarily Daytona, Atlanta, and Charlotte—was contracted to manage the team by Holman-Moody, Ford's powerhouse stock car operation.

The first race for the new team was the Riverside 500 on January 19, and the season opened with tragedy when the defending NASCAR national champion, Joe Weatherly, was killed during the race. He'd lost about twenty laps early while his team changed the car's transmission, returning to the track in hopes of earning a few points toward the defense of his title. He'd slid broadside into a concrete wall in Turn Six when his throttle apparently stuck open, dying instantly from head and chest injuries. He was one of an estimated 20 percent of the drivers who still wore only a lap belt, declining the option of a shoulder harness.

"I don't use a shoulder harness because it would snap your neck in a quick stop," he said in a radio interview with Chris Economaki just before the start of the race. "I'd rather flop around. My way of thinking is that I move around so much that I feel it's a hazard."[1]

At forty-one he'd been among the oldest drivers in NASCAR but had no plans to retire. "I'll keep goin' until I can't turn those corners anymore," he said. "I like racing and I think I've got as good a chance as anybody at winning the championship this year."[2]

Helped by caution flags, Foyt moved up from his twelfth starting position to challenge leader and eventual winner Dan Gurney with about thirty laps

◄ The Dinosaurs: Parnelli Jones and A.J. Foyt. *IMS Photography Archive*

remaining, only to spin off the track. He later remembered "Little Joe" fondly as one of the first in the NASCAR garage to welcome him, saying he enjoyed bantering with the driver who once called him "Balloon Foot."

· "He was a character, he was always joking with me," Foyt said quietly when asked about Weatherly, adding, "He got killed at Riverside."[3]

"LET'S BEAT THEM."

Told the rear-engine Huffaker car was nearly ready for testing at the new Phoenix International Raceway, Foyt decided to add a pair of January 26 sprint car races at the Phoenix Fairgrounds to his schedule. He'd already committed to attending the annual dinner of the Houston Racing Hall of Fame the night before, where he would pick up the driver of the year award. The award didn't mean much to him, but the dinner also honored astronauts Scott Carpenter, Gordon Cooper, and Wally Schirra. With NASA based in Houston, Foyt was friendly with many of the astronauts and insisted on attending, staying until nearly midnight before heading to the airport for a flight to Phoenix.

Despite complaining the Chevrolet V8 engine in his sprint car never ran properly, Foyt won one of the two fifty-lap races and finished second in the other to take the overall victory. A tired Foyt spent most of the time after the races complaining about his car, to the point that one Phoenix reporter called him "grumpy." It wasn't the first time the adjective was used in reference to Foyt, but the reporter also called him "chunky." Once noted for his athletic build or, at worst, labeled barrel-chested, stories were increasingly referring to him as "hefty."[4]

His first chance to drive Joe Huffaker's new rear-engine car came a few days later. He'd already tested once at the facility, driving his roadster to a one-mile track record of more than 112 miles per hour over the smooth and freshly paved surface, unofficially breaking the previous one-mile mark set by Jim Clark in a Lotus at Trenton.[5]

Despite the brakes not working properly, he was able to better that mark and predicted a 160 mph lap in the car at Indianapolis. Afterward, Bignotti confirmed the team's order for one of the new machines.

The car featured a unique hydraulic or "liquid" suspension. Rather than the springs, shock absorbers, or torsion bars found on a traditional automotive suspension, it basically used air and fluids in rubber bags to act as the car's shocks and springs. Huffaker was backed by San Francisco import car dealer Kjell Qvale, a major importer of MG production cars that featured a similar suspension concept. The car was known as the "MG Liquid Suspension Special."[6]

Although it wasn't unusual for different teams to share a track during testing, Foyt was surprised to see Bobby Marshman behind the wheel of a Lotus with a new Ford dual overhead cam engine (DOHC) at the track. It was a marvel to behold, with an intricate "bundle of snakes" exhaust pipe system. Marshman made a few slow laps and then parked the car, the team unwilling to display its full capabilities with Foyt present.[7]

Landing a new Ford engine was proving much more difficult than coming up with a rear-engine car. The company had developed the V8 specifically for racing, replacing the production-based engine used in 1963. Due to the complexity of the powerplant, however, Ford decided only company engineers could work on them. With only about twenty-five engines available, Ford capped the number of cars it would support at ten.

Three of these were the Team Lotus entries, updated versions of the 1963 car now labeled the Type 34. Jim Clark and Dan Gurney would return as drivers. The Lotus Type 29, crashed in practice the year before by Gurney, had gone to Marshman and car owner Lindsey Hopkins. After more than a thousand miles of testing in the car, doing development work for Ford and tire tests for Firestone and Goodyear, Marshman was so at home in the machine that Colin Chapman dubbed him "an American version of Jimmy Clark."[8]

Another engine was promised to Rodger Ward and crew chief A.J. Watson. Both had been helpful when Ford first decided to enter the 500. Another would go to Eddie Sachs. A proven winner and fan favorite, Sachs had a new rear-engine car designed and manufactured by Ted Halibrand—who'd made his name producing lightweight magnesium wheels, drivetrains, and other race car components—and assembled with the help of Wally Meskowski. The master dirt car builder would also serve as crew chief.

There'd been discussions within Ford about supplying engines to Foyt and Parnelli Jones. At first glance it seemed like a no-brainer. A few argued, however, that if one of those drivers won, they'd get most of the credit, not Ford. Their attitude was "First let's beat them."[9]

While Ford's racing management debated how to allocate the remaining engines, the decision was made for them. Mickey Thompson was to receive engines for all three of his cars. A Southern California hot-rodder, Thompson at one time held more than 295 land speed records and liked to be known as "The Fastest Man on Wheels." The master self-promoter also was well-known for his backdoor access to Detroit's Big Three automakers. He'd simply bypassed Ford's racing department and went direct to Charles Patterson, the executive vice president who oversaw the company's North American operations and was third in line on the corporate ladder behind Henry Ford II and company president Arjay Miller. Patterson promised him the engines.

Unable to decide between Foyt or Jones, the decision was made to only support nine teams. The third Lotus—controlled by the team under the contract signed by Chapman and Ford—would go unassigned until at least Clark and Gurney were safely in the field.

SPORTS CAR WINNER

The Daytona Speedweeks kicked off in 1964 with the American Challenge Cup. The sports car race run on the oval in the rain the year before was shifted to the road course and featured an eclectic mix of sports cars and production-based racers. Gurney captured the pole in a new Lotus 30 sports car with Foyt alongside in Mecom's Scarab. Fireball Roberts was third in a prototype Ford Falcon from Holman-Moody.

Foyt and Gurney were unsure how the fragile sports cars would handle the 250-mile race moving between the high banks and demanding road course and agreed not to race each other hard at the start while trading the lead to keep the fans happy. They put on a show, officially swapping the lead sixteen times at the start/finish line during the first twenty-eight laps and multiple times at other points in the course. Gurney's Lotus was strong on the track's infield portion with Foyt's big-block Chevy roaring back on the oval. Gurney stalled during a pit stop and when it took more than thirty seconds to restart his car he fell from contention, eventually withdrawing with a broken transmission. With Gurney out, Foyt cruised home to a three-lap win over Roberts.

"It got pretty lonely out there after Gurney left," Foyt said. He also hinted at their agreement. "I intended to wait until there were only twenty laps to go, then turn it on. I think Gurney had the same idea. I wasn't afraid of him, because I knew I could make up more on the oval than he could on the road course."[10]

Foyt said the victory was sweet because of the Scarab. "It's an American car, American built and everything on it is American."[11]

He was supposed to race again the next day in the two-thousand-kilometer Daytona Continental in a decidedly un-American car, a Ferrari 250 GTO, one of ten such cars entered in the event. Foyt qualified fifth, third among the Ferraris and behind a pair of Cobras. An hour before the start, however, his car was ruled ineligible. It was the newest version of the GTO with a slightly larger engine and officials ruled it a prototype. Foyt made a fuss, trying to get the other car owners and drivers to sign off on a paper saying his car was a production model. The effort got no further than the North America Racing Team with Ferrari factory drivers Phil Hill and Pedro Rodriguez refusing to sign. Foyt started the race anyway, running ten laps before pulling into the pits and being disqualified. Afterward he blamed Hill "for doing a job on me."[12]

The antics didn't sit well with Hill, the eventual race winner, who led a Ferrari sweep of the first three positions.

"He kept striding up and down in front of the pits with about ten guys trailing after him," said Hill, the only American-born Formula One world champion. "He had a paper in his hand which stated that his car met the qualifications for the race and he was trying to get all the other owners to sign it. It was as if Foyt wanted to race a 6-liter car at Indianapolis when the limit is 4.2. I mean who's kidding whom?"

A week later at the Daytona 500, Foyt was joined by a host of other champ car drivers. Almost all were in Fords and found themselves well behind the Chrysler products powered by a new engine dubbed the Hemi. Foyt finished fourth in his qualifying race behind three Chrysler products, the highest-placed Ford. He then joined a contingent of the USAC regulars, including Parnelli Jones, Johnny Rutherford, and Marshman, who went to Memorial Stadium, a quarter-mile oval dirt track just a couple miles from the Daytona Speedway.

NASCAR was staging a series of midget races as part of its Speedweeks activities and Bruce Homeyer, the prominent car owner they'd all driven for in the past, had entered his midget. Homeyer wasn't able to attend and asked the group to check and see how his new driver was doing, the kid from Pennsylvania, Mario Andretti. Homeyer was worried Mario was on the wild side.

An immigrant from Italy, Andretti had been competing with some success in the United Racing Club (URC), which staged races primarily in the Northeast. He'd raced against several of the drivers, including Foyt, in a couple of USAC sprint car events at the end of 1963 but hadn't met them yet. Foyt didn't recall the night, but Andretti remembers it vividly.

"It was just before the feature and here comes Foyt and this gang of drivers. They were checking my car, asking about my weights, making sure my setup was right. They were really nice to me and seemed to agree with what we'd done. That really seemed to intimidate the field. Then I went out and won the feature."[13]

In the 500, Foyt was the only Ford driver to lead a lap and he ran second or third for much of the first half, which surprised winner Richard Petty. "I don't know how he got that close," Petty said. "He must have been drafting a lot to stay up there at all." Foyt lasted until the race's halfway point before dropping out with a blown engine.[14]

Back in Phoenix the next day for more testing with the Offy-powered Huffaker, Foyt upped his unofficial one-mile track record to nearly 116 mph. All was not well, however, as the signs continued to mount that Ford would be sending its engines elsewhere.

The next stop for Foyt and the Huffaker was Indianapolis, and although rain limited track time, he averaged more than 150 mph during a one-hundred-mile run. He thought the car was too fragile for the Speedway, however, and returned to Phoenix with his roadster, where he again raised the track record.

His relationship with Ford was on increasingly shaky ground. The company's hopes to counter the Hemi with a DOHC engine of its own were turned down by NASCAR, and rumors started that Foyt was looking to make a move to one of the Chrysler teams. Not long afterward Ford announced it would not provide Indianapolis engines to Foyt or Jones, saying it preferred to win the 500 "on its own." Despite the announcement, Foyt still held out hope of driving the third Lotus, for which no driver was listed on the entry form.[15]

The relationship with Ford wasn't helped when he turned up at Sebring to drive Mecom's Corvette against a fleet of Ford Cobras and Ferraris. There was confusion from the start as Foyt was listed as a driver for the Ferrari NART team, ironically the same team that blocked him from competing in the Daytona Continental. He quickly set the record straight: he was driving the Corvette.

He may have regretted the decision. After arriving Thursday and running a couple of laps, he declared the car undriveable. Ripping into Mecom's crew, he worked on the car through the night, stripping it down and starting from scratch. The car was in no shape for qualifying the next day, failing to post a time. He was given the sixty-second starting position in the sixty-seven-car field. Foyt pulled another all-nighter, rebuilding the engine and changing the jetting on the carburetors. He got a couple of hours sleep and returned to the track for the 10 a.m. start without the benefit of a warm-up lap.

"If we had about two weeks to work on this we would really have something," he said before the start. "Keep everything crossed and hope that it will last twelve hours."[16]

As usual he jumped the Le Mans start and was one of the first to his car, although it did little good as he struggled to get it started. Finally away, he put in a spectacular first lap, weaving his way through the field and into the top ten by the end of the 5.6-mile circuit.

Sharing time with road racing veteran John Cannon, they were still running in the top ten after nine hours and keeping pace with the Corvette entries, although they were fourteen laps behind the race-leading Ferrari. Shortly after a pit stop for tires, refueling, and a driver change, with dusk setting in and Foyt back in the driver's seat, the car lost a tire, spinning wildly to a stop on the far side of the circuit. At the time cars were not towed back to the pits and could only be repaired by one of the drivers. Foyt ran across the infield and back to the pits, about two miles.

With an Indy car race scheduled for the next day at Phoenix, no one would have blamed him for heading to the airport, where a Goodyear Lodestar waited for him. Instead, he "berated everyone in sight," according to a reporter who happened to be in the pit, grabbed a tire—"for a moment it looked like he intended to brain a mechanic"—and headed back to the car, where he replaced the tire in the dark. The team managed to finish the race in twenty-third, although forty-six laps behind the podium-sweeping Ferraris.[17]

Foyt grabbed a quick shower and a change of clothes and then boarded the Lodestar. Flight time for the slow plane was about thirteen hours, including two refueling stops. He dozed and munched on snacks during the flight. Lucy was meeting him in Phoenix and hoping to spend a few days relaxing at the Wigwam Hotel, one of their favorites in the area.

Fighting buffeting head winds, the flight arrived early and Foyt was able to take another shower before qualifying second to Jones. Both elected to race their roadsters, as did almost everyone else, despite expectations the race would mark the debut of new rear-engine cars.

Foyt got a good start and took the lead going into Turn One. Too good, according to Jones, who claimed later, "he jumped me!" For a moment officials considered black-flagging A.J. but decided against it. From then on there was no stopping Foyt as he led all one hundred laps and took the checkered ahead of McCluskey and Jones. Afterward he seemed refreshed, even attending a Goodyear victory celebration.

"He's a human dynamo," said Goodyear's Tony Webner, the company's general manager for racing. "I've never seen him tired. He's the greatest race driver in the world."

Hopes for a few days in Phoenix with Lucy were dashed, however, by a March weather system sweeping across the country and forecast to hit Indianapolis later in the week. The Speedway would close on April 1 in preparation for the 500 and not reopen until May 1. The Huffaker car was already at the track, and the decision was made to begin testing immediately.

Typical Indianapolis March weather—wet, with temperatures in the thirties and gusty winds—disrupted practice, but the team did manage to get in more than one hundred laps. Foyt had nothing but praise for the Goodyear tires, saying he'd run the same set more than seven hundred miles and declared them ready for the 500. Neither Bignotti nor Foyt were happy with the car, however. Both were trying to come to grips with how to adjust the liquid suspension.

"There are just too many things to correct," Bignotti complained. "We need more time."

"I'm not sure those Lotus-Ford jobs can beat the [roadsters]," Foyt added. "I just don't believe they can. It'll make things real interesting. That's the way I like it. Competition makes racing great."

Marshman, testing a pair of year-old Lotuses, thought he had the hot ticket.

"This car feels real, real good. It really gives out down the straightaways— faster than I've ever gone before. I'm convinced this is the direction to go. I'm beginning to feel part of this car . . . more secure."[18]

Before the storm front came in, Foyt also managed a few laps in the Novi being driven by Bobby Unser and was surprised by the power of the supercharged engine.

"Man, I hope they never get it running right."[19]

Staying one step ahead of the storm, Foyt was in Reading, Pennsylvania, for a sprint car race on Sunday, March 30. After setting a fast time early in qualifying, he and Rutherford were watching McCluskey on his qualifying run when the defending series champion's car began to slide, caught a rut in the dirt surface, and launched into a series of barrel rolls, turned on its nose, and flipped end over end several times before coming to a rest on its wheels.

Foyt and Rutherford ran to the car, pushing aside the safety crew. Rutherford held McCluskey's head while Foyt hoisted him from the car and carried him to the ambulance's gurney for the trip to the hospital.[20]

In the race Foyt led all thirty laps, although he was pressed hard by Jim Maguire, the twenty-two-year-old newcomer who'd captured an eastern regional sprint car championship the year before. He was attempting to make the jump to USAC and recently entered in the 500.

The word on McCluskey from the hospital was better than could be hoped: he was in serious but stable condition with a concussion, a compound arm fracture, and other injuries. He wasn't the only one to visit the hospital. Don Branson also suffered a compound arm fracture. Marshman and Bud Tingelstad each crashed heavily into the fence, escaping with minor injuries. Speculation started immediately that McCluskey and Branson would miss the 500.[21]

Foyt was grilled by reporters on why he ran sprint car races paying about five hundred dollars to win, when an injury could cost him tens of thousands of dollars. Car owners were already saying they wanted their drivers to stop driving in sprint car races, at least until after the Indianapolis 500.

Chuck Barnes, whom Foyt worked with on promotional activities, tried without success to talk Foyt out of running the sprinters. "Sprint racing is the most dangerous of all racing, with the highest proportion of accidents and fatalities," Barnes said. "Maybe he'll break down and win nothing. Maybe he'll crash. Maybe . . . who knows."[22]

Foyt wasn't hearing it.

"A good racer, a real race driver, can drive any kind of machine," he said. "I really believe this. If you're a racer, you drive anything that races. And you drive it to the hilt, as fast and hard as she'll go. That's the only way to be. There are plenty of times things get real hairy, but that's part of the game."[23]

One of Foyt's car owners, Bill Ansted, knew better than to even ask.

"How are you going to restrain a national champion from racing?"

———

Most of the top sprint and Indy car drivers showed up the following week at Eldora Speedway in Ohio, but Foyt was in Atlanta, back in Matthews's stock car. The updated Ford engines had found the speed to challenge the Chrysler Hemis. He qualified second and was chasing Paul Goldsmith in the early going when the leader blew a tire and flipped, Foyt taking evasive action and spinning down to the inside of the track. His car never ran well after that and eventually retired with a blown engine.

The next week he was back in his sprint car at Williams Grove Speedway. After qualifying sixth he fought his way to the front, passing Maguire and then pole sitter Johnny White with twelve laps remaining for the victory.

At Trenton a week later he again entered the roadster rather than the rear-engine car. It proved the right move as he qualified on the pole, with Ward in the new Watson rear-engine Ford alongside. Ward led into Turn One, but Foyt immediately passed him back and led all one hundred laps. Ward hounded Foyt for the first half of the race before being taken out by the spinning car of Andretti.

One reporter wrote Foyt was "rapidly turning into the Babe Ruth of American auto racing," and another asked, "How can you improve on perfection?" Most, however, wanted to talk about what car he was going to drive at Indianapolis.

"Right now my choice would be the one I drove today," Foyt said of the Watson roadster Rose had driven the year before. "You can't get a car that would perform better than that. It couldn't have been easier. But I'll run the rear-engine job out at Indy and make my decision after that."[24]

He skipped a sprint car race in which the promising Maguire, only a few days after receiving his USAC license in anticipation of racing at Indianapolis, lost his right arm when it was severed between the shoulder and elbow in a rollover accident. Chuck Hulse, second to Foyt in Indy car points and slated to drive Clint Brawner's new lightweight Watson roadster at Indianapolis, was involved in another accident, flipping more than ten times and ending up in the hospital with serious back and head injuries.[25]

With the opening of practice at Indianapolis approaching, Foyt didn't deny rumors he'd test a Lotus-Ford at the Speedway.

"I have talked with Ford about driving one of their Lotus-Fords, but it won't be definite until sometime this week," Foyt said. He used his stock car contract as a bargaining chip. "I also have talked with the Plymouth people concerning the stock cars. But that will have to wait for the decision on the Lotus-Ford. If I get the Lotus seat, I'll naturally drive a Ford in the stocks."[26]

Foyt also said he wasn't ready to bury his roadster just yet.

"Even though I will try the Lotus-Ford, I want to emphasize I'll only drive the fastest car for the 500—whether it's my roadster, Offy rear-engine car or the Lotus. All I want is to win."[27]

FOYT WINNER IN 500
SACHS, MACDONALD DIE
7th EXTRA

CHAPTER 15

THE MAGNIFICENT AND THE MACABRE

1964

Two weeks after A.J. Foyt said he expected to have things worked out with Ford to test a Lotus at the Indianapolis Motor Speedway, no such deal existed. Sixty-one cars were entered for the 500, twenty-three of them rear-engine machines.

Several drivers had their choice of both types of cars, including two of the sport's three biggest names, Foyt and Parnelli Jones. The third, Rodger Ward, made his decision before reaching the Speedway.

"I'm not going to switch back and forth from a roadster to a rear-engine car every day like some of these drivers," Ward said. He was also one of the lucky few with a new Ford engine. "So far as I am concerned, they can take the roadster, run it off a boat and use it as an anchor."[1]

As a result, A.J. began the month of May focused on his Watson roadster, the same car he ran the two-hundred-mile-per-hour lap with at the Goodyear proving grounds. George Bignotti had worked hard to improve and lighten the car, and some of the changes, especially a large air scoop on the nose, made it look remarkably like the car Jones drove to victory in 1963. There was also the Offy-powered rear-engine car built by Joe Huffaker at Foyt's disposal.

With all its engines assigned, Ford did reach out to Foyt regarding the third Lotus-Ford, but several problems persisted. One was money. Ford and Chapman wanted fifty thousand dollars for the car and engine support. Although that was roughly a third of its estimated value, Foyt felt the company should be paying him. In addition, Ford wanted a commitment from him to drive its stock cars and the new GT40 sports car. The company was at war with Ferrari for sports car supremacy and wanted Foyt to drive in the major events, including the 24 Hours of Le Mans.

◀ Mixed emotions in Victory Lane. *Associated Press Photo Archive*

The biggest problem was timing. Foyt wanted to take delivery immediately so he could spend the first two weeks of May getting comfortable with the car. Ford said its hands were tied; Chapman wouldn't give up the car until after his two drivers qualified. They pointed to Gurney's 1963 crash as proof of the need to retain the backup machine.

Tall and slender with a pencil-thin mustache, Chapman was a doppelganger for British actor David Niven. Publicly he was the perfect Britisher, polite and refined. Behind the doors of the Lotus garage, he could be every bit as demanding, driving, and irrational as Foyt on a bad day.

Chapman felt secure in playing hardball with Foyt. He reasoned if Ford really wanted the driver to have a car or an engine, the company could certainly get him one. There was another Type 29 like Marshman's available. And there'd been no pressure from the Blue Oval suits to meet Foyt's demands. It was as if the company wanted Chapman to play the heavy, a role he was happy to take on. He ordered the third car partially disassembled so it appeared unavailable to prying eyes.

Beginning with the first day of practice on May 1, Foyt focused on his roadster, turning the fastest lap on each of the first six days on the track, earning free dinners for two at the nearby Red Carpet Restaurant. The success was a little misleading, as Jones spent most of his time in his rear-engine car and Team Lotus was yet to arrive. When Jones finally took the roadster he called Calhoun on the track, he jumped to the top of the speed charts, setting an unofficial record in the process. Afterward, he couldn't resist tweaking Foyt, who'd been bragging about his Goodyear tires.

"I don't think you can put the reason for the big jump in speed on anything but the tires," Jones said. "We haven't been putting on soft tires like those Goodyear cars. My crew had been needling me just before I went out, claiming that Foyt drove in deeper [in the turns] than I did. That probably helped me too."[2]

"Just another record to be broken," A.J. shot back.

Unknown to Foyt, Firestone was urging Jones's team to use higher levels of nitromethane in its methanol fuel blend. Normally "nitro" was used only for qualifying. It provided a short-term power boost but could damage an engine if too much was used. Firestone promised to pay for any broken engine and offered a five thousand dollar bounty for outrunning Goodyear's lead car. The company hoped Foyt would get frustrated running second to Jones, blame the tires, and return to the Firestone fold.

Foyt was already upset with Goodyear. The tires he'd been using were different from the ones he'd spent the past year developing. A new group of engineers was now running the program and didn't believe the original tires would last for five hundred miles. Foyt argued he'd already put 1,500 miles on the tires. When Victor Holt Jr., Goodyear's president, came to visit the Speedway, Foyt complained directly to him, warning he might switch back to Firestone.

"I'll sign any kind of certificate because I know those tires will do what I want them to do," Foyt said. "If you let me run the tire I tested and did all the work with, I'll be glad to run it."[3]

Holt, six-foot-seven and a standout high-school and college basketball player, wasn't easily intimidated. He explained that it was a matter of safety, and that company policy gave the last word to the engineers when it came to safety. Foyt said he had no love for Firestone but would switch back if he necessary. "It means more to me to win the race."

He'd yet to try his rear-engine machine on the track when Huffaker's own team arrived at the Speedway, more than a week behind schedule. Just one of the cars was ready and it lasted only a day before rookie driver Pedro Rodriguez spun and hit the wall. The car was badly damaged, and Rodriguez ended up in the hospital with a chipped vertebra.

The next day Foyt took his Huffaker out for the first time. He ran only a few laps before returning to the pits. "We got some problems—handling, engine, fuel—everything," Bignotti said, sending the car back to the garage for further work. As far as Foyt was concerned, it could stay there. He drove Sachs's backup car for a few laps, an Offy-powered rear-engine Halibrand, but didn't like it either.

"Just didn't feel comfortable," he said of the rear-engine machines. "My roadster has been pretty faithful to me. I want to go with something I know."

Having even bigger problems in his rear-engine car was Jones. Saying it "felt really weird," he slowed moments before the right-front suspension collapsed. That was it for Jones, who said the rear-engine car was being shipped back to California and "It's back to Old Calhoun for me."[4]

As qualifying approached, Marshman emerged as the pole favorite, with a lap of nearly 159 mph. Clark was close behind. The success of the Lotus drivers only increased Foyt's frustrations and he stepped up his lobbying efforts, finally getting an indication from Ford he'd be able to test the Lotus the day before qualifying started. He didn't want to wait until after Clark and Gurney were qualified to make his run, but if the Lotus proved impressive, he'd have to consider it.

"I'm going to take the third team Lotus out for a test," he told reporters on Thursday, May 14, two days before pole qualifying. "That is if they can get it put back together in time."[5]

He was right to be concerned. The third Lotus was still in pieces and the door to the garage open for all to see, although it looked worse than it was. If necessary, the Lotus mechanics could quickly put it back together. But when a Ford representative came to arrange Foyt's test, Chapman simply pointed to the car and shrugged.

"Well hell," a disgusted Foyt told the Ford rep who broke the bad news. "We'll just race you."[6]

Foyt had one more decision to make: which tires to use. Rules required a car race on the same tires used in qualifying. He'd practiced on the Firestones and felt they were better than the Goodyears he'd been using, but not as good as the ones he'd developed. He called Holt, who'd given Foyt his home phone number.

"Vic, you gotta tell those guys to let me use that tire," he said. "It's the only chance we've got, and we've all worked too damn hard to blow it now."

Holt reiterated that company policy wouldn't let him override the engineers.

"Well, they may be experts about building tires, but they're sure as hell no experts about driving them, that's my job," Foyt countered. He offered again to sign a release form and take full responsibility for the decision. "It's my judgement and my ass."

Holt said he was sorry, it was out of his hands.

"Okay," A.J. said, "I'm running Firestones."

Having struck out with Ford and Goodyear, some said A.J. was getting his due.

"Foyt has a habit of badmouthing people," Hopkins said. He still felt burned by Foyt in 1962, when the driver had jumped to his team then back to Bignotti after a few winless races. "He badmouthed Firestone and then wanted to come back. He badmouthed Ford and now he wants back. He changes his mind constantly. He's a magnificent driver, the best of our time, but he's an impossible man to deal with."[7]

There was one last meeting of Ford racing and corporate executives and Lotus management the morning of qualifying. Lee Iacocca, Ford Division president, and Benson Ford, Henry's brother, who'd be driving the Mustang pace car, were in attendance, having flown in the night before on the company plane. They gathered on the bottom floor of the Speedway's scoring tower, Ford having rented it for office space and media hospitality.

Chapman said the team wanted to qualify on Dunlop tires, as they were faster. Someone asked about durability, and he said he was confident they'd go the distance. Just in case, they'd be ready to change tires. Thanks to the fuel economy of the Ford engine running on gasoline, the team planned on making only one pit stop while the roadsters would be making at least two.

"What about Foyt?" somebody asked. "What *about* him?" was the general response. The Speedway was buzzing with word of Marshman's 160 mph lap in morning practice. He and Clark had everyone covered. Although Sachs had crashed in the practice and the Thompsons were struggling, the cars driven by Ward and Gurney were also considered better than the Foyt or Jones roadsters.[8]

A huge crowd of about 250,000 turned out for qualifying, forcing the Speedway to close infield parking for the first time. Foyt was first on the track but quickly pulled into the pits, complaining there was too much wind. Most thought it was too much nitro. Jones was next and it was more of the same, the nitro-heavy fuel blend burning a piston before he could get started.

After that it was all Ford, Clark taking the pole with four laps at nearly 159 mph, seven mph better than Jones's record. Marshman was second, having pushed too hard on his opening lap. Ward in third completed an all-Ford front row. Jones came back to qualify fourth and Foyt fifth with Gurney in sixth. Dave MacDonald managed to qualify a Thompson in fourteenth. Sachs, his car repaired overnight, topped the second-day qualifiers and would start seventeenth. Safely in the field, Foyt sold his rear-engine car back to the Huffaker team.

A week later A.J. was startled along with the rest of the racing community by the news of Fireball Roberts being badly burned and near death following a gruesome stock car crash at Charlotte.

"The one thing that runs through my mind all the time I am in a race car is being trapped in it and burning to death," Foyt said. "Physical discomfort and even broken bones don't bother me. But damn fire scares me. It would be an awful way to go."[9]

Despite the seemingly long odds against him, *Sports Illustrated* featured Foyt on its cover the week before the race, under the headline "Champion of the Old

Guard." Calling him "the hottest property in all of racing" and "the best all-around American driver in history," the article said, "Against the opposition's superior speed, Foyt must draw deeply upon his incandescent will to win to repel the invaders."[10]

Foyt eventually reached a familiar conclusion. Ward and Jones were the drivers to beat. The Team Lotus cars were too fragile and were experiencing chunking problems with their Dunlop tires in practice. He dismissed the Hopkins team and Marshman. "That operation never had a good record of finishing races," he said. "I went over there and sat on the pole, but I never could win a race. Something always happened."[11]

The pace would be fast, and he'd have to run hard in the early going, but he had a chance of winning and that's all he ever asked.

"Maybe I'll get beat," he said, "but they're going to have to do it over 500 miles—not 100."[12]

Fuel was a major topic of discussion the week before the race. Ford was committed to using gasoline, which provided less horsepower but better fuel economy, and planned only one pit stop. The Offys needed to use a methanol blend for the added horsepower. To counter the fuel economy advantage, several of the roadster teams indicated they'd install larger fuel tanks in their cars capable of holding up to one hundred gallons, which would allow them to make only one stop. Jones and Jim Hurtubise installed massive fuel tanks in their cars. Bignotti hinted there'd be a big tank in Foyt's car, too, although he didn't follow through on it. There was a price to pay for added fuel—a heavier and slower car—and most everyone decided to go with a traditional fuel load of forty-five to fifty gallons.

While the cars were set for race day, Foyt almost didn't make it. He'd bought Lucy a Welsh pony to use on her daily ride with Mari George, but the horse showed a tendency to rear up. With no activity at the track, he decided to break the horse of the habit.

"A guy told me to take a whisky bottle filled with water and when it rears up, break it between its ears. He'll think its blood and will stop rearing up. I hit that son of bitch hard, but it still reared up and I went over backwards. I hurt my back so bad I could hardly walk."[13]

"I was in the men's restroom laying on a bench and George [Bignotti] came in and said, 'Aren't you a big cowboy. You know we got a race in two days.'"

He seemed to be his old self by race morning, walking up and down the grid, waving, and playing to the crowd, stopping to pose for photos and to sign autographs. He participated in a pit-stop drill, teasing the crew member who had trouble adding fuel during the 1961 win. He hammered away to tighten the knock-off hubs on each wheel, a not-too-subtle reminder of the problem from 1962.

He bounced from car to car and driver to driver, trading barbs with some, needling others, the mental race already underway. He reminded Sachs of a newspaper article in which MacDonald said he was concerned about the track's walls and still "learning to walk" at the Speedway. "That's the guy you're followin' out there today, Eddie boy," Foyt said, patting Sachs on the chest. Then he was gone, looking for his next target.

He was especially hard on a young Firestone representative, H.A. "Humpy" Wheeler. It was Wheeler's job to get each driver to sign a release form so their photo could be used in the company's "win" advertisement the next day. He offered each driver a buck for luck and most signed mindlessly. Not Foyt. He was wearing the same Goodyear uniform he'd been wearing all month, despite having switched to Firestone.

"He was giving me hell, but that's just Foyt," Wheeler said. "He said he needed more than a buck. I told him he'd better take the money; he might need it. He laughed, signed the form, and took the dollar."[14]

Foyt even admitted to having "little bitty butterflies" to the track announcer but said they would disappear when "the green flag falls."[15]

It was a good start, Clark jumping ahead with Jones right behind him. Foyt tried to follow Jones, but Marshman moved between the roadsters with Ward and Gurney just to the outside. Coming down to the start of the second lap, Marshman was in second and Ward and Gurney passed Jones and Foyt. The Fords were in the first four positions and already pulling away.

Coming out of Turn Two and running right behind Jones, Foyt saw Clark's arm shoot up and initially thought something must have broken on the Lotus. Then the yellow light flashed on, and he saw a huge black cloud growing in Turn Four.

"It looked like an atomic bomb had been dropped," he'd say.[16]

Along with the other leaders, Foyt slowed to a crawl by the end of the back-straight. Several cars were parked on the track between Turn Three and Turn Four. He started to pick his way through the maze before being waved to a stop by other drivers. The main straight before the pits was completely blocked by a black wall of smoke, orange flames breaking through.

MacDonald had been moving up fast and was trying to pass several cars when the Thompson suddenly veered left and out of control, turning 180 degrees as it slid backward and broadside toward the inside wall. At impact it burst into flames and ricocheted back across the track, drawing a curtain of black smoke and fire behind him.

Exiting Turn Four and closing fast was a four-car freight train led by Sachs, followed by Johnny Rutherford and Ronnie Duman running nose to tail, with Bobby Unser a car back.

"The whole track was blocked," Unser would say. "I didn't know if it was one burning car or ten. It looked like ten."

Unable to stop, Sachs tried to beat the sliding MacDonald to the rapidly narrowing gap between the Thompson and the outside wall. He didn't make it, hitting MacDonald broadside, causing a second, even bigger explosion. The cars driven by Rutherford, Duman, and Unser plowed into the inferno and all three emerged on fire.

For the first time, the Indianapolis 500 was stopped by an accident. Drivers gathered in twos and threes in Turn Four, wondering who'd been involved. Many feared there were injuries and deaths in the grandstands, a possible devastating blow to the future of the race.

For the most part Foyt kept to himself. He knew it was bad, and he knew people were probably dead. He didn't want to know anything else.

He did talk to Donald Davidson, an eighteen-year-old British lad making his first trip to the 500. He'd amazed Foyt and the rest of the Indy car community with his knowledge of the race and his ability to answer seemingly any question about the event. He'd received full credentials for the race, and Foyt spotted him milling around the drivers, coming up behind him and spinning him around.

"Look, even the tree's on fire," Davidson remembered Foyt saying, as he pointed to the smoldering sycamore tree that stood as a distinctive landmark near where MacDonald first hit the inside wall. Davidson recalls thinking Foyt was in denial. Then the driver was gone.[17]

It wasn't long before track announcer Tom Carnegie told a hushed Speedway, "It is with deep regret that we make this announcement. Driver Eddie Sachs was fatally injured in the accident on the main straightaway." All around the track the crowd rose in silence in tribute to Sachs, who'd always been a fan favorite. Foyt would say he didn't hear the announcement, didn't see the crowd, that he blocked it out. MacDonald died a short time later at Methodist Hospital.

"There would be a time to know, but right at that moment, I didn't really want anybody to confirm what I already knew," he'd say.

It took workers an hour and forty-two minutes to clear the track of wreckage and firefighting chemicals the best they could. There'd been no discussion of cancelling or postponing the race. When drivers were told to return to their cars, everyone responded.

"It became, grimly and awesomely, a 500-mile race of men brave enough to stay in it and see it through," wrote *Sports Illustrated's* Bob Ottum, who spotted A.J. standing alone.[18]

"Foyt pulled on red golfing gloves, banging his fists together like a boxer to tighten them across his knuckles." He was one of the first to climb back in his car, waiting patiently while others did the same. Among the last was the leader, Clark, followed by Eddie Johnson, who was driving a Thompson-Ford that was a twin to MacDonald's car.

Clark led a single-file line of cars at the restart. Each time the cars passed by the accident site they kicked up large dust clouds of the powder put down to absorb the spilled fuel, oil, and firefighting chemicals.

"Of course I thought of the crash at first, going by where it happened," Foyt said. "Each time we would go through there, the dust would go up. So I found myself thinking about the crash those first couple of laps because of the dust. But you can't think of too many things out there, you can't let things bother you. After a while I forgot about it."[19]

Marshman soon passed Clark and, turning incredibly fast laps, pulled away from the field. At the end of thirty laps he was averaging 155 mph, shattering the previous record by more than ten mph. He repeatedly ignored pit signs pleading with him to "Cool It," and seeing Foyt and Jones ahead, he picked up his pace.

Glancing in his mirror on the front straight, Foyt was surprised to see Marshman closing fast. He'd been running hard while having a good battle with

Parnelli, and although the race wasn't even a hundred miles old, he was about to be lapped. Even more surprising was the speed at which he was closing on the car in front of him, the roadster driven by Johnny White. Unknown to Foyt and the rest of the field, White was driving the one car starting the race with one hundred gallons of fuel. As a result, he was heavy and slow, and already one lap down to Marshman.

Jones went high and Foyt barely missed White, diving to the inside going into Turn One. Now it was Marshman who was surprised. He was forced even lower on the track and felt the car bottom out as it hit the apron. Although Marshman retained control, the car was soon smoking badly. Both the oil plug and water flange had been knocked off when the car bottomed out. Marshman's race was over.

"It was my fault," Marshman told his father, George. "I just wanted to pass Foyt and see the look on his face."[20]

With Marshman out, Clark moved back in front, but only temporarily. He was already slowing, feeling a vibration in the rear of the car as the Dunlop tires started to come apart. The vibration soon caused the left-rear suspension to collapse, and Clark did a masterful job of guiding the crippled machine to a stop in Turn One. Gurney, who'd been experiencing his own challenges, was eventually called in and parked over concerns about the same problem.

Ward also was having trouble. The team had ignored Ford's directive to use only straight gasoline in the race, feeling it needed a fuel blend to keep up with the Lotuses. Instead, it was using a fuel mixture concocted by Watson.

The problem arose when Ward tried to adjust the blend. After changing the adjustment valve the morning of the race at Ward's request, Watson failed to communicate the change clearly to the driver. As Ward tried to lean out the mixture, he was actually making it richer, hurting both the performance and fuel economy. He'd already made two pit stops and would make three more before the end of the race.

That left Jones in the lead. He and Foyt had been thrilling the crowd with their own private race, passing and repassing each other on every lap. Jones, however, was beginning to experience his own difficulties. The team had left the larger fuel tank in his car, filling it only about halfway for the start. But the fuel sloshing around loosened the tank from its mounts, and it was shifting in the car. As the level dropped, fuel wasn't reaching the pickup points, and the engine was cutting out. Foyt would move temporarily ahead in the turns, with Jones repassing on the straights and leading at the start/finish line.

Thinking he was running out of fuel, Jones came in early for his first pit stop and as he pulled away, an explosion ripped off the top of the tank. Jones later theorized the buildup of fumes in the half-full tank caused the blast. Realizing he and the car were on fire, he aimed his roadster toward the pit wall, bailing out the right side of the car just before impact. The safety teams, still on edge from the second-lap crash, responded immediately and put out the fire before it could spread. But Calhoun was out of the race and Jones was headed for the hospital.

From there it was all Foyt as he led the final 146 laps. He was so far ahead he even maintained the lead during pit stops. Toward the end of the race he came up to lap second-place Ward. He waited until he was on the front straight, in front of tens of thousands of fans and, more importantly, the Ford executives who'd been unable to arrange the deal for him to drive the third Lotus. As he pulled alongside Ward, Foyt flipped him the finger, although it was really aimed at the Ford execs.

"I wanted to make sure they knew who was number one," Foyt quipped later. Coming down to the checkered flag his pit crew held out a simple sign board: "$$$."

Watching from the tower with Mari Hulman George, Lucy had turned away, unable to watch the final laps. She'd been good friends with Nance Sachs, better friends than A.J. and Eddie. When the cheers of the crowd indicated the checkered flag, she let out a sign of relief.

"Thank God it's over," she said. Later she'd tell a reporter she hoped it was A.J.'s last 500.[21]

The celebration in Victory Lane started as if there'd been no crash, nobody killed. Foyt's face was covered with grime, the outline of his goggles clearly visible. The right elbow of his Goodyear uniform was ripped open, frayed by the buffeting winds. His lips, hidden behind his red bandanna, were nonetheless cracked and raw and he pushed away the bottle of milk, saying he needed ChapStick and water first. His request fulfilled, there were kisses for both the race queen and Lucy and the bottle of milk to drink, all captured by a scrum of photographers.

"I feel great," Foyt said. "I really enjoyed this race. My crew did a terrific job. We planned the race just like it went. I'd say they got fooled. I think we're here to stay. I like Old Betsy."[22]

Next came the traditional newspaper proclaiming Foyt's victory. The *Indianapolis Star* printed a front page each year proclaiming the race winner and helicoptered it into the track for photos with the winner.

Foyt held it up, smiling and posing for more photos with Lucy. Then he caught a glimpse of the headline, and the grin froze.

FOYT WINNER IN 500
SACHS, MACDONALD DIE

From that moment on the celebration changed. A.J. glanced at Lucy for confirmation and saw the slightest nod of her head. He struggled with his emotions, trying to balance the crush of congratulations and well-wishers with thoughts of the dead drivers. He admitted the crash "shook him up."

"I hated to see it. Before every race I ask the Good Lord to take care of all the drivers. I regret the accident. Both were real fine people."

Firestone's Wheeler worked his way through the crowd and thrust a hat in Foyt's direction.

"A.J. you've got to put this on for me," Wheeler pleaded. He'd just become the first race winner to complete the five hundred miles without a tire change. At first Foyt balked. Then he spotted Ray Firestone, the company's soon-to-retire chief executive, standing on the edge of crowd. He put the hat on and thanked "Mr. Firestone" over the radio broadcast for everything he'd done for racing. Then just as quickly he flicked the hat away.

Foyt would say later he didn't cash Firestone's award check, "but Bignotti probably did." He would accept the Mustang pace car but eventually turn it over to his housekeeper.[23]

Returning to Gasoline Alley, Foyt and car owners Shirley Murphy and Bill Ansted stopped at Sachs's garage, the red-carpet welcome mat still in place. They offered their condolences to his car owners, who were also Indianapolis businessmen. Inside the garage the destroyed race car was covered by a tarp, and the only comforting words were that Sachs must have died instantly.

A subdued celebration was underway in Foyt's garage when he arrived. Ward came by to congratulate him. A lawn chair was opened in the middle of the small room, and he held court from his new throne, clutching an empty champagne bottle as his scepter and harping at reporters with what became a familiar theme.

"Some of the writers sort of implied Parnelli Jones and I were idiots for sticking with the old-style machinery in this race, but them antiques has made me an awful lot of money the last few years."[24]

"You guys didn't come right out and say it—but you sort of hinted I would lose. You thought this so-called antique front-engine roadster couldn't hack it against the high-powered Ford, against the rear-engine cars. We just didn't think the Fords would make it. We were right."

Foyt was still in his driving uniform when his entourage prepared to leave Gasoline Alley late that afternoon. He'd been fond of the fun-loving Sachs and impressed with the young MacDonald. The *Sports Illustrated* reporter asked him how he was able to keep going.

"Looky here," he said. "You can't let this get you down, about those guys getting killed. You got to carry on in racing. You can't let anyone get too close to you in this game; if they get killed, it breaks your heart. Maybe you haven't noticed it about me, but I haven't got any close friends in racing. If you are going to race, you've got to race alone."[25]

That evening the group visited several victory parties, but at each stop they'd been too late for food. Near midnight they headed to White Castle for fifteen-cent hamburgers. It suited A.J. fine, but Lucy was more self-conscious in a mink stole he'd bought her.

Up early the next morning for a prearranged breakfast with reporters, Foyt admitted, "I didn't sleep too well last night. I tossed and tumbled all night and was up by six o'clock. I couldn't get the wreck off my mind.

"I am real sorry those guys died. That's racing. Eddie was there way before me, but he was always nice to me. Eddie Sachs was good for racing. We all got mad at him at times, but he had more guts than any of us. He probably was one of the hardest race drivers there ever was. When he buckled himself in his seat you had to beat him. He was a helluva race driver."[26]

He talked about roadsters versus rear-engine cars and the use of gasoline, which was being blamed for the intensity of the fire.

"You have more room in a front-engine car and you can get out quicker," Foyt said. "That fuel is not all around you like it is in the rear-engine cars. I just feel safe in this type of car.

"I think the rear-engine cars have a future in the 500, but I'm not sure. If I drive one, it won't be on gasoline, you can be sure of that. I am scared of having all that gasoline around me in that type of chassis. I can carry just as much fuel in my front-engine car—my so-called antique car—with a much greater safety margin. Maybe it would be wise to ban gasoline and also limit the amount of fuel in a car and make it mandatory to make either two or three pit stops. This would make the race safer and more interesting. What would a race be without pit stops?"[27]

After breakfast A.J. and Lucy went across the street to the Conkle Funeral Home to pay their respects. A crowd was already gathered. Nance Sachs hadn't arrived yet, and the couple couldn't wait. A.J. was entered in a thirty-lap sprint car race later in the day at New Bremen Speedway in Ohio. Although he'd decided against driving in the race, he agreed to drive the pace car rather than completely disappoint the fans. Jud Larson would drive his car.[28]

Soon after arriving at New Bremen, and wearing a white dress shirt and red cardigan, Foyt was up to his elbows working on the engine. With the race attracting many of the top drivers from Indianapolis, he was having second thoughts about not competing.

"I wanted to drive it," he'd say, "but Jud kept begging me to let him drive. I had promised him, and well, finally I let him drive it in the race. It hurt me more than anything, but I let him drive it."[29]

Larson held off a hard-charging Mario Andretti to win the feature event, earning $850. Back in Indianapolis that evening, Foyt picked up a check for more than $150,000 at the Victory Banquet, which went on as scheduled. Having escaped the hospital, Jones presented the winner's ring.

"It's a great pleasure to present this ring to you, because you're the greatest race driver that ever lived," Jones said. He'd later expanded on his comments. "A.J. Foyt is the greatest of the many drivers I've raced against. All the good ones I've faced had their own styles. Some of them have been chargers, some waiters. Some were at their best qualifying, some in traffic. But they've all got the basic tools.

"In the end, I think you come down to desire. You take ol' A.J. Foyt. I don't think he's as talented as Don Branson. He's not as smooth as Jim Clark. Or as patient as Rodger Ward. And no one could be braver than Jim Hurtubise. But A.J. will do anything to learn, to get ahead, to succeed. He has such great desire; it hasn't left him even now when he's won so much. He maybe has more determination than anyone that ever went into racing. More than me, even."[30]

Foyt said it was his decision to choose the roadster. "I felt there had not been enough time to test and prepare the rear-engine cars. I was confident they would not finish the race and they didn't."

Gurney, for one, took exception with the comments. He'd started calling Foyt "Cassius" after Cassius Clay, the boxer who'd won the world boxing heavyweight title three months earlier with a surprising knockout of Sonny Liston. Clay (who was in the process of changing his name to Muhammad Ali) called himself "The Greatest of All Time."[31]

"That's Foyt with his hindsight 20/20 vision," Gurney said. "The crystal ball expert. That's why the crowd loves Foyt. He's never wrong. Well, let me tell you, he was the most worried guy in the world before the race. He knew he had chosen the wrong car. He was crying the blues. 'My car's too slow,' he said. 'I don't have any chance at all. I don't know what I'm going to do.'"[32]

Sports Illustrated had the final word, noting it was Foyt's "iron nerve and matchless skill . . . that brought him out of it a winner. Of all the drivers, [he was] the man most unshakably immune to the clash of cars and the smoke of death. He drove calmly, icily . . . through an atmosphere of high tension that made this year's race—more than any other 500 in history—a spectacle of the magnificent and the macabre."[33]

CHAPTER 16

EUROPEAN VACATION

1964

A.J. Foyt's name was everywhere in the days following his Indianapolis 500 victory, from being hailed as America's greatest race car driver to his comment comparing driving a rear-engine car to "lying in a bathtub of gasoline."[1]

Ferrari entered a car for him in the 24 Hours of Le Mans, although he had no intention of racing there. BRM offered him a ride in the United States Grand Prix at Watkins Glen in October, which he said he'd consider. He told John Mecom Jr. he'd race the Scarab in England in August. More immediate, Holman-Moody wanted him to replace Fireball Roberts in the team's Ford for the Atlanta 500 and the July Fourth Firecracker 400 at Daytona.

His name also came up Monday morning at Ford's "Glass House" world head-quarters in Dearborn, Michigan, as Lee Iacocca convened a meeting of Ford's racing executives. Iacocca had already faced members of the company's executive committee, some looking to take the high-flying executive and architect of the Total Performance program down a notch. He finally walked out on the meeting, yelling, "If you can't stomach it, pull out!"[2]

Iacocca, who was from the same hometown as Eddie Sachs—Allentown, Pennsylvania—and sat with the driver at dinner the night before the race, was still on edge. He told his managers to get control of Colin Chapman and to find out what happened with the tires. He asked how Rodger Ward found a way around Ford's gasoline directive. And he ordered the group to disassociate itself from Mickey Thompson.

He also was furious over Foyt's antics, demanding the company terminate its relationship with him. Someone started to explain that the driver was under

◄ Guards Trophy sports car race, Brands Hatch, England, August 3, 1964.
Revs Institute, The George Phillips Photograph Collection

contract to drive Ford stock cars, but Iacocca cut him short. He didn't care; he wanted Foyt out, no matter what it took.

Foyt had already turned down Holman-Moody regarding Atlanta; there was an Indy car race at Milwaukee that day, June 7. He decided to make a quick detour to Canada's Mosport Park for a sports car race the day before. Driving the Mecom Scarab, he challenged eventual winner Bruce McLaren before being forced to the pits with tire troubles. He arrived in Wisconsin too late for a practice session, in which Marshman crashed and his Lotus caught fire. Although Marshman was uninjured, his car couldn't be repaired in time for the race. Parnelli Jones, still recovering from the burns at Indianapolis, wasn't entered.

That left Ward with the lone rear-engine Ford, and he qualified on the pole, with Foyt second and Jim Hurtubise third. Ward and Foyt swapped the lead from the start with Hurtubise never more than a car length away in third, the three cars snaking nose-to-tail through traffic.

With Ward leading at the halfway point of the one-hundred-mile event, he suddenly slowed when something in the rear of the car broke. Foyt braked and darted to the right to avoid Ward, but when Hurtubise tried the same maneuver, it was too late. His left-front tire climbed over the right rear of Foyt's, catapulting Herk's car into the outside wall, where it exploded on impact. On fire, the car spun wildly down the straight, coming to a stop in front of the pits.

Knocked out in the initial impact, Hurtubise slumped in his seat, his arms and bare hands hanging over the side of the flaming cockpit. His brother and chief mechanic, Pete, was the first to reach the car. Spotting the motionless Herk, he dropped the two fire extinguishers he was carrying and waded into the flames to unbuckle the safety belts and pull his brother from the car.[3]

Hurtubise had been one of those putting an extra fuel tank in his car for the Indianapolis 500. Although it wasn't needed for the short Milwaukee race, the team discovered during practice that the car handled better when the auxiliary tank was full. Hurtubise later said the car carried more than eighty gallons of methanol, and although the auxiliary tank remained intact in the crash, the nozzle broke free, spewing the fuel that caught fire. In addition to not wearing driving gloves, Hurtubise didn't treat his uniform with fire-retardant chemicals as was recommended—but not required—by the rules. Like many drivers, he thought the chemicals smelled and made the uniform uncomfortable.[4]

Foyt was never challenged after his two main competitors were eliminated. Climbing from his car in Victory Lane he saw the damage and black tire marks left by Hurtubise's car. He was told Herk was at a local hospital in critical condition, with second- and third-degree burns over 40 percent of his body, although the hospital report also said he was "doing fine."[5]

"The wreck wasn't anyone's fault, it just happened," Foyt said. He called the racing "hairy," then made a surprising confession. "I don't mind racin', but what Rodger, Jim, and I were doing really was too dangerous. I know the people liked it, but we could have all three been killed very easily riding on each other's tailpipes like that. Herk was the innocent bystander. If he hadn't hit me, I might have really gone out of the park as he knocked me away from Ward. I only thank God that Herk isn't hurt any worse than he is; he's a close friend of mine, probably the closest among the drivers. Something like this happens and it scares you and even makes me think of retiring."

Then Foyt headed to the hospital. Marshman and Jones were already there. Hurtubise was in surgery to reinflate a collapsed lung and for doctors to clean the burn wounds the best they could. Foyt offered the use of his plane but was told plans were already underway to move Hurtubise, a Coast Guard veteran, to the US Army Burn Center at Fort Sam Houston in San Antonio, Texas. A US Air Force evacuation team and C-131 medical transport plane were already on the way to Milwaukee to handle the transfer.

The Milwaukee crashes and alcohol-fed fires involving Marshman and Hurtubise further complicated the next day's meeting of the USAC rules committee that met to investigate the deaths of Sachs and Dave MacDonald.

In open forum at the Speedway Motel's restaurant, the committee heard testimony from oil company representatives that gasoline and alcohol-based fuels were equally dangerous. Foyt wasn't in attendance, having returned to Houston for his first trip home in six weeks. Ward served as the drivers' spokesperson.

"It's getting pretty hairy around here," Ward said, mimicking Foyt's Milwaukee comments. "There is no way to build an absolutely safe race car. If we are to improve the breed, we will have to gamble once in a while. There is no way to build fuel tanks to protect drivers under all circumstances. Almost everybody is going to build rear-engine cars and they are going to be light. Roadsters are pretty much on the way out."

"Except A.J. Foyt's," he cracked leaving the podium, bringing a needed laugh to the group.[6]

In the end, no decisions were made, and a subcommittee was formed to look at various issues, including the size and structure of fuel tanks, refueling hoses and techniques, and mandatory pit stops. There was no need to make an immediate decision on gasoline versus alcohol, as the remaining races were shorter events, making the use of gasoline for its fuel economy benefits moot.

In Houston, Foyt visited his daddy's garage, saw friends, and met with local reporters. His views on rear-engine cars were already softening.

"If we can work out the fuel problems, I'm all for it," he said. The fuel choice should be left up to the teams and drivers, although he called for a maximum onboard limit of forty-five gallons. He said a minimum car weight was a good idea and hinted he was looking at an enclosed cockpit design, something Holman-Moody considered prior to the 1964 race.

"We'll be trying out something different next year because we're always checking out different cars and approaches in racing."[7]

He came to the defense of the 500, under attack on several fronts by the news media. Shirley Povich, influential sports editor of the *Washington Post*, wrote: "There is a new revulsion toward the speed carnival. The deaths and injuries will be listed as accidental, but the trappings for accidents are built into the whole senseless spectacle." The *Chicago Tribune* called for an end to the 500, and the *Detroit Free Press* ran a column headlined "500 Suicide: Has it gone too far?" An editorial on the local CBS-TV affiliate in Detroit, WJBK, said: "We say the

Indianapolis Memorial Day race should be discontinued. It has killed fifty-six people. This is enough. Memorial Day is a time to pay our respects to those who have defended our country and right to freedom. It is not a day to kill people."

Foyt countered by saying auto racing was no more dangerous than boxing, football, and boating—or the local freeway.

"At least on the track we don't have a bunch of drunks to contend with," he said, pointing out that a record 405 people were killed in traffic accidents over the three-day Memorial Day weekend. "We got people behind the wheel that know what they're doing."

The stay at home was short-lived and any talk of retirement long forgotten as Foyt headed to Terre Haute for the June 14 sprint car race, which was notable for three reasons.

After setting a record in qualifying, Foyt led all thirty laps, his eleventh consecutive open-cockpit victory dating back to the second race of the year in January. Second in qualifying and continuing to make a name for himself was Mario Andretti, a "rising eastern driver on the USAC trail," although his car failed to finish the race.[8]

Then there was Johnny White, the driver Foyt tangled with (on the same track) the year before. Voted Rookie of the Year in the Indy 500 just two weeks earlier, White lost control of his car during time trials, sliding into the guardrail and launching into a series of barrel rolls along the top of the railing, before tumbling outside the track. White survived the crash but was paralyzed from the neck down and would never race again.

Foyt donated half his winnings to a fundraiser for Ronnie Duman, recovering from his Indianapolis burns and destined for a lengthy hospital stay. He encouraged others to give and convinced Goodyear officials to match his contribution.

Bob Renner of the *Indianapolis News* used the occasion to contrast the two Foyts.

"One, a man who pushes to the extreme as he duels his opponents down every straight away, through every turn, in all races, with but one thought in mind: victory. The other, a man of rare gentleness and tenderness, in a violent business whose true feelings toward friends and fellow members of his exclusive fraternity may shine through only during a time of misfortune."[9]

HERK

Another week brought another victory, this time in a June 21 champ car race at Langhorne. He didn't qualify on the pole this time, Johnny Rutherford taking that honor, but Foyt grabbed the lead in the first corner and never looked back, leading all one hundred laps. It was his fifth consecutive Indy car win, virtually wrapping up the national championship halfway through the season. The only challenge on the hot day came when his car's power steering went out just thirty-five miles into the race. Afterward, a reporter asked why he hadn't accepted Ferrari's offer to race in the 24 Hours of Le Mans that was being run in France.

"Heck, over there you drive twenty-four hours for half of three, four thousand dollars. Here I drove fifty-eight minutes for $7,000. You don't have to be smart to see where the percentage is."[10]

From Langhorne he flew to San Antonio and the Brooke Army Burn Center. After being moved from intensive care, Hurtubise was able to have visitors for short periods of time. The first round of skin grafts on his badly burned hands was done and Hurtubise was upbeat, happy to see A.J., and promising to race again. At times he was also in a great deal of pain, singing "You Are My Sunshine" as loudly as he could while the dead skin was scrubbed from his body.[11]

Foyt wasn't prepared for what he saw at the hospital. Hurtubise was in a ward with sixty other patients. With the Vietnam War ramping up, he was surrounded by badly burned and dismembered pilots and soldiers.[12]

"I went there to see Hurtubise and the people I seen there that were in the army that had no arms and no legs and had been burnt in helicopters back then— I was sick to my stomach. I said, 'Man, I gotta get outta here.' It was terrible. I said, 'Man, why would you even wanna attempt to live?' I know they probably didn't want to live. Why would they let something like that just go on?"[13]

He told reporters Herk was "improving and in good spirits. He feels really lucky, although he got burned very badly."[14]

When doctors told Hurtubise his hands would never be fully functional, he famously told them, "Just shape them so I can grab a steering wheel and hold a bottle of beer." It would be nine months before Hurtubise would be released from the hospital and, incredibly, return to racing shortly thereafter.

Everyone, except perhaps Foyt, knew Foyt's streak couldn't last forever, and it ended the following week in a sprint car race at Indianapolis Raceway Park. He lost nine laps in the pits while a suspension joint dripping hot grease on his foot was repaired. He returned to make up two laps, finishing eleventh.

FIRECRACKER FIRSTS

Iacocca's edict to terminate Ford's relationship with Foyt must not have worked its way down to the Holman-Moody stock car team, as A.J. was initially named to replace Roberts for Daytona's Firecracker 400. Foyt was out of the ride almost as soon as it was announced, however, although it didn't take him long to line up another car. It came from an unlikely source, Ray Nichels, his old car owner he'd upset the year before when he jumped to Smokey Yunick's car.

Nichels, having switched from Pontiac to Dodge at the start of the year, was still looking to field the brand's first NASCAR winner. He finished a new car for Foyt in three days, to go with entries for regular team drivers Paul Goldsmith and Bobby Isaac. Foyt and Nichels decided to forgo a traditional contract, agreeing with a handshake to split any winnings fifty-fifty.

Holman-Moody also moved quickly, replacing Foyt with Rutherford. After tangling with Foyt early in his career, Rutherford had earned A.J.'s respect by not backing down. Rather than being upset after hearing Rutherford was taking his seat at Ford, he offered the driver a ride to Daytona on the private plane of one of his sponsors.

"I learned early on you never go talk to A.J. when he's got some of the press surrounding him, because he will cut you to ribbons," Rutherford said with a laugh when asked about his initial interactions with Foyt. "If A.J. has a crowd around him, don't try to talk to him. He'd let them know what your faults were. That was just A.J. It's just something he would do."[15]

Away from the crowd of reporters, Foyt treated him with respect, and the trip gave Rutherford a glimpse of what life was like on top of the racing world.

"In those days we raced three or four times a week," Rutherford said. "Young drivers today ask how we stayed in shape back then and I tell them we didn't have to work out, we were always racing. We had three races over the Fourth of July. A.J. arranged for the Purolator corporate jet to take us down there after a race at Raceway Park. We get there and Bill France Sr. is waiting for us at the airport, and he takes us to his house for dinner."

It was a somber evening, word coming earlier in the day that Roberts had succumbed to complications from the burns suffered in the Charlotte 600 back in May. It was a stark reminder of what might have been for Rutherford, whose neck was still covered by scabs from his Indianapolis burns.

On the track, Foyt, Goldsmith, and Rutherford were involved in a multi-car accident in a Firecracker qualifying race. Goldsmith's car was destroyed, knocking him out of the main event, while Nichels's crew worked through the night to repair Foyt's Dodge.

Forced to start deep in the field, Foyt, followed closely by Rutherford, somehow avoided a first-lap crash and he was up to sixth by lap fifty. Richard Petty was out front and making a mockery of the event, lapping the field and dominating the first 250 miles before being sidelined by a blown engine.

"It looked like Petty was long gone," Foyt said. "The way he was traveling, I didn't think I had much of a chance. But anything can happen in a race. Of course luck has something to do with it. You make a lot of your own, but ol' Lady Luck was sitting there too. Bad for Petty, good for me."[16]

With Petty out, Foyt and Isaac battled in their identical Dodges, swapping the lead nine times during the final fifty laps. With two laps remaining Isaac pulled alongside his regular teammate, Goldsmith, who'd moved into another car as a relief driver, although two laps down. Going into the last lap it appeared the two had the track blocked but somehow Foyt went low enough coming out of Turn Two to pass both cars, holding on for the victory. He was the first non-NASCAR winner in the series and it was the first victory for Dodge.

"Give A.J. a couple more years and he'll be a pretty good racer," said a tearful Isaac, who was still looking for his first major NASCAR victory. "I had hoped to be in second place on the white-flag lap and then try to slingshot on the fourth corner. But when Paul got there, I decided between the two of us, we could keep Foyt trapped back there. I thought I was going to win. I thought Goldsmith and I had the track blocked. I figured A.J. couldn't get around."

"He did."

Foyt said he knew what was going on when Isaac pulled alongside Goldsmith. "I would have done the same thing. That's racing. If you're a racer you wanta win. Bobby's a racer.

"So I just played possum. I think I'm beginning to figure this track out. Knowing when to pass and how and when to draft here is the difference. I thought I could get by Bobby, but I didn't really know until it was over. When Bobby and I kept swapping back and forth, I decided to try to come in behind him on the last lap. I knew he could do the same thing, so I was glad when he stayed out front with one to go."[17]

With Chrysler products sweeping the first six positions—Rutherford in seventh was the top Ford—Foyt wore a button proclaiming "Total *What?*" a slam at Ford's Total Performance slogan, and he couldn't resist taking a shot at his former car supplier.

"It's nice to be back on a winning stock car team. I won four or five straight races with Chrysler and then changed to Ford. After that, I finished only one race. I never did do too hot with Ford."[18]

Foyt became the first driver to win at both Indianapolis and Daytona, accomplishing the feat in the same year. Chrysler featured Foyt's victory in full-page ads running in newspapers across the country the following week.

After pocketing about $6,500, half of the first-place prize money, A.J. headed for the airport with Rutherford in tow for another corporate jet ride back to Indianapolis. Both planned to race in a thirty-lap sprint car race the next day in Eldora, Ohio. First-place prize money: about one thousand dollars.

More than six thousand spectators turned out at Eldora, many to see Foyt. After winning his heat race, he could do no better than fifth in the main event. Upset about his second consecutive sprint car loss, and with winner Jud Larson passing him in the series point standings, he didn't bother to pick up his check for $379.

It took two weeks for things to return to normal. At Williams Grove Speedway for a sprint car race, Foyt qualified on the pole, winning his heat race and then the main event. It wasn't easy as Andretti, from nearby Nazareth, nearly stole the show to the delight of the crowd.

Seventeenth in qualifying and barely advancing to the feature from his heat race, Andretti sliced through the field in the main, taking the lead from Foyt on lap seventeen. It lasted only four laps as Andretti spun. Foyt avoided him, but third-place Branson couldn't, knocking both drivers out of the race and allowing A.J. to cruise to an easy win.

The next day in Trenton the Indy car race proved to be a test of resilience for both man and machine. Foyt qualified fourth, the lone roadster among the first seven cars, with Jim McElreath on the pole, followed by Ward and Marshman.

With air temperatures hovering around one hundred degrees and track temps topping 130, Marshman was the early leader and one of the first out with car troubles. Ward took over and was close to lapping Foyt, who'd lost his brakes. Ward suddenly pulled into the pits, overcome by the heat. He was replaced by Marshman, although the car lost several laps in the change. McElreath inherited the lead and appeared on his way to victory until he was also overcome by the heat. Another driver, Troy Ruttman, managed to pull his car into the pits before passing out from heat exhaustion. Foyt moved into the lead, lapping the remaining cars and setting a track record for 150 miles.

"I just wish you Ford guys would hold together once so I wouldn't have to keep backing into these victories," said a seemingly fresh Foyt, who said the lack of brakes kept him from thinking about the heat. "It was pretty tough without brakes in traffic. I'd just hang on and say a little prayer. The breaks were with me. I guess I'll stay with this old antique, it sure has made me a lot of money."[19]

No one was more impressed by the performance than his crew chief, who thought he'd seen everything.

"The guy won because a blowtorch couldn't melt him," George Bignotti said. "He doesn't know how to quit."[20]

EUROPEAN VACATION

Foyt delayed his departure for Europe with the Mecom sports car team in order to fulfill a promise he'd made to the fans at New Bremen Speedway. After begging out of the race the day after winning the 500 and before committing to the European trip, he'd told the crowd he'd be back for the July 26 sprint car event. The decision to honor the commitment also ended discussions with BRM about driving in the August 1 German Grand Prix at Nürburgring, there being insufficient time for practice on the fourteen-mile circuit.

For Foyt and Bignotti, the races in Europe were secondary. The main goal was to check out the different racing machinery.

"We're not so much looking for something to buy," Foyt said. "What we're after are ideas that we can incorporate in the new cars we're going to run next year. We definitely plan to have two cars for next year's 500. We have some ideas of our own about what we want to use. If we see them incorporated in something over there, we may be in a buying mood. But I think George and I will probably wind up building our own cars."[21]

Before he left, Foyt tried to squash any talk about future races for him in Europe.

"I'd rather race at home. I think we've got a tougher circuit over here. In Europe you've got [Jim] Clark, [Dan] Gurney, [John] Surtees, and a couple or three others who will win races. Over here there are at least fifteen drivers who can beat you any day.

"I don't think you can call that the world driving championship—world road racing championship would be better. I don't see how you can call a man the world's champion of all racing when he only drives one type. Now I don't want to take anything away from Clark, but I would like to see him try to drive a championship car at someplace like Springfield [Illinois] or a sprint car or a midget at Terre Haute. Actually I don't look on this trip as too much of an adventure. I raced against these guys at Nassau in this same car and beat them—set new records doing it too. I can do it again if things go right."

Although Foyt earned the pole position at New Bremen, Larson owned the race, leading all thirty laps. It was Larson's third straight victory at the track, having jump-started his season driving Foyt's car to victory in the May race.

Foyt and Bignotti left the next day for London, where they joined the rest of the Mecom team, including drivers Walt Hansgen and Augie Pabst, for the Guards Trophy sports car race at Brands Hatch, just twenty miles outside the city. A former motorcycle track and, for a short time, an Indy-type oval, the track had been reconfigured as a tight 2.65-mile road course with sweeping high-speed curves and short straights winding through a wooded area, a new experience for Foyt. Site of the European Grand Prix three weeks earlier, most of the top F1 drivers were back, including GP winner Clark, McLaren, Denis Hulme, Jack Brabham, and Graham Hill.

Things went wrong from the start. The Scarab that performed so well on the wide-open Bahamas airport circuit and high banks of Daytona was a handful in England. The car's monster Chevrolet engine—the biggest in the race—was of little use on the tight course, and the car needed a much stiffer suspension. The team brought a limited number of spare parts and the Scarab's uniqueness made it difficult to find replacements. Starting well back in the field, Foyt parked the car after just three of fifty laps, citing a suspension problem. McLaren led all the way to win. Gurney wasn't critical of Foyt for dropping out but seemed to enjoy watching him struggle.

"Everything was passing him," Gurney told Robert Daley, the *New York Times* motorsports correspondent in Europe, who was working on a profile of Foyt for *True Magazine*. "Jaguars, MGs, everything. He was so mad. All he could do was try to set his tires on fire by spinning his wheels coming out of every corner. If he couldn't win, at least he wanted to put on a show. But he couldn't even do that. After a while he drove into the pits and retired. You can't blame him for that. As USAC champion, he didn't want to be passed by all those small cars. But anyway, at least it's a chink in the story that the guy can do it in anything."[22]

The race wasn't a total waste of Foyt's time, as he reconciled with Phil Hill. A group of drivers were talking and Foyt, still miffed at Hill for the Daytona Continental incident, was ignoring him. Daley wrote about what happened next. Like many racing journalists, he was an admirer of Hill, referring to him as a "thoughtful, gentle man."[23]

"A girl came up and invited Hill to a party after the race," Daley wrote in his 1965 profile. "'Don't you think you should invite A.J. too?' asked Hill. The girl did so, and Foyt, who loves parties, loves to belong to the 'in' group, immediately became very cordial to Hill, and thanked him profusely for arranging the invitation."[24]

The party was held at McLaren's rental house in southwest London, known as "The Castle" because of its size. Pre- and post-race parties often reached legendary status, with drivers competing in jousting tournaments using cardboard swords and armor, with abundant "fair maidens" in attendance. Mecom accompanied Foyt to the party, which A.J. didn't recall.

"The respect that he commanded in Europe among all the F1 guys was incredible," Mecom remembered. "At the party, A.J. was the center of attention the entire time. But I'm not sure if he appreciated how important he was. He had this façade—he would tell you how good he was–but he didn't believe it as much as everybody else did. He always felt like he had to prove himself."[25]

From London, Foyt, Mecom, Bignotti, Pabst, and Hansgen flew to Modena, Italy. The area was a favorite of Mecom's, who visited often. A number of the top Italian specialty automotive manufacturers were based nearby and the group spent several days touring the factories, including a stop to see Alejandro de Tomaso, who'd built Mecom a beautiful but impractical Indy car prototype.

Highlight of the trip for Bignotti was a meeting with Enzo Ferrari and a visit to the Ferrari factory. Mecom was a top customer of Ferrari production cars in the United States and was friendly with "the old man" as he called Enzo. Ferrari had tried to fight the rear-engine revolution in Formula One, arguing the oxen belonged in front of the buggy. He admired what Foyt had accomplished with the roadster but admitted the switch to rear-engine cars was now inevitable. The meeting went well and there was talk of a Ferrari Indy car, with Foyt driving for the company at both Indianapolis and in F1.

"The old man was dying to meet A.J. and really wanted to bring him on board," Mecom recalled. "I think the idea of driving for Ferrari had an impact on A.J.—it would on anybody. Ferrari approached us about the possibility of doing an Indy car. I think the old man considered it, but George wanted to build it himself and Ferrari didn't like that so much."[26]

Initial media reports out of Modena quoted Foyt saying Enzo "was extremely cordial." The article from *United Press International* also said Foyt would stay in Europe until October, and quoted him saying "I intend to compete in Europe with Ferraris of the North American Racing Team."[27]

Something was lost in translation, as not only did NART not race in Europe, but Foyt was also back in Houston the following night for a quick change of clothes. He had a sprint car race at Terre Haute in two days.

"A.J. was different," Mecom said of the confusion. "I often found myself trying to think ahead of him, but I was usually about four laps behind. If I tried to figure out what he was really thinking, I'd probably have hit a wall."

Foyt had gotten a dose of the politics constantly surrounding Ferrari and his teams back in February when his car was protested by the other Ferrari entries at Daytona. But what really turned him off was the possibility of team orders, that he might be told to let someone else win a race or finish in front of him because it was important for world championship points.

"I told them I wasn't interested, I didn't want to race that way," Foyt said years later. "What I didn't like about Formula One, they kind of tell you where you got to finish. You might have to run second or third. When Ferrari told me that, I just told them I don't race that way. I'd rather run my midget or sprint car. That's the reason I was never interested in Formula One or anything like that."[28]

No Foyt meant no Ferrari Indy car—a long shot anyway, as the factory was reluctant to give up control. Chapman refused to sell his main competitors a new Lotus, although with Ford's assistance they did manage to land one of the year-old cars "for a nominal fee." Bignotti also placed an order for a new Lola, although it might not arrive in time for the 1965 500.

CHAPTER 17

THE YEAR OF FOYT

1964

Back in the States, A.J. Foyt still held out hope of winning the sprint car championship. He'd won more races than anyone else, but Don Branson and Don Larson were ahead of him on points, having run more races.

Although he missed a sprint car race at Salem while in Europe, his car didn't. Parnelli Jones, who hadn't driven a sprint car in more than nine months, "borrowed" the car along with engine guru Herb Porter. They won in dominating fashion, with Foyt reading about it in a newspaper after he returned.[1]

"I wondered what the hell was going on," A.J. said. "They had nothing to do that weekend and just decided to go racing. They took my car there and blew everybody away."[2]

It ended up helping Foyt, as it kept Branson from winning the race and piling up more points. The engine was damaged in the process, however, and Foyt didn't discover the problem until he arrived to drive the car at Terre Haute. It didn't stop him from capturing the pole and battling Branson for the lead before making a rare mistake and spinning out of the race.

"I'd rather eat nails than spin out," he said. "I was diving low trying to pass Don and hit a rut and simply went around. I was missing on one cylinder for some reason and couldn't get the power in the turns."[3]

His slim hopes at the sprint car title ended the following week in Allentown, Pennsylvania, but the race was important for another reason. More than ten thousand people converged on the half-mile dirt track to see local favorite Mario Andretti take on USAC's best. Andretti had moved into the sprint car owned by Rufus Gray, one of the better rides in the series, and he didn't disappoint, qualifying on the pole for the first time in a national series event. Foyt was the obvious

◀ Foyt's big year saw him win in multiple cars. *Revs Institute, Albert R. Bochroch Photograph Collection*

target for any young driver on the rise, and although Andretti had competed in ten races with the veteran, he'd finished ahead of him only once while A.J. won six of them. This was Mario's chance to end that string.

Andretti brought the field down for a fast start—too fast, as he slid high going into Turn One. Seeing an opening on the inside, Foyt went low from his fifth-place starting position and nearly grabbed the lead before he bounced up the track as well, bumping into Andretti.

"Like the cagey veteran he is," the Allentown newspaper reported the next day, Foyt "swung fast into the first turn and literally bounced Andretti out of his way, causing the Nazareth driver to nearly lose control and fall back."[4]

Larson recovered first and went on to win the short thirty-lap race with Foyt third. Andretti struggled to get going again and was a lap behind when he did. Upset by the move, Andretti set off after A.J., running Bobby Marshman off the track in the process but coming up just short of Foyt at the finish.

Nearly sixty years later, Andretti perked up when the race was mentioned. The anger was long gone, and he said he'd learned a valuable lesson.

"He cheated on the start!" Andretti said, a broad smile on his face. "He spun me. I was on fire that day, and even though I was last and a lap behind, I caught him and I was going to do it to him. I felt I had to show off to my own people there and I think I would have done something stupid. It would have been the stupidest thing in my life. Luckily, just as I closed up behind him, the race ended. Even now I think back to that race and say, 'Thank God, *thank God* I didn't get close enough to him.' I would have regretted that the rest of my career."[5]

One of Andretti's cousins approached A.J. afterward and complained, but Foyt seemed not to understand nor care. He said he didn't recall the incident. Throughout his career, Andretti said he never confronted Foyt.

"I was always afraid of him. He was so much bigger than me. But I figured I could outrun him if I had to."

Branson's victory ended Foyt's fleeting sprint car championship hopes and he turned his attention back to the big cars for one of his favorite weekends of the year, the Saturday night dirt car race at the fairgrounds in Springfield, Illinois, followed the next day by the race on the paved Milwaukee track.

At Springfield it appeared his string of champ car victories would end at six as a faulty magneto in qualifying relegated him to sixteenth starting position in an eighteen-car field. Foyt fought his way past Andretti, Jones, Rutherford, and Bobby Unser, but Marshman seemed to have the race under control until he was forced to the pits for a new tire. Foyt moved into the lead, and while Marshman challenged, he was able to hold on and keep the streak intact.

The race was marred by a fiery crash that took the life of Bill Horstmeyer, an experienced midget and sprint car driver who was making his first big-car start. He hit the wall early in the event, sending the car into a series of flips and rupturing the fuel tank, the car landing upside down and fully engulfed in flames. For more than twenty laps the cars slowly passed the wreck under caution as firefighters battled the blaze in windy conditions before finally extinguishing the fire and pulling Horstmeyer from the car. He would die the next morning.[6]

The following day in Milwaukee, Foyt was set to make his debut in a rear-engine Lotus. It had all come together quickly, Ford's frustration with Colin Chapman apparently overcoming hard feelings and Iacocca's ban.

The company was insisting the Lotus team run the final two paved oval races of the year at Milwaukee and Trenton in preparation for the 1965 season. With Clark and Gurney competing in the Austrian Grand Prix, Lotus lined up Jones and Hansgen to drive at Milwaukee.

Hansgen, A.J.'s teammate on John Mecom's team, was a successful sports car driver with limited Indy car experience, although he'd driven a Huffaker car—like the one Foyt tested—up to third place in the Indianapolis 500 before dropping out.

Jones and Hansgen tested at Trenton the week before Milwaukee, both having minor accidents. When the team moved to Milwaukee for another test session, Hansgen crashed more seriously and ended up in the hospital with a concussion. With a backup car available and the team in need of a driver, a call was made to Foyt, who somewhat surprisingly agreed to a test. After a two-hour session he decided to drive it in the race.

"I feel this is the right time to make the change to a rear-engine car," he said. "I've got the championship almost wrapped up. They are the fastest and the safest of the rear-engine machines. I am definitely going to have one at the Indianapolis Speedway next year."[7]

In an indication of the importance Ford and Lotus placed on the race and its two guest drivers, Chapman was on hand rather than in Europe for the grand prix. Jones, driving the green Lotus that Clark had driven in the 500 but carrying the No. 98, put his extensive testing in the car to good use, qualifying on the pole ahead of Ward and Foyt, who was driving the white Lotus backup car with the No. 1.

At the start of the race Foyt jammed the transmission when he tried to shift up and couldn't get it out of first gear. Fuming, he pulled into the pits at the end of the opening lap and behind the pit wall for repairs. Although it was an easy and quick fix, he was disqualified for pulling behind the wall, missing out on an opportunity to further test the car for the remainder of the race. He wasn't happy, saying, "I'll never drive another one of those funny little cars."

Jones cruised to victory, finishing two laps ahead of Ward. Not surprisingly, he had a different view of the car.

"A Lotus makes this race driving easy. In fact, this is the easiest race I ever drove. Why, I never even gave it full throttle until the finish."[8]

Within a few days Foyt also changed his tune, hopeful of driving the car again a month later at Trenton.

"It looks like next year we will be running a Ford engine. I was sorry this freak thing happened. But I just grinned and walked away, because I knew that I was going to have some bad luck this time. The engine proved real successful—it really surprised me how it ran."[9]

He no longer seemed concerned about the safety of the cars. "I've seen them crash these cars two or three times and I've never seen one catch fire yet. It made me feel real good about it. We're out to win and we are trying to get the best equipment money can buy. And the winner next year? Lotus-Ford."

In Du Quoin for the annual Labor Day weekend slate of races, he was back on dirt, back in the seemingly unbeatable Meskowski-Offy, and back in a midget for the first time in twenty months. He was also back in Victory Lane.

In the midget race he led the first fifty-five laps before being sidelined by a fuel line problem. There was no stopping him in the Indy car race, as he led all one hundred laps for a runaway victory, his fourth in a row in the event. It wrapped up his fourth Indy car season championship and pushed his earnings for the year above two hundred thousand dollars, both records. He also tied Ward for the most series victories.[10]

Two days later he was at the Indianapolis Fairgrounds for festivities marking the last day of the state fair. While he'd been dominating the Indy car series, Jones was nearly as dominant in the USAC stock cars. Driving a Mercury, he was well on his way to the series championship while Foyt struggled to finish races in his Dodge. The Wednesday event was a rare open date on the racing schedule and attracted a top field of Indy car drivers in addition to the regular stock car pilots. Ford even brought in NASCAR's Ned Jarrett, its top dirt track driver.

Before the cars took to the track, a special harness horse race was set up for Jones and Foyt. Jones had been doing some promotional work for the fair, and after lapping the track earlier in a sulky he challenged Foyt to a race, who was quick to accept.

Foyt was behind a horse named Redstone Ranger and Jones's horse was named Pokey, quickly dubbed "Slow Pokey" by A.J. It was all in good fun and Jones thought he and Foyt had agreed to cross the finish line side-by-side for a tie. He should have known better. Foyt went to the whip coming to the finish, taking a slight lead before Jones could react and winning by three-quarters of a length.[11]

Things started poorly for Foyt in practice for the actual race when the engine in the Dodge blew. With no time to replace it before qualifying, he hatched a plan to get back in the event.

While Joe Leonard qualified one of the three identical Ray Nichels Dodges in second, Len Sutton, still hurting from an Indy car crash at Milwaukee three weeks earlier, spun on his qualifying lap and failed to make the twenty-car starting field. Foyt started taking the doors off his car, hoping to put them on Sutton's car, which he would then try to qualify as his own No. 47.

Henry Banks, USAC's director of racing, was alerted to the ploy and put a stop to it. Foyt then went to work on the race promoters and convinced them, "in the interest of a better show," as it was announced to the crowd of fifteen thousand, the field would include all thirty cars attempting to qualify. Foyt was allowed to sub for the ailing Sutton but would start last. Few gave him a chance. They should have known better.[12]

Reports have Foyt passing between nine and fourteen cars on the first lap, in the top ten after seven laps, and hounding leader Jones by the halfway point of the one-hundred-mile race. Jones was struggling with his brakes, and they failed completely on lap fifty-nine, sending him into the guardrail and eliminating another front-runner, Lloyd Ruby, in the process. Foyt barely missed the two crashing cars and lost several spots before regaining control, and soon the lead. He went on to lap the field except for the second-place finisher.[13]

As if to prove it wasn't a fluke, four days later he took control from the start of a grueling 250-mile stock car race at Langhorne, putting nearly two laps on Marshman in the second-place Ford and four on third-place Sutton. If Foyt was looking to improve his relationship with Ford with an eye toward Indianapolis, he went about it in an odd way.

"I could have gone much faster," he said. "I would have liked to put another lap on Marshman, but I kept getting an 'E-Z' sign from my pit crew. I was just playing with those Fords. They couldn't have caught me in a million years."[14]

It was Foyt's eighth victory at the track considered by many to be the most dangerous in the country. But it was a bittersweet victory. In an attempt to make it safer, the track was scheduled to be reconfigured and paved during the off-season. Foyt would never win another race at "The 'Horne."

MORE DRIVER THAN HOOD

By mid-September Hurtubise was able to leave the hospital for several days at a time and journeyed to Indianapolis for the Hoosier Hundred Indy car race. Heavy overnight rains turned the track into a quagmire, and although Foyt and Bobby Unser said they were ready to race, the rest of the field deemed it too dangerous, and the race was postponed by a week.

The delay only heightened fan interest, and a record 29,185 were on hand, only 150 short of the combined number of people who'd turned out to see two shows by the Beatles at the Fairgrounds three weeks earlier. They were treated to the same show that had been running all season, a commanding performance by Foyt.

After predicting "I'll lead the thing all the way," he qualified on the pole and then took a hacksaw to his tires, cutting a special tread design more to his liking. He came up short of leading every lap, out front for only ninety-four of one hundred. He wore a cowboy hat to Victory Lane where he picked up a record dirt track payout of more than eighteen thousand dollars. He'd become the winningest driver in Indy car history, and his ninth champ car victory of the year set another record.[15]

Bignotti stood on the fringe of the crowded victory celebration, allowing Foyt to bask in the limelight. They still argued more than any other crew chief and driver, "because we both want to win so badly," he said, but winning had a way of smoothing things over. Someone told Bignotti while he had a good driver, there must also be something special under the hood.[16]

"Yes," he said with a grin, "but I've got more driver than I've got hood."[17]

Because of the initial postponement, the Indy drivers and teams were forced to hustle to Trenton for a race the next day. The plans for Foyt to drive the Lotus again were dashed when Clark, with no conflicts on his European schedule, decided he wanted to run the race. He took over his primary car and Jones moved to the car Foyt drove at Milwaukee, relegating Foyt to his antique roadster.

It didn't seem to matter which Lotus Jones was driving, as he put it on the pole. Foyt was fourth, the only roadster among the top five, while Clark, with little practice, could do no better than seventh. Turning in one of his best drives of the season on the track where he'd won five consecutive races, Foyt hounded Jones from the start, jumping ahead early on a restart and leading for nine laps before the Lotus moved back out front. Foyt eventually retired with a bad clutch and Jones went on to win by more than a lap.

Jones complained about Foyt jumping the restart, then praised his only challenger.

"Foyt is fantastic," he said, shaking his head. "He's fantastically strong. He's got fantastic reflexes. He never gets in trouble. He's thinking all the time. He's just fantastic."[18,19]

The following week Jones and Foyt skipped the biggest sprint car event of the year at Salem to run a stock car race in Missouri, Jones winning with Foyt coming in fourth. Foyt's sprint car was in action, however, driven by Roger McCluskey on the high banks.

The defending sprint car champion, McCluskey was finally recovered from the serious injuries he'd suffered in the March race, but he was having trouble lining up a car to drive. When Foyt heard about the problem he offered up his car, just as he had with Larson at New Bremen. While McCluskey dropped out early with a blown engine, he proved himself capable of running up front and other owners came forward. Offering his car to another driver in need was something Foyt continued to do in the years ahead.

Andretti made the big news at Salem, winning his first USAC feature race, just as Foyt and Jones had done years earlier. It wouldn't be his last.

With the final USAC races of the year not scheduled until late November, Foyt entered the October 11 sports car race at Riverside. Mecom had commissioned a new car called the Hussein 1, a tribute to his friendship and oil dealings with King Hussein of Jordan. The king was a car fanatic and Foyt met him at Mecom's Houston shop earlier in the year. The car was basically an English-made Cooper Monaco chassis with new bodywork and a mammoth NASCAR Chrysler Hemi engine in the back.

Foyt waited and stewed at the track while parts for the car were late arriving. He missed the time trials entirely, forcing him to start from the back of a qualifying race. He went from thirty-fourth to sixth to make the field, and then got as high as second in the main event. The race again attracted the top drivers from around the world, with Bruce McLaren on the pole, followed by Hansgen in the Scarab Foyt drove the year before.

More than eighty thousand spectators turned out on race day and watched as Jones led from the start, out front for seventy-five of seventy-seven laps and besting Roger Penske and Clark, with Foyt dropping out early. Jones then faced the same questions Foyt did earlier in the year about racing in Europe. His answers were also similar.

"I don't think they pay the kind of money over there that we can race for here," he said. "And I'm not interested in traveling for fun."[20]

Unhappy with the Hussein, which some were calling the "Insane 1," Foyt decided to compete in a NASCAR race at Charlotte the following week rather than the sports car event at Laguna Seca.

It was Foyt's first time at the Charlotte track, and teammate Paul Goldsmith took great delight in painting the bumper of his car yellow, warning others of a rookie driver. It was also Foyt's first NASCAR start since his victory at Daytona, and he soon discovered the win had earned him increased scrutiny. NASCAR inspectors sent his car and others back to the garage several times because the front end was judged to be too low. After finally passing tech, he was next in line to qualify when the track was closed for the day, ending his hopes of earning the pole position. Foyt wasn't happy.

"I quit, I'm going home," was his immediate reaction when officials blocked him from driving onto the track. He eventually calmed down, if only slightly. "I know they got rules, but my goodness. All my crew's watches still had three minutes to go. We had been sitting out there for ten minutes. We were on the line. But you can't argue with them. You just have to do what they say."[21]

When rain washed out the final two rounds of qualifying, Foyt was forced to start eighteenth. He passed eight cars on the first lap and eventually moved into second behind leader Petty, only to drop out before the halfway point with car trouble.

It had been more than a month since Foyt's last victory when he arrived on October 25 at the California State Fairgrounds for the final champ car dirt race of the year. He turned in only one of the normal two qualifying laps and pulled off the track, complaining about his car's engine and setup. Bignotti changed the fuel pump, while Foyt went to work on the suspension, finishing up just minutes before the start.

Jones, limping badly after crashing at Laguna Seca, made one of his rare dirt track starts, qualifying on the pole and leading early. But Foyt caught and passed him before the race was a third over, Jones eventually dropping out. Foyt led the final seventy laps, completing a sweep of the year's five dirt track races. Ward then surprised many, announcing he was retiring from the dirt tracks.[22]

"Championship dirt track racing is for fellows a lot younger than me," said Ward, who at forty-three was fourteen years older than Foyt. "I really hate to give it up because I've always had a lot of fun on the dirt. But I noticed this year I was a little more tired after a one-hundred-mile battle on dirt than the same distance on a paved track. And when you're battling A.J. Foyt, you've got a fight on your hands every foot of the way. So for 1965 I'm going to leave the dirt tracks to him and concentrate on trying to beat him on the paved ones."[23]

Foyt was already looking ahead to the coming year, deciding a rear-engine car was the way to go. Bignotti took delivery of the Lotus that A.J. drove at Milwaukee and Jones took to victory at Trenton. Agajanian received the Lotus that Clark drove at Indianapolis and Jones won with at Milwaukee.

Marshman was continuing his extensive testing in his Lotus for Ford and for both tire companies. He'd set unofficial track marks at Indianapolis and Phoenix but fell short of Foyt's closed-course record of more than two hundred miles per hour at Goodyear's test facility when windy conditions disrupted his effort. Foyt also was testing a rear-engine car, although it wasn't the Lotus, Bignotti having decided to beef up its suspension prior to putting it on the track.

"While we don't see much point in messing up a good thing, George and I would rather be fifty pounds heavier and know the car is going to hold up than shave a few pounds and hope," Foyt said of the decision.[24]

With his Lotus parked, Foyt used a Halibrand-Offy at Phoenix, similar to the one Eddie Sachs was driving when he was killed at the Speedway. After running laps a second below the track record, he decided to use the car in the season finale.

With more than a month before the race at Phoenix, Foyt agreed to run a trio of much-hyped races at Ascot Park. Promoter Agajanian billed the events as a face-off between the sport's two best drivers—Foyt and Jones—hinting the races could be the pair's final sprint car and dirt track events, a story widely reported as fact. Foyt had, in fact, sold his sprint car while Jones was openly questioning his future in racing. Jones handled the prerace promotional work and found himself mostly answering questions about Foyt.

"We're friendly, but not buddy-buddies," Jones said of their relationship. "We rarely see one another except when racing. And then, all too often, I'm looking at his back. Foyt has it all: strength, stamina, nerve, fantastic ability, and a Texan's determination to do everything better than the next guy. All I know is that if I ever get enough money to quit driving and own a racing car, I'd want Foyt to do the driving for me."[25]

The races were anticlimactic, McCluskey winning one sprint car event and Bobby Unser the other, Foyt finishing second in one and Jones taking the runner-up spot in the other. Jones won the tiebreaker, a stock car race, after Foyt captured the pole but was slowed by car problems.

Later, while in Phoenix for the final Indy car race of the year, Foyt participated in a special Goodyear test, lasting only five laps before his rear-engine car darted up the track and into the wall, badly damaging the front suspension. Determining there was more damage than could be fixed at the track, the car was loaded on a trailer and sent back to Ted Halibrand's shop in Los Angeles. Working into Saturday night, Halibrand grafted a new front end on the car and had it back in Phoenix for qualifying Sunday morning.[26]

With limited practice, Foyt qualified second to the Lotus of Jones. Getting a good start—Jones would again say A.J. jumped the green flag—Foyt took an early lead but couldn't hold Jones back. Trying to keep the leader in sight, he eventually spun and dropped out. Jones dropped out with engine problems while Lloyd Ruby, driving another Halibrand, won his second champ car event.[27]

THE DEATH OF MARSHMAN

There was one USAC race remaining, a stock car event at Hanover Speedway in California. Foyt was in good spirits, holding up a "Go Now" pit sign for teammate Leonard during practice. The mood soon changed, however, when word spread that Marshman, who'd stayed behind to test in Phoenix, had crashed. Details were sketchy, but apparently he'd been burned in the wreck. Foyt went on to qualify on the pole with Jones second. The pair traded the lead in the race before Foyt took command, leading 103 of the 134 laps, Jones finishing second.[28]

Returning home, Foyt learned Marshman's situation was much worse than initial reports indicated. He'd crashed on the backstraight at Phoenix, the car catching fire on impact and sliding one hundred feet before coming to a stop, fully engulfed in flames. Marshman was struggling to get out of the car when a firefighter in an asbestos uniform arrived and tried to assist him. The seat had been jammed forward in the impact and slowed their efforts, and it took more than a minute to get him out of the burning car. Some reports said Marshman wasn't wearing a flame-retardant uniform, although it was never confirmed. Nor was a cause of the accident.

Taken to a hospital in Phoenix in critical condition, he'd been airlifted to Brooke Army Medical Burn Center in San Antonio with second- and third-degree burns over 90 percent of his body. In comparison, as bad as Hurtubise's burns were, they had covered only 45 percent of his body. Hurtubise was still being treated at the hospital and sat vigil with arriving members of Marshman's family.[29]

Although less than two years younger than Foyt, Marshman was considered *the* young up-and-comer, "the caliber of Jim Clark, A.J. Foyt, and Parnelli Jones." He'd shown good speed in various cars and on different types of tracks but with only a couple of victories. Some said he was a hard-luck driver. He'd been leading the Ford and Lotus development efforts and was considered a top challenger heading into 1965.

George Marshman, Bobby's father, arrived in San Antonio soon after his son. The elder Marshman knew well the dangers of auto racing, having been a driver himself and owner of the racetrack where his son started his career. Doctors cautioned the family "not to get their hopes up," and warned Bobby's vital organs were likely to begin shutting down. Despite the warnings, George Marshman couldn't help but sound hopeful when he talked to his local newspaper.

"Mentally he's all right," he told *The Pottstown Mercury*. "I'm relieved now that everything which can be done is being done. This place is the best. You can just tell they're professionals. Don't get me wrong, he's still in very, very serious condition and if he makes it, the recovery period is a long, long time. But I feel certain that he'll get the very best care that there is."[30]

The elder Marshman telephoned Foyt and it was a gut-wrenching call for A.J. to take. He'd considered going to the hospital but was scheduled to depart for the Bahamas and Nassau Speed Week. And he was haunted by images from his visit to Hurtubise. He attempted to comfort Marshman's father, trying to balance a parent's hopes with the reality of what the doctors were saying.

"His daddy called me and said, 'They tell me my boy is gonna die within a day or two.' He was burned terribly. I said, 'Mr. Marshman, where's there's life, there's still hope. At the same time, they are very brilliant doctors there.'"[31]

As the doctors feared, Marshman's organs began to shut down and the end came quickly. Wednesday night he lapsed into a coma and Bobby Marshman died the following evening. He was the second driver from Pennsylvania to die from burns that year, and a third, Andretti, sounded amazingly fatalistic when asked to comment.

"We'd be fools not to expect something like this," he said. "We can't let ourselves be too surprised and just hope that it doesn't happen to you. He was a very careful driver. You find some reckless guys out there, but Bobby took care on the track."[32]

NASSAU 1964

Foyt was already in Nassau when word came of Marshman's death. He'd run some slow practice laps and was disappointed to find few of the problems he'd identified with Mecom's forty thousand dollar Hussein 1 sports car had been addressed. He began to tear down the car himself.

"No brakes, the engine isn't right, and I don't like the way it handles," he said. Nichels, who'd made the trip, went to work on the Dodge engine. Foyt and the crew worked through the night, and although the brakes were still the weak link in the heavy machine, it was more to his liking for the first feature event, Friday's Governor's Trophy race. It was a new experience for Mecom's crew, but Nichels had been through it before.[33]

"A.J. sure doesn't mind working," he said, any thoughts of a few days on the beach long gone. "That's what makes the real great race drivers. He'll try anything and he'll work from sunup to sundown to get the job done. If it's not finished then, he'll work around the clock. He goes all the time. He can't slow down. He *works* at being a great race driver."[34]

Penske, no longer Foyt's teammate at Mecom and now driving a Chaparral for Jim Hall, was unbeatable in the week's preliminary events. Yet Foyt nearly pulled off a stunning upset victory for the second straight year. He watched Penske and Dan Gurney in a Lotus sports car swap the lead before Gurney retired with handling problems. Then Penske pitted, concerned about a loose wheel and unaware he was starting the last lap. Foyt took the lead as Penske's crew waved him back onto the track, where he caught and passed Foyt before the checkered flag.[35]

In the week's finale, Sunday's Nassau Trophy race, Penske led from the start but dropped out early with a broken suspension, Foyt taking the lead. Penske then took over the car of teammate Hap Sharp, and when Foyt's brakes finally gave out, causing him to slide off the course, he retook the lead. Foyt continued, two laps back, and fell even further behind when the engine started losing power. This time he didn't quit, soldiering on to finish nineteenth, eight laps behind Penske.

"He went by me so slow I thought he was out for a Sunday drive," said one course worker. Foyt said there was a good reason he continued. "I didn't have any brakes to stop in the pits so I figured I might as well keep going. I knew I had blown the race, but an old friend had bet me five dollars I wouldn't finish. I wasn't about to lose that bet."[36]

After sweeping the week's big events, Penske announced he was retiring from driving. Foyt did manage to post a victory in the Volkswagen Grand Prix, a mostly-for-fun short race for stock VW Beetles. More important than the victory, the race went a long way toward creating a link between Foyt and Gurney.

The two had never been particularly friendly, sometimes trading barbs at the track and in the press. Foyt had called him "just another driver" at a stock car event and Gurney continued to call him Cassius. Even occasional words of praise were often a backhanded compliment.

"Foyt's got a tremendous amount of skill," Gurney said earlier in the year. "[He's] also driven an awful lot of miles. He drives much more than anybody else, so it stands to reason he's usually sharper than most of the others."[37]

Three-year-old A.J. Foyt in his first race car. He already has his game face on.
Foyt Family Collection

Tony Foyt (center) with friends and A.J. (left). At twenty-nine with three dependents, Tony went to enlist on December 8, 1941. He eventually became a sergeant in the US Army Air Corps recognized for being "a skilled mechanic." *Foyt Family Collection*

A.J. teaches his sister Marlene and a friend how to drive. *Foyt Family Collection*

The Houston Heights must have been a neighborhood full of racers. *Foyt Family Collection*

A.J. and his sister Marlene. *Foyt Family Collection*

With his "Daddy" and others at Tony's garage. *Foyt Family Collection*

School photo. *Foyt Family Collection*

A.J. in car No. 2 at Playland Speedway. *Foyt Family Collection*

Foyt's No. 2 ready for the start of a race at Playland Speedway. "Skyrocket," at the time the world's longest wooden rollercoaster, is in the background.
Foyt Family Collection

Getting ready for a road trip with the midget. *Foyt Family Collection*

With Sonny Morgan, another driver on the IMCA "Fairground Circuit." *Foyt Family Collection*

With Lucy (middle) and a friend, ready to go racing. *Foyt Family Collection*

Lucy Foyt, sometime in the mid-1950s. *Indiana State Library*

A.J.'s 1957 win in Les Vaughn's sprint car on Salem Speedway's high banks caught the eye of Indy car owners. *Foyt Family Collection*

A.J. and Lucy at the Illinois State Fairgrounds in Springfield in 1958 for his first Indy car race. *Foyt Family Collection*

Working alongside Clint Brawner in Gasoline Alley. *IMS Photography Archive*

1960 Golden State 100 winner. *Revs Institute, The Bruce R. Craig Photograph Collection*

Both Foyt and Parnelli Jones earned the right to use No. 1 after winning regional sprint car championships in 1960. Here they battle on the high banks of Salem in 1961. *Steve H. Shunck Photo Collection*

BOWES "SEAL FAST" CORPORATION

5902 East Thirty-Fourth Street, Indianapolis 18, Indiana   LIBERTY 7-5245

the famous "500" line of car care products

3-28-61

AGREEMENT

It is hereby agreed between A. J. Foyt, Jr. and Bowes "Seal Fast" Corporation of Indianapolis, Indiana, that A. J. Foyt, Jr. will drive the car, or cars, owned by Bignotti-Bowes Racing Associates and sponsored by Bowes "Seal Fast" Corporation in all championship races in 1961 for the following consideration:

1. Bowes "Seal Fast" Corporation agrees to pay A. J. Foyt, Jr. the sum of $6500.00. A. J. Foyt, Jr. will then purchase a 220 Offy for this sum and it will run under Bowes "Seal Fast" colors.

2. A. J. Foyt, Jr. agrees that 50% of all 220 prize money be delivered to Bignotti-Bowes Racing Associates; Bignotti-Bowes in turn promises to keep the car in good racing condition during the season and guarantee that after the season the car will be in the same condition as at the start of the season.

3. In case of any accident involving injury or permanent disability or death, Bignotti-Bowes Racing Associates and Bowes "Seal Fast" Corporation agree to purchase 220 Offy for $6500.00, payable to A. J. Foyt, Jr., or his estate.

4. A $10,000 life insurance policy on A. J. Foyt, Jr.

5. A. J. Foyt, Jr. agrees in consideration for the above mentioned $6500.00 to allow Bowes "Seal Fast" Corporation to use his name and picture in promoting their products during the year 1961.

6. Bowes "Seal Fast" Corporation agrees to furnish A. J. Foyt, Jr. with gasoline credit cards for use in his traveling in connection with the 220 Offy, and to furnish him uniforms and other necessary accessories used in connection with racing.

_____
A. J. Foyt, Jr.

_____
for Bowes "Seal Fast" Corporation

Witnesses:

Foyt's 1961 contract with Bowes Seal Fast provided for the purchase and expenses covering a "220 Offy" or sprint car for A.J. to drive. *Photograph by Ed Justice Jr.*

A.J. helps push the Trevis Offy down pit road at Indianapolis for the start of practice in 1961. *Revs Institute, The Bruce R. Craig Photograph Collection*

Foyt's 1961 win came while the front straight was still paved with bricks.
IMS Photography Archive

A victory lap with Lucy in 1961. *The Henry Ford, David Friedman Collection*

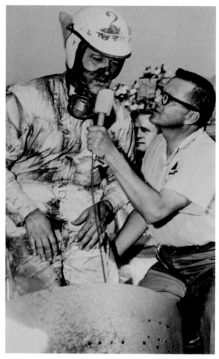

Foyt is interviewed in Victory Lane at Langhorne Speedway in 1963 by Chris Economaki. *Revs Institute, The Bruce R. Craig Photograph Collection*

A determined Foyt waits for the restart of the 1964 Indianapolis 500. *Revs Institute, The Tom Burnside Photograph Collection*

Foyt leads Parnelli Jones during the running of the 1964 Indianapolis 500.
Revs Institute, Robert Tronolone Photograph Collection

Foyt prepares for his first laps in a Lotus at Milwaukee in August 1964. Parnelli Jones is behind him in a second Lotus. Foyt would drop out on the first lap of the race, while Jones would go on to win. *Revs Institute, The Bruce R. Craig Photograph Collection, photograph by C.V. Haschel*

Foyt and Gurney were the two biggest names in the VW race and went in different directions at the start. Gurney was clearly in the fastest car, Foyt the slowest. That's when Gurney made a move that would establish their friendship. He fell back in the field, trying to provide a draft for Foyt. When that didn't work, he dropped behind A.J. and started pushing. Gurney knew what the others didn't: his car was illegal, equipped with aftermarket speed parts.[38]

"I was running dead last," Foyt recalled. "The car I had wouldn't outrun shit. Dan's was so much faster, and he pushed me past everybody because he had that much more horsepower."[39]

"I realized my car was much faster, and not wanting to take off, I decided to push A.J.," Gurney would say. "We'd come to a turn, and he'd shake his hand in the mirror, giving me the high sign to back off. Right before the checkered I blew by him and won the race. But they pulled my engine apart and found some parts that weren't the way they were supposed to be. I got disqualified and A.J. won the race."[40]

"They told me I'd won because they disqualified him," Foyt said. "Then they gave me the trophy. I'll never forget that."

He never would, and it proved to be a turning point in their relationship. Throughout his career Foyt returned kindness with loyalty—at least until he felt he'd been wronged. Gurney never crossed that line, and the pair would eventually share one of racing's great victories.

The victory didn't stop Foyt from giving a cringe-worthy interview to a local radio reporter that had the sponsoring tourist board wondering if the event was worth it.

"And how do you like Nassau A.J.?" the reporter asked.

"I've been better places," Foyt said.

When the startled reporter asked why he would say that, Foyt responded, "Because I've been in better places."

FAMILY MAN

The racing year finally over, Foyt returned to Houston victorious but exhausted. By his own estimate he'd spent nearly three hundred nights away from home for the second year in a row. He'd run fifty-eight feature events, driven thousands of test miles, and made a whirlwind trip to Europe. It took a toll on him, and he sounded like a man contemplating his future.

"That's just too much time away from my family," he said. "I've been going night and day, and frankly, I'm just plain tired. Driving is a harder life than people realize. I wouldn't want my son to live this way."[41]

Foyt's success on the track also focused unwanted attention on his family, whom he worked hard to shield and protect from the media. He talked about cutting back on his sprint car and midget racing in order to spend more time at home. Yet he was torn by the need to prove he was the best, week after week, no matter what the track or car. At times he was brutally frank in acknowledging his inner drive and its impact on his family.

"You have to love this business to get into it. And once you're in it, you love it so much, you fight like hell to stay in it. I've neglected everything for it, my education, my wife, my kids, my home. That's bad in one way, but it's the reason I'm on top too. I love racing. It's the only thing I've ever studied, the only thing I've ever really understood."[42]

Not everyone grasped what drove Foyt. One columnist joked A.J. would be spending the holidays in a hotel. Others took a darker look. Among those was Jack Kofoed, who wrote a popular general interest column for the *Miami Herald*.

"Foyt has an attractive wife and three children. Yet, he is so in love with the roaring road he rarely sees his family. The family worries itself sick every time the phone rang, figuring pop had had it. The man lives with a compulsion for speed. A compulsion as gripping as that of drugs or alcohol. No doubt in his particular way, Foyt loves his family, but it isn't the kind of love most women could live with. Worry and lonesomeness would kill it, just as the track sometime probably will kill A.J. Foyt."[43]

With those kinds of comments, it's little wonder Lucy was withdrawing further from the racing world and the media covering it. She'd been available to the press in the early years, but that was changing. She'd go to Indianapolis during the month of May and spend time with her good friend Mari Hulman George, but trips to other races were becoming increasingly rare. She'd never been a race fan and would sit in the grandstands reading a book until A.J. was on the track, then stay laser-focused on his car. Years later she often said she never worried about A.J. when he was racing, but in 1964 she felt differently.

"I suffer at the track," she admitted. "I always worry when A.J.'s racing. That's something you cannot help."[44]

"I don't want to be there nervously clutching a handkerchief before every race."[45]

The main reason she stayed home, however, was the children, dating back to the agreement she'd reached with A.J. shortly after Tony's birth. Now eight, Tony was considered old enough to attend a race, but he shied away from the track, frightened by a crash he'd seen several years earlier and complaining the cars were too loud. Daughter Terry, six, had no interest in racing, and when she broke her leg while A.J. was away racing late in 1964, Lucy worried what would have happened if she hadn't been home. Jerry was just two. They'd hired someone to help at home, but the three kids were becoming too much of a handful for either of the grandmothers to take care of when Lucy traveled. So she mostly stayed home.

It's not that Foyt completely neglected his home life. They moved into an eighty-thousand-dollar, four-bedroom home (easily a million-dollar home in 2024 dollars) spread out over four lots in one of Houston's toniest suburbs. There was a swimming pool in back and the driveway and garage were clogged with cars and motorcycles. Foyt owned five of each. There was no trophy room in the house, and with about seventy-five scattered around or in storage, Foyt found himself increasingly giving trophies away. Lucy also was being overwhelmed trying to maintain the scrapbooks of news clippings she'd kept on A.J. since early in their relationship.

"We spend a lot of time around the pool," she said. "A.J. is out of town racing most of the time and with the exception of occasional family visits, we spend plenty of time at home. I keep most of the clippings that I can find because A.J.

is very much interested in them. Fans and friends send us clippings and that helps a lot, but we can't get copies of them all."[46]

Most of Foyt's extended home time coincided with the Christmas holidays; always a festive time for A.J. and Lucy when they were growing up, they carried the tradition on with their family. The house served as a holiday gathering point for family and friends as Lucy oversaw the decorating and kept an ample supply of baked goods on hand. They seldom went out but entertained socially, A.J. often the life of the party. Always a sharp dresser away from the track or shop, he favored sports shirts, golf sweaters, and dress slacks, at times replacing his cowboy boots with expensive Italian alligator shoes.[47]

With the year coming to a close, Foyt left it to others to sum up his achievements in "The Year of Foyt," as the *Indianapolis Star* called it. He'd won in USAC's Indy cars, sprinters, and midgets, on paved tracks, dirt tracks, and road courses. He'd won in sports cars and stock cars, becoming the first non-NASCAR driver to win on the southern circuit.

He'd won a record four national Indy car championships in just five years. His seven consecutive champ car victories and ten in one season are both records that stand today (Al Unser would also win ten in 1971, but it took him more races to do it). He won $245,000 in USAC races and another fifty thousand dollars in outside competition, putting the total close to a record three hundred thousand dollars. That didn't include the appearance "expenses" paid by Agajanian, France, and others, nor the four-year, one-hundred-thousand-dollar contract he'd signed with Goodyear, the first driver to enter into such a deal.

In comparison, baseball's Willie Mays was the highest-salaried American athlete in 1964 at $105,000. Joe Namath, who'd led Alabama to the 1964 national championship, would stun the sporting world in January 1965 by signing a three-year, $427,000 contract with the upstart New York Jets of the American Football League, at that point the largest contract for a professional athlete. Brazilian soccer sensation Pelé was considered the world's highest-paid athlete at $150,000. Foyt had them all covered.[48]

Some tried to compare Foyt's accomplishments to those of other athletes.

"Foyt's ten championship wins in thirteen races is like a golfer winning ten of thirteen major tournaments, Willie Mays batting .770 on the season, and Johnny Unitas having a pass completion average of 77 percent," wrote Wilbur Adams, sports columnist for the *Sacramento Bee*. "His skill at the wheel has made him the all-time leading money winning driver in the history of American automobile racing."[49]

Years later Foyt would look back on the 1964 season and talk about it as a team effort. Long forgotten was the constant bickering between him and Bignotti and the harsh words for crew members. The burning desire to win, however, clearly remained.

"I felt like I was pretty good, but I had a good team, too. Bignotti and the crew were very good. When you've got a good combination going, I don't care if it is football, baseball, hockey or whatever it is, and you all get to clicking, it is hard to beat that kind of team.

"We all worked hard together on trying to win. That was our big deal, trying to win. Not run second. Like I used to say, 'You show me somebody that is happy about second and I will show you somebody that has never won a race.'"[50]

While many of the year-end stories focused on Foyt's remarkable season, it could not be overlooked that 1964 was also a horrific year on the racetracks. Seven drivers at the very top levels of the sport had been killed, four in USAC (Eddie Sachs, Dave MacDonald, Bill Horstmeyer, Bobby Marshman) and three in NASCAR (Joe Weatherly, Fireball Roberts, Jimmy Pardue). Countless others had died on the country's short tracks and around the world. Sachs, MacDonald, Roberts, Horstmeyer, and Marshman all died horrible deaths as a result of fiery crashes. Hurtubise, Foyt's closest friend among the drivers, was still recovering from his burns. Another friend and fellow Texan, Jim McElreath, also had been badly burned. As the country's most famous and visible racer, it again fell to Foyt to defend the sport.

"If I considered auto racing dangerous, I would quit," he said. "You can see persons hurt every day on the highways of our country. I just don't consider auto racing dangerous. Of course there are slips sometimes, but you are racing with competent drivers and they all know their business. But auto racing is a good, clean, honest sport."[51]

Foyt had yet to celebrate his thirtieth birthday and already he was the ultimate survivor, winning more races, championships, and money than anyone else. He seldom put a wheel wrong on the track and had never been involved in a major accident, nor badly hurt in a crash.

That was about to change.

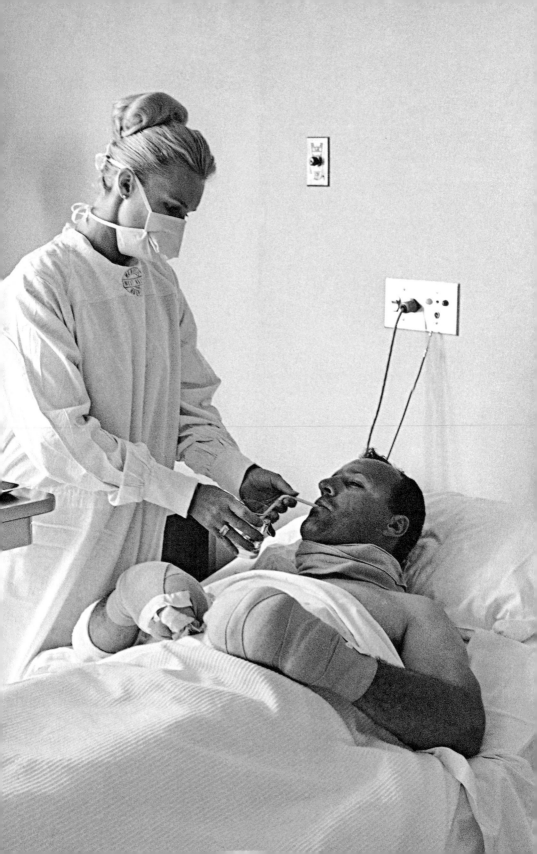

CHAPTER 18

SHEET TIME

1965

Although the calendar flipped to 1965, the sporting world was still debating who'd receive the Hickok Belt for 1964, presented annually to America's top professional athlete. Established in 1950 to honor Rae Hickok—a sports fan and founder of belt maker Hickok Manufacturing—first prize was an alligator belt with a solid gold buckle. The buckle was covered with diamond and gem chips and valued at ten thousand dollars.[1]

Voted on by journalists, past award winners were typically "mainstream" athletes, with baseball players winning belts in eight of the previous years. Sandy Koufax took the honor in 1963 and another pitcher, Bob Gibson of the St. Louis Cardinals, was considered one of the favorites for 1964, along with football's Johnny Unitas, golf's Ken Venturi, and basketball's Oscar Robertson. For the first time, a race car driver was part of the mix, and A.J. Foyt's accomplishments were generating significant support, although he was facing an uphill battle.

"It will be the biggest robbery since Brink's if it doesn't go to A.J. Foyt," wrote racing reporter Dave Overpeck in the *Indianapolis Star*. "The Texan dominated his sport as no man ever has before. He dominated auto racing like no man dominated ANY sport since Bobby Jones was the beginning and the end in golf in the '20s."[2]

"If A.J. was a baseball player or a football player or a golfer with this kind of record, he'd be a shoo-in for the Hickok belt. But A.J. is a race driver and that automatically puts two strikes against him. Unfortunately race drivers are often characterized as more akin to movie stuntmen than athletes. Too often the athletic skill and condition required in racing is forgotten."

Chief among the anti-racing journalists was Dick Young, the abrasive columnist of the *New York Daily News*, whose column was widely syndicated and read across

◀ Lucy always led the recovery team. *Associated Press Photo Archive*

the country. Young wrote with "all the subtlety of a knee in the groin," the *New York Times* said in his obituary.[3]

"If a bunch of kick-seekers want to risk their lives in a race for money, fine, go ahead," Young wrote. "If a bunch of sadists want to watch them break their necks, and maybe be cremated, that's all right too. Just don't go calling it a sport.

"It's dangerous, no doubt exciting to large numbers of people, and the driving of the cars requires a certain amount of sensitized reflexes. I just don't think that's enough to make it a sport, nor do I think that makes A.J. Foyt an athlete. It is the machine that does the job, not the driver."[4]

It was a polarizing subject, and even columnists for the same newspaper didn't agree.

"I am casting my vote for A.J. Foyt as the professional athlete of 1964," wrote Gene Ward in the *Daily News*. "It will be a sad miscarriage of justice and should be appealed all the way to the Supreme Court [if Foyt doesn't win].

"He [dominated] auto racing as it never had been dominated before. In fact, as no sport has been dominated in the memory of man. And . . . Foyt performs under the most pressure-cooker conditions an athlete can be called on to face— the ever-present threat to life. A.J. Foyt is a pro athlete if there ever was one, the very best of the breed in the year 1964. I make him my winner of the Hickok belt hands down and a whole hoot-and-a-holler ahead of all other contenders."[5]

Another with a vote and lobbying for Foyt was Hank Hollingworth, the executive sports editor of the *Long Beach Independent Press-Telegram* in California. "Few men in history ever dominated a sport so completely as did Foyt. The men in his trade say he is destined to go down in sports history as a legend in his time. One gentleman boasts credentials that history may never view again and thus he will be our choice."[6]

Car owner and promoter J.C. Agajanian was especially outspoken. "In my 30 years of auto racing and promotion of the sport, Foyt has achieved the greatest record. It isn't conceivable in my mind, with the competition that he has had, that a record such as his will ever be equaled. He has competed in all types of racing and on all types of tracks. Few take on all-comers in this game. If Foyt wins the award, I know he would be beating out quite a few of the greatest men in sports today. It is also a fact that a race driver has never before received this tremendous honor. If this young guy from Texas doesn't receive some sort of national acclaim for his 1964 feats, no one in the sport ever will."[7]

Despite the efforts of Agajanian and the writers, Foyt finished second to a surprise winner, Jim Brown of the Cleveland Browns and the National Football League. Virtually unmentioned in pre-vote stories, he'd led the Browns to a stunning upset win over Unitas and the Baltimore Colts in the NFL championship game on December 27, and the effort was still fresh in the memory of many voters. It was the closest tally ever: Brown totaling 161 points to Foyt's 154. The driver received significantly more first-place votes—thirty-eight to twenty-six for Brown—but as feared, some writers, who cast votes on a 3-2-1 basis, refused to vote for Foyt.[8]

Foyt gave no indication he was aware of the hubbub surrounding the Hickok award, although he'd eventually weigh in on the question of whether or not drivers were athletes.

"I've watched a lot of football games, and you know a player gets a rest whenever the coach thinks he needs one. When you start a 500-mile race, you don't have no rest periods. It's just a man and a machine. You call all the shots yourself. The biggest thing is just concentrating for three or four hours. You don't have anybody sending in the plays. Take a baseball pitcher. He can have a bad day and if his team's hitting, you can still win. If a driver's having a bad day, he has no chance of winning anything."[9]

BACK TO WORK

As they had in recent years, Elmer and Mari George visited the Foyts the week after Christmas, and the two families watched the New Year's Day college bowl games together, especially the Cotton Bowl in nearby Dallas. Then it was time to get back to work and Foyt headed for the Phoenix racetrack and a Goodyear tire test, his vacation having lasted exactly one month.

He still planned on cutting back his sprint car and midget schedule and suddenly found himself without a NASCAR ride. Chrysler announced it was pulling out of the stock car series after the organization banned the Hemi engine. Ray Nichels would run his Dodges in USAC but not NASCAR. As a result, Foyt had no car for the first race of the year, the Riverside 500.

The trip to Phoenix was part of his new deal with Goodyear to test and develop tires for the Indy car circuit. He was driving the same Halibrand he'd used at Phoenix the past November, now equipped with the Ford DOHC engine. George Bignotti was continuing to work on the year-old Lotus. Colin Chapman had warned them the Lotus 34 would need significant updating to handle the more powerful Ford engine, and the crew chief was working to stiffen and strengthen the car. Yet to arrive was the Lola chassis.[10]

The test team insisted on using an alcohol/methanol fuel blend instead of gasoline in the Ford. There'd been no pushback; Bobby Marshman's fiery crash and death had ended discussions on the use of gasoline.

The test was barely underway on Tuesday, January 5, when one of the Goodyear reps was called to the telephone. He returned ashen and with terrible news. Billy Wade was dead. He'd been killed driving a stock car during a Goodyear NASCAR tire test at Daytona. Any hope that a new year would end the string of racing deaths had been quickly dashed.

While friends from Foyt's early days of racing in the Houston area in the early 1950s, Wade, five years older and starting a family, had been content to dominate the Houston jalopy and stock car racing scene, including three track championships at Meyers Speedway. It wasn't until he won the modified championship in 1961 in a car built by Tony Foyt that he decided to give NASCAR a try, moving his wife and four daughters to Spartanburg, South Carolina, and earning 1963 Rookie of the Year honors. He won four consecutive races in 1964, was extremely popular with fans and drivers, and seemed on the verge of becoming a NASCAR star.[11]

Just five foot seven and 148 pounds, Foyt called Wade "Mighty Mite" early in their careers and the nickname stuck. Like Foyt, he'd been in Houston over the holidays, although the pair failed to connect when Wade went to Daytona as a last-minute replacement for a driver who'd been injured in an earlier test.

Foyt called a reporter looking for more information, but details were sketchy. Wade was the only car on the track and lapping at about 170 miles per hour when the right-front tire blew going into Turn One, shooting him up the thirty-two-degree banking and into the track's new concrete wall. The impact tore the seat from its moorings and his shoulder harness was unbuckled.

The diminutive driver was known for not liking to wear a harness, and although required in NASCAR races since the death of Joe Weatherly, it was unclear if Wade was wearing his during the test. Some thought a first responder may have unbuckled the harness. The car also was not equipped with a fifth belt that Foyt and some drivers were starting to use, a so-called "crotch" or "submarine belt," designed to keep a driver from sliding forward in a frontal impact.

"You won't find a better guy than Billy," Foyt told the reporter. "He was a real buddy to me. He had everything it took to make a great driver. This year, he was going to make it big."[12]

While Wade was the third driver killed during tire testing within five months, Foyt decided to continue at Phoenix, as the tires were completely different than those used at Daytona. Near the end of the session, he was approached by a Goodyear engineer. Although Ford would face no Chrysler challengers at the upcoming Riverside stock car race, Goodyear and Firestone were very much in the middle of a NASCAR tire war. As a result of Wade's death, a Goodyear-equipped Ford stock car was available. Was Foyt interested?

"I kinda liked Riverside," Foyt recalled thinking, having raced both stock cars and sports cars there in the past. "It was a dangerous racetrack, but I liked it. So I said fine."[13]

RIVERSIDE, 1965

While a road course, the most dramatic feature of Riverside International Race-way was the 1.1-mile back straightaway that doubled as a drag strip, the first half of which was downhill. Stock cars topped 150 mph before braking hard for Turn Nine, a nearly flat 180-degree right-hander, bringing the course back to the pit straight and the start/finish line. The outside of the turn was guarded by boilerplate steel guardrails backed by sunken telephone poles. Nine drivers had been killed at the track since it opened in 1957, four of them in Turn Nine.

Foyt's ride was a new Ford Galaxie, built and entered by Holman-Moody, "one of the most powerful forces in racing in the 1960s." In addition to building most of Ford's stock cars for other teams, it ran its own two-car operation and was getting involved with Ford's sports car program. It was both the front and back door to Ford's stock car racing operations with Ralph Moody, a former NASCAR driver, running things at the track and John Holman overseeing the business operations.[14]

For Riverside, Foyt was paired with team leader Fred Lorenzen and newcomer Dick Hutcherson, a rookie making the jump from IMCA and ARCA. Lorenzen was one of NASCAR's elites and a bit standoffish, but A.J. immediately bonded with Hutcherson. It was the first step in a relationship that would grow and prosper in the years ahead.

Foyt's car was No. 00, which raised eyebrows as it looked the same upside down as it did right side up, considered unlucky by some. Foyt wasn't concerned, asking only that a submarine belt be added to the safety harness, a request Moody, who'd pushed NASCAR to adopt the feature, was only too willing to meet.

Dan Gurney and Foyt turned in the two fastest times during practice, both breaking the track record, but they were relegated to starting eleventh and twelfth as the speeds came a day too late for the pole. After celebrating his thirtieth birthday the night before the race, Foyt chased Gurney from the start. The pair worked their way through the field and into the top spots when Parnelli Jones, who'd led early, dropped out. From there Gurney and Foyt battled nose to tail, Foyt pulling alongside at times, but never able to complete a pass, eventually spinning and falling behind the leader.

Gurney pulled away to a fifty-second lead with only twenty laps remaining when a caution flag bunched the field as allowed under NASCAR's rules. Gurney's teammate Marvin Panch was second, followed by Junior Johnson and Foyt. There was time for one more run at the leader.

Pulling to the inside of Johnson at the end of the backstraight on lap 169 of the 185-lap race, Foyt waited until the last moment to brake for Turn Nine. He'd struggled with the new self-adjusting brakes throughout the race and this time "the pedal went clear to the floor." He tried pumping the brakes to build pressure without success and then considered trying to make the turn but, he said, "I knew I'd take Johnson and Panch with me if I did."[15]

"I wondered what happened," Johnson said. "[Foyt] came shootin' by me forty miles an hour faster than I was going."[16]

Foyt veered to the inside of the course, where the ground dropped thirty-five feet away from the track surface so quickly and steeply it was known as the "Turn Nine Canyon." The car left the track at an estimated 100 mph and flew about forty feet in the air before disappearing into the canyon. The first impact popped the windshield out of the car and kicked up a huge dirt cloud, the car emerging in a series of rapid end-over-end flips. The Galaxie stopped just short of the track, pointing at the middle of Turn Nine, having carried so much speed it nearly hit the cars Foyt was trying to avoid. Panch would say he felt the impact of the car's final flip.

"I was watching from the pits and I could see right away what he was trying to do," said Leonard Wood of the Wood Brothers team and co-owner of the cars driven by Gurney and Panch. "His car just started cartwheeling. It was a terrible accident. He went so far he nearly came back up on the track and hit Panch."[17]

The first to arrive at the car found Foyt unconscious, covered in dirt, and hanging limp but secure in his seat. Someone supposedly told others not to rush, the driver was dead. The wreck quickly attracted a crowd and another person noticed movement in the cockpit. A Holman-Moody crewman arrived on the run and climbed into the car, asking Foyt if he was okay. He nodded, dazed and unable to talk, but very much alive.[18]

One of the myths surrounding Foyt—and Jones—is that Parnelli was the first to spot movement, climbed in the car, and cleared dirt from Foyt's mouth so he could breathe. Extensive media reports of the day mentioned only the Holman-Moody crew member and early biographies of Jones make no mention of the incident. With good reason. Jones says it never happened.

After dropping out of the race, Parnelli was watching from the entrance of Pit Road, near the exit of Turn Nine. Like others, "he ran to see what he could do, which amounted to watching the rescue crew extricate Foyt and load him in an ambulance." No one knows how or why the story of his expanded role in the rescue started.[19]

Foyt says he'd obviously heard and repeated the Jones story, but was in and out of consciousness and has no actual recall of the accident's immediate aftermath. "The only thing I could hear was a strange wheezing, then I realized it was my gasping for air," Foyt said. "That's all I remember." He did recall the moments before the crash in various accounts over the years.

"You don't exactly reason it out," he said soon after the crash. "Hell almighty, there's no time for debate. If you've been doin' this thing for a while, you get the picture right away and you react, almost by instinct.

"Maybe I could have missed Johnson, but not Panch. If I'd of hit him from behind, I'd have rode him up into the wall. I might've gotten away with it, but I don't think he could've. I didn't think I could cut underneath them and stay on the track, but that's what I figured I had to do, so wham, away I went. I hit a bump though and got airborne. That's about all I remember."[20]

Taken to Riverside Community Hospital, initial reports that evening downplayed Foyt's condition, saying he'd suffered a "foot injury, cut hand" and had some chest pain. Those coming to check on him discovered otherwise. Richard Petty was one of the first to arrive at the hospital. He'd been unable to drive in the race because of the Chrysler boycott, driving the pace car instead.

"It was a bad wreck," said Petty, who was on his way to the Los Angeles airport. "Before we flew out, me and Dale [Inman, Petty's cousin and crew chief] went by to see him at the hospital and he was pretty beat up. It looked bad. But he's a hard head."[21]

Jones and Agajanian also visited the hospital. The heavily sedated Foyt remembered little of those first hours, only that he was desperate to reach his mother, who'd recently suffered a heart attack. He wanted to assure her that he was okay.

"I remember coming to in the hospital, not really coming to, but off and on. I kept saying I need to talk to my momma. They finally got her on the phone and she said, 'Ah honey, are you real bad off?' And I said, 'Momma, I'm fine. I'm bruised up pretty good, but I just wanted you to hear my voice. I'm fine. Now I'm tired and I'm sleepy and I'll talk to you later,' and I went back out."[22]

It wasn't until later in the week that the extent of Foyt's injuries was known. Lucy arrived from Houston to find the left side of his face and chin scraped and cut where his helmet twisted during the crash. He had two black eyes. He complained about pain in his lower extremities and she gasped when she lifted the sheet. He was black and purple from the waist down. The submarine belt had worked, but had left its mark.

Another round of X-rays discovered that he'd cracked his ninth vertebra in addition to the compound heel fracture. The broken back had been hidden in earlier X-rays by swelling and was the cause of the pain. He was also diagnosed with a bruised aorta. He'd been lucky, doctors said—an inch or two either way and he'd have been paralyzed, or worse. They said the upcoming races at Daytona were out, and Phoenix and Trenton were doubtful. Even Indianapolis was questionable.[23]

It took ten days for Foyt to convince the Riverside doctors he could travel. Ford sent one of its company planes to move him to Houston, where he entered Memorial Hospital. It was another ten days before doctors there let him go home.[24]

It was Foyt's first extended "sheet time," as he called hospital stays. Once at home, Lucy discovered what doctors and nurses already knew.

"He is a horrible patient," she said. "Horrible. It was like, God, I'd almost rather do this myself. I'm a lot better patient than him. He's no fun when he's sick. If I could send him off, that's what I would have liked to do. But he always got home as soon as he could."[25]

He spent much of the downtime studying for his pilot's license. Part of his deal with Goodyear included the use of an airplane, and there was a new Beechcraft Bonanza waiting for him. Feeling hemmed in by the rapid growth of Houston and saying "I want to have something else to do" other than racing, he purchased a ranch in Hockley, an unincorporated area about thirty-five miles northwest of downtown Houston and, at the time, in the middle of nowhere. He'd spend long hours at the ranch working alongside his daddy, which would become a favorite part of his rehab routine and a vital part of his life in the decades to come.[26]

Film footage of the Riverside crash was featured in the opening credits of the movie *Red Line 7000*, which premiered in late 1965. "I tried to stop them from using it, but I guess because I'm a public figure they could," he'd say. It didn't help that Ford was involved in the movie, and had supplied many of the cars and much of the racing footage.[27]

Although he passed a physical allowing him to race in the Phoenix Indy car event, A.J. was vague regarding his plans, and news reports varied on if he intended to compete in the USAC opener. Waiting for him when he arrived at the track was the Lotus, resplendent in a new pearl white Dean Jeffries paint job, accented by a red, white, and blue nose similar to the 1964 roadster.

It had been completely reworked by Bignotti and Lujie Lesovsky, one of the best body and chassis men in the business. The pair strengthened everything from the body shell to the suspension, using stronger steel and heat treating many of the components. Bignotti said only the steering arms, wheels, disc brakes, and rear sway bar remained from the original car. It came at a cost, adding 50 pounds to the car.[28]

"You won't be able to tell it from last year's Lotus-Ford," Lesovsky said, "but the car is 95 percent new."[29]

"It's been Americanized," Foyt said. "Let's just call it a Lotus-Lesovsky."[30]

He couldn't help but brag about his recovery, saying, "The doctors tell me nobody has recovered from that type of break so fast. They said I could probably go on my head again without any extra risk to my back."[31]

He wasn't the only driver returning to the track; so was Jim Hurtubise, completing his recovery from life-threatening burns just seven months earlier. Missing from the field was Jones. His team was still awaiting parts from Lotus in England.

Any question about Foyt being ready to return was answered when he qualified on the pole and took the lead at the start of the race. But Rodger Ward passed him after eleven laps, followed by Mario Andretti and others. He eventually parked the car, the rear sway bar broken.[32]

"That damned bracket was one of the few original limey parts that we didn't bother to change," Bignotti said, promising to replace them for Indianapolis.[33]

A week later Foyt was in Atlanta, where he planned to get back in a stock car for the first time since Riverside. A new Holman-Moody Ford was waiting for him, to be crewed by the Wood Brothers. Moody said he doubted Foyt would be able to drive the whole race. A 150-miler at Phoenix was one thing. Five hundred miles on a high-banked track like Atlanta was another.[34]

Even Foyt acknowledged the challenge. "We'll just have to see how I'll do over that distance."[35]

Unlike his first appearance at the track, he was warmly welcomed back by many in the NASCAR garage. Among the first to spot him was Johnson.

"Thanks for not runnin' over my ass, Cassius," Johnson said. Few dared to call Foyt "Cassius" to his face. To most Foyt was Tex, Super Tex to some—mostly those who didn't know him well—and to his crew he was simply "boss." Gurney also called him Cassius and Foyt seemed to embrace the moniker.[36]

"That's what we call drivers who do something spectacular," he laughed. "The doctors said I wouldn't make it here to Atlanta. Carroll Shelby said I wouldn't make it to Indianapolis. And Chris Economaki just thought I wouldn't make it. And you know something, after I saw films of the wreck, I didn't even think I'd make it."[37]

Not everyone thought he should be back on the track. Panch, the regular Wood Brothers driver, told a reporter, "The pain's so bad, he can't sleep nights. He shouldn't be driving again, but he won't admit it." Foyt caught a break and additional recovery time when the rain postponed the race for a week.[38]

Eventually qualifying sixth at Atlanta, and despite promising to "take it easy," Foyt moved into second place behind Panch before the race was a third old. Then he suddenly shot past his teammate and up into the wall, the result of a sticking throttle. He was able to regain control and shut down the engine, his race over.[39]

Or so he thought. After explaining what happened to the Wood Brothers, he was packing his uniform in the garage area when Glen Wood sent word Panch needed relief. Despite dominating the race, he was complaining of a painful neck and the heat, with temperatures in the mid-80s. Foyt ran back to Panch's pit and took over on lap 212 of the 334-lap event. Back in the race, he had more than a lap lead and was never challenged.

"I was beginning to believe this was a hex year," Foyt said. "I quit sprint cars because my family and friends said they were too dangerous—switched to the *safe* stock cars. Well I done near got killed in a stock car. Today, when the throttle stuck in the first car, I almost went out of the park. I said to myself, here I go with another Riverside. It made me gun shy."[40]

Buoyant after returning to Victory Lane, Foyt entered a pair of races the following weekend, including a sprint car event at Reading, Pennsylvania. He was brought back to earth when he failed to qualify because of mechanical problems. He put the Lotus on the pole for the Trenton Indy car race the next day and led twenty-five early laps before being sidelined with transmission problems.

With the Lotus continuing to prove fragile and the Lola yet to arrive, Foyt insisted on entering his roadster in the 500, even though it was slated to be on display at a children's museum during May. Absent from the Sheraton-Thompson Indy entries was the Halibrand, which Foyt had deemed too frail for the Speedway.

POLE WINNER

The accidents and mechanical problems had Foyt in a bad mood when he arrived in Indianapolis. Things got worse when he discovered the Lola was still a no-show, more than a month overdue. Also yet to arrive were the new and stronger ZF transmissions, being shipped from Germany. When officials announced additional changes would be required to the Lotus steering box in the name of safety, he exploded, barking at everyone in sight. His reputation took a hit, but he didn't care.

"A lot of guys, reporters, photographers and racing fans, think I'm a real bad guy when I won't stop and pose for pictures or interviews or sign autographs," he said. "I'll do those things for anybody at the right time. When I pull that car out on the apron to run, or I'm working on it over in the garage, I just can't stop or drop everything to be a nice guy. I've got a job to do."[41]

When a reporter overheard Foyt saying he might retire if the team didn't get the Lotus straightened out, A.J. found himself explaining the comment the next day.

"I said in a joking way that I was thinking of retiring if I couldn't get my funny car to run safely. But then I've told some reporters hello and been misquoted."[42]

When he finally did take to the track, A.J. found himself chasing Jimmy Clark's new Lotus 38. Foyt had just run his fastest lap of the month on Wednesday, May 5, when his car veered right exiting Turn Two and hit the outside wall, sheering off the right-rear wheel. The car was airborne for a moment, thumping back to the track and going on a long slide, coming to rest against the inside fence. Although he'd spun cars in the past at the Speedway, it was the first time he'd hit a wall. He immediately thought of his back.

"I laid my back against the seat as straight as I could," Foyt said. "When I hit the wall, the first thing I did was try and move my legs and I said, 'Oh God I can move!'"[43]

His next thoughts were of fire, and he ripped his uniform and skinned his knee scrambling to get out of the car before it came to a stop.

"I told myself this thing may be on fire, but it's not going to be Foyt that's burning. I had my seat belt undone when that thing hit the inside wall."

He called the car "unsanitary," which drew the ire of Bignotti. Thinking the transmission had failed, he said, "I'll never drive another one of these cars until we get some gears in them. These were special gears we had made for this car, but they're just not built to handle the 500 horsepower this engine produces."[44]

Car owner William Ansted indicated the team's original plan was to race the Lola. "A.J. says the thing isn't safe and I don't blame him a bit for thinking that. He hadn't planned to qualify the Lotus anyway."[45]

The next day it was determined the crash was caused by a failed rear hub carrier, which helps connect a wheel to the suspension. The discovery set off a wave of finger pointing with Agajanian complaining the hub carriers came directly from Lotus. The English company countered that its older cars had been "extensively altered in private hands." Because the cars were heavier and had increased torsional stiffness, Lotus warned "some components may be operating at stresses in excess of their designed conditions."[46]

Until the hub carriers were strengthened or new ones made, USAC decided to park all the Lotuses—old and new—along with the Lolas for good measure. It didn't take long, as Clark was back on the track in less than a day. Jones also took his Lotus out, but had a wheel come off while warming up.

Foyt wandered down to Jones's garage to check on the car and driver. Sitting in the corner was "Calhoun," Jones's 1963 race-winning roadster. It hadn't been driven since the explosion during the pit stop in the 1964 race, and while the crew swarmed around the broken Lotus, Foyt climbed into Calhoun.

"If you'll drive yours, I'll drive mine," he said when Jones walked in. "Let's don't even paint 'em. Won't that make 'em mad, to get beat by a roadster with a year-old paint job."[47]

Jones asked where A.J.'s "Old Faithful" was. Foyt said he didn't know, but when reminded it was still on display at the Children's Museum, he wondered "if they'd consider a trade for [his] Lotus."

Despite the moaning and groaning, by Thursday, May 13, there was nothing but smiles as Foyt, in the Lotus, turned his fastest laps ever on the track at more than 161 mph. Later in the day he took the Lola, which had finally arrived, out for a few laps and then parked it, saying there wasn't enough time to sort out the car. He'd qualify the Lotus.

Foyt also announced he'd be using Goodyear tires, the culmination of three years of development work. The tire company was hedging its bets, backing a new team formed by Gurney and Shelby called All American Racers (AAR) and running a new Lotus 38. Team Lotus, which had tested both Goodyear and Firestone tires, said it would use Firestones, as did Jones.

For the first time, the Speedway used a blind draw to determine the qualifying order, and Foyt drew the fourteenth spot, while Clark was thirty-first or last among the drivers expected to make an attempt. Foyt's car was late arriving on pit lane, however, and moved to the end of the line behind Clark. He gave several different reasons for the delay, eventually admitting he'd been "stalling" in order to be put at the back so he could see what time he needed to beat. The delay was not without risk. Rain was in the forecast, and if it arrived before he could take to the track, it would wash away his chance of capturing the pole or even starting up front.[48]

The rain stayed away and, in one of the most exciting pole position days in Speedway history, the more than 150,000 spectators had already heard track announcer Tom Carnegie's famous call of "It's a new track record!" twice, as first rookie Andretti and then Clark set qualifying marks.

Among the throng in Gasoline Alley and in the pits was Charlie Gray, who was overseeing Ford's drag-racing programs. He'd been at Indianapolis Raceway Park's drag strip and decided to visit the Speedway for qualifying. He was surprised to see Connie Kalitta, known as the "Bounty Hunter," who was the driver of a Ford-powered Top Fuel dragster.

"Foyt rolled his car onto Pit Lane and you could smell the nitro," Gray recalled. "I asked Connie what he was doing there and he said he'd been working with A.J. on his fuel blend. They were both really good with fuel. As soon as A.J. started that engine, oh man, it starts cackling. Everybody was crying because of all the nitro in the air. But the thing held together for four laps."[49]

Foyt says he doesn't remember getting help from Kalitta, but aided by the special witch's brew of methanol and nitro, he set one- and four-lap records, claiming his first Indianapolis pole position. He was joined on the front row by Clark and Gurney, with Andretti and Jones on the second row.

"I wanted to bring the honors back to the United States," a beaming Foyt said, twice referring to Clark as a "furriner." He admitted to "sandbagging all week" and said he could have gone faster, if not for a mix-up with his crew, which caused his first and fastest lap to be missed. He also complained about his engine being down a few rpm and admitted if he'd gone before Clark, he probably wouldn't have accepted the time.[50]

Foyt often listed the pole run as "one of [my] biggest memories. He [Clark] was on Firestone and we were on Goodyears and it made us real happy."[51]

The next day a new Foyt roamed the pits, reveling in the attention afforded a pole winner. The "non-cooperative" Foyt was gone, replaced by the affable and relaxed Foyt. He looked ready to hit the Speedway's golf course in his light blue slacks and sports shirt, posing for photos and signing autographs. He walked out to Turn One, one of his favorite vantage points, and chatted casually with fans. Word got back to him that Clark was upset about the "furriner" comments.[52]

"Aw shucks, I was just kidding," he said. In reality, Clark was the one foreign driver he'd come to respect. "He drove hard, but he drove clean, and I had a lot of respect for him because he raced at Milwaukee and Trenton, too. He was kind of quiet, not a smart ass or a jerk. Yeah, we were rivals, but I liked him — and I wasn't real fond of the Brits."

Clark wasn't around to hear Foyt's semi-apology. He was back in England, where Queen Elizabeth presented him with the Order of the British Empire (OBE), a step on the way to knighthood.

The playfulness lasted one day. On the track Monday with a full load of fuel to test fuel economy and tire wear, Foyt was in the pits with chunking tires before the run was completed. Several other Goodyear-shod cars experienced similar problems. It didn't help when a Goodyear representative said the company may have to withdraw its tires from the race.

Foyt also used more fuel than expected in the short run and that worried him more than the tires. He'd done the development work and run hundreds of miles on the tires. It was probably a manufacturing problem that could be corrected. But the fuel usage was troubling. If he needed to make more than the two required pit stops, his chance at back-to-back wins was gone.

By Tuesday the uncooperative Foyt was back—and then some. He chased a *Sports Illustrated* reporter out of his garage. "Get your ass out of here and keep your god damn paper out of here too," he yelled before explaining to others present, "The bastard wrote something bad about me."[53]

His mood swings were beginning to have an impact on his relationships with reporters.

"As far as the press is concerned, the fellow ranks as a genuine cad," wrote Rich Roberts in a biting column in the *Long Beach Independent Press-Telegram*. He'd often talked with Foyt in the past when J.C. Agajanian was promoting an Ascot event, but this was different. "He's the toughest interview, the hardest to get along with, and the most difficult to catch. Possibly the only thing bigger than the Houston Astrodome is Foyt's swelled head.

"He's always been that way," Roberts wrote, quoting another writer who asked to remain anonymous. "He was pretty cocky when he came out of Texas, but then when he made his success, it really made him difficult. He's just a very obstinate s.o.b. You want to write a column on him? If you do, just write that he's a bastard."

As expected, Goodyear quickly identified a production problem and started building replacement tires. The fuel economy situation was more challenging. At first Foyt said he'd run on gasoline, surprising many as he'd been an adamant opponent since the previous year's fires. After running some slower laps using gasoline, he again changed his mind, saying he'd add another fuel tank to his car so it could carry the maximum seventy-five gallons of methanol, reminding some of Foyt's initial comments comparing the original Lotus to "lying in a bathtub of gasoline."[54]

The other option was a blend of about 80 percent alcohol and 20 percent gasoline. The trick was getting the engine set just right to operate on the blend. Foyt's first test ended quickly with a sticking throttle. Told it was fixed, he went back on the track but lasted less than a lap before he was forced to pull off on the backstraight with the same problem. Back in the garage Foyt erupted. In a flashback to 1962, he and Bignotti exchanged barbs.[55]

Having an even tougher time was Jones, who crashed his Lotus during practice, although damage to the car could be repaired in time for the race. X-rays showed a slight neck fracture for Jones but doctors said he could race—if he wanted to.

Foyt also spent time in the Lola, preparing it for another driver to qualify. He'd originally offered it to NASCAR's Lorenzen, who decided to stick with stock cars. When Hurtubise destroyed his rear-engine car in practice, Foyt talked with him about the Lola, but Herk said he felt more at home—and safer—in a Novi. Bobby Unser put in a good word for his younger brother, Al. There were other options. Fellow Texan Lloyd Ruby was looking for a car, having crashed his in practice and unsure if it could be repaired in time for the race. Ward was having all sorts of trouble getting the new rear-engine Watson up to speed. Both of those drivers were potential race winners in the Lola. Instead, Foyt made a surprising choice.[56]

AL UNSER

Al Unser figured he'd blown his last chance at making the Indianapolis 500 when the engine in his Weisman-Maserati, hyped with nitro, exploded during Saturday practice on the final qualifying weekend. He'd scrambled from the car while it was still moving and watched it burn before the fire crew could put it out. Not that it mattered, it was the team's third and last engine. He made a last-ditch run in another one-of-a-kind car, an Eisert-Chevrolet, but was unable to get it up to qualifying speed.

Now he was packing up his gear to return home to Albuquerque. He didn't have enough money to stay and watch his brother Bobby drive a Novi in the 500 a week away. He'd never been so dejected. Ten other rookies were already in the field.

That's when Foyt walked through the door of Unser's garage. He paused for a moment and looked around, his eyes adjusting to the light. The two had never met, although they'd been at the same track many times. When he spotted Unser, he walked over and stuck out his hand.

"I was in the garage with my head between my legs because I thought I was through," Unser recalled. "In those days when you missed the show at the Speedway, you were put on the back burner. You weren't thought about again.

"He said, 'Al Unser?' And I said, 'Yes sir.' He said, 'I got my Lola and I'm willing to put you in it. Come over to my shop if you want to drive it.' He walked out the door and I walked out touching his back. I wasn't stupid. I was a young kid, but I don't have to be knocked in the head to take that deal."[57]

Bignotti was upset when Foyt returned with a rookie driver. He wanted one of the veterans in the car. "George was against it," Unser recalled. "He told Foyt to go hire another driver. Foyt said it was his team, his car, and he'd hire whoever he wanted. He said, 'Leave us alone, George.' Bignotti would have nothing to do with me after that. I just tried to stay out of the way."

Foyt took the car out first, to show Unser it was capable of qualifying speeds. After several laps between 153 and 155 mph, it was Unser's turn. After running about twenty laps at just under 150 mph, right on the borderline for qualifying, Foyt waved him in from the pit wall. He told the crew to take the car back to the garage. He wanted them to make a few changes and then refuel it.

Unser said he remembered it "like yesterday. We went back to his garage and I'm sitting on the bench and he said, 'Are you ready to go?' I thought I was gonna pass out. I was surprised he had that much confidence in me. I said yes sir. What are you gonna say?"[58]

Foyt grabbed a sheet of paper and sketched out a crude map of the track. Then he launched into a five-minute Brickyard 101 lecture.

"He said, 'Don't do anything different than what I'm telling you to do,'" Unser recalled years later. "He drew the whole course out. In those days you had to lift going into all the corners. Not like it is today where you run wide open."

Foyt said, "The secret of this place is driving deep into the corners and getting back on the throttle quick. Use the power. Under power you can do almost anything."[59]

Coming down the front straight, Foyt wanted Unser next to the outside wall—no more than a foot or two off the barrier. There were braking markers on the fence for reference points approaching the first turn, 3-2-1. Unser should back off after passing the second sign. He'd be going about 190 mph at that point, and Foyt warned, "It gets to looking awful narrow."

Foyt told Unser to diamond the corners, to touch the brake slightly to settle the car and turn smoothly into the turn. Take it down to the white line at the apex—a wheel inside was okay—while getting back on the throttle and letting the car drift back up to the wall between one and two, before turning back down the track to the Turn Two apex and then hard on the accelerator onto the backstraight.

"I have no definite point to get back on it," Foyt said. "It's as soon as possible, according to how the car feels."

Turn Three "gives me the most trouble because of the wind," which he said "moved me all over the track" during his qualifying run. He said to check the wind sock above the grandstands while driving down the backstraight.

"The wind is normally blowing across the curve from the southwest," Foyt said. "I pinch the car in a little more and hold it to keep the wind from pushing me out. It pushes real strong here," he said of an alley between the grandstands on the inside of the track, which funneled the wind across the turn. He said to let the car slide out to the wall again between three and four, ease off the accelerator for a moment, then go hard over the bump in Turn Four, letting it release to the wall.[60]

"Let the car go here," he said of the Turn Four exit. "Pull it back and the car gets excited."

Told the Lola was ready to go, Foyt decided to push it directly into the qualifying line. If something went wrong during the first attempt, there'd be time for a second run. If Unser went out and practiced first, there'd be time for only one attempt.

Whether it was the lesson on driving the Speedway, changes to the car, or perhaps a little added nitro, Unser needed only one attempt, easily turning his fastest laps of the month, including one at just under 156 mph. He'd be starting back in thirty-second because he qualified on the last day, but he was in the 500.

"Without him taking the chance on me, I probably would have never made it," Unser said. "I often wonder why he asked me. He had probably fifteen drivers trying to get that ride and he walks over and offers it to me, a rookie."[61]

Foyt made another addition to his team, Unser's brother Lloyd, who'd worked as a mechanic on his other cars.

"The man has a kind heart and an eye for talent," Al Unser said. "I'm not trying to brag about myself, take me out of it. Foyt always had a knack about putting good people around him. It opened doors for me and the next year Andy Granatelli and Chapman hired me for Team Lotus. I would have never got it without the Foyt ride."

It's hard to imagine Al Unser not eventually making it at the Speedway even if he didn't qualify in 1965, but it's something he firmly believed. He'd go on to match Foyt's four Indy 500 victories and record ten wins in a single year. His thirty-nine Indy car victories, ironically many in later years with Bignotti as his crew chief, rank sixth overall. He proved himself a winner in multiple cars, including sprint, stock, sports cars, and the IROC series, and Foyt often pointed to Unser as his toughest challenger. Both Unser and his son, Al Unser Jr., would drive for and with Foyt in the future.

On July 20, 2021, nearly two months after Hélio Castroneves became the fourth driver to win four Indianapolis 500s, he joined the other three members of the special fraternity—A.J. Foyt, Al Unser, and Rick Mears—at the Speedway for a special roundtable interview session and film.

Unser had lost weight and looked gaunt. His brother Bobby had died earlier in the year. Al had been quietly battling cancer for nearly twenty years, and few people knew it was back. Those who did were surprised he had traveled to the Speedway.

"I only came because *you're* here," Unser told Foyt before the session. The comment and obvious sincerity surprised Foyt and for a moment he stumbled for words. "Well, I gave you your start—so don't forget it," he said. Al laughed and patted him on the shoulder. "I know it," he said. "Boy I know it."[62]

Unser died a few months later, on December 9, 2021. Reached in Texas by an Indianapolis television station, Foyt gave an emotional response.

"I lost a damned good friend," he said, his voice cracking. "What I liked about Al was that he didn't blow his horn that much, but he was a helluva race car driver. I would rather have a friend of mine be a four-time winner than someone I don't like—and Al was a good friend of mine, so I was happy he made it. You had to take care of a car back then and Al knew how to do that, where a lot of people didn't."[63]

THE WOOD BROTHERS

While Bignotti and the crew were preparing the cars for the final Carb Day test, Foyt spotted Leonard Wood and several Wood Brothers team members entering Gasoline Alley. He ran up to Leonard and insisted on showing them his car, all of which made Wood increasingly uneasy.

Unknown to Foyt, the Wood Brothers, known for the speed and precision of their pit work in NASCAR, were there at the behest of Ford to handle the pit stops for Team Lotus, whose pit work the past two years resembled a Keystone Cops routine. "If Clark loses this race, he'll lose it in the pits," one driver had said.[64]

"Foyt is showing us his shop, showing us his race car and how he's got his gas tank fixed special for refueling," Wood remembered. "Then he asked, 'What are you guys doing up here anyway?' I looked around and finally broke the news we were going to pit for Clark in the 500.

"I can't tell you exactly what he said, but he called me a SOB and everything else you can think of."[65]

In the final practice session, Foyt was in the pits most of the time, complaining about his car's handling. He finally got out of the Lotus, took the right-front wheel off, and, grabbing a hammer, started pounding on the suspension, much to the dismay of Bignotti. The three-hour practice session over, the team pushed the car back to the garage, where they worked well into the night making changes Foyt demanded.

Sports Illustrated predicted the race would be "more perilous than any so far," and it was billed as a battle between Clark, the European gentleman farmer and OBE, against Foyt, the American high school dropout.[66]

It didn't disappoint—for three laps.

Clark led the first lap, with Foyt passing him on lap two to the roar of the crowd. "I didn't mind when Foyt passed me," Clark said. "I wanted to see how fast he was going to go and that's how I learned I could beat him."[67]

They ran wheel-to-wheel on lap three and then Clark started pulling away. He was the first to pit and was in and out in just twenty seconds. The stop was so fast, many thought the vaunted Wood Brothers had made a mistake and didn't completely refuel the car. In reality the pit crew had performed flawlessly.[68]

Chapman would go even further. "They were bloody great," he said, admitting he first argued against using the NASCAR team. "The best thing we did all month was to get the Woods up here. Their performance was fantastic."[69]

Foyt led for nine laps before making his stop, but only after running completely out of fuel. The stop stretched to more than forty seconds as the team struggled to restart the engine. Bignotti later said Foyt ignored a signal to pit. Foyt blamed Bignotti. Regardless, Clark went past Foyt as he was returning to the track, putting him a lap down. Running the fastest race laps of his career at that point, A.J. caught and repassed Clark, becoming the only driver on the same lap as the leader at the halfway mark. He continued to cut the margin by as much as a second a lap, but it was all for naught, as on lap 116 he was back in the pits, the transmission shot. Climbing from the car, he headed straight for Gasoline Alley.

"When my pit crew gave me the sign that Foyt was out of the race, I was very glad, of course," Clark said. "I knew I could best him anyway from our earlier running together."[70]

In Gasoline Alley, Foyt spotted Gurney, who'd been running a close third until blowing an engine after just forty-two laps. "The big guy," as Foyt often called him, was already in street clothes. They went back to Foyt's garage to commiserate, Gurney grabbing a soft drink from the cooler while A.J. slumped in a chair.

"Will someone close the door?" Foyt said when reporters began to arrive, wanting to know what happened. "I don't want to see anyone." It was left to co-owner Ansted to face the media.

"He's all in a dither," Ansted said. "We were in beautiful shape. Tex was just beginning to move up the way we had planned. The thing that knocked him out of the race is the same thing that's happened to us three times this month. The gear box just let go."[71]

Foyt briefly considered taking over for Unser, but decided against it when told the engine in the car was down a cylinder. After Gurney departed, Foyt showered and headed to Turn One to watch the rest of the race, returning to Unser's pit in time to congratulate the young driver on his ninth-place finish.

Clark cruised home, leading 190 out of 200 laps—the third most in 500 history—and winning by nearly two laps over Jones. It was the fastest 500 ever, the first victory at the Speedway by a rear-engine car, the first for Ford, and the first by a foreign driver in forty-nine years. Andretti finished third, earning Rookie of the Year honors. Perhaps most importantly, it also turned out to be the safest 500 in more than thirty years, with less than twelve minutes run under the caution flag.

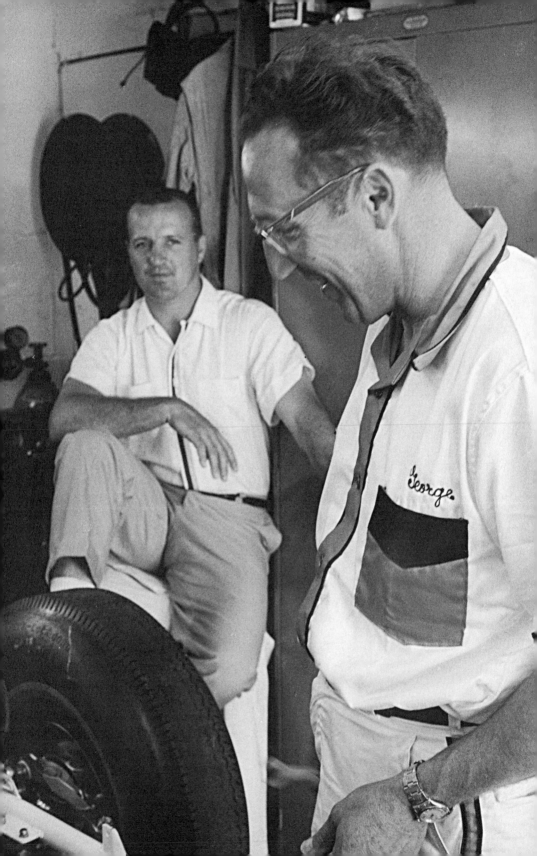

CHAPTER 19

THE BREAKUP

1965

Throughout May the rumor mill focused on one story—A.J. Foyt would retire if he won the 1965 Indianapolis 500. Despite the loss, the stories started again, this time fed by Foyt himself.

"I sure am thinking about it," he said of retirement. "I've got a couple of people to talk to here before I take off to Houston, and that may decide it. Nothing has gone right for me the whole year, and I just don't know. I should know soon, however, what I'm going to do."[1]

While Lucy said she thought her husband would retire, others close to him doubted it.

"He's a millionaire," noted one friend, "but he doesn't live for money alone. He could be far richer than he is, but he won't even endorse products he doesn't like. That's the way he is. Same way in a race car. He thinks he's cheating the public if he lets a foreigner win this race."[2]

The argument Al Unser witnessed between Foyt and George Bignotti was mild compared to some of the others during May. They'd increased in frequency and intensity as the month wore on and the problems with the Lotus mounted. Foyt was unhappy with the car's preparation and the delay in getting the Lola on the track. His comment about driving his 1964 race-winning roadster had been more than a longing for the good old days but was shot down by the owners and Bignotti, who'd invested tens of thousands of dollars in the rear-engine cars. Still, he seemed to talk himself out of quitting as quickly as he mentioned it, and the competitive fires still burned.

"There's always somebody coming along who's a little better than the guy before him," Foyt said. "I want to beat as many of those as I can. I want to be the best

◀ Foyt and George Bignotti. *Revs Institute, The Tom Burnside Photograph Collection*

in any kind of racing on any kind of track. I guess it's competition that makes me keep going. It makes me sick anytime I lose. Sometimes it makes me mad. Why shouldn't it? I want to be the best in my profession. Doesn't everyone? People keep asking me when I'm gonna quit. Now, I ask, how do you quit doing the thing you love most. I'd go crazy if I quit racing. What would I do with all my time?"[3]

Bignotti, for one, didn't think Foyt would go through with his retirement threats.

"He has led every race he ran this year before something went wrong. He is a bit disgusted. I would have liked to see him quit had he won Monday's race [the 500], but you can say he isn't going to retire—now."[4]

Bignotti also tried to lower the tension between himself and Foyt, with a minimum of success, admitting he was probably a more conservative crew chief than others.

"A.J. is one of the few drivers who understands everything about cars. He could build his own cars and they'd be competitive. This is both bad and good. He can tell you what's wrong with a car he's testing and how to fix it and a lot of drivers can't. He's always right about what's wrong. But he's not always right about how to fix it.

"Because he's a good mechanic, he won't let his mechanic alone. Because he's the best driver doesn't make him the best mechanic. There are differences between good mechanics just as there are between good drivers. A lot of us are good at what we do. Some are better. Some are more imaginative, some more conservative. Striking a balance is the big thing. You don't just want the fastest car or the one that will run the farthest, but the one that will run the fastest and finish. Some guys always have to be fancy. If something isn't far-out, they're not happy. I won't try something radically different until I feel it's better.

"Foyt and I are always at odds. But in the past we decided we could do better together than we would apart. I decided it's better to fight with Foyt all week and win on Sunday than have peace with somebody and never win."[5]

As Bignotti predicted, Foyt was back in the car six days later at Milwaukee. "I guess I was wrong," Lucy said. "A.J. has to keep going all the time. He doesn't even like to take a day off."[6]

It was more of the same, however, as he put the Lotus on the pole for the fourth straight race and led twenty-eight laps, only to drop out just past the half-way point of the one-hundred-miler, the transmission again the culprit. Making matters worse, Parnelli Jones drove his similar car to victory.

Foyt begged off Ford's Le Mans team, where he'd been listed as a driver for Carroll Shelby. He hadn't scored a single USAC championship point and couldn't afford to miss a race, he argued. He also severed his relationship with John Mecom Jr., saying he was unhappy with the Hussein sports car.

"He was unhappy with it, but he was the only one he'd allow to drive it," Mecom said. "As far as he was concerned, nobody else could get in it. It was his. A.J. had a choice of any car he wanted to drive, but that one fit his style more than any others. It was a beautiful car but needed a lot more development, to say the least. Way too much horsepower."[7]

Desperate to jumpstart his championship defense, Foyt headed to Langhorne, a track where he'd won eight times in an assortment of cars during the past four years. He'd once joked if they ever closed Langhorne he'd have to retire. Although the track was still open, they'd done the next worst thing—paved it. The new track was as foreign to Foyt as the French road course, and he found himself on equal footing with everyone else.[8]

In place of Puke Hollow and the rutted, potholed dirt circle, universally feared and hated by most drivers not named Foyt, was a D-shaped asphalt track. Bignotti brought the team's Lotus for the race and most other teams also brought their Indianapolis cars, although there were some roadsters and even a few dirt track cars entered.

Nearly everyone struggled with the new configuration, including Foyt, who wanted multiple changes made to the car. He adjusted the brakes, springs, and camber, but nothing seemed to satisfy him. His demand for adjustments wasn't new, but the intensity was.

"You never know how good you can get a race car to feel unless you try everything possible," he'd say about his constant changes. "You put more weight on here, raise this side, lower this side and pick up a little. Then you try to do something else to squeeze a little more out. Sometimes it works and sometimes it doesn't."[9]

Nothing worked at Langhorne. He continued to push the team and Bignotti began to push back. Disgusted after a practice session and saying the car was undrivable, Foyt told Henry Banks, USAC's competition director, he was withdrawing the car and going home. When he ordered the crew to load the car on the transporter, however, Bignotti confronted him. Saying Foyt was free to go home, Bignotti pointed out there were plenty of others who wanted to drive the car, including Joe Leonard, who was standing nearby. Foyt questioned Bignotti's work ethic, which, not surprisingly, he took personally.

The two went toe-to-toe, yelling at each other in language and volume reaching new heights, even for them. Foyt was on the verge of losing control and clenching his fists. Even though Bignotti was nearly fifty—and nineteen years older than the driver, wore glasses, and had never been known as a fighter—crew members were afraid they'd come to blows.

"If Foyt had said some of the things to me he'd said to Bignotti, I'd have taken after A.J. with a monkey wrench," Leonard would say.[10]

Eventually, they yelled themselves hoarse and Foyt relented, qualifying the "undrivable" Lotus fifth, although behind one of the roadsters.

They went at it again race morning, Foyt threatening to quit and Bignotti egging him on, saying, "Go ahead and quit." Foyt started the race but pitted after thirty laps, complaining the engine was overheating and walking away. Bignotti called co-owner Bill Ansted and turned in his two-week notice. Then he told the press he was leaving the team.[11]

"I told A.J. I was done. Life is too short, and I couldn't take his continual complaints about the running condition of the car. The final blow came when he claimed we hadn't been working on the car enough and that it wasn't working right, when the truth was we had been. We worked darn hard, even late Saturday night, to fix it. And then he complains.

"It was just too much and I thought it best for all concerned just to step out of the picture. This is it. I've had it this time. I end up with nothing. A.J.'s the driver for car owners Bill Ansted and Shirley Murphy in the Sheraton-Thompson car and they'll keep him. So old George is on the outside."[12]

Ansted called Foyt, who seemed upset and surprised by Bignotti's decision. Later the car owner made it clear he didn't fault his former chief mechanic.

"I don't blame him a damn bit," the normally soft-spoken Ansted said. "I wouldn't have taken that kind of treatment either.

"I'm certainly sorry to lose George. Nobody can come close to his record, and I admire him for this step if that's the way he feels. Nobody shoots sevens and elevens all the time. The racing business is a bouncing ball and at the moment it has been bouncing the wrong way."[13]

The Foyt/Bignotti split was big news in Indianapolis, the story running on the front page of the *Indianapolis News*. Foyt would only say "Bignotti is losing interest in racing and he's not giving it his fullest attention."[14]

Few blamed Bignotti. "Foyt is quick to anger and also quick to criticize when things go wrong," wrote one columnist. "This misfortune has not been the fault of Bignotti, and no one knows this better than Foyt. Troubles have arisen from a new type race car with a powerful engine, strong rear tires and a weak gearbox. Bignotti has probably taken more abuse from his driver (than anyone else). It will be a tough job to find someone who will take as much. A first-class mechanic, he will also have to have the patience of a saint."[15]

Bignotti was "on the outside" for only three days. That's when it was discovered that he was in Houston, finalizing a deal to become part of a new super team being put together by Mecom and including driver Rodger Ward.

After talking about forming an Indy team for several years, Mecom worked quickly to make it a reality. He acquired a Halibrand chassis from Lindsey Hopkins as well as J.C. Agajanian's Lola, which he sent back to England for updating. He signed a deal for Ford engines and announced plans to run in the next champ car race, a month later in Trenton.

Ward's decision was as surprising as Bignotti's. The so-called "Flying Ws" of Ward, chief mechanic A.J. Watson, and car owner Robert Wilke was the longest continuous driver-mechanic-owner team on the Indy car circuit, having formed in 1959. They'd won the 1959 and 1962 Indy 500s and national championships, finished second in the 1960 and 1964 500s, and won seventeen other big car races.

The move to rear-engine cars, however, was proving a challenge for the team and things came to a head when Ward was unable to qualify for the 500, the first time he'd missed the race in fifteen years. He'd been slow again at Langhorne and when Watson asked Leonard to try the car, he'd immediately turned laps two seconds faster than Ward's best time. The scenario was similar to the Foyt/Bignotti situation, Watson blaming Ward and Ward blaming the car, only at lower decibels.

Ward took the opportunity to weigh in on his rival. "I think Foyt's troubles occur mainly because he drives a race car to its maximum capabilities. He literally abuses a car. And if you have a problem—like the rear-end troubles in his car—maybe driving with a little more caution would be the solution."[16]

The quick teaming of Bignotti, Ward, and Mecom seemed to indicate that discussions were underway prior to the faceoff at Langhorne. With the deal finalized, Bignotti unloaded on Foyt to his hometown newspaper.

"I've had it with Foyt. He's got the big head and wants to run the whole show—driver, mechanic, the whole bit. Only trouble is, he's not the mechanic he thinks he is.

"Ever since the first week of May, Foyt has been saying, 'Change this, change that' and when I did the car failed him and then he would turn around and claim it was my fault. [We] worked hard and long on Foyt's car and always tried to have it in first-class shape. Most of the time he would show up on race day and order things changed that I knew from past experience would only make the car either hard to handle or suffer a breakdown. For a while he let us handle the pit end and we won ten of twelve starts, including four national crowns for him. Now he can win his own races. I've had it."[17]

BIG GEORGE NOTTI

"If there was ever a period in my life that stands out above the others, it was the Bignotti years," Foyt said in his autobiography. "And I bet it stands out in George's too. And in the minds of just about everybody around racing. It started off on the quiet side, but it didn't stay that way long."[18]

It's a common belief that if Foyt and Bignotti had somehow managed to coexist there's no telling what they might have accomplished. In their five years together, they won thirty-two races (twenty-seven champ car events), two Indianapolis 500s, and four national championships. Bignotti would have a hand in winning five more Indy 500s and three USAC national championships, finishing with an incredible eighty-five race wins.

"As far as I'm concerned, George and I are still friends," Foyt said at the time. "We just decided that it would be better for both of us if we went our ways."

They'd continue to clash in the years ahead. Both also would battle with their counterparts, Foyt running through a series of crew chiefs and Bignotti an equally large number of drivers. Their egos and personalities were simply too much alike to allow for any long-term relationship. In later years, as time dulled memories and healed wounds, the two spoke fondly of their time together.[19]

"I'd say he was one of the greatest mechanics that was ever at the Indianapolis Motor Speedway," Foyt said, following Bignotti's death in 2013. "We had a close relationship, even though I went on my merry way. We were still close up to his death. We did so much racing together and in '64 we were just unbeatable. We had a lot of arguments up and down, but they weren't arguments like people think. We both respected each other a whole lot. I damn sure respected him for what he was doing on the cars, and I think he respected my driving ability."[20]

Bignotti did. "A.J. was a great driver. He could drive just about anything, and he wasn't bad to get along with. We never raised our voices at each other in the garage, though in front of the public, he would blow his top."

Caught in the middle through it all was Mecom. His venture into Indy car racing would be short-term, and in 1967 he'd dissolve the team, turning his attention to professional football and purchasing the New Orleans Saints.

"A.J. had a bad habit of getting mad real quick and sometimes letting his mouth overload the moment," Mecom said. "But by God, normally after about twenty minutes, he'd forgotten why he was mad. Then there was the case with George. Maybe he just didn't want to admit that he'd made a mistake. That's how George came to join my team. But I don't think they were enemies for the rest of either one's career."[21]

Although their racing relationship was over, Mecom remained friendly with Foyt, the two eventually owning a business together, sharing a financial advisor, and serving together on the board of several Houston-based companies.

"It was a sincere pleasure to have been associated with A.J., much less call him a friend. Even with all his quirks and temper tantrums, he was still a friend. He just had—as they say in the entertainment industry—he had 'it.' Every time he was in the car was exciting to me. There wasn't anybody like him. Everybody says that and it probably seems trite, but it's not at all. I don't know a damn thing he couldn't do except, sometimes, keep his mouth shut."

JOHNNIE POUELSEN

With any possibility of a Foyt/Bignotti reconciliation eliminated, focus shifted to who would become the new chief mechanic on the Sheraton-Thompson Special. The name mentioned most often was Johnnie Pouelsen, the head wrench for Agajanian and Jones. While Foyt lobbied for Pouelsen, his car owners weren't so sure.

The fact Pouelsen was being considered for the job spurred speculation Jones was getting ready to retire, otherwise the team would never allow the mechanic to leave. Pouelsen had been a top sprint car driver on the IMCA circuit in the mid-to-late 1950s, besting both Foyt and Jones on occasion. He'd made the move to full-time mechanic with Jones and Agajanian in 1960 and had been with the team ever since.

On the surface Johnnie Pouelsen ranked with A.J. Watson, George Bignotti, and Clint Brawner among the top crew chiefs in the sport. In reality, his days with the team were numbered. Agajanian had long ago soured on him, blaming him for the car's poor finishing record. On the surface Jones remained loyal to his crew chief, although he'd spent the night before the recent 500 secretly changing things on his car without Pouelsen's knowledge.

When word began to leak that Pouelsen was in the running to replace Bignotti, it put Agajanian in an awkward position. Although Foyt was a competitor, he was also a friend, and Aggie took the unusual step of cautioning it might not be a good match. The warning fell on deaf ears, however, and in the end Foyt got his way, Pouelsen coming on board in time for the Trenton race.

"We didn't hire Pouelsen away from Aggie," Ansted clarified in making the announcement. "He had notified Aggie he was quitting. Since he was available then, we took him."[22]

With a month until the Trenton Indy car race, and desperate to return to Victory Lane, Foyt made his first sprint car start of the year. Having sold his sprinter at the end of 1964, he reunited with Wally Meskowski, but the magic was gone. When the car arrived for their fourth race together with an engine oil leak, Foyt refused to wait for Meskowski to fix it and said he was going to find another car. The two exchanged words and Foyt told him to find another driver. Furious, Meskowski climbed in the car and challenged Foyt, although he had no prior driving experience. Cooler heads prevailed and Meskowski and his car were parked. Foyt jumped in the car he'd sold the year before but lasted only eight laps before dropping out—with an oil leak. Rather than jumpstart the season, the year hit rock bottom.[23]

It took a trip to the south before Foyt found a brief respite from the on- and off-track drama of Indy car racing, returning to Daytona to defend his Firecracker 400 title on July 4. He was paired with the Wood Brothers, Foyt apparently forgiving them for their dalliance with Jimmy Clark. It was a nearly all-Ford affair, with the factory Chrysler teams continuing their boycott over rule issues.

For most of the race, he ran in a pack following leader Cale Yarborough, who was making his first start as a factory Ford driver. Eventually, Foyt went low to pass Yarborough, just as the engine in Yarborough's car blew up, setting off a chain reaction crash and taking out four of the front-runners. Foyt later said he had a premonition to go low.

"I don't really understand it, but coming down the straightaway on that lap something told me to get around Cale. If I had stayed on his rear bumper I would have been involved in that wreck, because I would have been the first car to his oil slick. I truly believe I had a premonition that something was going to happen. I was almost around Cale when I heard a noise and glanced in my mirrors and saw smoke and cars dodging everywhere."[24]

Home free after that, Foyt won by more than three laps. He saw the irony in winning his first race of the year after most of the other front-runners crashed or dropped out. He also indirectly addressed Ward's comments that he "abused" his race cars.

"It's been that kind of year," Foyt said. "This is the second time I've finished a race this season. I nursed the car along. I simply do not believe in pushing one all the way, all the time. I do this because at the end, if it is close, I have the best of it over the guys who have been doggin' all the way."[25]

The race was notable, as it featured Foyt's first experience with Goodyear's new tire inner liner, the safety feature Billy Wade was testing when he was killed at the track in January. Foyt suffered a blown tire early in the race when he ran over some debris but had made it safely to the pits.

"That safety shield in the Goodyear tire was a lifesaver," he said. "I ran over something and my rear tire popped. The car hardly even wobbled. I would have been in trouble had I been using the old-type tires. The car swayed just a little bit and I was able to drive to the pits. That new tire is the best thing in racing in many years."[26]

Foyt's talk of a premonition to go low around Yarborough was not the first, nor the last, time he'd talk about having a premonition in a race car. He also said he'd gone to see "Weegie," a psychic who often traveled to Indy car races, about his troubles. Many drivers would visit Weegie, but few admitted to believing what she had to say.

"This lady astrologer told me to expect some trouble," Foyt acknowledged. "She said I'd have hard luck until late July or early August and warned me to check all the parts of my race car. Of course I don't believe in astrology or things like that. But I've always believed in checking out the equipment."[27]

———

If ever Foyt wanted to do well, it was July 18 in Trenton, the first meeting of the new and reconfigured champ car teams. Once again he qualified on the pole. The Mecom team's updated Lola wasn't back from England and Bignotti prepared a Halibrand-Ford for Ward, who spun in qualifying and failed to make the field. Also missing the race with car problems was points leader Mario Andretti.[28]

Even though it'd been a year and a day since he'd finished an Indy car race on pavement—a victory at Trenton—Foyt seemed to be his old self on race morning, cocky and ready to go. At the drivers' meeting, he interrupted the instructions on how to get to Victory Lane, saying, "Never mind the others, I know where to go." Good on his word, Foyt led all 150 laps, finishing more than a lap ahead of second-place Jim Hurtubise.[29]

"I could feel it in my bones when I woke up this morning," he said. "It was a good feeling, the kind I haven't had for a long, long time. I don't know how to describe it, a kinda happy feeling I guess you'd call it. I just knew it was going to be my day."[30]

He went out of his way to praise Pouelsen, drawing a comparison to the unnamed Bignotti.

"Johnnie deserves as much credit for the win as I do. He worked day and night on this car with the rest of my crew, changing things I thought should be changed. I guess that was why I felt so confident."[31]

The honeymoon lasted one week, until the next race at Indianapolis Raceway Park, the first road course event for Indy cars in more than a quarter century. Foyt missed all but thirty minutes of a three-hour practice session when he ordered a last-minute gear change. He still qualified second to Andretti and promised to do better after more changes were made to the car. Foyt also had one of only three cars in the race equipped with a multi-speed gearbox while Andretti's had the traditional two-speed transmission.

Forced to pit early to replace a loose wheel, Foyt reentered in sixteenth, well behind leader Andretti. Moving quickly through the field, he was able to close up under a caution flag. On the restart Andretti ran off the course, allowing Foyt past, who stretched his lead to more than ten seconds. Coming down to the white flag, however, the engine in Foyt's car coughed. He was running out of gas. Andretti passed him as did two others, A.J. chugging home fourth. Pouelsen protested that officials missed a lap and Foyt should have been flagged the winner, but USAC saw it otherwise and proclaimed Andretti the victor.

"I thought I was seeing a miracle when I saw him slowing down," said Andretti afterward. "But I guess one man's misfortune is another's fortune."[32]

The big winner was the race itself. *Indianapolis News* sports editor Wayne Fuson wrote it "was such a thriller that there seems little doubt now that other road courses will get into the act and schedule races."[33]

The next week the Indy cars went to another track for the first time, the high-banked 1.5-mile circuit at Atlanta Motor Speedway. At 250 miles and paying more than $12,000 to win, it was the second-longest and -richest race on the schedule. Foyt was one of the few who'd driven the track in the past, having run several NASCAR races there. His experience showed as he qualified the Lotus three miles per hour faster than anyone else, setting a speed record for tracks of that length. He also freely provided advice to anyone who asked about how to set up their car for the track.

Foyt led from the start, although he was pressured by Johnny Rutherford, who'd taken over Ward's old ride with Watson. He was ahead of Rutherford by five seconds on lap 107 of the 162-lap race when the right-rear suspension of the Lotus collapsed, sending him into a series of wild spins. Rutherford went on to his first Indy car victory, but afterward all he wanted to talk about was Foyt.

"A.J. has been a lot of help to me. He's given me a lot of tips on this car and has it where it will almost run as fast as his. I was right behind Foyt when his car went. It looked like something gave way and he handled it like the champion he is. He could have really been hurt out there."[34]

"Racing with A.J. was the highlight of the day for me," Rutherford would say of his first big car win. "Anytime I raced with A.J. it was good. He's such a strong competitor, and he ran the rest of us so clean, it was fun to race him."[35]

BUS DRIVER

As it became apparent Foyt had no intention of cutting back his schedule, promoters began jockeying to get him in their race. He's "by far the biggest gate attraction on four wheels," one lucky promoter said.[36]

Foyt landed a new sprint car ride, moving into the machine of Babe Stapp that Rutherford drove early in the season with some success. Bumped from his ride, Rutherford jumped into the Meskowski car. While Foyt finally was able to finish a few races, Rutherford was winning them, reeling off five victories in the next eight events and setting a track record at Winchester. For once, Foyt's uncanny ability to jump from car to car and make it pay off let him down.

It wasn't until late August and the start of the fair season that Foyt's year began to turn around, and it included one of the more amazing weekends in Foyt's amazing career.

It kicked off on Saturday, August 21, at the Illinois State Fairgrounds and Foyt's first champ car race of the year on dirt. After qualifying fifth, it took him only fourteen laps to pass Rutherford for the lead and pull away. An hour-long rain delay turned the fast track into a quagmire, but it didn't slow Foyt, who lapped everyone but the second-place finisher.

After picking up his winnings—$4,609—Foyt loaded the mud-caked car on the trailer and made the two-hundred-mile drive to Milwaukee for a pavement race the next day. He expected to meet Pouelsen and the team there with the Lotus, which was being fitted with a new oiling and cooling system.

At the track, however, the Lotus was nowhere to be found. There'd been problems with the update, and when the crew fired up the car it blew oil out the exhaust. The car and crew were still in Indianapolis. Foyt found himself at the track without a race car or a team—just the dirt track car, his dad, and a few buddies. The answer was obvious: pull the dirt track car off the trailer.

"We came to race and that's what we've got," Foyt told his friends. "So let's get with it."[37]

The first chore was washing the mud from the car. They also needed wheels and tires. The knobby dirt track tires wouldn't last long on a paved circuit, and Foyt borrowed wheels to fit the pavement tires. He had only a few practice laps, driving the car like he would on dirt, sliding around the corners and picking up the left-front tire off the track in the turns, before pitting to check his lap times.

"Foyt came in and asked how he was running and I said you're almost a second quicker than anybody," recalled Steve Stapp, one of the drafted crew members, the son of sprint car owner Babe Stapp and a driver himself. "He cussed at me and said I didn't even know how to read a damn stopwatch. So I handed it to him before he went out for more practice and said, 'You do everything else perfect, go time yourself.'"[38]

Foyt put the dirt car on the pole with Dan Gurney, driving his Lotus 38, in second. "Pretty damn impressive as I recall," Gurney would say.

After Foyt led the first couple laps, Gurney passed him and Andretti moved into second. Most assumed Foyt would fade back into the field, but he hung on in third and when the two leaders experienced car troubles, he moved back in front, the crowd showing its approval. It was only a matter of time, however, as Foyt knew the smaller fuel tank on the dirt car would require an extra pit stop. The stop was further delayed while the crew struggled to change a tire, although he still managed a second-place finish to Gordon Johncock.

It was a remarkable turnaround for Foyt, who'd been roundly booed at the track just three years earlier when he clashed with Milwaukee promoter Tom Marchese. Now the fans were cheering him as if he'd won the race—and Foyt was mad because he didn't.

"A.J. was pissed off because he hadn't won so he didn't talk all the way home," recalled Stapp, who rode back to Indianapolis with Foyt. "He wasn't mad at me or anything, he was just mad he hadn't won."[39]

Years later Foyt would call it one of the most rewarding races of his career.

"I looked like a greyhound bus against all those little itty-bitty rear-engine cars," he said. "I'd have to say that was one of my career highlights."

TIM DELROSE

Typical of Foyt's patchwork crew that day was Tim Delrose, who'd driven to Milwaukee from the Chicago suburb of Joliet, Illinois, where he owned midget and sprint cars and was a regular at the local dirt tracks. He'd met Foyt in 1961, and they'd been friends ever since.

"I was a big fan of Bob Tattersall, who raced midgets in the Joliet area and the Midwest. I thought he was the best driver by far. Then I went to Terre Haute in 1961 for a sprint car race and saw A.J. Foyt. I thought right then, there's the champ. That guy knows what he's doing."[40]

At Indianapolis that year Tattersall introduced Delrose to Tony and A.J. Foyt.

"Later that day I was in the Speedway restaurant when Foyt came in. The place was packed. He came over and said, 'Hey, didn't I just meet you?' I said, 'Yeah, sit down,' and we talked for a while. Then he said, 'When you're done, come on back to the garage,' which I did. We talked some, and he asked about my family. I told him about my car, and he knew my mechanic. He invited me to Milwaukee, put me on the pit list, and we've been friends ever since."

Delrose became part of a small but trusted entourage of friends Foyt could relax with. They'd attend races with him, visit the Foyt ranch, and go hunting with the driver. Delrose's successful media distribution business would allow him to travel widely with Foyt, including trips to the Kentucky Derby and to Europe when the Indy cars raced there. They'd eventually own several thoroughbred race horses together.

The key to a long and successful friendship with Foyt? Honesty.

"When he asks me something, I tell him what I think. I don't tell him what he wants to hear. He asks me what I think and I tell him. A couple of times he's gotten mad at me. He'll say, 'Hey, it's my money, I'll do what I want.' I tell him you're right, do what you want. But if you're asking me, I'm telling you.

"You don't want to lie to him. If you lie to him at any time, I don't care who you are, if you lie to him, you're fired, you're out of there. And do what you say you're going to do.

"He's smarter than you think he is. He may give you that dumbshit act every once in a while, but that's bullshit. He's a smart dude. He's tough and he's smart."

––––––––

By September the problems and bad luck of the first half of the year were forgotten as Foyt won four of five races in four different types of cars over a one-month period. He won a USAC stock car race when the two leaders ran out of gas on the last lap. A week later he captured the Hoosier Hundred, becoming the first driver to win the top-paying dirt track race four times. He won again at Trenton, leading all two hundred circuits and lapping the field. For good measure he ran his first midget race in nearly a year, driving a new Pouelsen-built car and coming from seventeenth starting position to win the Hut Hundred, the year's richest midget race.

On a roll, he headed for Charlotte and the last big NASCAR race of the year. There he tried to explain what it was like to drive the different types of cars.

"I don't much care what I'm racing or what type of race I'm running as long as the machine will go," he said. "You're always on pins in one of those open-air cars. They cut quicker, more like a go-kart, and the wind sometimes bothers you.

"In a stock car you're on pins too, but you have a roof over your head and the wind isn't as bad. In a sprint car you want the windshield at eye level. If you get it any higher it will slow you down, and if it's any lower, the wind whipping against your face can wear you out.

"At Indy where we're running pretty fast, I've had the wind whipping so strong against my shoulders that it would rip my uniform. After the race my eyes and face are usually swollen from the wind pressure against my goggles.

"I love to race down here, and I love to drive the stocks, but then again, I love to drive anything."[41]

Ford pulled out all the stops, adding both A.J. Foyt and Curtis Turner to the Wood Brothers team and fielding eight factory cars. Turner was a legend in the South, known for his hard living and hard driving.

"For my money," Turner said when told Foyt was to be his teammate, "he's the finest race driver around."

The event was marred by a five-car accident on the first lap that stopped the race and took the life of driver Harold Kite, who served with distinction in World War II and Korea and was making his first speedway start in ten years.

Once restarted, it became a battle of Foyt versus the NASCAR regulars. Curtis Turner, Cale Yarborough, LeeRoy Yarbrough, Fred Lorenzen, Dick Hutcherson, and Ned Jarrett all led, but more often than not it was Foyt out front, leading twice as many laps as anyone else. With one hundred miles remaining, Lorenzen, NASCAR's leading money winner, winner of the Daytona 500 earlier in the year and the last two races at Charlotte, emerged as the primary challenger. It had also been Lorenzen to whom Foyt offered his Indy 500 backup car to earlier in the year.

"It was everything racing is supposed to be—and more," wrote one reporter. "Every person present was standing, waving, shouting. It was one of the greatest duels the sport has ever known."[42]

With ten laps remaining, the two series stars began running side-by-side with Lorenzen in the middle of the track and Foyt up high, Hutcherson occasionally diving low to make it three wide. With six laps to go, Foyt slid up the track, touching the wall and going into a half spin as Lorenzen went on to win. Like Rutherford earlier in the year, Lorenzen only wanted to talk about Foyt.

"I've always wanted to beat A.J. Foyt, that has been a personal ambition for a long, long time," Lorenzen said. "He is the king of racing. He comes down South a couple of times a year and smokes everybody off. I beat the king, and this may be the best race I have ever driven."[43]

Although Lorenzen denied it, the Wood Brothers and others said he pushed Foyt up the track and into the wall. For his part, the USAC invader was uncharacteristically restrained, saying only, "Maybe he hit me, maybe he didn't. There will be other races."[44]

Later Foyt came to Lorenzen's defense.

"I never worry when I'm running side by side with him, both of us going all out. He's a sportsman and a damned smart one. He's thinking ahead of you every minute."[45]

————

For the season-ending sprint car races at Ascot, Foyt made another car change, moving to the top West Coast team owned by the Morales Brothers. It was called the "Tamale Wagon" because the brothers owned a Mexican food company. Andretti took over the Stapp ride. Foyt led the first race before being hit by Bobby Unser, knocking his car on its side and out of the event, Andretti coming home the winner. Taking no chances in the second race, Foyt led from start to finish, Andretti taking second. The big winner was Rutherford, who captured the national sprint car title driving the Meskowski car Foyt abandoned early in the year.

By the Indy car finale at Phoenix, Andretti had already clinched the national championship and the new pecking order was on display as he led from the start, Foyt chasing in second. When Andretti's rear axle cracked near the end of the race, Foyt got by for the victory, pushing him into second in the final point standings, a remarkable comeback for a driver who had no points in the first half of the year. While Andretti won the title, matching Foyt as the youngest champion at twenty-five, A.J. won five races, tops in the series, to just one for Mario.

"Well at least he's consistent," Foyt said of Andretti. "But if we'd [Foyt and Pouelsen] gotten together sooner we'd have beaten him. I think with Pouelsen we can go good next year."[46]

Despite the late-season surge, some thought Foyt was a changed man after the year-opening Riverside crash. It was the first time he'd been badly hurt in an accident and spent extended sheet time. He didn't know how to handle the downtime, rushing back before he was fully recovered. His tantrums came with more frequency and intensity. Joe Scalzo, a top chronicler of the era, was a leading proponent of the crash having changed Foyt. Not his skill on the track, which was still evident for all to see. He'd had the type of season any other driver would have loved. He was still the king of the track. But as a person, "A.J. is in mean pain with a smashed back," Scalzo wrote. "To me, A.J. was never the same."[47]

Andretti said the championship marked one of two turning points in his career involving Foyt, and even though he was fortunate to win the title, it proved to him he could compete with A.J.

"When I was breaking in, and especially when I got to drive for Al Dean and Clint Brawner, Foyt was setting the standard. He was only five years my senior, but he was the established champion. Let's face it, he was the yardstick, the guy who was winning most of the races.

"I depended a lot on Clint and Jim McGee. Clint's wisdom was very good for me. He was cooling me down. I didn't need to be nudged to go fast, I needed to be settled down so I wouldn't kill myself. Clint and Jimmy kept saying, 'As fast as you go, that's good enough for us.' It was great for me to hear that. I'd make some mistakes, but I was always thinking, 'I've got to bring this baby home because I've got to face those guys.'"[48]

At one point during the season, Andretti's obsession with beating Foyt began to concern Brawner. While the exact timing of their conversation varies, Andretti clearly recalls the lecture his crew chief delivered.

"'You know, kid, forget about beating Foyt, you ain't gonna beat him now,'" said Andretti, doing his best to emulate Brawner's gruff and gravelly voice. "'You ain't gonna beat Foyt now. The only way you'll beat Foyt is if some son-of-a-bitch jealous husband shoots the bastard.'

"That comment really resonated with me, because I had to work hard just to be competitive with A.J. If I was to win any races, I would have to find a way to beat him. In 1965, when I won [the championship] as a total rookie, the biggest thing for me was that somehow, I did better than he did. That gave me so much encouragement.

"I look back at A.J.—he was so good for me. For me to feel like I belonged, I had to beat somebody like him. Winning over A.J. was a phenomenal day. Finishing second to A.J. was a helluva a day. That's the way I always looked at it."

CHAPTER 20

WILY COYOTE

1966

During the short off-season between 1965 and 1966, there was no mention of A.J. Foyt's possible retirement. He went in the opposite direction, deciding to add a teammate and enter two cars in the Indy car pavement races.

For all its early problems, Foyt's Lotus had become the winningest car of its kind in Indy car history. Now he assembled an all-star team in Los Angeles to update the Lotus. Johnnie Pouelsen and Lujie Lesovsky were back. They were joined by Eddie Kuzma, who'd been responsible for reworking the Lotus of Parnelli Jones, and Dean Jeffries, best known for his paint jobs, but who was also a top-notch designer and fabricator, having just completed something called the "Monkeemobile" for a new television show. Gil Morales, of "Tamale Wagon" fame, was hired to serve as crew chief of the team's second car.

Both Foyt and George Bignotti had considered the Lola the team purchased the previous year to be a better car than the Lotus. When it arrived too late to prepare for the Speedway, it had been shelved for the year. Now the team was pulling from both cars to create a heavily modified car of its own.

Having joked before about calling his old car the "Lesovsky Lotus," Foyt decided there'd been so many changes on the new machine he could justify renaming it entirely. He wanted something to reflect his home state of Texas.

"We were looking for a name and Dean said, 'Well, you got a lot of coyotes in Texas,'" Foyt recalled. He liked the idea and asked Dean to come up with a design. "The first Coyote picture he drew was a real friendly one. A real polite one."[1]

Foyt had already obtained the Lotus 38 Bobby Johns drove to seventh in the 1965 500, the sister car to Jimmy Clark's race winner. There was another 38 on

◀ Nose of the first Coyote, painted by Dean Jeffries. *Revs Institute, The Bruce R. Craig Photograph Collection*

order, and he figured he had more than $120,000 invested in machinery. He grabbed No. 82 for his second car, the number Clark had driven to victory.

The big question was, who'd be the team's second driver? Al Unser, who'd done such a good job driving his second car at Indianapolis in 1965, had signed with Andy Granatelli to drive an STP-sponsored Lotus as a teammate to Clark in the 500. Once again, Foyt's choice was a surprise, especially to the driver.

"I'd been part of the Firestone test in December and turned some pretty fast laps," recalled George Snider, who'd taken over J.C. Agajanian's car from Parnelli Jones midway through 1965 when Jones decided he wanted a break.[2]

"I had raced against him all year, but I'd never really *met* A.J.," Snider said. "I had just finished tire testing for Firestone, and he had just come in with Goodyear. We just kinda met in the alley of the garage area. I was leaving and he was coming.

"Then during the holidays, I got a call from him wanting to know if I'd be interested in driving for him. I said, well *yeah*. We met at a motel near the Los Angeles airport and I ended up signing a contract."

From the Fresno area, Snider had a solid background driving modifieds on the West Coast and had responded with a steady, if unspectacular, season as a replacement for Jones. His best performances came on dirt, finishing second to Foyt in the August race at Springfield. He'd qualified second to Foyt for the Hoosier 100 and led the first fourteen laps before A.J. got by for the victory. He'd also earned Poulsen's seal of approval from their time spent together with Agajanian.

The Foyt deal "is a real big break for me," Snider told the *Fresno Bee*. "A.J. knows he can win the 500 and I believe I can. And A.J. believes I can too. He has offered me a top car and everything he does is first class. He's a great mechanic and chassis man and has already taught me a great deal. I really considered it a very flattering offer to drive for him. I have been given such great opportunities and I think Foyt will put the frosting on the cake."[3]

HARDBALL

Contract negotiations were ongoing with Ford and Foyt wanted the company to step up its funding and support of his two-car operation. He knew the company had decided not to renew its contract with Lotus and, as a result, additional money should be available. Much of the Lotus savings, however, was earmarked for Ford's Le Mans sports car program.

When negotiations slowed, Foyt played hardball, hinting to reporters he might sign with Chrysler for NASCAR and at the possibility of running a new super-charged Offenhauser engine at Indianapolis. The engine boasted more horsepower than the Ford, and Jones had run record laps with the new Offy during Phoenix testing. Rodger Ward was rumored to have one, too. Foyt's hand was further strengthened when Lotus announced it would use BRM engines in the 500.

In danger of losing the top Indy drivers and teams to the competition, Ford eventually agreed to a deal, including a $100,000 parts credit, but it came with strings attached. In NASCAR, Foyt would drive for a new team headed by the recently retired Junior Johnson. The cars would still be built by Holman-Moody, but Johnson and crew chief Herb Nab would be responsible for preparing and maintaining the cars. Ford also insisted Foyt join the Le Mans program, and drive a Mustang in the new Trans Am series when he was available.

At first glance the teaming of Foyt with Johnson seemed a good combination. Both were hard-nosed racers and got along well on and off the track. Foyt would be paired with Johnson's regular driver, Bobby Isaac, his old teammate from the Ray Nichels days.

Their first race together came at Riverside, scene of Foyt's crash the year before. He denied having any second thoughts about returning to the track and enjoyed rehashing the accident for the large number of reporters who thronged around him.[4]

The mood didn't last long. After only a few practice laps, he hit the wall in Turn One, damaging the bright yellow Ford No. 48 enough to sideline him the rest of the day.

"I really went in a little too hard and had to hit the brakes," he said, indicating that the brakes jerked the car into the wall and not trying to hide his frustration. "You shouldn't really need them at all in the turn, but when you need them, they should work." Things didn't improve on day two. "The brakes still don't feel right and the engine is missing coming down the straightaway."[5]

He made no secret that he preferred being with the Wood Brothers, whose cars qualified two-three-four. He finally made it in the field, despite engine troubles during his qualifying run. On race day he pulled into the pits after a few laps, said he had a head cold, and got out of the car. Another driver took over but didn't last long before dropping out with a busted transmission.

Things got worse at Daytona. NASCAR had certified the Chrysler Hemi engine for competition and the Plymouth and Dodge products held an advantage. Foyt complained loudly and often about the performance of his car before going under the hood himself to work on the engine. That didn't set well with Nab, a renowned engine builder who'd already won twenty-six races as a NASCAR crew chief—twelve alone in 1965 working on Johnson cars—and was well on his way to winning multiple Daytona 500s and championships in a career that would end up in the NASCAR Hall of Fame.

None of that mattered to Foyt at the time. After qualifying thirteenth, several miles an hour slower than Richard Petty's pole speed, he insisted the car be withdrawn from the race. He tried Johnson's backup car, but said it wasn't any better. Ford eventually offered him the car driven by Jack Bowsher in winning the 250-mile ARCA race earlier in the month for upcoming and second-tier drivers. Foyt went to work alongside a startled Bowsher to rebuild the car to meet NASCAR specifications.

The race itself was forgettable. The car failed to start, Ford engineers managing to get it going in time for the green flag. Foyt lasted less than one hundred miles before a head gasket blew and he was already on his way home when Petty took the checkered flag for his second Daytona 500 victory.

USAC's traditional Indy car series opener in Phoenix on March 20 gave an indication of how much the sport was changing. A year earlier there'd been only a handful of rear-engine cars and a roadster winner. The numbers were now reversed; only a few of the old roadsters made the field. An even bigger change was the driver getting the most attention. A year earlier Foyt was coming off his record-breaking 1964 season. Now reporters surrounded Mario Andretti, who'd come from Indianapolis, where he'd been running record laps during testing.

Andretti claimed the pole, breaking Foyt's track record in the process. After qualifying fourth, Foyt moved up behind Andretti at the start and hounded the leader, pulling alongside at several points but never able to pass. Less than a third of the way into the race, they began lapping slower drivers, and as they did, their two cars touched. Both cars spun, Andretti's sustaining enough damage to knock it out of the race. Foyt was able to continue, but eventually dropped out with engine problems. He was surprisingly restrained afterward.

"We were racing," he said. "Don't blame anybody."

Nearly sixty years later, Andretti was the first to bring up the incident.

"I feel so bad, to this day, about a race in Phoenix," he said. "I was going into Turn Three. I was too ambitious, and we got together. I felt so fricking bad. Of all people, that I go out there and crash, it had to be A.J.

"The thing I really remember is that he never said a word. I went over to him, and he didn't really talk to me, but he didn't say, 'Hey, you asshole,' either. He didn't call me any names or anything. I learned something from that. That was on me, that was a stupid mistake on my part, and I feel, to this day, so fricking bad about it. But he didn't say a word."[6]

From Phoenix, Foyt went to Sebring. On Friday he started in the inaugural Trans Am race. He was by far the biggest name in the field and battled for the lead in the Mustang before dropping out midway through the four-hour event.

The next day's twelve-hour race was his first chance to drive a Ford GT MK II. He was teamed with Ronnie Bucknum, who'd made the unlikely jump from SCCA amateur champion to driving for Honda in Formula One. The pair was in one of two Holman-Moody entries and saddled with an experimental automatic transmission. Sebring is known for being hard on brakes, and without the help of a transmission to slow the car, the team changed brake pads at nearly every stop on their way to a twelfth-place finish.

It was a tragic race, with Canadian driver Bob McLean, in a privately owned Ford GT40, killed in a fiery crash early in the event. That night four spectators were killed when they wandered into a restricted area and were hit by a spinning car that had collided with a Ferrari driven by Andretti, although Mario wouldn't be aware of the deaths until reading about them the next day. A few days later Walt Hansgen, who'd finished second at Sebring, was killed at Le Mans during a rainy test session. It was turning into another bad year for racing.

Although he wasn't entered, Foyt flew from Sebring to Atlanta for the NASCAR stock car race the next day. He was joined by Lloyd Ruby, who'd been the surprise Sebring winner along with Ken Miles.

They were in Atlanta to support Jim Hurtubise, who was driving a Plymouth. Despite being under contract to Ford and saying he was "worn out" from the Sebring trip, Foyt volunteered as a relief driver, telling Herk he could go "an hour or so." He wasn't needed for anything more than cheerleading as Hurtubise captured what he called "the biggest race I've won."[7]

It didn't bother Foyt afterward when Ford announced it was pulling out of NASCAR in a disagreement over rules. He'd already told the company he wouldn't drive for Johnson again. Despite their disagreements, Johnson would later call Foyt "The greatest driver that I ever knew. The best all-around. He could drive anything, anywhere, anytime."[8]

Returning to Phoenix for another test session, Foyt's two-car plans suffered a blow. Unhappy with the performance of the Lotus 34 he'd driven the year before and that Snider was now driving, he told Pouelsen to test it. Pouelsen was a successful sprint car driver and had driven Indy cars in the past. This time he lost control and crashed, emerging unharmed but with a badly damaged car and Snider would miss Trenton. Despite the setback, Foyt was able to joke afterward.

"We've taken away his beginner's driving permit," Foyt quipped of Pouelsen. "I guess I just let him solo too soon."[9]

Foyt stayed in Los Angeles working on his new Indy cars, although he found time to win a midget race at Ascot. The new car was now officially called the Coyote 1 (some of the early spellings had *Coyotte*) and the team was joined by Klaus Arning, a suspension engineer who'd been dispatched by Ford to work on the project. Arning had done much of the development work on Carroll Shelby's Cobras. Foyt called him "our computer. He told us where to put our mounting points and figured our angles. He told us why and it made sense." The car's dramatic suspension offset was the most notable feature, four inches to the left, compared to two and a half inches on the factory Lotus.[10]

Waiting until Friday night to fly cross-country, Foyt arrived in Trenton in time for a few practice laps and qualifying. Although he'd said no one was to blame for the Phoenix mix-up between him and Andretti, others were quick to point a finger.

Andretti "spun out and took Foyt with him," said a preview story in the *New York Times*, adding Mario "is haunted by the specter of Foyt. This big, brawny Texan is the Babe Ruth of the sport and everyone else is measured against him. If you can beat Foyt, you can win the race, it is that simple."[11]

Andretti tried to defuse the situation, with minimal results.

"A.J. and I are not exactly intimate," he admitted, "but I respect him, and I'd like to think he respects me. In the Phoenix race, we were both running hard. Each of us expected the other to lift. Neither of us did and we clashed a little bit. But there is nothing deep or lasting about our rivalry. It's something that some people like to build up."[12]

Fanning the fires were promoters, hoping to drive up ticket sales, and the local press, hoping to sell more papers. In the past it had been Eddie Sachs and A.J. Foyt. Now it was Andretti and Foyt. "Foyt vs. Andretti Means War," was the headline in the *Philadelphia Daily News*. Although noting "A.J. Foyt says a racetrack is no place for a feud," the article warned, "When these two tangle on a racetrack, they put on one of the hottest impressions of a feud you ever saw."[13]

Andretti again earned the pole, setting a record in the process. Ruby, debuting Gurney's new Eagle, was second, Foyt fourth. It took Foyt just seventeen laps to work his way around Ruby and then, in traffic, past Andretti and into the lead. He stayed out front until lap thirty-nine, when Andretti made an impressive pass around the outside. Foyt said later his engine was starting to go away and by lap eighty-five he was out entirely.

Andretti pitted early, having burned a tire off in the battle for the lead. A freak rain shower hit shortly after he returned to the track and ended the race with Ward out front, giving the team of Bignotti and John Mecom their first victory.

————

When practice started for the Indianapolis 500, it was all Andretti as he repeatedly turned the fastest lap of the day. By the time the first day of qualifying rolled around he was running more than five miles per hour faster than anyone else, with an increasingly unhappy Foyt in second.

A.J. spent part of the month with a pair of rookies: Ronnie Bucknum, his teammate from Sebring, and Cale Yarborough, who was looking for work because of Ford's NASCAR boycott. When A.J. spotted Yarborough, he took him around the garage area, introducing him to other drivers and pointing out where things as basic as the track restaurant were located, repeating tips Pat O'Connor had given him nearly ten years earlier.

Yarborough found the atmosphere in Gasoline Alley with its closed garages different from anything he'd experienced in NASCAR. While the drivers he met were civil, only Foyt and Ruby seemed friendly. There was none of the close interaction and horseplay common on the NASCAR circuit. He wondered if it was unique to Indy or if the entire series was run that way. He was grateful to Foyt for his help.[14]

"I ain't never seen that place before, and I needed some help," Yarborough recalled. "He gave me *a lot* of help. We'd kinda hit it off a bit when we first met in NASCAR. I already had a lot of respect for him. No matter which circus you drove in, you had to respect A.J. He had more talent in his little finger than most of us other drivers did in our whole body. He was just a natural-born race car driver. He could drive anything.

"He walked me around a bit and then he took me in a car and drove me around the track. He gave me the layout and told me how to get into the turns and how to drive the short chutes. Anything he told me I'd listen to. He said it was *his* opinion. But it was good and I really appreciated that."[15]

Given the intensity of the tire wars, some were surprised that Foyt, a Goodyear driver, would give so much help to Yarborough, aligned with Firestone. Not Yarborough.

"We weren't talking tires," he said. "We were talking racing."

There was less need to spend time with Snider. Although making just his second start at the Speedway and with only a little more than sixty race laps under his belt, he'd run about four thousand miles during tire tests and was doing what Foyt valued the most, turning consistent laps. The pair often practiced together, taking turns leading so each could see the impact of air on their car.

Neither Foyt's Coyote nor Snider's Lotus was running as fast as A.J. wanted, but that was a car problem, not a driver problem. Andretti was turning his fast laps on Firestones and with qualifying approaching, they used Snider's connections with the company to run some laps on its tires with one caveat. The Firestone engineers insisted on mounting and removing the tires on Pit Lane, not allowing Foyt to take them back to his garage. It didn't matter, there was no significant change in the speed of the cars.

It's not that they were slow—Foyt turned in the second-fastest practice speed of the month and Snider was in the top ten—it was that they were considerably slower than Andretti, and that wouldn't do. Andretti himself switched between a Lotus 38 and the Brawner Hawk he'd run in 1965, eventually deciding to stick with the Hawk.

When qualifying started, Snider, one of the first to take the green flag, was the big surprise. Running laps faster than he had all month, he broke his car owner's one- and four-lap track records.

It was Foyt's turn a few spots later, and his first lap was faster than he'd gone all month, but slower than Snider and well below the speed Andretti was expected to post. Coming around on lap two, he pulled in, not willing to concede the pole just yet. He'd say later it was one of the biggest mistakes of his career.

Andretti proved he was in a different speed zone when he qualified with a record four-lap average of nearly 166 mph. Foyt said he wanted to try one more thing and returned to the track for practice when there was a pause in qualifying. He'd run a couple fast laps and was headed to the pits when the Coyote slid higher than normal in the short chute between Turn One and Turn Two. The right rear grazed the wall, just enough to turn the front of the car into the wall for a harder hit, knocking the right-front wheel askew. At that point, Foyt said, "All I could do was go along for the ride," as the car ground to a halt against the wall. He was at a loss to explain what happened.[16]

"I was driving my usual pattern," Foyt said. "I wasn't doing anything different because I always drift close to the wall. But all of a sudden I pushed into it. I thought for a minute I could keep it under control and maybe I'd just brush the wall. But I went in good and solid. When the front end went in, too, and the wheel sorta collapsed, I knew I'd had it. Maybe it was the wind and maybe it wasn't. But something pushed me out and that's all there is to it."

In his garage Foyt surveyed the damage and considered the options. Eighteen cars were already qualified, there was no way Foyt could do better than that. The car he'd spent the last eight months building and fine-tuning was badly damaged. There was no way it could be repaired in time to qualify on Sunday. Waiting another week would push him even further back in the field.

That left the team's Lotus 38 backup car. There was only one problem. It had come not from the Lotus factory, but from the Lotus Components Group, which meant it was mostly in crates and boxes with more than some assembly required. It wasn't exactly in a million pieces, but it was close. With no other viable option, Foyt and team went to work. He was too busy to talk with reporters and Snider wasn't sure what to say.

"It feels pretty good to beat the boss," he finally said sheepishly.

Andretti was on the pole with Clark alongside and Snider a surprise on the outside of the front row. Others already in the field included Jones, in fourth, and all three Mecom/Bignotti cars for Rodger Ward, Jackie Stewart, and Graham Hill. In the row in front of where Foyt hoped to start were three rookies.

After two weeks of practice without a car hitting the Speedway's walls, more than half a dozen cars crashed during the first day of qualifying. Foyt was one of the lucky ones. Chuck Rodee, getting his big opportunity in an A.J. Watson car, lost control while warming up, hit the Turn One wall, and was killed instantly. He lived only about a mile from the track, where his wife and four kids, ages thirteen, twelve, three, and two, were waiting for him.

Foyt and his team worked until about 3:30 a.m. Sunday before taking a break for a few hours' sleep, returning later in the morning to finish the car. By 2:30 p.m. the Lotus was ready to test. It was a stark refrigerator white and carrying No. 45, with a handful of stickers on its sides. After just seven laps, the fastest at 159 mph, he pulled into the pits, added a bit of nitro to the fuel mixture, and pushed the car to the qualifying line. Four laps later, one above 162 mph, he was the day's fastest qualifier and sixth fastest overall, but would start nineteenth.

He didn't try to hide his disappointment.

"[The Coyote] was built for the 500-mile race and that's all," he said. "I think we can borrow some pieces off it and put it on the Lotus and have time to make the car ready for the race. In fact, I know we can. It's just a shame. We had our chassis working well and I was real pleased with it. But they say everything that happens has a purpose. Maybe this did too. I guess we'll find out."[17]

Later in his garage Foyt was handed a card.

"Congratulations to the B-Team," it read, signed, "the A-Team."

While Foyt was disappointed, others were amazed he'd been able to take an untried car and turn his fastest laps ever at the Speedway. An "unbelievable performance by the unbelievable A.J. Foyt," Andretti said, "perhaps one only a race driver could understand."[18]

Safely in the field, Foyt and Pouelsen went back to square one, taking his Lotus apart, replacing some parts with those from the Coyote, and strengthening others when possible. They determined the crash had been caused by an A-arm suspension failure and worked on beefing up the area on both cars. Jeffries came in to paint and letter the car. Renumbered with No. 2, the car looked nearly identical to the Coyote and even carried a "Coyote Jr" on its nose.

It wasn't until the end of the week that Foyt got back on the track, but only for a few laps. He admitted he would be starting the race with his fewest practice laps ever for the 500, yet he sounded extremely confident.

"I've completely reworked this car and it will be just like the Coyote. I figure I can maybe run up on 'em [the leaders] within ten laps. After all, I'm only six car lengths out of the lead when they wave the green flag, unless the birds up front pull a quickie on us. I sure am glad I'm on the inside. That gives you a little more operating room and I'll need it on race day."[19]

When the final field was set, however, Foyt actually moved up one spot when another driver was bumped from the field as too slow. That put him in eighteenth, on the outside of the sixth row alongside two rookies and behind Hill, another rookie.

Also in the field was Yarborough, who'd learned his lessons well, turning in the second-fastest rookie time behind Jackie Stewart and the fastest times of anyone in the corners. He sounded like a person who'd found his future.

"Man, I love this kind of racing," Cale said. "This is real racing. I've just fallen in love with it. Open cockpit racing is for me. Driving one of these cars is like riding a streak of lightning. Man, you are really flying."[20]

By the final practice session, Carb Day on Friday, Foyt was putting the finishing touches on the Lotus. He spent the first half of the three-hour session making minor changes, and then was ready for a fuel-economy run. After a quick couple of laps, however, he was black-flagged for leaking oil.

Foyt was irate when he climbed from the car and laid into his crew for leaving a fitting loose. He grabbed a wrench and crawled under the car, emerging a moment later and calling for a USAC official. When the official was in reach, Foyt grabbed him by the neck and mentioned where he was going to shove his head. Then he told the official to "go on, get down there and see if you can show me any oil leaking." Unable to find any, Foyt was able to run a few more laps before the practice ended.[21]

Still surly the next day, Foyt attended a small media gathering in a downtown Indianapolis hotel. Several writers who weren't regulars on the racing beat were in attendance, and it didn't help when all they wanted to talk about was Andretti. The pole sitter was the talk of the town and featured in the 500 preview issue of *Sports Illustrated* with the headline "Fastest Hee-ro at Indy." Chief among the cheerleaders was Andretti's car owner, who just happened to be Foyt's former car owner.

"He is the most exciting driver I have ever watched," said Al Dean. "The finest driver ever to come to the Speedway."

Foyt had heard enough.

"Who's Mario Andretti? What'd he ever win? Mario's got a near perfect car—everything's been working just right for him. But what'd he ever *win*?

"One race," he answered. "One race. That's all he's ever won."[22]

He was also critical of the risks he felt Andretti was taking.

"Four times Andretti has sent his car out of control with his tactics, such as cutting in from the right going into a turn. He's got enough experience and too much finesse to act that way. It's not necessary. But I'll tell you this. If anyone messes around with my life—and I don't care who it is—I'll punch him right in the nose."

By the next day he'd calmed down enough to joke with Snider about the start of the 500, urging his teammate to "make sure they come down nice and slow, we want a lovely start." Snider gave no indication he was listening to his boss.[23]

"I just plan to really go at it, try and jump out front if I can," he said, noting Clark had taken the lead ahead of Foyt from his second-place starting position the year before. "I figure the way to beat Andretti, Clark, Jones and Lloyd Ruby is to beat them around the first turn."[24]

Snider couldn't have asked for a better start as the eleven rows of cars were tightly bunched behind the red Mercury Comet pace car at the prescribed ninety mph. Some would later say the speed was too slow and the cars too close together. As the pace car pulled into the pits, starter Pat Vidan immediately began waving the green flag. Some would later say it was too soon and some drivers were caught by surprise. There'd been no chance for the cars to accelerate as they approached the starting line. Andretti moved cleanly away, but Clark, who said, "I never saw a green light," lagged behind. Snider got a good jump, pulling down in front of Clark and putting a nose ahead of Andretti going into Turn One.[25]

Behind them pandemonium broke loose.

Starting on the outside of the fourth row, two rows in front of Foyt, was Billy Foster, who'd missed the first thirty minutes of the drivers' meeting and the warnings to take it easy at the start. Foster darted to the inside of the car ahead of him, driven by Don Branson, a respected veteran racing in his eighth 500 but a notorious conservative starter. Taking advantage of his five-speed transmission, which allowed for quicker acceleration than most of the other machines in the race equipped with two-speed gearboxes, Foster quickly moved past Branson and alongside Gordon Johncock, starting on the outside of the second row. All just as the cars were passing the start/finish line.

Foster was nearly past Johncock when his car moved back up the track. Nearly. Foster would say he was bumped up the track. Branson was quick to disagree.

"No one forced Foster into Johncock," he said. "He just ran over him. Some guys ought to have more sense. You'd think when they get in this race they'd have some sense, but they sure as hell don't show it."[26]

The limited video footage, crude compared to today's multi-camera broadcast, was inconclusive. The cars touched, Foster careening into the outside wall. The impact sent the right-side tires and nose from the car bounding across the track, forcing others to take evasive action and turning the fifty-foot-wide front straightaway of the world's most famous racetrack into a smoky pinball machine of spinning race cars, bouncing tires, and flying car parts. At one point ten tires could be counted bouncing high into the air.

Caught in the middle of it all was Foyt, attempting to knife his way through the melee while at the mercy of less experienced drivers, not that any amount of experience would have prepared them for the free-for-all they now found themselves in.

There was little rhyme or reason for who was able to get through and who was caught up in the accident. Hill, starting behind Foster and in front of Foyt, paused for a moment and then accelerated through a small hole and somehow made it through. Mel Kenyon, who started next to Foyt, made it through. Just as he thought he might follow Hill and Kenyon, Foyt, who initially slowed when Hill did, was drilled from behind by Al Miller, who somehow made it forward from his thirtieth starting position. Foyt was pushed into the outside wall and a flash fire quickly extinguished itself; the self-sealing rubber fuel cell in Miller's car had done its job.

Cars were still spinning and sliding, but Foyt was already out of his and scrambling up the twelve-foot fence that separated the track from the spectators, barrel-rolling over the top into the relative safety of the grandstands. Even that was not without danger, as fourteen spectators were injured by the raining debris. Foyt's knee hurt and spectators pointed to his hand, where blood dripped from his red glove. In his haste to get out of the car, he'd bruised his knee on the instrument panel and a sliver from the windscreen had cut through his golf glove and lodged in his knuckle.

"Blood was running all down my left hand, going all over," Foyt said. "I thought, man, my hand must be in bad shape. I pulled the glove off and there was this little ole bitty nick. I really thought I was hurt a lot worse. It was embarrassing. I thought, man, I ain't even gonna show it to nobody."[27]

With the track blocked, the race was stopped by an accident for only the second time in history, but also the second time in three years. It wasn't long before Foyt was stomping down the front straightaway through the carnage, looking like a boxer tracking down his prey. His driver's uniform, crisp and sparkling white just moments earlier, was open at the top and now grimy and blood splattered from top to bottom. He'd somehow lost his right shoe in the confusion.

He spotted Gurney, whose car had also been destroyed, walking zombie-like back toward the pits, helmet on and white fireproof scarf still covering his nose and mouth. His goggles hung down around his neck, a look of disbelief and disgust in his eyes. They spoke briefly and then were approached by Chris Schenkel, covering the event for ABC's *Wide World of Sports*. Gurney went first and while it was against his character to publicly criticize another driver, he didn't hesitate to unload on the group as a whole.

"Collectively, I don't know, really, who is to blame. I don't think you'll be able to blame it on any one person. But they were all using very, very poor judgment," he said, his cadence quickening and his voice raising an octave. "It's not very difficult to drive down a little straight piece of track here with a few cars on it. There shouldn't be any trouble at all. We're supposed to be good drivers, but I don't think they have the judgment of a flea as far as I'm concerned."[28]

Gurney was just getting warmed up. Clark sought him out and tried to console him. Gurney also spoke with Hill before being approached by several print reporters.

"Everybody has a brake and an accelerator and should be able to drive down a straight-away without running over each other. In this case I think enthusiasm took precedence over judgment. The cars were bunched, but I don't feel you can blame that. I think the drivers were at fault. These guys are a bunch of clowns. This is ridiculous."[29]

In comparison, Foyt was rather subdued when he spoke with Schenkel.

"What happened today, there was no call for. One of the guys was just too eager and I don't think had enough experience, just caused a lot of cars to get tore up. It was really ridiculous what happened. Just glad nobody got hurt real bad."

Then Foyt faced the print reporters and began naming names. Some surprising names.

"That Hill's foot came off the pedal, that started the troubles. I've been telling them those blankety-blank midget drivers from overseas would cause something like this," Foyt said, apparently unaware that, at six feet, Hill was an inch taller than he was.[30]

"I was very fortunate," A.J. said. "I seemed to be in the middle of it. I was very busy trying to avoid the cars and the wheels and various other bits that were flying around. I thought I was being bombed. I had to look up in the air as well as on the track."[31]

"Man, I thought I was home free. I got all the way through the mess without anyone or anything hitting me. I thought I was in the clear and boom! Miller hit me and I went into the wall. I'll never start this far back in the pack again. I had a sneaking hunch about it. From now on, if I don't qualify the first day, I'll forget it."[32]

It took ninety minutes to clear the track and those watching on closed-circuit at theaters across the country were entertained by repeated showings of Foyt scaling the fence, the crowd roaring with laughter each time. After Foyt had a chance to watch the crash footage several times and talk with other drivers, he changed his tune, joining the chorus of those pointing a finger at the Canadian driver.

"I saw it all happening. Foster made a [blankety-blank] fool of himself. Foster tried to move up and had nowhere to go. He went from the outside to the inside and then back outside again and he and Johncock collided. He wiped out a bunch of good cars. I said yesterday there were five guys in the race I was worried about and Foster was one of them."[33]

He said he decided to climb the fence after being sprayed by fuel and oil from Miller's car.

"I was drowned in alcohol. Then hot oil hit me and I thought I was burning. I got out of that car and over the fence while they were still having wrecks."

Many thought Foyt would replace Snider in the second car when the race restarted. The drivers, however, said it was never discussed, never considered.

"I never thought about replacing Snider," Foyt would say. "He had more talent, when he wanted to apply it, than most race drivers. He was a very good race driver."[34]

There were no heroics for Snider on the restart as he followed Andretti and Clark for the first fifty miles. Jones and Ruby passed Snider, and Chuck Hulse was gaining on him when he suddenly lost control coming out of the second turn.

"I was looking down at my dash coming out of the turn and all of a sudden I was, 'What the hell, I'm in the grass.' I don't know what it was, but Hulse told me it was the quickest spin he's ever seen."[35]

With both his cars out and the race only twenty-two laps old, Foyt changed into street clothes and joined Gurney in Ruby's pit. His fellow Texan was running second when Clark spun on lap sixty-four and Ruby took the lead at Indy for the first time. He led a race high sixty-eight laps and was nearly a minute ahead approaching the 400-mile mark when his engine started smoking and he was black-flagged by officials. Foyt walked onto Pit Lane and was the first one to console him.

With Ruby out and Clark having spun again, Stewart was in front, with Clark second and Hill third. Three British drivers in three British-made cars were running one-two-three. Stewart would drop out and Hill would pass Clark, although the Lotus driver didn't realize it was for lead. Even Hill found himself a bit surprised in Victory Lane.

"I had a pretty steady run and very uneventful," he said in a classic British understatement. "I'm a bit surprised to have won, but naturally I'm very pleased to have done so."[36]

Foyt said he wasn't going to the Victory Dinner. "You call that a race? Who'd Graham Hill beat? I don't mind losing a race, but I don't like to be put out before I make the first turn."[37]

At the dinner Hill initially dismissed the European trio running up front as a "coincidence," the result of so many top cars and drivers having been knocked out of the race. He couldn't resist, however, rubbing a little salt in the wounds of the American drivers while accepting a seemingly endless number of checks provided by various accessory companies to the winner for using their product. Hill pocketed $15,000 from Firestone, more than $8,000 from Autolite spark plugs, $1,000 from Prestolite, and on and on it went. Grateful, yet amused by it all, Hill's dry and very British sense of humor took some in attendance off-guard.

"Jimmy and I are thinking of sponsoring an award for the top-finishing American next year," he quipped. Many laughed, although few drivers joined in.[38]

Stewart said he wanted to contribute to the prize, too. Later at a Grand Prix event he went even further, saying he believed rear-engine cars demanded more finesse than American drivers, used to wrestling roadsters and stock cars around in circles, may have.

"The A.J. Foyts were good for American racing for a while," he said, "but they are hurting it now."[39]

Stewart later tried to walk back the statements when a *Sports Illustrated* article implied he had little respect for American drivers.

"It's ridiculous. Everybody knows that Foyt is a great race driver. If you take the top four or five American drivers and pit them against the top four or five Grand Prix drivers with equal equipment in any type of racing you will see some great competition."[40]

Not seeing anything funny about the race was Ward, the two-time 500 winner and the all-time leading money winner at the track. He'd dropped out early, citing slippery track conditions. He felt slighted by the amount of attention given by the Mecom team to Hill and Stewart during the month and used the banquet to announce his surprise retirement.

"I always said that when it wasn't fun anymore I would retire. Well yesterday it just wasn't fun."[41]

In its race report, *Motor Sport*, Europe's leading racing publication, implied it had been a rather easy event and warned, "If regulations are not imposed on foreign entries there may be many more road-racing drivers and cars at the 1967 race. If this happens, then the myth of Indianapolis will become history and live only in the minds of those who can remember the 'Golden Days.'"[42]

CHAPTER 21

BAD BREAKS

1966

Given Graham Hill's comments at his Victory Dinner, it was probably a good thing A.J. Foyt wasn't in attendance. With only six days until the next race at Milwaukee, he was in his Gasoline Alley garages with three wrecked race cars. The damage to George Snider's car could be fixed, but repairing his own Coyote would take at least a month and it was doubtful the Lotus wrecked on the race's first lap would ever run again.

Once more Foyt turned to Colin Chapman. With Jimmy Clark back on the Formula One circuit, his second-place Lotus 38 was available. It took only a day for Foyt to write a check for $50,000 and take delivery of the car, the type of business deal Lotus had come to expect and appreciate when working with him.

"A.J. was regarded with much affection by everyone at Team Lotus," said Andrew Ferguson, the team's competition manager. "Both he and his father were perfect customers. If payment was not made upfront prior to order confirmation—usually because we were unable to price items instantaneously—subsequent invoices were always paid by return. As a result, everyone involved, from accountants to store-keeper, responded instantly to A.J.'s requirements. Not so much Chapman, who kept insisting Foyt put the Lotus emblem back on his cars, although the demand was ignored by those working directly with Foyt."[1]

Even though the car had finished second at Indy, it was a testament to Clark's skills more than the machine. Built at the end of 1965, it was nicknamed "The Old Nail" and Clark said it "handled like a pig," especially on cold tires. He'd

◀ Aldo and Mario lean in to hear what Foyt has to say after A.J. led the first ninety-seven laps at the Hoosier Hundred, only to snap a brake pedal and finish second. "I asked him why he was using his brakes," Mario recalled. "I think it pissed him off." *Revs Institute, The Bruce R. Craig Photograph Collection*

spun twice during races and said, "I actually spun six times, but I caught four of them." He joked sponsor STP stood for "spinning takes practice."[2]

Foyt knew all that when he purchased the car, but it was the best he could do on short notice. There wasn't time to do more than change the car's settings from the slightly banked 2.5-mile Indianapolis Motor Speedway to the flatter, one-mile Milwaukee track and slap the No. 2 on its sides and nose. The car was still painted STP's dayglo red, or "Granatelli Green" as the Lotus crew called it.

After checking to make sure Snider's car was running okay, Foyt waited for more than an hour after the start of practice before taking to the track himself. "If I keep it in the pits, I can't get it banged up," he joked.[3]

He'd run less than a dozen practice laps when, entering the second turn, he felt the right-rear suspension buckle and the back of the car begin to slide toward the wall. He knew better than to turn into the slide as was the natural tendency; the car could suddenly grip the track and go head first into the wall. Instead he yanked the steering wheel to the left, hoping to spin it harmlessly in a circle without hitting anything. It didn't work. He was in trouble, sliding backward toward the wall and powerless to do anything more than brace for the impact.

Foyt's head snapped forward as the car hit the wall, but the safety harness held his body in place. Now it was time to get out. Only the car was still sliding, and as he released the belts he hit the wall a second time, this time nearly head-on. It wasn't much more than a bump, but it was enough for him to drop back into the cockpit and slide forward, his feet now tangled in the pedals. He could smell methanol. While the car's main fuel cells remained intact, a small overflow tank located under the driver's seat had ruptured, its contents quickly spreading onto the car's floor.

The Lotus did another half spin and came to a stop, all four wheels askew. He felt the heat first and then saw the smoke as the clear methanol flames began to burn the car. He attempted to push himself up from inside, only to fall back in the seat again. Some of those watching said later they saw Foyt fold his arms and slump back in the seat. They thought he'd given up. With the flames engulfing the Lotus, he was actually gearing up for one last effort to get out.

"I knew I had to get out or just fry," he said. "I gritted my teeth and put my hands into the burning fuel to raise myself out."[4]

A leader in driver safety more by example than his words, Foyt was one of the first to regularly wear a racing uniform and used lap and shoulder belts and a submarine belt before they were required. Now he was wearing a new Hinchman driver's suit made from a recently introduced fabric, Nomex, rather than a cotton-treated uniform. Hinchman even provided him with a trademark red bandanna made out of Nomex.

Unlike some of the other drivers who'd begun using fire retardant driving gloves, however, Foyt didn't like the feel of the thick gloves on the steering wheel. He'd long worn red Ben Hogan–branded leather golf gloves, and that's all that covered his hands as he reached outside of the car's cockpit and into the flames lapping at its side. He pushed himself up again, kicking his feet to try to escape the pedals.

It worked. He pushed himself up and out of the car and stumbled away, rolling on the ground to try to extinguish the flames on his driving suit. He got up and ran a few steps toward a fire truck, which had arrived at the scene. He'd later call the response of safety crews "Mickey Mouse" and criticized the track for having only one truck on hand for practice.[5]

"I'm okay, I'm okay," he yelled, running toward the firemen and waving his hands. "I think it's just my hands."[6]

The golf gloves were all but melted away and his skin, "like on a chicken bone, slid off both my hands." As the firemen fumbled with their hoses, the first people to reach him had only a wool blanket and they wrapped him in it to snuff out any remaining flames. The wool fibers on the raw skin caused excruciating pain and he lost consciousness.[7]

At Milwaukee's West Allis Memorial Hospital, doctors who'd treated Jim Hurtubise the year before were relieved to see that Foyt's burns weren't nearly as bad. They quickly determined there was no need to try and move him to the burn center in San Antonio and listed him in "fair condition" with second- and third-degree burns. The Nomex uniform had done its job: the burns were limited to areas not covered by the suit, primarily his face, neck, wrists and hands, ankles, and feet. The crash was big news in Indianapolis, the story running under a page-one banner headline in the *Indianapolis Star,* knocking an article on a planned space walk from the top spot.

His hands were the major concern and heavily bandaged. For the first time since he was an infant, he needed help doing everything, including going to the bathroom. He said he was too proud to let the nurses help and waited for Lucy to arrive at the hospital later that night, which seems like it might be part of the A.J. Foyt lore.

Foyt wasn't the only driver to miss the Wisconsin race. Lloyd Ruby crashed his plane while taking off from Indianapolis on his way to Milwaukee, suffering a compressed spinal fracture. Parnelli Jones, the defending race champion, ran only a few practice laps and decided to step away from racing. Johnny Rutherford was still recovering from two broken arms. With A.J. Foyt, Parnelli Jones, Lloyd Ruby, Johnny Rutherford, and the retired Rodger Ward on the sidelines and only a dozen cars making the start, Mario Andretti qualified on the pole and led all one hundred laps to score his first Indy car win on an oval. The following week at Langhorne, facing another depleted field, Andretti scored another sweep.

After originally being told he'd be in the Milwaukee hospital for several weeks and out of action for a couple months, Foyt convinced his doctors to let him return home to Houston on Tuesday, with the understanding that he'd check into a hospital there. Back in Texas, he decided his recovery could continue at home, with outpatient trips to the hospital for his bandages to be changed. His arrival at the house, however, was not without incident.

"My kids started screaming and running because they thought I was a mummy," he recalled. *The Curse of the Mummy's Tomb* movie had recently been released in the United States. For ten-year-old Tony, it was the first time the dangers of what his father did for a living struck home.[8]

"That tore me up, when he got burnt real bad, where he got his hands and face burnt. We went to the airport to pick him up and he looked like a mummy, all wrapped up. That was kind of scary," Tony recalled.[9]

"There wasn't even a place to give him a kiss," said daughter Terry, who was eight.[10]

That weekend word came that Jud Larson and Red Riegel had been killed in a sprint car race at the Reading Fairgrounds in Pennsylvania. It was Larson whom Foyt let drive his sprint car at New Bremen the day after winning the 1964 Indianapolis 500. Larson had gone on to win thirteen feature events since then, and Foyt called the fellow Texan "the greatest dirt track driver in the United States."[11]

Larson and Riegel had been battling for the lead along with Bobby Unser on the second lap of the thirty-lap feature when they came together, both cars flipping outside the track. The race was stopped for forty-five minutes and won by Unser when it was restarted.

"Jud Larson was one of my heroes," Unser said. "He could make magic on dirt. Everybody wonders how you could keep racing when you just lost two guys ten feet from you. Well it's not hard. It's the way we live. We're race car drivers. Did I like to see Jud get killed? Lordy mercy no. Did it bother me? Yeah, sure it did. But somebody's gonna win that race. I needed the money and I'm there to race. We all lived that way."[12]

Unser pocketed just under $1,000 for the victory.

Foyt also missed the 24 Hours of Le Mans in mid-June where Ford finally beat Ferrari in the endurance classic. Missing Le Mans didn't bother him, and he hoped Ford's victory would ease the pressure on him to drive there in the future. Andretti's big lead in championship points was more concerning, and he was eager to get back in action as soon as possible.

His hands were healing well, although it was a painful process.

"You can break bones and you can do a lot of stuff, but I don't think there's nothing no worse than burns. Peeling the skin off and scrubbing it with iodine and all that. Man, it hurt."[13]

He agreed to speak with reporters during one hospital visit and showed his sense of humor hadn't been injured. The Lotus was a complete write-off, he said, noting, "Fifty-thousand is a lot to spend for ten laps."[14]

He confirmed having worked a deal with Gurney to take over the Eagle being driven by Joe Leonard. Gurney's All American Racers operations was stretched thin with him driving in Europe, and Foyt would operate the team with Leonard continuing as the car's driver. He also had another car on order from Lotus.

"I'm healin' up faster than we can put race cars back together," he quipped.

The team still had only one car available for the June 26 Atlanta race and when "George (Snider) told me he didn't care to run the high banks," Foyt decided to give it a try. In retrospect, just about any track would have been better for his return than high-speed Atlanta Speedway, but it did have the second-biggest purse next to Indy and the winner earned 600 points toward the championship, also second only to Indy.

Plans for an extra day of practice evaporated when the car arrived late. When he finally got on the track, he was unhappy with its handling, chewed out Johnnie

Pouelsen, and could do no better than seventh in qualifying, five miles per hour off his record pace of a year earlier.

He lasted only five laps in the race, all of them under a caution caused by another driver's spin in the first turn. He got out of the car complaining about its handling, while one crew member said it was a gear problem and another that the car was overheating. Foyt also pulled off his special gloves made of muslin gauze to display his blistered hands, which were already beginning to crack and bleed. "My hands just weren't ready," he said. "I couldn't hold them down [on the wheel] for any time at all. The blood rushing to them would make the pain unbearable."[15]

Outwardly he was philosophical about the crashes, saying, "It's just racing luck. You take the good with the bad and I've had my share of good luck. It's just the same as when you're in business, you have your ups and downs. If I was spinning and crashing into walls, I might really give it some serious thought. But mechanical failure and that wreck on the first lap in the 500 weren't my fault so I simply consider it as bad luck."[16]

Once back in a race car, however, there'd been a new experience he hadn't felt before. He was "petrified."

"Every time the car kind of jumped sideways, you know, it petrified me," he admitted years later. "You knew you were going to hit the wall. You knew it was going to blow up."[17]

With Foyt out, Andretti rolled to his third straight flag-to-flag victory at Atlanta, lapping the field. He'd led 500 consecutive laps over three races and held the track record on every paved course on the circuit. There'd be no more questions about how many races Andretti had won.

BACK IN ACTION

With Ford still boycotting NASCAR events, Foyt had a full month to rest before the next Indy car race on the road course at Indianapolis Raceway Park. The down time also allowed Pouelsen and team to prepare two cars for the race. The Coyote was back, featuring a hodgepodge of parts, including some salvaged from the wrecked cars. They'd also continued to work on the car raced at Atlanta.

Foyt's hands were much better when he arrived for the race, bright pink in color but no longer bleeding. He gave Snider, making his second road course start, the choice of cars and George picked the Coyote. Both struggled in qualifying and ended up starting next to each other back in the seventh row. Foyt dropped out after just five laps with ignition problems and then replaced Snider, losing a lap during the process but coming back to finish sixth.

Andretti saw his string of laps led snapped as he spun out in the first corner, dropping to last in the twenty-four-car field. Much as Foyt had the year before, he battled back to take the lead and, unlike Foyt, held on for his fourth straight win.

Nobody in the Foyt camp was happy afterward. A.J. didn't like the car preparation and Pouelsen took exception with the complaints. Snider was unhappy with both the chassis setup dictated by Foyt and being bumped from the car.

The turmoil simmered for two weeks as the team prepped for Langhorne, scene of the breakup between Foyt and George Bignotti the year before. A reporter asked Bignotti about Foyt's troubles on and off the track since their split.

"I really couldn't say if it's because I left him, though he probably wouldn't have had quite as much trouble if I'd stayed. A.J. can be the nicest man in the world, or he can be the meanest. Foyt is a good mechanic, but he's not meticulous. He's not a watchmaker. And he's not really capable of making all the decisions. Every time he did something, we had to re-do it."[18]

Foyt took the unusual step of entering his dirt track car at Langhorne, but that didn't work out either. He ordered the car loaded up and taken home after practice, and this time no one stood in his way.

"Everything I did today was backwards," he said. "Every other time that's happened this year, I've wound up crashing. So I decided, 'Why take the chance?' The car was fine. I just didn't want to run it."[19]

Snider at least started the race but ran poorly, finishing seven laps behind winner Roger McCluskey. Things didn't improve during the two weeks prior to the annual Springfield-Milwaukee weekend. Pouelsen and Foyt continued to battle. Snider argued with his crew chief, Gil Morales, and presented Foyt with an ultimatum over his car's setup. Foyt said he was free to leave, which he promptly did, signing on with Bignotti to drive Jackie Stewart's car from Indianapolis at Milwaukee. Morales was let go, and a few days later the team's engine man, Leroy Neumeyer, walked out, having heard enough complaints about the powerplants.[20]

More than fifty years later, both Foyt and Snider said they didn't remember the incident nor why they split up in 1966. They would reunite in several years and become close friends, Snider often driving a car for Foyt at Indianapolis.

On Thursday evening, two days before the August 20 Springfield race, the simmering volcano erupted. Unhappy with the engine in the dirt track car, Foyt said, "We're gonna stay right here until we get this thing straightened out."[21]

Pouelsen, no stranger to hard work and agreeable to staying through the night if necessary, said he needed to get something to eat first.

"I said we're staying right here until we get it fixed," Foyt countered.

Pouelsen shrugged, said "I'm going to eat," and walked out. He returned Friday morning to pick up his belongings, sold his tools, and left for his California home. They would briefly get back together before the end of the year, but any relationship they had ended that night in the garage. Pouelsen would die in a private plane crash in 1967.

Despite the departures, Foyt's car was finally running right when he took it to Springfield, although Don Branson led all one hundred laps. Foyt challenged at times, but Andretti passed him for second near the end of the race, A.J. coming in third.

The next day's race at Milwaukee was rained out, although the extra week of preparation didn't help. His season hit a low point August 27 as he qualified the Coyote twenty-second in a field of twenty-six cars and finished twenty-fourth, lasting just fourteen laps. Only Leonard seemed to be able to run consistently for the team, finishing third in the Eagle.

Three consecutive dirt track races were next, two in his Meskowski champ car and another in a sprint car. The first was at Du Quoin, where Foyt had won five of the past six events.

The situation between Andretti and Foyt had worsened, and the more Andretti won, the more annoyed A.J. became. Both drivers traveled with an entourage who reported on what the other driver was doing or saying. Someone would tell Andretti that Foyt said he was reckless. Someone else would tell Foyt that Andretti said he was over the hill. Race promoters and the media were only too happy to fan the flames.

"I believe that many of our problems were caused by people who like to gossip and stir up controversy, thus creating situations that might never have existed otherwise," Andretti said in his 1970 autobiography, *What's It Like Out There?* "Naturally we had some scrapes. He thought they were my fault; I thought they were his. Neither of us would give an inch on or off the track."[22]

It reached a point where Andretti says he felt the need to reach out to Foyt for a meeting. He spoke of it often over the years and recalled it happening prior to the 1966 Du Quoin race, during Fair Week. Foyt says he "kinda" remembers a meeting, but none of the specifics about where or when it took place, not even what year it happened.

The most specific account of the meeting comes from an unusual source, a syndicated publisher of a religious column called Lenten Guideposts. It issued a bylined article by Andretti titled "My Race against Hate," in which he recapped the competition with Foyt and how it had become a "vendetta." In the column Andretti said he was at the drivers' meeting about an hour before the Du Quoin race when he spotted Foyt.

I was by myself. I happened to look up across the room and there was A.J. standing there alone. Suddenly from somewhere deep within myself came the conviction that it was wrong to let rivalry turn into bitterness. Somebody had to put an end to the bad feelings. So I walked over to him. "Maybe we should talk," I said.

"Sure," he said.

We walked out to the parking lot, just the two of us. We talked, openly and frankly. We didn't say much, just covered the important things, talking objectively, without anger.

We admitted to a mutual love—racing. And we knew if we kept going the same way, we would divide our world into two camps. We decided that it did nobody any good for us to nurse a grudge.

The air was cleared and we walked out of the lot together, each minus a ton of weight.[23]

Neither driver fared very well in the race, although at least Foyt finished, in seventh, while Andretti dropped out. Five days later in the Hoosier Hundred, they matched up in a race both would long remember, although for different reasons.

It was the Foyt of old as he qualified on the pole and led the first ninety-seven laps. Andretti was right behind for most of the race but had faded to a three-second deficit near the end. Foyt seemed to have the race wrapped up when he suddenly slowed. At first his crew thought he'd run out of fuel, but when he slid up against the wall, they knew something else was wrong. Andretti went by and on to the victory, Foyt recovering to finish second.

The cause of Foyt's problem soon became apparent. As he pulled slowly into his pit, he reached inside the car and pulled out the brake pedal, which had snapped off, tossing it at the feet of the crew.

"I couldn't catch Foyt," Andretti admitted afterward. "I knew if I ever won this race, something was going to have to happen to his car, because I couldn't catch him."[24]

One newspaper article said Foyt "proved he has what it takes to be a champion as he quickly regained composure and walked to the winner's circle to congratulate the still shocked Andretti."

Mario remembers it a little differently.

"A.J. came over [to Victory Circle] and wasn't very happy. He told Bill Marvel [a USAC official interviewing Andretti] he would have won if his brake pedal hadn't broke. He was right, but I said, 'Why were you using your brake pedal? I never used my brakes.' I think it pissed him off."[25]

Andretti later called the race a turning point in his career—and in his relationship with Foyt.

"That day I beat the king—I passed him right at the end," Andretti wrote years later in a first-person account for *Motor Sport*'s My Greatest Rival column, leaving out the part about Foyt breaking his brake pedal.[26]

The race did mark a turning point in their careers and especially their relationship. Andretti and Foyt were clearly on equal footing on the racetrack. Despite the Du Quoin meeting, their relationship, never close to begin with, was changed.

"Did we fall out?" Andretti repeated the question. "Well, he did with me, always had some kind of snide remark, but I just let it go. There was some tension between us outside the cockpit, but on the track he was always correct. I never felt he would do something to really hurt me."[27]

Chris Economaki, a leading auto racing journalist who knew both men well, said, "The Foyt-Andretti rivalry was epic, and very good drama. The two men were different in almost every way: their personalities, their backgrounds, their temperaments. The rivalry sometimes became bitter. In all my years, I've never seen two performers who were so bitterly divided.

"To their credit, they were always gentlemen away from the track when they interacted with one another."[28]

More than fifty years later Foyt was quick to point out that even though he finished second, he still made more money in the race than Andretti.

"I hated it," he said when asked about the race. "I led it all day long. And I still made more than Andretti, 'cause they were paying lap money. People are gonna read that and say, 'Bullshit, you don't make more money running second.' Look it up."[29]

A check of the record shows Foyt was right. He earned $17,068 to Andretti's $10,100.

RESET

The next day Foyt finished third in a sprint car race at Terre Haute. He'd been challenging for the lead when he made a rare mistake, sliding high in Turn Four. He regained control to finish third, but that wasn't good enough. He said he was through for the year and would pass up the final three champ car races and an exhibition race in Japan while getting ready for 1967. He got testy when asked if he was considering retirement.

"Why would I be building race cars if I was thinking of quitting?" he snapped. "I'm going to stay right here in Indianapolis and work on the cars and run them during tire tests, so we'll be completely ready for the first race next year."[30]

The broken brake pedal was still bothering him.

"Why the hell couldn't that thing have lasted three more laps? It had gone all that way, why wait until the ninety-seventh lap and snap? You can't understand something like this when you get in a streak of bad luck. But that's racing. You have to take the bitter too. I've had some good breaks too, remember."

It took him less than a week to start walking back his comments. He talked cryptically about a new Ford engine he was testing and that he might race it at Trenton, "if it meets with our approval." He also heard from promoters desperate for him to keep racing. He was still the sport's biggest draw, and a Foyt-Andretti matchup was the best opportunity to sell tickets they'd had in years.[31]

A few days later A.J. took the unusual step of calling reporters from the Speedway where he was testing to let them know he'd race at Trenton. He'd admitted coming back too soon from his Milwaukee injuries.

"This year, with all the wrecks and trouble, I was hurting. And when you don't feel right that kind of knocks the racing spirit out of you. I was, I admit, down in the dumps and blue. But right now, I feel like racing again.

"The story of my retirement really was wrong," he said. "I just said I wouldn't race again until my cars were capable of running a lot of miles. We got caught up on our two cars and everything's fine."[32]

Everything may have been fine, but it wasn't good enough to stop Andretti at Trenton, where he put two laps on the field. Starting back in thirteenth, Foyt showed flashes of his old self, driving to third place and happy "to finish a race again." He confirmed he'd run the final two Indy car races of the year after all (although not the exhibition in Japan), along with the NASCAR Charlotte race and a Can-Am event at Riverside.[33]

After settling its differences with NASCAR, Ford found a new stock car home for Foyt. Cale Yarborough, who'd been driving for Banjo Matthews prior to the boycott, was moved into the Wood Brothers' car, paving the way for Foyt and Matthews to reunite. Matthews embraced the "Cassius" nickname, putting it on the signboard where the driver's name normally went.

"That's because A.J. talks so much," Matthews joked. He said he was happy to get another hard charger in the car.[34]

"That's the only way I want to race," he said. "Conservatism may win point championships, but I like to look up and see my car out front. I think A.J. is one of the greatest racers ever. I don't know anyone who has more talent than A.J. He is so versatile he can drive anything from a go-kart to a prototype, and he'll win more often than not."

The return to NASCAR didn't go smoothly. One of the five fastest in practice, Foyt was turned away twice from a qualifying attempt because the car was judged to be too wide. After the second attempt he confronted official Norris Friel, with whom he had clashed in the past.

"What is the matter with the car?"

When Friel tossed the tape measurer at Foyt's feet and turned his back on the driver, A.J. launched into a tirade and had to be restrained from going after Friel.

"Everyone talks about my temper and I thought I kept it pretty well," Foyt said later. "I asked a simple question and I'm entitled to an answer. When he acted like a child and stomped off, it ticked me off. I've got a right to know what was wrong with the car. His behavior just hacked me off."[35]

Not having any problems was Gordon Johncock, who qualified second after signing with Junior Johnson to replace Foyt. After finally qualifying tenth, Foyt ran only twelve laps before his engine let go, one of sixteen cars to retire with engine problems.

The best thing coming from the trip was the new color Matthews was painting his cars. Gone were the mostly blue-and-white paint schemes he'd used in the past when Foyt drove for him, replaced by a bright orange/red combination he'd started using earlier in the year. Foyt liked it so much he asked what it was, discovering it was called "Poppy Red," a Ford factory color introduced on the Mustang.

DISAPPOINTMENT, DEATH, AND VICTORY

From Charlotte, Foyt went to Sacramento and the California State Fairgrounds, where he'd won three of the past four years. He was never in contention, qualifying twelfth, dropping out early, and finishing seventeenth, or next to last. Andretti led the most laps but also dropped out, although he scored enough points to clinch the championship, becoming the youngest driver to win two titles. The race was won by Dick Atkins, Jones's protégé, driving J.C. Agajanian's car.

Nothing good was to come from the October 30 Riverside Can-Am event. The new Can-Am series for unlimited sports cars was attracting a wide range of interest from both manufacturers and drivers. Like most in the series, Foyt was driving a new Lola T70. While most used Chevrolet engines, Foyt was saddled with the same Ford engine used by the victors at Le Mans. Fine for endurance races, it was too heavy for the Can-Am sprint events.

Foyt and Jones each received appearance money just to show up, and when neither qualified, the organizers waived the rules, allowing them to start in the back. It didn't do much good, as both were out before the race was ten laps old.

Foyt remained at Riverside the following week to help test Ford's new J-Car. The company had decided to return to Le Mans in 1967 and defend its title against Ferrari. The new car had been conceived, designed, and built at Kar-Kraft, Ford's racing skunkworks in Dearborn, Michigan. In theory it was lighter, more aerodynamic, and of course, faster. However Ken Miles, lead development driver of the Le Mans program, had been killed at Riverside in August testing the car. While Bruce McLaren took over the lead development role, Ford wanted its top two American drivers—Foyt and Andretti—more involved in the program.

McLaren and Andretti spent most of their time in the J-Car. The winning Le Mans Mark II, featuring numerous updates, was used for comparison and driven primarily by Foyt and Ruby. Ultimately, all four drove the J-Car and signed off on the machine, while submitting a long list of suggestions. Another test session was planned for late in the year at Daytona.

Still without a victory as the end of the year approached, Foyt agreed to run a couple of sprint car races for Agajanian. The first was at Ascot and attracted a top field, including Andretti, Atkins, Branson, and McCluskey, the series champion.

Don Branson, forty-six, the 1959 and 1964 national sprint car champion and eight-time 500 starter, was telling friends he planned to retire at the end of the year. Dick Atkins, twenty-eight, had seen his career skyrocket since winning the Turkey Night Grand Prix at Ascot in 1965. He was coming off his first big-car win just three weeks earlier at the California Fairgrounds and had established himself, alongside Andretti, as one of the sport's promising new stars.

Foyt took the early lead. As typical of such a short race, the pace was frantic, cars sliding up the track coming out of the turns, then diving down toward the corner, searching for a way past the car ahead. The crowd was still on its feet on lap five when Branson's car suddenly drove straight ahead into the Turn One wall, flipped on its side, and slid back into the middle of the track, where it was rammed by the car driven by Atkins, who had no place to go.

Branson died immediately, his neck broken when he hit the wall. Although speculation centered around a failure in the vehicle's steering system, the car was too badly damaged to tell for sure. Atkins was pulled from his machine by bystanders as a fire spread, following the flow of leaking fuel. The fuel pooled at the bottom of the track and continued to blaze for more than ten minutes, eventually stopping the race. Despite initial news reports, Atkins escaped major burns, but was unconscious and rushed to a local hospital where he would die the next day.

It took more than an hour to clear and clean the track, and once racing resumed, Foyt remained out front until lap seventeen, when he stopped with engine problems. McCluskey moved into the lead and won, followed by Andretti.

The victory "celebration" was nonexistent. Branson was well-liked, one of the best ever on dirt, and his retirement plans were well known. Both drivers were married and had three children. Atkins had a fourth on the way. They were the fourth and fifth drivers to be killed in sprint cars since the start of the year, most considered among the very best in the series. Even the relentlessly upbeat Agajanian, who owned Atkins's champ car, had a hard time addressing the crash.

"What can you say? That's the business and it's hard to stay with it sometimes. But you stay or you get out. I stay."[36]

Having an even harder time was Jones, who'd spent his entire career racing against Branson and had handpicked Atkins as his replacement. In his private life Jones was ending one relationship and beginning another—and considering retirement.

"The death of those two guys," Jones would say, "I mean, how bad can you feel? Whatever it is, I felt it. It had been the worst year of my life. I didn't know what the hell to do. But I still didn't want to quit. If I left racing, what the hell would I have left?

"I love racing. I always have and I always will. And I'm no more afraid of it than I ever was. But I've been through some things and I've seen some things that have made an impression on me. I know that if you keep on with this thing, the odds begin to run against you."[37]

The remaining sprint car teams made the nearly ten-hour overnight haul to Altamont Speedway in northern California near Stockton for another race on Sunday. Snider was hurt in his heat race when the throttle stuck open and he hit the outside wall, his car flipping three times and bursting into flames. Snider "managed to wriggle free and stagger a few feet away before collapsing."[38]

With Andretti in Las Vegas for a Can-Am race, Foyt took over Mario's ride in the Wally Meskowski sprinter and, facing a small field, scored his only feature victory of the year, beating Bobby Unser and Roger McCluskey in the process. Years later he seemed confused by a question about how he was able to race the next day after seeing Branson and Atkins killed.

"That's what we did," he said with a shrug, sounding a lot like Bobby Unser after Allentown. "I needed the money and there was a race to run."[39]

Andretti's response was similar, but more expansive.

"It happened. It was happening way too often. It seemed like you had to accept it. If you dwelled on it and allowed it to interfere in your objectives, then you had to get out of the business. It's not that we didn't have feelings. I mean, Doug Atkins was my teammate [in the race]. You had to put it aside. That year was a terrible time. Terrible time. We lost some really good friends. A lot of times when those events happened, you had to just go out and keep going."[40]

One race remained on the Indy car schedule, November 20 at Phoenix, and Foyt was a nonfactor, qualifying seventh and dropping out on lap forty-seven of two hundred. The star of the show was Jones, who'd overcome his questions and concerns to drive Atkins's car. After a problem at the start left him in last, he put on "a virtuoso display by a man it had become fashion to downgrade," before being taken out in a crash, Andretti going on to win.[41]

———

Foyt missed the Turkey Night Grand Prix at Ascot where Jones drove to an emotional victory. Ford was making a last-ditch effort to revive its Can-Am program and wanted Foyt and Andretti in the Bahamas for Speed Week.

Initial reports said the two cars were "nearly identical," which Foyt quickly corrected, noting Andretti was driving a Holman-Moody car, while he owned and prepared his own machine.

"It is my car, and it was my idea," he said, when asked about being teammates with Andretti. "We get together on some things, but Mario and I aren't really teammates. Mario doesn't even own the other Lola-Ford."[42]

There was another difference. While several Andretti sightings were reported at the local casino, Foyt spent most of his time under his baby-blue car.

"To novice race goers . . . Foyt is a rarity among professional athletes," wrote the reporter, who interviewed A.J. while the driver was changing a tire. "He owns the racing car he drives and oversees the repair operations. Foyt spends more time flat on his back with grease smeared across his face than behind the wheel."

It didn't matter who owned or worked on the cars, they shared the same problem: neither one was very good. Foyt was able to win a four-lap heat race, besting Mark Donohue in Roger Penske's Chevy-powered Lola, but it was the only race either Ford finished. A.J. then sold his car to Bob Bondurant, who, along with Andretti, Gurney, Jones, and others, would make a handful of starts in various Ford-powered Can-Am machines in the coming years with limited success.

The 1966 Speed Week marked the end of the annual event. Unnoticed by most of the racers during the week, the Bahama parliament was dissolved, and with it went many of the event's supporters. Foyt, who'd found his first road-racing success on the airport track—and was tied with Stirling Moss and Hap Sharp for the most victories in the series—was one of the few who wasn't sad to see it go.

"You've got to be realistic," he said. "First prize here is $5,000, which isn't so hot. And after that the prize list is pretty small."

J-CAR

Before Foyt and Andretti could go home for the holidays, they had to make a couple more stops at the behest of Ford, the first at the Daytona International Speedway. There was tension in the air as the updated J-Car was rolled out. Gone was the cockiness displayed by the Ford team since the Le Mans victory. Company spies had observed the recent Ferrari tests of its new 330 P4 prototype at the track and by all accounts it was impressive. All four of the Scuderia's Grand Prix drivers were on hand and took turns lowering the track record. Ferrari was obviously coming back with a vengeance.

McLaren and Andretti again focused on the supposedly new and improved J-Car while Foyt and Ruby established a baseline in a Mark II that had been undergoing continued development. It was immediately apparent the J-Car was a disaster. Most of the drivers' suggestions from the Riverside tests had been ignored.

"They do not have practical experience and rely solely on slide rules," complained one unnamed driver about Ford's engineers. "As a result, it takes longer to test and correct new cars and components than it does small, more flexible operations."[43]

The car was difficult to control at anything near high speeds and there was a problem with cracking wheels. Worst of all was a failure of the unique "honeycomb" chassis the car was built around. Foyt and Ruby ran the Mark II hard, faster than the J-Car, but couldn't match the speeds of the recently departed Ferraris. By the end of the test, however, all four drivers agreed. The J-Car was undrivable. The updated Mark II would have to do for February's 24 Hours of Daytona.

From there they went to Detroit for a year-end media party and holiday gala and the presentation of a new honor, the Ford Award, recognizing the top driver using the company's products. To nobody's surprise Andretti received the honor.

Andretti was clearly auto racing's new Golden Boy. He had company executives and reporters fawning over him, and Ford announced he'd be part of the Holman-Moody factory team for the 1967 Daytona 500.

"Andretti to me isn't the next Foyt as he has been billed," wrote Bob Myers in the *Charlotte News*. "He has already arrived, and there is little question that Foyt, plagued by misfortune, has been psyched by the achievements of the new king."[44]

It didn't help that Foyt had become increasingly difficult for reporters to talk with.

"It would be wrong to say that he was unpleasant when things were going badly," one columnist noted. "The fact is, he was downright mean."[45]

Not everyone was ready to declare the king dead, least of all Bignotti and Andretti.

"Don't put Foyt down because he's having a lousy year," Bignotti said. "He's had a helluva streak of bad luck and some guys are loving every minute of it. You can bet your last buck on this. When A.J. gets a new car that will go and it's what he wants, he'll be right up front again. Foyt is too great a driver to do anything else."[46]

Asked if Foyt was through, Andretti responded, "Are you kidding? That guy is having bad luck this year, but he is plenty tough. When you are in a race and you are leading, you know one thing for sure. You know that sooner or later he'll be up there challenging you."[47]

The year mercifully over, Foyt retreated to Houston to contemplate his future. For the second year in a row, he'd spent substantial sheet time, missing about a month of the season and returning too soon, hurting his overall performance. He'd won just one feature event, and for the first time since 1960 he'd failed to win an Indy car race, finishing only four. He'd fired his crew chief and watched as other crew members walked out. One former crew chief—Bignotti—had won the Indy 500 and another—Clint Brawner—had won his second straight national championship.

"I reckon I learned more about life in general last year than ever before," he'd say. "This is a funny business. One day you are on top and the next day you are so far down you can't even look up. And you don't even know how you got there.

"I think if I had got hurt any more I would have quit. Man, when you're getting hurt you think about a lot of things. But I love racing. I don't think I have anything to prove. I just enjoy the competition."[48]

CHAPTER 22

———

SCARED SHITLESS

1967

Having made the decision to return in 1967, A.J. Foyt set about making wholesale changes to his racing operation.

He rejected an offer from Andy Granatelli to drive a new turbine-powered car that the STP maven said he'd secretly been building the past two years. "Why the hell would I want to do that?" he barked at "Granabelli," as Foyt liked to call him. "I'm building two new cars of my own."[1]

The Coyotes—one all-new car and an overhauled version of the original—were under construction in Houston instead of Long Beach, California, where the "Lesovsky Lotus" and original Coyote were created. "Nothing was getting done out there when I wasn't around," he said. "So I decided to move everything to Houston."

Family friend Jimmy Greer, whose Houston business empire was taking off, had acquired several warehouses to support his operations and rented one on Toledo Avenue to Foyt. He decided to run a two-car team again, with Joe Leonard in the second car. Victor Morales returned to serve as Leonard's chief mechanic and brought several of the "Tamale Wagon" crew with him.

Leonard was a holdover from the second half of the 1966 season, having clicked for five top-five finishes in the races he'd started in the Eagle for Foyt. A.J. called him "Pelican Joe" because "All he did was swoop in and take our money." More importantly, "he liked to race, he knew how to race, and he was a hellofa racer."[2]

Two and a half years older than A.J., Leonard had started racing motorcycles in the early 1950s, winning three American Motorcycle Association (AMA) championships and twenty-seven national AMA events on road courses and dirt and paved ovals. He'd twice won the Daytona 200, the Indy 500 of motorcycle racing.

◀ "I wanted to win, but I wasn't sure it was worth it." *Revs Institute, Robert Tronolone Photograph Collection*

He began transitioning to four wheels in the early 1960s, running mostly USAC stock car races. He'd been working and driving occasionally for Ray Nichels when Foyt joined the team in 1964. Leonard had run a couple of Indy car races without a top-ten finish, but he remembered Foyt encouraging him to give it another try—in A.J.'s own unique way.

"Hey [Joe] you're good," Leonard recalled Foyt saying, "but I bet you're afraid to drive an Indy car." Foyt helped arrange for a ride at Phoenix late in '64, a fifth-place finish. A.J. put in a good word with Dan Gurney, who was starting his team and looking for drivers. Leonard then went to work for Gurney and gave All American Racers its first Indy car victory before ending up back with Foyt.[3]

Four cars were entered in the Indianapolis 500, two under the banner of Ansted-Thompson Racing for Foyt and, for the first time, two by A.J. Foyt Jr. for Leonard. All were sponsored by Sheraton-Thompson.

In NASCAR, Foyt signed on to drive a new Ford Fairlane in a handful of races for Banjo Matthews. In sports cars, Ford and Goodyear shifted him from the Holman-Moody team to one run by Carroll Shelby, which suited A.J. fine. He felt Holman-Moody's strength was in stock car racing, while Shelby's strength was sports cars. He was also happy to learn he'd be paired with Gurney for the upcoming 24 Hours of Daytona, although others questioned the wisdom of teaming two notorious hard chargers for an endurance race. As a result of Gurney's recent signing with Mercury to drive its stock car and Trans Am entries, and the possibility Foyt might also run several races for the brand, their GT 40 Mark II would carry the Mercury logo at Daytona.

Finally—and most importantly—A.J. named "the only man I can trust" to oversee the entire operation. His father, Tony Foyt, had been serving as de facto crew chief since the departure of Johnnie Pouelsen, and the announcement made it official. Reluctant to make a full commitment to the role in the past because he didn't want to give up his repair shop, Tony agreed to convert it to doing body work and other work for the team. The first race of the season was NASCAR's Riverside 500, where the year got off to a bad start. Billy Foster, whom many blamed for the first-lap accident at Indianapolis the year before, was killed when his brakes failed in practice and he hit the Turn Nine wall.

After qualifying seventh, Foyt moved to the front and was among the early leaders before rain stopped the event and postponed it until the following Sunday.

During a week of inaction, a small pool of oil formed under Foyt's car. Rules said a car couldn't be worked on during the red flag period and when the race restarted under yellow, Foyt came into the pits. While the crew added oil, Banjo crawled under the car and did the best he could to plug the hole. It worked for a while and Foyt moved toward the front again, until a telltale cloud of smoke began to trail the car and he parked it for good, Parnelli Jones going on to win the race.

Despite failing to finish, it was an encouraging start to the season. Foyt seemed to be his old self, joking with drivers and crew members and yelling at reporters who'd written his racing epitaph during the offseason. Only one problem remained.

"I was scared shitless every time I got in the car," Foyt said in his autobiography. "The start of the 1967 season was the worst of any for me. I made myself come back. I could have retired at that point and lived very comfortably for the rest of my life. I was in good enough financial position to do it. But I wanted to race.

"I had mixed emotions. I wanted to win, but I wasn't sure it was all worth it. I made myself drive harder than I really wanted to. I made myself get back on the horse that threw me."[4]

————

The California rains delayed the arrival of Foyt, Gurney, Mario Andretti, and others in Daytona for the 24 Hours race. When they did show up, it was obvious things were not going well. The new Ferraris were every bit as fast as rumored. Even faster was the Chevrolet-powered Chaparral 2F, featuring a high-mounted wing on the rear of the car. Often referred to as the "flipper car," it looked to be the pole winner, followed by the three Ferraris as qualifying drew to a close.

That's when Shelby ordered a set of special Goodyear "gumball" tires mounted on the Foyt/Gurney car and sent Dan out for a last-ditch effort. The tires were good for only a couple of laps, but Gurney needed just one. Told to ignore the previous engine rpm limits, he shattered the track record, although the engine did have to be changed afterward. If nothing else, the Ford/Mercury was on the pole.

There would be nothing else. Foyt started the race and dropped back as planned. Andretti, teamed with American Grand Prix driver Richie Ginther and starting in fifth, was the designated Ford rabbit. It was Mario's job to take the lead and set a fast pace, hoping the Ferraris would give chase and prove fragile.

The plan immediately fell apart. Phil Hill, starting second in the Chaparral, jumped out front and, despite his best efforts, Andretti was unable to keep pace, pulling into the pits before the twenty-lap mark in need of new tires. A few laps later another of the Fords was in the pits with a busted transmission. Then another. And another. It was apparent the cars shared a transmission problem, later traced to defective heat treatment during the production process.

The Ferraris refused to take the bait, content to maintain a pre-set pace and let the Chaparral and Fords battle for the lead. The Chaparral dominated for the first three hours until Hill skidded into the wall entering the banking, damaging the car beyond repair. With the Chaparral out, two of the Ferraris moved to the point, followed by the Foyt/Gurney car in third. While slowed by battery and clutch problems, it was the only Ford still running with the original transmission.

It was only a matter of time until the Foyt/Gurney car required a new gearbox, and when it did, the mechanics put an older-model tranny in the Mark II. It was 1:00 a.m., they were thirty laps behind the leaders, and they were given the green light to run as fast as they could. With both drivers turning near-record race laps, they were still going at the eighteen-hour mark, having moved up to fifth and having cut the margin to eight laps. The strain was too much on the engine, however, and it exploded shortly thereafter, knocking them out of the race and ending dreams of a Ford miracle.

The Ferraris were so far ahead as the race entered the final hour, they slowly circled the track three abreast, emulating Ford's botched finish from Le Mans the year before. Rubbing salt in Ford's wounds was Chris Amon, who'd shared the winning Mark II at Le Mans in 1966, and now led the Ferrari parade across the finish line.

"It's rather like driving a truck compared to a car," Amon said when asked to compare the Ford to the Ferrari, calling attention to the one-thousand-pound weight difference between the cars.[5]

The beatdown complete, the Ford team huddled. The transmission failures were a production problem and would be fixed, but Ferrari was a bigger challenge. Le Mans was a little more than four months away and the new Italian cars were clearly faster than the Mark II. Typical of management by committee, the group failed to make a decision. The race teams would continue to develop both cars. There'd be no more talk of a scaled-down effort or budgets. Work to reduce weight and add horsepower to the Mark II "B" would continue. And somehow, someway, *someone* needed to fix the J-Car.

That someone was Phil Remington, officially Shelby's head of research and development, unofficially the team's "chief engineer, chief mechanic, fabricator and all-purpose nuts-and-bolts wizard."[6] He'd been asking for a chance to take on the J-Car since before Ken Miles was killed at Riverside.

During the lengthy November and December J-Car and Mark II test sessions, Foyt had worked at length with "Rem" for the first time and came away impressed, as almost everybody did. They'd worked closely again with Gurney at Daytona, and he was confident if anyone could resurrect the J-Car, it was Remington.

"He was very brilliant, and I had all the respect in the world for him," Foyt said. "When he told you the car was going to do something, it did it."[7]

While Remington headed for Dearborn to make over the J-Car, Foyt stayed in Florida for the start of Daytona 500 practice and pole day qualifications, turning in the seventh-fastest time. Curtis Turner surprised everyone by qualifying Smokey Yunick's Chevrolet Chevelle on the pole.

In his qualifying race, Foyt quickly moved to the front and led a race-high nineteen of the forty laps before a late-race caution flag set up a four-lap sprint to the finish. LeeRoy Yarbrough got a good start on the green flag and used lapped traffic to box in Foyt and win the qualifier, with an unhappy A.J. second.

"Where and to whom do I protest this race," he asked as he climbed out of the car, saying Yarbrough jumped the start. "I'm so disgusted with the place that I'm ready to tell them to tear up my entry.

"They specified in the rules meeting that if anyone passed before the green came on that it would cost them a lap. When the man got done saying that he looked at me and said, 'You too, A.J.' Rules are fine, but don't anybody try penalizing me some other time for doing the same thing that was done to me here. I still don't know if I'll run Sunday."[8]

Yarbrough disagreed. "The green was on two seconds before I started moving by Foyt. They said in the meeting that anytime the green comes on the racetrack—you're on your own."

The finish meant little. Yarbrough won $1,360 and the third starting spot in the 500, while Foyt won $650 and would start fifth, one row back. It was being robbed of a victory that bothered him. While A.J. and NASCAR founder Bill France remained close, he didn't have the same relationship with Bill France Jr., who'd taken over much of NASCAR's management, and Foyt wasn't afraid to call him out when he felt he'd been wronged.

"Everybody in the place but Bill France Jr. knew that was what happened. I'm so disgusted I don't know if I'll go in the 500."

No one took the threat seriously; he'd used the tactic too often in the past. Everybody knew the car could win the race and Foyt wasn't about to pass up that opportunity.

Racing in the other qualifier was Andretti, who was having an interesting Daytona Speed Week. Driving a Holman-Moody team car to Fred Lorenzen, he'd been complaining about his engine being underpowered since the start of practice.

"The car felt good," Andretti said. "Very balanced, right in the sweet spot." There was only one problem. "It was slow. Nobody would tell me what revs I should be turning. I tried to find out from the other drivers, but nobody would tell me.

"I asked to see the dyno sheets and was told, 'They're all within five horsepower.' Each engine crate was tagged with a driver's name, so I took my tag and swapped it with A.J.'s and they said, 'Oh, you can't do that!' That answered my question."[9]

Holman would eventually come up with a new engine for Andretti, whose driving style was creating a stir. He'd dive low into the turns and then slide up against the wall in the straightaways. The car was "loose" in NASCAR terms, the rear end dancing around on the edge of control. None of the NASCAR regulars wanted to draft with him.

Off the track, and in contrast to Foyt's "I'm going to take my ball and go home" manner, Andretti launched a PR offense, winning over much of the Southern media who'd had little previous contact with him.

"Unlike many athletes, Mario is his own best public relations man," wrote Bob Collins, sports editor of the *Indianapolis Star*, already aware of Andretti's charisma and amused at the fawning NASCAR media. "He has been charming his way around Daytona with a mixture of candor and good humor, spiced with just the right blend of self-deprecation."[10]

Come race day it took Foyt only four laps to move into the lead, where he stayed for seven laps before dropping back, content to run in the tightly bunched lead pack, which included Andretti. The race was marred by several early accidents involving multiple cars and Foyt found himself in the middle of one after just forty-four laps, burning out his clutch while trying to avoid the chaos that claimed several other leading cars.

There were thirty-seven lead changes, and late pit stops made things interesting, but it was a dominating performance by Andretti, who led 112 laps, more than three times that of any other driver. It was Andretti's biggest victory to date, and the media was ready to crown him racing's new king.

"Unmistakably, Andretti is the hottest item to come along in auto racing since A.J. Foyt," wrote Bob Myers of the *Charlotte News*. "Andretti is also developing into the most versatile race driver in the land and there are those who feel he might have reached that lofty plateau."[11]

MARK IV

From Daytona, Foyt went to Indianapolis for the first round of Goodyear tire tests. The rebuilt Coyote was on hand, but weather limited track time. So when the Le Mans development team started testing at Daytona and asked him to come down, he was only too happy to oblige.

It was Foyt's first look at the car—now called the Mark IV—and for the first time he thought it *looked* like a racer. Working around the clock and mostly from Remington's eyeball recommendations, a team of Kar-Kraft and Ford corporate design studio modelers had dramatically reworked the front and rear of the car. Gone were the original "lobster claws" that protruded from the front fenders and the boxy "bread van" back end. Refined in Ford's wind tunnel, it looked like a cross between the original GT and the Chaparral, with only hints of the J-Car remaining. The results were startling. Drag was down by one hundred pounds at just 120 miles an hour, the wind tunnel's top speed. The team knew that meant speeds approaching 220 miles an hour on Le Mans's Mulsanne Straight.

The car's first real-world test was even more encouraging. It came on Saturday, March 4, just four weeks after the Daytona debacle. With Bruce McLaren in Europe getting ready for the start of the Formula One season and Foyt in Indianapolis, Andretti handled the Mark IV while Lloyd Ruby drove the Mark II for comparison. The test was held at Ford's Kingman, Arizona, proving grounds, a five-mile oval using runways from an abandoned World War II Army Air Corps base.

Even Andretti, who'd worked enough with Remington to know his capabilities, was surprised by the new car. "Phil Remington designed the car inside his mental wind tunnel," he'd say. Despite wind gusts of up to 30 mph, Andretti pushed it to a track record of 215.82 mph, faster than he'd ever gone in his life. Ruby in the Mark II could do no better than 212.[12]

The Mark IV was judged ready for the upcoming 12 Hours of Sebring and trucked back to Daytona for a final sign-off, where troubles immediately cropped up. McLaren was back and no matter what he and Andretti tried, the car was once again unstable and jumping around on the straights at anything approaching high speed.

They'd changed the rear differential and other rear-end components several times without success and finally put in a call to Foyt, who flew down from Indianapolis. It didn't take him long to identify the problem, supposedly needing less than half of Pit Road. As he accelerated toward the track, he shifted through the gears and felt the car dart slightly sideways, not enough to notice, but enough for a driver to feel.

"When I backed off to shift gears going down the Pit Road, the car darted, and I knew immediately what it was," Foyt said. He stopped, backed up, got out of the car, and told the engineers to check the stagger of the rear tires. "You've got two different size tires on the rear," he told the engineers. "That's your problem."[13]

At first the Goodyear engineers protested. That had been the first thing they'd checked and the markings on the tires were identical. They also realized Foyt was the best tire tester they'd ever worked with, and when he insisted they measure the tires they did, discovering slight—but significant at speed—size differences.

"Indy cars were running a locked rear end, which won't let one wheel go faster than the other one," Foyt explained. "Sports cars were running an open rear end and the tire sizes needed to be identical. It's hard to build tires the same size, and at 200 mph you can really tell it, if you know what you're looking for."[14]

This is an often-repeated story by Foyt admirers and included in his autobiography. At first glance it seems ripe to be a bit of Foyt folklore. Andretti doesn't recall it and McLaren and Shelby never mentioned it. However, the official Ford test report from the session highlights the darting problems and although not mentioning Foyt by name, stresses the need for tire suppliers to verify sizes before shipment and for engineers to measure stagger, rather than go by tire markings alone. That, and Foyt's vivid recollection of the event, warrant its inclusion.

With matched tires fitted to the car, it performed flawlessly, Andretti turning a lap three seconds under the record set by Gurney in February. It was decided to take both cars to Sebring and continue the comparison under race conditions. The two lead development drivers, McLaren and Andretti, were paired in the "Springtime" yellow Mark IV, wearing No. 1 and managed by Shelby. Foyt was loaned to Holman-Moody and teamed with Ruby in the No. 2 dark "Guardsman" blue Mark II, which now carried a "B" designation to reflect its continued development.

It was hardly a fair match, nor was it meant to be. The Foyt/Ruby car, although featuring a range of new upgrades, was making its fifth endurance start, having raced at Daytona, Sebring, and Le Mans the previous year, and in the ill-fated Daytona event in February. The car was also equipped with the automatic transmission none of the drivers liked. Still, it was a good car, the one Gurney and Jerry Grant co-drove to within a straightway of victory at Sebring the year before, and it still carried the bulge in the roof created to provide Gurney more headroom.

Both Foyt and Andretti were doing double duty, racing at Sebring on Saturday and in NASCAR's Atlanta 500 on Sunday, a Ford corporate jet shuttling them back and forth for practice and qualifying. Gurney had done the double in the past and didn't envy the two drivers.

"It's a killing experience," Dan said. "I'll never try it again. It dilutes both efforts too much."[15]

Skipping the race were the Ferrari factory and NART teams. Having already made its point at Daytona, Ferrari decided to focus on the Le Mans practice session the following weekend. That left the two Chaparrals as the only real challengers for the Fords and the underdogs were clearly the fan favorites.

With Andretti in Atlanta qualifying for the NASCAR race, McLaren put the Mark IV on the pole, matching the lap-record time posted by Andretti in practice and more than two and a half seconds faster than the Chaparral 2F. Having already qualified for Atlanta, Foyt was able to remain in Sebring and qualified the Mark II B third ahead of the Chaparral 2D. The Chaparral team was forced to shake up its driver lineup at the last minute when Hill was rushed to the hospital for an emergency appendectomy, car owner Jim Hall taking his place.

Foyt was up to his usual shenanigans on the Le Mans–style start and was one of the first to reach his car, while many drivers were still only halfway across the track. As expected, the race turned into a battle between the Fords and Chaparrals, and while the flipper car led at times, both Chevy-powered machines were out by the seven-hour mark. McLaren and Andretti motored to the finish unchallenged. The Foyt/Ruby machine was forced to the pits with an engine problem with thirty minutes remaining on the clock but was far enough ahead of the third-place car to be credited with second. It was a one-two sweep for Ford, and more importantly, the Mark IV proved itself ready for Le Mans.

The victory celebration was cut short as Andretti and Foyt were soon on a plane for Atlanta. The two had remained civil since their meeting at Du Quoin, and the trip was a quick one, less than two hours. There was small talk between the two, but nothing memorable.

Foyt started fifth at Atlanta, and raced with the leaders before dropping out with a blown engine just past the halfway mark, his car grinding to a halt against the wall. Running the high line around the track, Andretti worked his way to the front after starting twenty-second, taking the lead on lap 152. It was short-lived, as he blew a tire moments later, tagging the wall and knocking him out of the race, ending his hopes of becoming the first driver to win major races on subsequent days.

Following Atlanta, Foyt shifted his focus to the Indy cars, with the first races of the season coming up at Phoenix and Trenton. He elected to keep the new Coyotes under wraps, entering a pair of year-old Lotus 38s for him and Leonard to drive. Foyt drove the No. 84 in both races, Leonard the No. 82. A.J. qualified and finished fifth at Phoenix and, "driving like a demon," pushed Andretti for the lead at Trenton before he dropped out with suspension problems. Andretti went on to win in a new Brawner Hawk, having destroyed the original car at Phoenix.[16]

Leonard finished alongside his boss in both races. Still unsure of his own schedule after the 500, Foyt told "Pelican Joe" he planned to run him for the national championship.

With each passing race and practice lap, Foyt felt more comfortable in a car. Gone were the early-season fears. And just in time. Next stop, Indianapolis.

CHAPTER 23

THE TROUBLE WITH TURBINES

1967

Any lingering doubts others may have had about A.J. Foyt's commitment to his team and Indy car racing ended when his four cars unloaded in Gasoline Alley in advance of the track opening. For once the cars were early and ready to run.

The Coyotes were immaculate and striking in their simplicity—"elegant" in engineering terms. They were also a new color, Foyt having eschewed the gleaming pearl-white finish with red and blue pinstriping he'd been using for several years, complaining that everyone else was copying his paint scheme.

It was the same color as Banjo Matthews's stock cars, "Poppy Red," according to Ford's color palette, although Foyt repeatedly called it "Poppycock Red." A red-and-yellow mixture gave it more of an orange look than Ford's more traditional "Rangoon Red" and it had first appeared on a Mustang being introduced at the 1964 New York Auto Show. It carried Ford paint code M1730 and would be used by the company throughout the 1960s and '70s on numerous vehicles under several different names, including "Calypso Coral," "Competition Red," "Competition Orange," and "Mexicalia Red." In the racing world it became known as simply "Foyt Orange."

Some fifty years later Foyt said there was another reason for the color change.

"We were doing all the touch-up painting when Dean [Jeffries] wasn't there, all the pinstriping and everything," he said. "The paint wasn't very good back then, and you were constantly touching it up. You had to do it by hand. We were doing all that work when we should have been doing something else. I finally said, 'Shit, let's pick one damn color and then when we touch it up, it'll be a lot easier.' I liked the color of my stock car, so we went with it."[1]

The resemblance between the Coyote and Lotus entries was unmistakable, but the differences also were noticeable. The exterior of the Coyote was smooth

◀A.J. in 1967. *Associated Press Photo Archive*

and sleek, interrupted only by a couple of NACA air ducts to direct airflow to the brakes and radiators. An engine cover, small chin spoiler, and upswept rear lip were integrated into the body work, all of which were fabricated at Tony Foyt's Houston shop with the help again of Lujie Lesovsky and Eddie Kuzma.

"Where the Lotus's fuselage is all rivets and seams, the Coyote's skin is glass smooth and unbroken," noted one writer.[2]

Less apparent were the changes to the chassis and suspension, made more important by the first complete repave of the Speedway in the track's history. Gone was the prior year's significant suspension offset. The chassis mounting points were relocated, with the front and rear track narrowed more than four inches to increase straight-line speed. Ford played a significant role in developing the suspension, once again led by Klaus Arning. He received help from Kar-Kraft's chassis experts including Bob Riley, who was also working on the Le Mans program and would be intimately involved in future Coyote designs, although he wouldn't meet Foyt for several more years.[3]

"I remember when we first got Foyt's Lotus," Riley recalled. "The bump-steer [the way a tire and wheel react to changes in the track surface] was terrible. We could get rid of bump-steer in front, but on the independent rear [suspension] cars, we didn't exactly know how. That's what drove a lot of them, that rear steer, which was really quite bad. Ford had just gotten into the computer age when we did the Le Mans cars. I think we went through sixty or seventy computer runs [on the Coyote] and almost by accident we found out how to get the rear steer out [by putting] castor in the rear uprights."[4]

It took only a few laps in March tire tests for Foyt to notice the improved straight-line stability and speed of the car. He put a blue Ford oval sticker on the nose of his cars in recognition of the company's help.

"They were way ahead on suspensions for the rear-engine cars," Foyt said of Ford and Arning. "When other teams saw what I was doing, they tried to do the same thing to their cars. But they'd just screw them up to where they couldn't drive them."[5]

The new Coyotes featured a first for Indianapolis: an onboard fire extinguisher system. Developed by DuPont, it was activated either by a heat sensor or manually, with an actuator switch located next to the gearshift lever. The system provided about fifteen seconds of fire retardant through three nozzles aimed at the driver.[6]

Foyt was justifiably proud of the cars, pointing out, "The magnesium castings for the rear uprights are the only parts that were made in Europe."[7]

"We had only eight men to build two completely new race cars and rebuild two others," he said, noting that the team's move to Houston had paid off. "We just worked eight hours a day, but I didn't give anyone time to goof off."[8]

"The fact that we came here with all four cars ready when the track opened shows we have a fine operation. Our cars are brand-new. I read books on rear-engine cars and studied design and construction and I think we have the best cars here. I know Mario has great success, but they've been working with that chassis for three years. Ours is new and different, but I think it will prove itself in the next couple of years."[9]

Even the Lotus team was impressed by the new Coyote. In his history of Lotus during the 1960s, Doug Nye noted, "Ayjay [*sic*] and his father had modified the cars almost beyond recognition by replacing much of the Cheshunt magnesium with Texas chrome-molybdenum, beefing up the monocoque, and adding new body paneling."[10]

A leading European racing publication, *Motor Sport*, was not as impressed, continuing to refer to the car simply as a Lotus.

The new cars also carried new numbers, No. 14 on Foyt's and No. 4 for Leonard. USAC numbers were primarily based on a driver's finish in the previous year's point standing, although car owners were free to choose any available number. Some team owners always used the same number every year, for instance J.C. Agajanian's cars always carried No. 98.

Leonard's No. 4 represented his finish in the 1966 standings. Foyt finished thirteenth in 1966 and as much as he denied being superstitious—he'd driven the No. 13 car for Smokey Yunick after all—he wasn't about to tempt fate for a whole season. Mel Kenyon had finished fourteenth and Rodger Ward fifteenth in 1966, and with Ward retiring, Foyt and Kenyon simply moved up one notch, Kenyon taking No. 15.

Over time, Foyt gave other reasons for choosing the number, including honoring drivers who'd used it in the past, among them Wilbur Shaw, Tony Bettenhausen, and Bill Vukovich. He also pointed out that he'd won with the number at the end of 1962 after reuniting with George Bignotti. In 1967, however, it was simply the next number in line.

The team even showed up at the Speedway with a live coyote. One of the crew had trapped it back in Texas and they displayed it in Gasoline Alley in a dog cage. But not for long. Speedway officials weren't amused, and the Indianapolis Zoo soon took delivery of a donated coyote.

Among the crew members was Frank Lance, who'd known the Foyts since the mid-1950s, when he was one of those visiting the B & F Garage to see whatever race cars might be there. He and A.J. had worked at different dealerships for "Big" Jim Hall in Houston. Lance later worked for the other Jim Hall at Chaparral, and for Carrol Shelby and John Mecom when Foyt drove the team's sports cars. He'd been part of Mecom's Indy team in 1966, before joining the Foyt crew at the start of the 1967 season.

So happy was Foyt with the preparation of his cars he decided to participate in the annual jockeying to see who would turn the first lap on the opening day of practice. It was a ceremonial event, as officials enforced a speed limit, but each year a couple of drivers lined up to see who got on the track first and dominated media coverage for at least a day.

Opening day, usually May 1, was moved up to Saturday, April 29, in 1967 to give the record ninety entrants two full weeks of practice before the first day of qualifying. It was also good for the bottom line, with more than ten thousand fans turning out.

George Snider, driving for Vel Miletich, put his car in prime position when he parked at the locked gate between the Gasoline Alley garages and the pits at 4:30 p.m. on Friday afternoon. It was soon followed by Cale Yarborough's car, whose sponsor, Bryant Heating and Cooling, had been on the first car in five of the past six years.

Snider and Yarborough had been sitting in their cars for more than an hour Saturday morning when Foyt was pushed into line just as chief steward Harlan Fengler announced, "The track is open for practice."

Rules required that cars be moved onto Pit Lane before using an electric motor to start the engine, and all three teams began pushing their cars, Snider followed by Yarborough and Foyt. Eager to get ahead of the others, Foyt popped the clutch in his Coyote and jump-started the engine. Hearing Foyt's car come alive, Snider did the same in his, and when it momentarily bucked, he was hit from behind by Yarborough, breaking the nose cone off the second car. Foyt motored past both, leaving Lance and a photographer tumbling in his wake.

The track, however, wasn't really open. Fengler had jumped the gun and there were emergency vehicles still circling the Speedway. Foyt was stopped at the end of Pit Lane by an official holding a yellow flag, and he was soon joined by Snider and Yarborough, the latter's car missing its nose. All three started to creep ahead and into the first turn before thinking better of it and stopping, their crews forced to retrieve their cars and push them back to their pit.

While Snider climbed out of his car in disgust, Yarborough refired his machine and headed back onto the track, ignoring the yellow flags. Foyt took off in pursuit, both drivers completing a lap. Fengler was having nothing of it, disallowing the laps and fining each twenty-five dollars. When the track was finally opened for practice, it was a bemused Leonard who officially became the first driver to make a lap.

Along with the record number of entries was a record number of rookie drivers, twenty-three in all. The rookie ranks were swelled by an influx of grand prix and sports car drivers drawn by the success of Jimmy Clark, Graham Hill, and Jackie Stewart and an unusually early May 7 race date for the Monaco Grand Prix, which meant it wouldn't conflict with qualifying for the 500. Fourteen drivers with Formula One starts were entered, including newcomers Chris Amon, Lorenzo Bandini, Lucien Bianchi, Bob Bondurant, Ronnie Bucknum, Richie Ginther, Denis Hulme, Jochen Rindt, and Pedro Rodriguez joining previous starters Masten Gregory, Dan Gurney, Clark, Hill, and Stewart.

The big draw was the huge pot of gold at the end of five hundred miles.

"It's almost ridiculous in comparison to what I normally get paid for winning in Europe," Graham Hill, the 1962 World Champion, said after cashing his check for winning in 1966. "The financial rewards of Indianapolis outstrip anything else in motor racing today."[11]

Clark, hoping to make his fifth consecutive start in the 500, made it clear that if it weren't for the money, he'd be elsewhere.

"It's very simple. The European courses offer a much greater challenge. It's an entirely different style of racing. It doesn't take too much imagination and ingenuity to keep turning left."[12]

As he often did, Foyt was working with a couple of the rookies and took Wally Dallenbach out for his first laps around the track in a Camaro pace car. As a favor to car builder A.J. Watson, he did the same with Pedro Rodriguez, who'd won the opening Formula One race of the year in South Africa. The Mexican driver had been trying since 1963 without success to qualify for the 500, and Watson's car provided him with the best shot yet.

Also undergoing a rookie evaluation of sorts was the turbine car, making its first appearance on the track since March tire tests. Parnelli Jones, who'd been considering retirement, had been enticed by Andy Granatelli to drive the turbine for a reported $100,000. While the 1963 Indy winner was anything but a rookie, Fengler decided the car's unique design required it to run through the same series of gradually increasing speed tests as a first-time driver. Other cars, including those of Mickey Thompson and Smokey Yunick, had been forced to do it in the past. Granatelli and Jones didn't like it, but the turbine quietly and effortlessly completed the test.

Foyt and other drivers were already complaining about the turbine. It was too wide. It was too low. It had an airplane engine. The heat waves caused by the engine's exhaust were too hot, smelled bad, and were difficult to see through. The air brake that popped up on the back of the car distracted trailing drivers and blocked their vision. Officials eventually forced Granatelli to take the STP sticker off the air brake and install an air diffuser on the exhaust, but otherwise the car was declared legal.

Things got so bad between Foyt and Granatelli that at one point A.J. demanded more money to put STP stickers on his car, wanting double the going rate of $2,500. Granatelli refused, telling Foyt, "Remember, you're just one of thirty-three cars in the race."[13]

"Yeah, but there's just gonna be one winner," Foyt shot back.[14]

Despite the driver grumbling, fan sentiment was clearly behind Jones and the Swooshmobile, Whooshmobile, or Silent Sam, as it was being called, depending on the reporter. Rainy and cold weather didn't stop the crowds from turning out in record numbers for a glimpse of the car. Powered by a Pratt & Whitney helicopter engine rated at 550 horsepower and featuring four-wheel drive, Jones seemed to effortlessly turn laps in the mid-160 miles per hour range and other drivers accused him of sandbagging. In reality, Granatelli's team had discovered the car's weak link. The torque from the turbine was destroying gearboxes at an alarming rate, and Jones was told not to exceed 165 mph on the track.

There were no such limits on Andretti, and he picked up right where he left off the year before, turning "unofficial" record speeds and predicting a possible lap of 170 mph. Just a tick of the clock behind was Gurney, with Foyt and Leonard a little farther back.

Also attracting attention, although for the wrong reasons, was the contingent of foreign drivers, all of whom were struggling. The Lotus cars driven by Clark and Hill, who'd left his winning Mecom team to drive for Colin Chapman, were designed for a BRM powerplant that failed to materialize and the team was trying to adopt Ford engines to the cars. Others having even bigger problems were Rindt and Amon, both suffering significant crashes during practice.

Against this backdrop an estimated crowd of 225,000 people turned out in blustery and damp weather on the first day of qualifying to see Jones and the turbine take on all challengers. With a two-hour rain delay, it wasn't until early afternoon that Leonard got qualifying off to a fast and surprising start when he set new one- and four-lap records in his Coyote. It didn't last long as first Gurney and then Andretti upped the ante, although Jones qualified slightly slower than Leonard.

Foyt's first run was cut short on his third lap when the engine lost power and he coasted into the pits. With time running short and weather closing in, he pulled the engine cover off and spotted a cracked distributor cap. He took off on the run back to his garage, removed the cap from a backup car, and ran back to his pit. He installed it and, good as new, helped push his car back into the qualifying line. He was able to get back on the track late in the afternoon and qualified fourth, just ahead of Leonard, although much of the crowd had left after Jones's run.

"Heresy of heresies," noted one columnist sarcastically, "the crowd didn't wait to see A.J. Foyt in action."[15]

Disappointed his first run was cut short, Foyt was relieved to qualify on the first day after pledging the year before he wouldn't race if he didn't.

"I'm disappointed that I'm not further up because I had been sandbagging all week. I could go out and run fast whenever I wanted to. The car just stopped running.

"If something had gone wrong and I hadn't made it the first day, I would have had to seriously consider trying to qualify at all. But I'll admit, I'd probably have gone ahead and tried it because I want to race so badly."[16]

A record twenty-five drivers qualified on day one as Americans swept the first five rows. Clark was the top foreign driver in sixteenth, and Hill didn't even attempt a qualifying run, leading team owner Chapman to apologize for the poor performance of his cars.

"I think we're ahead of them now," Foyt said. "Take nothing away from their driving because Jimmy Clark, Hill and Jackie Stewart are great race drivers. But I don't think they're going to win this time."

Reminded of his offer of a contingency prize for the top finishing American, Hill said, "I think we struck a nerve."[17]

Years later Foyt still recalled Hill's words. "They gave me a lot of drive. I knew I wanted to beat them awful bad."[18]

Hill was having more trouble than any foreign driver and things looked bleak when he blew the team's last available Ford engine. It would take several days to get another powerplant from Detroit, and Hill would lose valuable practice time.

Help came from an unexpected source—Foyt. Despite his past problems with Granatelli and Chapman, Foyt had an extra Ford engine and offered it to Hill. He wanted the defending champion in the race. With the new engine installed, Foyt wandered out to Turn One with a stopwatch to time Hill through the corner. He was quickly surrounded by reporters and fans and someone asked if Hill and the other foreign drivers were better than the Americans.

"I can't buy that," he said. "I'll admit they caught us with our pants down when they first came here with the Lotus-Ford. Nobody had driven cars like that on this track before. It was a radical new design with a new motor. But when you analyze it, all they did was take a car built by a huge American company, a superior car nobody else was familiar with, and win with it."[19]

Foyt ignored the fact both of the past two winners, Lotus and Lola, were built in England and only the Ford engine was American, but his point was the same.

"Now everybody's equipment is equal, and where are they? Most of 'em are still trying to qualify. We'll whip their pants off this year."

It was just another indication of the odd dichotomy that was A.J. Foyt. He desperately wanted Hill and the other foreign drivers in the field so he could beat their asses.

"He harbors no personal prejudice against the British or any other non-American race drivers," one columnist wrote. "But A.J. Foyt is fiercely dedicated toward 'returning the Indianapolis 500 trophy to the United States.' He has assumed the role as 'Yankee Doodle Dandy' quite willingly. . . . A.J. feels almost personally responsible for allowing [foreigners] to wheel into Victory Lane the past two years."[20]

There was another driver ready to uphold America's honor. Jones and the turbine had been established as clear favorites, and if there were any doubts, he erased them during the final practice session on Carb Day. Jones put on a show, darting in and out of traffic and passing other cars at will, even those who'd qualified faster than him. No one had ever turned race laps above 160 mph, but Jones was capable of doing it with ease. "He could win by five laps," Andretti said.[21]

"Can you see this race next year if Parnelli wins?" Foyt asked. "There'll be nothing but jets and empty stands. No piston engine can keep up with a jet. And when he uses that wing flap in the back to help in the cornering, it looks like the whole thing is ready to fall apart and a driver starts thinking the wrong thing. It might cause a serious incident."[22,23]

Jones was enjoying the psychological advantage and said, "I was quite surprised. It was very easy. If I don't have any problems, I don't see how they can catch me."[24]

"I went by old A.J. and flapped it [the airbrake] a couple of times like a playful porpoise. Did he get mad! I told him later to get that noisy thing out of the way."[25]

While Jones and the turbine were the fan and race favorite, Andretti remained the media darling. *Sports Illustrated* billed the 500 as "Mario vs. the Whooshmobile." Its coverage focused on the "Tiny Tiger," as it called Andretti, with only a passing mention of Foyt. In the biggest public relations coup yet for auto racing, *Newsweek* magazine put Andretti on the cover with a four-page spread inside—one week after rising politician Ronald Reagan received similar treatment.

Proclaiming "Motor racing is in a golden age," the article quoted Chuck Barnes, Andretti's manager, who also worked with Foyt and Jones.[26]

"Auto racing is exploding and he's the champ at the right time," Barnes said of Andretti. "He's like Arnold Palmer was when golf took off. He has the magic name and the magic looks that attract people."

The article listed Foyt, Jones, Clark, and Gurney as primary challengers to Andretti, calling A.J. "a fearless freewheeler" and the antithesis of the "quiet and introspective" Clark. However, "none of these drivers has achieved quite the charisma in the U.S. as Mario Andretti."

One local newspaper even launched an effort to come up with a nickname for Andretti. "Super Wop" and "Super Dago," were the early leaders, although both were deemed offensive by Italian American groups. The paper eventually settled on variations of the Italian word *paisano*, loosely defined as a "friend or brother," as in the "Fearless Paisano" or "Flying Paisano." It didn't matter much to Andretti.

"A.J. called me 'Wop' and Bobby [Unser] called me 'Dago,' or maybe it was the other way around," Andretti said with a grin and a shrug when asked about his nicknames. "It didn't bother me none. Everybody had nicknames for everyone else. That's just the way it was."[27]

UNDER THE RADAR

With prerace attention focused on Andretti, Jones, and the turbine, Foyt flew under the radar and avoided the demands of journalists for much of the month. Anxious to keep his chassis setup secret, "Keep Out" signs were plastered on the doors of his Gasoline Alley garages.

"For the first time in years hardly anyone has mentioned A.J. Foyt," noted one writer.[28] It wasn't until a few days before the race that Ray Marquette, a reporter with the *Indianapolis Star*, approached him about an in-depth story.

Marquette was one of the best in the business, respected by everyone in the garage area, including Foyt. He'd later serve as president of the American Racing Writers and Broadcasters Association and be inducted into its Hall of Fame. Three times he'd receive the "Best Sports Reporting Award" from the Indianapolis Press Club. He'd add the Indiana Pacers to his beat later in the year and excel there are as well, serving as executive director of the United States Basketball Writers Association and receiving a Distinguished Service Award from the National Association of Basketball Coaches. He'd eventually become vice president of public affairs for USAC in 1977, only to be killed the following year in a plane crash returning from a race.

In 1967 he was the right reporter in the right place at the right time when he approached Foyt. He found a relaxed, introspective, and surprisingly confident driver. So talkative was Foyt, Marquette broke the interview into a two-part series.

"The legend of A.J. Foyt is a many splendored thing, full of contradictions, a fierce competitiveness and a basic honesty and drive that makes him somewhat unique among men," wrote Marquette in his lede.[29]

"No one can be around the Texan very long without being affected by him. He has the drive of a tyrant, the mind of a successful businessman and a spirit that is unquenchable. He also has a temper that can explode in blinding fury, and other times a personality that can melt icebergs. But above all else he is a race driver who operates with only one objective—to win."

Foyt's willingness to sit for the interview with Marquette was an indication of the confidence he had in the team's preparedness. He also was willing to reflect on what he called, "the worst year in my career."

"After last year I know there were a lot of people who said Foyt is through—but I certainly don't feel that way. It was the worst year in my career. . . . Yet I consider myself fortunate in getting through the year alive."

He admitted to thinking about retiring following the first lap crash at Indianapolis and then the accident and burns suffered at Milwaukee.

"When I was lying there hurting so bad, I did think for a while that maybe someone was trying to give me a message and [my] morale was low. But that was only when I was hurting so bad.

"I think I can race until I'm thirty-five or thirty-six years old at least. But even after I quit as a driver, I'll keep a couple of cars going for Indianapolis. I'll never be all the way out of racing, even though I could quit right now and never work another day in my life. I was fortunate in making some investments, so money is no problem anymore. When the time comes that I do decide to quit, I'll make the decision right then and stick to it. If I decided right now it was time to retire, I'd put my helmet on the wall and that would be it. There will be no dilly-dallying around or retire and then coming back.

"And I won't race just at Indianapolis. I don't think you can do a good job by racing just once a year. I'll keep on the full championship circuit. I'm having a new sprint car built now so I can keep my hand in there, too. I've been offered a good car for the Grand Prix circuit—but I'm not going to run over there. My career is here in America. But I may, if the dates work out, try a Formula One race in Europe. I'd like to go over there and win one for the United States."

It was his first mention of running an F1 race since his dalliance with Ferrari in 1964. He didn't say so, but Gurney had asked Foyt to drive his second car in the Netherlands Grand Prix at Zandvoort on June 4, the week before Le Mans, and the Belgium Grand Prix the week after Le Mans at Spa on June 18. It was too late to enter Foyt's name on AAR's Zandvoort entry, but Gurney had already filed an official entry for Foyt at Spa and hoped A.J. would run both races.

In part two, Foyt opened up about his relationship with Andretti, saying, "Mario and I have never had a feud the way some of the newspapers tried to blow it up."[30]

He'd spent much of the past six months with Andretti, at Daytona for the sports car and stock car races and shuttling back and forth between Sebring and Atlanta, not to mention the Indy car events. Andretti's two big victories—in cars other than the Indy machines both drivers normally drove—had influenced Foyt. They'd never be good friends or pal around together, but Andretti had earned something even more important.

"I have great respect for Mario now," Foyt told Marquette. "He's a good driver, he knows how to step on the gas and go. His start was a great deal like mine, I guess. I know when he started, he chopped me off a few times and I got mad at him. But I was young and running fast when I started and guys got mad at me, so I guess we're of the same breed. I told him a couple of times to knock it off, but that's as far as it went. Since then, he never cuts me off. I've run wheel-to-wheel with him, and we've had no trouble.

"We're closer today than we ever were. We get along real good. I have great respect for him. I respect him just the way I hope he respects me."

There was one other person exceedingly confident in the team's chances: the new man in charge, Tony Foyt.

"He was wanting me to do it a couple of years ago, but I didn't care much to," Tony said of taking on the role of crew chief. It wasn't until his son decided to build his own cars that he agreed to take on the challenge full-time. "He was having so much trouble, he thought by building his own he could eliminate it. The biggest part of 'em [the Coyotes] are his ideas. There are some changes I've made. We'd just get disgusted and find a way to make 'em work."[31]

The team was in the process of taking both cars apart and putting them back together in preparation for the race. A.J. was never far away, questioning something or someone, or telling a crew member to do something else.

"He's awright," Tony said of his son's tendency to stick his nose in whatever the team was working on. "He just don't like nothing patched up. He wants it right or he don't want it. I was usually the same way. I don't like nothing patched."

Did they have a chance against the turbine?

"I'll tell you, he's pretty dang hard to beat," Tony said of his son. "Anything he puts his mind to, he makes a go of."

CHAPTER 24

THERE HE IS!

1967

May 30 dawned cool and gray, with rain forecast throughout the day. Few thought the Indianapolis 500 would be run, although more than 250,000 clogged the roads and filled the seats just in case.

Arriving late at the track was A.J. Foyt. He'd overslept and didn't awaken until 8:15 a.m. when astronaut Wally Schirra knocked on his door at the Speedway Motel for a prearranged meeting. Schirra, the command pilot for the upcoming Apollo 7 moon mission, was a silent partner on Joe Leonard's car—silent because NASA frowned on the highly visible interest a number of astronauts had shown in what it considered the dangerous sport of auto racing.

The meeting was cut short and the cars were already lined up on the track when Foyt finally arrived. Striding down the grid still in his street clothes, he waved to the fans while most drivers shuffled nervously about. He was relaxed and unrushed when he finally started to change into his uniform just thirty-five minutes before the start.

"A lot of guys popped up," Foyt said to no one in particular as he dressed, noting the acrid smell of "pop" or nitromethane surrounding the cars. In an attempt to keep pace with the turbine of Parnelli Jones, some teams were using more nitro in their fuel blend than normal. Others were starting with a lighter fuel load and hoping for caution flags to stay close. Foyt said he was going with a normal blend of methanol and nitro and a full load of fuel.[1]

"Maybe I've guessed wrong about strategy, but I hope not," he said. "I still think you have to go 500 miles and that's just what I aim to do."

Lujie Lesovsky was brought in to assist Tony Foyt and oversee things from a perch at the timing table behind the pit. On the signal wall between Pit Lane

◄ There he is! *Steve H. Shunck Collection*

and the track was Frank Lance, who'd get information from Lesovsky on what to write on the chalkboard to show Foyt.

Anxious to avoid a repeat of the 1966 first-lap fiasco, chief steward Harlan Fengler held a private meeting with the drivers, warning them any attempt to jump the start would be severely dealt with. As pole sitter, it was incumbent on Mario Andretti to bring the field down for a smooth and fast start. As the pace car pulled off the track, he surged ahead, taking a four-car lead at the start/finish line. Then he seemed to hesitate, allowing the other front-row starters to catch up going into Turn One.

Starting fourth, Foyt watched as Gordon Johncock and Dan Gurney dropped down the track and into line behind Andretti going into Turn One. Out of the corner of his eye, Foyt spotted the red turbine high on the track, normally no man's land. Jones was having no problems, however, as he passed Gurney on the outside in the first turn and Johncock on the outside of Turn Two. Then he ducked down to the inside of Andretti and was gone. It took half a lap for Jones to take the lead, and by the end of the circuit there was a new first-lap speed record.

Andretti almost immediately began to fall back, having damaged his clutch on the herky-jerky start. Foyt moved into third behind Gurney, and teammate Joe Leonard followed him into fourth. Only rain could slow the turbine and as it started to fall, the race was stopped on lap eighteen.

Officials waited until 4:10 p.m. before postponing the event, setting up the first time the Indianapolis 500 would be run on two separate days. Told the race would restart an hour earlier on Wednesday, Gurney had a new plan. "We'll start at ten and Parnelli starts at eleven."[2]

"Regardless whether they finish today or next week," noted the *Indianapolis Star*, "it is quite apparent that thirty-one cars [Lloyd Ruby was already out] have a giant task trying to catch the flying Jones."[3]

––––––––

Despite the turbine's early dominance, one driver remained confident: Foyt. He often dined with Tony Hulman the night of the race and they decided to go ahead with the meal as planned.

"I'm so sure I'm gonna win this race," Foy said he told Hulman, "I ought to charge you for keeping my money overnight.

"That's how confident I felt," he said later. "But I was confident only because I didn't think the turbine would last. There's no way any of us could run with it."[4]

More than 175,000 were back on Wednesday, down only slightly from the Memorial Day crowd. Local school districts closed for the day as their buses were needed to transfer race fans. Businesses closed. Vendors were especially happy. No beer sales were allowed on the holiday, but now the lines were long, despite the early morning start and cool temperatures.

Although confident the turbine would break, Foyt had no illusions about outrunning it.

"It has twice the horsepower we're running," Foyt told ABC's Jim McKay prior to the restart. "It's hard to compete with a car that has that much advantage. But I really feel in my own mind it will break. I feel it will have gearbox trouble."[5]

Sitting in the turbine and chain-smoking, casually flicking the ash over the side as if he were in a passenger car at a stop light, Jones was amused by it all.

"If the car lasts through the race, she'll beat everybody, easy," he agreed. "And if she don't, you ain't got a thing to worry about."

Several teams were tipping the can even further, adding more nitro to the mix. Rules of the day allowed Andretti's fried clutch to be replaced overnight, but he'd restart six laps behind the leader. Gurney went with both a higher nitro mix and a light fuel load to try to pressure Jones. Both the Jimmy Clark and Graham Hill Lotus-Fords were over-juiced and would soon be out.

Only Foyt among the front-runners seemed to be playing it safe, sticking with the 5 percent nitro blend and carrying a full fuel load. He also went with a higher final gear than most, banking on improved fuel economy at racing speeds on the track scrubbed clean by a day of rain.

Following Hulman's call of "Gentlemen, re-start your engines," Foyt was content to watch Jones pull away, gamely chased by Gurney. Andretti, hopelessly behind, turned the fastest laps of the race before dropping out after losing a wheel. Gurney was knocked out at the three-quarter mark with a burned piston, the result of the lean fuel mixture. All the while Jones pulled farther ahead.

Even though Foyt was turning race laps of more than 160 miles per hour, better than the race record, Jones and the turbine were just too fast. Only a series of spins, crashes, and the accompanying yellow flags kept Foyt on the same lap as the leader, his ultimate goal.

Foyt took the lead on lap 130 when Jones made his final pit stop for fuel, and he held it until his own stop on lap 148. Waving off a "Want Tires?" sign board, he heard the cheers as Jones moved back in front. After the pit stops were completed and with little more than one hundred miles to go, Jackie Stewart moved up to dice with Foyt, until A.J. was informed the Scot was a lap down and to let him go. A few laps later Foyt spotted Stewart's smoking car, pulling off the track in the fourth turn. Fully a third of the field was out with engine troubles.

Through it all Jones continued to pull away. With twenty laps to go, he saw the Coyote ahead and realized he could lap Foyt. The STP crew, which had been holding out an "EZ" pit sign without getting much response, began showing one saying "Save Fuel" in hopes of slowing Jones down. Seeing the sign, Lance signaled his driver, "J May Pit."

Another caution flag on lap 181 was the only thing that slowed Jones. Foyt barely dodged the spinning cars as a tire carcass flew over his head. It took seven laps to clear the track, and no sooner had it gone green than Johncock, running fifth, shredded a tire and crashed. There were now wrecked race cars and debris scattered around the track, and it appeared the race would finish under caution.

"That seems to lock it up for Parnelli Jones," said Rodger Ward, providing color commentary on the *Wide World of Sports*. "This race could conceivably end under a yellow flag," agreed McKay.[6]

As Jones went past the start/finish line to start lap 196, Dolly Granatelli, Andy's wife, began to lead a contingent of STP executives and family toward Victory Lane. The crowd roar from the north side of the circuit stopped everyone in their tracks. In an era before viewing screens were scattered around the Speedway, crowd noise was often the first indication something was happening. The roar was still rising when Tom Carnegie's booming voice broke through on the public address system.

"We understand Parnelli Jones is coasting, coming around the number four turn," Carnegie said, his voice rising with every word. "Parnelli Jones is coasting to a stop coming around the fourth turn! Parnelli Jones is coasting, coming down, out of the fourth turn!"[7]

Foyt's first indication something was happening came on the backstretch when he saw fans rise in unison in the Turn Three bleachers. Some were looking and pointing toward Turn Four, out of his line of sight. Others were looking his way and waving him onward. As he got closer, he could hear their cheers above his engine.

Coming out of Turn Four, Foyt spotted the turbine rolling slowly toward Pit Lane. He could still see heat waves from the exhaust, so he figured it was something other than a lack of fuel. He raised an arm to salute Jones as he flashed past and gave the universal "okay" sign when he spotted his team's hastily scribbled "Jones Out" pit sign.

Granatelli met Jones as the turbine crept down pit lane. It was still running, but there was no connection to the drivetrain. A six-dollar bearing in the transmission had failed.

Now Foyt was hoping the race would finish under caution and was surprised when, coming down to start the final lap, Vidan suddenly waved the green flag, barely catching Foyt as he went past. The race was on again. Not that he had anything to worry about; he was two laps ahead of second-place Al Unser and could practically coast home.

He slowed approaching Turn Three and even more as he got close to number four. He pulled low coming out of the final turn and allowed a car close behind to swing around and pass. Then his arm shot up, not in recognition of the cheers, but as a warning to drivers behind him. There was a crash on the track.

The car driven by Bobby Grim, running thirteen laps in arrears, broke a half shaft coming down the straight, tossing the car sideways. Running behind Grim was Carl Williams, who saw what happened and slowed. But Chuck Hulse, in seventh and still going hard, rammed Williams from behind and shoved him into Grim, sending the three cars spinning like tops down the straight.

Next on the scene was Bud Tingelstad and Larry Dickson, and each spun to avoid hitting the other cars, the track seemingly blocked by spinning cars, smoke, flying tires, and car parts.

"Smoke and dust was flying everywhere," said Lance from his position on the pit wall. He was certain there was no way Foyt could get through.

Carnegie was keeping the fans around the track informed of the leader's progress when all hell broke loose. He'd later say it was the most dramatic call in his career.

"Foyt should be moving into the number four turn. And there he is! And there's a spin right in front of him! A spin right in front of him! There's one, two, three cars involved. Where is A.J. Foyt? Did he get through? Did he get through? Did he get through?"[8]

In the television booth McKay could see nothing on the monitor and looked out the window to find his view obscured by the smoke.

"Where's Foyt!?!" he asked Ward. "I don't know whether he can get through or not. Foyt's only got a couple of hundred yards to go, but where is he!?!"[9]

It was almost as if Foyt could hear the frantic cries of the announcers as he burst through the smoke and spinning cars, waving his arm from side-to-side like an anxious schoolboy, as if to say, "Here I am!"

On different floors in the control tower, Carnegie and the TV broadcasters spotted him at nearly the same time and had the same response.

"There he is!"

After downshifting into second gear, Foyt had moved to the inside of the track and then veered toward the middle to avoid a sliding car. He spotted Vidan in his gleaming white coat and knew the yard of bricks was close. Despite the still-spinning cars, the flagman was, incredibly, in his normal spot for the finish, fifteen yards onto the track, waving the checkered flag as Foyt went past. He then retreated to the pit wall where he was handed a yellow flag and then a red one to stop the race. At the time, the race was normally continued for five minutes following the checkered flag, but not in 1967. It was the first time only the winner completed the full five hundred miles in a race not ended early by rain.

"How do I feel?" Foyt repeated when he arrived in the raucous Victory Lane. A wreath of red and white carnations was placed over his head. "Happy as hell. Personally, I felt sorry for Parnelli, but things have happened to me before when I had a race won too. They all seem to even up eventually."[10]

Lucy arrived amid all the commotion and was knocked into the race car, her dress smudged with grime, although she seemed not to notice.

"I honestly thought I was out of it," A.J. said. "Before the race was restarted, I figured the turbine would be out of business within 100 laps. When the darn thing was still going, I figured he had won and there was nothing I could do about it. I just tried not to let him lap me."

He said he had a premonition to slow down entering the final turn.

"Somehow, I had an instinct not to accelerate coming out of the fourth turn. I had been driving real careful and staying back out of traffic so I could keep out of trouble. Then I came out of the turn, looked ahead and there was the mess.

"The first thing I did was hit the brakes and then looked over my shoulder to see if anyone was close enough to ram me from behind. The only car I saw behind me was Art Pollard and he was slowing down, so I came to an almost complete stop. I could have walked faster than I was moving. I shifted into low gear, went down close to the inside wall, and accelerated as I threaded my way through. There was only one car sliding back across the track at me and I knew I could get through."[11]

Over the years Foyt would add another element to his last-lap story. "I said to myself, 'I don't know who I'm gonna hit, but I'm gonna carry him past that start/finish line.'"[12]

Back in Gasoline Alley, a dazed Jones, speaking softly and slowly, took journalists' questions, although his answers often trailed off unfinished.

"I was going into the third turn. It felt just like pulling the car out of gear. I was running all day soft on the throttle, not trying to abuse the transmission . . .

"I couldn't say this was my biggest disappointment. . . . But if you're only four laps away and running under the yellow, well I guess you're not supposed to win . . ."[13]

Jones would come to blame himself for the turbine's transmission failure, saying he'd been too hard on the car accelerating away after his second pit stop. "Stupid me, if I had just taken it a little easier going out of the pits, we'd have won it hands down."[14]

Despite ten caution flags, the incredible pace set by Jones when the cars were at speed helped Foyt set a race record of 151.207 mph, breaking the mark set by Clark in 1965.

"There was no time during the race I tried to run with the turbine," Foyt said. "I never even got close enough to the thing to see if the exhaust or heat bothered me. I think the closest I got was about eight seconds. I couldn't race him."[15]

It was every bit as big a victory for Goodyear, its first at Indianapolis in forty-eight years, as Foyt ran the full 500 miles without a tire change. It was only fitting Foyt was the one to give Goodyear its first victory, having encouraged its return to the Speedway in 1963.

The Victory Banquet was typically held the night after the 500 but because of the rain delay it was held the evening of the race in 1967. Thanks to the early start and record pace, there was just enough time for Lucy Foyt to dash out and buy a new dress. Just as she had in 1961, she'd already shipped most of her clothes home.

A.J. was having his own challenges getting ready for the banquet as Granatelli repeatedly called his room at the Speedway Motel. When the STP head refused to meet Foyt's demand for $5,000 to run his company's stickers on his car, Foyt had refused to display them. Now, Granatelli was desperate to get Foyt to put the stickers on his car before the annual morning-after photo shoot so it could be featured in STP advertisements.

"His room was below mine at the Speedway Motel," Foyt recalled more than fifty years later. "He called my room four or five times, and I said, 'Andy, I'm trying to get dressed. I got to get cleaned up and go to the awards.' He kept saying I got to put his sticker on the car. I said, 'Well, I run your product,' which I did, but I wasn't gonna run his sticker. He said, 'What can we do?' I said, 'We can't do nothing, you've got to give me what I want.' Then he came up with a Studebaker and gave me the money I wanted and I let him put a sticker on it."[16]

Foyt also picked up a $10,000 accessory award check from STP as the race winner. Granatelli later said the agreement with Foyt was reached the morning of the race, but the stickers didn't get put on the car in time. They were on in time for the photo shoot, and A.J. and Tony eventually appeared in an ad, although Granatelli would be questioned as to whether Foyt really used STP in the car.[17]

Not everyone stuck around for the banquet. Clark, Hulme, Rindt, and Gurney all left immediately for Holland and the Dutch Grand Prix. Hill, ever the gentleman and as the defending race champion, stayed behind to honor the new winner, saying, "It's a pleasure for me to be in a position to award the winner's ring to A.J. Foyt, who drove a great race in a beautifully prepared machine."[18]

Foyt relished his time at the podium, at one moment combative, the next gracious. He noted he now had a ring for each of his children and as a result, must be a pretty good father. He accepted the keys to the Camaro pace car, saying he planned to trade it in on a Ford Thunderbird.

"Some people said I was over the hill," he said. "I wish to thank those who had faith in me. You have to finish this race to win it, and I guess this was just my day. I've brought the race back to America, it's up to you young guys to keep it here."

Someone yelled out Foyt was "lucky." Thinking it came from Jones's table, he shot back that "cheaters never win." Surprised, Jones answered with "Next year, Andy is going to build *ten* turbine cars, so there'll be a lot of cheaters."[19]

In a quieter moment, Foyt and Jones shook hands. "I deeply regret that Parnelli didn't win," he told a reporter. "It was one of those days."

CHAMPION'S BREAKFAST

Foyt met a handful of reporters for breakfast at the Speedway Motel's Checkered Flag restaurant the next morning, including Bob Ottum of *Sports Illustrated,* and Corky Lamm and Dick Mittman from the *Indianapolis News.* In front of him was his favorite breakfast: steak and eggs, potatoes, and toast. Waiting at the track for him were photographers and a spotless Coyote.

He'd had trouble sleeping, bothered by the sometimes acrimonious tone of the Victory Banquet and reliving the final lap over and over as he tossed and turned. Their table overlooked the first tee of the Speedway's golf course, and as they talked Foyt spotted Jones getting ready to tee off, resplendent in white saddle-shoe golf spikes.[20]

"I'm sorry for Parnelli," he said with a nod. "He's one of the great competitors. Has lots of ability. But I'm not sorry about the turbine. Indianapolis is a proving ground for autos—not airplane engines. The turbine just has too much horsepower and torque for any piston car to catch it. They either have to get it out of the race or put it on a dyno and get its horsepower down to ours. They say it's 550 [horsepower], but I won't buy that. If they don't restrict it, I'd definitely have to consider it."[21]

He was in a reflective mood, thinking aloud at times about what the future held for him. One thing was apparent, he wasn't a driver considering retirement.

"I wanted to win more championship races than any other driver and I did that before I was 30. It's a great honor to have my name alongside Mauri Rose and Louie Meyer," he said, either forgetting or ignoring Wilbur Shaw. "Now I want to be the only four-time winner of the 500 and this puts me a little closer to my goal."[22]

He surprised the writers by saying he was thinking of skipping the four road courses on the 1967 Indy car schedule, up from the single road race in previous years. "My car isn't set up for that kind of racing," he explained. "It was built just for Indianapolis. I don't even know how we'll do this Sunday in Milwaukee."

In the next breath he surprised them again, revealing he'd considered entering the upcoming Dutch Grand Prix rather than the race in Milwaukee. But the rain delay and the responsibilities of winning the 500 changed that. He also was leading in the season-long points championship, and if he decided to seek another title he couldn't afford to skip Milwaukee.

"I thought seriously of dashing over there," Foyt said. "But it would have been too much of a crash program getting things cleaned up here. I do believe some American drivers could blow them off over there."

He seemed resigned about his upcoming trip to the 24 Hours of Le Mans and said he wasn't looking forward to the event. It was part of his agreement with Ford, however, and something he was committed to do.

"I really don't enjoy those kind of races as much. But I've got a job to do. It's not really a race, but a durability run."

One writer asked about the reports that after his two big accidents, A.J. had lost the will to win.

"What other people have said never bothered me," he responded. "I've never been ashamed of anything I've done on a racetrack. I've always figured I had a chance to win out there. The day I don't, that's the day I quit."[23]

HELP WANTED

After the breakfast and photo session, Foyt found himself facing a unique challenge for someone who'd just won the Indianapolis 500. After paying bonus money to his and Leonard's crew members, many of them had turned in their notice, including those recruited from the "Tamale Wagon" sprint car team that called Los Angeles home. With the Indy 500 won—and the bonus money in their pockets—those who weren't excited about moving to Houston or Indianapolis in the first place wanted more money before embarking on the road for the rest of the season. Foyt thought they were already overpaid and turned them loose.

Foyt later said he'd made a mistake he never repeated.

"You learn lessons through the years, and I learned an important lesson then. After that, nobody gets their bonus until after Christmas. If I have to split it twenty ways and two people leave, then I split it eighteen ways. I've had a couple of people who quit and ask about a bonus, and I'll say, you forfeited it to your friends who still work here. If you work for me, you'll get your percentage, but it comes after the season is over with, not after a big race. You live and learn."[24]

Among those leaving was Lance, whose bonus was 5 percent of Leonard's earnings, or $2,700, a fair amount of money in 1967.

"I'd been doing it for ten years," he said. "I'd been away from home for more than a month and we were going to work out of Indianapolis for the rest of the season. I decided I needed to be in Houston where I had a wife and four kids trying to get by."[25]

There was another reason for Lance's decision.

"Tony didn't care for me for some reason. I'd known him since before I went to work for A.J., but he didn't like my attitude. I thought my attitude was good, I wasn't a smart aleck or anything like that. Maybe he just didn't have much confidence in me. I'd worked mostly with sports cars and didn't really know what I was doing with Indy cars.

"I never had a problem with A.J. I liked him and we got along fine. Never had an argument or cross words or anything like that. But then I wasn't his chief mechanic, Tony was, and I was working under Tony."

With both his cars headed for the Milwaukee race, Foyt needed replacement crewmen and needed them fast. One of those recommended to him was Jack Starne, who'd spent the month as a "stooge" or gofer for RCG racing, a team formed by 1960 500 winner Jim Rathmann and astronauts Gordon Cooper and Gus Grissom. In tribute to Grissom, who'd been killed in a launch training accident earlier in the year, the team had kept its original name. It only ran at Indianapolis and struggled all month with new Mongoose race cars, a new supercharged version of the Offenhauser engine, and two drivers with limited experience at the Speedway. As a result, both team cars failed to qualify.

Foyt played with Rathmann in the charity golf tournament and, always on the outlook for new workers, asked about the RCG crew. Rathmann said Starne was green, but a hard worker.[26]

Starne had stayed in Indianapolis to attend the 500 and see a girl he'd met in the city. With the race over, he was packing up the team's garage and getting ready to return to Southern California and his job at Crower Cams.

"I don't think A.J. knew who I was. He came into the garage and introduced himself and asked me if I wanted to go to Milwaukee and work for him part-time. He's the Indy 500 winner and here I am—I don't know nothin' about anything. I guess he couldn't find nobody else. I said, yeah, okay, I'll go."[27]

JACK STARNE

Starne's decision to join Foyt's team was the next step for the Southern California boy who recorded the Indy 500 radio broadcast on a reel-to-reel tape machine so he could listen to it over and over. As a teenager he'd spent his evenings in Bruce Crower's shop, doing whatever odd jobs they'd allow. Crower's Cams produced high-performance engine camshafts, and there was a constant flow of hot rods and race cars through the facility.

He'd been mesmerized when a Kuzma Indy roadster, the Helse Special, showed up in early 1959. It was the car Jerry Unser would crash in practice for the 500, eventually succumbing to the effects of his burns. The badly damaged car shook Starne when it was returned to the shop, but it didn't dampen his interest in racing.

Eventually he went to work for Crower's Cams, and when Crower was hired to service the RCG car at Indy, Starne was added to the crew. He'd enjoyed his month at the Speedway, working for crew chief Bob Dickson, who'd already turned down Foyt's job offer. A.J. was "too much of an ass," Starne remembers Dickson saying. Starne had nothing better to do, however, and took the job. Tony Foyt pointed him at Leonard's car and told him to strip the tape from the car.[28]

"Back then Tony wanted everything on the car taped over," Starne said. "He felt it helped keep things tight. I started gathering the tape and gathering it and pretty soon I had enough tape that it looked like a basketball. It was a little bit of a struggle, but we managed to get through [the first weekend].

"I got along with Tony right from the very beginning. If I needed help, all I needed to do was ask. I've always been the type of person who tries to learn from people who have been through it, have experienced something," Starne explained. "I just listened and watched and learned.

"Tony was an excellent engine man. He could do transmissions, drivetrains, everything. He was very, very good at it. He'd get all the parts together and make it happen. You'd think, 'he can't do that,' but he always could."

Starne learned another important lesson, one Lance had learned before him.

"Tony was the type of person that if he liked you, it was great, he'd do anything in the world for you. If he didn't like you, you'd better stay away from him."

Tony took an immediate liking to the easygoing Starne, and while the job was supposed to be temporary, he kept showing up for work every day. At the end of the season, he moved to Houston and before long convinced his then-girlfriend from Indianapolis to join him. A.J.'s mother also took a liking to Starne, who was about five years younger than A.J.

"Tony became like a father to me, and Evelyn was one of the nicest ladies you'd ever want to meet. She was like a mother to me and my girlfriend. Not sometimes, *all* the time. They were super, super, great people."

That included words of motherly advice for his girlfriend.

"A.J.'s mother said to her, 'He needs to marry you, period. Either that or find somebody else. Don't give your life up for him.' So we got married."

A.J. served as best man and Lucy the maid of honor. Tony Foyt gave the bride away and the reception was held at the elder Foyt's home. "We packed the washing machine with ice and then filled it up with champagne bottles. It was quite a deal."

The Starnes were invited to the weekly Foyt family Sunday dinners at Tony and Evelyn's house. Other crew members were often included. Starne says A.J. became the brother he never had—a sentiment echoed by Foyt. And like typical brothers, they'd have their share of run-ins.

"We had our moments," Starne says. "I'd stand up to him and he'd stand up to me. A.J. was more hot-headed than his daddy. He'd blow off real quick. Sometimes he'd know to back off someone who made a mistake, but not often.

"You'd immediately know how he felt and what he was upset about. Five minutes later it was over with, and you'd go drink a beer. Let's move on. Let's go win some races. That's what it was all about."

Starne would have opportunities with other teams and job offers, but would never leave Foyt's operation, although A.J. was concerned he'd gone too far at times.

"I never really threatened to leave. But there were times when he thought I was going to quit. He'd run to my wife for help and say, 'This time he's really mad,' but it would eventually go away."

At one-point "Little Jack," as everyone called him, came off the road, while remaining a fixture in the race shop, taking on special projects and personally overseeing the racing careers of Foyt's children and grandchildren.

For more than fifty-five years, Starne remained a fixture with the team.

"I guess I'm still just temporary help."

CHAPTER 25

LE MANS

1967

The 24 Hours of Le Mans is the oldest, most prestigious road race in the world and was, in 1967, "the most dangerous race in the world," according to Mario Andretti. "One long accident waiting to happen."[1]

First run in 1923, it's held on what's known as the Circuit de la Sarthe, named after its local governing "department" located about 130 miles southwest of Paris. At the time it was 8.36 miles long over mostly public roads, connected by short stretches of dedicated racetrack. Its main feature was the 3.6-mile Mulsanne Straight, where speeds topped 200 miles per hour for extended periods of time.

Although Le Mans was on equal footing with Formula One's Monaco Grand Prix as Europe's most famous race and, along with the Indianapolis 500, considered one of the three top events in the world, it was far from a favorite of most American drivers. The international travel was a challenge, coming in the middle of the busy racing season. A field of up to fifty-five cars was spread over three classes, ranging from those with 1.0-liter engines putting out less than 100 horsepower to the monster 7.0-liter, 500-plus horsepower Ford and Chevrolet powerplants. Speed differences between the cars could reach 100 mph on the Mulsanne.

It was especially dangerous at night, when cooler temperatures allowed cars to run at peak speeds and the fastest threatened to outrun their headlights. There is always the possibility of rain, and few of the American drivers at the time had experience racing in "the wet," not to mention the ground fog that seemed to rise near dawn every year as temperatures began to warm. And with 110 mostly European drivers in the field—including some amateurs—many of the competitors were unknown to the Americans. Besides that, it paid very little to win.

Ford had finally beaten Ferrari at Le Mans in 1966 after three years of trying, and in 1967 was out to prove it wasn't a fluke. It decided to follow its successful

◄ The start of a tradition. *The Henry Ford, David Friedman Collection*

race-winning strategy, splitting cars and drivers between the same two teams, Shelby American and Holman-Moody. Each team was provided with a pair of the new Mark IVs and a Mark II B for the race.

Assembling a driver lineup proved a little more challenging with the pairings partially dictated by tire contracts. At Sebring, Goodyear and Firestone had turned a blind eye toward the proceedings, but Le Mans was different. Both brands were pouring untold millions of dollars into developing dry- and wet-weather tires for the race and all contracted drivers were expected to toe the line. Shelby's team would be on Goodyears, Holman-Moody on Firestones. Ferrari also was committed to Firestone.

At Shelby American the powers that be—Ford, Goodyear, and Shelby—again paired A.J. Foyt with Dan Gurney. They'd gotten along well at Daytona, and there was an obvious respect between the two. While it was Foyt's first trip to Le Mans, it would be Gurney's tenth start, which included a class victory and fourth-place finish overall in 1964. He knew the track as well as any driver in the field, and it would be his responsibility to set up the car. In a sign of respect, they were assigned the No. 1 machine. In perhaps a sign of disrespect, it was painted Ferrrai red.

In Shelby's second Mark IV was 1966 Le Mans co-winner Bruce McLaren, who was paired with Mark Donohue. The third Shelby car, the Mark II B, was assigned to Ronnie Bucknum and Australian Paul Hawkins.

Leading the Holman-Moody and Firestone lineup was Andretti, the Daytona 500 winner and Sebring co-winner when he'd been on loan to Shelby. He was paired with Lucien Bianchi, the Belgian he'd driven with the year before. A solid endurance racer, with a couple of class victories in eleven Le Mans starts and an overall win at Sebring, he was no match for Andretti in sheer speed.

In the team's second Mark IV was Lloyd Ruby, also making his first Le Mans start, and F1's Denis Hulme, who'd just won Rookie of the Year honors at Indianapolis. In the team's Mark II B was the odd couple of Roger McCluskey and Australian road racer Frank Gardner. It was a week of firsts for McCluskey, a last-minute addition to the team. He was making his first trip to France, getting his first look at the Le Mans circuit, having his first drive in a Ford GT, and meeting Gardner for the first time.

The three USAC Le Mans "rookies," Foyt, Ruby, and McCluskey, made their way via commercial flights to Europe, where a Ford charter was waiting for the short hop to Le Mans. The plane was a Beechcraft Baron, a twin-engine, five-passenger model similar to Foyt's own Cessna 310. After takeoff Foyt glanced at the gauges, noticing the tachometer needles were past their redlines and their air speed was much higher than he thought it should be. He asked the pilot what had been done to reinforce the plane for the higher speed. The pilot shrugged, "Nothing."

"I thought, 'Holy shit.' I was waiting for one of the wings to come off the whole trip," Foyt recalled, deciding then and there the entire return trip would be on commercial aircraft.[2]

After arriving near Le Mans, the trio was whisked to a luncheon for drivers and news media at Henry Ford II's hotel. According to the *New York Times*, it didn't take long for Foyt to cause a commotion when "he made the waiter remove an excellent trout amandine because he could not bear the thought of eating fish with the head still on."[3]

"They split the fish down the middle, kept the head and tail intact, fried it, and then put almonds on it," Foyt explained later. "Everyone was telling us how good that trout was. But I didn't like the looks of it. It wasn't done and was kinda raw. So I sent mine back.

"I guess you might say I'm a funny eater. What I really like is fried chicken, hamburger and steaks. About the only thing I found in France that I like was the homemade bread."[4]

Foyt also discovered he wouldn't get along with European reporters any better than he did stateside media. "Do you think it's a big honor to get killed racing?" one reporter asked in broken English. Foyt looked at him incredulously. "What?" The reporter attempted to rephrase the question, but Foyt cut him short.[5]

"I think you're a goddamn fool to get killed racing," he said. End of interview.[6]

Things didn't go much better when the drivers lined up for their race physicals. The eye chart was the largest Foyt had ever seen. When asked his blood type, Ruby drawled, "Red," the attendant dutifully writing it down. Afterward, Foyt went in search of a Ford exec and demanded they have an American doctor available. He was happy to learn the company had taken the precaution the year before and again would have an American medical team on hand.[7]

In fact, Ford's Le Mans racing program was by now a finely tuned machine. The race team contingent topped one hundred, not including the large number of Ford executives. In addition to the fourteen drivers, Shelby had nineteen crew members on hand and Holman-Moody twenty-seven. Thirty-five more came from Kar-Kraft and other Ford-run operations.

Most team members were housed at the Hôtel de Paris in the heart of Le Mans, a short way from the track. Nearly everyone was expected to share a room, although Foyt and Gurney were allotted singles.

Ford again rented the service garage of a local Peugeot dealership as the team's primary base of operations. Holman-Moody shipped a transporter packed with equipment to be used by both teams as a machine shop. A British catering company was hired to feed the small army, with a kitchen open around the clock to provide meals on demand, although by all accounts the hamburgers were marginal. Because of complaints about the strong French coffee, a Café Americana machine was brought in, along with another dispensing Coca-Cola.

PRERACE

During pre-practice inspection, or "scrutineering," as it's called in road racing, the Mark IV's cockpit rearview mirror was ruled insufficient, and the Ford teams were ordered to mount rearview mirrors on the front fenders.

A potentially more serious problem with the Mark IV's ride height was averted, at least for the time being. Regulations called for a car's ride height to be at least 10 centimeters, and each car was rolled over a wood box during scrutineering to ensure it met the minimum. In testing, the Ford team had discovered a significant improvement in performance and stability when the nose of the Mark IV was set at just under the limit. Phil Remington was credited with coming up with a shim that was placed in the front springs of the cars to increase the ride height enough to pass scrutineering and would then break up or fall out once the car was on the track. Years later and unprompted, Foyt said the shims were his idea, a trick he'd picked up in NASCAR, where "you had to cheat to eat."[8]

"I don't want to blow my own horn, and I really don't care if you put it in the book, but I'd seen them do this in NASCAR and I told Phil and Dan about it," Foyt said more than fifty years later. "Cut a rubber hose and wrap it with friction tape. You jack the car up and tape rubber blocks into the springs. It would hold for a lap or two, then the friction will push it out of the way. It was illegal, but it wasn't *illegal*. Everybody else was cheating too."[9]

Not until Wednesday prior to the race did drivers get their first laps on the track. While there was an entire month of practice before the Indianapolis 500 and two weeks prior to the Daytona 500, Le Mans held one test weekend in April and then allotted just two days of limited practice time before the race. As a result, McLaren had spent considerable time carefully setting up the Mark IVs at Riverside, signing off on each car prior to them being sent to France.

The Holman-Moody cars were among the first on the track, but not for long. Andretti and Hulme were soon in the pits with windshield cracks directly in the driver's line of sight. The Ford engineers wondered what the NASCAR team had done to cause the cracks.

Gurney took the No. 1 car out for a short shakedown run then turned it over to Foyt. A.J. completed only a couple of laps before pitting with an almost identical crack. McLaren was told to pit and as the car sat in its stall, a crack spread across the windshield. A sinking feeling swept through the area. The windshields were clearly the problem. Only two replacements were available. In four years, Ford had never replaced a windshield.

A quick call was made to Ford engineers in Dearborn, who contacted the windshield supplier, Corning Glass, in upstate New York. The windshields in question had received extra tempering or heat treatment to decrease the risk of chipping. They'd apparently been over-treated, however, and as a result were now proving brittle. Replacement windshields were ordered, but wouldn't arrive until after practice and qualifying.

The teams jury-rigged a Plexiglas backing to the windshields to hopefully keep them from falling into a driver's lap and released the cars for limited practice. Foyt, Ruby, and McCluskey all made tentative laps around the track, Ruby asking afterward, "Y'all remember which way to go?"[10]

A LAP AT LE MANS

Following the abbreviated practice session, Ford asked Andretti to talk with his Indy car counterparts. Mario had driven in the race the year before and, despite the track's dangers, had fallen in love with it. Thanks to his extensive testing, he'd also spent more time in a Mark IV than the other three drivers combined.

Nothing about a lap around the Le Mans course in 1967 was easy. More than 80 percent of the lap was driven with the accelerator flat on the floor, putting a huge strain on the engine. The other 20 percent put an even bigger strain on the brakes and transmission.

Just pulling on the track was treacherous. Only a double white line separated the pits from the racing surface, and as cars accelerated, they were being overtaken by others at the end of their lap, the fastest approaching 190 mph.

The pit straight was the scene of the worst tragedy in auto racing history in 1955 when two cars collided, catapulting one into the crowded grandstands, killing the driver and more than eighty spectators. The racing surface and pit entrance were widened slightly the following year and the earthen barrier protecting the grandstands enlarged, but it remained a dangerous portion of the track.

Coming out of the pits and watching his mirrors for fast-closing cars, a driver immediately faced a blind, uphill, and off-camber right-hand bend under the track's iconic landmark, the Dunlop Bridge. Bursting from under the bridge at speeds topping 180 mph at full song, cars then plunged downhill like a rollercoaster ride toward the esses.

The approach to the "S" turns was one of the few areas of the track lined by barricades or earth barriers on both sides. Drivers are hard on the brakes and downshifting, hugging the right side of the track before diving left and then right again, exiting the turns at less than 100 mph in second gear. Then it was back on the gas for a short straight under a smaller Dunlop Bridge to Tertre Rouge, trying not to be distracted by the lights of the popular carnival area on the outside of the track, driver's left.

At first glance, Tertre Rouge, or red knoll, appeared to be a precise but relatively simple corner, a tight right-hander taken in second gear. Yet most considered it the track's most important turn, as it led to the Mulsanne. A sandbank guarded the outer exit and drivers starting to accelerate too soon often dropped a wheel off the surface, kicking up sand onto the track and turning it into an ice-skating rink.

Pulling onto the Mulsanne a driver was greeted on the left by a line of more than two dozen pine trees standing like sentries, spaced a few feet apart and a few yards from the pavement, their trunks painted white in warning.

"At night the lights reflected off the trees and ought to blind me," Foyt would say in his autobiography. "Goddamn, if you went off there, you were in trouble."[11]

The Mulsanne Straight is neither straight nor flat. In 1967 it was about three traffic lanes wide and there were no chicanes to slow the cars—those would come later. The fastest cars normally stayed to the left, while the slowest hugged the track's right border. The middle was up for grabs, where overtaking cars from both lanes might try to pass a slower machine. At various points the road was lined by houses, restaurants open for business, telephone poles, trees, and drainage ditches, but no real guardrails or fencing. Fire hydrants were marked by hay bales. There were no lights illuminating the track surface at night, only darkness.

The fastest cars covered the ground in about ninety seconds, which can seem like an eternity. Early in the event, with a full field of cars jumbled by the footrace at the start, it's a madhouse of darting machines. In the early morning darkness, with the field shredded by mechanical problems, a driver might find himself alone on the straight, struggling to keep his mind from wandering.

At one point Foyt and the other newcomers were warned that spectators sometimes wandered across Mulsanne at night, some drunk, others looking to force drivers to take evasive action. Foyt was having none of it.

"I told Ford, if somebody wanders in front of me, I'm not gonna kill myself and go in those trees. I said I don't wanna hit nobody, but I'm not going into those trees to kill myself if somebody is staggering across the track."[12]

A gradual and barely noticeable rise in the Mulsanne turned into a series of gentle waves, until a full-blown hump two-thirds of the way down the straight got a driver's attention and alerted him that a bend in the road—known as the Mulsanne Kink—was fast approaching. The cars were nearing their maximum speeds at that point, with the quickest topping 210 mph and covering the length of a football field in about a second.

The kink could be taken flat out, but only by the most skilled and courageous. Make it through in a Mark IV without lifting and you'd be hitting about 215 mph on the other side. Drivers then started braking for the Mulsanne Corner, the tightest and slowest part of the track, where brake-killing temperatures hit 1,500 degrees Fahrenheit.

Andretti told the others he was taking the kink without lifting. So were McLaren, Gurney, and a couple of the Ferrari and Chapparal drivers. Mario would say he went "from one shoulder of the road to the other, grit my teeth and do the kink flat."[13]

The three USAC drivers had all been breathing the throttle at the kink and some could have taken Mario's comments as a challenge, although Andretti said it wasn't meant that way. Gurney pulled Foyt aside afterward and told him to ignore what Andretti, McLaren, and the others were doing. There was no need to run flat-out through the kink. It had taken him ten years to realize it, but now Gurney said it was more important to ease up and save the brakes and transmission as you approached the slowest point on the track—the Mulsanne Corner.[14]

"If you went down deep into the turn at the end of the straight and put the brakes on, you would kill the brakes," Gurney said. "At the end of the straight I was backing off about 250 yards before I needed to and letting it coast down on the engine. Instead of slowing down from 212 mph, I was slowing down from maybe 170, 165. The difference was much better for the brakes."[15]

Foyt took Gurney's message to heart. He'd later call the kink a "little 200 mph soft right-hand dogleg," while acknowledging, "You've got to suck everything up tight. Back off a bit and hit the brakes, really mash down, then drag it down to first gear and breathe the brakes."

The entry to the corner was bumpy, just to keep things interesting. If you were going too fast, there was a runoff road that would take you all the way to the village of Mulsanne. Try to make the turn while going too quickly, and you were likely to end up buried in a huge sand mound on the outside of the corner's exit.

It's not a traditional corner, although not quite the hairpin some call it. More of an elbow or V-turn. "Suddenly you're going in the other direction," Foyt noted.

Adding to the challenge, the turn was little more than two traffic lanes wide and soon covered with sand, gravel, and dirt as one car after another clipped the apex or left the braking until too late. There was often a car stuck in the sandbank, the driver frantically trying to dig it out.[16]

Pulling away from the corner, the signaling pits were on the right. A quick glance informed a driver of his lap time and team instructions. Miss a "PIT" sign and a driver was in danger of running out of fuel if forced to run another eight miles. A short straight then led to a series of bends and turns known as "Indianapolis" because it was originally paved with bricks. From there it was another tree-lined drive to Arnage Corner, a hard right-hander leading onto the backstraight toward Maison Blanche.

Named for the white house standing alongside the track on a bend in the road, the area was a favorite of campers. Early morning smoke from campfires, combined with the ground fog prevalent in the area, added to the difficulty. There were no Porsche Curves or Ford Chicane to slow the cars in 1967, and the approach to Maison Blanche was the second-fastest part of the track, with some cars reaching 200 mph. Drivers slowed only slightly for the bend in the road around the house, which was guarded by concrete abutments. Andretti warned the others to be careful, saying, "Miscue there and you're smithereens."[17]

Clear of the white house, drivers accelerated past the pits to start another lap, all the time watching for cars entering and leaving the racing surface. "You had better be hitting 180 and climbing as you go past the pits," Foyt would say, "or everybody will think you're a tourist."[18]

While Foyt struggled to learn the track, Gurney struggled with the car setup. Every change he made seemed to make the car slower. Crew members recall the two drivers bouncing up and down on the fenders of the carefully calibrated car to test the springs. They changed the camber and caster, springs and spoiler settings, even the carefully set ride height. At one point Ford engineers took the unusual step of asking Holman-Moody for a set of its springs and shocks for the Shelby American driver to try.

Thursday evening, with the end of practice and qualifying approaching, Gurney asked McLaren to test hop the car. The two were closer friends than most drivers, but McLaren was still surprised when someone of Gurney's stature and experience asked for help.

Agreeing to run a few laps, McLaren was back in the pits before completing one circuit, saying he found the car impossible to drive. He suggested Gurney put the original setup—McLaren's setup—back on the No. 1 machine. As if to prove a point, McLaren got back in his car and turned the fastest qualifying lap, five seconds faster than Gurney's best effort, and fast enough to capture the pole. Gurney ended up ninth, behind the other three Mark IVs, a Chaparral, a pair of Ferraris, and even two of the older Ford Mark II Bs.[19]

Shelby waited until his two star drivers departed for the hotel after qualifying, then sent the No. 1 machine back to the Peugeot garage. He'd become increasingly frustrated by the performance of the car and told crew members to return the suspension to its original settings. He allowed only for Gurney's spoiler change, which McLaren also requested for his car. The mechanics were sworn to secrecy; not a word was to be said to the drivers.

––––––––

The prerace Le Mans festivities are every bit a match for those at Indianapolis, with marching bands, beauty queens, and dignitaries from around the world clogging the track and pits. Wedged between grandstands on one side and the pit-side viewing boxes rising three stories high on the other, the crush of people matched anything the drivers had seen at Indy. In front of the grandstands was a terraced viewing area, allowing spectators to stand twenty-five rows deep, crammed shoulder to shoulder, to watch the famed running start. As the French tricolor wouldn't be waved until 4:00 p.m.—versus the 11:00 a.m. green flag at Indy—the excitement, anticipation, and tension built throughout the day to a fever pitch.

An estimated crowd of more than 350,000 was even larger than Indianapolis, drawn by an epic rematch between two heavyweight champions, Ford and Ferrari, and what promised to be a slugfest among the world's best teams and drivers. Just as at Indianapolis, race time approached with the main straight still jammed with people ignoring pleas from the announcer to clear the grid. It remained that way until an hour before the start, when a small army of French police, the famous *gendarmes*, stretched across the track, linked arms, and began to walk toward the start/finish line, sweeping everyone and everything before them.

The classic Le Mans start, where the race began with drivers running across the track, jumping into their cars, and roaring away, had been banned in England since 1962 as too dangerous. Not in France, however, and a few minutes before four, fifty-four drivers began to line up. Each driver stood in a small circle designating their starting position, twenty-five yards across the track from where their car was parked at a sixty-five-degree angle facing the Dunlop Bridge.

As the second hand approached 4:00 p.m., many of the drivers crouched in what could loosely be called a runner's stance. Several stood with hands on hips or slouched in a practiced nonchalance.

While the roar of the cars coming down to the green flag at the start of the Indy 500 is nearly drowned out by the cheering crowd, the starting line at Le Mans quiets to a near silence as the clock approaches the magic hour. As the second hand hits 4:00 p.m., the French tricolor waves and the announcer issues a simple "Go!" The footsteps of the drivers echo as they run across the track. Invariably, someone jumps the start and is well ahead of the rest. The sound of a single engine breaks the silence, and a moment later more than fifty cars roar to life and scream away.

First off in 1967 were the older Ford GT Mark II Bs of Gardner and Bucknum. Neither driver made any effort to fasten their belts, convinced the safest start was to get a jump on the horde of cars. They were followed closely by Pedro Rodriguez, who didn't have to worry about fastening his belts. His Ferrari didn't have any.

Gurney was quick on his feet, his long strides getting him to his car ahead of nearly everyone else. He buckled his belts and pulled away, accomplishing what he'd been unable to do during qualifying, passing the Mark IVs, Ferraris, and Chaparral as they sat in line. But he was in for a surprise when he reached the Mulsanne.

"It's really something when you drive around the first corner and onto the Mulsanne Straight and then glance down and discover that your seat belt is not locked," he'd say. "I began to steer with my knees—I held the speed down to about 195 or so—and I buckled myself in. Then I *really* stood on it."[20]

The otherwise good start created an interesting challenge for Gurney. The car felt great, the best it had since the start of practice. By lap three he was in third, behind only Gardner and Bucknum. He was tempted to give the No. 1 its head, to push it into the lead and see what the car could do. But he remembered his talks with Foyt about Le Mans being an endurance test, not a race. If he ran a few blistering laps now, Foyt might try and match the speeds later.

With that in mind, Gurney went into endurance mode, content to run in place and allow Gardner and Bucknum to lead. In his mirror he caught a glimpse of McLaren's yellow car moving into fourth place, also seemingly happy to hold position.

The two Hulman-Moody Mark IVs, however, were already having problems. Hulme made an early ten-minute stop to fix a sticking throttle. Bianchi, who started the No. 3 after Holman-Moody decided it wanted Andretti in the car at the end of the race, stopped with a chipped windshield, afraid it might indicate a return of the problem they'd experienced in practice. It was quickly identified as simply a stone mark and he was sent on his way.

While the thirsty Fords were expected to refuel about every ninety minutes, the first stops were planned for the one-hour mark to double-check gas mileage. Drivers were scheduled to run two segments or "stints" before changing. Gardner had already been in and out of the pits a couple of times when midway through Gurney's second stint, about ninety minutes into the race, Bucknum suddenly slowed on the Mulsanne and pulled to the right. Gurney went past and into the lead, although he didn't know it was for the top spot until he reached the signal station.

"We didn't pay attention to what the competition was doing," Dan said. "I was really surprised that we were leading so early."[21]

When Gurney brought the car into the pits for the first scheduled driver change, he told Foyt everything was good, helped him get belted in, and then sought out Shelby. Yelling above the noise of the cars, he told the team boss, "I think we finally got it set up the way we want it."[22]

As Foyt pulled on the track, the midnight blue No. 4 Mark IV shot past. Just a few minutes earlier, A.J. had been talking with Ruby, one of its co-drivers. So Foyt knew it was Hulme in the car.

The New Zealand driver was on his way to winning his first F1 driver's championship but was still an unknown to many race fans. Following his performance at Indianapolis, he'd joined the short list of foreign drivers earning Foyt's respect. A.J. knew Hulme probably should have won Le Mans the previous year when paired with Ken Miles, and, most importantly, Ruby spoke highly of him. If

Hulme was good enough for ol' Rube, he was good enough for Foyt. He fell in behind the blue car and started to follow it around the track.

Hulme was several laps behind because of the early pit stop and a second one for tires after he'd spun avoiding a slower car. He was in full catch-up mode, the fastest car on the track, topping McLaren's pole speed and setting a lap record in the process.

"I followed him for about four or five laps," Foyt said. "That's kind of how I learned the course." He later passed Hulme and pulled away, as the Kiwi slowed to pit and turn the car over to Ruby.[23]

Foyt turned out to be a good student. Watching A.J. go through the Mulsanne Corner and coming away impressed was leading European journalist Denis Jenkinson. "Foyt doesn't make mistakes," he wrote in his notebook.[24]

The next time Foyt saw the No. 4, it was stuck in the sandbank at Mulsanne Corner, Ruby pawing at the ground, trying to free the car. "I told him later he looked like a dog digging in the dirt," Foyt recalled. He made a mental note to not let that happen to him. "I wasn't gonna stand there and get my ass run over."[25]

Champing at the bit to start his run was Andretti. Bianchi's pit stop and leisurely pace had dropped them two laps behind the Foyt/Gurney car. Andretti immediately jumped to the top of the speed charts and matched Hulme's track record. By the four-hour mark, he was up to second and finally eased off. Foyt and Gurney were still more than a lap ahead, but Andretti was ecstatic after his run.

"I couldn't believe we would smoke off the Ferraris like this. I can pass any of them, anytime I want, anyplace on the track I want," he said, scoffing at the idea the Ferraris were running slower by plan. "People may say they're holding back. All I know is that Chris Amon is really winging it, because his back end gets all squiggly when he goes around corners. He is obviously going as fast as he'll go."[26]

The McLaren/Donohue car was doing well to stay in touch with the leaders. They'd made one unplanned stop when one of the fasteners on the rear bodywork of the car came loose, but Donohue noticed a vibration and pitted to have it repaired before any damage was done. They'd lost a lap with the added stop but were content to cruise between third and fourth, swapping positions with the Chaparral on pit stops.

The one-lap cushion the No. 1 Ford enjoyed disappeared in a flash as Foyt rolled into the pits just after 8:00 p.m., holding the door open and yelling, "The car's out of goddamn gas." The team's scorers had somehow lost track of its lap count and run the car out of fuel. Crew members were unprepared for his arrival, and he fumed while waiting for servicing to be completed.

"It wasn't like NASCAR or even Indy," he recalled. "Everyone took their goddamn time." It could have been much worse. He'd been fortunate the car started coughing as he approached the pits, not on the other side of the track where he would have had to hike back to the pits for a can of gas, then return to the car to refuel it and hope it started.

Despite the slow stop, the Foyt/Gurney car still led as darkness settled in and shortly after 10:00 p.m. the fastest of the Ferraris, the P4 Spyder of defending race co-champion Chris Amon, was out. Slowed by a flat tire and unable to change it, he'd tried to drive slowly back to the pits. Flapping rubber shreds severed a fuel line, however, and the car burned to the ground.

While the McLaren/Donohue and Andretti/Bianchi cars continued to swap second and third depending on pit stops, by the eleventh hour Andretti was getting antsy. When Andretti was at the wheel, the No. 3 car was the fastest on the track. When Bianchi took over, it was the slowest of the leaders.

Even though they were good friends, Andretti and Bianchi, unlike the team of Foyt and Gurney, were not on the same page—and hadn't been since the start of the race. They weren't even reading from the same book.

Bianchi, like most European drivers, saw Le Mans as an endurance event, pure and simple. Their team had dropped out with a blown engine less than a third of the way through the race in 1966, and he was determined to avoid that fate again.

For Andretti, Le Mans was also simple. Like everywhere else, he wanted to lead. If he went out, he'd go out in a blaze of glory. Matched against Foyt, he took big chunks out of the lead car's margin. Bianchi, running against Gurney, gave it back.

"I busted my ass putting time between us because Lucien would go against Gurney and Dan was quicker than Lucien," Andretti said. "But I was miles quicker than Foyt. I had one stint where I put a lap and a half on him."[27]

By early morning Andretti was in the zone, consistently lapping near his own track record. He noticed a slight vibration in the brakes but ignored it, continuing to close on Foyt. He knew from thousands of miles of testing that the beryllium disc brakes used to slow the big Fords would warp slightly and create a vibration, but they wouldn't fail.

By the time Andretti pitted about 3:00 a.m., he'd clawed his way into second place on the same lap as the Foyt/Gurney car and ahead of McLaren/Donohue. For the first time since the start, the leaders were within reach. He turned the car over to Bianchi, hoping the other driver would realize now was the time to pick up the pace. But a lap later Bianchi was in the pits, complaining about the brake shudder.

Amped up from the brilliant dark-of-night stint, Andretti was still debriefing in the No. 3 pits when Bianchi pulled in. Mario stuck his head into the cockpit, assuring his friend the brakes were fine and explaining his testing experience. Bianchi nodded and rejoined the race but was back a lap later, asking for the brake pads to be changed.

Holman-Moody had developed a quick-change system for the 1966 race and perfected it to where they were able to change the pads in a matter of minutes. Bianchi, however, elected to exit the car during the process. That was too much for Andretti, who grabbed his helmet, buckled back in the car, and roared off as soon as the team gave the okay.

He didn't make it far. Up the hill and under the Dunlop Bridge he went, where on a normal lap a Mark IV would be approaching 190 mph and the driver preparing to brake for the esses. Since Andretti had just left the pits and was nowhere near top speed, he waited a moment longer before hitting the brakes. When he did, the car made a vicious right turn.

"It jerked the wheel right out of my hands," Andretti said. "It was heavy with a full load of fuel and there was so much weight on the wheels that it just turned right, head-on into the wall."[28]

The car slammed into the barrier and pinballed off the walls before coming to a rest farther down the track. Dazed and in a great deal of pain, Andretti pulled himself from what was left of the Mark IV and stumbled to the side of the track, the car sitting in the middle of the road.

That's where McCluskey found it nearly half a minute later as he crested the hill at full speed. There'd been no warning signals.

"I came over the hill and saw a black blob in front of me on the track," McCluskey said. "So I went into the wall to avoid hitting anyone. I ricocheted off both walls and really tore my car up."[29]

Almost immediately a third car arrived at the crash site, the Ford of France Mark II B. It spun and hit the wall but somehow managed to avoid the other two cars.

It could have been worse. McLaren, having just left the pits, was soon on the scene. He was moving slowly, checking the just-completed transmission and brake repairs, and able to pick his way through the carnage, puncturing a tire but making it back to the pits. Then it was Foyt's turn, on his last lap before pitting to turn the car over to Gurney. By now the yellow lights were flashing and there were people on the track. He also made his way carefully through the mess, but couldn't tell who was involved.

Two theories emerged on the cause of Andretti's crash, but with the front of the car ripped away and destroyed, it would be unable to tell for sure. The initial report in 1967, and the one Andretti says he was told and believes, said a brake pad was installed backward. When those reports emerged, Holman-Moody was quick to say it was physically impossible to install a brake pad backward and took the unusual step of providing a personal demonstration for *National Speed Sport News* editor Chris Economaki. Still, in the haste of the early morning pad change, the chance of some sort of an improper installation was a distinct possibility.

Others suggested Andretti failed to properly "bed" the new pads and lightly test them before heavy application. Yet all the pads were supposedly bedded before the race, and it seems unlikely a driver, especially one of Andretti's caliber and testing experience, would make such a mistake. Still, he was frustrated with Bianchi and had only a few minutes of rest from his previous three-hour stint when he went back on the track. So the possibility does exist.

Regardless, there was pandemonium in the Ford pits, with crew members trying to account for lost cars and drivers and executives demanding to know what was happening. McLaren came in for new tires and said it looked bad. In the midst of it all, Foyt arrived for his scheduled driver change. He was actually two laps earlier than originally planned, the team deciding to bring him in early as a precaution against running out of fuel again.

Foyt was never so ready to get out of a race car. The compromised seating position was taking its toll and his arms and shoulders ached more than he could remember. "Get me out of here," he yelled as a mechanic reached in to help undo the belts.[30]

Out of the car, Foyt was surprised by the confusion and crowded pits. Up and down pit row, only skeleton crews manned the positions of opposing teams. The only person Foyt didn't see was Gurney.

"Where's Dan?" he asked one of the crewmen, who did a quick scan of the area and shrugged. "I don't see him."

"Well goddammit, go find him, it's his turn to drive," Foyt half yelled, half begged as the crewman ran out the rear of the pit building. The drivers had a number of trailers, or caravans as the Europeans called them, staged in back of the pits to rest. It was team manager Carroll Smith who reported back to Foyt. He said both Andretti and McCluskey had been involved in the crash and while their cars were badly damaged, they appeared to be okay. Then he dropped the bad news.[31]

"We can't find Dan," Smith said. "You'll have to do another stint."

Foyt expressed his displeasure but reluctantly got back in the car and rejoined the race. A few minutes later Gurney arrived in the No. 1 pits and insisted he was on time. No one had told him of the plan to bring the car in early and when the crewman came looking for him, he'd already left his motor home. He'd been walking with Evi Butz, Porsche's public relations representative, and stopped briefly at Shell's hospitality site before going to the pit box.

No one was happy about the situation, least of all Gurney. He wanted the car called in, but rather than make another stop, the decision was made to let Foyt try and run the full ninety minutes.

FERRARI STANDS PAT

Shortly after the 4:00 a.m. halfway point in the race and a few hours before dawn, when things are normally at the quietest around the Le Mans circuit, there was new life and—for the first time since the start—excitement in the Ferrari pits.

Word of the Andretti crash and subsequent carnage filtered in as driver changes took place. The yellow No. 2 Ford, one of two remaining Mark IVs and the car Ferrari considered its primary challenger, had been in and out of the pits several times for lengthy stops. Despite the loss of Amon, Ferraris were running two-three-four, the Michael Parkes/Ludovico Scarfiotti car in second. Just like Daytona, the Ferraris were lined up, waiting for the final shoe to drop on the leading Ford team, the unlikely combination of Foyt and Gurney.

The Parkes car, under team orders to run slower lap times than it was capable of, was fluctuating between four and five laps behind the front-runners and that concerned the English driver. At Daytona, Ferrari's successful plan had allowed for the Fords to be as much as five laps ahead. But this was different. A lap at Le Mans was more than three times longer than at Daytona. And Foyt and Gurney were incredibly consistent.

Gurney's pace puzzled Parkes. Whether in a prototype or F1 car, Dan was the driver Parkes often measured himself against. Gurney's pace was still fast, just not *Dan Gurney* fast. The Ferrari driver had followed him several times during the race and Dan was slowing at points on the track where he'd never let off before. Foyt was also surprising. The oval track driver was much better than Parkes expected. Not as fast as Gurney, but no slouch and maddeningly consistent. In fact, Scarfiotti had been unable to make up any time on the Indy 500 winner.

Parkes sought out the Ferrari team manager and asked for approval to start running faster. They needed to press the No. 1 car, he argued, add to the panic in the Ford pits, and force them to make mistakes. If something were to happen to Parkes's car, there were two other Ferraris backing them up.

The team manager thought for a moment and shook his head no. There was no need. The plan was working. The timers indicated the lead Ford was slowing its pace by nearly twenty seconds a lap. Of all the Fords, no one thought the Foyt/Gurney car would be the one to finish. Parkes should maintain his conservative pace.

He was still upset as he prepared to replace Scarfiotti. He saw Gurney get in the No. 1 and pull away. The hell with team orders, Parkes thought, and set off after the red Ford.

Gurney wasn't happy either, still upset over the confusion regarding the pit stop. Back on the track he noticed the flashing headlights behind him for several laps, coming hard. Even in the dark he could tell the car was using every inch of the track, darting from side to side, the front end diving under hard braking. Now, as he entered the Mulsanne, the other car was close—close enough for Gurney to recognize the distinctive Ferrari headlights. Then the flashing headlights began again, a rather rude but widely used signal on the autobahns and high-speed highways of Europe: "Move over, coming through."

Down the Mulsanne they went, both accelerators flat to the floor. The Ford pulled ahead as both cars reached their top speeds and cruised through the kink—both cars flat out. Gurney figured it must be Parkes. With Amon out, he didn't think any of the other Ferrari drivers were capable of running the kink flat. Gurney had the utmost respect for Parkes, both as a driver and as an engineer. Only now he was becoming a pain in the ass.

Parkes had pulled the flashing lights stunt several times already, attempting to goad Gurney into racing him, trying to get the American to run harder and put more strain on the Mark IV. Each time, Gurney resisted the urge, slowing and allowing the Ferrari to pass, although it was becoming increasingly difficult.

"My first instinct always was, 'Okay, let's get it on.' But I had resisted it so far," Gurney recalled. Every bone in his body wanted to show what he and the Ford could do.[32]

Yet again he lifted early toward the end of the straight to save the brakes, as he had been doing since the race's first laps. The headlights behind kept coming as Parkes left his braking until the last moment and then he was hard on them, the front end of the car nosing down and the lights showing the slightest of wiggles as it took all of Parkes's ability and the Ferrari's brakes to slow the car from 200 mph.

Tight behind the Ford once again, Parkes began flashing his lights. Gurney cursed the French scrutineers who'd forced the fender-mounted mirrors to be added to the cars. If there'd been only the interior mirror, he could have simply turned it down. But the incessant flashing lights were being reflected in the fender mirrors, something he could not control.

Around the Mulsanne corner they went, and Gurney pulled to the right as he accelerated away more slowly than normal, checking his sign board and leaving room for Parkes to pass. Parkes followed him to the right, continuing to flash his lights. Through the right-hand bends at almost 185 mph they went, and then the sharp right-left turns at Indianapolis and short straight to Arnage, with both drivers dropping down into first gear. Exiting the turn, Gurney pulled to the right, followed once again by Parkes, lights flashing.

More than a little annoyed, Gurney did something he'd never done on any race course. He pulled over and stopped. Parkes did the same, coming to a rest a few yards behind the leader. The first- and second-place cars in the 24 Hours of Le Mans sat idling, nose-to-tail, on a distant and deserted part of the racetrack. Parkes occasionally flashed his lights, as if to say, "Come on, let's see what you've got."

Finally, after what seemed like an eternity, but in reality was little more than fifteen seconds, the Ferrari pulled back on the track, paused alongside the Ford, and then took off, tires and V12 engine screaming eerily into the night. Gurney waited a few more seconds—enjoying the sound of the Ferrari—and then returned to the track and resumed his pace. A few laps later he spotted a Ferrari's tail lights and slowly closed in. Parkes was back to running his more conservative pace, his spirit seemingly broken with the realization Gurney wasn't going to be goaded into a car-breaking race. He followed for most of a lap before pulling out to repass the Ferrari. "I never saw him again," Gurney said.[33]

By morning, it was Foyt and Gurney who were asking to run quicker. They'd been ordered to slow down following Andretti's accident and now both drivers were complaining it was more difficult to run a 3:50 lap than one at 3:30. They were losing focus at the slower speeds and making mistakes. Foyt had missed a shift "when a little Porsche or something spun out in front of me" and thought he'd damaged the engine. The drivers and Shelby worked out a compromise and they started running laps in the 3:40 range.[34]

The No. 1 car settled effortlessly into its new pace. With the field thinned by attrition, it was easy for Foyt and Gurney to pick their way through the remaining cars. There was one remaining moment for Foyt, however.

About 10:00 a.m. he pulled onto the Mulsanne and spotted the bright-yellow tail section of the No. 2 car alongside the road. He slowed, looking in vain for more yellow among the whitewashed trees. "Holy shit," he thought, "where's the rest of the car?"[35]

He drove to the pits to alert the team and was relieved to see the other car already there, minus its rear bodywork. The tail section had worked its way loose again and flown off completely as McLaren started onto the Mulsanne. Donohue recalled Foyt being "animated and really upset."[36]

The remainder of the race was anticlimactic, the top seven positions unchanged. As planned, Foyt drove the final stint but wasn't sure what to do as he took the checkered flag. He spotted Gurney running toward the car, and Dan climbed on the car's nose. Foyt popped open the door and asked, "Did I win rookie of the year?"[37]

Crew members began to scramble aboard until there were nearly a dozen riders as Gurney directed his co-driver toward the winner's podium.

"Man, that last hour was long," Foyt said. "I thought it was never going to end."[38]

It was a crowded and jubilant podium, in stark contrast to the nearly empty and subdued aftermath of the 1966 race. Foyt and Gurney were greeted by Henry Ford and his wife, Christina, who kissed Foyt on the cheek. At Gurney's urging, they were soon joined by the drivers of the second-place Ferrari, Parkes and Scarfiotti, Parkes seeming almost as happy as Gurney. Also coming onstage were Jo Siffert and Hans Herrmann, who'd driven their Porsche 907 to fifth place overall and first in the 2-liter class, although thirty laps behind the winners.

Jean Marie Dubois, a Moet Chandon representative, stepped forward and handed Gurney and Foyt each a magnum of champagne, which they cradled in their arms while the ceremony took place. Once the formal festivities were completed, Gurney went to open the bottle, but the cork proved balky. As an amused Parkes looked on, Dubois returned, offering a suggestion as to how to release the cork and telling Dan to point the bottle skyward so he wouldn't injure someone. When the cork finally blew, champagne began flowing out of the bottle. At first Gurney tried to drink the bubbly from the bottle but was soon overwhelmed. He next tried to stop the flow by putting his thumb over the top, but the pressure proved too much, and the champagne was soon spraying all those around him, to his and Foyt's amusement. Gurney enjoyed it so much he took another bottle, shook it, and began purposely spraying those around him.

Siffert, one of Gurney's F1 buddies, grabbed a bottle and was soon spraying the crowd, before turning it on Dan. The Fords were thoroughly soaked and retreated from the stage. Foyt got in on the action, returning fire in defense of his teammate. Suddenly there was champagne spraying everywhere on the podium and the crowd below.

Foyt spotted a friendly face, Ray Marquette of the *Indianapolis Star*, one of several reporters Ford public relations had brought to the race. Foyt's initial reaction was that it had been one of the most dangerous races he'd ever driven in, citing the speed variances of the different cars and the incident with the spinning Porsche. He also had a message for the folks at home.

"It does me good to come over here and take a victory away from these guys like they have done to us at Indianapolis," he said. "But I'd still rather run the 500. I think it is a tougher job than the 24 hours we run here."[39]

Both Parks and Scarfiotti wanted their pictures taken with A.J. and he happily obliged. Seeing this, a European reporter noted that Foyt was now famous.

"Famous? You think this race made me famous?" Foyt said. "Listen, I'll tell you what made me famous. You see this here right foot? Well that there foot is what made me famous."[40]

———

It was several hours after the finish before Foyt and Gurney found a moment of relative quiet together. In winning they'd run farther and faster than any car in race history to that point, covering 3,251 miles at an average speed of 135.48 mph. They finished thirty-two miles ahead of the second-place Ferrari. Only sixteen cars were still running at 4:00 p.m.

They were thoroughly enjoying the team's raucous party. Both understood it was more than a celebration of their race victory; it was the culmination of more than five years of hard work since the launch of the Le Mans program. It was a victory by American drivers in an American car. It was for Walt Hansgen and Ken Miles, who'd been killed testing. Gurney thought of his friends Phil Hill and Richie Ginther, who played vital roles early in the program. It was rare for such a celebration to take place—there was seemingly always another race to run. But this was different. Most knew they were unlikely to return. No one wanted to leave.

Both men were still in their racing uniforms, having donned quilted, dark-blue Ford racing coats on the victory podium against the cold and dampness, Gurney putting his over the Goodyear jacket he'd been wearing in the pits. They both had Moet magnums in their laps, Foyt occasionally sipping from his bottle. Gurney's remained corked; he'd already had plenty.

They wore the same "We did it!" grins they'd been sporting since Foyt crossed the finish line. Now they sat together, their backs against one of the team's caravans, a handmade sign behind them proclaiming Foyt "Rookie of the Year." At one point Gurney asked Foyt about Spa. He was still hoping A.J. would drive the second Eagle in the Belgium Grand Prix, one week off.

Foyt said he was honored to be asked and had seriously considered the offer. He still hoped to drive some F1 races and believed that in the right car, with the right amount of preparation, he would be competitive. But the timing wasn't right. After the Indy win he was now leading the Indy car points championship with teammate Joe Leonard in second. A host of Firestone drivers were close behind, however—including Andretti—and Goodyear wanted the championship to go with the Indy victory. In a bit of unusual scheduling, Foyt would miss two races if he stayed for Spa. Andretti, Ruby, McCluskey, and most of the others were already headed back to the states.

Foyt was ready to go home. He'd slept only about an hour since the start of the race and hadn't eaten well since he'd been in France. Given the time difference and spotty telephone service, he'd had trouble calling home. Although the grin never left his face, Foyt slowly shook his head no. He was going home. Gurney nodded his understanding.

"It would have been very interesting," Gurney said. "A.J. was a legitimate superstar at the time. He was at his zenith. A truly legendary driver. Not a road race specialist, but he was, nevertheless, a great racing driver."[41]

Even the hard-core European racing media agreed with Gurney.

"Are there still people who think A.J. Foyt is just 'a wild USAC track driver?'" asked Jenkinson. "We did not see Foyt in the sand, or spinning round, or breaking the Ford and he did more than his share of driving. Who else has won Indianapolis *and* Le Mans, and in the same year?"[42]

RETROSPECT: LE MANS 1967

While it was certainly a big deal in 1967, over the years the victory by Foyt and Gurney at Le Mans took on mythical proportions. Sandwiched between two great individual victories, Foyt at Indianapolis and Gurney's F1 triumph the following week at Spa, the three-week period came to mark the height of what *Newsweek* called the "Golden Age" of auto racing.

Over the years several backstories and sidebars emerged that didn't detract from the victory, but simply added to the intrigue and mystique. Many of the stories came to light during celebrations of the fiftieth anniversary of the victory. Foyt and Gurney appeared several times together to mark the occasion and Foyt journeyed to Le Mans for the race, although Gurney was physically unable to make the trip and would die on January 14, 2018.

The biggest issue was the slow lap times turned in by Gurney during qualifying and the condition of the Foyt/Gurney Mark IV prior to the race. In later years Gurney was adamant he didn't push the car in practice and that accounted for his slowest qualifying time of the Ford teams.

"I never once drove one lap within about three or four seconds of what I could have. Never," Dan said in 2016. "Practice and qualifying and in the race, the same program. I set a mark that A.J. could equal very easily. I think within about an hour I was leading and hadn't changed a thing about what I was doing. That took care of what might have been a 'who can drive the fastest' contest because it wasn't as important."[43]

Others, including crew members, Ford executives, and Shelby told a different story.

"Gurney was a fiddle fuddler," Shelby said in a 2011 interview. "By the time they finished practice at Le Mans the goddam car was a disaster. After each one of them made their changes to it, the son of a bitch wouldn't even go down the straightaway. I told the mechanics to take the car back to the base plate and set it up just like it was brought over on the boat. Foyt and Gurney didn't know about it. I just said fuck it, let them drive it in the race that way."[44]

Part of the confusion stems from Shelby himself. Another master storyteller, he never hesitated to adjust his story depending on the audience.

"The brilliant thing was the way Dan Gurney managed A.J. Foyt," Shelby told an interviewer doing a tribute to the two drivers on another occasion. "A.J. didn't have the experience on road courses, but naturally a race driver's ego will not let somebody else go faster than they went. Gurney just went at a normal pace all during practice, he worked with A.J., showed him the ins and outs and never got in competition with A.J. to see how fast they could go because Le Mans is an endurance contest."[45]

On many occasions, although not specifically in regard to Le Mans, Gurney would acknowledge he was a tinkerer. "Sometimes I'm my own worst enemy," he'd say.[46]

There seems little doubt that Gurney and Foyt made numerous changes to their Mark IV, and Shelby and other team leaders blamed those changes for the slow lap times. There also is little doubt that McLaren, who was killed in a 1970 testing accident, drove the car and found it atrocious. He wrote his father about the occurrence, and it's recounted in several books. He had no reason to make up such a story and in fact was Gurney's good friend. McLaren drove the second F1 Eagle later in 1967 after Foyt declined the opportunity, and Gurney later drove McLaren's F1 and Can-Am cars.

Perhaps it was the euphoria of the victory, but in a sport notorious for its inability to keep secrets, no one apparently told the drivers of the reset, either before or after the race. Nor did Foyt and Gurney apparently read any of the articles or books—including Shelby's authorized biography—that reported on the reset. It didn't appear on the drivers' radar screens until they were asked directly about McLaren's test hop and resetting of the car's setup during interviews surrounding the fiftieth anniversary. Gurney took it personally, never accepted it, and wrote to several racing magazines, including this note to *Vintage Motorsports* in early May 2017.

"When we got to Le Mans in 1967 the car was great, neither one of us fiddled with it. I never ran a really hard lap in practice, qualifying or the race. That is what A.J. and I agreed to do.

"We didn't change any of the set up. If the car came to Le Mans with McLaren's set up, that's how we raced it. The car cornered very well, and we did our best not to overstress the brakes, it was a real pleasure to drive and it was the fastest car in the race.

"I did adjust the rear spoiler height and got the car to where it was just enough to get through the kink flat-out. Any more than that would have cost lap time."[47]

Foyt didn't recall any specific problems with the car, or McLaren driving it. "I don't remember that," he said in 2019. "Dan did most of the running [in practice]. I know he wasn't happy with it. But come race day we were pretty happy. We run off and left everybody."

Of that there is no doubt.

———

Also getting a great deal of attention in later years was the driver-change pit stop when Gurney either arrived late or Foyt arrived early. Foyt would sometimes say, as he did in his autobiography, "Dan did it on purpose . . . he knew all about road racing, and he knew the early-morning shift is the worst, with the fog and later with the sun in your eyes."

Gurney's efforts to point out he believed he was where he should be, when he should be, fell on deaf ears.

"I still don't know why Foyt came in early, but he did," Gurney would protest with little success. "I know what time I had to be back, and I was carefully watching on my watch."[48]

Because of the missed stint, A.J. sometime says he drove "eighteen or twenty hours—something like that." Records show Foyt drove an extra ninety-minute shift and his final tally was about 13.5 hours compared to 10.5 for Gurney. In his race report, Marquette wrote the two drivers split time, "almost right down the middle."[49]

Much was later made of Foyt calling the 8.3-mile track "just a little old country road . . . I had driven roads like that all my life," as appeared in his autobiography.

European journalists often took exception with Foyt's comments, just as American journalists challenged Clark when he called Indianapolis "rather boring." In 1967, however, there were no such utterings by Foyt before or after the race, just a healthy respect for the track.[50]

When he returned to Le Mans for the fiftieth anniversary, Foyt was asked about the "little old country road" comment. "Those weren't *my* words," he said, an indication of another time Bill Neely may have taken some editorial liberty in the autobiography.[51]

———

One thing Foyt wasn't impressed with on his return visit was the new track configuration or style of racing.

Beginning shortly after the 1967 race, the Circuit de la Sarthe underwent significant changes, mostly in the name of safety. Virtually no portion of the track remains unchanged. In 1968 the so-called Ford Chicane was added between Maison Blanche and the pit area to slow the cars coming onto the straight. Armco railing was installed in many places around the circuit prior to the 1969 race and in 1971 was finally used along the start/finish straight to separate the pits from the track. In 1972 the Porsche Curves dropped speeds on the backstraight even further and the Maison Blanche was bypassed entirely, although the white house remains. Urban sprawl forced some of the changes, the Mulsanne Corner moving in 1986 when the original intersection was turned into a roundabout. The Dunlop Chicane was added before the Bridge in 1987 and multiple changes were made between the bridge, the esses, and Tertre Rouge—what Foyt called the tunnel. Nothing changed the character of Le Mans more, however, than the installation of two chicanes on the Mulsanne in 1990 when the FIA ruled no straight could be longer than two kilometers, or 1.2 miles.

"They don't have the White House, they don't have the Mulsanne Straight like it used to be and there's no tunnel," Foyt said in 2017. He'd been driven around the track by Patrick Bourdais, the father of Indy car champion Sébastien Bourdais and a former driver himself. "What kind of racing do you call that? I couldn't believe there was air conditioning in the goddam cars! And we didn't have no four or five drivers like they have now. It was just me and Dan. And that made it that much better."

He was also asked why he'd never gone back and couldn't help but take a shot at Andretti.

"They kept inviting me back, but like I told 'em, I came over, I won it, I had no reason to go back. Mario went back five or six times. I had nothing to prove."[52]

Still, he enjoyed the anniversary trip. "It was a big honor."

While Gurney had been unable to attend, he put the hoopla around the anniversary in perspective.

"The feeling of having a Yank group of guys and a Yank car was just fabulous. I just loved it. It was a little like the Olympic spirit, where you might try and do a little bit more for your country, if you felt that way, and I think we generally did. It was a special, special, brief period.

"It's wonderful to have a little spot in history and an appreciation for that era."[53]

CHAPTER 26

RETURN OF THE KING

1967

Back in the states following the Le Mans victory, A.J. Foyt basked in the attention heaped on him by the media.

"The sun once more is shining on A.J. Foyt's world," wrote Bob Collins in the *Indianapolis Star*. "He is back in the only spot that counts to him, the place where he fervently believes he belongs.

"He's No. 1 again."[1]

Bob Myers of the *Charlotte News*, who'd six months earlier proclaimed Mario Andretti the new king of auto racing, added his mea culpa.

"The triumph establishes that Foyt is still the nation's most versatile race driver, perhaps the world's," he wrote. "Foyt has bolted out of Mario Andretti's shadow and is Foyt again."[2]

A.J. seemed to take special delight in sitting down with Myers to help promote the upcoming Firecracker 400 NASCAR race at Daytona. He made no mention of Myers's previous column announcing Andretti's coronation, but gave every indication he knew about it.

"I guess a lot of people thought I was through," Foyt said. "They said Andretti bugged me, but he didn't. I just got tired of hearing that I was finished while Andretti was winning. I guess a lot of people are eating their words about my being through."[3]

"Indisputably, this year he is the king returned to the throne."[4]

At times, especially when other drivers were present, Foyt seemed embarrassed by the attention, pointing out, "There's very little difference between champ and chump."[5]

While Foyt decided not to race at Spa, he'd still be driving an Eagle in his next race, thanks to a late schedule change. With USAC continuing its efforts to increase the number of road races, it jumped at the opportunity to stage the first Indy car

◄ The King. *Bernie Thrasher Collection, A.J. Foyt Racing Website* event in Canada on Saturday, June 17 at Mosport. The only problem: there was already a race scheduled for Langhorne the next day. Some teams had different cars available for the two races. Others faced a twelve-hour overnight tow and scramble to convert their car from a road course setup to one that only needed to turn left.

With Goodyear's assistance, Foyt acquired two of Dan Gurney's Eagles that raced at Indianapolis. For Mosport, A.J. would drive the "Smoked Eagle," the car prepared by Smokey Yunick and driven by Denis Hulme at Indy. Joe Leonard would pilot the car Gurney drove at the Speedway. While there'd been time to paint Foyt's car Poppy Red, Leonard's still sported the blue-and-white colors of All American Racers. Gurney, who held the track record at Mosport, set up both cars. The Coyotes, designed for oval tracks, were sent to Langhorne.[6]

Little worked out as planned. At Mosport, Foyt, Leonard, and the cars all arrived late and missed qualifying, barely managing a few familiarization laps on the track. It didn't matter, as the race was rained out the next day and rescheduled for July 1.[7]

Langhorne was uneventful, as Foyt qualified eighth and finished fifth, with Leonard starting tenth and finishing seventh. Lloyd Ruby won his second race of the year.

Word arrived before the race of Gurney's victory at Spa, making him the first American driver to win a Grand Prix in his own car. The victory was big news to Foyt, who thought it should have been even bigger news in Europe.

"I'll tell you what, Gurney didn't get the credit he deserved," Foyt would say. "Here's an American guy, an American car, and had his own motor. Who else had ever done it? Nobody. At least not from the United States. He didn't get recognized for it. That's one thing I didn't like. I believe when people do something, recognize it."[8]

CHAMPIONSHIP RUN

In the rescheduled Mosport race, Foyt came from seventeenth to finish seventh in one Eagle with Leonard ninth in the other. Bobby Unser, who was beginning to live up to his promise, won his first Indy car race somewhere other than Pikes Peak.

Foyt was first in points—200 ahead of Firestone's Al Unser—but more than two-thirds of the season remained and A.J. still wasn't sure if he wanted to run for the overall title. Andretti was further back in eighth. Things got more challenging when Leonard, fourth in points, was approached by Parnelli Jones and Firestone with a significant offer to move to the team of Vel Miletich. Foyt was working on a deal for Leonard with Goodyear, but "Pelican Joe" decided to take the money on the table.[9]

Leonard also knew that as much as Foyt said he disliked the Formula One system of having a number-one driver, there would never be any doubt who the lead driver was on the team. The two remained friends in the years ahead as Leonard went on to win six Indy car races and national championships in 1971 and 1972, although at times Foyt changed his nickname from "Pelican Joe" to "Vulture Joe."

"That's the reason I went out and ran for the championship," Foyt said later. Rather than hire another driver, he decided to consolidate his team, moving Starne to work on his car and telling him, "Well shit, Jack, we need to go run for the championship now."[10]

The decision also meant any hope of a Grand Prix start late in the season was gone for good. He'd continued to talk with Gurney about running the United States and Mexican grands prix, but both conflicted with Indy car events. Gurney then hired Bruce McLaren to finish the year in his second car.[11]

With Leonard gone and as many road races on the schedule as dirt track events, Foyt decided to convert one Coyote for the upcoming races at Indianapolis Raceway Park and Circuit Mont-Tremblant, outside Montreal. He finished seventh at IRP and was lapped just past the halfway point by Andretti, who credited a new four-speed transmission. Afterward, Tony Foyt decided to build a multi-speed transmission for the Canadian race, where Starne was treated to his first father-son blowup.

"Before we'd only run a two-speed gearbox and Tony built a four-speed," Starne said. "A.J. wasn't happy with it and kept hollering, 'That ain't gonna work' and 'This ain't no good' and on and on and on. He took the car out, and he's still complaining about this and that. Tony kept saying, 'It will be fine, it will be fine. You just try and break it.'"[12]

Foyt finished second in both heats to Andretti. Between races Foyt pulled Starne aside.

"I tried to break it, but I can't," Starne recalled Foyt saying, careful not to let Tony hear. "They used to get riled up all the time. Five minutes later it was over and done with, and we'd move on to the next thing."[13]

The second-place finishes at Mont-Tremblant were the best Foyt could manage during two long summer months in an assortment of cars, although it was enough to maintain his lead in the points battle. Andretti won four in a row during the period to move into second. The winless streak was beginning to bother Foyt and he blamed himself, admitting he was having a hard time driving the Coyote on the smaller oval tracks.

"I just haven't been able to figure out why I'm not winning," he said. "The only thing that's for sure is that I can't set one of these things up right on the day of a race. But I guess that's just the way it goes sometimes."[14]

It wasn't until the series moved from road courses to dirt tracks on August 19 that Foyt got back in the victory column. Driving his four-year-old Meskowski at the Illinois State Fairgrounds, he led all one hundred laps to beat Andretti by ten car lengths. The next day it was Mario leading all two hundred laps at Milwaukee with Foyt eighth, allowing Andretti to close within sixty points in the championship. That set up a string of four Indy car races in four weeks, three of them on dirt.

The run kicked off at the annual Labor Day race at Du Quoin on September 4, when Foyt battled Roger McCluskey for the first half of the race before taking the lead and the victory. Andretti also got past McCluskey to finish second and was just eighty points behind Foyt.

The following week was the Hoosier 100, where Foyt's 1966 season had reached a low point. The outcome was the same, although this time Andretti scored a dominating victory and Rodger Ward said Mario had become "a finished dirt track driver." After two weeks the point spread was back where it started at sixty points and with a pavement race next on the schedule at Trenton, Andretti couldn't help but celebrate.[15]

"This gives me a sort of special glow," he said. "I run to win, but as bad as I dislike losing, I can accept a second place behind Foyt on dirt. He's a master on dirt, just like everyone says. I guess this was just my day. He's had days on me when everything went his way and this time I was on top."[16]

With a week off before Trenton, Foyt decided to run the USAC stock car race at Milwaukee. He arrived late after breaking the landing gear on his plane prior to take-off and being forced to rent another plane. He made it with just ten minutes left in qualifying, and as another driver had already qualified his car, he was directed into the Holman-Moody Ford normally driven by Andretti, who was off racing in a Can-Am event. Foyt qualified second and went on to win the race over Parnelli Jones.[17]

There was only one problem. Holman-Moody used Firestone tires and Foyt was under contract to Goodyear. When Goodyear executives heard about the indiscretion, they terminated Foyt's contract, worth an estimated $100,000 a year, for "repeated violations" of the driver's commitment to exclusively use Goodyear tires. "It's not the first time he's switched on us," complained one Goodyear executive. "He's a man of whimsy."[18]

It was especially bad timing for Foyt, as it came two days after Firestone announced it was slashing the amount of money it spent on racing. While Firestone said it would honor existing contracts like the one it had with Andretti, it wouldn't be adding any new drivers.[19]

Foyt claimed he was "a victim of circumstances." With the Indy car championship still in doubt, cooler heads prevailed and Foyt was back in the good graces of Goodyear by Trenton. Andretti took his fourth consecutive pole position at the track, Foyt qualifying alongside. Andretti and Foyt were running one-two when Ruby tried to pass them both but slid up into Andretti, sending both cars spinning into the fence.

Foyt deliberately spun to avoid the other two, sliding into the infield and stalling his engine. Somehow two spectators ran out and were able to push-start the Coyote. Foyt was in last place, but on the same lap as the rest of the field.[20]

"How I got through that thing I'll never know," he said. "When I put it into the spin, I looked on both sides of me and there was Andretti on the right and Ruby on the left. I guess Lady Luck was with me. I knew the only chance I had was to get a lot of yellows."[21]

Fortunately for Foyt he got six of them, four for spins directly in front of him. Each time the field closed up under the caution, and each time Foyt passed several cars on the restart. It still took a mechanical problem for Al Unser, who led more than half of the two hundred laps, to move Foyt into the lead. Once out front, he lapped the ten cars still running in what one reporter called "one of the most outstanding races of his brilliant career."[22]

"I don't know if this was one of my better races," Foyt said, "but it was my most exciting."[23]

The victory celebration was interrupted by news that Gary Congdon, who'd worked for Foyt and Johnnie Pouelsen and attempted to qualify Foyt's car at Indy earlier in the year without success, had died in a sprint car crash at Terre Haute. Congdon's death came a little more than two weeks after Pouelsen himself died in a small-plane crash.

On dirt the following week at the California State Fairgrounds in Sacramento, it took Foyt one lap to move from third to first, passing Andretti in the process and leading the final ninety-nine circuits. Afterward, he passed around credit for the victory, saving some for himself.

"My car drove strong down the chute, anybody could have drove it. The only difference between me and the other guys is our control mixture—secret fuel, sort of—my daddy—he's a great mechanic—and my crew. Another thing I think helps is I do most of my own work on my car."[24]

———

Foyt, Andretti, and Gurney weren't the only drivers having a great year: Richard Petty and his Plymouth were rewriting the NASCAR record books. He'd already won twenty-seven events and was on a ten-race winning streak heading into the Charlotte National 500 on October 15. Foyt was already planning on racing at Charlotte as he had the past couple of years, but Ford made a big deal of bringing him and Andretti in for the race.

The Charlotte promoters billed it as a match between Foyt and Petty and both played along. Petty challenged Foyt to put up his winnings for the year and he'd do the same, winner take all. Foyt didn't take the deal—his winnings were much higher thanks to the Indy 500 victory.

"I didn't come here just to beat Richard Petty," Foyt said. "I plan on outrunning anyone who's in front of me. I came here to win, no matter who's out front."[25]

Neither was around at the finish. After starting on the front row, Foyt ran with the leaders and led one lap before blowing an engine past the halfway point. Petty lasted a few laps longer before also losing an engine as Dodge driver Buddy Baker scored his first superspeedway victory.

Two weeks later Foyt made his first trip to Rockingham Speedway, a tough one-mile banked track in North Carolina. Joining the NASCAR circus for the first time in another Ford was Jimmy Clark, fresh from victory in the Grand Prix of Mexico.

Foyt led twenty-five laps but minor problems slowed him in the second half of the grueling five-hundred-lap event and he finished fourth. Clark moved up from his thirtieth starting position to thirteenth but lasted only 144 laps before being sidelined with engine problems. It was enough to leave an impression on Foyt, who'd always said he respected the Scottish driver.

"His car wasn't too good, but he ran a hell of a race," Foyt said of Clark's effort. "Half these Formula One drivers would be lost on tracks like that. Rockingham was a hard track. For him to do what he did with only a limited amount of practice was pretty amazing. I had a new level of respect for him after that."[26,27]

———

Sandwiched between the two NASCAR races was an Indy car race at the new Hanford Speedway in California. Foyt finished an uncharacteristic and uneventful fourth, a lap behind winner Gordon Johncock. He did, however, take a commanding points lead when Andretti failed to score any points for the second consecutive event. Foyt's lead of 740 points with two races remaining "just about guaranteed him a fifth national driving championship," according to the *Indianapolis Star*.[28]

Involved in an accident at Hanford was McCluskey, his Eagle badly damaged. Hearing McCluskey and car owner Lindsey Hopkins might miss the final two events of the year due to a lack of parts, Foyt sold them the "Smoked" Eagle.

On the way to Phoenix for the Indy car race, Foyt stopped in Las Vegas for the presentation of the new American Driver of the Year award, presented by the Italian spirits company Martini & Rossi and voted on by US racing writers. Despite Foyt seeming to have a lock on his fifth Indy car championship to go with his Indianapolis and Le Mans wins, not to mention Petty's amazing season, Andretti was named the winner.

At Phoenix, Foyt needed only a fifth-place finish to clinch the title and planned to play it safe. It all came undone when he clipped a car he was lapping, spun, and brushed the wall, damaging his rear suspension and knocking him out before the halfway mark. Andretti came back to win and score maximum points and—combined with Foyt's failure to score a point—cut the margin in half. With Foyt's lead at 340 points and 600 points available to the winner at Riverside, the championship would go down to the finale.

It was the first time for the Indy cars to run at Riverside and the first time the championship would be decided on a road course. The race was set for 116 laps around the track's 2.6-mile "club course," making it the second-longest race of the season after the 500. While Foyt often ran well at the track—aside from his accident in 1965—most gave the advantage to Andretti.

It also was a key battle between Goodyear and Firestone. Foyt and Goodyear had wins at Indianapolis and Le Mans, with Gurney at Spa, and recently added Hulme's F1 championship. Firestone had big victories with Ferrari at the 24 Hours of Daytona, Andretti in the Daytona 500 and at Sebring, and Petty's record NASCAR season. The Indy car title would tip bragging rights toward the winning tire manufacturer. Both companies brought in their road-course ringers, including Gurney for Goodyear and Clark and John Surtees for Firestone. Fifty cars were entered, although only thirty would start.

Foyt entered a second car, his remaining Eagle, for Jim Hurtubise to drive. Although no road-racing expert, Hurtubise was expected to stay out of trouble and the car would serve as backup insurance. Under USAC rules, should Foyt's car fail, he could take the wheel of the second car, and accumulate points in that machine based on the finish and number of miles he drove. McCluskey, in another Goodyear-shod car, with many of the parts from the Eagle Foyt had sold the team, offered his car if needed. Foyt said there'd be no more taking it easy as he'd tried to do at Hanford and Phoenix.

"I wanted to wait until the last 100 miles or so before I let loose," he said of Phoenix. "I won't try that again. I'm going to run flat out. All out at all times. If I break, then I break. We'll just put this thing on 'may the best man win' basis."[29]

Gurney captured the pole with Clark alongside. Surtees and Bobby Unser shared the second row, while Andretti and Foyt lined up side-by-side in the third row. Gurney led at the start, hounded by Clark, who took the lead on lap twenty-three. That lasted just one lap when he made a rare mistake, missing a shift and damaging the engine, knocking him out of the race and putting Gurney back out front.

While Gurney battled Clark and then Bobby Unser up front, Foyt briefly dropped out of the top ten before closing back on Andretti after twenty laps. The two championship contenders ran nose-to-tail, Foyt content knowing that unless Andretti won, he would win the championship if he finished within three spots of Mario.

That's the way they were running on lap fifty when Andretti moved to pass Al Miller, who was already four laps down. The move startled Miller, who lost control and spun, hitting Foyt and knocking both cars out of the race.

"I tried to go by him," Foyt said, "and he started looping. So I went off the course to miss him, and he still hit me!"[30]

Foyt took a quick look at his car and started running. Thinking A.J. was coming for him, Miller flinched and turned away but Foyt only glanced at him and didn't break stride. He was headed back to the pits as fast as he could run. The dirt infield, turned into a quagmire by several days of rain, slowed his pace. He tried to spot Hurtubise on the track without success and stumbled several times. His legs were covered in mud—"I must have stepped in quicksand," he joked later—and the run was more of a walk by the time he reached his pits. "Staggering from exhaustion," is how the track's press notes put it. That's where he found his insurance policy with a pool of oil under it, Hurtubise having been black-flagged at the same time as Foyt's spin.[31]

The "Foyt Out" signal had already been given to McCluskey, who'd taken the lead during a series of refueling pit stops. He didn't hesitate and stopped the next lap, surprising Foyt, who asked him, "Couldn't you have waited one more lap until I caught my breath?" It was a tight fit and the bottom of the steering wheel was bent as Foyt struggled into the car. Through it all he lost only one lap and most of another, but was back on the track by lap sixty-three.

It didn't help when Gurney lost the lead and nearly a full lap when he was forced to the pits to change a flat tire on lap seventy-two. Andretti moved into first, with Firestone driver Bobby Unser running in second as his wingman. With Foyt in fifth, Andretti could win the title by winning the race.

That's where Mario was running five laps from the finish when his engine began to stutter. He was running out of fuel and forced back to the pits. "Just a miscalculation, I guess," he'd say. The stop took only twelve seconds, but it was enough to drop him to third behind Unser and a flying Gurney, who was closing at a rate of two to three seconds a lap. Gurney passed Unser as they approached the final lap, winning the race with Andretti third. Foyt was slowed by a broken half-shaft the final fifteen laps but with a four-lap margin over the sixth-place car, held on for fifth, one spot better than needed.[32]

Then the fun started.

Over the public address system and in the press box it was announced Andretti was the new champion. The teams knew otherwise, and officials quickly realized they'd overlooked Foyt's 160 points from the shared McCluskey ride. That put A.J. eighty points to the good and he was declared champ, only to have his finishing position protested by a Firestone team. Gurney's car was also protested, and a counter-protest was filed against Andretti's machine. It took three hours after the race before the final positions, and Foyt's championship, were upheld.

"He told me before the race that if anything happened, he'd give me the ride," Foyt said of McCluskey. He'd be upset later at suggestions he'd bought McCluskey off.[33]

"You don't buy off McCluskey. Roger and I have been friends for a long time. He came to me before the race and said that if anything happened to my car, I could drive his. That's all there was to it."[34]

"I know if I was in A.J.'s shoes he'd do the same for me," McCluskey said, noting the assistance Foyt had provided not only with the Eagle, but several years earlier when he'd driven A.J.'s sprint car after coming back from an injury.[35]

"I would have done the same for Andretti if the situation was different. Mario and I are good friends, but as far as tire companies go, A.J. and I have the same interest [Goodyear]."[36]

Goodyear honored McCluskey along with Foyt and Gurney at its year-end banquet and provided him with a bonus estimated at $35,000. Still, McCluskey denied Goodyear had any role in making his car available to Foyt.[37]

"Definitely not! It was our own doing. The only people who have anything to say on that car is the owner, Lindsey Hopkins, [crew chief Jack] Beckley, and myself. Nobody even knew that we had talked about it. Hell, A.J. and I didn't even talk about it until after the drivers' meeting, fifteen minutes before the race."[38]

While Andretti initially said "I wish I had friends like that," he later admitted to making similar plans, including having approached Jones to drive one of his cars if necessary.[39]

"I don't blame him [McCluskey]," Andretti said. "I had a couple of backup cars in that race too. It could have turned out the other way."[40]

Even though Foyt won five races to Andretti's eight, he'd been more consistent over the length of the season to win his fifth driving title. No one else had won more than three. His $250,000 in winnings was a record, topping the one he'd set in 1964. That didn't include the money he received from Goodyear, Ford, and other manufacturers, estimated to push his total to about a million dollars for the year, on par with the leading golfers and boxers of the era.

With the season concluded, only the honors remained. The biggest was the annual Ford dinner, where Foyt was named the company's Driver of the Year in front of more than five hundred attendees. His first words silenced the room.

"I think I should have received this award last year," he deadpanned. Everyone knew Andretti had rightfully received the honor in 1966. With timing that would have made Bob Hope proud, he added, "Just for staying alive."[41]

"There are good years and bad years in auto racing," he went on. "When you're having a bad year, everything happens. When you're having a good year, things seem to fall into place.

"I never think of the hazards of racing. We all must go sometime. When my time comes, I'd just as soon it be in a race car, because that's where I love to be."[42]

Ford's Donald Frey, who'd played poker with the French scrutineers at Le Mans, announced that in addition to the trophy and a Continental Mark III passenger car, the company was giving Foyt a Mark IV.

"No one connected with auto racing has done more to give it stature than Foyt," Frey said. "I don't know anyone who has done more to create a professional image for the sport, or to provide it with a big-league aura."[43]

Foyt surprised many when asked what his biggest accomplishment of the year was.

"Winning Le Mans!" he said, relegating his third Indy 500 and fifth national title to supporting status. "Being a rookie and being on the first all-American team in an American car."[44]

The Mark IV given Foyt was painted to look like the race-winning car and included a "Gurney Bubble," but was actually one of the other cars. The race winner was at the Henry Ford Museum in Dearborn, Michigan. After a couple of 200 mph runs down Houston freeways, Foyt eventually sold his Mark IV. "We liked to have a wreck a couple times. I said I better get rid of it because somebody is gonna get killed."[45]

While he was inducted into the Texas Sports Hall of Fame at the end of the year, one honor Foyt didn't receive was the Texas Pro Athlete of the Year. The prize went to Tommy Nobis, the outstanding University of Texas linebacker, who'd just completed his second year with the 1-12-1 Atlanta Falcons. Second place was Rusty Staub, an outfielder with the Houston Astros. Foyt, who received more first-place votes than anyone else, finished third overall when some reporters left him off their ballot entirely.

CHAPTER 27

TAXICABS AND TURBOS

1968

Phoenix, April 7, 1968. A.J. Foyt was in a foul mood. He'd been stunned earlier in the day by news of Jimmy Clark's death in a minor Formula Two race at Hockenheim, Germany. Just a week earlier Clark was testing a new Lotus turbine at Indianapolis and came away so confident he uncharacteristically predicted victory. The normally quiet Clark was one of the few foreign drivers Foyt could stomach and he was visibly upset by the news, managing only short whispers in response to reporter questions. "It's terrible," he told one. "It makes me sick," he said to another before turning away.[1]

"Clark was a good guy," Foyt would say. "He wasn't cocky like Graham Hill or Jackie Stewart. He drove hard, but drove clean, and I had a lot of respect for him."[2]

"The way I look at it, in all of the years I ran against Formula One guys, I think in my lifetime the best driver was Jimmy Clark."[3]

Now Foyt was standing along the inside guardrail of Turn Three at Phoenix International Raceway. For the second time in six races, his car had failed to complete a single lap before blowing its engine. Phoenix didn't yet have an access tunnel under the track, and as a result, he was trapped inside the course until the race was over. Not wanting to face reporters back in the garage area, he'd stayed where the Coyote rolled to a stop to watch the race.

And a pretty good race it was. Eighty laps into the 150-lap event, Roger McCluskey looked unbeatable. He'd stretched his lead to nearly seven seconds over Mario Andretti and was about to lap Johnny Rutherford for a second time. That's when Al Unser, running just ahead of both cars, blew his engine, dumping oil on the track and setting off a chain-reaction accident.

Rutherford hit the oil and spun, sliding up to the top of Turn Three. McCluskey did the same, sliding into Rutherford. Andretti arrived on the scene and lost control,

◄ "Jimmy Clark was a super man." With Clark in 1966. *IMS Photography Archive*

spinning up the track and crashing into both cars. The last impact ruptured the fuel tank in Rutherford's car, sending up "a wall of flame around all three cars."[4]

The accident happened right in front of Foyt. He jumped the guardrail and ran up the track, finding a way through the fire. McCluskey and Andretti were nearly out of their cars, and he turned his attention toward Rutherford, lifting the struggling driver out of his cockpit and guiding him away from the flames as safety crews arrived. Like Foyt, Rutherford wore golf gloves while driving, and he was moaning and holding up both hands, the gloves shredded and melted. But it wasn't his hands that were hurting.

"A.J., my feet are burning," Rutherford yelled. Foyt dropped to his knees and pulled the smoldering laces away and then the shoes. He ran to check on McCluskey and Andretti, who seemed shaken up but okay, and medics were placing McCluskey on a stretcher and preparing to put him in the lone ambulance. Seeing Roger wasn't seriously hurt, Foyt took charge.[5]

"Sorry, Roger, you're not hurt bad enough," Rutherford said he heard A.J. saying. "Look at Rutherford over there."[6]

Foyt ordered the attendants to replace McCluskey on the stretcher with Rutherford and then climbed in the ambulance for the ride to Good Samaritan Hospital. He told nurses he was Rutherford's brother so he could stay with the driver. Having been through his own hand burns two years earlier at Milwaukee, he peppered doctors with questions. About every thirty minutes, he made a reassuring phone call to Betty Rutherford, who was pregnant and at home in Fort Worth.

Fortunately for Rutherford, his burns weren't bad and he was treated, bandaged, given meds for the pain, and released to Foyt. Lucy, making one of her rare trips to a race, arrived at the hospital with a car, and the couple started to drive Rutherford to their hotel. On the way, Rutherford began to feel the effects of the medications.

"I became nauseated and told A.J. to stop the car," Rutherford recalled. "He immediately pulled off to the side of the road and ran around to the passenger side so he could hold my forehead while I threw up. Once he was convinced I was okay, he sped back to the hotel. A.J. and Lucy kept an eye on me overnight and took good care of me. He made arrangements for me to fly home to Fort Worth and put me on the plane the next day.

"This is a side of A.J. that a lot of people never get to see."[7]

It was Foyt's second trip of the year to Good Samaritan, having visited the hospital following his own crash early in the year during a secret Phoenix test of a new turbocharged Ford engine. A rock had somehow jammed the throttle open entering Turn One.

"I locked up the brakes, but both front tires popped," he said. "The left front popped first, turning the car to the left. That saved me from going into the wall headfirst."[8]

It was still a big hit, the car pounding the inside guardrail and both front wheels breaking away. The impact pushed the monocoque back in the cockpit and tore off a fuel tank cover, causing a flash fire.

The new engine Foyt was testing was Ford's response to the success of the turbine and the new turbocharged Offenhauser. Despite air inlet restrictions,

Clark's comments indicated the turbines would continue to be competitive. After talking with Ted Halibrand about the possibility of building a turbine, A.J. decided against it, instead sharing development duties on the new Ford with Andretti and George Bignotti. After a late start to the testing, Foyt doubted the engine would be properly vetted in time for Indianapolis.

The crash in testing was just one of the early-season problems for Foyt. He'd done no better than a pair of fourth-place finishes, one in a stock car on the Phoenix road course, the other in an Indy car race at Hanford. He'd failed to finish the other four races, including the Daytona 500, where his car lasted only three laps.

Ford was pushing Foyt to compete for the USAC stock car championship, which had been dominated by Chrysler products in the past. He was paired with car owner/driver Jack Bowsher for the title run and his first victory of the year came in one of Bowsher's cars, although it was anything but easy.

More than half the entries for the May 5 Yankee 250 on the Indianapolis Raceway Park road course failed to pass technical inspection prior to qualifying, including those of Bowsher and Foyt. Officials then decided to let drivers draw for a starting position and Foyt ended up twenty-sixth—and last. It wouldn't have mattered, as his car arrived late on race day and was still going through final tech inspection when the field pulled away on the pace lap. When the new Torino came up forty-six pounds light, the crew tossed a fifty-pound bag of sand in the back and Foyt took off in pursuit of the field, led by pole sitter Al Unser in a Dodge. He was at full speed when he caught the pack as it approached the green flag and just kept going, climbing to sixth by the end of the first lap.

"I took a couple of pretty good chances," he admitted. "When I got to about the middle on the first lap, I got a little nervous because I was going about seventy miles per hour faster than some of those guys."[9]

Still to come was a flat tire, a spinout, and a skirmish that left another car in the tire barrier. "I gave him a little boost," Foyt said. "I really felt bad about that." So bad he pulled off the track and stopped the next lap under a yellow flag to make sure the driver was okay. Foyt eventually took the lead on lap sixty and pulled away, winning by nearly a lap.[10]

When questions continued about the legality of the car's engine and size of the fuel tank after the race, Foyt took it apart himself for all to see, inspectors ultimately declaring it legal.

———

The IRP victory was a momentary respite. At the Speedway, Foyt experienced nothing but trouble. He entered three cars in the 500, two under the Ansted-Thompson banner and carrying Sheraton-Thompson sponsorship. The third car listed Foyt family friend Jim Greer as the entrant and sponsor, a role he'd take on often in the future. They picked fellow Texan Jim McElreath to drive the Coyote that Joe Leonard steered to a third-place finish the year before.

Carrying Foyt's No. 1 was a new machine, one of the lightest cars entered in the 500. It featured a narrower tub and a symmetrical suspension, a concession to the increased number of road courses on the USAC schedule. It was equipped with an automatic transmission, and there were turbocharged and normally aspirated Ford engines from which to choose. A.J. proudly showed off how the automatic was operated by switches on the steering wheel, a forerunner of future high-tech designs. But despite having tested the car extensively, nothing seemed to be working at the Speedway.

"This place has its own set of characteristics," Foyt said. "You never know how anything is going to act here."[11]

Meanwhile the turbines were proving more than competitive. Graham Hill and Mike Spence, Clark's Lotus replacement, consistently set fast times in Colin Chapman's new wedge-shaped cars. Jones briefly tested his old Swooshmobile, before deciding it would be uncompetitive and saying he wouldn't run in the 500.

It wasn't until Leonard tested the original turbine and promptly crashed and destroyed it that problems began to arise on Andy Granatelli's team. Spence, after setting an unofficial track record, crashed while testing another of the turbines and was killed in the accident.

Distraught after losing his second driver in two months, Chapman returned to England. Despite the crash a line of drivers formed to test one of the remaining turbines. Foyt said Granatelli asked him several times to drive one.

"I could have had one, and one of the best ones too," he said. "But I just don't think they have any business here. It's impossible to race with two formulas. There is no way to equate a turbine with a piston engine."[12]

Five days before qualifying, an updated version of the Ford turbo was delivered and Foyt set the day's fast time, although he doubted the engine would last long in the race. Thursday evening before qualifying he elected to go with the tried and true, having the normally aspirated engine installed and switching to a manual transmission and an offset suspension. He qualified eighth, fastest of the cars not powered by a turbine or turbocharged engine. Like the year before, he was counting on the other cars not being able to go the distance.

"I honestly don't think the turbo-Ford will last half the race," he said. He bet Andretti, who qualified a turbo-Ford fourth, fifty bucks Mario would be out before the halfway mark. "Too many people forget this is a 500-miler. You have to go the full 200 laps to win, and that's what I'm banking on. I can run with everything in the race except the turbines. There's no way anyone can beat them if one of them goes the distance."[13]

FIGHTING MAD

There was talk throughout the month of a new Foyt—a calmer, more relaxed Foyt—following his victory the year before. That ended a few days before the race when he was named, along with McCluskey, Jack Beckley, and two others, in a lawsuit filed in federal court. Court officials were at first blocked from entering the Speedway to serve the summons, allowed in only after they threatened to close the track.

In the suit filed by Einar Jonsson, an alleged brawl took place at 1:30 a.m. on March 21 in the cocktail lounge of the Northwest Holiday Inn, stemming "from an argument over the merits of turbine versus piston-engine powered race cars."[14]

Jonsson had engineered the transmission for a pair of new turbines developed by Ken Wallis, the designer of the original Swooshmobile. The cars, entered by Carroll

Shelby and heavily backed by Goodyear, had been testing in March at the Speedway along with other Goodyear teams, including those of Foyt and McCluskey.

The suit said Jonsson was "overpowered and maliciously beaten and cut" by the defendants, causing "numerous bruises and contusions." It said Foyt struck Jonsson with "a sharp and deadly weapon." The suit said Jonsson was treated at Marion County General Hospital where it took thirty-stitches to close his wounds. Jonsson was seeking $200,000 in damages.[15]

McCluskey and Beckley denied being involved, and Foyt said he wasn't the one who cut Jonsson. It also came to light Jonsson had been arrested and charged with being drunk and disorderly, although those charges had already been dismissed.

The lawsuit would eventually be thrown out on technical grounds, the federal court ruling it had no jurisdiction in the case. However, there was no more talk of a mellower Foyt.[16]

The Wallis/Shelby cars were already long gone, having disappeared from the Speedway in the dark of night following Spence's death. A statement at the time implied the turbine cars were unsafe. It was later revealed Wallis had incorporated an illegal air inlet that had been discovered by the team, which caused Shelby to withdraw the cars.

In the 500 Foyt failed to lead a lap and spent most of the first two hundred miles swapping fifth and sixth positions with Dan Gurney. Knocked out by a broken connecting rod before the race was half over, Foyt sat perched on the roll bar of his car like George Patton on one of his tanks as the crew rolled it back to the garage, to the cheers of the crowd. He'd already won his bet with Andretti, who didn't last two laps before burning a piston in the turbocharged Ford.

Foyt returned to his pit in his driver's uniform but said he had no intention of relieving either McElreath or Carl Williams, who'd qualified a third Coyote.

"Everyone wanted me to get in Jim's car," he said. "But that's not the way I do business. When I sign someone to drive for me, it's his car. I've won this race three times and a lot of guys have never won it. This is my team and that's the way I run it."[17]

He pitched in on pit stops, helping to repair the cars when they suffered damage, although both would drop out late in the race. Foyt stayed to watch as Bobby Unser took the lead when Leonard's turbine broke nine laps from the finish.

He was still there when Denis Hulme, driving one of Gurney's Eagles and pitted next to Foyt's now-empty slot, surprised his team by stopping two laps from the finish with a flat tire. When Hulme's crew struggled getting the jack under the car, Foyt dashed around to the right rear to help manually lift it.

Afterward he told reporters he wouldn't compete for the Indy car championship. In five years, the schedule had grown from a dozen races to twenty-eight, and it was restricting Foyt's participation in other events.

"I may only run four or five more championship races this year," he said. "But I'm going for number four [500]. I'm not giving that up until I get it, even if I'm ninety!"[18]

What he didn't say was he had no intention on cutting back his overall racing schedule. In the upcoming weeks, he'd run the Indy car race at Milwaukee, his first sprint car race of the year, and both USAC and NASCAR stock car events, although he failed to finish any of the races. It would be a month before he saw a checkered flag, and when he did, it was in victory, ironically in an Indy car race he hadn't planned on running.

It came July 7 at Continental Divide Raceway in Castle Rock, Colorado, the first Indy car race at the 2.66-mile road course. Ford had taken over development of the Coyote chassis for road racing, converting the car Williams drove at the Speedway. For once, the project was ahead of schedule.

After qualifying fourth, Foyt trailed road racing expert Ronnie Bucknum until the leader suffered mechanical problems. He then fought off a challenge from Leonard in the turbine and stretched his lead to nearly a lap over second-place Lloyd Ruby at the finish.

"This is the first time this year I've come to any racetrack knowing the car was really ready to run, and boy did it run well," Foyt said. "I didn't know the course so all I wanted to do was keep the leader in sight, put the pressure on him, and try and stay out of trouble. I was honestly worried about Leonard late in the race. But when he closed up on me, I stepped on it again and got right back to a 40-second lead with no trouble. Then I knew I could handle him."[19]

The following week he took Bowsher's stock car to victory at Milwaukee, where his stiffest competition came from the ninety-one-degree temperatures that had many drivers, including McCluskey, asking for relief.

"I was dying," Foyt admitted. "It was the hottest race of my career." Earlier in the year he'd turned down an opportunity to use an experimental "cool suit" for just such occasions. "They threw water on me when I came into the pits, but that was good for only four or five laps."[20]

The victory moved him into first place in the stock car driver's championship standings, and the rest of the summer he upped the lead with consistent finishes. Despite his comments on running a reduced Indy car schedule, he made most of the events and did especially well on the road courses, finishing with a pair of seconds at Mosport. At Indianapolis Raceway Park he started seventeenth after missing the primary qualifying session and drove through the field to finish fourth. He then took exception with the attention being paid second-place Andretti compared to winner Al Unser, who was in the midst of a six-race winning streak.

"Look at that, half the people at the track are down there trying to get a look at Mario," he complained to a reporter. "Al Unser wins the race, and most people don't even recognize him. Mario finishes second and they wanta elect him president. He's something else. Even when you outrun him, you can't beat him. Far as the crowd's concerned, he don't ever lose."[21]

––––––––

It wasn't until the stock and Indy car series moved back to the dirt tracks that Foyt once again hit his stride, taking both races at the Indianapolis State Fairgrounds and then a taxicab event at Cincinnati. It was enough for him to secure the stock car championship with four wins and thirteen top-five finishes in fifteen races.[22]

He also won the late-season California Indy car races at the Sacramento Fairgrounds and Hanford Speedway, his hundredth USAC victory and fortieth Indy car win, extending his own records. The victory at Hanford was the first for a turbocharged Ford engine as he ignored rpm limits late in the race and "just let her whistle."[23]

Two weeks later at Phoenix, he was battling with Andretti when he hit an oil slick exiting Turn Four, hit the outside wall, and spun down the front straight before being rammed by Mario, who had no place to go. The race was stopped as Foyt's car caught fire and he burned his hands getting out of the car, enough to require his third trip of the year to Good Samaritan, where he was listed in satisfactory condition and spent the night.[24]

He started the final race of the year at Riverside wearing a bandage on one hand, but was out before it was fifty laps old. He still finished sixth in the final point standings, not bad for someone who skipped several races and didn't score a point at Indianapolis.

Despite the late-season surge on the racetrack, it was a difficult period for Foyt. His mother, Evelyn, hadn't been feeling well and suffered another heart attack. A.J. started shuttling back and forth between Houston and various races, flying into a track the morning of a race and departing immediately afterward. Thanks to his friendship with Dr. Denton Cooley and Lucy's connections, they were able to ensure the best of care for Evelyn and her health would stabilize, but she would never again be the vibrant head of the household and rock of the family she'd once been.

CHAPTER 28

DRIVER OF THE DECADE

1969

Ford Motor Company boasted it was putting together a "Million Dollar Team" of eight drivers for 1969, with A.J. Foyt and others being joined by Richard Petty, who'd been enticed away from Plymouth by Ford's mega dollars. When Chrysler's advertising theme positioned its drivers as the "Good Guys" complete with white cowboy hats, Ford handed out black hats to its drivers. Foyt embraced the "bad guy" theme and took it a step further, getting the black cowboy hats to his Indy car crew.

Following their championship season, Ford decided to pair Foyt and Jack Bowsher in both USAC and NASCAR events and at the Riverside season opener they got off to a good start. Carrying the No. 1 on his white Ford Torino as the USAC champion, Foyt claimed the pole position on his thirty-fourth birthday. After coming down with a 104-degree temperature the night before the race, he caught a break when it was rained out. It took two weeks for the rains to subside and the track and spectator areas to dry sufficiently to stage the race, and when it did, Foyt led until his brakes began to fade, eventually finishing second to Petty.[1]

At Daytona he ran well again and finished fourth, although his biggest contribution may have come during the prerace drivers' meeting. Several teams expressed concern about a decision to allow television reporters to interview drivers during pit stops.

"I'll tell you how to stop them," Foyt said. "When they stick the mike in your face just let 'em have . . ." and he proceeded to string together a series of expletives that impressed even the hardest of the NASCAR regulars.[2]

Two weeks after running the fastest track in America, Foyt returned to Houston for the first Astro Grand Prix—a pair of one-hundred-lap midget car

◀ The 1969 Indy 500 pole-winning team of Tony and A.J. Foyt. *Revs Institute, The Bruce R. Craig Photograph Collection*

races to be held on successive nights on a quarter-mile dirt track laid out inside the Houston Astrodome, not far from where Playland Park once stood.

With $60,000 at stake, the races attracted entries from more than sixty drivers. Twenty-one had made Indianapolis 500 starts, including Mario Andretti, Johnny Rutherford, Lloyd Ruby, Jim McElreath, Bobby and Al Unser, and Mel Kenyon, the USAC midget champion three years running.

After spending the week before the race testing at Indianapolis, Foyt was unhappy with his car. Driving a midget reportedly first raced in 1946, he failed to qualify for the opening-night twenty-car feature and was saved the embarrassment of missing his hometown event only after receiving one of four "invitational" spots added to the field.

Starting twenty-third, he didn't disappoint, passing everyone except winner Gary Bettenhausen. He wasn't as fortunate the second night, spinning with Bobby Unser on lap five and, under the rules of "spin out, stay out," watched the remainder of the race.

The event proved to be a success, with more than thirty thousand fans turning out each night, the largest crowds for an indoor motorsport event up to that point.

ROGER MCCLUSKEY

With the Indy car season fast approaching, Foyt announced he was adding McCluskey in a second car. Although Foyt didn't like having season-long teammates, he made the move in response to the escalating costs of auto racing in general, and Indy cars in particular.

"If you break even in racing, you've got to be luckier than Dick Tracy," Foyt car owner Bill Ansted said, referring to the comic book detective.[3]

Many considered McCluskey a hard-luck driver, others thought he was simply too hard on his equipment. For the past three years, he'd driven for the well-financed team of Lindsey Hopkins but, like Bobby Marshman and Foyt before him, had experienced minimal success.

"To be frank about it, I did get discouraged," McCluskey said of his time with Hopkins. "The harder we tried, the more things went wrong. Last year everything went to hell."[4]

Toward the end of the 1968 season, McCluskey had approached Foyt about the possibility of the Hopkins team acquiring a Coyote to run. The discussion evolved to McCluskey joining with Foyt and bringing longtime sponsor G.C. Murphey department stores to the team. There was no signed contract, just an agreement that McCluskey and his team would keep 100 percent of its winnings. As McCluskey was already signed to drive a Plymouth stock car, it meant the two would battle again for the taxicab championship.

In making the decision, McCluskey said he'd been impressed when Foyt refused to replace McElreath in the previous Indy 500 and by A.J.'s dislike of the Formula One system of tiered team drivers.

"There are no number-one or number-two drivers in these garages," McCluskey said, and seemed to believe it. "We don't operate that way. We work hard on both cars and there is no favoritism. A.J. stressed this. He said he didn't just want another car to tag along. This is flat-out racing at this place. I wouldn't expect any quarter from him, and he wouldn't expect any from me. We just cut down the cost, using the same crew, the same equipment. It also gives me the advantage of added technical knowledge that wouldn't be available otherwise."[5]

Things got off to a rough start as the cars arrived late for the March 30 Phoenix season opener. Foyt qualified sixth, with McCluskey seventh, and they were running in that order when a rock pierced the oil cooler in A.J.'s car, McCluskey spinning in the oil. The next race was at Hanford. Foyt lasted only a lap while McCluskey was involved in an early crash.

The opening defense of Foyt's stock car title didn't go any better, as he qualified last because of car trouble at the tiny Tri-County Speedway near Cincinnati. He was booed when the field was inverted, putting him on the pole, and then decided against making the start. He still collected his $1,000 appearance money as the defending series champion, more than all but the race winner received.

Trenton was supposed to be the final tune-up before Indianapolis, and Foyt found himself again in the center of controversy when the race was delayed for a week because of ripples in the track's new surface. The delay put the race in conflict with qualifying for a stock car race at Indianapolis Raceway Park, an event Foyt said was more important to him.

"I'm under contract to Ford and have agreed to run at IRP," he said. "If my stock car is ready to run, I'll be at Raceway. There's no way I'll be an alternate starter or start at the back of the pack. If Trenton is run on Saturday, then I don't see why I can't withdraw my entry."[6]

When USAC threatened to penalize any Indy car driver who did not run at Trenton, Foyt followed through on his threat and withdrew his entry. It wasn't just Foyt caught in the fix; McCluskey and the Unsers faced the same problem. Adding to the tension, Foyt had reluctantly taken on the role of driver representative on USAC's board and now found himself speaking on behalf of other drivers.

While a confrontation was avoided when the Trenton race was again postponed, the incident indicated that not only was racing becoming more expensive, it was becoming more political. Never one to shy away from speaking out if he felt wronged on the track, Foyt was becoming increasingly outspoken off it. Although it was a role he neither sought nor relished, he was beginning to leverage his position in the sport to affect its management and direction, for better and for worse.[7]

———

The new Coyotes arriving at the Speedway in 1969 once again stood out for their simplicity, eschewing the trendy wedge-shaped designs influenced by the turbine success and the wings that seemed to cover every inch of other cars. The bulkier turbocharged Ford engine, and new rules allowing for wider tires, had required significant body and chassis changes to the cars. Eddie Kuzma shaped the bodywork while Ford engineers and computers refined the chassis. Most of the suspension pieces and other parts were custom made by the team. Foyt and McCluskey drove hundreds of test miles at Indianapolis and Phoenix, and the cars spent many hours in Ford's wind tunnel.

Many of the top drivers had new four-wheel-drive cars developed by Lotus and Lola at their disposal, including the new team of Roger Penske and Mark Donohue. Foyt and McCluskey considered and decided against incorporating four-wheel drive, saying the systems were too heavy and complex.

"The thing uppermost in my mind with these machines was would they last," McCluskey said. "A.J. and I talked quite a bit about four-wheel drive, the wedge design and we honestly felt the two-wheel drive with the rubber we have now would not be at a disadvantage. We felt to make the four-wheel-drive car strong enough, it would be too heavy."[8]

Missing from the Foyt cars were and shapes sprouting up all over Gasoline Alley. A new term was being used—ground effects. Engineers were talking about the impact air moving under the car had on its handling characteristics and how the wings directed air and created downforce. Foyt, however, said he preferred to run without the benefit of the aerodynamic aids.

"I don't want to have to race with those things on," he said of the wings. "I think the more simple you can keep the thing the better off you are."[9]

"Everyone was convinced after last year that the wedge design was the way to go, and that four-wheel drive was a great advantage. I don't happen to believe that. I concentrated on making my car as aerodynamically sound as possible with the least clutter I could get. Simple and sleek. And with the design of our car, we can keep it stable and straight, and don't need the fins and elaborate spoilers other guys have. Maybe I'm wrong, but after less than twenty laps I was going faster than I've run at Indianapolis."[10]

Foyt identified engine cooling and fuel economy as two problem areas for the turbo-Ford and secretly worked with fuel injection wizard Stuart Hilborn to develop a special system for the engines in his cars. He shared the package with Smokey Yunick for the car driven by Joe Leonard, and then test hopped the car to make sure it was operating smoothly.

Although the first weekend of qualifying was rained out, Foyt went ahead with his plans to add George Snider to drive a third entry. Snider had bounced between several teams in the three years since he'd split with Foyt, continuing to run well on dirt and in sprint cars but struggling at times in champ cars. It was something of a homecoming for Snider, and there'd never been a problem with chassis setup at Indianapolis—whatever Foyt wanted was good for him.

In a speed class of his own all month was Andretti. Following the death of car owner Al Dean at the end of the 1967 season, he'd taken over running the team in 1968, discovering ownership and management wasn't for him. He'd sold his equipment to Andy Granatelli and, along with crew chief Clint Brawner, became one of eleven entries running the STP dayglo red colors for 1969. Brawner and Andretti had taken delivery of a new $75,000 Lotus but insisted on running a separate operation from the other STP teams.

While nominal teammates Hill and Jochen Rindt struggled with the exotic Lotus, Andretti was the only driver above 170 miles per hour, several miles an hour faster than anyone else. That was until late Wednesday afternoon, May 21, when Foyt's Coyote grew wings, two front winglets and three separate wings spread across the rear of the car. He surprised himself, jumping to the top of the speed chart with an unofficial record lap of more than 172 mph.

Andretti, who'd been sitting in his Lotus waiting for Foyt to complete his run, immediately returned to the track. All eyes were on the exit of Turn Four, looking for the red Lotus to come flying out of the corner as Andretti attempted to retake the speed mark. What they saw was an airborne Lotus, with a tire and various body panels filling the air. The right-rear wheel had come off as Andretti entered Turn Four, sending him careening into the outside wall. The car bounced off the wall and was momentarily airborne, shedding body work as it went, before landing right side up. Andretti was already getting out of the car when a flash fire broke out, and he suffered superficial but painful and nasty-looking facial burns that quickly blistered. Foyt was one of the first to the infield care center to check on him.

"A.J. talked mostly about the problems he was having with his car and the fast lap he had just run," Andretti remembered. "But he didn't fool me. He was trying, in his own way, to say he was sorry. I will always appreciate it."[11]

Despite an engine that went "thunk" in the middle of his qualifying attempt, Foyt still captured the pole position, although he fell short of the one- and four-lap speed records set the year before by Leonard in the turbine. He'd briefly considered pulling off and trying again later in the day, remembered the problems a similar move created in 1966, and "decided to play it safe."[12]

"I was real disgusted," Foyt said immediately after his run. "We should have broken the record." Later, the pole secured, he changed it to "Kinda disappointed."[13]

"I made no secret about coming here to win the pole," he said. "I told everyone in Houston that's what I was going to do and I meant it. The way the car had been running I figured I'd have a lap in the 173s and an average at 172-plus. I was going for Leonard's record."[14]

Andretti surprised nearly everyone by qualifying second in his backup Hawk. McCluskey qualified slower than he'd practiced, in sixth, with Snider a few rows back in fifteenth. The Lotus machines driven by Hill and Rindt were withdrawn over continued concern about the wheels and just three of Granatelli's entries managed to make the race. Foyt gave a rare nod to Andretti and said the Hawk gave him a better chance of winning.

"Mario won't give up, he's worse than I am," A.J. said. "I'd rather see Mario in the race with his four-wheel-drive car than the one he's in."[15]

The McCluskey and Snider cars qualified without the spoilers and Foyt said he wasn't sure if they did any good. "I honestly don't know if they help or hurt my speed. But I think they might help me compete with the four-wheel drive cars when the track gets slippery race day."[16]

One reason Foyt had set his sights on the Indy pole was to give his father some recognition. Each year the chief mechanic of the pole-winning car was honored at the 500 Festival Pole Mechanics and Racing Awards Banquet prior to the race. George Bignotti had received the award following Foyt's pole-winning run in 1966. Now Tony Foyt shared the dais with his wife, Evelyn, and was coaxed into saying a few words in accepting the honor.

"Anybody on the crew could be a chief mechanic, we all just work together," Tony said. "I'd like to thank everyone who made this possible, and I guess I'd better thank my driver too."[17]

Sitting in the audience, A.J. expressed surprise. "That's the first time I ever got a thank-you from him," he told a reporter.[18]

Another prerace event was the premiere of *Winning*, a movie starring Paul Newman, Joanne Woodward, and Robert Wagner, much of which had been shot the previous year at the Speedway. Foyt had filmed a scene, donating his stipend to the family of driver Ronnie Duman, who'd been killed at Milwaukee. He'd been asked by director Jim Goldstone to react as if he'd just been beaten in a close race. Most of the scene, however, ended up on the cutting-room floor.

"Foyt asked me for a script, and I said there wasn't any, to just say what he'd normally say when he'd just lost a race," Goldstone explained. "Well he did. I was able to keep one piece of it which only had one 'damn,' but the rest had to be cut."[19]

———

As the pole sitter and odds-on favorite to win, Foyt was in demand by the media and he ran hot and cold, embracing some questions, turning on others. Often a difficult interview even for reporters who regularly covered auto racing, he had little patience for the hundreds of writers from around the country who covered one race a year and showed up a few days before the 500 looking for a story.

"If you're not in this business, you couldn't possibly realize what it's like to get out there on the track and compete," he told one group. "I'm undoubtedly more intense overall than most about that. But if you don't feel that way about competing, you'd better not get behind the wheel in the first place."[20]

The questions typically dealt with the dangers of the sport, and if Foyt would retire if he won his fourth 500.

"Sure, I'm conscious of the danger involved out there. Any driver who isn't, or says he isn't, either doesn't belong behind the wheel or is a damned liar. Mostly it's just the chance of fire that I think about. But new equipment and clothing and the like has cut down that hazard considerably.

"Will I be back next year? Hell, I got no time to think about that now. I've got a race to make—and maybe win—and that's the only thing I'm thinking about right now."[21]

———

The final practice session on Carb Day erupted into a war of words with Brawner, Andretti's crew chief, threatening to withdraw the Hawk after being told to remove an exterior radiator the team added overnight. Chief steward Harlan Fengler admitted giving initial approval for the installation but said after conferring with other officials he'd made a mistake—the radiator did, in fact, change the car's qualifying "configuration."

Brawner blamed Foyt for the fuss. One report said, "The smuggest smile at the Speedway Wednesday belonged to A.J. Foyt." While Fengler said, "There were many who complained," the pole sitter didn't shy away from taking responsibility.[22]

"Sure I screamed," Foyt said. "I asked last week if I could add a radiator after I qualified. I was told absolutely not. So my guys were up until 1 a.m. one night making the things so I could qualify with them. I might have gone faster without them because they do create extra drag. When they added their radiator after they qualified, I wanted to know why they could, and I couldn't. If they'd gotten away with it, I'd have taken the wings off my car."[23]

The turbocharged Ford engines were running hot and, prior to qualifying, Foyt had added small radiators—one an oil cooler and the other a water cooler—on each side of the driver's cockpit of all three Coyotes. Concern about overheating increased as weather forecasts called for race day temperatures of more than ninety degrees.

"A.J. anticipated this heating problem a couple of weeks ago and we gave up some speed in qualifying to be sure we would have them on race day," said Lujie Lesovsky, who'd crafted the coolers.[24]

Another way to cool an engine is to use more fuel, and several of the teams, including Andretti's, had gone that route. While fine in practice, it presented a potential problem during the race. Each car was limited to seventy-five gallons of fuel on board at the start, with another 250 gallons in the Pit Lane fuel tank. Fuel economy was becoming an issue. Word of Foyt's proprietary fuel system also leaked out.

"There is a real problem of running out of gas," Andretti admitted. "It could become extremely critical whether we make it or not. We are getting only 1.68 miles per gallon. Figure it out and you can see that's too close. Foyt has a different fuel distribution system than the rest of us and if it's hot on race day, he'll have quite an advantage."[25]

Andretti said he'd need to average at least 1.8 miles per gallon and benefit from caution-flag laps, the slower speeds providing improved fuel economy. Foyt boasted he was getting upward of 2.5 miles per gallon from his fuel system, although not everyone trusted him.

"Don't believe those stories," Brawner said. "He's just trying to psych us out. I bet we can slow down to their [Foyt's] speed and still beat them."[26]

Few others agreed.

"Foyt arrived at the Speedway in May better prepared for practice, qualifying, and race day than any other team," wrote Shav Glick in the *Los Angeles Times*. "[He] seems to have done everything perfectly. In a year when the wedge-look chassis gives the car a visual sameness, Foyt's Coyotes stand apart. They, like Foyt himself, are throwbacks to another era in a game where each idea is followed so quickly it develops instant duplicity."[27]

Andretti remained the fan favorite and the crowd roared when he took the lead on the first lap. By the sixth lap Andretti's water temperature was already too high and he slowed slightly, allowing Foyt and then McCluskey to get past. Brawner had secretly rigged a radiator in the interior of the car for some additional cooling, warning Andretti to keep an eye on the temperatures, and to slow early in the race if necessary.

For the first one hundred miles, Foyt and McCluskey ran one-two, A.J. setting lap records and running a couple seconds ahead of his teammate, with Andretti another second back in third. As the first pit stops approached, the Coyotes appeared to be in a class of their own.

All three leaders headed for the pits on lap fifty-two, but McCluskey ran out of fuel on approach and coasted into his pit. Foyt's crew put their driver back on the track well ahead of Andretti, whose team had decided to make deliberate, if longer, pit stops. By the time McCluskey was back on the track he was more than two laps behind. His crew later insisted there should have been plenty of fuel in the car.

Before long Foyt was back in the pits. After leading sixty-six laps, his engine showed a wisp of smoke and he slowed noticeably, losing almost a second a lap to Ruby, who took the lead on lap seventy-nine. Foyt made two quick stops trying to adjust the troublesome turbocharger without success. On the third stop he climbed out of the car and with Jack Starne went over the turbo unit, discovering a cracked pressure line clasp allowing turbo-boost pressure—and horsepower—to leak away. It was a freak failure; no one could recall having the problem before. It took nearly twenty-four minutes for a crew member to take the part back to the garage, weld the crack, and for Starne to reinstall it. A television reporter came looking for a comment and Foyt tossed him out of the pit area, but there was little else he could do except watch, his hands stuck in his pockets.

While this was going on, Snider's crew forgot to call him in for refueling and he ran out. Unlike McCluskey, however, he didn't make it back to Pit Lane, rolling to a stop between Turn Three and Turn Four. It took fifty-one laps to retrieve Snider's car and get it back on the track.

Then it was Ruby's turn for trouble on a pit stop as he tried to leave with the fuel lines still connected, ripping the tank open and flooding the pit area with methanol. Andretti was home free.

Foyt eventually returned to the race, and along with McCluskey, the Coyotes were easily the fastest cars on the track, running laps consistently at 165 mph while Andretti cruised at 160. McCluskey made up one lap and got as close as third place before a header on the engine cracked, knocking him out. Foyt made up three laps on the leader and finished eighth, though nineteen laps behind. At one point he played leapfrog with Andretti, trying to incite him to race.

"I was a little worried by A.J.," Mario said before being alerted by his crew to Foyt's troubles. "[When] I knew how far back he was I let him go. I wasn't going to start racing when all I had to do to win was finish."[28]

After taking the checkered flag, Foyt pulled alongside Andretti and acknowledged the winner with a wave. He was reserved in the garage area, saying he had ordered the pressure line stiffened but not the clasp, and that it probably cost him the race.

"It was a little ten-cent clasp that failed," Foyt said. "Everything was peachy until it started leaking. Just one of those things, a part of racing. I was running just as fast as I wanted to run. Nobody was passing me."[29]

"I was almost hoping something else would break after I went back out. If something big had gone, then I could have said it just wasn't meant to be my day. But the thing ran like a dream. It was only that little nit-picking thing. Everything else worked just beautifully."[30]

Foyt's late-race efforts didn't go unnoticed.

"By the time they got it fixed there was no way in the world he could even hope to win," Parnelli Jones said. "Yet he went back on the track and drove the hell out of his car. It would have been easy for him to park the car for the day and say, 'to hell with it, I don't need the money so why go out and take a chance.' Or he could have stroked it the rest of the race. But he's not made that way. He drives only one way—to win. I don't care if he is ten laps down with eight to go, he still thinks he can win, and he'll do his darndest to win."[31]

Over the years Foyt would say he won some 500s he shouldn't have, and lost a few he should have won. The 1969 race was one he always felt he should have won, perhaps even more so since it was Andretti's lone victory.

"I still tease Mario about that one," he said fifty years later. "I tell him, 'Andretti, I gave you that race. You know I did.' But I won a couple I should not have and then lost three or four I should have won. That's racing. Just like ballgames or anything. You hate it, but it happens."[32]

Following the race, questions about Foyt's retirement made the rounds again, this time fueled by an unlikely source—Tony Foyt.

"I'm getting tired of racing," Tony told a Houston television station. "In fact, I'd like to see him get out of it. I'm thinking of getting out myself."[33]

A.J. was standing alongside his father when he made the comments and for the second time in a month he was surprised by something his daddy said. He quickly told the reporter he had no intention of retiring.

———

Foyt spent the rest of the year trying to retain his USAC stock car championship. Often traveling with McCluskey, it was in some respects a return to the barnstorming days of the 1950s. Except rather than towing his midget or sprint car from race to race, Foyt flew his own plane into a track the morning of an event, practiced, qualified, raced, and flew out before the crowd had left their seats, sometimes using the straightaway as a landing strip.

It wasn't until June 21 that he posted his first victory of the year, a stock car race at the Indiana State Fairgrounds. He'd won ten previous events on the track, but never the stock car race, and it broke a winless streak of more than six months.[34]

His change of fortune lasted exactly one week. In Memphis for a stock car race on a new road course, he qualified on the pole but blew the Ford engine in practice. After installing a new powerplant, he dominated the race run in blistering heat, with track temperatures estimated at more than 130 degrees. He led 110 of the 118 laps and was holding an eight-second lead when he blew a tire three laps from the finish and ended up second to McCluskey. He collapsed after climbing from the car and crew members poured water on him and administered oxygen. He said later he'd never race again at Shelby County International Raceway.

"I felt sorry for A.J.," said McCluskey, who stopped to check on Foyt before talking to reporters. "He's OK now. It was a bad break. I was fortunate beyond your imagination. You never give up hope, but when it's as hot as this you're thinking primarily about just finishing what you came here to do. It was so hot you couldn't see for the sweat pouring down your face."[35]

Foyt continued to find unique ways to lose races. He broke the gearshift of his Ford stock car off in his hand and ran several slow caution laps with a mechanic in the car fixing the shifter, dropping him off in the pits after the repair was completed. He finished second to McCluskey on July 4 after suffering another late flat tire while leading. Two days later he was challenging Gordon Johncock in the final laps of the Indy car race on the Continental Divide road course, where he was the defending champion. This time his engine seized up with two laps remaining, sending him into a spin. The next week, in a stock car race at Milwaukee, he led the first eighty laps, only to be hit by a spinning car.

He then made a rare appearance at a Trans Am event, Ford calling him in to supplement Parnelli Jones and George Follmer, Carroll Shelby's regular Mustang drivers. The team was having a hard time beating Donohue, who was dominating the series in Penske's Camaro.

The effort didn't last long. Foyt ran only a few practice laps at the Circuit Mont-Tremblant in Quebec before he stopped, complaining about the car's handling. Jones took it out and promptly crashed, damaging the car too badly to be repaired in time for the race, which Donohue went on to win.

As the August 3 stock car race approached at the new high-banked track in Dover, Delaware, McCluskey had a seemingly insurmountable lead of nearly 500 points. But Dover was Foyt's kind of track—fast—the one-mile oval reminding many of "the Hills" of Salem and Winchester. He led 154 of 158 laps and was two laps ahead of everyone except second-place McCluskey when rain stopped the event.

For the upcoming fairground season, he took delivery of a new dirt track car designed by Wally Meskowski and powered by a non-turbocharged version of a Ford engine he'd played a key role in developing. It replaced the six-year-old model that had served him so well, and he passed it on to McCluskey.

Its first appearance wasn't on dirt, however, but on the paved track at Milwaukee when his Coyote suffered problems in practice. Rather than bump McCluskey out of the other Coyote, Foyt switched to the dirt track machine, which had yet to turn a race lap. Although there was no repeat of the dirt car histrionics of 1965 when he nearly drove to victory on the same track, he did manage to finish ninth, twelve laps behind winner Al Unser.

The next day on dirt at the Illinois Fairgrounds, he battled eventual winner Andretti for the lead until pitting for a new tire. The car backfired and ignited a small cockpit fire two laps from the finish, but Foyt brought it home fifth, stopping at the local hospital on his way out of town to have the burns on his feet treated.

It wasn't until the fairground season got underway in earnest that Foyt won again, taking the August 31 stock car race at Du Quoin. Following a month of consistent finishes while McCluskey struggled at times, Foyt retook the point lead with the victory.

He was well on way to making it two in a row at Du Quoin the next day as he led Andretti and Al Unser in the Indy car race with just three laps remaining. That's when they came up on the slower car of Jerry "Scratch" Daniels. Several laps behind, Daniels suddenly slowed, out of gas. Foyt locked up his brakes and slid high just as Daniels moved up the track trying to get out of the way. Both Foyt and Andretti were blocked, allowing Unser to get by from third place for the victory.

"Son of a gun, he just plain cut me off," Foyt said. "I should have run right into Daniels and piled up all four of us. I had no chance to do anything but lock the brakes."[36]

He'd nearly missed the race entirely. Event promoters had brought in one of the lions from the popular *Daktari* television show as a gimmick and staked it in the infield. That's when A.J. and the animal's trainer came up with an idea to create a little excitement.

"They told me to run from it and it'd jump on my back, but wouldn't hurt me," Foyt said at the time. "So I took off running and that big old thing came galloping up behind me and when it jumped on my back, it plain flattened me. That thing weighs 400 pounds and when it hit, I went down.

"That son of a bitch knocked me to the ground harder than I ever hit the ground in my life. Knocked the crap out of me. The trainer said it might play with me a bit, but when it nuzzled my back, it brought blood. I guess I finally found something I shouldn't have challenged."[37]

His uniform ripped and bloodied, Foyt changed into a new one for the race.

"The lion was a bit testy, not unlike A.J. now and then," said Rutherford, one of the drivers nearby when Foyt and the trainer hatched their plot. "Everything was going okay at first. A.J. was petting the lion and clowning around. Then the lion swatted at A.J., and he backed up and turned around like he was going to run. Suddenly, the lion pounced on him. It wrapped one of its paws around A.J. and slammed him to the ground. The lion wasn't gnawing A.J., but A.J. was certain that was going to be the lion's next move. When the handler finally pulled the lion off, A.J. was more somber than I've ever seen him. He got up and dusted himself off, and it seemed like he didn't know whether to laugh, cry, or throw up."[38]

Not even a lion could have stopped Foyt a week later as he passed Andretti at the halfway point of the Hoosier Hundred and went on to win nearly $20,000 in the richest dirt track race on the schedule. It was his eleventh victory on the track, a record sixth Hoosier Hundred win, and pushed his total winnings in the race to more than $200,000. To hear Foyt tell it, the Hoosier Hundred was surpassed only by the Indianapolis 500.

"I think it's about time for me to get title to this place," he said. "I'll tell you right now, I'd settle for winning the 500 and this one and to heck with the rest of the races—and I mean it. People never remember you when you lose, but they sure do when you win, and I wanted to win this one."[39]

What Foyt didn't realize at the time, what no one would have bet on, was that it would be his last victory at the track and his last in a championship dirt car. USAC was taking steps to remove the dirt tracks from the Indy car schedule and create a separate series just for them.

With five races remaining in the USAC stock car season, McCluskey held a slim 165-point lead over Foyt, with Dodge's Don White, a former series champion, another 347 points behind. With points awarded depending on the number of miles in a race, any of the three drivers could win the title.

On the road course in Brainerd, Minnesota, Foyt led fifty-seven of the sixty-seven laps in the two-hundred-mile event and held a ninety-second lead when he suffered two late flat tires. It dropped him to third at the finish behind White and McCluskey and put McCluskey back into first in points.

A week later he led from start to finish in a one hundred–miler at Nazareth, with White second and McCluskey third. He won again at New Bremen Speedway in Ohio and at the Missouri State Fairgrounds as both McCluskey and White had problems.

The victory moved him into first place in what was originally the final points race of the season. USAC, however, had elevated a race initially scheduled as an invitational to regular status and dubbed it the Race of Champions. It was to be held at Shelby County International Raceway—the track Foyt said he'd never race at again.[40]

He hadn't originally planned on racing in the event, filing an entry for a NASCAR race at Rockingham set for the same day. His late-season surge into the points changed things, and with Ford pushing hard for another championship, he was forced to enter after all. Less than one hundred points separated the three drivers, and he'd win the championship by finishing at least fourth, even if McCluskey or White were to win.

McCluskey said it was "the most important race of [his] career" and that he'd prepared "more for this race than [he had] for any in a long time." Five-time champion Foyt tried to low-key it.[41]

"It is just another race, and I am not preparing for it in any special way," he said. "Competition? I can't single out anybody in particular that will give me fits."[42]

Foyt led early but spun out of the race on lap eighty of the 118. He then got in the car of Jack Bowsher and drove it from fourth place to victory. The rules had changed, however, since he'd used the tactic to help win the Indy car championship, and he earned no points for the effort. White crashed out and McCluskey won the title with his second-place finish. An upset Foyt took the victory wreath and tossed it in the back of his passenger car, then left the track without talking to reporters.

Less than a week later McCluskey announced he was splitting with Foyt at the end of the Indy car season. He was joining a new team being formed by fellow Arizona natives Brawner and Jim McGee, who were both leaving Andretti over disagreements with Granatelli.

"I wouldn't say that the partnership with A.J. was not successful—we had a pretty good run at it and we were always competitive and a contender," McCluskey said. "But we worked with one crew and two different trains of thought—that made it tough on the crew and tough on us. We were both seeking the same thing—victory—but we had separate ideas on how to get it."[43]

At Riverside for the finale, Foyt crashed heavily in practice, destroying his car and knocking the wind out him. It was a dismal end to a dismal season, one that began with such promise. He'd started fifty races and won eight, not bad for most drivers, but not up to Foyt standards.

That didn't stop the Associated Press from naming Foyt its Driver of the Decade. In USAC alone he'd started 488 races during the 1960s and finished in the top three an incredible 233 times, winning forty-two champ car races, twenty-six in sprint cars, twenty-two in stock cars, and nineteen in midgets. The *Indianapolis News*, however, pointed out that since Andretti and Foyt started going head-to-head in USAC competition in 1964, Mario had won the most races in the six-year period.

Despite the successes and accolades, some noted he was also becoming increasingly belligerent and difficult to work with, straining his relationship with McCluskey and others.

"Foyt is many things to many people," started one year-end review. "The fans adore him. Most of A.J.'s competitors hate his gaudy guts. Car builders and mechanics eye him with heavily mixed emotions. For track promoters, Foyt's presence always means fatter gate receipts."

ENGINE MANUFACTURER

Late in the year Foyt found himself in another situation having nothing to do with the happenings on the racetrack. The Big Three auto companies were facing the challenges of the upcoming 1970 Clean Air Act, the latest in increasingly stringent national environmental standards being set by Congress. To address the new regulations, the companies needed to divert research dollars and engineering manpower that in the past supported racing programs.

As part of its cutback, Ford wanted to exit the business of building Indianapolis-type engines. Production had been farmed out since 1965 to a company run by Louis Meyer, a three-time Indianapolis winner, but the contract was up at the end of the year, and Ford said it wanted to further reduce its involvement. The company would continue to work on development and make some of the parts, but wanted Meyer to take on more of the production responsibilities. Ford said it would sell its inventory for about $400,000, less than half its estimated value, but it was too high for Meyer.

The company then offered the opportunity to Foyt, who'd played a key role in the development of Ford's turbocharged engine and its dirt track powerplant. Foyt had the resources, but when word of the possible deal leaked out, most warned him against taking on the role, concerned he'd keep the best engines for his own team.

"The money would be nice and so would the position, if A.J. wasn't shooting for a fourth [Indy 500] win," summed up Ron Lemasters in the *Muncie Star Press*. "The only way A.J. can come out of the deal unscathed is to walk away now. Even if he did run the operation with no discrimination whatsoever, treating each and every request, including his own, fairly, there would be those who would refuse to believe it."[44]

Jones, whose own two-car team used Ford engines, warned, "A.J. doesn't know what he's letting himself in for.

"I'm not even driving, but as a car owner, I wouldn't take the job on," Jones said, although privately he'd expressed an interest in doing just that to Ford. "Even if he does as honest a job as possible, there is going to be talk every time one of those engines fails. But there's also another problem. A.J. wants to win that fourth 500 in the worst way possible. But he's going to spend all this time talking to people with engine problems. Every time somebody wants something for a Ford, they're not going to go to the guy he has servicing the engines. They are going to go to A.J."[45]

It was a seemingly no-win situation, one Foyt nonetheless decided to pursue.

"It is taking on something that can be quite a headache," he admitted. "I've got some good men here and I'll still race and sort of be the boss overseer. I think this is going to be the winning engine for the next couple of years."[46]

CHAPTER 29

TURNING POINTS

1970

The dawn of a new decade marked a major turning point for the sport of auto racing and its leading protagonist, A.J. Foyt.

The popularity of the sport had more than tripled in 1969 according to a Lou Harris poll of sports fans. Attendance at all types of racing events topped forty-one million, just behind horse racing and ahead of the combined pro and college football numbers—although much of the growth was traced to young fans flocking to drag strips. Racetracks around the world had paid out more than $5 million and several drivers were among the top-earning athletes. Thanks to his victory in the Indianapolis 500, Mario Andretti had record winnings of more than $350,000, while Foyt's earnings of about $200,000 pushed his career total to over $3 million.

The boom did not go unnoticed. Television networks, having taken the first tentative steps toward broadcasting races live, were clamoring for more. USAC signed a contract to televise eight races in the coming year and NASCAR signed a three-year, $1.4 million deal.

"Viewer interest in the sport confirms our belief that the time is ripe for auto racing's expansion on television," said Roone Arledge, president of ABC Sports. "Auto racing has been one of the mainstays of *Wide World of Sports* since the program debuted nearly nine years ago and has continued to be among our best-rated shows."[1]

The growth in popularity and attendance also triggered an explosion in the building of racetracks. A new track in Michigan had just completed its first full year of operation and attracted more than fifty thousand spectators to its inaugural Indy car race. A twin track in College Station, Texas, gave the state its first superspeedway. NASCAR's Bill France opened a high-banked track in Talladega, Alabama, although its first event was steeped in controversy as many drivers boycotted, concerned about the high speeds. An $8 million speedway patterned after Indianapolis

◀ Victory Lane at Riverside. *Photograph by Ed Justice Jr.*

was nearing completion in Ontario, California. A new road course at Sears Point in Sonoma, California, was planning its first race and other existing tracks clamored for more events.

More tracks meant more races, and even with an airplane helping him get from track to track, Foyt was already complaining about the increase. Running for the USAC stock car title had been a grind. He'd felt a responsibility as the defending champion to run as many races as possible, but he admitted the travel wore him out late in 1969.

"Making these long hops to races can get you down," he said. "They are the worst part of racing, even more than driving the long-distance events."[2]

There was no talk of retiring, or even slowing down. "I race year-round. I plan to race a good many more years and then maybe I'll consider retiring. But it won't be for some time."[3]

There were other warning signs that despite the boom in popularity, challenges remained. The sport's biggest corporate supporters, the tire and automotive companies, were continuing to trim spending. Having already announced its Indy car cutback, Firestone said it was pulling out of NASCAR entirely.

RIVERSIDE BREAKTHROUGH

Foyt was back for a third year driving cars built by Jack Bowsher in both USAC and NASCAR. After fading brakes cost Foyt a possible victory at Riverside the previous year, the team came up with a new plan. The Ford's self-adjusting brakes were set so Foyt wouldn't be able to use them up in the first half of the race, and a higher gear ratio was installed to ease wear and tear on the engine and transmission. Bowsher decided not to tell the driver about the plan.

Parnelli Jones in the Wood Brothers car was the fastest qualifier. He was moved to the rear of the field, however, when NASCAR ruled his Firestone tires were ineligible because of the company's failure to make them available to the entire field, a series requirement. Foyt started third behind odds-on favorite Dan Gurney and David Pearson.

Pearson took the early lead and Gurney was out of contention almost before it started, making an eleven-minute pit stop on the fourth lap to adjust his brakes and suspension. Jones put on a show as he drove through the field, passing eighteen cars on the first lap and taking the lead on lap forty-three. Foyt was seemingly biding his time, although complaining about his brakes on every pit stop.

It wasn't until after the halfway point in the race—when Bowsher went under the car and gave Foyt full use of the brakes—that A.J. began moving up. Whether or not he had anything for Jones or Pearson is doubtful, but they took care of themselves, Pearson dropping out on lap 148 with a busted transmission, Jones rolling to a stop twenty laps later with a fried clutch.

Foyt was then able to handle his nemesis from the year before, Roger McCluskey, making a dramatic pass around the outside going into Turn Nine, scene of his near-fatal 1965 crash. Earlier in the race he'd been trailing Jim Cook, who slammed into the barrier while attempting a similar move. "It struck head on, then knifed up in the air and came back," Foyt said of the crash, which left Cook in a wheelchair for the rest of his life.[4]

"I never thought I'd live long enough to have this racetrack give me any luck," said an ecstatic but exhausted Foyt. "I thought Riverside was a hoodoo for me. After it put me in the hospital for six months in '65 I was determined to do something here. Then last year when we led for 300 miles before having to slow down, I knew it was a hoodoo."[5]

He'd spent closer to six weeks in the hospital in 1965 and led about 150 miles the year before, but no one called him on the numbers, least of all Bowsher, who explained the race strategy.

"Our first objective was to finish," Bowsher explained. "Our plan was to keep the car running and keep the brakes holding. That seemed the way to win, to be still in there when the other fellows started dropping out."[6]

Foyt embraced the strategy after the fact.

"This race has been a nightmare for me. We decided a change in strategy was in order. I've tried to outrun 'em and outsmart 'em, but this year we just tried to run a steady race and stay in all the way."[7]

A month later the team arrived at Daytona looking for a second consecutive NASCAR victory, but for Foyt it was the sideshows that made news.

As a favor to France, he'd agreed to compete in a Formula Super Vee race, the first event for the small Volkswagen-powered open-wheel cars at Daytona. Arriving early for qualifying, it was apparent he'd never fit in the car's narrow cockpit. Jim Hurtubise replaced Foyt, and although he failed to qualify, it didn't stop him from taking a shot at his friend.

"Foyt is rich, old, and fat," Herk joked. "He isn't hungry like me."[8]

In another preliminary race, this one run by the Automobile Racing Club of America (ARCA), Foyt joined Bowsher and Junior Johnson crew chief Herb Nab in the pits for Louis Wusterhausen, an Austin race promoter, sometime Bowsher crew member, and would-be race car driver. He'd bought a Holman-Moody Ford for the event and prepared it at the Bowsher shops, complete with the team's trademark blue-and-white paint job and No. 21.

Wusterhausen was running fourth on the same lap as the leaders when he headed to the pits in response to a signal from his crew. When the caution light came on, Foyt jumped over the pit wall and waved the driver back on the track, Wusterhausen ignoring an official's stop sign at the end of Pit Road. Two laps later he was black-flagged and back in the pits.

Foyt charged down Pit Road "at a dead run," according to news reports. He "collared chief NASCAR steward John Bruner, the two arguing heatedly for a couple of minutes while Wusterhausen sat helplessly in his car listening." Bowsher eventually pulled Foyt behind the wall and Wusterhausen was penalized a lap, costing him any chance at victory.[9]

In the 500 Foyt was a nonissue, battling engine problems in both the qualifying and main events. It would be his last NASCAR start of the year, Ford announcing after the race it was cutting back on funding for the series.

DONNIE ALLISON

Back in Texas, Foyt reached out to another NASCAR Ford driver affected by the cutback, Donnie Allison. The two had become friendly when both were driving for Banjo Matthews, Allison filling the driver's seat in events Foyt couldn't make. He'd been bugging Foyt ever since about a chance to drive at Indianapolis and A.J. finally decided to give him an opportunity.

"Every time I saw Foyt I'd say, 'Why don't you let me drive one of your Indy cars?'" Allison recalled. "Well, in 1970 at Daytona he said, 'You really want to drive one of those don't ya?' I said, 'Yup.' He said he'd call me, but I'd heard that before.

"This time he did call and asked me to come to Houston. He took me back in the shop to meet his dad, Tony, who I knew a little bit. A.J. pointed to a car up on the rack and said, 'That's the car you're gonna drive. We'll get it down, and you and Daddy can put it together.'"[10]

The shop itself was impressive and immaculate compared to some of the NASCAR garages he was familiar with. Off to one side was the red No. 1 Mark IV Foyt had been given by Ford. In a corner was a speedboat with a 427 Holman-Moody Ford engine in the back. On one wall was a sign: "Luck is where preparation meets opportunity."[11]

The car was the 1967 Eagle that Gurney drove at Indianapolis and Foyt later used on road courses. It was last driven at the end of 1967 by Hurtubise at Riverside and then put up on the storage rack, where it had remained since.

"They were having a test in Phoenix and I went, not to drive or anything, just to go, although I always traveled with my helmet and fire suit," Allison said. "At one point A.J. looked at me and said, 'Do you want to take a ride?' and I said, 'Yes, I do.' So he said, 'Go get your uniform.'"

The cockpit was configured for the six-foot, two-hundred-pound Foyt, and swallowed up the five-foot-nine, 165-pound Allison. The crew put a couple of large Goodyear blankets in the driver's seat so Allison wouldn't bounce around too much.

"A.J. just said, 'Watch yourself.' He didn't give me any other instructions about what to do or what not to do. I went out and after about three laps, he's out there on the racetrack motioning for me to come in. He said he was really mad at me. Said I'd cost him $500. I asked him how the hell I did that. Well, he'd bet the Goodyear guys I wouldn't break twenty-nine seconds and my second lap was a 28.70."[12]

Allison was thirty at the time, four and a half years younger than Foyt. Raised in Miami, Florida, he was the third oldest in a big family, three years younger than Eddie and a year behind Bobby. Although smaller than most kids his age, he was the family's natural athlete, playing all sports and shining in the swimming pool, winning the Florida AAU swimming and diving championship at fifteen.

Even more than swimming, he loved being around horses and spent much of his free time at Miami's famous Hialeah racetrack, where he became an excellent rider and dreamed of being a jockey. A high school motorcycle accident that nearly took his leg, followed by a growth spurt, ended those hopes. He was still slight, but too big for a jockey.

He dropped out of high school and, like his older brothers, worked at his father's garage and junkyard. He followed them into auto racing and, along with Red Farmer, rose to the top of the Miami racing scene. Seeking more competition and richer purses, the "Miami Gang" moved to Alabama for the 1961 racing season. Donnie, with Eddie serving as his crew chief, won a 1962 track championship and started picking up NASCAR rides. He raced mostly modifieds, including events at several tracks hosting Indy car races, Trenton and Langhorne among them. When he won one of the premier modified races at Martinsville driving for the Wood Brothers, he graduated to the Grand National circuit—NASCAR's highest level at the time—taking over the Matthews Ford that A.J. drove in the 1968 Daytona 500. He'd since accomplished something Foyt had failed to do—driving the car to victory at Rockingham and Charlotte. Donnie also had a reputation as someone you didn't mess with.

"He could be very belligerent," Eddie said. "He was four times wilder than Bobby and me put together. You cross Donnie Allison, and you're likely to see a fist in your face. You didn't want to fight [him] because he'd whip your butt. He was lightning fast and so strong."[13]

Which, in 1970 at least, was fine with Foyt.

ASTRO GRAND PRIX

During this period Foyt was also busy helping to promote the second running of the Astro Grand Prix for midget cars in Houston's Astrodome. More than sixty entries again were filed for the March 14 event and Foyt arranged for a charter flight to bring drivers from Indianapolis.

The race itself turned into a fiasco. The temporary quarter-mile dirt track rapidly disintegrated during practice, leaving the racing surface badly rutted. A huge dust cloud overwhelmed the Astrodome's ventilation system and made it hard for drivers to see. Pole sitter Mike Mosley withdrew, saying it was too dangerous. Nine drivers were involved in a crash on the formation lap, although many continued. Four cars were knocked out in a lap-six accident.

There were no inside guardrails on the track, just flimsy half tires marking the turns. Halfway through the one-hundred-lap race, drivers started cutting corners. Officials briefly tried standing at the turns, but when Foyt took the lead on lap sixty-three, bouncing off Billy Vukovich Jr. and nearly hitting the flagman in the process, the race was stopped.

Officials announced they were canceling the remainder of the race and declared Foyt the winner. Threatened by a fan riot, they agreed to finish the event, Foyt holding on to win. Vukovich was disqualified when he tried to pass Foyt by cutting a corner, and later fined for arguing with officials. He also exchanged words with A.J.

"There's nobody I'd rather thumb my nose at as I went by than that guy," Vukovich said of Foyt. "It's not that I don't like him, it's just that he's the best there is—certainly on dirt."[14]

For his part Foyt said, "I didn't start that business of cutting corners, but once they did and I started losing ground, I joined right in. I know as many short cuts as anyone, and if you had to do that to keep up, I was willing."[15]

In addition to promoting the midget race, Foyt discovered taking on the Ford engine program was as challenging and time consuming as others had warned. He added six thousand square feet to his race shop to handle engine development and production. To oversee the program he brought in Howard Gilbert, a long-time chief mechanic and car builder who'd been part of three Indy 500–winning teams and a major force in the building of the laydown roadster Sam Hanks and Jimmy Bryan drove to victory in 1957 and '58.

"If I had it all to do over again, I'd never tackle the job," Foyt said. "My own racing program has suffered because we've spent so much time and effort getting the engine business straightened out. We'll be lucky to have a car ready by May 1—and there's no way I like to be that far behind going into the 500. But this is part of it, and I can accept it.

"What's really hurt the most is all the talk about me getting the good engines and everyone else suffering or me holding up parts for someone or even refusing to supply them. I think I've surprised people because we've organized the business pretty doggone well and we're making improvements all the time. I'll have a pretty complete stock of parts built up by the time May gets here—and they'll be available."[16]

Despite being behind schedule, he decided to go ahead with a hunting trip and for the first time he sounded fed up with racing.

"I've about had it. I don't care what problems I'll be leaving behind or how much work it'll take. I know I need to get away from it for a while."[17]

Foyt was headed for Alaska, where he was to hunt polar bears for an episode of *American Sportsman,* a popular outdoor sports program sponsored in part by Ford. Not surprisingly, he found the March weather in Alaska harsh.

"I don't intend to go back," he said. "We were snowbound for seven days, and it was so cold [forty-five degrees below zero, with winds up to sixty miles per hour] that when we took our mittens off to shoot, our fingers turned blue in two seconds."[18]

Saying his previous hunting experience consisted of "practice shooting out at my ranch," the group hunted their prey by air, landing when they spotted bears. Foyt eventually shot a ten-foot, 1,200-pound polar bear. Houston Ford dealer Luke Johnson, who was also on the hunt, joked the first thing A.J. did "was to rush up and put an STP sticker on it."[19]

Even the hunting trip would eventually add to Foyt's worries. It attracted the ire of Warren Bush, producer of the film *Say Goodbye,* an Academy Award–winning documentary about the impact of man on wildlife, who cited them as an example of "sportsmen" hunting polar bears.[20]

The bear would be displayed at Foyt's dealership in coming years and then moved to his house and finally son Tony's ranch. "I did it once and that's it," Foyt would say. "I'm just not a big-game hunter."[21]

MEANWHILE, BACK AT THE RANCH

While A.J. was on the hunt, he left his father behind to manage the race team and Tony wasn't happy about it.

"It really bothers me the way he's always on the go," the elder Foyt said. "He's got too much on his mind. He's racing stocks, he's racing championship cars, he's got some oil-well stuff going for him down in Texas. That keeps him busy.

"Now he's taken over this Ford engine deal and it's bound to chew off some more of his time. That's our big problem right now. He is trying to do too much. He really doesn't have the time for all of these things, and I sure wish he'd get rid of some of them. We didn't start using our own stuff until four years ago and he's been going full speed just about every hour of the day ever since. There's something about racing that's hard to explain. I guess you can't help diving in over your head."[22]

The trip came right in the middle of Indianapolis tire testing, which he entrusted to the rookie Allison, something he'd never delegated in the past. He didn't miss much as heavy rains limited Allison to only four laps.

"I think it's any driver's ambition to come here," Allison said of the Speedway. "It was my first time on the track and they won't allow you to run over 120, but I accomplished what I wanted. It's just like I dreamed it would be. I know I want to go back."[23]

Back from Alaska in time for the start of the champ car season on March 28 in Phoenix, Foyt finished fourth as Al Unser drove to victory over his brother Bobby. Driving for the team of Jones and crew chief George Bignotti, the younger Unser brother was becoming a major force in Indy car racing, finishing second to Mario Andretti in the 1969 championship and proving himself a serious contender on paved ovals, road courses, and dirt tracks.

Unser was driving a revised and updated Lola, and the team, taking a page out of Foyt's playbook, rebranded it a Parnelli Colt. It featured a striking bright-blue paint job with gold lightning bolts, reflecting the team's new Johnny Lightning (a Hot Wheels competitor) sponsorship.

Ironically, Foyt complained about his engine in both qualifying and the race while Unser and Andretti said their Ford powerplants ran flawlessly.

TERRY FOYT

The next day was Easter Sunday and the Foyt family was at the ranch, which had grown to about five hundred acres. Everyone in the family had their own horse, and A.J. admitted "playing cowboy" helped him relax away from the track. He saddled the horses for the kids and sent them on their way. There was hay for him to pitch.

While Tony, fourteen, had really taken to horses, both Terry, twelve, and Jerry, seven, also enjoyed riding. Terry was a tomboy in every sense of the word and the most competitive of the kids.

"I remember I got some Barbie dolls for Christmas," Terry says. "They were pretty and all, but when Tony got a new go-kart, I started crying. I told Mom to take back my Barbie dolls, I wanted a go-kart. Dad took me over to the shop, and he had another one there. I remember I outran Tony, but we were running around the neighborhood and I almost got hit, so I got grounded."[24]

Foyt had just started his chores when the boys returned.

"Tony rode up and said, 'Dad, Terry fell off the horse,'" Foyt said. "I figured she had just fallen off and gotten right back on. Tony came back about five minutes later and said, 'Mom says to hurry, Terry isn't moving.' That really scared me."[25]

Terry had hit her head in the fall and was unconscious.

"My younger brother [Jerry] and I were racing down the road," Terry would say. "I had this thoroughbred, and she used to spook sometimes, and she'd stop on her front feet. The last thing I know, we were racing down the road, and I guess she spooked, and I went over her head and hit my head."[26]

Foyt drove her to the local doctor, who said she should wake up in about forty-five minutes. She'd already been out about an hour, and A.J. wasn't about to wait around.

"She just wasn't moving," he said. "We got back in the car and took a wild ride into Houston. I had the Thunderbird and it was wide open. We ran about 125 or 130 and ran stop lights, everything. It's a wonder we weren't all killed."[27]

Once again Lucy's family medical connections came in handy. A leading neurosurgeon at St. Joseph's Hospital in Houston told them he was confident Terry would be okay, but couldn't tell them when she would come around.

Terry did regain consciousness, and when her condition was upgraded to fair, Foyt headed for California and the new Sears Points road course. Shortly after he arrived, however, he learned Terry had lapsed back into a coma, and he immediately returned to Houston. She'd been tossing and turning, and he didn't like what he found at the hospital.

"She was unconscious and in intensive care, and they had her restrained," Foyt said. "I didn't want to see her tied down. So my wife and I, we'd take turns and stay there with her, just lay there with her."[28]

Foyt put his racing plans on hold, canceling a return trip to Sonoma for a stock car race. Even Indianapolis was at risk.

"That's the first time in my life my back has been against the wall," he said. "I was standing there and couldn't do anything. Right then I began to think I really might not be back for the month of May.

"I told Lucy that if Terry lives through this, she's going to be a girl. No more Levi's and cowboy boots. She gonna start wearing dresses."[29]

Terry emerged from the coma, although her left side was slow in responding. "It was a long, tough recovery," she says. Eventually, she returned to the ranch and riding, although her dad told her Lady, the horse that threw her, had died. Various reports listed colic or a heart attack as the cause of death.

"I never believed it," Terry said. "I never did find out what happened to my horse. I don't know if he sold it—or what."[30] In an interview for this book Foyt admitted to shooting the horse, although he bought Terry a new one when she felt better.

"Pretty Girl was the first one I got back on," she said, "but Dad made me ride in a helmet after that."[31]

By April 18 Terry had improved to the point Foyt felt he could make a quick trip to Phoenix for a stock car race, where practice, qualifying, and the race were all squeezed into one day. He battled with McCluskey throughout, each leading about half of the two hundred laps before he gained a five-second advantage during the final pit stop and held on to win. Two weeks later on the road course at Indianapolis Raceway Park, he beat McCluskey again, this time in dominating style.

Saying beforehand "I didn't come here to run second," he set a track record in qualifying and led eighty-two of one hundred laps. Don White hounded him for much of the race before his engine let go.[32]

"I don't feel sorry for anyone," Foyt said of White, although he admitted, "I had all I could handle until he went out."[33]

Despite earlier warnings that he might not have any cars ready for the start of practice at Indianapolis, Foyt arrived with four, an updated or "new" Coyote for himself, the Eagle for Allison, listed as the Foyt-Greer entry, and a pair of backup cars. If all went well, one of the backups, the car he'd put on the pole in 1969 and led the race with, would go to George Snider.

A.J. was something of a numerologist, especially when the numbers added up in his favor, and now they never looked better. His first three Indy victories had come at three-year intervals, 1961, 1964, and 1967—a good sign for 1970. He put No. 14 on one of his cars for the first time since he'd won with the number, although he'd be driving lucky No. 7. He also brought back the helmet he wore in the '67 race.

"I think it's sort of in the cards or it isn't, for a driver to win here," he said about the three-year cycle. "You have to be prepared, but you also have to have some breaks too. I've had my share of breaks here, and I've had bad luck too.

"I'm not superstitious, I'm just careful."[34]

Allison found out in a hurry the Speedway can bite you at any time as he spun his second time out on what was supposed to be a slow warm-up lap. A few days later he hit harder, caught by a gust of wind going through Turn Three that sent him into the outside wall, damaging the nose of the Eagle.

"I told him it was gonna happen," Foyt would recall. "He wanted to run a different nose cone with a trick spoiler on it and I said, 'Don't do it. You'll spin and hit the wall.' So he goes out there, spins and hits the wall. We gave him a hard time over that."[35]

Foyt piled the broken parts up in the corner of the garage as a reminder, although the pair continued to get along well.

"Even after those two spins, he made it clear that he still believed in me and that did a lot to build my confidence," Allison said. "Experience is still the greatest teacher."[36]

Al Unser, who'd been the fastest driver all month, won the pole position with Johnny Rutherford second and Foyt third. A.J. sent a case of Lone Star beer to Rutherford's team but refused to shake a reporter's hand who offered him congratulations on the run.

"I got nothing to say," he barked. "I fouled up. That's all there is to it."[37]

For the most part Foyt's takeover of the Ford engine program was turning out to be a nonissue. He'd held the line on cost at about $28,000 for a new engine and $22,000 for a rebuilt one, although it was still higher than the cost of a turbocharged Offy. He said he'd sell parts to anyone who wanted to build their own powerplant, an option Bignotti elected for the engines of Unser and Joe Leonard. Bignotti also decided to use a more traditional version of the engine, while Foyt, Andretti, and others were using a "short stroke" model Foyt had helped develop.

During the month a Learjet was used to shuttle between Houston and Indianapolis, delivering engines and parts as needed. When Bignotti needed a turbocharger, Foyt provided one originally designated for his team. Even General Motors dealer Roger Penske decided against using a Chevrolet stock-block engine in favor of the Ford. Penske seemed happy with it and the service, saying, "It's been reliable, and we've gotten lots of help from the factory people and from Foyt."[38]

In fact, the only one having a problem with the new Ford engine provider was Foyt himself. A parts shipment for his team was mishandled by Delta Airlines, costing him a day of practice. Allison's engine problem during qualifying was the last straw. Once Allison finally qualified on Sunday, Foyt dressed down Gilbert, collected the other driver, and headed for the airport. They were going back to Texas to build their own race engines.

"We weren't running like we needed to," Allison remembered. "A.J. got mad at the engine people and said he was going home to build his and mine engines. So he and I got on an airplane and flew to Houston, built two engines, put them on an airplane back to Indy and that's what we run in the race.

"How many people ever done that? It was just us, the drivers of both cars. We put the block together and assembled the whole engine, tracked them on the dyno, then told the people there to pack them up and send them back. We did that in two days."[39]

Back at the Speedway, Snider qualified a third entry and Foyt was finally happy with the performance of his cars as the third day of qualifying drew to a close. He said he "was going home" after driving all three cars and signing off on them, adding, "If I had four cars in this race, I'd commit suicide."[40]

That was before he was approached by fellow Texan Jim McElreath, who'd just been bumped from the field.

"Jim goes by with his chin hanging down," Foyt said. "He asked me how many hours work were left on the car [the No. 14 Coyote, which hadn't been run]. I said about four and he asked if he could drive it. I decided, hell, why not?"[41]

Rather than head home, Foyt and the team worked into the night preparing the car. He took it out Sunday morning for a few laps and, when the crew spotted metal shavings in the oil filter, ordered the engine changed. Two hours later he ran ten break-in laps before turning it over to McElreath.

"They were still bolting the car together when they brought it out," said McElreath, who called the Coyote "the finest race car I've sat down in." After six practice laps he got in line for a qualifying attempt and easily made the field, making Foyt the first owner in twenty years with four cars in the race. Eighteen turbocharged Offenhauser engines qualified compared to fifteen turbo Fords, but four of the five fastest were Fords.[42]

Back in the garage afterward, Foyt watched on television as Allison, with late relief help from LeeRoy Yarbrough, drove to victory in the Charlotte 600 stock car race. On Carb Day A.J. drove all four cars, complaining the other three felt better than his.

The addition of a fourth car put a strain on crew members, and Foyt brought in additional help for race day. Wally Meskowski was to serve as Allison's crew chief and members of Banjo Matthews' NASCAR team helped with the car. McElreath had his own pit crew, and Gilbert was assigned to oversee the effort while Tony Foyt, as usual, would captain his son's car. All four stalls were lined up on Pit Lane, with Foyt's at the head of the line, closest to the pit exit. It made for a lot of chefs in the kitchen, and after several slow practice stops by the crews, Foyt insisted the teams do it his way.

"It didn't work, did it," he snapped at one of the other crews. "Now do it my way this time, or go back over in that area," he said, motioning to Gasoline Alley. By the end of practice, all the crews were in the seventeen-second range, on par with the previous year.[43]

From the start of the race, it was apparent that Al Unser, as he had been all month, was the best car on the track. Only Foyt was able to keep him in sight, typically several seconds back, occasionally closing up behind the leader.

"I was trying to cool it," he said. "I wanted to stay six or seven seconds behind Al, then go after him following the last pit stop. I knew the race was between the two of us."[44]

That all changed on the next round of stops. Foyt came in and found Snider being serviced behind his spot and Mosley in the pit in front of his. He was forced to make another lap before stopping, falling "too far behind [Unser] to catch him." Things went bad again on the next stop when he left the pits with the jack still under his car. It wasn't a rules violation at the time, although it slowed his exit.[45]

Despite the pit problems, he was still running second, ahead of Mark Donohue and Gurney on lap 172, when five cars tangled in front of him, forcing him to take evasive measures.

"When I downshifted, I screwed it up and had to run in second gear the rest of the way," he said. "It was just one of those days. The car was running beautifully until the wreck."[46]

Forced to hold the lever in the lower gear, he put added strain on the engine, running laps with his tachometer showing more than 11,000 rpm, well over the engine's redline. It wasn't long before the temperature gauges were pegged and he was out of water. With ten laps to go he slowed to a crawl, hugging the inside of the track.

Once Unser took the checkered flag, Foyt pulled in the pit exit, waving as Al drove past to Victory Lane. Confused in part by the three Poppy Red cars running among the leaders, scorers initially had him in second, but he knew better. He was tenth in the final results, five laps behind the winner. Allison finished fourth, with McElreath fifth, both completing 500 miles.

Most car owners would be ecstatic with three cars in the top ten but not Foyt, who made more money than everyone except the first two finishers. He spoke briefly with reporters and then retreated to his garage, ordering the doors closed and telling the crew to keep everyone out.

It wasn't until A.J. Watson came by that Foyt allowed a visitor. Mosely was one of Watson's drivers, and he apologized for any problems they might have caused on Foyt's stop. Then he walked over to Allison, who'd passed both Andretti and Bobby Unser late in the race.

"I was sitting on the bench changing out of my uniform and putting on my street clothes when he walked over to me and stuck out his hand," Allison recalled. "He said, 'You're the only stock car driver I ever saw that could drive one of these cars.' Then he turned around and walked out of the room.

"I thought that was quite a compliment coming from him. It was probably the best compliment I was ever paid in racing."[47]

While Foyt told reporters Allison "did a helluva job," there was limited praise back in the garage. "I think A.J. told me a couple times I'd done good," Allison said. "For a taxi driver."

Allison won $35,000, nearly as much as he'd made the week before in winning the Charlotte 600, and was named Rookie of the Year. For Christmas he received a box from Foyt.

"He sent me a big package COD," Allison recalled. "I opened it up and inside were all the broken parts from the car I'd crashed."

UNSER AND BIGNOTTI RULE

Like the 500, the rest of the Indy car season belonged to Al Unser, who gave much of the credit to his crew chief, Bignotti. As a rookie at Indianapolis in 1965, Unser saw firsthand the tenuous relationship between Foyt and Bignotti. While Foyt and other drivers often clashed with Big George, Unser found a way to work with him.

"He was easy for me to get along with 'cause I let George make all the decisions," Unser said. "He was a brilliant man and I let him do his thing. I wasn't one of the drivers who said I know more than you know. Foyt would try to tell George what to do and George didn't like that.

"Foyt won enough as it was. But if they had stayed together, he would have continually won. But Foyt is a racer, he's hard headed."[48]

For only the second time in ten years (1966 was the first), Foyt failed to win a champ car race, although he came close on several occasions. He ran out of gas at IRP after leading, and twice on dirt tracks he lost big leads because of traffic.

At Du Quoin on September 7, he built a four-second lead over Al Unser before being blocked by traffic, Unser getting past. Trying to take the lead back, he slid up the track and hit the outer guardrail, flipped several times, and landed upside down. It was one of the first times anyone could remember him making a mistake while chasing another driver. It took a while to get Foyt out from under the car, and he limped away with a badly sprained ankle. Blaming the Goodyear tires, he sought out the company rep, picked him up, and threatened to throw him in the track's infield lake.

The next week in the Hoosier Hundred, Foyt led a race-high fifty-four laps before being balked by traffic. His engine was already going sour and he ended up third. Al Unser emerged the victor in each case, launching him on a five-race winning streak, matching another Foyt record, and on a sweep of the year's dirt track events.

Foyt did post a victory as a car owner, with McElreath winning the inaugural California 500 at Ontario. Among several features of the new track was an electronic scoring system, with tiny transmitters placed in each car. Foyt didn't like the idea from the start, saying the transmitters could play havoc with a car's electrical system, although officials assured him they were designed to operate at low frequencies and power levels that would not affect the cars.

With Unser running away with the race, Foyt pitted, complaining of electrical problems. With Tony at home recovering from ongoing stomach pains, A.J. got out of the car and spent twenty minutes changing the spark plugs himself. Preparing to rejoin the race, he grabbed a ball-peen hammer and knocked the transmitter from the front of the car, forcing officials to manually track his progress.[49]

He was back on the track when a busted transmission forced Unser into the pits with fourteen laps remaining, turning it into a new race. Art Pollard was holding a comfortable twenty-second lead over McElreath, who was driving the same Coyote he'd run at Indianapolis. That's when Foyt, running fast but more than sixty laps behind the leaders, spun—"I ran over a broken wheel and blewey went two tires," he said—bringing out the caution light and bunching up the field. He jumped out of the car and helped push it off the track.[50]

When the green flag came out with three laps remaining, McElreath and Pollard traded the lead, McElreath eventually taking the checkered flag. Some questioned the timing of Foyt's spin, although Pollard wasn't one of them, saying a tire leaking air cost him the win.

"I knew they were running one-two at the time and I would just hate to see it end under a yellow," Foyt said. "That's why I was down there trying to drag my car off the track."[51]

Car owner Foyt took a victory lap with McElreath in the pace car, but when the post-race activities stretched on he left, stranding the winner without a ride back to the Holiday Inn. Actor James Garner eventually stopped to pick up the hitchhiking driver, who'd just won more than $150,000 and was still in his uniform.

Foyt did manage to win three of USAC's biggest stock car races of the year. He started both halves of an Indy car/stock car doubleheader at Michigan, leading all one hundred laps to win the taxicab event. He followed it with a win at Dover for the second straight year, then kicked off fairgrounds season by winning at Milwaukee on August 20.

His season came to a premature end a month later, however, when the stock cars returned to Milwaukee. He was running among the leaders when a car losing power attempted to cut across the track, clipping the rear of Foyt's car, turning it hard right and sending it head-on into the outside wall. Complaining of neck and back pain, he was taken to the local hospital, where doctors said his back was badly sprained. They reluctantly released him, urging him to take the rest of the year off.

For once Foyt followed doctors' orders. He retreated to his ranch, although his idea of rest was to stay constantly busy working on one project or another, including adding more horses and cattle. Helping keep him close to home were his father's continued stomach problems, as Tony was back in the hospital while doctors searched for a cause.

When the Foyt team failed to show two weeks later for the Indy car race at Trenton, rumors spread he'd been hurt much worse than originally reported and was considering retirement. The medical problems of his father and daughter added to the speculation and a Charlotte newspaper reported Allison was being groomed to replace him. Several days later Gurney announced his intention to retire at the end of the season.

"I have always maintained that part of being a successful race driver is in knowing when to quit," said Gurney, who was four years Foyt's senior. "I guess this is it. I'm bowing out while I'm still in one piece.

"I guess most drivers think about retiring at one time or another. I always wondered how it would be. You know, would I be full of tears and cry about it? But I don't feel that way. I found that I was devoting more time to All-American Racers than racing. Driving has to be a full-time business—you can't be successful on a part-time basis. Now I want to put something of myself back into racing. I made many friends in racing and the thing I treasure most is the fact that I was held in high esteem by my fellow competitors. That means a lot to me."[52]

After Gurney's announcement the Foyt retirement stories started again. Some called on him to retire, most notably Rodger Ward. As the publicity director for the Ontario track, he'd been in the midst of the controversy over the scoring transmitter and was unhappy with the way Foyt had acted.

"A.J. Foyt should say, 'It's been nice, but so long.' I hope he does before he gets himself skinned up," Ward said. "Foyt hasn't been acting like a man who wants to race. I know what he's going through. It isn't so bad once you get out there on the track, but it's getting there that's tough. At Ontario A.J. was finding all kinds of excuses why his car couldn't make the race, like saying that scoring device would harm his engine. When a driver starts doing this, he really doesn't want to race."[53]

The normally well-connected and pro-Foyt reporter Ron Lemasters wrote: "It is the opinion of this writer that Foyt is ready to call it quits. . . . It is clear he has his best racing years behind him. . . . If he should happen to win the Indianapolis 500, expect an almost immediate announcement of retirement. If he doesn't win his fourth 500, this writer figures he will announce 'semi-retirement,' driving a few select stock cars races and the three 500 milers on the USAC schedule next year."[54]

At times even Foyt sounded like he'd had enough, telling a reporter in one breath, "You want to throw your helmet away and run. It hurts like hell. You get sick. There is so much ache and so many pains in life." In the next breath it sounded as if he'd never quit. "You stick around. Who knows why? It's your life, that's all.

"I like the idea of being alone with a car and getting the most out of it. Nobody but you is guiding the car and only you can control it. That's what I like."[55]

———

By mid-November he couldn't resist the itch to get back in a race car any longer, although technically he wasn't racing. He joined Pearson on a joint Ford/Goodyear stock car test in Southern California, bouncing between the oval track at Ontario and Riverside's road course.

They were nearing the end of the three-day test on Friday, November 20, having mounted new tires for one last session at Riverside following a lunch break. They'd only run a few laps when they were flagged into the pits and told to report to the track office. A Ford executive in Michigan was on the speakerphone and waiting to speak to the drivers and company engineers.

"He told us just to pack up and go home," Pearson said. "He said Ford was withdrawing from its racing program and that testing was to end immediately. That's all he said, nothing else. A.J. was in shock and I just couldn't believe it. One minute we've got factory backing, all the money and parts we could want, and then the next minute we're on our own. I felt like an orphan. Nobody wanted me."[56]

Late that afternoon, Ford issued a statement attributed to Matthew S. McLaughlin, the company's vice president of sales. "For some years Ford has spent considerable money and energy to the support and sponsorship of various automobile racing activities in North America. We believe these efforts have been worthwhile as an aid to promotion of both the sports and our products. We are proud of the records achieved by the drivers in Ford and Lincoln Mercury products. However, we believe our racing activities have served their purpose."[57]

What the statement didn't say was after nearly ten years of massive spending on the company's "Total Performance" program and victories at Indianapolis, Daytona, Le Mans, and virtually everywhere else its cars raced, Ford had failed to move the sales needle. The company was still locked at a 29 percent market share, while General Motors, the only one of the Big Three not officially in auto racing, continued to grow. In addition, increasing federal safety, fuel-economy, and emission regulations were proving to be a drain on corporate finances and engineering manpower, refocusing the company's research and development budget. The company had just introduced the Pinto and its advertising was focused on miles per gallon, not miles per hour.[58]

The announcement also didn't mention an internal Ford audit, which found widespread fiscal malfeasance throughout the racing program. Henry Ford II, a driving force behind the motorsports program, who once famously said there were no budget limits on winning at Le Mans, made the final decision. Shut it down. A three-year contract with Kar-Kraft was terminated with two years remaining and the doors to the Ford-owned building padlocked. Jacque Passino, head of Ford's racing program, was allowed to resign immediately, while several other company executives were terminated. Phone calls like the one to Foyt and Pearson went out to Ford racing executives and engineers, telling them to return to Dearborn immediately.[59]

Foyt had been aware for some time of Ford's plans to cut back its racing program but had been offered a new contract with the company and told earlier in the month there would be a limited NASCAR schedule. He'd put off signing, saying he would do it at Daytona, only now that opportunity was gone. Still, while Ford's announcements made things more challenging, it also presented some opportunities.

Overnight he went from Riverside to Phoenix, where he qualified third for the final Indy car race of the year, although a brake problem forced him out early. Al Unser also failed to win, meaning he ended the season with ten Indy car wins, tying Foyt's 1964 mark, although he'd been in eighteen races compared to Foyt's thirteen.

Ford's withdrawal was the talk of the paddock. Foyt assured everyone he was already building engines for the coming year and would continue to do so.

Then he headed back to Houston to put his plans in motion.

CHAPTER 30

FORD OUT, FOYT IN

1971

Back at his race shop, A.J. Foyt's first calls were to his contacts in Dearborn, Michigan, to confirm what he already knew—Ford was out completely. Since 1965 he'd been one of the company's top drivers and major benefactors of its corporate largesse, on the receiving end of significant financial and technical support. Kar-Kraft had routinely worked on Foyt projects at Ford's behest, not the least of which was helping turn the Lotus into a Coyote. One Ford team or another had supplied his stock cars for the past five years. Now it was all gone. He was on his own.

It was just the type of challenge Foyt relished. In the face of Ford's move and the calls for his retirement, he did the last thing anyone expected. He doubled down.

Rather than reduce his schedule, he'd increase it. He'd run the full Indy car season and some races in the new dirt track series. He started discussions with two designers to replace his aging Coyotes. Because of Ford's restrictions he'd run only two NASCAR races in 1970, but now he went to work lining up sponsorship with plans to double or triple that number.

Ford had announced that Holman-Moody, the Wood Brothers, and its other NASCAR teams could keep the cars and equipment in their possession, although there'd be no further financial or engineering support. The company also agreed to provide Foyt with the remaining inventory of Indy engine blocks, parts, castings, and manufacturing dies, everything Ford had relating to the Indy engine program. It even sent engineers to help install the new equipment. For legal reasons Foyt would have to purchase the inventory. The total cost was one dollar, and then he set about creating the Foyt Engine Corporation.[1]

◀ When Ford dropped out of racing, Foyt took over engine development.
Revs Institute, The Bruce R. Craig Photograph Collection

Foyt hadn't been the only one interested in the Ford equipment, however.

"We wanted to give part to Parnelli Jones and part to A.J., but we didn't have enough pieces to go around," said Charlie Gray, who'd been Ford's NASCAR program manager before the withdrawal. He was one of the few from the motor-sports department still around after the purge and was charged with distributing what was left to the race teams. "I made the decision and it was not very popular. I gave it all to A.J. and he went from there. P.J. was a very good friend of mine, but he didn't get any Ford equipment. He was upset and he should have been. But a decision had to be made. There simply wasn't enough to go around."[2]

Foyt didn't get everything he wanted.

"All the [USAC] stock car equipment went to [Jack] Bowsher," Gray said. "Foyt called and asked if he could have one of the cars. I said, 'Jack built those cars, he takes them to racetracks, you get in them and drive them, get out, and then he takes them home, rebuilds them, and gets them ready to go. Those are his cars.' A.J. wasn't upset, but he didn't like it."[3]

Foyt was also getting calls, one of the first coming from Cale Yarborough. He'd won thirteen races, including most of NASCAR's major events, while driving for the Wood Brothers the past five years. A potential sponsor had backed out, however, leaving the team's future uncertain. "I might run a couple of races and see if I can make a profit," Glen Wood said. "If not, I'll quit."[4]

Offered a full-time ride on the Indy car circuit by Gene White, the Firestone distributor in Atlanta, Yarborough wanted A.J.'s opinion. Foyt told him White ran a good team and was switching to Ford engines in the coming year. He encouraged Cale to make the move and Yarborough decided to take the advice.

"I needed to have a job," Yarborough said. "I owed a lot of money and I needed a way to make some. We had a discussion about it and he was all for it."[5]

Donnie Allison called. His car owner, Banjo Matthews, was also looking for a sponsor without success and preparing to go back to building race cars. Allison wanted to know if he could drive for Foyt in the coming champ car season. The answer was less encouraging. Foyt said he'd made a mistake the previous year running four cars at Indianapolis and he would start the season running only one. Indianapolis was a possibility, but no promises.

Foyt chose an interview at the end of 1969 with Bloys Britt, who covered the sport for the Associated Press, to make his plans known. The lengthy article was picked up by newspapers across the country during the slow holiday season.

Britt had interviewed Foyt many times and noted a difference in the driver, writing that A.J. was "plumpish, rich, apparently mellowed. The silent, brooding, morose, abrupt, tough, quick-tempered, heavy-handed Foyt of the past smiles a lot now."[6]

There was a good reason for the smiles. Foyt knew there were major sponsors looking to get involved in auto racing. The Public Health Cigarette Smoking Act took effect on January 1, 1971, banning television cigarette advertising. With millions of marketing dollars to spend and nowhere to spend them, the tobacco companies were turning to racing. Marlboro announced it would spend $300,000 in USAC.

"There's a lot of prize money floating around next year and I want my share of it," Foyt said. USAC had added two new 500-mile races with large purses at Ontario and another new track in Pocono, Pennsylvania, calling it the Triple Crown of Indy car racing. Foyt said he'd talked with Allison, Jim McElreath, and others about driving for him but, he explained, "We spent too much time last year looking after two or three other cars. We'll concentrate on one—*mine*—in 1971 and I think we'll be better off."[7]

Britt asked Foyt about his reputation for being hard on crew members.

"Racing is still my business and like anything else there is no room for errors—either by the driver or the crew. Racing is dangerous. You're alone out there in the car. A mistake back in the garage or in the pit could end it all for you. I'm not anxious to hurry death along. I want to be happy when I go.

"That's the name of the game, being happy. And you're happiest when your car is performing well, when you know that the crew and yourself have put everything together right. Racing is a business. It is my livelihood. To be successful, you have to pay attention to detail. I won't allow sloppy work in my garage or at the track. I never have, and I never will."

Britt also quoted several former crewmen who didn't want to be identified.

"Racing is his food and drink," said one. "Without it he would die. With it he will perhaps do the same. But he is sure he will survive until he is ready to quit. He has been seriously hurt several times, but he is sure he will not be hurt again, for he is the total master of his fate on the race course. He has to drive to live and win to be happy."

Foyt hinted at the possibility of a new Indy car, inspired by Jim Hall's Chaparral 2J that was blazingly fast on the Can-Am sports car circuit in 1970. The car had movable front, rear, and side skirts to block airflow under the chassis. It also used fans driven by an auxiliary motor to pull air out from underneath, creating a vacuum and "sucking" the car to the ground. While most focused their attention on the fans and nicknamed it the "sucker" or "vacuum" car, the skirts were the real key to the car's primitive "ground effects."[8]

While the 2J was often the fastest car on the track, it failed to finish a race, and at the end of the year the series, known for its lack of regulations, outlawed it for 1971. That didn't mean a similar machine couldn't run at Indianapolis, and after being slow to move to rear-engine cars and lucky to beat the turbines, Foyt wanted to be ahead of the curve if a suction car was the next big thing. He hired Chaparral engineer Don Gates to design a new Coyote. Others were thinking the same thing: Roger Penske was looking at a similar machine for Mark Donohue, hiring another Chaparral engineer to develop their car.[9]

To cover his bases, Foyt hired a second designer, Bob Riley, a Ford employee. Assigned to Kar-Kraft prior to its closure, Riley was back in the company's engineering department working on emission controls. He'd been recommended by Klaus Arning, the Ford chassis engineer who played a key role on the race-winning 1967 Coyote. The recommendation was backed by Ron Fournier, another Kar-Kraft alum who'd worked for Roger Penske's Trans Am team before joining Foyt and proving to be an outstanding fabricator.

Foyt asked Riley to come to Houston and their first meeting was over lunch at a Mexican restaurant. The two had never met, even though Riley worked on the suspension and chassis of the Mark II and Mark IV sports cars, and for Arning on the Coyote chassis.

"A.J. said he wanted a strong car, a strong tub, and that he was tired of getting burned," Riley recalled. "I told him some of my ideas. I had done some designs and wind tunnel tests for a Super Vee and Formula Ford. This was before full ground effects had really been developed, but because of my aerodynamic background, I was already experimenting with it."[10]

Foyt liked what he heard and asked Riley to design an Indy car. Despite the recommendations, it still took a leap of faith to entrust Riley with the next Coyote. Super Vee and Formula Ford were primarily series for amateur racers and crude in comparison to the cars raced on the Indy car circuit. And although Riley had been to the 500, he was really a road racer at heart. None of that seemed to concern Foyt.

Returning to Detroit, Riley told his bosses about the opportunity. The project was a whole lot more exciting than emission controls, and he was prepared to quit if necessary. He discovered Foyt's network of friends at Ford ran to the very top and included Gene Bordinat, the company's chief designer and vice president of styling. He'd already agreed to a one-month leave of absence and a "loan" of Riley.

"They were all enthusiasts, but at the time there was absolutely no racing supposedly going on at Ford. So they had to keep quiet."[11]

Asked what he thought of the Chaparral 2J, Riley said he told Foyt, "That's going to be a lot of trouble, a lot of development there. Foyt said he'd try to get USAC 'to ban it.'"[12]

By now A.J. knew the political ins and outs of dealing with USAC, and rather than simply going to the organization and asking it to ban the 2J concept, he presented Gates's plans for approval. The legality of the concept came to a head at the annual USAC board meeting in late January. Having finally put the turbine issue to bed, the board was in no mood for another controversial and expensive car, ruling it violated the spirit of USAC's rules, which said no part of the car could drag on the track. The concept was dead, at least for the time being.

Which was fine with Foyt, who thought the design too radical.

"We actually hadn't gotten into construction," he admitted after the ruling. "We had the blueprints and everything drawn and I wanted to know one way or the other before we went any further. I'm building two cars for this season and the second one was the ground effect job."[13]

Gates moved on, later creating the Antares for Indy car racing, an innovative but odd-looking machine that failed to win a race.

Foyt set Riley up with an apartment and car in Houston, and a drawing board in the middle of the race shop, where he received plenty of advice from crew members.

"I was on a pretty steep learning curve," Riley said. "A mechanic would come up and say, 'Be sure to do this.' Then a fabricator would come by and say, 'You know, you always want to incorporate this.' A.J. was observing all of this and finally told me, 'I want you to listen to everybody, but I want you to do what you think is best.' That was quite an influence on me and really very good advice."[14]

THE WOOD BROTHERS

With work started on the new Coyote, Foyt's next move was to call Glen and Leonard Wood. He'd last driven for the small family team in 1965, co-driving to victory at Atlanta and then scoring an outright victory in the Firecracker 400 at Daytona. Even after Yarborough became the team's regular driver in 1966, the brothers and Foyt had remained friendly.

With Yarborough headed for a full season of Indy car racing, the Woods needed a driver and, more importantly, a sponsor. Foyt knew where they could get both for the first two races of the year, at Daytona and Ontario, and they quickly reached an agreement.

"A.J. is a great driver and we feel he can win both races for us," Glen Wood said in making the announcement. "He has driven for us before and this means we won't have any problems getting adjusted to each other.

"We'll just have to see how we do at Daytona and Ontario. A.J. can't drive for us past those two races, so we'll just have to wait until then to make any kind of decision about the rest of the year. If we can convince [the sponsor] to help us the rest of the year or come up with another sponsor, then our decision will be made for us."[15]

It was a dream come true for Leonard Wood, who'd first seen Foyt drive in 1958 while he was in the army and stationed in Germany, and Foyt raced in the World of Champions event in Monza, Italy. While Glen Wood served as the team's spokesperson—"I'm the one who does the talking, but it's Leonard who does most of the work," Glen would say—it was Leonard who looked after the cars and engines, and to whom Foyt naturally gravitated.[16]

"We had several world class drivers in our cars over the years, but I remember how proud I was when we had the race car in the shop with A.J. Foyt's name on the door," Leonard said. "I was fifteen years old when I started racing, and I never dreamed I'd be setting cars up for the world's greatest driver."[17]

He'd appreciated Foyt, the driver, from the very first time A.J. drove for the team at Atlanta in 1965.

"I loved the way he came off the corner," Wood recalled fifty-five years later. "He'd come off a turn right up against the wall. That means he's using all the racetrack, letting the car free up coming off, rather than pinching it down. A guy comes off on the inside, well he ain't using all the benefit of the racetrack.

"We also used blackboards to signal drivers back then, before radios, and sometimes drivers didn't acknowledge their signs. If we gave A.J. a blackboard he would turn his face straight at you and gave you an okay that he'd read the sign."[18]

Foyt, the person, was also a hit with Leonard. The driver had risen to sports royalty status since those races in 1965, but he was still A.J. to Wood.

"He was a very classy guy, one of the classiest guys I've ever known," Leonard said. "One thing he would always do, whenever he would meet up with you at the track, didn't matter if he had a movie star with him or some other important person, the first thing he'd do is introduce you to them. No other driver ever did that. No matter who it was, the first thing out of his mouth was to introduce you to them."[19]

While Foyt was making his deal with the Wood Brothers, NASCAR was pulling off a major one of its own. Chrysler had followed Ford's announcement by cutting back its NASCAR support to just two cars, a Plymouth for Richard Petty and a Dodge for Buddy Baker, both to be run out of the Petty Enterprises shop. With the country just emerging from a recession, sponsors were in short supply and it wasn't just the former Ford teams looking for money.

Faced with the loss of significant manufacturer financial backing, the series went looking for a major corporate sponsor. The timing couldn't have been better, however, and NASCAR found a sugar daddy in its own backyard.

R.J. Reynolds was based in Winston-Salem, North Carolina, little more than an hour from NASCAR's outpost in Charlotte. RJR's major brand, Winston cigarettes, was the best-selling cigarette in the world but coming under increasing pressure from its major competitor, Marlboro. Like Marlboro, Winston was looking for a place to spend its marketing dollars and NASCAR was the perfect outlet. It was a marriage, if not exactly made in heaven, that gave birth to the Winston Cup Series at the start of 1971.

The new team clicked from its first practice laps at Daytona.

"He fit right in with our team," Leonard Wood remembered. "There was no problem. Sometimes a driver and crew don't hit it off. He got along great with everybody. He'd pick somebody out of the crew to pick on. He'd make up a story that wasn't true and tell it like it was true. He used to pick at my brother Glen a lot."[20]

The team discovered Foyt was sought after by the news media and wasn't about to hold back when answering their questions. The big controversy at Daytona centered around the first use of a carburetor restrictor plate, a device designed to limit the airflow going into an engine's combustion chamber, cutting horsepower and a car's top speed. Early practice speeds were under 180 miles per hour, down nearly fifteen mph, and Foyt didn't like it.

"It's a shame to put blinders on it like you would a horse," Foyt said. Glen Wood was forced to walk a fine line, trying to keep both his driver and NASCAR happy. "In a way it seems a shame to put shackles on a good race car and a good driver like that," Glen said. "But in the long run, I think it will help the sport. I think we'll have a better race at that speed because more cars will be able to run together."[21]

Despite his complaints, Foyt qualified on the pole, nearly two mph faster than the second-fastest car but almost twelve mph slower than Yarborough had been in the same car the year before. While Foyt admitted to sandbagging during practice, he didn't believe the factory Chrysler products of Petty and Baker were holding back. "I think if they could have been on the pole, they would have," he said. "It paid $5,000!"[22]

Although guaranteed the first starting position, Foyt elected to run his entire qualifying race, swapping the early lead with Petty, Fred Lorenzen, and Pete Hamilton. The Wood Brothers gave him a big lead on their pit stop—too big, in fact, as Petty and Hamilton teamed up in a draft and moved to Foyt's bumper with a lap to go. When a caution light came on, Foyt lifted instinctively for a moment, while Hamilton kept his accelerator floored and shot past for the victory.

"I backed off just a little because I didn't know what was ahead," Foyt said. USAC rules required cars hold position when the caution light came on, but NASCAR rules at the time allowed drivers to race back to the finish line. "That was all it took. I backed off just enough for the kid to get by me."[23]

Afterward, Hamilton, who was twenty-nine, came face-to-face with Foyt in the garage area.

"Nice finish, kid," A.J. said with a grin. "You did everything perfect."[24]

"It gave me a feeling like I've never had," said Hamilton, a transplanted Yankee from Massachusetts, and the defending Daytona 500 champion. "Here was A.J. Foyt, my hero since I was a kid, telling me that I was perfect. You know, I almost shed a tear."[25]

Glen Wood's prediction of tighter racing proved to be right, and the 500 featured forty-eight lead changes among eleven drivers. Foyt was leading Petty going into Turn One with about one hundred miles left when both cars received signals to pit for their final fuel stop. The Wood Brothers car, however, ran out of gas coming out of the turn and Petty swept by. He was completing his stop when Foyt rolled silently into his pit. The normal stop of about twenty seconds stretched on to fifty-three as the engine failed to refire and Leonard went under the hood to prime the carburetor.

While this was going on, there was a blown engine and crash on the track. The yellow flag was displayed, and somehow the pace car got between Foyt and Petty, putting A.J. a lap down.

It was a rare mistake by the acknowledged best pit crew in auto racing, the team having failed to completely refuel the car on its previous stop. It was so unusual, Leonard Wood at first expected sabotage, although he later discarded the idea. He said Foyt never said a word to him about the incident, never questioned what happened.

When racing resumed Foyt was able to pass Petty and Baker and get back on the same lap as the leaders, but the electric blue Plymouth fell in behind the Mercury and drafted his way home to victory, with Baker second, Foyt third. Foyt and the Woods challenged the finish, saying they were never passed by the leaders on the track and shouldn't have been put a lap behind during the caution. An official scoring review satisfied the team, if not the driver.

"Between you and me, I think I won," Foyt told a reporter. "I had Glen and Leonard recheck the tape after the race to make sure some error in scoring hadn't been made. They said they were satisfied. Me? I don't think I'll ever be convinced. But Petty made the biggest bank deposit, so he must have won."[26]

Petty acknowledged Foyt had the fastest car, and the worst luck. "If it had come down to the wire between Foyt and myself, it would have been a tough one to win. A.J. had the fastest car in the race and I probably had the second fastest. But he had an unlucky break or two."[27]

"That was wild out there today," Foyt said. "I guess the man upstairs just said, 'Foyt, you'll run third today.' I wish I could have won, but you've got to take the good with the bad in this game. We could have wrecked."[28]

He had nothing but praise for Petty.

"If there's one guy at this track that I don't mind running right on my bumper, it's Petty. He's smooth. When Petty's back there it's more like we're driving one car. I don't worry when we're side-by-side either."[29]

Petty was also generous with his praise.

"It's remarkable how that guy can handle a car. I'd hate to see him run an entire season down here on the NASCAR circuit. He's at one disadvantage when racing down here. I know the other drivers running. I know their driving habits and what they will probably do under various situations. Foyt doesn't and I would say this is a disadvantage."[30]

The next race for the team came two weeks later on NASCAR's first trip to the new Ontario track, and it included a little prerace drama. When several reporters wrote Foyt was being replaced in the car by series regular Charlie Glotzbach, an angry A.J. confronted Glen Wood.

"I ran out of gas and didn't win the 500, so I guess I'm fired," Glen Wood recalled Foyt saying. "There were reports that Foyt will not drive our car at Ontario and it upset him. Foyt will be driving our car at Ontario and maybe at Atlanta and maybe some others, too."[31]

Foyt skipped USAC's first Indy car race of the season in Argentina in order to run at Ontario. The Argentina race was originally scheduled as an exhibition, but when A.J. and others said they weren't going, it was switched to one counting toward the national championship. Foyt held his ground, officially protesting the change and saying he was already committed to the Wood Brothers and Ontario. The race was paying more money to win than the Daytona 500, plus bonus money for every lap led, just like Indianapolis. For the first time, a NASCAR race would start with the cars three abreast.

Foyt put the Wood Brothers car on the pole and led more than half the race, fighting off the challenges of Petty, Baker, and Lorenzen.

At one point Foyt thought he had a flat tire, something plaguing the team in practice. When a caution flag flew shortly thereafter, the team radioed for him to pit if he thought it necessary to change tires. He elected to stay on the track.

"He got to thinking about the $150 he was picking up for every lap he was leading and decided the tire didn't feel too bad after all," Leonard recalled. Foyt also took advantage of the slowdown to signal Baker to check the tire.

"A.J. kept motioning to his right tire, asking me if it was flat," Baker said after the race. "Like a fool I said no. Then he took off."[32]

In a reverse of the Daytona finish, Petty slid through his pit box on his last stop and under the rules of the day was forced to make another lap, allowing Foyt to cruise home to the victory.

"It was one of the best races I have ever driven," Foyt said. "Race driving is getting to be hard work, but I get the same kick out of winning as I did fifteen years ago. It always helps the adrenalin when you win a big one like this. The money is good, I don't deny that. But racing is hard and it gets harder as the years go by. They say this speedway wasn't built for stock car racing, but let me tell you, it's a wild racetrack for any type of machinery."[33]

Foyt won $51,800 in lap and prize money. Al Unser, winner of the Indy car race in Argentina, pocketed $20,000, although Unser also picked up 600 points toward the national championship. Afterward, Foyt received a phone call from Yarborough, who finished a respectable eighth in Argentina.[34]

"Cale called me and said, 'Man, I checked my mailbox. You could at least send me a crumb.'"

QUESTOR GRAND PRIX

Following the success at Ontario, Foyt and the Wood Brothers decided to add a third race to their schedule, the five hundred–miler at Atlanta. That was six weeks off, and first up was a tire test at Indianapolis, followed by a busy last weekend in March, running his first Indy car race of the year at Phoenix on March 26, and a new event the next day on the Ontario road course.

With work continuing on Riley's new Coyote, Foyt arrived at Phoenix with the year-old car he'd been running at Indianapolis. Shuttling between practice sessions at Ontario and Phoenix, he qualified fifth for the Indy car race. A new rule required a fuel stop and most of the leaders elected to pit early, allowing Foyt to lead for twenty-six laps before pitting. When his stop ran long, he reentered at the rear of the field and, with a cooling system rigged for the high speeds of Indianapolis, the engine began to overheat, forcing him to withdraw.[35]

He departed immediately for Ontario and the Questor Grand Prix, a unique race pitting Formula One cars and drivers against the best American drivers in Formula A cars. The $250,000 purse made it the richest road race in history.

While the F1 drivers were in their regular grand prix machines, many of the top American drivers, including Foyt, had never driven a Formula A car before the first practice session. Formula A was an open-wheel series that evolved from the mostly amateur ranks of the Sports Car Club America (SCCA) and was still considered a lower-level series. The cars were more powerful but heavier than their F1 counterparts, in theory making them an even match.

Foyt's car was entered by Agapiou Brothers, who'd worked on Carroll Shelby's Le Mans winners. It was a several-years-old McLaren and powered by a Chevrolet engine, while the Ford Cosworth was the Formula A engine of choice. Still, $250,000 was $250,000, and A.J. was joined by Al and Bobby Unser, Mark Donohue, Swede Savage, and others. Mario Andretti, who was transitioning to the F1 circuit and had won the South African Grand Prix earlier in the year driving for Ferrari, would again have a blood-red car at Ontario.

Promoters had brought in Jackie Stewart to hype the event in advance, and he didn't disappoint, saying Europeans considered it "the greatest race ever held across the pond." He made it clear he hadn't forgotten about the Indianapolis 500.[36]

"Road racing takes more intelligence," Stewart said. "We expect to win. Can you imagine what the fellow down in Texas is planning to do to us? I hate to think what he would be like if he beat us."[37]

Foyt was a favorite target of Stewart, who told another reporter, "I'm going to show that gentleman from Texas how a long-haired Scotsman can come over here with a nervous, high-strung, delicate car and beat the brawn of America. They're going to cry when I take away all their money."[38]

At the request of the Agapious, Stewart drove Foyt's car while A.J. was in Phoenix and he took the opportunity to tweak him further.

"They asked me to give it a few laps. I've got some road racing experience. Foyt had been able to get only ten laps on the car and they didn't have any idea of what gears to use. I helped them set up the camber and the gears. I was very impressed with it."[39]

It was apparent from the opening of practice that the F1 cars were faster. Foyt, Andretti, Donohue, the Unsers, and Savage chartered helicopters and a Learjet for the trip from Phoenix but still arrived too late for the first round of qualifying, not that it mattered. Stewart captured the pole, with F1 cars taking the first six places and eight of the first ten. Foyt qualified ten seconds behind Stewart, thirtieth in the thirty-three-car field and started last when the last three withdrew.

The battle between American and European drivers never materialized, although Andretti in the Ferrari came from twelfth to beat Stewart, giving the Americans a partial victory. The highest-finishing Formula A car was seventh. Foyt was out after ten laps with engine problems, although at least one report lists his failure to finish as "Gave up, deliberately blew engine."[40]

Andretti was quick to point out the race was not a fair comparison.

"They had no chance at all," he said of the Formula A machines. "But you put guys like Foyt and the Unsers in good Formula One cars and they'll be right up there. Let's face it. The Formula One cars are faster, lighter, more agile, and have the right power-to-weight ratio. The 'A' car is only a trainer, it doesn't belong in a big meet like this."[41]

It was one and done for the Questor Grand Prix. "The greatest race ever held across the pond" was never held again.

CHAPTER 31

A.J. FOYT VS. TIME INC.

1971

Next on the schedule was the NASCAR Atlanta 500, and with regulations varying for different size engines, the Wood Brothers elected to run a smaller powerplant than most of the other Ford teams despite the high-speed nature of the track.

Before running any fast laps, Leonard Wood asked his driver to run a couple of slow circuits so he could make sure everything was right with the new engine. When the team returned to the garage after the warm-up, a buzz went through the area. Foyt was several seconds off the pace.

"Well there's one time the great A.J. Foyt and the Wood Brothers have gone and over-engineered themselves," said Harry Hyde, one of NASCAR's oldest and best crew chiefs and a longtime Chrysler campaigner.[1] His driver, Bobby Isaac, had finished second to Foyt in qualifying for the two previous races. Hyde was also one of the gruffest characters in NASCAR, and years later served as the model for the crew chief played by Robert Duvall in the movie *Days of Thunder*. He'd been calling the smaller Ford motor a "lawnmower engine."

"He had beautiful race cars," Foyt said of Hyde. "He said, 'You're not going very fast here, are you? That lawnmower motor won't get the job done here.'"[2]

Foyt went to find Leonard Wood. He wanted to prove a point.

"You get me one second and I'll get the other," A.J. said. Good to his word, Foyt put the Mercury on the pole, edging Hyde's car for the third straight race.

"I saw Harry and said, 'That goddamn lawnmower ran pretty good.'"

After the pole run Foyt was relaxed and downright chatty with reporters.

"I've had a lot of people ask me why I race, why I go through nearly a full schedule of racing when I don't have to. I tell them that I love racing and a person

◀ Foyt had a special relationship with NASCAR's Bill France Sr.
Associated Press Photo Archive

has got to have something to do. I like to keep busy. I'd get restless if I had to sit around and do nothing. When I don't feel comfortable racing, I'll quit. It's as simple as that.

"Many of my friends—Fireball Roberts, Joe Weatherly, Eddie Sachs, Jimmy Bryan and others—have been killed racing. I don't mind saying that the loss of some of my friends hurt a lot and so now I make it a policy not to get too close to the drivers. It's not that I'm unfriendly; it's just that I don't want any close ties in this business."[3]

He certainly made an impression on Al Thomy of the *Atlanta Constitution*. "For a guy said to be temperamental and bombastic, he was in a genial mood. For a guy said to be a loner, he did not resent the company. For a guy said to be a millionaire, or more, he was down to earth."[4]

Foyt even agreed to join other drivers for a reception at the Georgia governor's mansion, the type of event he normally avoided at all costs. He and Petty talked with the recently elected Jimmy Carter, who said, "You two have been my heroes for more than ten years."[5]

The mood didn't last and Carter may have thought differently if he'd been a *Sports Illustrated* reader.

As practice continued Friday and Saturday, a different buzz began working its way through the Atlanta garage area. The new *SI* edition, delivered to subscribers and available on newsstands Thursday afternoon, carried a statement Foyt supposedly made after winning the Ontario stock car race and before the Questor Grand Prix that was generating more than a little conversation. Foyt was quoted as boasting, "Now that I've taken care of these hillbillies, I'm looking forward to beating those long-haired European fags."[6]

The quote was in an article recapping the Questor race. A reporter showed it to Foyt, who reacted about as expected. He was furious.

"I never said that," A.J. claimed. "And if they don't print a retraction, I'm going to sue them. They're a bunch of liars. I've never said anything like that. I enjoy racing against the NASCAR guys and have always felt great when I've beaten them. It's something special to me when I come down South and beat these guys.

"I know there's a lot of them who won't read the story in the magazine. But I feel I have to apologize because I didn't say those things. I've never used the word *hillbilly* in my life. If I ever considered the Grand National drivers hillbillies, I certainly wouldn't have one of them driving a car for me at Indianapolis," he said in a reference to Allison.[7]

He also claimed never to have used the word *fag*. "I'd just come right out and call 'em queer," he said. It wasn't politically correct in 1971, but it was A.J.'s attempt to show the magazine had misquoted him.[8]

Others weren't so sure. Jackie Stewart, on his way to a second Formula One World Championship asked sarcastically, "Can you imagine A.J. saying a thing like that?"[9]

Sports Illustrated responded to Foyt's outburst by saying it was standing by the writer, Gwilym Brown, a Harvard grad and respected veteran associate editor. By race day Foyt was so fired up he asked to address the drivers' meeting.

Problems between Bignotti (left) and Foyt were already apparent at Indianapolis in 1965. *The Henry Ford, David Friedman Collection*

An unhappy Foyt watches the action at Langhorne in 1965. Before the weekend was out he would split with crew chief George Bignotti. *Revs Institute, Tom Burnside Photograph Collection*

After being forced to qualify his dirt track car when his primary rear-engine machine failed to arrive, Foyt captured the pole and led the field down to the green flag at Milwaukee, August 22, 1965. He'd finish second behind Gordon Johncock. *Revs Institute, The Bruce R. Craig Photograph Collection, photograph by C.V. Haschel*

Leading Mario Andretti in the Hoosier Hundred. Andretti won the race, but Foyt won more money. *IMS Photography Archive*

Foyt enjoying himself in the Bahamas in 1965. *The Henry Ford, David Friedman Collection*

Dan Gurney pushed Foyt to victory in a 1965 Volkswagen race held during the Bahamas Speed Week. *The Henry Ford, David Friedman Collection*

Dirt track helmet and goggles. *Bernie Thrasher Collection, A.J. Foyt Racing Website*

In 1967, A.J. makes a point to Parnelli Jones (right)—no doubt about the turbine—as Lloyd Ruby (left), Mario Andretti (middle), and Norm Hall look on. *The Henry Ford, David Friedman Collection*

An early 1967 practice session at the Speedway. The front-lip spoiler has yet to be added to the Coyote. *The Henry Ford, David Friedman Collection*

Foyt and the Coyote were no match for Jones and the turbine, but they had everyone else covered. *The Enthusiast Network*

In Victory Lane for number three with his mother, Evelyn, and Lucy. *Associated Press Photo Archive*

The triumphant trio: Dan Gurney, Phil Remington, and Foyt during a Daytona test session. *The Henry Ford, David Friedman Collection*

At Le Mans's Mulsanne Corner in 1967. Leading European journalist Denis Jenkinson wrote in his notebook: "Foyt doesn't make mistakes." *The Henry Ford, David Friedman Collection*

Gurney and Foyt and their "we did it" grins. *The Henry Ford, David Friedman Collection*

The Le Mans celebration winds down. *The Henry Ford, David Friedman Collection*

Father and son ready for qualifying at Indianapolis in 1968. *The Henry Ford, David Friedman Collection*

Signing autographs for a Boy Scout troop at Indianapolis in 1968. *The Henry Ford, David Friedman Collection*

A.J. and George Snider seem happy during a 1973 practice session. Foyt would take over for Snider when Swede Savage's accident stopped the race and George said he didn't want to continue. *Steve H. Shunck Collection*

At a 1974 driver's meeting, pole sitter Foyt and defending champion Gordon Johncock share a laugh. Behind Foyt is Wally Dallenbach and Mike Hiss; Mario Andretti and Mike Mosley are behind Johncock. *Steve H. Shunck Collection*

On his way to victory in the 1970 Astro Grand Prix midget race in the Houston Astrodome. *Photograph by Ed Justice Jr.*

Donnie Allison checks with Foyt during practice at the Speedway in 1971. *IMS Photography Archive*

No one could run with Foyt and the Wood Brothers' Mercury in the 1972 Daytona 500. *ISC Archives*

The debut of the Bob Riley–designed 1973 Coyote/Foyt. Note the high-mounted radiators toward the rear of the car. Riley would leave the team at the end of the year. A.J. continued to develop the design, and when he moved the radiators forward "the car came alive" according to Riley. *Revs Institute, The Bruce R. Craig Photograph Collection, photograph by Jack Fox*

Foyt in 1977. *Steve H. Shunck Collection*

Foyt's final pit stop in 1977. Evel Knievel (above the word *TEAM*) urges him on.
Steve H. Shunck Collection

Foyt was greeted on Pit Lane after his fourth win by crew members and other drivers. *Steve H. Shunck Collection*

Gordon Johncock waves his congratulations. *Bettmann Collection*

The Ride. *Steve H. Shunck Collection*

"I just want you to know it's a damned lie," he started, telling the drivers much of what he'd already told the media. "I have never used the word *hillbillies* in my life and I don't even know what it means. I've had some guys checking into the situation and I understand the guy who wrote the story wasn't even at the race. Somebody at that outfit is going to apologize to me or there will either be legal action or fist city.

"I just want you to know that I respect every one of you drivers and I think you are the greatest stock car drivers in the world. I consider it a great honor to come down here and run against you men. And I think every one of you understand me well enough to know that if I have something to say about you, I would say it to your face."[10]

After facing his competitors in the drivers' meeting, Foyt went out and thoroughly destroyed them on the track, although at times it wasn't easy. He led the first forty-eight laps before cutting a tire and being forced to the pits, dropping a lap behind in the process. Thanks to quick work by the Wood Brothers during later pit stops, he was able to get back on the lead lap and beat Petty at the end for the victory. A spin by Sterling Marlin in Turn Four as Foyt came to the checkered flag made things interesting. At Daytona he'd lifted during the qualifying race. He didn't make the same mistake twice.

"I didn't slow down very much because I thought I saw the cars spin out of the groove. Anyway, I figured I could work my way through the situation as well as anyone else, and I saw other cars getting through."[11]

Petty was impressed.

"It's been a long time since I have seen anyone outrun everyone like that. He could outrun me by three car lengths down the straightaways and these straightaways are only a quarter of a mile. That shows how strong he was."[12]

"Like I've always said, anytime you can run with these boys and get lucky enough to beat 'em, you've done something," Foyt said. "You've beaten the best in the world. They are gentlemen and they race you wheel-to-wheel just as hard as you want to run. They're true racers."[13]

If Foyt's magazine article or drivers' meeting speech were an issue with his fellow competitors at the time, no one seems to remember it. Years later not one person—not Leonard Wood, Donnie Allison, Yarborough, or Petty—remembered the incident. Even Stewart said he had no recollection of the hubbub, although Foyt certainly did.[14]

A.J. FOYT VS. TIME INC.

When no apology or retraction came from *Sports Illustrated* by mid-August, Foyt followed through on his threat and filed a $500,000 libel lawsuit in Houston federal court against *SI*'s parent company, Time Inc., charging the magazine attributed false statements to him. The lawsuit claimed the article defamed and endangered him as the story caused "animosity which could carry over to the race track and cause physical harm to come to the plaintiff."[15]

When there was no movement by the publishing house after a year, his lawyers raised the ante to $1 million dollars.

"They basically said, 'We're Time Life, just do whatever you think you're big enough to do,'" Foyt recalled. "I said, 'Okay, you sons of bitches, I'll see you in court.' All I asked them to do was retract that statement. They said they weren't gonna retract nothing. You do what you want. They were very rude to me. Everybody knew I didn't talk like that. I might have said something, but them weren't even close to my words."[16]

The case finally went to trial in June of 1973 and Foyt's lawyer, Houston attorney Larry Bass, argued the term *hillbillies* could cause Southern race drivers to want to fight.[17]

Time initially defended the story, saying it believed the quote to be accurate. Brown testified that Stewart, who'd mocked Foyt when the reports first appeared in print, was the unnamed source of the quote. Brown said Stewart, who'd been at the stock car race as a commentator for ABC Sports, told him of the winner's comments. Brown said he confirmed the quote with Monty Roberts, an executive at Ontario. A fact checker for the magazine testified she verified the quote with Roberts.

In a deposition provided to the court, however, Stewart said he didn't hear Foyt make the statement, rather someone recited it to him and he'd simply mentioned it to Brown. Roberts then said he didn't actually hear Foyt make the remark.[18]

Chris Economaki of National Speed Sport News testified that Southern drivers would find being called hillbillies offensive, adding the statement was out of character for Foyt.[19]

It took two years, but a federal jury eventually found in Foyt's favor, although he was awarded only $75,000.

Foyt wasn't surprised to learn Stewart was the source of the quote. As a rookie at the Speedway, Stewart had taken shots at Foyt and A.J. never forgot it. An uneasy truce existed between the two while Stewart was a commentator for the 500 and other races on ABC Sports, a role he took on beginning in 1971. At times he said Stewart was "just as good" a driver as Jimmy Clark and, "They're as good as any drivers I've ever ran against," as he did in his autobiography.[20]

Fifty years after the court case, however, Foyt didn't try to hide how he felt about Stewart.

"I never cared for him when he first came over. I didn't like him and I think he knew that. He was a big jackass, as far as I was concerned. He still is. I didn't think he was much of a race driver. He almost backed into it [winning the 500 in 1966]. He wasn't outrunning nobody.

"He just thought he was above everybody. He wasn't close to Jimmy Clark, as a gentleman or a race driver. Jimmy Clark was a super man. Jackie Stewart was just full of bullshit."[21]

After the Atlanta victory, Foyt decided to skip the next Indy car race at Trenton to focus on finishing his new cars.

He also took the opportunity to get into the car business, completing the purchase of MacRobert Chevrolet in Houston. It was one of the largest Chevy dealers in the state, but struggling to make a profit. Foyt's budding business empire was up to eleven companies. As if there weren't enough on his plate, he was also overseeing construction of a new six-bedroom family home on Sandringham Drive in the upscale Memorial section of Houston, one of the toniest neighborhoods in the city.[22]

"It was a good chance for me," he said of the dealership purchase, adding in typical Foyt fashion, "Our customers are going to get service or I'll fire people until they do. When someone gets his car fixed, he's going to get it fixed and not just a bill. I decided to build my reputation that way."[23]

More than a few noted that Foyt now owned a Chevrolet dealership while building Ford's Indy engines. "Only A.J. could get by with it," wrote *Indianapolis News* sports editor Wayne Fuson. "And only A.J. would try."[24]

COYOTE II

The new Coyote was unveiled April 28 in Houston, a day before the team departed for Indianapolis. Two of the new cars were built and entered in the 500, along with Foyt's cars from 1969 and 1970. Allison was named the team's second driver for Indy.

To emphasize the difference from previous generations, Foyt initially called the new car Coyote II, although the II was soon dropped. While many of the suspension mounting points remained the same, only the Poppy Red color, now commonly called Foyt Orange, remained of the car's appearance.

Designer Bob Riley had started with one absolute: the car must carry a full allotment of fuel, seventy-five gallons. The driver/owner also wanted a four-speed transmission and better brakes.

With a better understanding of aerodynamics than most, Riley said he went "bat shit over [reducing] the frontal area" and strived to narrow the cockpit. He incorporated all the aspects Foyt wanted and brought the car in seven inches narrower and about two hundred pounds lighter than the 1970 Coyote. Other changes included a fifteen-degree recline in the driver's position, and less chassis offset.[25]

He'd been horrified, however, when Foyt first struggled into the slim cockpit prior to the unveiling. The gearshift lever was located on the right side of the cockpit as normal, but the fit was so tight A.J. couldn't draw his right arm back far enough to change gears.

"I guess I turned white," Riley recalled, "because he looked up and said, 'Don't worry about it, Bob, I'll just shift with my left hand.'" Riley would go on to a become a very successful race car designer and builder with a career spanning fifty years and often told the story to drivers who wanted their gearshift lever moved a quarter inch forward or back.

Ron Fournier and Eddie Kuzma did most of the work on the car. The smooth and beautifully rounded lines of the Lotus-turned-Coyote were replaced by a wedge-shaped design with straight and jagged edges. At the back of the car were small "winglets" on each side of the engine. Big rear wings were the rage in F1, but they'd been outlawed by USAC after 1969 and Riley counted on the wedge-shape design to help keep the car planted on the ground.

"The fabricators were so talented," Riley said. "A.J. wanted a car he would be proud of and he took more time with the detail work, to make everything very nice. It's just unbelievable all the beautiful work those guys did. They even made their own radiators and they were usually brass, because brass cooled a little better."[26]

One writer said the car was "unlike anything Foyt has driven before. Two giant wedges. Flat on top, flat on the sides and flat on the bottom."[27]

Riley wasn't in attendance for the unveiling, having returned to work at Ford. And while race car designers were becoming increasingly recognized for their work, his name wasn't mentioned. Instead, Foyt said the new car represented "all the things I've learned, put into one package."[28]

He said he'd spent about $75,000 to build the car and that development was continuing on the turbocharged Ford engine, with the engine putting out 800 horsepower, 125 more than the previous powerplant.

"This car should be ten miles an hour faster than last year's down the straight," he said. "I should be able to do 240. If it's not fast enough, I'll have it torn down and rebuilt."[29]

Despite the unveiling, there was still work to do on the new Coyote, and it wasn't until May 5 that the car made its first tentative laps around the Indianapolis Motor Speedway. Foyt gradually built speed in the car, and Riley, who'd taken vacation time to spend a few days at the track with the team, was impressed watching him work.

"He was so damn good sorting out a car," Riley said. "He had just fantastic feel. I was used to working with not a very high level of driver [in Super Vee and Formula Ford]. You'd tell the driver to watch for understeer and then they'd go out and run right off the track. Wham! They'd come back and say, 'It understeered!'

"The first few days with Foyt and the new car I'd say something like 'It'll probably be a little loose.' The mechanics would look at me and giggle."[30]

Foyt typically ran one slow lap, followed by several faster laps, running the car hard in one or two corners but seldom putting together a full lap. After returning to the pit, he'd walk back to the garage to debrief, not wanting others to overhear.

"He'd talk this, that, and the other with the crew, and then we would sit down in the back of the garage. He was a very fast thinker. He would say, 'We should go to this spring,' and I'd have to think about it a little while and say, 'Yep, that's right.' I was always a few steps behind. Maybe I was a little more of a deep thinker. He mostly knew what to do and we were just bouncing things off one another. I enjoyed working with him. He was so talented."

Foyt often made the changes himself, impressing Riley with his skill and speed around the car nearly as much as he did in it.

"He used to work very fast with a speed wrench. Some of the crew would just stand back and watch him, he worked so fast. If you had a problem, you had to fix it that day or that night."

After several days of practice, Foyt topped out at 168 miles per hour. A day later Riley said he was out of vacation time and had to go back to his job at Ford. Foyt asked him to stay, there was more work to do.

"Let me call Henry and see if I can't get you a few more days," Riley remembered A.J. saying. "I called my boss and told him that and he said, 'Oh my god, don't let him call Henry Ford, take as much time as you want.'"[31]

Foyt's concern centered around another new car, a McLaren, especially the one owned by Roger Penske and driven by Mark Donohue.

The McLaren team had entered its first 500 in 1970 with modest results, starting work on a new car immediately afterward. The death of team founder Bruce McLaren, in a June 1970 Can-Am testing accident, threw the team into turmoil, although two of his disciples, Teddy Mayer and Tyler Alexander, were determined to carry on with entries in F1, Can-Am, and Indy-type racing.

That's where Penske and Donohue came in. They'd been running a McLaren on the Can-Am circuit and wanted the new Indy car to replace the Lola they'd raced at the Speedway the previous two years. Penske offered to take over development of the Indy car, agreeing to share everything he learned with the factory team.

Having already earned a reputation for meticulous and immaculate preparation, no one was surprised when the Penske team was the first on the track when it opened for practice. It was a beautiful car, "Sunoco Blue" (after the car's sponsor), with gold pinstriping. Much of the body work was done by Lujie Lesovsky, the master fabricator who'd been most responsible for transitioning the Lotus into a Coyote, and Foyt's 1967 race winner. He'd joined Penske in 1970.

Officially a McLaren M16A, the flat-sided, wedge-shaped design was not unlike the Coyote II or Dan Gurney's new Eagle. The most dramatic and controversial feature of the car was a large wing that stretched off the back of the machine and spread between the two rear tires. USAC had sought to regulate wings by requiring that an airfoil be integrated into the bodywork of a car, and no higher than the rest of the machine. Lesovsky had crafted a roughly foot-wide strip of aluminum that stretched from the rear of the cockpit, over the engine, and to the wing, calling it an engine cover. Penske claimed the wing was thus integrated into the bodywork and USAC officials reluctantly agreed.

The car was specifically designed by McLaren for the turbocharged four-cylinder Offenhauser engine, which was narrower, shorter, and about one hundred pounds lighter than the V8 Ford. With new development dollars and engineering support from Champion Spark Plugs—its primary competitor on the track and in the consumer marketplace was Ford-owned Autolite—the turbo Offy was proving more than competitive.

"We first ran the McLaren at Phoenix without the wings," Penske said. "We wanted to make sure everything was right mechanically. When we put the wings on the car it was just amazing."[32]

Amazing was the right word. After the first few days of practice, Donohue was running six mph faster than his closest competitors, the team McLaren cars driven by Peter Revson and Denis Hulme. After running his first laps at speed in the new Coyote, Foyt took Allison down to Turn One to watch Donohue in action.

"It's not difficult to see what he [Donohue] is doing," Foyt said after returning to his garage. "He's running through the turns faster and coming off across the short chutes faster. The whole car is in perfect balance. Mark's not carrying the car and the car is not carrying him."[33]

He'd liked Donohue since the first time they met during the Ford Le Mans program, although they couldn't have been much different. After attending college prep school on the East Coast, Donohue earned a degree in mechanical engineering from Brown University and the nickname "Captain Nice." He'd joined Penske in 1967 and won three Trans Am championships, a Can-Am title, and 1970 Indianapolis rookie of the year honors. Foyt and Donohue often shared the track at Indianapolis, Ontario, and Phoenix during Goodyear tire tests and A.J. appreciated the other driver's mechanical knowledge, attention to detail, desire to learn, and ultimately his driving skill. Foyt was effusive in his praise following Donohue's record laps and even stopped to tell the driver directly.

"Mark is doing a wonderful job," he said. "And he worked hard in testing for the things he has gained. Indianapolis is a very demanding track. You have to be exactly right."[34]

At first Foyt seemed unconcerned by the McLarens' speed, saying "We're gonna be all right, there's still plenty of time." But after a week of chasing Donohue and falling further behind—ten miles an hour behind—Foyt had enough. He tried a different nose on the car that didn't help and finally decided he wanted a wing too, and he wanted it now.

"You couldn't just go to the airfoil book and pick one out," Riley said of Foyt's demand. "During the day I designed an airfoil and Ron [Fournier] built it that night over at Steve Stapp's sprint car shop. I think it was 48 inches because that happened to be the size of the piece of metal they had. Tony [Foyt] painted it the next morning and we put it on the car."[35]

With Penske and Donohue off running a weekend Trans Am race in Lime Rock, Connecticut (Donohue won), Foyt debuted the now winged Coyote, which also featured a new nose and front winglets. When others complained the wing wasn't integrated into the bodywork, Foyt took a one-inch strip of scrap metal and stretched it from the rear of the cockpit to the wing. It certainly wasn't nearly as elegant as the McLaren's design, but as far as the USAC inspectors were concerned it met the letter of the law.

"I'm sure Roger thought they were going to get away with the unfair advantage," Riley said. "But when A.J. did that, they didn't know how to take the wing away. That was a very exciting time. I kind of miss the '70s at Indy."[36]

Foyt immediately began turning faster laps and within a few days gained a full six mph. Allison was struggling, however, as was Jim McElreath, who'd been added in a third car, the No. 14 he'd driven to victory at Ontario the previous year. Allison was driving the car Foyt had qualified third in 1970, but he was having trouble getting it up to speed. There was a second new Coyote in the garage, although Foyt wanted to keep it in reserve.

"I couldn't drive it," Allison said of the year-old car. "I mean it was *really* bad. He had the new car he was running and a second straight-sided car but he wouldn't let me drive it. He and I got in a helluva argument."[37]

Further complicating matters, Foyt had worked out a deal with his sponsor, Purolator, to put Allison in the Wood Brothers car for the major NASCAR races A.J. couldn't run. As a result, Allison was shuttling back and forth to Talladega,

Alabama, the week before qualifying at Indianapolis. He'd qualified the Woods' car on the pole for the Sunday race—the sixth straight for the car—and Allison needed to qualify for Indianapolis on Saturday or wait until the second weekend, which no one wanted to do. Foyt, however, was adamant about holding the second new car in reserve.[38]

Third in line to qualify, Foyt set one- and four-lap speed records of 174.656 and 174.317 mph, bettering his previous personal best by more than four mph and surprising Riley.

"I thought the whole month we were in trouble," he said. "One thing about A.J., he was the best sandbagger of any driver I've ever worked with. He would run three corners and not run the next corner. He would seldom put a whole lap together. He didn't want anyone to see how fast he was truly going. But when it came time to qualify, he put it all together."[39]

Foyt, Riley, and the other 250,000 people at the Speedway knew the marks wouldn't stand and five minutes later Donohue was the new record holder, another four mph faster than Foyt. Even that wasn't fast enough as Revson was the surprise pole winner, with one lap of more than 179 mph.

By the end of the day, Foyt was sixth and joined in the field by Allison and McElreath, although neither was happy. McElreath made it on his third and final qualifying attempt for the car, and both were six mph slower than Foyt. They were the two slowest qualifiers of the day, back in twenty-second and twenty-third positions, and both knew they were in jeopardy of being bumped from the field.

Immediately after returning from the Talladega 500, where he'd scored a dramatic car-length victory over brother Bobby, Allison started in on Foyt about getting the second new Coyote ready for him to qualify. The more Allison pushed, the more Foyt pushed back, as he continued to work on the race setup of his own car and suggested Allison do the same. At midweek, after setting a fast time with his race setup, A.J. told reporters the second Coyote II would stay in the garage, even if his other cars were bumped from the race.

It wasn't until Friday, May 21, the day before the final qualifying weekend, that Foyt took the No. 84 backup Coyote onto the track. He'd already been out in his primary car, running laps in race trim almost as fast as he'd qualified. He wasn't the only one running fast, and it was clear both McElreath and Allison would be bumped from the field. By Saturday morning things reached a boiling point between Foyt and Allison. Adding to the drama was a forecast for rain on Sunday, possibly wiping out the last day of qualifying.

"The new car was just sitting there in the pits," Allison recalled. "He and I got in an argument about my car. He kept saying, 'I ran that car such and such last year.'"[40]

Allison finally challenged Foyt to drive the older car and see if he could match his speed from a year ago.

"I moved everything back like he ran it, except the windshield, and he complained about it. I said I'll give you a mile an hour for that. So he turns to Jack [Starne] and says, 'Give me a half-inch wrench,' and he puts a turn of boost into the wastegate. He went and ran three laps and came in and looked up to me and just says, 'See.' Starne had the pit board and he said, 'You'd better see this, you didn't run within a mile an hour of what he ran.' So he jumped out of the car and said, 'Go ahead and take that new car for a ride.'"[41]

Despite a cockpit set up for the much larger Foyt, Allison ran three laps, the fastest at nearly 174 mph, before A.J. waved him in. He'd proven his point and Foyt sent the car back to the garage to be fitted for the smaller driver.

Late in the afternoon the car was rolled out and placed in the qualifying line, there being no time for practice laps. There was only one problem. Allison's first car hadn't been bumped yet.

"It's going to get bumped, no question," Allison said. "So they put me in the qualifying line and Foyt comes over. He says he's going to withdraw the other car, and I would qualify the new one. Mind you, I had run three laps in it."[42]

Withdrawing a non-bumped car, fairly common practice in later years, hadn't been done since 1946. Rules regulating the procedure were vague, and not everyone thought it was legal.

"Foyt goes up to the USAC stand and all I can see is arms flying and him and [Andy] Granatelli [who also owned a car trying to qualify] screaming and yelling at each other," Allison recalled. "He finally walked back and said he got that done."[43]

Foyt told Allison to run as hard as possible leaving the pits. Since time was short, the team would time him on the out lap and, if it wasn't fast enough, wave off the run, make a few changes, and put him back in line for one final attempt.

"If you ain't fast enough, I'm gonna throw the yellow flag," Allison remembers Foyt saying. "I said, 'A.J., you can stick that yellow flag up your butt because I'll be fast enough.'"

One of Foyt's crewmen, Cecil Taylor, rigged a stopwatch in the cockpit with crude pie-shaped brackets, to indicate 172, 173, and 174 mph, an effort to give Allison an idea of his speed on the out lap.

Coming down to the start/finish line, "I'm not in any of the brackets," he said. "But I've got a tachometer and I know I'm going way faster than I ran in practice. So I put my hand up [to start the run] on my own."

His opening lap was nearly 174 mph, faster than Foyt's first lap a week earlier, although his speed tailed off from there. He still qualified nearly four mph faster than he had the weekend before, fastest of all qualifiers on the day and holding on to his twenty-second starting position.

"When I came in, they didn't say congratulations or good job," Allison said. "A.J. said, 'Why the hell did you slow down so much that last lap?' That's just the way he was."

McElreath wasn't as fortunate. He'd been bumped, then reinstated when Allison's original car was withdrawn. He was bumped again and qualified a car for another team, only to be bumped once more, becoming the first driver bumped three times from one 500.

The media called Foyt's decision to withdraw the car a "masterful move" and Allison had nothing but praise for his car owner.

"I want to thank A.J. for putting up with me all month. He has to be the best guy in the world to give me his own car for another chance. I'll never forget it."[44]

Both cars ran well on Carb Day, and Allison was among the fastest before departing for Charlotte, where he qualified the Wood Brothers Mercury for the World 600. Foyt had hoped to drive the car himself in the race, to be run the day after the 500, but his request was turned down by USAC because it wasn't an FIA-sanctioned event. USAC reasoned if it opened the door for Foyt, it would be hard to close it on others.

Foyt also wanted the Wood Brothers to pit his car at Indianapolis, as they'd done for Jimmy Clark's win in 1965. Leonard Wood said they seriously considered the request but there'd been a full week between the races in 1965, not less than a day, and they eventually decided against it. Instead, A.J. brought in Smokey Yunick, a former Indy 500–winning crew chief, to oversee race day operations.[45]

"He's my ace in the hole," Foyt said. "With Smokey in the pits it's like money in the bank. He's a master strategist in planning races. We're going to use him in every stage of our planning from here on."[46]

While Foyt was considered a prerace favorite, second only to Donohue, he never challenged for the lead. Donohue had a two-car length lead before the start/finish line and disappeared, lapping all but the second-place car before the race was fifty laps old. Only a broken gearbox while working lap sixty-seven stopped him from one of the most dominating victories in 500 history.

From then on, it was Al Unser in control, with an occasional challenge from brother Bobby, teammate Joe Leonard, Lloyd Ruby, and Peter Revson. After Bobby Unser was taken out in a crash, and Ruby and Leonard suffered car failures, Al coasted home for his second consecutive 500 victory. Ironically, his Colt was one of the machines to race without a rear wing.

A faulty turbocharger, a problem Foyt says he noticed on the first lap, spoiled his race before it started, although he was able to run to the finish. He made five pit stops, two more than required, as Yunick and Tony Foyt tried to fix the problem without success. He was more than two laps behind when Unser took the checkered flag but, thanks to the high attrition rate, finished third. Only twelve cars were running at the finish, two of those more than fifty laps behind.[47]

Allison drove a steady, if unspectacular, race for sixth. He flew to Charlotte that night and finished second to brother Bobby the next day in the World 600, returning to Indianapolis to attend the 500 Victory Banquet.

It wasn't a bad weekend of work for the duo, as Foyt pocketed $65,000 at Indianapolis and Allison $45,000 for his two finishes.

Allison convinced Foyt to allow him to drive in more races, but both drivers dropped out early with engine problems the following week at Milwaukee. The engine situation was becoming a concern. Although Al Unser won his third straight race powered by Ford, it was different from the one being run by Foyt's team and built by Unser's own engine man.

Both Foyt and Allison planned a busy Fourth of July weekend, running the Pocono 500 for Indy cars on Saturday and NASCAR's Firecracker 400 on Sunday. Foyt had made a late decision to race in the Firecracker, and rather than bump

Allison, the defending race champion, from the Wood Brothers ride, he was entered in a second Holman-Moody car as a teammate to Bobby Allison.

The Pocono race was the first to be staged on the new triangle-shaped, 2.5-mile speedway and USAC allowed for two weeks of preparation and a special qualifying weekend, although the Foyt cars arrived late and missed the first few days of practice.

Despite the outward appearances, all was not well between Foyt and Allison. The more at home Allison felt in an Indy car, the more he wanted to set it up for his own style of driving, something Foyt wouldn't allow. Although both qualified relatively well for the short time they'd been at the new track—Foyt in eighth and Allison fifteenth—they continued to argue about car setup into the following week.

"I kept telling Foyt I wanted to change my car and he kept saying no," Allison recalled. "He'd do things to his car first and then do it to mine. He wouldn't let me do things to my car."[48]

A big issue were the rear springs being used on their cars. The Coyotes were originally designed to run with rear springs rated at about 350 pounds. When Foyt learned the McLarens were using 600-pound rear springs, he ordered both his cars fitted with 500-pound springs. Allison didn't like the way the car handled with the bigger springs in back.

"I can honestly tell you," he said fifty years later, "that when I drove down Pit Lane [with the bigger springs], I never felt like I was gonna drive back home. I felt like I was going to come back on the end of a wrecker.

"So we got in a hell of a bad argument about the cars. He kept saying I didn't know what I was doing, that I was just a taxi driver. I said it didn't make no difference if you were driving a cab or a limousine, if you get into a corner, it's got to turn."

At one point Allison said he was through, he wouldn't race the car and left the track, hitching a ride back to the resort where the team was staying. Unable to get a flight out that night, he booked one for the following morning and packed his bags. Foyt called twice that night trying to work things out but Allison was adamant. He was going home.

"Five o'clock the next morning he calls and asks me to come to the coffee shop," Allison recalled. "He said, 'I think we got too strong of springs in the back, let's go to the racetrack and we'll fix them.' I said, 'you'll let me change them?' and he said yup."

Foyt tried the lower-rated springs first and then told the crew to fit them to Allison's car. "I put them on and my first timed lap was six miles an hour faster than I qualified."

Donohue, who'd qualified on the pole, was unstoppable as he drove to victory, Penske Racing's first Indy car win. Foyt led nine laps and finished third. At the start Allison quickly worked his way forward, passing Johnny Rutherford and moving into the top ten in the first one hundred miles. Following a yellow flag for a blown engine, however, he made an admittedly rookie mistake.

"I went into turn one and they'd put oil dry down in the corner," he said. "I should have went wide and stayed up high, but I went in low, which was wrong. I spun and hit the wall."

Several times Allison tried to get out of his car, only to drop back into the cockpit as other cars approached at speed.

"After the race I'm in the garage and the entire entourage was there. Foyt's normal procedure was to belittle you. He said 'Allison, what the hell were you doing, you looked like a turtle with your head popping up and down out of the car.' I said I was trying to keep those crazy son of a guns from running over me.

"Then he asked what the heck I did. I just said I f-ed up. I didn't make no excuse. And when I said that it really made him mad, because he couldn't say nothing else.

"That's just the way we were."

Afterward, the pair flew together to Daytona. Foyt qualified tenth but wasn't happy with his car. It was the one Mario Andretti drove to victory in the 1967 Daytona 500, having been reworked several times since. He never did get it to his liking and ran just thirty laps before stopping, one media outlet listing his reason for dropping out as "quit." Allison also struggled at times on his way to a fifth-place finish.

The USAC victory drought continued through the summer. It had been nearly two years since Foyt's last Indy car triumph, on dirt in the 1969 Hoosier Hundred, and nearly three years since his last victory on a paved oval. Despite the streak he was still in the running for his sixth national championship and became defensive when asked what was wrong. Much had been made of him passing the $3 million mark in career earnings and some wondered if he was still hungry.

"Money hasn't affected my driving at all. I run just as hard for a dollar as I would for a million dollars," he said. "There's only one objective in anything you do—that's to win. If you're not a winner, who cares about you. With me, each race is a new race and I try not to remember the wins. I don't have to prove anything to anybody."[49]

It wasn't until August 19 when he drove Jack Bowsher's Ford to victory at Milwaukee that he broke into the win column again, although it had more to do with gas mileage than speed. There was no doubt three days later, however, when he made his first start in the new Dirt Track Championship series (eventually called the Silver Crown Series) at the Illinois State Fairgrounds.

Qualifying tenth, he took the lead on the twentieth of one hundred laps around the mile-long oval. He pitted for a new tire at the halfway mark, returning to the track seventeenth and last of the cars still running. From there it was vintage Foyt as he knifed through the field, passing leader George Snider with eight laps remaining.

Despite the triumph, the pressure of the season, especially of overseeing the Ford engine program, was taking its toll. Making matters worse, the points-leading team of Parnelli Jones and Al Unser announced it was switching to an Offenhauser engine for the next race at Ontario. Jones was still bitter about Ford's decision to give its spare Indy engine parts to Foyt.

"We're going out there to win, that's why we changed," Jones said. "We didn't want to go and just stroke it. Sure, we could have finished and probably pretty high with the Ford, but we want more than that. We were getting outrun, and we didn't like it.

"I hated to part with Ford. We had been loyal to them for a long time. So I went to A.J. and asked him if he planned to make any major changes to combat the improved Offys. When he said he didn't, I went to Ford Motor Co. and asked them. They said, 'We're not in racing.' So I suggested they loan us some money so we could develop our own engines. They didn't like that idea either.

"Now I've got two Offy engines and twelve Ford engines—and all twelve are for sale. The engines will run forever, so they'll be popular with a lot of fellows who will keep them in their cars and fill up the fields and run in the back of the pack. It'll be embarrassing to us Ford dealers."[50]

Although Offy-powered cars swept the first seven qualifying spots, it was Jones's other car, driven by Joe Leonard and still using a Ford engine, that won the race as the Offys broke and Fords took four of the five top spots. Leonard took the points lead in the process. Foyt led seven laps before experiencing rear-end problems and dropping out, while Allison dropped out early with another engine failure.

Despite Leonard's win and Unser's problems, Jones didn't let up after the race, saying, "Anybody who'd run a Ford next year is an idiot."[51]

Foyt did make one announcement, saying he would run a single car in the coming year.

"I'm going to concentrate next year just on me," he said. "I built these new cars but I haven't had a chance to test them and I'm just cheating myself."[52]

That meant Allison, whom Foyt earlier in the year called "a helluva a race driver" and "probably one of the best up-and-coming drivers there is," was without an Indy car ride. He'd get other offers, but Ontario would be Allison's last race in an Indy car.[53]

"I got phone calls from several people who wanted me to drive their cars," Allison remembered five decades later. Crew chief Wally Meskowski also tried to line him up with a ride. "But I didn't feel like any of them were better than A.J.'s cars, so I wouldn't do it."[54]

Older brother Bobby would be outspoken in his belief that Donnie wasn't brought back because he'd outperformed Foyt on the racetrack.

"Donnie idolized A.J.," Bobby said. "At least that's the way I saw it. He thought everything about him was great. A.J. was a good driver and a good mechanic, and a promoter's dream. He bragged a lot, but he backed it up.

"Anyway, my version of the deal is he gave Donnie a worse car [at Indy in '71] because Donnie had done better than A.J. and you don't do better than A.J. I felt like Donnie got short-changed. That's my opinion. A.J. didn't want him around because how can this little kid from Alabama take A.J.'s car and do better than A.J.?"[55]

One person who didn't buy into the theory was Donnie Allison.

"I don't feel like I didn't run the car after that because maybe A.J. didn't want to share the spotlight," he said. "I think I probably talked myself out of a ride.

"To this day I have the utmost respect for that man. I thought he was probably the best race car driver at the time. I know some say Andretti was the best. I don't feel like that. Andretti was a good race car driver, but I don't think he was a better driver than A.J., or my brother Bobby. Andretti is a tremendously good race car driver, but he's not as good as Foyt. That's *my* opinion.

"I don't think A.J. ever went to a race in his life he didn't think he was going to win, no matter how he was being outdone. He let you know that. He was always very, very, *very* confident in his own ability. I think good race car drivers have to be that way. He could do about anything he decided to do, and you never doubted him, he'd show you he could do it.

"I know he's an ornery old SOB. He's also the smartest, or one the smartest, people I've ever been around a race car with, and he's an all-around good guy. Believe me, it was a treat driving for him.

"You just have to overlook the little tantrums he has sometimes."[56]

Allison and Foyt continued their friendship and even shared stock cars again in the future when both drove for Banjo Matthews and Hoss Ellington. Allison would win ten races in the Winston Cup series and numerous short track races before retiring in 1988.

Foyt called Allison "underrated" and said "Donnie is one of the best stock-car drivers around. He was a lot better driver than people give him credit for. I took him to Indianapolis with me because I felt he was one of the very few NASCAR drivers who could adapt to Indy cars."[57]

———

After Ontario, Foyt moved to head off the revolt against his Ford engine program, saying there was a more powerful engine under development with a new turbocharger and fuel system.

"I'll sell them if somebody wants one, but I'm not going to push them," he said.[58]

Despite pledging his allegiance to the Ford Indy engine, Foyt broke with the company in stock cars after Bowsher said he could no longer afford to run two cars. He signed to drive a Plymouth Road Runner in USAC and a Chevrolet Monte Carlo in NASCAR. After Ford's withdrawal, NASCAR had been courting General Motors, and the Chevrolet Division was making its first tentative steps to return to the sport, providing technical support to the entries of Junior Johnson and Banjo Matthews that were otherwise considered "independents."

At Charlotte for the October 10 race, he had to sit and watch for two days while the Matthews crew finished the car. It was worth the wait as he set a qualifying record, although he'd have to start twenty-third. He also lost $100 to Donnie Allison when he was unable to run flat out without lifting off the accelerator.

Making his first NASCAR start in a Chevrolet since 1963, Foyt passed sixteen cars on the first lap. The handling soon deteriorated and after a number of pit stops, he eventually dropped out.

The performance was strong enough for Foyt to sign on to run the car two weeks later at Rockingham, which meant he'd spend another week flying between racetracks as the last Indy car race of the year was being run at Phoenix on Saturday.

He was among the fastest in practice for both races, but when qualifying at the Rock was rained out he left for Phoenix, where he qualified a surprising third.

The race was even more surprising as he quickly moved to the front and led 107 of 150 laps for the victory and enough points to finish second behind Leonard in the national championship. He said he'd been using the new engine and that the Ford "still has a lot of potential left."[59]

The season over, Foyt took the opportunity to review the year, saying it was a disappointment despite the early- and late-season wins, second place in the Indy car championship, and earning nearly $300,000.

"It has not been the kind of year A.J. Foyt is used to," he said. "I've spent too much time with my businesses and haven't concentrated on my racing. I've made up my mind to say the heck with everything but racing in 1972. I'm building some super cars for Indianapolis, which I should have won this year."[60]

He admitted buying the Chevrolet dealership while taking on the Ford engine program was more work than expected. He said the dealership's profit/loss reports didn't add up, noting, "I had to make a few changes."[61]

He faced the inevitable questions about retirement.

"I guess I'm a fool to keep driving," he said. "But it's a challenge. I'm like an alcoholic. I'm hooked on racing and I love it, even though one day you're a hero and the next day a chump. I dread the day when I have to quit. I really don't know how I'll accept it."[62]

CHAPTER 32

DAYTONA TO DU QUOIN

1972

Despite the promise the new Chevrolet Monte Carlo showed at the end of 1971, A.J. Foyt elected to reunite with the Wood Brothers to start the new season, beginning with the first race of the year in their Mercury at Riverside.

They picked up right where they left off, with the No. 21 car on the pole, although Bobby Allison, now behind the wheel of Junior Johnson's potent Chevy, broke the track record on the second day of qualifying. It was Foyt's first trip back to the track since winning the 1970 race.

"After I won, I said I'd never come back," he said. "It was a last-minute decision, and the crew had to work some long hours to get the car ready. This place is one of my favorite road courses, and I enjoy road racing, but I've had an awful lot of bad luck at this track."[1]

He led from the start and cruised while Allison quickly worked his way through the field. Allison caught and passed Foyt on lap five and from then on the two traded the lead six times, Foyt bumping Allison out of the lead in the esses at one point, a favor soon returned. The pace eventually knocked Foyt out with a busted transmission after 107 of 149 laps, and slowed Allison enough to allow Richard Petty to get past for the victory.

"I saw Allison and Foyt rippin' at each other up ahead, so I decided I'd stay behind a bit and watch what was going on," Petty said. "I didn't figure there was any reason for me to get with them and knock out three cars. I figured I'd wait and see, and sure enough something happened to both of them."[2]

Next up was the Daytona 500, a race the Woods and Foyt felt they should have won the year before, and a race Foyt still thought he *did* win. He was grouchy from

◀ With the Wood Brothers, Glen (standing) and Leonard (right, seated).
Photograph by Ed Justice Jr.

the start, complaining about the new Mercury body style the Woods were running, saying it "looks about two miles an hour slower on a super track like Daytona."[3]

Not buying Foyt's comments was Lee Petty, winner of the first Daytona 500 and head of his son's team. "He'll outright lie to you," Lee said. "Nobody never knows how fast A.J. can go until it's nip and tuck in a race. Then you know he's faster."[4]

Both seemed to have a point in qualifying as Foyt was second by nearly two miles an hour to Bobby Isaac, who'd played second fiddle in 1971 when it came to pole runs. He'd won major Cup races, NASCAR's national title in 1970, and had set more than twenty national speed records at the Bonneville Salt Flats, but said beating Foyt for the pole was his biggest racing thrill to date.

"You figure Foyt never goes for second place," he said. "So when you beat him in a speed dash, you figure you have beaten the best there is."[5]

Foyt jokingly blamed himself, saying, "I shouldn't have told him about the dream."[6]

"Foyt told me just before I went out [to qualify] that he had dreamed last night I would beat him out for the pole," Isaac explained. "So I took him at his word. Anybody who can dream that way and have it come true could make a pile of money. He doesn't need to race for a living."[7]

Struggling in qualifying was Mark Donohue, who was making his first Daytona stock car start in a new American Motors Matador from Penske Racing. The car was built by Holman-Moody with Dick Hutcherson serving as crew chief, but Donohue was more than thirteen miles per hour slower than Isaac in qualifying. He needed to finish high enough in his qualifying race to secure a place in the field, no easy feat with fifty-nine cars entered for forty spots. As a favor to all, Foyt took him out on the track and tried to work with him on drafting, but the boxy Matador had trouble keeping up. Donohue also said he was having trouble being accepted by the NASCAR regulars, a problem Foyt didn't have.[8]

"We all get along pretty well," Foyt said of his relationship with the taxicab drivers. "The past couple of years I feel like I'm one of them. I look at it this way—several of them have taken some money from USAC racing. So I'm merely squaring things up.

"Guys like Petty and Allison are great drivers and they like to face the best. Now, I'm not pumping up my own ability, but I know they like it even better when I'm here and they beat me. It makes them feel they've earned it."[9]

Isaac won the first qualifying race in an event marred by a twelve-car crash that took the life of Raymond "Friday" Hassler. Bobby Allison won the second qualifier over Foyt as A.J. had handling problems and hung back to help pull Donohue along in the draft. Donohue eventually finished fifth, qualifying for the 500.

After the races everyone wanted to talk about Hassler, whom Foyt barely knew. He was popular among NASCAR drivers and a close friend of the Allison brothers, who'd traveled the Southern short tracks with him. He was also the father of four sons.

"It broke my heart," said Bobby Allison, who was asked to tell Hassler's wife her husband was dead before starting the second qualifier. "I thought about

Friday every lap. You've got to realize there's danger in what you do, but it's never easy to accept."[10]

"He told me it was the hardest thing he's ever had to do," said Foyt, who was sharing media interviews with Allison. "It's something you have to live with. Some guys can, some can't. Some break out in a sweat and never drive again. But I realize that what happens, happens, and you can't do anything about it."[11]

"The way I look at it, the way I have to look at it, is that the Lord put us here and when he is ready for us to go, he will take us away," Foyt said, repeating a refrain he used often over the years. "That's what I call a square deal. You can't ask for anything more than that.

"You have to put it out of your mind completely. We all know what happened to Friday and we all care. But we can't dwell on it. I really don't believe racing is any different from anything else when it comes to that. We take risks, sure. But it can happen on the highway just as quickly."[12]

Foyt took the lead on the opening lap of the 500, with Bobby Allison coming up to challenge. The No. 21 Mercury was loose in the qualifying race—the rear end of the car moving around in the turns—and Allison moved close to the rear bumper of Foyt's car, trying to aggravate the problem.

Allison wouldn't make public his thoughts on brother Donnie's time with the Foyt Indy program until years later, but he and A.J. were never friendly. Like Foyt, he thought he was the best driver, knew best how to set up a car, and had a chip on his shoulder every bit as big as A.J.'s. It wasn't just Foyt; he'd had run-ins with Cale Yarborough, Petty, and most of the team owners he'd driven for.

"They're more acquaintances than friends," Donnie said of his brother's relationship with Foyt. "They were too much alike."[13]

Foyt slowed and Bobby Allison went past. This was the Daytona 500, however, not a qualifying race, and Leonard Wood saw a different response from his driver.

"A.J. was very much one of those people who could take care of himself, on and off the track," Wood said. "Bobby got behind him and was making his back end wiggle. So he backed off, let Bobby pass him, then ran right up behind him and gave Bobby the same medicine. A.J. then dropped down and went by. Bobby didn't bother him again."[14]

Allison's lead lasted two laps before he began to fade back in the field, his car later running on seven cylinders. Petty, having to start thirty-second because of trouble in his qualifying race, appeared to have the only car capable of challenging Foyt and charged through the pack to take the lead on lap twenty-one. They traded the front spot ten times over the next sixty laps before Petty slowed with a blown engine, out before the halfway mark, as were most of the other expected contenders.

There was only one more tight moment, on lap one hundred; Foyt was coming up to lap Jim Hurtubise when the engine blew in Herk's car.

"That one really could have been bad," Foyt said. "I was coming up fast on Jim and when the engine blew and the next thing I know, bloop, my whole windshield was covered in oil. The only daylight I had was a tiny little hole down near the bottom of the windshield. I didn't think I was going to make it back around to the pits."[15]

The race itself was never close after that as Foyt led 167 of the 200 laps. Near the end he was two laps ahead of the second-place car, and at least five laps ahead of everyone else.

"Most of the spectators would have to nominate this 500 for the most monotonous award in the history of NASCAR," wrote one reporter. To keep things interesting, Foyt made a surprise pit visit, sliding to a stop in front of the team.[16]

"How am I doin', boys!?!" he asked before pulling back on the track, still laps ahead. In later years he'd enhance the story. "I was just having some fun with the boys and told them to say hi to that pretty girl standing in our pits. They didn't think it was too funny, but I enjoyed it."[17]

Later he tried to describe how difficult the race was with a straight face.

"It may have looked easy because so many guys went out, but let me tell you, it wasn't. Anytime you have to run 500 miles it's not easy. Seems like every time in the past when I've had a long lead something has happened. You're just sitting out there hoping nothing goes wrong and it gives you too much time to think about it.

"I'd just as soon run a whole race the way I did with Richard and Bobby in the early part of this one. We were going all-out then. I backed off when I got a two-lap lead, and it seems in cases like that, something happens."[18]

Adding the Daytona 500 to his Indianapolis and Le Mans wins accomplished another of Foyt's goals. "This is another dream I always wanted because it's the biggest stock car race in the world."[19] No one called it the Triple Crown of auto racing at the time, although some would in later years. Others would point to wins at Indianapolis, Le Mans, and Monte Carlo on the Formula One circuit as the Triple Crown, a feat accomplished by Graham Hill. Years later, when Mario Andretti won the F1 World Driver's Championship to go with his Indy and Daytona wins, some called that the Triple Crown. Foyt loyalists argue F1 and Indy cars were similar open-wheel racers, while Indianapolis, Le Mans, and Daytona represented three distinct types of cars and therefore represented auto racing's true Triple Crown.

There was no doubt what was next on Foyt's bucket list. "I'll never retire until I win number four," he said. "My biggest thrill in racing will be when I win for the fourth time."[20]

After his dominating victory, *Sports Illustrated*, the magazine Foyt was suing for libel, featured him on the cover of the next issue, the first Daytona 500 winner to be so honored.

Two weeks later, Foyt and the Woods were back at Ontario, where they'd won in dominating fashion the year before. The team brought an all-new car to the track, and Foyt was unhappy with it on the first day of practice. The next morning the No. 21 Mercury was first in line when the track opened.

"We worked ourselves hard this morning," Foyt said later. "We had to keep changing one thing and another, trying to find the right combination. I kept taking a lap or two and coming in and trying another gear ratio, a new suspension, anything we could think of.

"Glen and Leonard are easy to communicate with. When I had an idea, they knew exactly what I meant and did it right away. It sure makes my job easier to work with a crew like the Woods boys."[21]

Nearly fifty years later Leonard Wood remembered the day and shed light on the process of working with Foyt to sort out the new car.

"He wasn't the type of driver who you told, 'Look, this is what we're going to do,'" Wood said. "You tell him why you're going to do something. He said, 'We should change the right-front spring.' So I changed the spring and he came in and said, 'Now that really feels good.' I said, 'Yeah, but you run half a second slower.' A.J. says, 'Then put it back like it was. I'll drive it.'

"It's how you connect with people that determines how you get along," Wood said. "You just have to connect with him one-on-one. We had a great understanding. We got along great with A.J."[22]

With a purse topping $200,000, Ontario was the second-richest race on NASCAR's schedule and a record 111 cars entered, bolstered by a large number from the series' Pacific Division. Foyt drew the number-one qualifying position, and Leonard Wood, watching from the pits and using a handheld stopwatch, figured he'd run fast enough to earn the pole. Only the electronic scoring system, the same one that gave Foyt fits in the Indy car race eighteen months earlier, failed to record his time.

While Foyt sat in the car and steamed, the Wood Brothers jacked it up and poured water over the tires to cool them. Returning to the track he ran even faster, breaking his own track stock car record by more than two mph, but he wasn't any happier.

"Was I mad?" he repeated after his qualifying run. "I sure wasn't real happy. When you qualify you really hang it out. I drive right on the edge. You try to get everything you can out of the two laps. When it's over you just feel lucky to be back and have it over. Then to be told you've got to do it again—that's too much."[23]

The race featured thirty-six lead changes among seven drivers. Foyt was the one constant, turning back one challenge after another and leading 132 of 200 laps. Bobby Allison was second and led the second-most laps—twenty—followed by Buddy Baker and Petty. The three NASCAR regulars worked together throughout the race, drafting and taking turns pushing each other past Foyt and into the lead, all for naught in the end.

"The only way the rest of us could keep up with Foyt was to hook up and push one another around," Allison said.[24]

Racing for the first time with two-way radio communications with the team, A.J. regained the lead each time. Petty was the strongest challenger but fell behind when a tire came off following a late pit stop.

"When it's your day, it's your day," Petty said, sounding a lot like Foyt. "And when it ain't, it ain't."[25]

Foyt didn't try to hide his annoyance when reporters asked about his "easy" victory.

"I don't know why you gentlemen would call any race easy," he said. "I've never run an easy race in my life. You can get killed at 160 miles per hour, just like you can at ten. It was a warm day [high of eighty-nine degrees] and a tough race all the way. I couldn't put two or three laps together the way I wanted to. Maybe it's because I was trying so hard—we wanted to win this one real bad."[26]

———

A.J. wanted to try to make it three in a row at Rockingham a week later but had already committed to run the Astro Grand Prix midget race in Houston, which he was again helping to promote. In some respects it was a flashback to the 1950s as Johnny Rutherford, Hurtubise, Bill Vukovich Jr., and others gathered in Foyt's garage the week before the race.

More than twenty-five thousand fans turned out to see Foyt, Rutherford, and several other Indy 500 starters compete with the best from the midget ranks, although the defending national midget champion, Danny Caruthers, had been killed in a late-1971 crash. His brother and runner-up in the title chase, Jimmy Caruthers, was entered in Houston, along with Gary Bettenhausen, the fast-rising USAC star and son of Tony Bettenhausen.

ABC's *Wide World of Sports* was on hand to cover the event. Chris Economaki was part of the broadcast team, and a local reporter asked him who was the world's best driver.

"If you would have asked me that a year ago, I would have said Mario Andretti," Economaki said. "But today I have to say A.J. Foyt. A.J. has had his ups and downs. But sometimes you get him in a racy mood. Well, A.J. got in a racy mood in 1970 and he's been going ever since. He's quite a driver."[27]

Racy mood or not, Foyt didn't make it past the first corner in his opening heat race before he was clipped by another car, sending his thirty-year-old midget into a slow roll, coming to a rest on the recently added roll cage covering the driver's cockpit. With the race stopped, he crawled from under the car and ran to another owned by former midget champion Mel Kenyon in time to restart the heat, dropped out again, and was forced to start near the back of the field in the main event. He finished fifth in the feature as Bettenhausen lapped the field. The night's activities were marred by numerous accidents and rollovers and the final checkered flag didn't wave until after 2:00 a.m. in what would be the last Astro Grand Prix.[28]

Despite the late-night finish, the next day Foyt held a "Texas-style" barbecue at his ranch and invited much of USAC's racing community, Tony Hulman, and his former car owner, John Mecom, among others.

March 18 marked the start of the Indy car season at Phoenix, and most of the teams brought their year-old cars, including Foyt. The lone exception was Dan Gurney's All-American Racers, which had a new Eagle for Bobby Unser to drive.

The new car was immediately impressive, Unser qualifying on the pole, shattering the previous record. In practice Unser and Gurney discovered what became known as the "Gurney Flap," a small strip of metal on the upper trailing edge of the car's wing that improved downforce and handling without a major increase in drag. Amazingly, the team was able to keep the flap a secret for much of the year, and Unser lapped everyone except second-place Andretti, putting three laps on Foyt, who was never in contention and finished eighth.

––––––––––

The hype surrounding the Wood Brothers and Foyt renewed a month later in Atlanta, where they were again the defending race champions. A.J. was clearly enjoying himself, saying, "I get my kicks knockin' around in a stocker. It's a lot of fun and a change of pace."[29]

"Leonard and Glen are great. They make you try to drive a better race. I'm amazed with the speed in which they get me in and out of the pits."[30]

Glen Wood was equally effusive when talking about Foyt. "A pit crew always looks forward to having the best guy available in the car. And I can't think of anybody who is better than A.J. Foyt. You like to pay attention to what the driver says because, after all, he's the man who has to handle the car. Foyt knows about the car. That's what makes him so great. You have to go along with a driver like him."

The constant Foyt, Foyt, Foyt media drumbeat, however, was beginning to wear thin on some of the NASCAR regulars.

"Beating or losing to A.J. Foyt means no more than losing or beating anybody else," Isaac said. "That No. 21 has won a lot of races no matter who was driving it."[31]

Asked if NASCAR should ban USAC drivers, an obvious reference to Foyt, Buddy Baker shot back, "No, but it should ban the Wood Brothers."[32]

The Wood Brothers had obviously found "something" and most of the speculation centered around the 429-cubic-inch engine that Leonard had elected to use rather than the time-proven 427 powerplant. Others thought it went further than that. Bobby Allison was the most outspoken, implying the Woods had found a new way to cheat.

"I guess you could say that somebody has found a secret in that engine," Bobby said after Ontario. "I would go deep into a turn and I would be coming out and heading down the straight and starting to catch Foyt. Then I could see him get on it and he would just start to pull away, like that. It takes real horsepower to be able to do that."[33]

Despite his concerns, Allison put Junior Johnson's Chevrolet on the Atlanta pole with Isaac second. Foyt qualified fourth, his worst NASCAR start in two years. Allison and Isaac were the front-runners and battled for much of the race, swapping the lead back and forth. With about sixty laps to go, all the leaders pitted under a yellow flag for fuel and tires. Allison stopped a second time at the end of the caution period to top off his tank, which dropped him about ten seconds behind Isaac and Foyt on the restart.

When racing resumed, Foyt followed Isaac until there were eleven laps remaining and then took the lead for the first time. It looked for a moment that Foyt might win his third straight, but Allison, with more fuel and fresher tires, was coming fast. He passed Foyt with two laps remaining, scoring the first victory for Chevrolet on a superspeedway in nearly ten years.

"I've never driven a harder race," Allison said. "It has to rate high among my greatest victories. I feel good about beating Foyt. I don't go out to beat anybody in particular, but when you beat Foyt, you know there aren't many better."[34]

With the Indy car season starting in earnest, the Wood Brothers hired David Pearson to replace Foyt in the No. 21 car. Darlington was his first event and Pearson qualified on the pole, led two-thirds of the race, and won by more than a lap over Petty. He would go on to win six of the next twelve races the team entered.

———

Bob Riley was already at work in Houston on a new Coyote, once again taking a monthlong sabbatical from Ford. He'd been bothered by the lack of public recognition he'd received from Foyt, who at one point said his father, Tony, had designed the car. At other times Foyt implied the car represented his ideas, fed into a computer. Riley's friends kidded him, wanting to know what he was really doing in Houston.[35]

"I have specialized people putting the information into computers," Foyt had said. "Sometimes we disagree and I've gone ahead and done it my way and a lot of times I've been right. Trial and error, practice, experience, that's still hard to beat."[36]

Jones, who was becoming as big a rival to Foyt as a team owner as he'd been an on-track competitor, also made off-season news. He hired Mario Andretti to drive alongside Al Unser and Joe Leonard for crew chief George Bignotti, creating the first Indy car "super team." Each driver had won an Indy car championship over the past three years. Jones also lined up a new sponsor in Viceroy, landing some of the big tobacco dollars for his team. And he said his team would only run Offenhauser engines during the coming year.

"Ford has sold all the rights to A.J. Foyt, and of course Foyt is a direct competitor of ours," Jones said. "I just don't think we're going to get all the latest equipment from him, so I don't think we really had much of a choice. I think the Offenhauser has a better foundation to start with anyway. I think it pulls more power, is lighter, and is just generally better in the long run."[37]

His new Indy car still not finished, Foyt decided to skip the April 23 race at Trenton, the final tune-up before practice started at Indianapolis. The race marked the debut of another new car, the VPJ-1, called the "Parnelli" by most. It was every bit as radical as rumored, with what the team called dihedral wings, or "a pair of stubby wings mounted at 45-degree angles on either side of the driver," in addition to the large wing in back.[38]

All three members of the super team struggled. Bettenhausen, who'd joined Penske Racing to team with Donohue, gave the updated McLaren 16B its first victory as Offenhauser engines powered the top-nine finishers.

Even as the new Coyote was being completed, Riley knew he hadn't pushed the envelope far enough. The 1971 McLaren had sparked a revolution in car design and Gurney's Eagle was a game changer. Unser had reportedly turned a lap above 190 mph in Speedway tire tests, ten mph faster than the pole speed just a year earlier. If it finished, the Eagle would be hard to beat.

USAC had given up on the charade of the wing being part of the bodywork and they'd grown in size. Also contributing to the increased speeds were new "slick" tires from Firestone and Goodyear.

"I wanted to do a good durable car [and] kind of played it safe," Riley would say. "It was just a run-of-the-mill car, almost a follow-the-leader car. It's the same old dilemma. How far out do you go?"[39]

The biggest challenge for Riley was dealing with the size of the turbocharged Ford V8. With Howard Gilbert continuing to lead development, it was rebadged a "Foyt" engine, complete with new valve covers carrying the designation. Its size and weight dwarfed the four-cylinder Offenhauser and limited Riley's options.

"The power was okay, but the engine was just so bulky," Riley said. "It's just a huge bulk with the air intakes here and there. [The Offy] was a nice, simple, straight-up engine. I wanted to run with an engine cover [but] people said, 'You'll never be able to run with them in the race. The engine just gets too hot.' There wouldn't be much room for the air to get back to the wing."[40]

For a while Foyt toyed with the idea of not building a new car. Along with Gene White, Lloyd Ruby's car owner, he ordered a car from a group of former McLaren team members who were building an M16 copy designed for the Ford/Foyt engine. The group completed only one car—called an Atlanta—before it went belly-up. When the car went to White, and after hearing of Unser's speeds, Foyt launched an around-the-clock effort to build Riley's new design.

Initially designated the R71 in deference to Riley, and called the Coyote III by some, Foyt later said it was the first of the 1973 cars. In addition to the new Coyote, he entered three older models in the 500, two under Jim Greer's name. For the first time he sold several of his old cars. Two, including the one Donnie Allison drove the year before, went to Hurtubise, who would drive a rear-engine car for the first time since 1967. Two more were sold to Lindsey Hopkins. Because of the late start building the new car, he'd been unable to do any testing before arriving at the Speedway for the first time in many years.

"I didn't plan to build a race car this year, but we started seventy-two days ago, working days and nights," Foyt said. "It's fantastic, unheard of to build one so late.

"I hope to run that fast or faster," he said when told of Unser's speeds. "A 200 miles per hour average is just around the corner. I'd like to be the first man to make it. I want to try and break my own records. All the other guys are getting younger—I'm getting older."[41]

Despite rumors about a Ford/Foyt engine development program producing more horsepower and improved durability, at least one team said there was no turning back.

"Sure Foyt won at Phoenix [in the last race of 1971] and looked impressive, but 200 miles isn't 500," said Andretti. "It really doesn't make any difference what A.J. does. We can't go back to Ford as long as Foyt is the distributor. You know you're not going to get the same Ford parts and pieces as he's using. You've got to be at a disadvantage from the start.

"You can't race against your parts supplier. It's as simple as that. Foyt is a pretty fierce competitor any time. Give him the advantage he has as a parts supplier and we're all behind the 8-ball."[42]

Many of the other teams agreed and switched to the Offenhauser engine during the off-season. Fifty-four of the eighty-one Indy 500 entries listed an Offenhauser engine, just twenty the Ford/Foyt. The year before it had been a nearly equal mix, thirty-six Offys, thirty-three Fords.

As expected, the Eagles topped the early speed charts, but unexpectedly it was one driven by Jim Malloy often setting the pace. Malloy was three years older than Foyt, but had run his first 500 in 1967. He was often fast, although still looking for his first USAC victory. His fourth-place finish for Gurney in 1971 had secured him one of the coveted new Eagles for '72.

With several of the Eagle and McLaren drivers turning laps above 190 mph, Foyt slowly built speed and crept closer to the mark as the first weekend of qualifying approached. The car seemed solid, only the engine was a question mark.

"We got an engine I feel can keep up with the Offenhausers," Foyt told anyone who asked. "Don't get me wrong, I'm not being stubborn about running this engine. If I thought the Offenhauser was really better, I'd be running one. I can't help but think that if an eight-cylinder engine can be close to giving the power that a four-cylinder engine does, the eight has to be more dependable. That's what I'm banking on. I think I can run with anyone else on race day and I think I'll still be running when it's over.

"I also think I'll be in the ball park with the other guys. I think it'll take 190 or 191 to win the pole and I feel my car is capable of it. My straightaway speeds are faster than anyone else. I'm working on the corners now, taking them one at a time and getting the feel of the car. The pole is no big deal anyway. I've been on the pole before. I'd just as soon get in the show the first day, then worry about the race itself."[43]

Like Gurney, Riley was experimenting with a flap on the wing, but unlike the Eagle, he was unable to hit on the right setting.

"We had an adjustable flap that you could put up," Riley recalled. "It [just] seemed like there was something wrong. Never really got it to work just right. But you know A.J., he could handle that sort of thing."[44]

Pole day was cold and rainy, and it wasn't until the afternoon that the track opened for practice. After several drivers waved off qualifying attempts, Foyt started his run with only a few minutes left before the track would close for the day. USAC rule changes now guaranteed any car in line would get at least one qualifying attempt at the pole, so there was no need for Foyt to make a run, but he decided to anyway. The forecast was for more rain on Sunday and if he was able to qualify now, he could spend the coming week working on his race setup. Just one official qualifying run would also save Tony Hulman from issuing rain checks to 175,000 ticket holders, only a few of whom were still at the track. At two dollars a ticket, that added up to about $350,000.

His engine had acted up earlier in the day, but after a warm-up lap of 188 mph and with the clock at 5:59 p.m., Foyt decided to roll the dice, raising his hand to signal the start of an official qualifying run. He didn't get far, as the oil cooler started smoking in the short chute between Turn One and Turn Two, forcing him back to the pits without completing a lap. It had cost him one of three official qualifying attempts, however, and any chance at the pole. No matter what his speed on subsequent attempts, he'd line up behind the other "first day" qualifiers still in line.

The next day got off to a terrible start when Malloy, one of the first cars on the course, entered Turn Three low and shot up the track, hitting the wall nearly head-on and at full speed. Operators of the Jaws of Life said it was the worst accident they'd seen, and it took ten minutes to cut Malloy out of the car. He'd never regain consciousness and died four days later when his life support was turned off.

Scattered showers followed the accident, and it wasn't until later Sunday afternoon that qualifying resumed. Bobby Unser won the pole with four laps at nearly 196 mph, seventeen mph faster than the record set just one year earlier. The strain of the high speeds and constant questions about a fourth win were beginning to have an impact on Foyt.

"Win a fourth one? Why don't you guys get off my back," he finally said. "Of course I'm here to win. If I wasn't, I wouldn't be here. But being the first guy to win four hasn't got anything to do with it. It's become more than just a race to me. This is a way of life which you people just don't know about.

"The first thing is to win. It's not the money anymore—I guess it never was. Sure, we take and use the money, who wouldn't? But the thing here, and everywhere in racing is the personal challenge of who is the best."[45]

Foyt would have to wait until the following weekend to qualify and worked on his race setup. He still averaged nearly 189 mph, the fifth fastest overall time, although he'd start in seventeenth.

"We couldn't get the pole anyway, so we went with a race setup," said Foyt, who figured he could "catch up with the leaders within three laps."[46]

He offered the No. 84 car to George Snider, with one string attached: he'd have to get his stylishly long hair cut. Freshly shorn, Snider qualified in twenty-first. Kenyon (twelfth) and Hurtubise (thirteenth) had also qualified their customer cars. The slowest qualifier, Cale Yarborough in White's Foyt-powered Atlanta, was still faster than the pole sitter from the year before. Eleven Foyt/Ford engines qualified, including one in the car driven by Dick Simon.

"I decided to stay with Fords because I do not have the money to jump from Ford to Offy and then back to Ford," Simon said. "I have enough confidence in A.J. that he is not going to stand back and let the Offys run away. He has tried to help us, but he has his own program and his time is limited. But he's been in our garage more than I've seen in the last two years."[47]

Because of the high speeds and buffeting wind drivers were experiencing, Foyt tested a plain white full-face Bell Star helmet for the first time during practice. He'd been partial to the open-face Bell Magnum for several years, but the tinted visor he liked to wear was being caught by the winds and jerking his head around. Introduced by Gurney at the Speedway in 1968 after using it in F1, many of the Indy car drivers had already switched to the Bell Star and Foyt elected to wear it in the race.

The new helmet may have been a godsend for the crew. When Tony Hulman called, "Gentlemen, start your engines!" thirty-two cranked up and one didn't—Foyt's. As the field pulled away to start the parade lap, Tony Foyt and Jack Starne tried to guide the car through the small opening in the wall near the start/finish line and were blocked by chief steward Harlan Fengler, who said the car must be pushed to the exit of Pit Lane. A.J. made a number of gestures and repeatedly tried to raise the helmet's face shield to yell instructions, only to have it fall back in place each time.

The team paused near the pit exit to try again to start the engine, only to hear Fengler on the public address system telling them to get the car off the track. They finally got it started as the cars came on the main straight a second time. When it appeared another pace lap would be added—all three front-row starter drivers had their arms raised—the team held Foyt in the pits, figuring he could take his position when the field passed. At the last moment, however, the pace car darted into the pits and the green flag was displayed. Bobby Unser jumped into an immediate lead and Foyt chugged onto the track. By the time he got up to speed, he was last, half a lap behind the leader.

Within twenty laps he was up to eighteenth, but his engine started popping and snorting and, before long, smoking heavily. He made several long pit stops, going back on the track each time to run a few laps before returning. Bobby Unser led the first thirty laps before his distributor failed, knocking him out of the race. Bettenhausen moved to the front, and as the leader approached the halfway mark, Foyt climbed from his car, having completed just sixty laps.

Bettenhausen dominated until his ignition failed with thirty laps remaining, handing the lead to Jerry Grant in Gurney's other Eagle. Grant had to pit for tires, however, Donohue taking over and leading the final thirteen laps for the win, the first at Indy for Penske Racing.

Offenhauser engines swept the top three positions and six of the top ten. Of the Foyt engines in the race, only A.J.'s had a terminal problem. The month had been tough on both engine manufacturers as they combined for more than sixty failures.

Foyt complained about the way USAC officials handled the start, saying they were "getting old and quick on the draw. We've got to have someone up there who will use good common sense.

"It was yellow, then went green, and I couldn't believe it," he'd say. "If I had pulled out you would have seen the damnedest wreck you'd ever seen. They all had their hands up for one more lap. Pat's [Vidan] as much to blame as anyone. Don't just blame Harlan. The starter has to wave the flag and he has to use some judgment.

"This was a cat-and-mouse game like they use on the midgets, hiding the flag until the last second. They don't have to do that to professionals. They saw me down there with my motor running and could have let me get in line. I probably draw as many people to that race as anyone. It was embarrassing to me and my sponsors."[48]

Vidan defended himself while throwing his boss under the bus.

"If the drivers were surprised, how do you think I felt?" the flagman said. "I was dumbfounded when Fengler yelled, 'Go Green,' while I was holding up a finger for another lap. I had no choice but wave the green flag. Harlan told me twice. I felt like a damned fool, but I don't like somebody pointing the finger at me when I was in the middle."[49]

Fengler said, "My back was to Pat and I didn't know his hand was in the air. There wasn't any mix-up as far as I was concerned. There was nothing the matter with it."[50]

Anxious to move on from the disappointing 500, Foyt entered the Dirt Track Championship race the next day at Du Quoin, along with a handful of other starters from the Speedway. After qualifying ninth in the one-hundred-lap event, he worked his way to the front by lap thirty and, with nearly a lap lead over the field, decided to play it safe and make a quick pit stop for a splash of fuel fourteen laps from the finish.

Everything went according to plan until Foyt started to pull away and he saw the gas can flip and felt fuel splash over him and the side of the car.

"I figured it would evaporate," Foyt said years later. "The exhaust pipes coming out the side, sometimes they burp fire, and when they did, I went up in flames like a Buddhist monk."[51]

Feeling the heat, he pointed the car toward the inside pit guardrail and tried to climb out of the moving racer only to fall to the ground, the left-rear tire rolling over his left ankle. On fire, his first thought was the lake in the middle of the infield. He turned in that direction, stumbling over the guardrail.

First to realize what was happening was Tony Foyt, who grabbed a fire extinguisher and set off in pursuit of his son, catching the driver as he fell over the guardrail. He emptied the extinguisher on A.J., who started struggling to unzip his uniform. Starne was close behind and with a knife sliced open the top.

"It just went whooff—like it was burning inside and it relieved it," Starne recalled. Then he noticed Foyt's ankle. "His foot was all the way around backwards, which was not a good sight."[52]

Foyt, who'd gone back to the open-face helmet for the race, was initially diagnosed with first- and second-degree burns over his face, hands, and legs, and a badly sprained ankle. Tony Hulman sent his plane to retrieve Lucy Foyt, who'd returned to Houston immediately after the 500. They spent the night at Marshall Browning Hospital in Du Quoin, flying to Houston the next day. As the swelling started to recede, doctors at St. Luke's Medical Center discovered a broken ankle along with severe ligament damage, requiring surgery. After the ninety-minute operation, Lucy agreed to do one of her least favorite things: talk to the media.

"He came in for fuel and when the crew was taking the hose from the tank, it jerked up somehow, and fuel fell on the hot tailpipe," she told reporters. "He jumped out immediately and the car ran over his left ankle. The burns aren't real bad. It's the broken ankle that seems to be giving him the most trouble right now. He's in no danger. He has some pain, of course, but he's feeling pretty good."[53]

One of the first to visit him in the Houston hospital was heart surgeon Denton Cooley, who'd attended the 500 but returned to Houston afterward with Lucy.

"I told Denton I was going to Du Quoin and asked him to stay," Foyt later recalled. "I said, 'I might need you.' He walked in my hospital room and said, 'Well, you didn't lie to me!'"

Foyt checked out of the hospital on Friday and when things at the main house got too hectic, he headed for the ranch. He spoke to fans at Sunday's Milwaukee

Indy car race via telephone over the public address system and gave them the bad news: doctors were saying it would be three months before he could get back in a race car. He talked separately with reporters about the crash.

"Dad came over the fence and saved my life," he said. "My crew feels the worst, but I told them it was just an unpredictable weekend. The hell of it is, if I didn't like the damn game and the challenge of it, I'd quit like everybody is yelling at me to do."[54]

CHAPTER 33

TAKING CARE OF BUSINESS

1972

If there was bright spot in A.J. Foyt's injuries and forced recovery away from the track, it was the time he could spend focused on his budding business empire. One publication named him among the richest men in sports with an estimated net worth of $7 million, more than $50 million in 2024 dollars. Topping the list were golfers Arnold Palmer and Jack Nicklaus at $20 million and $15 million respectively, while Foyt ranked just behind boxer Muhammad Ali's estimated $8 million.[1]

The acquisition of the dealership, renamed A.J. Foyt Chevrolet, was not only the most recent and visible aspect of the empire, it was also the one demanding most of his time. Located at 10306 South Post Oak, not far from Meyer Speedway, the dealership had struggled before Foyt stepped in to buy it from a Houston bank. He'd done his due diligence, but it was still worse than expected; even the bleak numbers didn't add up.

After bringing in a new management team, and thanks in no small part to the Foyt name, the dealership would grow to be the largest in the city, and the largest Chevrolet store in the state. With about 150 employees, it grossed more than $20 million the first year and would sell about six thousand cars a year at its peak. Foyt was ahead of his time, stressing customer service on a par with the top luxury brands. While coffee bars would become the rage for dealerships, Foyt put a full diner in his and it turned out to be a popular dining spot even for those not looking for a new car or a tune-up. And it bothered him when people thought the dealership was his in name only.

"Some people think I don't own that Chevy dealership, that I just stuck my name on it to help sell cars," he said. "But I call it two or three times a day to make sure that my people are doing the right thing. I've got good people, but you must stay on top of things or it'll go to hell."[2]

◀ Foyt in his "other" office. *Photograph by Ed Justice Jr.*

Early in his career, especially after winning his first 500 in 1961, Foyt had begun paying more attention than most drivers to his contracts and the business side of racing. When he reunited with George Bignotti near the end of 1962, the first task for new team owners Shirley Murphy and Bill Ansted had been to sign Foyt to a new deal.

"He may not have much education, but he certainly knows how to read a contact," Ansted said at the time, a comment repeated often in the coming years.[3]

At the center of Foyt's financial universe was Jack Trotter, a Houston lawyer and accountant best known for "making things happen."[4]

"I think I'm as knowledgeable about racing as any other individual, but I'd be the first to admit I don't know all there is to know about business and finance," Foyt said. "With Trotter's help, we started going places. Racing is a game with me, money is a game with Trotter, and we both play to win. I wouldn't accept a ride in a second-class race car and he wouldn't invest in anything that didn't look like a winner. So many sports figures have been badly managed, but I'd trust Jack with every nickel I've got."[5]

They'd met in typical Foyt fashion. Lucy's mother, Elizabeth Zarr, had married Elliott Flowers, a prominent Houston lawyer, and Trotter's company had been handling their taxes for several years. When A.J.'s taxes became more complicated, he went to Trotter's firm as well. The relationship almost ended before it started.

"His people did my taxes, and I wasn't happy and let them know it. I was walking out and said, 'If I got to tell you how to do it, then I don't have to pay you.' Jack heard me and came out of his office and said, 'I got to meet this guy.' From then on, he handled everything for me.

"He taught me probably everything I know about business," Foyt said. "He was very smart, very wealthy. We turned out to be like brothers, to be truthful with you. He came to Indy and all that. He did all my investments. A very brilliant guy."[6]

For the most part it was a conservative investment portfolio, built on dividend-paying blue-chip companies, including AT&T, Coca-Cola, and Mobil. Trotter also was a wiz at protecting Foyt's earnings with tax-friendly investments.

"Jack was real smart on stocks. He was probably one of the most important men in Houston. He was a top man and helped make Houston what it is today. Everybody loved Jack Trotter, except maybe the IRS."

Texas Monthly magazine would agree with Foyt. In an article entitled "Power" about those "deciding the fate of Texas," Trotter was on a list including H. Ross Perot and T. Boone Pickens, and called the "behind-the-scenes player setting the course of Houston's business community." He was politically astute, the article quoting a top state politician saying, "I've never seen Trotter on the wrong side of an issue."[7]

Foyt also was one of the first athletes to work with a sports agent. Chuck Barnes, a former Firestone public relations representative, quit the tire company and opened Indianapolis-based Sports Headliners Inc. For a business model he used the personal relationship between golfer Arnold Palmer and agent Mark

McCormack's International Management Group (IMG). After working with Foyt, he signed Rodger Ward, Parnelli Jones, Jimmy Clark, and Mario Andretti.

"I thought auto racing was a sleeping giant," Barnes said, noting it was a $50 million business. "Football players can endorse shoulder pads, footballs, but not much more out of that area. Racing drivers can endorse everything on a car from the front to the back bumper. It's good business to have A.J. using your stuff."[8]

Among the deals Barnes landed was one with a franchise company for naming rights to A.J. Foyt's Pit Stop Service Centers, which offered rapid service for minor maintenance such as an oil change in seven minutes. Foyt's responsibilities were mostly promotional, which at times proved frustrating and challenging for Barnes as A.J. would turn down appearance fees to compete in minor races that paid much less even if he won. Barnes also discovered what Ansted already knew.

"For a guy who quit school in the eleventh grade because he liked racing and wanted to work in his father's garage, A.J. is pretty good at reading the small print in a contract," Barnes said. Based partly on the success with Foyt, Sports Headliners branched out and signed athletes from other sports, hitting the big time when Barnes signed Heisman Trophy winner O.J. Simpson and negotiated his first pro contract.[9]

By the end of 1968, Foyt had become the first driver to pass $1 million in career winnings. That only scratched the surface. Along with his appearance fees and accessory earnings, Barnes put A.J.'s yearly income somewhere in the neighborhood of $350,000, or more than $3 million annually year in 2024 dollars. That put him on par with Simpson, who was about to sign professional football's largest contract ever.

In Houston, Trotter connected Foyt with a number of the city's movers and shakers, and at one point A.J. held minor ownership positions with the Houston Astros and Oilers. The group included Charles Duncan, Dale Cheesman, and Bobby Waltrip, all of whom attended the Indianapolis 500 as part of Foyt's entourage.

Duncan was the son of the founder of Duncan Coffee, where Tony Foyt worked maintaining the truck fleet in the late 1930s. Duncan merged the company with Coca-Cola in 1964, joining the board at Coke and rising through the executive ranks until becoming president. He'd later serve in the Carter administration, first as undersecretary of defense, and later as secretary of energy.

In 1962 Waltrip had founded Service Corporation International (SCI), a company that grew to be the country's largest owner of funeral homes. Foyt served on the SCI board and often joked about traveling with his own undertaker.

Cheesman attended Lamar High School a few years ahead of Foyt and went to the University of Texas. After starting in the family business trading oil leases, minerals, and royalties, he founded CICO Oil & Gas in 1965. Before long, two oil wells named after one of the original investors were pumping away, Foyt No. 1 and Foyt No. 2.[10]

One constant in the business inner circle was Jim Greer, who was often listed as a co-entrant or sponsor of one of A.J.'s cars in the 500. He'd built on his glass business with interests in real estate development, commercial construction, and banking. He bought several Marriott and Holiday Inn hotels along with Foyt, "mostly as tax write-offs" according to Greer, who urged A.J. to invest in land.[11]

Foyt started with the tract of land in Hockley. Its modest ranch house had become a major focus of his life, and he spent much of his free time there with his father and friends. He continued to buy surrounding land as it became available, with the ranch growing to a peak of about 1,500 acres. He wouldn't stop there and was constantly looking to acquire other acreage. He proved to have a good eye for property and took ownership of land in nearby Waller, site of his future race shop, in exchange for three used cars from his dealership.

"He'd buy property, improve it, and then hold on to it," Greer said. "He didn't get in a hurry and try to flip it right away. He'd wait until the time was right."[12]

Foyt sometimes joked about being "all hat and no cattle" when it came to ranching, eventually he'd have about 1,500 head of cattle at its peak and upward of one hundred horses, many of them thoroughbreds, spread across his properties.

"A.J. has always been interested in property," says Tim Delrose, the businessman and race car owner he'd met at the Speedway, who became a good friend. "He's probably owned about twenty ranches that he bought when they were junk. He fixed them up and made a lot of money that way. He's not a dumb person. He surrounds himself with fellows that will give him good advice."[13]

Thanks to people like Trotter, Greer, Waltrip, Cheesman, and Duncan, Foyt also became part of Houston's business elite, serving alongside them on the boards of various businesses and organizations. By all accounts he took his responsibilities seriously and was more than a celebrity board member, seldom missing a vote and typically well prepared for corporate discussions. On more than one occasion, he'd fly home from Indianapolis or some other racetrack to attend an important board meeting.

"You set out to build an empire, and all you can think about is keeping it from crumbling under you," he said. "Racing was a tool I used to build my empire. Now it's [racing] something I do because I love it. I don't have to race, not for money. I race for the challenge of it.

"I don't have to ask myself why I keep racing, because other people are always asking me that same question. I don't know just what to tell them, but I know if I get killed tomorrow, my family will be well taken care of. I've worked hard to get where I am, and now I can do the things I enjoy."[14]

Having proven himself adept at maneuvering his way through auto racing's political maze, Foyt was also an asset in Austin, where he made occasional lobbying trips, combining his name recognition with an easy, natural presentation skill. Several times he was asked to run for political office, outreach he quickly rebuffed. He did agree, however, to having his name listed on the Motorsports Committee for the Re-election of President Nixon.

"He became a very good businessman," Lucy said, with more than a little pride in her voice. "He had a lot of help and a lot of good advisors. He was a good listener. He learned by listening to people that could help him. He's done it his way and he's done it well."[15]

One of Foyt's business rules was to avoid debt. He used his winnings from his first 500 victory to pay cash for a home and a new Cadillac, a goal he'd had since his teenage years. When loans were necessary, they were typically short term and quickly paid off.

"If something happens to me," he often said, "I don't want to leave my family with a debt they have to pay."[16]

Cash was king in Foyt's business world, and he'd carry a large amount in an ever-present briefcase when he traveled to the races. Pocket change consisted of several thousand dollars. He reasoned you could never tell when being able to pay cash might sweeten or close a deal over someone else who needed to go to the bank.

Foyt's financial acumen was not lost on the other drivers. "You've got to make hay while the sun shines," said Joe Leonard after spending nearly a year with A.J. "Mr. Foyt is the smartest of all of us. It takes a highly educated person or someone who is highly educated to advise you on particulars."[17]

Despite an occasional hiccup, Foyt maintained a solid relationship with Goodyear throughout his career. Rather than take ownership of Goodyear stores, he preferred to buy the land and build the dealership, then lease it back for others to run. At one point he was carrying the lease on twenty-some Goodyear stores. He added Honda and Isuzu dealerships in the years ahead, with son Jerry taking on a key management role in their operation. By the mid-1980s, Foyt's interest in the Chevrolet dealership had run its course, and faced with the need to relocate the facility, he elected to sell it to Group 1 Automotive, in which Duncan was an investor. Group 1 was one of the largest dealership chains in the country, and Jerry Foyt would stay on with the new owners, serving as general manager at several of its luxury brand dealerships.

"I had a choice, either stay in the dealership business or stay in racing," A.J. said of his decision to sell the Chevrolet store. "I picked racing because I loved it a lot more than dealing with people. Dealing with people was a pain in the ass."[18]

There was also a philanthropic side to Foyt's business operations, especially in the Houston area. The dealerships often donated cars to fundraising efforts, but much of the charity work was done behind the scenes. He didn't like to talk about it then, and years later he still didn't like to talk about what he'd done for others. Some believe it's because he didn't want other people coming to him for handouts. Others think he was afraid of softening his image. It was probably a little of both.

If there was a shortcoming in Foyt's business style—and many wouldn't consider it a shortcoming—it was his dependence on personal relationships and the loyalty he showed those he was connected with. In addition to his small circle of Houston friends and advisors, he'd been with Ansted and Murphy since 1962, nearly ten years and a lifetime in most racing partnerships. They'd stood by A.J. during the split with Bignotti, and he'd stood by them as potentially bigger sponsors entered the sport. One key reason for their long-term success—Ansted and Murphy left running the race team to Foyt.

By 1972 the racing operation was up to twenty full-time employees working out of three buildings in Houston. With a new chassis costing about $100,000 to develop and engines pegged at $32,000 each, Foyt figured it cost half a million dollars just to run Indianapolis.[19]

Against this backdrop the racing sponsorship landscape was undergoing rapid change. The day when rich individuals could bankroll a race team was fast disappearing. It was becoming a corporate playground, fed by marketing dollars. Millionaire sportsmen like Lindsey Hopkins and J.C. Agajanian could still enter cars at the Speedway, but they were now plastered with sponsor names.

When it came to corporate dollars, Andy Granatelli's STP budget remained at the top of the heap and automotive companies like Purolator, Valvoline, and the gasoline brands continued to be prevalent. But new teams, including those of Parnelli Jones and Roger Penske, were tapping into large consumer brands including Viceroy, Samsonite Luggage, Johnny Lightning toys, and beer and soft drink companies.

The big money didn't come easy. America was still emerging from a recession and a corporate sponsor wanted to know what return on investment they could expect before paying to put their name on the side of a race car. It took time and patience to land large sponsors as they seldom made quick decisions. Jones estimated it took five months to seal the Viceroy deal. That was time and patience Foyt didn't have.

One thing was clear: money bought speed, and the twenty-mile-per-hour jump in speeds at Indianapolis didn't come cheap. The seventeen mph difference between qualifiers on the front row and the last indicated the difference between the haves and the have nots.

"The money you spend is in direct relation to the speed you'll get," said Phil Hedback of Bryant Heating and Cooling. Bryant was one of the longtime Indy 500 car sponsors being outspent by the newcomers. "When you get those kinds of speeds and that terrific jump in speed in just one year, you know there's a barrel of money being spent. A majority of sponsors just don't have that kind of money. How long can the little fellas stay around?"[20]

Change was coming to Foyt's sponsorship situation, and the handwriting had been on the wall since 1968. That's when Ansted and Murphy sold their company to International Telephone & Telegraph (ITT), a rapidly expanding international conglomerate in the process of growing from sales of $700 million in 1960 to $8 billion in 1970. While both men stayed on to run their businesses, they now had corporate bosses. ITT wasn't interested in running race cars. Ansted's death in 1970, followed by Murphy's retirement in 1972, spelled the end of the Sheraton-Thompson Special.

––––––––––

Unable to stay away from the racetrack any longer and wanting to continue development work on the Coyote, Foyt entered a car in the July 19 race at Michigan International Speedway. George Snider had already moved to a full-time ride for the rest of the season, so Foyt hired Sammy Sessions to drive the No. 84 in the two-hundred-mile race.

Sessions was Foyt's kind of driver. He started driving super-modifieds at the famous Oswego Speedway in New York where he won the track championship before graduating to sprint cars and an occasional Indy car ride. He was the defending national sprint car champion and, driving for Gene White, had placed fourth at Indianapolis, the highest-finishing car with a Foyt engine. He also used a Foyt engine in his dirt track machine, and when White decided not to enter a car at Michigan, Foyt stepped in.

With A.J. relegated to crutches and watching from the pits, Sessions drove a good race, finishing fourth again, as Foyt-powered cars took three of the top five spots. Foyt promised to enter Sessions in the upcoming five-hundred-mile races at Pocono and Ontario and he scored another fourth-place at Ontario. Contemplating his own future, Foyt talked with Sessions about running selected races in 1973, only to have the driver opt out when a full-time ride was offered him. Still, it was a memorable time for Sessions.

"I learned as much in six months with him than I have all the rest of the time," said the driver with more than a dozen years of experience.[21]

It wasn't until August 20 that Foyt was able to get back on the track himself, at the Illinois State Fairgrounds in Springfield, in the same dirt track machine in which he'd been injured and burned. He was limping around before the race, refusing to use the cane the doctors gave him. "I felt so damn foolish that I threw it away," he said. "It's healed up enough now so doctors say I can't hurt it."[22]

For a while it looked like a fairy-tale return as he went from sixth to the lead in eleven laps, only to be passed by Al Unser, who pulled away for the victory, Foyt finishing second. Unser then led the crowd in a standing ovation for A.J.

"When you've got someone like Foyt that comes back, you've got to give him a hand," Unser said. "He's done a heck of a job."[23]

A week later at Ontario, Foyt qualified the Coyote sixth as Jerry Grant's Offy-powered Eagle ran the first official 200 mph lap in Indy car history. When Grant's car failed to start, Foyt jumped out front, leading the first twenty-eight laps before his transmission locked up, sending his car into a spin and out of the race.

Overnight he flew back to Du Quoin for the annual Labor Day event, arriving early at the track to find only a single crew member standing guard over his car. Unhappy with the way the engine sounded, he went to work on it himself, getting in only a few laps of practice but still qualifying third. He took the lead on the fifth lap and pulled away, getting the victory when the scheduled one-hundred-mile race was stopped by rain just past the halfway point.[24]

He squared off again with Al Unser on September 9 in the Hoosier Hundred. He passed and led Unser for a time before being passed back and finishing second, Foyt engines powering the first four finishers. In the month since he'd been back, Foyt had run four races, led them all, won once, and finished second twice, good enough for the national Dirt Track Championship.

Only four races remained in his abbreviated season, two USAC Indy car events at Trenton and Phoenix and a pair in NASCAR. The Indy car races were forgettable, as he failed to finish either, although he did make his two hundredth start, fifty more than anyone else.

Reunited with the Wood Brothers at Charlotte, Foyt was teamed with David Pearson, who was having a spectacular year after taking over the No. 21 car, winning six events. The Southern racing media billed it as a matchup between two champions in equal cars, and both drivers played along.

"I want to beat A.J. anytime," said Pearson, who was the fastest qualifier. "I think I'll let him run off and wear everyone else out. Don't want to take any chances early and race A.J. Don't want to wreck two cars. But if it comes down to the last part and it's him and me, then it's going to be some race."[25]

Responded Foyt, who qualified the No. 41 car fourth: "I told Leonard and Glen to fix David's car for qualifying. But I'm going to blow him off on the first lap.

"Whenever I have run two cars, I tell my other driver just to look at me like another competitor. I don't believe in team cars. I am here for A.J. and the Woods. And David is here for David and the Wood Brothers. I plan to race him just like I would Buddy Baker, Richard Petty, Bobby Allison or Bobby Isaac."[26]

The matchup never came into play as Pearson's car broke a fan belt in the early going and lost four laps having it replaced. A late pit stop dropped Foyt from second to third behind eventual winner Bobby Allison, and he dropped another spot when a charging Pearson passed him in the closing laps.

"I didn't have any idea we were running for position," Foyt told Pearson when it was over. "I thought you were still a couple of laps behind me. If I had known third place was at stake I'd at least have raced you a little harder."[27]

That left only one race on the schedule, November 12 at Texas World Speedway. Although he'd previously practiced his Indy car on the track, it was his first race at the superspeedway closest to his home, having been rebuffed in previous efforts by sanctioning bodies and racing politics.

Pearson elected to skip the Texas race, saying, "A.J. had never raced in his home state and I thought it would be best for everyone to run just one car. Besides, I needed a vacation."[28]

Back in the No. 21, Foyt put it on the pole, helped by a timing and scoring error that failed to clock Baker's faster lap. The pole came with a special prize, one Leonard Wood remembered fifty years later.

"There was this bull tied up in the infield and the organizers said it would go to the pole winner," he said. "It was the meanest bull I'd ever seen in my life. They put it in a little pen and that thing kept running against a post and butting its head. There was blood flying everywhere. I couldn't believe it, but there was no way you were keeping A.J. from winning it."[29]

Baker thought the failure to capture his quick lap was a little too convenient. "Foyt has all the cattle he needs and I don't have any," he complained. "That bull would have been mine."[30]

In the race Baker showed just how fast he was, leading more than half the laps. Foyt lost a lap early when he ran out of fuel prior to the first pit stop. He continued to draft with Baker and Petty, but it wasn't until less than a hundred miles remained that he managed to get back on the same lap as the leaders. He made up nearly a full lap and pulled alongside Baker in the final turn, only to come up a quarter car-length short at the finish line.

"I will say Foyt did some brilliant driving to get back on the same lap after he had problems," Baker said. "I wasn't nearly as worried about Richard."[31]

Watching it from third was Petty. "I got to hand it to you," he told Foyt. "You sure can drive a race car. I'm tickled just to be in your league."[32]

Although Glen Wood announced the team would enter two cars in 1973 when Foyt was available, teaming him with Pearson, everyone involved was soon having second thoughts. The number of FIA-sanctioned NASCAR races was increasing, and Foyt indicated he wanted to run in at least ten, roughly half the twenty races the Woods planned to enter. They'd been stretched thin working on two cars at Charlotte and the thought of doing it for ten races was daunting.[33]

Neither driver liked having a teammate, and that was the real reason Pearson skipped the Texas race. They'd played nice at Charlotte, joking and ribbing each other, but there'd also been some "kidding on the square" about who had the best car, and comments with a sharper edge included more than a little truth. Two-car teams were a rarity at the time in NASCAR. Petty Enterprises tried it in 1972, but that relationship dissolved before the end of the season. It would be more than twenty years before the preponderance of multi-car teams in NASCAR began to emerge.

Foyt already was considering running his own car. Despite his success in the Mercury, he was impressed by the Junior Johnson Chevrolet that Bobby Allison had driven to the NASCAR championship. New regulations seemed to favor Chevrolet engines, and besides, he was a Chevrolet dealer. It made sense he should drive one.

Ultimately, it was Foyt's decision. A Wood Brothers car was his as promised, when and where he wanted to race. Instead, he decided to reunite with Banjo Matthews and run his own car, a Chevrolet. Purolator, where Foyt held the mostly honorary title of director of new product development, helped seal the deal, agreeing to take the unusual step of supporting two separate teams. Foyt would drive a gold No. 50 Chevy in 1973, marking the fiftieth anniversary of the company. A.J. Foyt Chevrolet would be another of the new team's sponsors, and once again Donnie Allison would drive the car in major events Foyt wasn't available for.[34]

Foyt drove twelve races for the Woods over several seasons (including Atlanta in 1965 when he relieved Marvin Panch), winning six (including Atlanta), finishing second twice, third and fourth once, and taking six pole positions.

"Sometimes you have a dominant car and sometimes you have to work at it," Leonard Wood said of the team's time with Foyt. "You go through stages where your car might have a little bit extra over everybody else. Then you might have a couple or three years where somebody else gets an advantage and have superiority over you. You don't always have the fastest car, but it sure feels good when you do."[35]

"A.J. came along at the right time. He knew how to drive a car and he knew how to win races. He fit the bill and it all just worked perfect."[36]

They remained friends, and the Wood Brothers continued to field winning and often dominant cars for Pearson and others in the years ahead. During 1973 alone, Pearson won eleven of the nineteen races the team entered—nine out of ten at one point.

Foyt, however, would never win another major NASCAR race. He'd made fifty series starts driving for other car owners since 1964, winning seven times and finishing in the top five twenty-three times. He'd continue to run up front and be competitive for the next eighteen years, but never again take the checkered flag first in a NASCAR event.

SPORTS IMMORTAL

At the end of the year Foyt was named one of the fifty greatest sports figures of all time by the Associated Press, the news service publishing a book entitled *Sports Immortals* just in time for Christmas. Foyt was the only race driver included, sharing a spot alongside Arnold Palmer, Jack Dempsey, Gordie Howe, Johnny Weissmuller, Babe Ruth, Willie Mays, Joe DiMaggio, and a host of others.

The chapter on Foyt was written by Bloys Britt, the AP motorsports editor.

"Never has there been a driver with such absolute urge to excel, the absolute need to win, fairly and honestly, gut against gut, skill against skill, flat out and belly to the ground. The total race driver, that's Foyt.

"Hardnose, sometimes violent, often truculent, always intense, sometimes boisterous, many times gentle, impetuous, rough, forceful, vehement, self-made, never vengeful. He would laugh with you one minute, completely ignore you the next. He was deliberately articulate one hour, purposely unresponsive the next. He could be moody, surly, happy, smiling, taut as a banjo string under stress, a model of charm when things were going 'according to Foyt.'

"He was a man of many facets and contradictions, gentleman rancher, breeder of fine horses and cattle, businessman, husband, father, auto salesman, penny pitcher at the state fair, high-stakes thrower at Vegas, practical joker and story seller, patriotic flag-waver, handsome, alert, a mechanical genius."[37]

The winners were honored at a New York City luncheon, and while Foyt had been to the city before, he tried driving there for the first time. "These cabs are something else," he said as he maneuvered a reporter's car through traffic for a story. "It's like being in a race with a bunch of rookie drivers. It's wild. I was the same way when I was a rookie. When I look back on what I got away with, some of the chances I took, it's scary. I drove race cars that were junk, and I just stood on 'em. It's been amazing, but right now, I'm glad just to be driving."[38]

Despite being a "sports immortal," Foyt was in Indianapolis running tire tests in mid-November when he got bad news. ITT was ending its sponsorship. A rumor Foyt was signing with a tobacco company was nothing more than that. Sponsors weren't exactly lining up at the door, and Foyt's reputation may have scared a few off. Having a soft drink with Gordon Johncock during a break in the tests, he mentioned ITT's departure left him "high and dry."[39]

Johncock suggested Foyt contact his former sponsor Jim Gilmore. Johncock had recently signed a lucrative contract to drive for Bignotti with backing from Granatelli and STP. While Gilmore had joined with Hopkins to sponsor Wally Dallenbach's car in 1972, he was eager to have his own car again. Foyt thanked

Johncock for the tip and called Gilmore, who didn't believe A.J. Foyt was on the phone.

Foyt said he was looking for a sponsor and Gilmore said, "I'm honored you thought of me." They made an appointment to meet in Houston the following week. After about ten minutes Foyt got to the point.[40]

"You think we can work something out?" Gilmore remembered Foyt asking. "I sure do," Gilmore says he responded. Gilmore handed him the draft of a basic contract, saying the driver could make any changes he wanted to, well aware of Foyt's reputation for studying the fine print. "Looks fine to me," Foyt said after a few minutes. "You want me to sign it here at the bottom?" So began a partnership that would take the team into 1973 and many more years to come.[41]

"We've had plenty of good drivers, but there's only one A.J. Foyt," Gilmore said in making the announcement. "He wants to be the first man ever to win four times at Indy. We'll give all the help we can to make that possible."[42]

CHAPTER 34

FIRE AND RAIN

1973

With his sponsorships squared away for at least another year and Banjo Matthews working on a new Chevy Monte Carlo for the upcoming Daytona 500, A.J. Foyt turned his attention to the latest Coyote creation from Bob Riley.

It hadn't been an easy process. Riley considered the 1972 car a failure and struggled in Houston to come up with a new design that would leapfrog the Eagle and McLaren. After a month at the end of 1972 without success, he told Foyt he needed more time.

"I went down there to do my usual thing," Riley recalled, "but I just wasn't happy with the design. At the end of four weeks, I could see that it was turning into another ho-hum car. So I wadded the drawings up and threw them away. I told A.J. what I had in mind and that I'd go home and finish them 'cause I had to go back to work at Ford. I did them at night. I guess I had an idea for the kind of car I wanted to do all along."[1]

While Riley was obsessed with reducing frontal area in the past, he decided to go in the opposite direction with the new car. Its most dramatic feature was what he called "a sports car nose," a low and broad one-piece design stretching from the middle of each front tire. He achieved a low center of gravity by moving a number of suspension mounting points and pushing the radiators to the rear of the car. Sidepods flanked the cockpit, which was tall and narrow, reminiscent of Riley's original design. A friend did a rendering for Riley to show Foyt, who liked it and decided to build two of the new cars.

With the next Coyotes under construction, Foyt headed for Daytona to run his first laps in his new Chevrolet. No one had ever won the Daytona 500 two years in a row and he wanted to be the first. "Actually, it should be three in a row," he said, clinging to the belief he'd won in 1971.[2]

◀ New Coyote hits the track. *Steve H. Shunck Collection*

When Ford withdrew from racing after 1970, Matthews had shifted from running a team to building cars for others. Smokey Yunick called him "the Henry Ford of race cars." When Foyt decided to run his own car in NASCAR, he knew where to find a crew chief. Having worked with Foyt before, Matthews knew what to expect.[3]

"He's intelligent, really smart, on or off the track," said Matthews, who was called "Banjo Eyes" as a kid because he wore thick eye glasses. "If we prepare the car in the right manner, A.J. will win races. When he's leading—up front or on the pole—he's easy to work with. But he's [not] when he's behind."[4]

It didn't take long for Foyt to let his displeasure with the new car be known. At one point he tried to buy the car of Cecil Gordon, an owner/driver who seldom ran up front but had a new Chevy. Rebuffed in his efforts, he turned his attention back to the Matthews car and gradually began to build speed.

He finished third in his qualifying race, riding in the draft the whole way with an engine running on seven cylinders. In the other qualifier, David Pearson started last in the Wood Brothers car after missing qualifying due to the death of his father and then drove to the front for the victory. Afterward, Foyt seemed to say he preferred racing in NASCAR and became one of the first to identify what would become known as "dirty air."

"Indy is so fast now the only place you can pass is on the straights," he said. "This is more competitive. You can draft and run two or three abreast in the turns. All in all, it's a hell of lot better racing here. Ours are so fast you just can't pass. With the front wings the air is so disturbed you can't steer around anyone."[5]

DARRELL WALTRIP

In addition to getting his own car sorted out, Foyt was trying to help a rookie named Darrell Waltrip, whom he'd met the previous year at a family function.

"A.J. was my hero when I was growing up, still is," Waltrip said of his early career. "He drove with red gloves and a red bandanna. So when I got my race car, I went to the golf store and bought me a pair of red gloves and I got me a red bandanna to put around my neck. I would ride around the track and visualize myself as being A.J. Foyt. I'd have my red bandanna flying in the air and had those red gloves on. I was badass.

"When you're a kid and starting your career, you have people you idolize and look up to, and people you want to be like. In your wildest dreams, you never think about ever meeting that person. It's just somebody you read about or heard about, maybe somebody you've seen race. But you never think about actually getting to know that guy. That's the way I was with A.J."[6]

Meeting Foyt happened sooner than Waltrip dreamed. He'd married Stephanie "Stevie" Rader a few years earlier. She'd been born in Harris County, Texas, and when the family moved to Kentucky they'd stayed in touch with Lucy Foyt's mother and stepfather. Both families attended the 1972 Daytona 500 and that's where Darrell met A.J. At the time Waltrip was a virtual unknown in the NASCAR world. He'd crashed out of the Daytona ARCA and late-model sportsman races earlier in the week and had yet to run in a Winston Cup event.

"When you finally meet someone you idolized, that's pretty special, a big thrill. He was like I thought he would be. He had a big ego and he was pretty outspoken. He was *A.J. Foyt* after all. He was good and he knew it. People say you're cocky, but I don't think you're cocky if you're really good at something and you know it. I just think you're confident."[7]

Fast-forward a year to Daytona 1973. After competing in five Cup races at the end of 1972 and winning a number of USAC, ARCA, and ASA (American Speed Association) events, Waltrip was planning to run for rookie of the year honors in NASCAR. But he was struggling in practice and not getting any help from the NASCAR regulars.

"I didn't know a lot and I was trying to learn as I went," Waltrip recalled. "I'd go out in practice with Richard Petty or Pearson or [Buddy] Baker, and I was trying to hang on and draft them. They kept giving me the finger and shaking their fist at me. I wondered what the hell was wrong with these people. I just wanted to follow them and learn what I'm supposed to do.

"So I go over to see A.J. and told him what was happening and asked him what I should do. He said, 'Let me tell you what to do, *boy*. Next time they take their hand off the wheel and start shaking their fist at you, hit 'em in the ass. I guarantee you they won't take their hand off the wheel no more and they won't give you the finger no more. Just hit 'em in the ass and that will stop all that.' So that's what I did."[8]

Waltrip managed to finish sixth in his qualifying race and on the same lap as the leaders. He dropped out early in the 500, but made an impression on others, including race winner Petty, who said, "The kid is already good. Give him the right management and he'll win a pile of money before he's through."[9] Foyt finished a disappointing fourth in the 500, four laps behind the winner and failing to lead a lap. He also praised Waltrip. "He shows a lot of promise and he's aggressive in my own style," A.J. said. He offered Waltrip his car to drive in the Charlotte World 600 while Foyt was at Indianapolis, saying, "With talent like that, he just needs a good car."[10]

By mid-March the new Coyote was ready for its first laps on the Speedway. It was low and wide, pushing the regulation limits at fifteen feet long and six and a half feet wide, and with a wheelbase of 104 inches. It was little more than thirty-two inches high and sat just three and a half inches off the ground. When asked about the fiberglass "bristles" under the car, Foyt grinned and said they were "to keep the track clean."[11]

"Nobody ever built a championship car this wide or this low," he boasted. "All the weight is distributed below the center of the wheels. It has the lowest center of gravity any race car ever had."[12]

The new car—Foyt called it the Coyote IV—also carried a new number. After missing five of ten races because of his injuries, he'd finished thirty-sixth in the final 1972 point standings and elected to use the No. 14 again. He'd last used the number in 1967 when winning the 500 and the national championship, but it had remained in the team's stable and used on several occasions, most notably during Jim McElreath's Ontario victory.

The car was fast right from the start, turning an easy lap at more than 193 miles per hour. Some said they'd clocked him running an incredible 240 mph on the backstraight. Whenever the car was stopped in the pits, the crew draped a mat over the front end, rear wing, and side pods to hide the new configuration from prying eyes.

Johncock was part of the Goodyear test and turned an even quicker unofficial lap, 199 mph in an Offy-powered Eagle. Despite Johncock's fast lap, his car owner, Andy Granatelli, was so impressed with the new Coyote he tried to buy one from Foyt, without success. One thing everyone seemed to agree on: this would be the year for a 200 mph lap at the Speedway.

From Indianapolis Foyt went to Atlanta for the next stock car race, where he continued to struggle with his new Chevy, dropping out early with overheating problems as Pearson won. He couldn't stop talking about his new Indy car, however.

"I designed and built the car," he told the NASCAR reporters. "I won't say this car will revolutionize racing, but it's got a lot of people worried. I think I can run it flat-out all the way around the track at Indianapolis."[13]

The Coyote wasn't the only thing sporting a new look. Self-conscious about his receding hairline, he'd followed the lead of Parnelli Jones and spent $600 and five hours in a salon chair for a hair weave, which was stylishly on the long side. He'd also started signing his autograph "A.J. Foyt—First or Nothing."[14]

Following the successful test, Foyt decided to enter the April 7 USAC season-opening doubleheader at Texas World Speedway, with both Indy car and stock cars in action. They were the first USAC races scheduled on the high-banked, ultra-fast track, and Foyt, who'd previously tested at the facility, sounded an alarm about the speeds the Indy cars would reach.

"It'll be one of the most dangerous races I've ever been in," he said of Texas. "If it weren't for the race being in my home state, I probably wouldn't race."[15]

Foyt said the cars were outrunning track and series safety standards.

"When you're running at speeds over 200 miles per hour you're just pointing. You're no more than a guinea pig. I'm sure you're going to see a lot of people hurt. These cars aren't designed to run that fast.

"It's time USAC did something," he said. "It's a shame that it always seems that somebody has to get killed before anybody will do anything. When you see some of your friends getting messed up because some people won't act, that takes some of the fun out of racing."[16]

He warned the wings had gotten too big, the engines too powerful. He suggested onboard fuel capacity be cut from seventy-five gallons to twenty-five, saying it would make racing safer and more exciting.

Once again Foyt's shops served as the base of operations for several teams while in Texas, including Johncock's stock car entry, which needed repairs and a new engine after Atlanta. Both races were run without incident, Al Unser winning the Indy car event and Johncock the stock car race. A.J. failed to finish either, although he'd battled Johncock in the stock car opener, trading the lead throughout before being knocked out by engine problems sixteen laps from the finish. The hairpiece also failed to survive the weekend, A.J. pulling it off and saying it was too hot.

After originally planning to run in the NASCAR race at Darlington the week after Texas, Foyt changed his mind, deciding to compete in the twin 150-mile Indy car races at Trenton. He said he needed to put more miles on his new car and besides, he didn't think he could beat Pearson. It was good news to the Trenton promoter.

"I would say Foyt would mean an extra 1,000 fans," said Bob Zera, predicting a sellout with news of Foyt's entry. At $12 a ticket, that added about $12,000 to the bottom line. "He still has magic about him even though he hasn't won in a while. He really generates interest around here."[17]

It was a good decision. One reporter noted the "often gruff and standoffish" Foyt was "absolutely gregarious" after qualifying second to Johncock, matching times with Bobby Unser in the process.[18]

In the opening race Foyt won going away, his first Indy car victory in nearly eighteen months. Between races "I out-engineered myself," he admitted later, changing the setting on the rear wing for more downforce. "Had the car pushing so hard I had to back off." He dropped to sixth in the early going before a caution flag allowed the crew to reset the wing. He charged back to second and was threatening eventual winner Andretti before blowing an engine.[19]

It had been even longer since Andretti's last Indy car victory, nearly three years, and afterward the two drivers celebrated together.

"This is more like it," Foyt said. "Maybe if I win at Indianapolis I'll retire, and I'll hire Mario as my driver."[20]

Despite his confidence in the new Coyote, Foyt continued giving mixed messages about the speeds expected at the Speedway. One moment he'd tell reporters he wanted to be the first to turn a lap at 200 mph, in the next he'd say the speed was "downright dangerous. I really expect there'll be a bad wreck one of these days."[21]

"The way things are going now, a driver just isn't able to react quickly enough to keep out of trouble at these way-out speeds," he told a group of reporters at a Goodyear luncheon in Chicago. His main target was the large rear wings on the cars. Johnny Rutherford, who'd joined the McLaren team, said the wings were "as big as picnic tables."[22]

"I believe that the wing size could be cut in half and you'd still have enough surface left to do the job—to provide the downward thrust you need for good cornering," Foyt said. "It would also do away with the turbulence. And the wings ought to be lowered. They're at a bad height and block the view of drivers moving up. It's a bad scene. The cars are moving too fast for safety's sake and you've also got a situation where your vision is partially screened."[23]

Turbocharger boost was unlimited, and he also warned engines were being overstressed. Roger Bailey, who built the Offenhauser engine in Rutherford's car, said it was putting out nearly 1,300 horsepower. "There could be a lot of car failures if they try to get up over 200 miles per hour and stay there," Foyt said. "If they don't detune to 196 or 197, they'll never run 300 miles. They'll never finish the race."[24]

At least one driver disagreed that the speeds were too high.

"I'm surprised at A.J.'s comments," said Bobby Unser, whom most expected to be the first to top 200 mph at the Speedway. "I don't feel that way. We are not guinea pigs in a car. It's a modern world and the driver has to be scientific to handle the speed. At one time 200 miles an hour was a magic number. We won't stop there. It's the American way of life that nothing ever stops. We have to do things bigger and better than the next nation."[25]

Taking a scientific viewpoint and differing with Unser was Dr. Steve Olvey, the assistant medical director at the Speedway. "At these speeds, it takes the equivalent of three football fields—about 300 yards—before the driver can even give any thought to what's happening. Anything within 300 yards is instinct—or luck."

FEAR

"Courage is resistance to fear, mastery of fear—not absence of fear," Mark Twain wrote.[26] While Foyt's remarks made headlines and drew comments from other drivers, it wasn't the first time he talked about being concerned, afraid, "petrified," or even "scared shitless" in a race car, and it wouldn't be the last. Yet he kept getting back in his car.

"It used to be that if you told somebody you were afraid, automatically you were branded a coward," Foyt said. "Today, people respect an individual who is not afraid to admit he has some fear. With the speeds and hazards we have at present in auto racing, you're not admitting that you are a coward when you say you have fear, you're just being honest with yourself. People can understand that.

"It's not that I'm any more afraid now than when I first started, but the older you get, the slower you react to certain situations. That's the only fear I have now. I'm afraid I may not be able to react as fast in certain situations."[27]

Few things bothered him more than hearing a driver say he wasn't afraid.

"You hear all these brave race drivers who have never been scared. When these guys talk, they are so brave. Well, A.J. Foyt was never that brave. I hear these other guys talking—I just shake my head. Why are you lying to yourself? Because that is all you are doing."[28]

"I don't know why people want to be brave in someone's eyes. It don't take being big and brave to drive a race car. It don't. And anytime you say you don't scare yourself, you're just kidding yourself. Every time I ever sit in a race car, even when I go out and practice, I thrill myself at least every now and then."[29]

Rain, wind, and cold temperatures limited practice time and held speeds down through the first two weeks of May, and Foyt was having a hard time getting above 190 mph, let alone 200. The new Coyote wasn't the problem: it seemed capable. But the team experienced one engine problem after another. Foyt's warnings about engines not lasting three hundred miles seemed optimistic—he was having trouble getting one to live for thirty miles. Along with teammate George Snider, who was driving the other new Coyote, No. 84, they'd gone through five of their eight engines before the start of qualifying. In the morning practice session before qualifying, Foyt damaged another one.

As a result, he wasn't on the track during practice when Art Pollard, who turned in the fastest lap on Friday and was one of the pole candidates, lost control of his car in Turn One and slid up into the wall. The car bounced off the barrier, caught fire, dipped down to the grass on the inside of the track, and then veered up toward the outside wall again, hitting it nearly head-on. The car then spun crazily down the track, on fire and shedding parts, coming to a rest in the second turn. The safety crew had the fire out almost immediately and Pollard, at forty-six the oldest driver at the track, was cut out of the car. It was too late—he was already dead.

Qualifying went ahead as scheduled, and it was Rutherford, one of Pollard's closest friends, who captured the pole with a record four-lap average of 198.413 mph in a McLaren. He was joined on the front row by Bobby Unser and Mark Donohue, each in an Eagle.

A new engine installed in his car, Foyt's first official qualifying run abruptly ended when he ran out of fuel, having cut the margin too close. On his second run he accepted a disappointing four-lap average of just under 189 mph, nearly ten mph slower than Rutherford.

"I wanted to qualify on the first day," A.J. said, recalling 1966 when he waited until the second day to qualify, started seventeenth, and was wiped out in a first-lap accident. "The car was handling beautifully going through the turns—it was just the engine. I don't know what the problem is, but we can't get the power. We'll tear it down and see if we can find [out]."[30]

At the end of the day Foyt found himself in twenty-third, second slowest of the first-round qualifiers. Afterward, car owners Dan Gurney and Granatelli called on USAC to reduce speeds and were joined by the new record holder.

"It wouldn't hurt my feelings a bit if they would bring the speeds down twenty miles an hour or more," Rutherford said.[31]

Unable to find any indication of mechanical failure on Pollard's car, USAC indicated it was probably driver error. Most thought he'd been caught by a gust of wind, similar to Jim Malloy's fatal accident in the same area nearly a year to the day earlier.

"Most of the time you can't even tell which way the wind is blowing or how to allow for it," said Swede Savage, the fourth-fastest qualifier. "But it really doesn't matter, because you don't have enough time to properly adjust anyway." Savage, Johncock's teammate, briefly held the track record and said, "This is the greatest day of my life. I honestly feel this is my year. I have confidence in the car, that it's safe, and confidence in myself."[32]

The winds dropped and car speeds picked up on day two of qualifying, and it became clear Foyt was in a precarious position. Six more drivers qualified, all of them faster than the No. 14. About fifteen additional cars were expected to make qualifying attempts on the final weekend and after three spots were filled, bumping would begin. As it stood, Foyt was second in line to be bumped. People were asking what was once unthinkable. Could A.J. Foyt be bumped from the Indy 500 field? Foyt himself asked a reporter, "Think I'll make the race?

"If for some reason we don't get bumped, I just don't think I'm going to run," he added. "I'll probably drop out of the race and forfeit my position if I have to start way back there. It's too dangerous to get out there and race. If I can't giddy-up-and-go with the rest of them, I would rather just watch."[33]

At the same time, Foyt talked with Gurney about acquiring an Eagle for a backup car before loading up his three best remaining engines and flying back to the Houston shop. Joining him was Herb Porter, a former crew chief and Goodyear engine guru. As Foyt's team had its own engine program, Porter worked primarily on Offenhauser engines and was a competitor in that respect. With Foyt being Goodyear's top driver, however, the company asked Porter to lend a hand.

"It goes much deeper than just business," Porter said of his trip to Houston. "It's a question of respect and friendship, and if you're in trouble, you help. We're family here. We respect each other. There were times in the past few years when I needed help and A.J. went to bat for me. If I can help him, fine. There's no money involved. It's something more than that. Nobody gets it done around here by himself."[34]

It wasn't until Thursday evening that they returned to Indianapolis, hopeful—but not positive—they'd solved the problems.

"We had to go home where we had the equipment to do the job," Foyt said. "We did a year's work in three days. It wasn't one thing, it was five or six things. We got the power, but it is a matter of keeping it."[35]

Friday morning Foyt ran his fastest laps of the month in the No. 84 car at more than 194 mph. In the pits Jim Hurtubise, who was having his own problems with a Foyt engine, walked up to A.J. and told him to "put it in the barn before you break it."[36]

He still preferred the No. 14 car and decided he would wait until it was bumped before moving to the backup machine, setting the stage for a pressurized final weekend of qualifying, especially for Snider.

"I won't pull it out," he said of his primary car. "I'll make a decision Saturday. A lot depends on how the motor performs on the racetrack. If we don't have the problems fixed and I can't go out and be competitive in the race, then I would rather sit in my suite and watch."[37]

The "suite" A.J. mentioned was one of several luxury units in a new facility the Speedway had built on the outside of Turn Two, not far from the Speedway Motel. It was three stories high, the bottom floor made up of VIP motel rooms going for $25 a night. The twelve second-floor suites went for $10,000 a year, and tenants included A.J. Foyt, Parnelli Jones, Roger Penske, and Mari Hulman George. There were eight larger suites on the third floor at a cost of $20,000 a year for a group that included Firestone, Goodyear, and Tony Hulman.[38]

The problems in Indianapolis were bad news for Waltrip, Foyt deciding not to enter his stock car at Charlotte.

"He got in a bad mood about the whole thing," Waltrip said. "Figured that Indy was taking too much money to justify running his stock car the same weekend."[39]

Few people believed Foyt would pull out of Indy no matter where he started, although at least one person hoped he would.

"Once or twice I've suggested that he ought to quit," said Tony Foyt. "His mother has tried to get him off the track too. She gets nervous, she'd like him to quit. But he won't listen to such talk. Racing always had been in his blood. He can't seem to get enough of it. He's well off enough now that he'd never have to touch another wheel if he didn't want to. But nothing can stop him."[40]

One reporter who'd been covering auto racing and Foyt for years, Bill Verigan of the *New York Daily News*, asked why he kept going. Foyt said it was hard for reporters to understand. "It is a very special feeling that goes deeper than satisfaction. Once you've tasted it, you keep coming back for more."[41]

It didn't help when more bad weather kept cars from qualifying on Saturday, pushing everything into Sunday afternoon. The No. 84 car would be kept in reserve until the last moment. If they played their cards right, Snider would be the last car to qualify. Foyt also made an unusual move of loaning an engine to Dick Simon, who could conceivably bump A.J. from the race.

"I know I've got a damn good poker hand, but I don't know how to play it," Foyt joked.[42] He spent most of the afternoon standing on the right-front tire of the No. 84 car in his driving uniform, ever-present Goodyear hat on his head and a stopwatch in hand, timing the competition. He nearly played it too close, Snider pulling on the track with less than two minutes remaining on the qualifying clock. Snider made it easily, turning in the fastest time of the day as Simon also qualified.

Given all the problems in practice, Carb Day turned out to be surprisingly clean, with Foyt turning laps at nearly 190 mph. Despite the poor starting position, no one was counting him out.

"Super Tex will have more eyes on him than there will be on me," said Donohue, the defending race champion. "The fans will expect him to make one of his classic charges, and I tend to agree that he will."[43]

Bobby Unser said, "That old grouch will need about two straightaways to get up where we are, and if his engine holds up, church will be pretty much out. Old A.J. wants to win his fourth one badly, and what Old A.J. wants, he usually gets."[44]

Even Tony Foyt sounded confident. "I don't see why we can't win it. Being in the eighth row means nothing to A.J. He could make that up in the first fifty laps."[45]

————

Two rain showers delayed the start of the 500 more than four hours, and when it finally got underway, it lasted only one hundred yards.

That's how far the leaders had traveled when the cars driven by Salt Walther and Jerry Grant, starting side-by-side in the sixth row, touched wheels, sending Walther's machine pinwheeling into the fence along the main straight grandstands. The impact broke several support poles and punctured a fuel tank, showering the crowd with fire and debris. Walther's car came back on the track upside down and spinning like a top down the front straight, seventy-five gallons of fuel spewing onto the track and a fire trail tracing its route. It came to a rest several hundred yards past the exit of Pit Lane, Walther's feet exposed where the front of the car used to be.[46]

Walther was transported to Methodist Hospital where he was listed in critical condition with burns on 40 percent of his body. Eighteen spectators were sent to area hospitals and five were held overnight, including two teenage girls with burns and listed in serious condition. All would eventually recover.

Although Foyt initially called it "probably one of the best starts in years," few agreed with him. It was a jumbled mess at best, "untidy" according to Jackie Stewart on the ABC telecast. There was supposed to be one hundred feet between each row of cars but in some cases there was virtually no gap. Numerous cars were a row or more out of position, with Steve Krisiloff, Peter Revson, and Foyt the biggest offenders. Video footage caught Foyt moving from the eighth to the seventh row while entering Turn Four and alongside Grant and Walther when they came together near the start/finish line.

"A.J. was supposed to be on the row with me, but suddenly he was gone, out of sight," said David Hobbs, who initially lined up to the inside of Foyt on the eighth row. "I hung back, but he was long gone."[47]

Mike Mosley, who started directly behind Grant in the seventh row, also called out Foyt for jumping the start.

"Nobody was in position behind the front row," said Mosley, whose car was damaged in the crash but would be repaired in time for the restart. "Both of A.J. Foyt's cars, Foyt and George Snider, passed me before we got to the green light. I am not saying it was their fault. Nobody was in position."[48]

Even a rookie driver with one year of Formula One experience, and making his first Indy car start, was critical.

"These drivers are yahoos," said Graham McRae. "I have never seen such antics among such experienced drivers. Something in their heads seems to go poof. Winning is all they seem to think about, regardless of the consequences. A.J. Foyt, for instance. Who does he think he is? He just said, 'Out of my way, A.J.'s coming through.' He could care less about the one hundred feet between cars."[49]

After watching video footage, chief steward Harlan Fengler fined Krisiloff, Revson, and Foyt each $100, saying they "improved their positions" before the green flag was displayed. For the second straight year Fengler found himself defending the decision to start the race, saying he'd been unable to see any cars out of position.[50]

The video footage showed Foyt pulling close to Walther and perhaps startling the other driver, which led him to move right. Some thought the two cars touched. While not denying he moved up, Foyt took exception with the television replays.

"They're wrong," Foyt said of the coverage. "I'm completely through with ABC. I'll never be interviewed by ABC again. I can tell you that.

"That camera they used was at a bad angle. The film was distorted. It may look like I was right on his tail, but actually I was ten or twenty feet behind Walther. I was a couple of rows up—you're damned right. That's the name of the game. You can't be a frontrunner if you sit back there and want to wait and wait, then all of a sudden say, 'Gee, I'd better go racing.'

"Sure, I was out of position and I thank God I was. I got fined $100 for it, and I was really happy to pay that fine. If I had been back in my own position, there's no way I would have been able to avoid hitting him. As it was, he went up on the wall and I thought sure he was going to come right back down on top of me. But somehow he stayed up there longer than I thought he could have. I scrunched down in my seat and stood on it. I wanted to get out of that mess."[51]

He was also critical of some of the drivers in the race.

"With the wing you can take anybody and put him in a car and they can run almost as fast as myself or Bobby Unser. It doesn't take talent today to run with wings the way it did years ago."[52]

Most saw the fines, the maximum Fengler was allowed to apply, as nothing more than a slap on the wrist.

"A hundred bucks," wrote one columnist sarcastically. "That ought to show old A.J."[53]

Walther, who'd spend nearly three months in the hospital and say he watched a tape of the crash more than fifty times, eventually talked with Foyt and absolved him of any blame.

"At the time I honestly felt someone bumped me," Walther said. "I never said publicly who I thought had done it but A.J. Foyt has taken a bad rap ever since as being the cause of it. When I saw A.J. I said let's sit down and talk about it. We did and A.J. convinced me he didn't bump me. He's a big enough man to admit it if he had done it, so I know he didn't."[54]

"I think I had a tire going low. So I think Foyt was unjustly condemned by some. I think he knew exactly what he was doing. Harlan Fengler should never have started the race. I want to get A.J. off the hook for good."[55]

———

Rain started to fall before the track could be cleared, and the race was postponed until the next morning. The restart didn't get past the pace lap before it was stopped again by rain. The second straight rainout was also taking its toll on crew members.

"It's exasperating," said Tony Foyt. "Up every morning at five, getting the car ready, hauling it back and forth between the track and the garage, fighting the rain. Pretty soon you get all whipped out."[56]

With a third consecutive day of rain showers forecast for Indianapolis on Wednesday, May 30, few expected the race to be restarted. Only about 25 percent of the Indianapolis police officers normally assigned to the track on race day were on duty. The Speedway opened only some of the access gates and refreshment stands because many of its part-time employees had returned to their full-time jobs. Some of the food stands reported they were out of hot dog buns and getting dangerously low on beer. Bathrooms hadn't been properly cleaned, and the health department threatened to shut the track down. There was talk of postponing the race until Saturday.

The scheduled 9:00 a.m. start came and went, and card games again started in the Gilmore Racing garages, which had become a regular gathering spot for drivers and crew members during the delays. Foyt played mostly gin rummy while others played poker and blackjack. Johncock was a big winner, pocketing about $150 playing blackjack. Foyt also spent about two hours arguing with Speedway officials over his hundred-dollar fine, to no avail.

It wasn't until after noon, when Bignotti and Roger Penske took a ride around the track and told Fengler it was safe to race on, that the process of moving the cars into position began and drivers were told to get ready. As the race had yet to complete a full lap, it was decided to start over and the now thirty-two cars were lined up three abreast. No lessons seemed to have been learned from the first-day debacle. Several cars had difficulty starting and pulling away, while others moved ahead of their assigned position.

The field seemed to be straightened out for the green flag, although Bobby Unser jumped ahead before the start/finish line just as he'd done on the first day, again without consequence.

It quickly became apparent something was wrong with Foyt's car, and he made the first of three early pit stops. He was several laps behind when he stopped for good on lap thirty-seven with a busted engine. Bobby Unser led early and then Savage, Johncock, and Al Unser took turns up front.

Foyt was still in the pits twenty laps later when several explosions ripped through the Speedway. Going for the lead, the back end of Savage's car slipped wide coming out of Turn Four before the rear tires suddenly gripped the racing surface, launching him toward the diagonal wall guarding the inside of the track. In an impact eerily similar to the one that led to the deaths of Eddie Sachs and Dave MacDonald nine years earlier, the car hit the wall nearly head-on, exploded in flames, and was ripped into two pieces, the cockpit and engine. Both pieces of the car ricocheted back toward the track, the four tires bounding skyward.

"I've never seen a car just disintegrate like that," said a shocked Chris Econo-maki on the ABC broadcast.

There was chaos on the track and in the pits. Unsure where Savage was, firefighters went to the closest piece of wreckage, which turned out to be the engine. Spotting him struggling in the cockpit near the outside wall, they ran toward him when another explosion engulfed it in flames a second time. Better prepared than they were in 1964 with asbestos suits, one fireman waded into the flames, pouring the firefighting foam directly on Savage. It still took about thirty seconds before the fire was extinguished and incredibly, Savage, who was wearing a full-face helmet and was one of only three drivers with a new safety uniform filled with a flame retardant, was not only alive, he was conscious.

The race was immediately stopped and some of those in the pits began running to the accident site, including Armando Teran, a member of the STP team assigned to McRae's car, a teammate of Savage and Johncock. Teran, twenty-three, ran onto Pit Lane and was hit from behind by a fire engine headed toward the accident, which was going the wrong way in the pits. Teran was thrown about fifty feet through the air and was unconscious when others reached him. He was pronounced dead at Methodist Hospital an hour later.

Foyt was among those who went to the accident site and then continued down the track to where the No. 84 was parked. Snider was out of the car and distraught. He'd worked his way up to fifth and was close enough behind Savage to see the fire. Foyt was talking with Snider when he grabbed Johncock, who'd also stopped nearby and was headed to check on his teammate. At five foot seven,

Johncock was sometimes called "Pee Wee" by Foyt and other drivers, but it took all of A.J.'s strength to hold him back.

"I knew he had to be hurt and the way the car looked, it was bad," Johncock said after the race. He'd been entering Turn Three when the accident happened. "I stopped about 200 yards from his car. I started to walk up there but A.J. stopped me. He wouldn't let me look. I felt like quitting right there and then. I didn't feel too much like racing anymore. There hasn't been a greater guy to work with than Swede Savage."[57]

In less than ninety minutes, the track was cleared and cars lined up in single file for a restart. Snider told Foyt he couldn't continue.

"I didn't want to drive after what I saw," he said years later. "I saw the big fire when I came around. It was just one of those deals that gets to you. Especially when they stopped the race and you sit around for a while. I didn't feel like getting back in.

"I asked him, 'Do you want to drive this thing? Because I don't want to drive it.' So I let A.J. drive it. That's the only time something like that happened."[58]

Unaware of the circumstances, some fans booed when it was announced Foyt was replacing Snider. He made it just past the halfway point in the race when the transmission seized in Turn Four, A.J. getting out and pushing the car to safety to avoid another caution flag. He and Snider were credited with twelfth as Foyt's prediction of mechanical carnage at the three-hundred-mile mark proved accurate. Only ten cars were running after 332.5 miles when rain mercifully stopped the race. Sixteen cars, nearly half the field, retired with engine problems.

Johncock, the last of the leaders still running, was named the winner while parked on Pit Lane and later gave some credit to Foyt, saying he probably wouldn't have restarted if he'd made it to the accident site.

The race over, Foyt didn't hold back, telling a reporter, "The speed is getting so fast, it scares me to death." The race winner also called for a reduction in speed.[59]

"They're getting too fast," Johncock said. "I would really like to see them slow these cars down. By slowing down the cars, you would have a much better race. They could do it tomorrow as far as I'm concerned."[60]

Some thought more should be done besides slowing the cars down.

"You can get off your knees, America," wrote Jim Murray in the *Los Angeles Times*. "They have finally stopped the Indy 500. That's got to be the best news since the armistice.

"This is the first time I have come 2,000 miles to cover a fire. I swear, this place has set fire to more vehicles—and people—than Hitler's army.

"They didn't give this one the checkered flag, they just put a lily on its chest. Someone named Gordon Johncock won it. It was the Indianapolis 332 1/2. God put a stop to it after 133 laps, which was not soon enough.

"Now if they can just cut it down another 332 miles . . ."[61]

For the *New York Daily News*'s Verigan, the reporter to whom Foyt had tried to explain why he raced, it would haunt him for years to come.

"I have seen too much dying in auto racing. I cover it now like a war correspondent in a battle zone, hating myself for the selfish satisfaction I receive from writing another big story about killing. And nowhere does that feeling haunt me like Indianapolis. I can only hope I never get so nonchalant about such scenes that I can overcome the churning in my stomach on race day in Indianapolis.

"I can still feel the blast of heat on my arms and face while Salt Walther's car exploded. I can still see them placing Swede Savage in the ambulance. . . . In no arena outside of ancient Rome has there been a spectacle comparable to that at Indianapolis Motor Speedway in May. But the barbarism in the coliseum ended some years ago.

"I ask them why. I wonder if the sport is worth the price. They tell me I don't understand.

"They're right."[62]

USAC moved quickly to head off a growing backlash from the media and drivers following the events at Indianapolis. It postponed the scheduled race at Milwaukee for a week and held an emergency Saturday morning meeting of its board of directors to rewrite the rule book. With Foyt on hand to argue his points, the board agreed to implement at least partially many of the measures he'd been calling for since the start of the season.

Effective for the next superspeedway race at Pocono on July 1, rear-wing width was reduced from sixty-four to fifty-five inches. Onboard fuel capacity was cut nearly in half, from seventy-five gallons to forty, with the right-side tanks to be filled with impact-resistant materials. The capacity of fuel tanks in the pits was lowered from 375 gallons to 340. With less available fuel, teams would be forced to detune engines to achieve better fuel economy, hopefully resulting in slower speeds.[63]

"I think USAC realized that an awful lot of drivers were upset over the whole month of May," said Johncock, who credited Foyt for his leadership in getting the changes made. "It seems like it always takes some guys to be killed or hurt badly to get changes. Instead, they should be looking into the future about new safety standards that are needed."[64]

Separately, the Speedway planned to remove the first twenty rows of seats along the front straightaway fencing. A change to the three-abreast start was discussed, but quickly rejected. The traditional start for the 500 would remain, along with stiffer penalties for those who jumped early.

Milwaukee's postponement created problems for Foyt. He initially planned to compete in the Indy car event on its original date, followed a week later by the NASCAR race at Texas World Speedway, which had received an international sanction. The delay put him in a tight spot of choosing one series over the other.

The politics of racing was becoming an increasing problem. USAC was threatening to withdraw from FIA and ACCUS (Automobile Competition Committee of the United States), auto racing's international and national governing bodies. It was upset over the granting of international rights to an increasing number of races, which allowed drivers from one series to race in another. Of the thirty-four races in the United States with full international sanction, NASCAR had fourteen, SCCA thirteen, and USAC seven. Part of the problem, however, was that many USAC promoters refused to pay the $3,000 application fee for international certification.

USAC saw it as a one-way trip, its drivers often racing in NASCAR events while Bobby Allison was the only NASCAR driver to enter the recent Indy 500. While there'd been a brief surge of NASCAR drivers racing in USAC in 1971–72 when Ford pulled out of racing, all had returned to the stock car series.

The relationship between USAC and NASCAR had never been very good, and sometimes that involved the Speedway. In 1954 the American Automobile Association (AAA), USAC's predecessor, had given Bill France the "bum's rush" out of Gasoline Alley, according to newspaper reports, ordering security to confiscate the NASCAR founder's "borrowed" credential. At the time AAA said, "We have a long-standing disagreement with NASCAR on what constitutes good racing." It didn't help when France had announced plans for a Memorial Day stock car race.[65]

Often caught in the middle was Foyt, the one driver who continued to jump from series to series. Promoters bartered for his entry forms, and he was on a par with NASCAR's big four—Richard Petty, Bobby Allison, Cale Yarborough, and David Pearson—receiving $3,000 in appearance money whenever he competed in a taxicab race.

He'd found himself in hot water with USAC after saying at Daytona he preferred the stock car series because it was more competitive. Now he was faced with a choice between Milwaukee, where he'd won six times in the past, and the Texas speedway he called his home track, and which he was negotiating to buy as it faced bankruptcy.

In the end he decided not to run in either race. He said he couldn't race at Milwaukee and make the rule changes required for Pocono, a more important race from a points and financial standpoint. A few days later he announced he wouldn't run at Texas, saying his car wasn't competitive. He wouldn't be buying the track either; the asking price was too high.

Foyt was forced to make the changes to his cars to meet the new USAC regulations without the help of Riley. The Coyote designer had been thinking about leaving the team prior to Indianapolis, and the race's death and destruction pushed him over the edge.

"The cars were so dangerous back then," Riley said, looking back nearly fifty years. "I asked myself what I was doing in this sport where so many people get hurt. What am I doing here? I said that to myself quite a bit."[66]

That wasn't the only thing bothering Riley. The fact Foyt never recognized him for designing the cars had continued to eat at him. And Riley was also one of those who said he never hit it off with Tony Foyt.

"During 1971, A.J. actually said his dad designed the car. Of course, anyone who knew Tony knew that he didn't design the car. He was a mechanic. Tony didn't really have much to do with the actual design, or anything to do with the actual cars. That kind of made me feel funny.

"I was a little upset that [A.J.] never mentioned my name for designing the car," Riley said, before rephrasing his statement. "Not upset. It became kind of embarrassing. People would come up and say, 'I thought you designed that car.'

"I decided it was time to change. I'm not so sure A.J. didn't think the same thing."[67]

Riley wasn't the only one who felt that way. Fabricator Ron Fournier, who'd done much of the work on the early cars, had already left the team for a similar reason.

"[A.J.] wasn't easy to work with," Fournier said. "He never gave me any credit. He liked to tell people that he and his daddy built those cars."[68]

While the new regulations would slow the cars during a race, Peter Revson set a track record in qualifying for the Pocono 500. The crew chiefs had simply trimmed three inches off each end of the rear wing, making up for the smaller wing by increasing the downward angle.

The fuel limits had an immediate impact during the race, however, McCluskey running out of gas in Turn Two on the last lap as Foyt swept by for the victory. A.J. had been careful from the start, monitoring his fuel mileage and making eleven pit stops for fuel, including the last one seven laps from the finish. As a result the race's average speed was down fifteen mph.

"I was being pretty cautious out there. I tried to run with Roger, but he made me back off a few times," Foyt said, admitting he "felt" for his friend and former teammate. "It's one of those misfortunate things. He gambled and lost. I won the gamble and the race.

"As for carrying less fuel, I believe it adds more to the race. The added pit stops give the fans more to see. And really, that's what they pay to see—action on the track and in the pits."[69]

McCluskey said, "It just isn't in my makeup to lose to anybody, but I'd rather lose to Foyt than anybody else. When you give way to him, you have been beaten by the very best."[70]

From there Foyt and Johncock, who'd led early at Pocono before crashing, flew to Daytona for the Firecracker 400. The next day, July 2, both were surprised to learn Swede Savage had died.

After spending several weeks in "critical but stable" condition at Indianapolis Methodist Hospital, Savage seemed to be improving before suffering a reversal, doctors saying his death was the result of lung and kidney complications. The Speedway's Dr. Steven Olvey would later say it was caused by contaminated plasma, with Savage contracting hepatitis B from a transfusion, resulting in liver failure.

Foyt refused to answer reporter questions, saying, "I don't want to talk about nothing like that." Johncock, who'd recently visited Savage, was a little more expansive.[71]

"He had been getting better the last four or five days," Johncock said. "He had been improving a little bit and joking. With the improvement, it was kind of a shock when I heard it this morning."[72]

Although Foyt dropped out early in the Firecracker, two weeks later at Michigan he drove the Banjo Matthews machine to its first victory in a USAC stock car race. He also led the Indy car portion of the doubleheader before dropping out seven laps from the finish.

Despite the victory, Foyt found himself back in USAC's doghouse for something he'd done at Daytona. A friend of his, Joie Chitwood Sr., had entered a car in the July 3 Paul Revere nighttime road race for Bobby Allison, who wasn't available for qualifying. Foyt agreed to qualify the car for the race, which was being run by IMSA (International Motor Sport Association), a relatively new organization closely aligned with NASCAR, but which did not have international certification for the race. Although Foyt didn't drive in the race, USAC officials were upset when they heard about his qualifying effort.

Two weeks later at Pocono he battled with officials who made him remove tape from the rear windows of his stock car that had been allowed in previous events. After threatening to withdraw from the race, he promised his crew he "would either sit on the pole or crash," before turning in the fastest qualifying time, more than a mile an hour faster than Richard Petty in second. Petty was one of several NASCAR drivers entered in the internationally sanctioned USAC event.

"Damn right I was mad," he said. "I guess the officials felt I was trying to cheat 'em a little bit. Looks like I showed 'em. The only reason I'm still here is because some of the other drivers asked me to stay and run with them."[73]

His fight with officials carried over to the race. After leading early and being shown in third place, but a lap behind with thirty laps remaining, he pulled over to argue with officials, passing the pace car in the process. He was penalized another lap and eventually finished seventh, two laps behind winner Petty. Afterward, he said he was tired of being "jacked around."[74]

"I'm not too happy with their stock car situation because to me, the way they run it, has been pretty Mickey Mouse," he said, promising to park his car.[75]

It wasn't until near the end of the year that he entered the stock car race at Texas. He immediately clashed with officials and went toe-to-toe with Jack Bowsher, his former car owner, after trying to qualify his car mounted with tires without the required safety inner liner, hoping to save a pound or two of weight.

"You think you're so good you have to run something different," Bowsher yelled at Foyt.[76]

"I've had enough of this," Foyt shot back. "You run your car the way you want and I'll run mine the way I want."[77]

After putting different tires on his car, Foyt went out and set a new stock car record, knocking Bowsher off the pole. In the race he battled for the lead before finishing second to McCluskey.

IROC

Not even a return to the dirt track series had helped Foyt as he failed to defend his title, dropping out of three straight races. As a result, he was in a sour mood when he showed up at Riverside International Raceway in late October for a new series put together by Roger Penske, the International Race of Champions, or IROC.

The series pitted twelve of the world's best drivers in evenly matched Porsches. Three forty-minute races would be held October 27 and 28 at Riverside, with the top six drivers advancing to the series finale at Daytona in February. The first three races would carry purses of $25,000 each, the winner getting $3,000. Each driver would be guaranteed $5,000 for the series, plus $1,000 in expenses.

At first Foyt declined the offer and was critical of the format, asking, "How can you determine a champion when you put these guys in a little car like a Porsche? Why not use several different types of machines—Indianapolis cars, stock cars, the Can-Am cars. And why all but one of the races on a road course? Why not different tracks? Mixing up the types of machinery and the tracks they use might give some indication of a champion. But not the way they're planning it."[78]

He didn't realize at the time even the Daytona race was planned for the road course. But there was another reason for Foyt's reluctance—money.

"They stand to make a bundle, and yet all they are guaranteeing the drivers is $5,000," he complained. "I told them how much I would come for, and they thought it was too much."[79]

While Foyt refused to say what it would take for him to participate, a crew member who heard the question wrote down "$50,000" on a sheet of paper and handed it to a reporter.

Instead, Penske lined up Roger McCluskey, Gordon Johncock, and Bobby Unser from USAC; Richard Petty, David Pearson, and Bobby Allison from NASCAR; Jackie Stewart, Emerson Fittipaldi, and Denis Hulme from Formula One; and Mark Donohue, Peter Revson, and George Follmer from American road racing. Goodyear was a major supporter of the event and as a result Firestone blocked its drivers, including Andretti and Al Unser, from participating.

Things began to unravel when Stewart announced his retirement following the death at Watkins Glen of François Cevert, his friend, protégé, and teammate. Dan Gurney turned down a request to come out of retirement and IROC organizers turned to Foyt as the only driver who could replace Stewart in terms of visibility and popularity.

"Had one of the road racers other than Stewart withdrawn, we probably would have replaced him with another road racer," said Les Richter, who was overseeing the event for Penske Productions. "But when Stewart retired, we decided we had to find the driver who would make the biggest impact on the American public. The people at ABC wanted Foyt, so we asked him again and he accepted."[80]

It took a major push by Goodyear to make it happen and there was no mention of what monetary incentive may have been involved, although Foyt later said, "I got what I wanted." It was also clear his feelings about the series hadn't changed.

"When they first asked me, I just flat told them no," he said. "I didn't want any part of it. All four races are on road courses and we'll be driving German-built Porsche Carreras, which most oval racers have never seen, let alone raced. Common sense told me you just don't give road racers that kind of edge and expect to beat them.

"I have never started a race in my life when I thought I was racing for second place, let alone seventh, and I'm too old to change my ways. When this thing is over I don't want some reporters saying one of the oval racers finished first in class. You'd better believe we won't be running for any class win."[81]

Gurney gave the road racers an "ever so slight edge," but didn't give his Le Mans winning teammate much of a chance.[82]

"I put Foyt, Pearson, and Johncock at the bottom," he said when ranking the competitors. "When Foyt replaced Stewart we lost a guy who could win the whole thing and got a driver with a big reputation in the United States but who can't keep up with these road racers. Foyt isn't in the same ball park. I just hope he doesn't beat the hell out of his car."[83]

Penske disagreed, although he ranked his driver tops.

"All things considered, all types of racing, there is only one other driver in the world as good as Mark, and that's A.J. Foyt."[84]

Despite concerns he'd break the Porsche, Foyt drove to a sixth-place finish in the first race, won by Donohue, and to fifth in the second, won by Follmer. Before the third race he joined Donohue on the grid. They had become increasingly friendly.

"I just hope an American wins this thing," Donohue remembered Foyt saying. Captain Nice said he thought Foyt, Follmer, and Revson all had good chances of advancing. "Peter I don't reckon is an American," Foyt said and Donohue asked him why not. "He's a good driver and all, but somehow he just gives you a feeling he's above it all."[85]

Foyt got his wish—at least if you counted Revson as an American—as Donohue won the third round with Foyt sixth, the two being joined by Follmer, Revson, Unser, and Pearson in advancing. Donohue, two years younger than Foyt, also won the Can-Am race later in the day and then surprised everyone by announcing the Daytona IROC finale would be his last race. Revson, Penske announced, would replace Donohue.

Only one race remained on Foyt's schedule for 1973, the November 3 Indy car event at Phoenix. A tough season that started with two wins in the first five races before falling apart was about to get worse, without Foyt turning a single lap on the track.

HEPATITIS

As Dr. Gary Friedman hustled the short distance from his office to the adjacent Houston Memorial Hospital where he served as chief of the pulmonary practice, he wondered what he had gotten himself into. It was less than two months since he'd completed his fellowship at Baylor University, opened his private practice, and joined the hospital.

A couple of days earlier, he'd been contacted by a doctor wanting him to look at a patient on the weekend. The doctor was a neurosurgeon, but he was calling about the father of one of his patients who was nauseated and couldn't stop vomiting. He was pretty sick and couldn't wait until Monday. Was Friedman willing to see him? The patient's name: A.J. Foyt.

Having grown up in Beaumont, Texas, about ninety miles south of Houston, and having attended the occasional race at local dirt tracks, Friedman knew who Foyt was and immediately said yes.

"A.J. was one of the most widely known sports figures in the world. He lived not far from the hospital, so of course I said yes," Friedman recalled. "When he arrived, he was a dark yellow color, about two shades darker than a pumpkin. It did not take a rocket scientist to figure out that he had a problem with his liver, most likely hepatitis.

"He was very sick, his blood test indicated a severe case of hepatitis, and I told him we needed to admit him to the hospital right away. A.J. has a mind of his own and said he had a race to go to. I told him that wasn't going to happen. I don't think anyone had ever told A.J. no before."[86]

Foyt was the latest casualty of what local officials were calling a "hepatitis epidemic" hitting Houston and already accounting for about one hundred cases in the city during the last week of October, five times the normal number. The outbreak had been traced to a shipment of oysters illegally harvested by poachers from polluted waters in Louisiana; there were more than one thousand cases nationwide. After confirming Foyt had dined on raw oysters several weeks earlier (hepatitis can have a long incubation period), Friedman explained the disease was highly contagious, and if not properly and promptly treated, including a week to ten days in the hospital, it could sideline the driver for months. He wasn't going anywhere.[87]

Checking on his prized patient during Monday morning rounds, Friedman found him irritable and refusing to eat or drink. He was mad about missing the race and complaining the food "tasted like shit."

"Part of the problem with hepatitis, along with the nausea and being on an IV, is you lose your appetite and everything you do eat tastes like cardboard or worse," Friedman said. "And hospital food also tends to taste like crap anyway. So this was my introduction to A.J. I discovered that what you see on TV is exactly what you get in real life."

Friedman said he'd talk to the hospital administration about the kitchen making anything Foyt wanted. He said he wanted a steak. The doctor said it might be a bit early for someone to find a steak at the local market, but he'd have one prepared for him as soon as possible. Friedman then finished his rounds and headed to his office to start the day's patient load.

That's where he was when he got a call from the hospital. Foyt had taken two bites of the steak prepared by the kitchen and flung the plate against the door, saying it tasted like shit and chasing the nurses from the room. He was threatening to leave the hospital. Could Friedman please come over and resolve the situation? Leaving a waiting room full of patients, he headed for the hospital.

"Here I am, a young doctor with a new practice, who has just been named head of pulmonary medicine for Memorial City hospital, with maybe six to eight weeks on the job," Friedman said, recalling his walk to the hospital. "I had to figure out what I was going to do. I had graduated magna cum laude from Baylor, one of the top medical schools in the country, but they don't teach you this kind of stuff in med school.

"I really liked A.J. from the moment I'd met him. We have pretty similar personalities. I came from a blue collar background and put myself through college and med school, so I related pretty well to him. And I can be pretty stubborn.

"When I got there, I sat on the edge of the bed and said that I think we can get along great, and that I intended to stay his doctor. I told him I know things taste bad because of the hepatitis, and that I didn't know if there was a lot we could do about it, perhaps try ice cream or something.

"I told him I wasn't mad at him for throwing the steak, but that I needed him to do me a favor. Would he please apologize to the nurses? Not for them, but for me. I told him I'm new here, and I've got to resolve this. Just tell them the truth, that you're not feeling well and you're sorry. Again, I'm not asking you to do it for them, I'm asking you to do it for me."

A contrite Foyt agreed and apologized. By the time he left the hospital a week later, he was signing autographs for everyone who asked—and everyone asked. In many cases hepatitis patients are prescribed three to four months of rest, which put the February races in doubt, although Friedman knew the chance of Foyt missing Daytona was minimal.

It was the start of a professional and personal relationship between Friedman and the Foyt family that would last the rest of their lives. Friedman went on to head a large pulmonary practice, establish the Texas Lung Institute, and bring the first hyperbaric treatment chamber to the Houston area. Having put himself through college working summers in the Texas oil fields, he had a special interest in treating gaseous and toxic fume illnesses and became nationally known for his efforts in this area. When legendary Houston oil-well firefighter Red Adair led a team to Kuwait to extinguish the fires started by retreating Iraqi soldiers during the 1991 Gulf War, it was Friedman who oversaw their medical care.

Through it all, Friedman would remain, in effect, the Foyt family doctor. Along the way he'd attend multiple Indy 500 races, watching the race from the Foyt suite, often alongside Foyt's mother and Lucy.

CHAPTER 35

DANCING WITH A BUZZSAW

1974

Although A.J. Foyt filed an entry for the 1974 Daytona 500 and said he was "rarin' to go" following several months of hepatitis-forced layoff, he admitted to enjoying his time at home with his family, to the point that he was thinking about retirement.[1]

"I'm very serious about it," he said a week after his thirty-ninth birthday. He was at Ontario to run tire tests for Goodyear, his first time back in a race car in three months and talking with the local UPI reporter.[2]

"I won't run much longer and this could be my last year. I enjoy the challenge as much as I ever did or I still wouldn't be at it, but my family and friends have been on me the last five years to quit. And really, there's not much left.

"My desire to win is as strong as it ever was, but I probably don't do some of the stupid things out there that I did when I was younger. If I have the car, you can bet your butt I'll try to be there. If I don't, I won't take stupid chances."[3]

Despite being "in bed off and on for almost a whole month," he'd been able to oversee changes to both his Indy and stock car operations while convalescing, and on occasion would sneak out while still hooked up to his IV. After a disappointing NASCAR season with Banjo Matthews as his crew chief, he picked another series veteran, Cotton Owens, to prepare his Chevrolet for Daytona.

He also was making changes to the Coyote as USAC announced a number of new rules, including trimming another foot off the rear-wing width. The most drastic move came in the further reduction of the fuel allotment. For five-hundred-mile races, fuel allocation was lowered to 280 gallons, down from 340 at the end of 1973 and a full 100 gallons less than was available a year earlier. Cars would need to average at least 1.8 miles per gallon in order to finish, up from about 1.2 gallons the year before. Officials expected the cut to result in a 25 percent reduction in

◀ The Buzzsaw. *IMRRC, Giminez Collection, photograph by Jim Rogers* horsepower as mechanics further detuned engines, and a seven-to-ten mile an hour drop in speed on the track.

In addition to reducing speeds, the move served as USAC's response to President Richard Nixon's call for Americans to reduce energy usage by at least 25 percent because of the Arab oil embargo. The embargo had been in place since October 1973 and the Yom Kippur War in the Middle East. Nixon also called for gas rationing and a fifty-five mph national speed limit. USAC noted the methanol fuel its cars used was organic—based on wood grain alcohol and not petroleum based—but realized the importance of showing support for the national conservation effort.[4]

Both the 24 Hours of Daytona and Sebring twelve-hour endurance races were canceled because of the energy crunch. NASCAR announced a 10 percent reduction in the length of its races, fewer practice days, and reduced field sizes. USAC said it would continue to run its events at pre-embargo distance, while limiting fuel for both practice and qualifying. The start of practice at Indianapolis was delayed from May 1 until May 6 and qualifying for the 500 would cover two days instead of four.

When Foyt arrived in Daytona, stories about his possible retirement were rehashed and received widespread coverage. He'd already made a 180-degree change in direction and spent much of his time denying the articles.

"I don't know where that stuff got started," he said. "All of a sudden, you newspaper guys started writing about me quitting after this year. All I did was answer a question. When they asked me when I was going to retire, I said it might be this year, or it might be ten years. And then it comes out in all the papers that I'm going to quit after this year."[5]

"I guess these writers have to have something to write about and I am a good subject to pick on. Really, I haven't considered retirement. When I have decided to retire it will come suddenly. I suppose that one day I will back off the throttle and when I do that, I will know that it is time to quit. I certainly will not go around telling anyone that this is my last season. It will make me mad that the time has come, but I will not be stupid enough to drive beyond that day."[6]

Foyt led early in his qualifying race and was the only driver running with eventual winner Cale Yarborough when his engine blew two laps from the finish. Bobby Isaac, driving for Matthews, won the other qualifier.

In the IROC finale he came from sixth to challenge for the lead on the first lap, but missed a shift and over-revved the engine on the second, putting him out of the race. Mark Donohue went on to win, following through on his decision to retire afterward.

As a result of the poor finish in the qualifying race, Foyt started the Daytona 450 thirty-fifth in the field of forty cars. He worked his way into the lead by midrace and traded the front spot with eventual winner Richard Petty before his rear spoiler loosened and he fell back, finishing fifth. It was a disappointing finish, but the first time he'd led a NASCAR event in more than a year.

Two weeks later at Ontario for the start of the Indy car season, only four cars were entered with Foyt engines. The season-long durability problems during 1973 led virtually all of the other teams not already running the Offenhauser engine to make the change. Only Foyt and his teammate George Snider, along with the cars entered for Dick Simon and John Cannon, were equipped with the V8 engine.

One of the unanticipated results of the new regulations, however, was to give new life to the Foyt engine. Handling unlimited turbocharger boost was a bigger challenge for the V8 engine than the four-cylinder Offenhauser and a major cause of the durability problems. The new fuel limits resulting in detuned engines, and the lower boost served as a savior of the Foyt powerplant.

From the start of practice, A.J.'s was the fastest car on the track, although many questioned if he could maintain the pace on the fuel allotted. Then again, maybe he wouldn't try.

"Someone could high-tail it out there from the start, going as fast as we did last year, and lead every lap for 300 or 400 miles," Foyt said. "If all the rest of us were geared down to a slower speed in order to finish, he'd have all the lap money to himself. We'd never see him—until he ran out of gas."[7]

With each lap worth $250 to the leader, Foyt figured someone could win about $40,000 in lap money before he ran out of gas. That was less than first or second paid, but twice what the third-place finisher would make.

While the reduced fuel allotment cut race speeds, it had done nothing to slow them during qualifying, where two of the three most recent deaths at Indianapolis had happened. So USAC came up with a pressure-relief or "pop-off" valve to control turbocharger boost pressure during qualifying, holding it to eighty inches of pressure. Cars were allowed to practice and race at any boost level the team wanted, but the valve would be fitted to engines by USAC officials prior to each qualifying attempt.

Throughout the week of practice, Foyt consistently ran about five mph faster than the next best car. Speculation in the garage area was that he was exceeding the eighty-inch boost level. Foyt clearly enjoyed being the center of attention again.

"No one knows but ol' A.J.," he said when asked about boost levels, "and he's not talking. But you know why I'm fastest out here? Because I've been putting in more work on it than anybody else."[8]

Although nearly ten mph slower than Peter Revson's track record, Foyt topped second-place Johnny Rutherford in qualifying by nearly five mph. It was his first pole in a five-hundred-mile Indy car race in nearly five years.

"I had the last laugh today," he said. "I ran with hardly any wing. My wing was almost flat. Everyone else had theirs slanted too much. That causes drag and robs horsepower."[9]

"I was really running all week with eighty inches of manifold boost. Nobody believed me when I told them, so I just started kidding around that I had one hundred inches of pressure. But you'll notice I was smiling all the time."[10]

It was more of the same the next day in the one-hundred mile qualifying race. Bobby Unser took the lead on the first lap, but Foyt went in front on lap two and never looked back, beating Unser by nearly seventeen seconds. The team managed the fuel allotment perfectly, A.J. running out as he crossed the start/finish line. Foyt admitted having something special.

"I've got a thing in my cockpit that lets me turn up the boost, or turn it down, during the race. When Bobby went past me, I decided it was time to show him something, so I turned it up. After I got way ahead, I backed off and cut the boost down the rest of the way."[11]

He certainly had the attention of the driver who won the second qualifying race.

"He was really something to watch, wasn't he?" Rutherford said. "I'd like to know his secret. It's obvious A.J.'s got the key to the bank right now."[12]

He was also winning the mind games.

"Old Tex has the other drivers so psyched out they don't know whether they are coming or going," one race official said. "If he went out with a pair of Texas boots mounted on his nose cone, you'd see a pair on all the other cars within five minutes. He's got 'em psyched good."[13]

Although Bobby Unser led the first lap in the 500, Foyt went past on lap two and started to pull away. He was catching the rear of the field by lap twenty when one of the cars lost a body panel. It hit Foyt's car, cutting an oil line and lodging in the suspension. His day was through.

"It was a one-in-a-million thing," he said. "I drove over some debris. I don't know where I picked it up."[14]

Later one of Foyt's crewmen pulled a two-foot piece of fiberglass from the suspension. "Walther" was partially visible on the part, indicating it came from the car of Salt Walther. Ontario marked his return to racing following the controversial and near-tragic crash at the start of the 1973 Indy 500.

"That's racing," Walther said with a shrug.[15]

Joining Snider's pit crew, Foyt changed a tire on one pit stop and later ran up pit lane to help push the car into its pit after it ran out of gas. Snider eventually finished eleventh, eight laps behind winner Bobby Unser. Afterward, perhaps aware of at least one of the reasons Bob Riley left his team, Foyt gave high praise to Howard Gilbert, whom he credited with the engine's revival.

"Gilbert has been the man who developed my Foyt engines when I first bought them from Ford. He's been working on them all along and we're real pleased the way he has it running."[16]

There was another, less evident reason for the Coyote's improved performance. The detuned engine required less cooling and Foyt removed the large radiators previously mounted vertically at the rear of each sidepod, replacing them with smaller versions in the front and nose of the car.

"They may have worked great in a wind tunnel, but that's not a racetrack," Foyt said. "Those things act like two sails. They take away from the effectiveness of the wing."[17]

Not only did the move enhance aerodynamics, it improved the car's weight balance. Riley, who designed a car for Roger McCluskey to drive in 1974, would go to work for George Bignotti beginning in 1975 and design a car called the "Wildcat" that looked similar to the Coyote. It would take several more years, however, for him to realize the benefits of Foyt's changes.

"The '73 car suffered, and the Wildcats I did later suffered from not having enough front weight," Riley said. "The '73 Coyote had too much weight in the rear, and it tended to understeer or push. Or as they say today, it was tight. A.J. had been able to drive it only because, well, he was A.J.

"When he put the radiator up front, I think that really brought that car alive. I did another couple of cars never realizing I needed more front weight. We'd even put a wing on the front of one of the Wildcats to give it more front downforce."[18]

The updated Coyote would receive the 500 Racing Design award presented by the Society of Automotive Engineers for "innovative features in [its] safety elements, suspension system, aerodynamics and engine." Tony Foyt would earn the D-A Mechanical Achievement Award for the car at Indianapolis. But at no point would Bob Riley's name be mentioned.[19]

––––––––

Foyt followed up Ontario by turning the fastest laps during the mid-March Goodyear tire tests at the Speedway. Missing from the test was Peter Revson, who'd been killed in a crash while practicing for the Kyalami South African Grand Prix. He'd run off the track and hit the guardrail at the end of the main straight, somersaulted end over end, and burst into flames at an area of the track so notorious drivers called it "Barbeque Bend."

A week later Foyt was at Phoenix where he qualified fifth and finished third, leading nine laps but making one more pit stop for fuel than winner Mike Mosley. He brought an updated car to Trenton April 7, but brushed the wall and did enough damage to keep him out of the race. This time he had no one to blame but himself. He'd arrived at the hotel about midnight the night before and agreed to meet some friends in the bar for a beer.

"Just one, I told myself, but just one turned out to be five or six," he admitted later. He didn't get to bed until about 4:00 a.m. and woke up at seven with a headache. "I don't usually drink since I had hepatitis, that's why I had the headache. In qualifying I wasn't as sharp as I should have been. That's why I kicked the wall. I could have said it was the thermostat or the cold weather tires. But deep down I knew it was A.J. Foyt's fault, period. Some guys blame the tires or the car or a little dirt. But when you start lying to yourself, you're in trouble."[20]

Despite the problem at Trenton, he was an overwhelming favorite for the pole position when practice started at Indianapolis. Many were complaining that the new rules gave the Foyt engine an unfair advantage, especially in qualifying.

"The new rules played right into his hands," Mario Andretti said. "When the Fords were winning over the Offys, the maximum turbo pressure was about eighty inches. Now we're back to that, and he's thriving on it. He's getting about 150 more horsepower, and that makes it tough."[21]

Most vocal of all was Bignotti, who said, "They've already allocated the qualifying money to Foyt."[22]

Only the McLaren driven by Rutherford—winner of the pole position the year before with the same car—seemed capable of running with Foyt, and by midweek he'd moved to the top of the speed chart at 192 mph. That mark lasted less than a day before Foyt turned a lap at more than 196, although few believed he'd been adhering to the eighty-inch boost limit he'd have in qualifying.

"You don't know what's going on in this little game of musical chairs, you don't know what he's doing to the boost," said Goodyear's Herb Porter, who'd helped Foyt with the engine but wasn't privy to the team's day-to-day shenanigans. "Some of it is a game of psychology. The only guys who really know are the driver and the chief mechanic and if you ask them, they'll all lie."[23]

Dan Gurney, Bobby Unser's car owner, agreed. "Foyt had a lot of people psyched at Ontario. I'm sure his speeds are having the same effect on some drivers here."[24]

Foyt's team was wearing a new red-and-white checkerboard-style shirt for qualifying, the creation of Jim Gilmore's wife, Diana "Di" Fell Gilmore, who shared her husband's passion for racing. It didn't take long for him to show off what he had for real as he was first on the track in qualifying. After two laps at more than 192 mph, wind gusts nearly put him into the wall on the third, dropping his four-lap average to 191.632 mph.[25]

He caught a break when Rutherford blew an engine practicing and wasn't in line to qualify when his turn came up. Under the new rules of the abbreviated two-day qualifying, Rutherford would be considered a second-day qualifier and start near the rear of the field no matter what speed he turned in.

That left it up to Wally Dallenbach, who was driving one of Bignotti's three STP-sponsored entries. The previous night, in a last-ditch effort to challenge Foyt for the pole, Bignotti installed an oversized turbocharger on the car's Offy engine. The big turbo circumvented the boost limit by overwhelming the pop-off valve. While others said it was cheating, USAC admitted there was nothing in the rule book about turbocharger size.

Bignotti wasn't the only one who considered the idea: the teams of Roger Penske and Parnelli Jones looked at using the big turbo. They'd been concerned about an engine's durability over five hundred miles, however, and asked USAC if they could change turbochargers after qualifying. Told that was against the rules, each decided against using the big turbo.

High winds hampered Dallenbach's qualifying run, and he ended up second to Foyt.

"I'm pretty happy about this," he said. "If you've got to be someplace, you might as well be next to A.J. Foyt."[26]

It wasn't until later that Bignotti approached USAC officials about switching turbochargers. Told that was against the rules, he exploded.

"This whole thing is sort of ridiculous," he said. "Everyone here knows that the pop-off valve was supposed to make things equal for everyone. But it doesn't. It definitely favors the Ford [he still refused to call it a Foyt] engine—yet no one screams about that. I don't like to go to a racetrack knowing I'm going to get blown off by five or ten miles an hour by another car like Foyt's."[27]

Gurney was one of the few who praised A.J.

"You've got to give Foyt credit, he figured out the best way to interpret the new rules," Gurney said. "I'm impressed with his engineering."[28]

Rutherford would eventually turn in the second-fastest time at more than 190 mph, though he would start in twenty-seventh. Even after turning the fastest lap on Carb Day, just a tick quicker than Foyt, few gave him a chance at winning.

Despite taking the pole, Foyt grew increasingly "irascible, irritable, and crochety" as one reporter wrote, upset with the constant complaining and whining. As he often did, he took the complaints personally, as if his ability as a driver and mechanic was being questioned.[29]

With the race a week away, Foyt had heard enough. He refused to reshoot the traditional "front row" photo after Mike Hiss surprisingly bumped into the third spot a week after a photo had already been taken with Gordon Johncock in third. Reporters and columnists from across the country started their annual migration to Indianapolis, and all their bosses wanted an interview with A.J., who was in no mood to answer hundreds of questions about the dangers of the sport and when he was going to retire.

"I built this car, I prepared the engine, I tested the car, I set up the chassis, I figured out how to make the fuel last, and I'm busy," he barked at one reporter. He told another, "There's not much Ford left [in the engine]. Call it a Foyt. And don't forget it."[30]

His father warned others to stay away. "Trying to talk to him has been like dancing with a buzzsaw." (This appears to be Tony Foyt's first reference to "dancing with a buzzsaw," although variations of the quote—often "dancing with a chainsaw"— would be used for years to come.)[31]

"With the way he has been performing here this month," Tony explained, "outrunning everybody in practice and qualifying and figuring he has the strongest equipment going, A.J.'s afraid if he doesn't win, everybody will start saying he's over the hill and finished. He's not that type of man. He doesn't want to go out that way."[32]

Tony himself was furious when he heard A.J. was going to drive in the Hoosier Sprints, a pair of fifty-lap sprint car races at the Indianapolis Fairgrounds two nights before the 500. One writer called them "nothing" races, and in fact they don't appear in many record books. Foyt hadn't started a sprint car race since June 1968 and while he'd entered a car in the race, he didn't originally plan to drive it.

"George Snider was gonna drive my car," Foyt remembered years later. "Then he got a chance to drive another car that was winning all the races and he told me he wanted to switch. I said, 'George, my car will run the hell out of that one.' He said, 'Your car can't beat it.' I said, 'Fine, off you go. I'll drive it.' Then Parnelli and me, we made a wager. He said, 'Bet you can't outrun those top guys who run dirt every week.'

"My daddy and everybody was mad at me. They were saying, 'You're on the pole, what are you trying to prove?' But I loved sprint car racing. Life's short, and if you can't do in life what you want to do, what the hell use is it being here?"[33]

He was facing a mixture of dirt track veterans and newcomers, including Duane "Pancho" Carter Jr. the son of former driver Duane Carter and one of the young guns, who was on his way to winning the 1974 sprint car championship. Starting eighth in the first race, Foyt was third by the end of the first lap but unable to close on Snider and Carter after that. A red flag allowed him to make changes to the car, and on the restart he quickly passed both drivers.

If the first race hadn't been stopped, "there was no way I could have beaten Pancho," he said afterward. "I went by him as hard as I could. Pancho drove a hell of a race."[34]

One of the changes Foyt made to the car got him in hot water again with a major supporter, Goodyear.

"I wasn't getting the traction I needed, so I put Firestones on the back and kept Goodyears on the front. Leo Mehl [Goodyear competition boss] got really mad. He said, 'A.J., you're embarrassing us.' I said, 'Listen, the Goodyears came home first. The Firestones chased them all night.'"[35]

In the second race he swapped the lead several times with Greg Weld, a veteran dirt-tracker. Well aware of Foyt's affinity for the high line, Weld stayed near the outside wall, forcing A.J. to go low. Foyt eventually made it past on lap thirty-nine for the victory.

"Why do I drive in 'nothing' races like this?" Foyt repeated afterward. "Well any race I drive, I don't call 'em that. If you call 'em that, then I've driven thousands of 'em. I figured this was a good way to take the tension off before the 500, to get away from the Speedway, to relax and take it easy."[36]

"It also helps sharpen your reflexes, keeps you on your toes. I wanted to see if I could still keep up with these kids. I've been away from sprint car racing for quite a few years and these kids are getting tougher all the time. I had my hands full."[37]

The crowd of nine thousand included many Indy 500 starters, some who'd never seen A.J. drive a sprint car or on a dirt track.

"This does my heart good," said Jerry Grant, a road racer starting seventeenth in the 500. "Everyone said A.J. was an old man, over the hill. All you have to do is watch that man drive wheel-to-wheel and you know he isn't over the hill."[38]

———

Tom Binford was the Speedway's new chief steward, having replaced Harlan Fengler following the 1973 debacle. He put the responsibility for a good start on pole sitter Foyt—ironic as he'd been one of those blamed for the problems the previous year. A new entrance to Pit Lane would take the pace car off the track sooner, and the field would be observed by Binford coming to the flag from a new flag stand overlooking the start/finish line.

"The pace car will leave the track much earlier than in past years and Foyt will take over as the pacesetter," Binford said at the drivers' meeting. "At the time the field should be going about eighty miles an hour and I hope A.J. will gradually accelerate to about 120 when he crosses the starting line." Binford warned that anyone jumping the start would be docked a lap.[39]

Foyt brought the field down for a near-perfect start. Dallenbach, riding the brake and trying to get the large turbocharger spooled up for the green flag, jumped ahead by two car lengths before the start/finish line. Although there was no penalty, it didn't matter—Foyt was back in front and Dallenbach out of the race by lap three with a burned piston. From there Foyt started pulling away from the field by more than a second a lap.

One car was running even faster, Rutherford's McLaren. Starting from the ninth row, he passed ten cars on the first lap and was fifth after six. He was benefiting from a high attrition rate, with six cars already out of the race, including three with blown Foyt engines.

By the fifty-lap mark, Rutherford was able to lead for the first time on an exchange of pit stops. The McLaren crew consistently got Rutherford out quicker on his stops and Foyt was forced to make up the difference on the track.

On lap 138 Foyt went into the lead again, but not for long. Rutherford's windscreen and face shield were immediately spotted by oil and the spray was getting heavier. USAC officials saw the same thing and black-flagged Foyt. He made a quick pit stop and returned to the track but, told his car was still smoking, drove straight to his garage, his race over. He'd led seventy laps, half the race up to that point. Twice he'd been passed in the pits, and twice he passed Rutherford on the track. But he'd been running too hard and knew it.

A crowd of reporters began to grow in front of his closed garage doors, and it was twenty minutes before he emerged in his street clothes and headed for his nearby motorcycle. Chris Economaki intercepted him and Foyt paused as the cameraman moved into position. But when told ABC was breaking for commercials and it would be a few more minutes, Foyt moved on and mounted his bike. "The scavenger pump broke in the turbo. That's all," he said, before heading toward the Turn Two suites.[40]

The quick departure bothered at least one writer, Joe Falls, sports editor of the *Detroit Free Press*, who'd been critical of Foyt in the past.

"I wondered as A.J. Foyt stormed away from the track, would he have stayed around and talked if he won?" he wrote. "Methinks A.J. thinks of only one thing: A.J.

"That's fine because everyone says he is such an intense competitor and you can't get down on a man for that. But I wonder how he would react if he were treated the way he treats other people. The time is coming when he won't be able to run and they won't want to talk to him. That's when so many of them change and become cooperative.

"By then, who cares?"[41]

It was left to Gilmore to provide some additional context. It had been a crushing defeat for the crew, many of whom were in tears. "Changing tires hurt us. We lost so much time A.J. had to put too much pressure on his engine."[42]

After that it was all Rutherford, as he pulled away to a twenty-second lead at the finish, the first time in eleven tries he'd completed five hundred miles. He confessed to having mixed feelings when Foyt dropped out.

As soon as his windscreen was covered by oil, "I knew A.J. had had it," Rutherford said. "I could catch A.J. at will but couldn't pass him. I could run all over him in the turns but he was faster down the straightaway. I know we had some tricks left with the boost, but I suspect they did, too.

"I hated to see it. You know A.J. is a close friend of mine. I knew how much he wanted this fourth win at Indianapolis and he had a good car and was going good. But I'm racing this guy and nobody knows better than me that when you go against A.J. you've got a race on your hands. I still would have rather won it with A.J. on the track all the way."[43]

Late in the afternoon a reporter intercepted Foyt going to his car at the Speedway Motel. He was more approachable and said he was skipping the awards dinner in order to attend his son Tony's high school graduation ceremony. He admitted it had been a tough loss but still didn't have much to say. The race had been his seventeenth Indy 500, more than any other driver, moving him ahead of Cliff Bergere, who'd made sixteen starts from 1927 to 1947.

"That's the first time I damn near cried after a race," he said. "I thought I had everything together this year. It was the biggest disappointment in all the years I've been racing."[44]

He started to turn away before adding, "If I couldn't do it, I'm glad Johnny won. He's one of the finest competitors I've ever run against, he has to be because he's from Texas, and he was long overdue at Indy."[45]

LONE STAR J.R.

Foyt's feelings were shared by nearly everyone and it was a popular victory among fans and other drivers. "He was the second choice of every driver in the race," chief steward Binford said. Rutherford credited Revson, his former teammate, with teaching him about "perseverance."[46]

It was also a desperately needed safe race after the horror and tragedy of 1973 and many thought "Gentleman Johnny" was the perfect Indy 500 winner for the time. The patient, articulate, "easygoing, always friendly" champion immediately went to work polishing the sport's reputation.

"I hope the world will realize now that Indianapolis really isn't the bad name in the sport, that we can have a safe race with all the thrills associated with racing but without the deaths and injuries."[47]

It had been a long time coming. Three years younger than Foyt, in the early 1960s he'd been driving mostly stock cars in the Dallas area with an occasional sprint car ride in a national event. That's when Smokey Yunick spotted him and invited him to drive his car in the 1963 Daytona 500. The performance attracted the attention of numerous car owners, and he made his first Indianapolis start later in the year. He'd won multiple sprint car races and the 1965 national sprint car championship, along with his first Indy car race that year at Atlanta. His future seemed as bright as another fast-rising USAC star, Mario Andretti.

Then came a sprint car crash at Ohio's Eldora Speedway in April of 1966. His car flipped over the guardrail and he suffered two badly broken arms and a head injury and was forced to sit out the rest of the year. When he was ready to return, many of the car owners who'd been calling him a little more than a year ago didn't answer the phone. He struggled in a series of different cars and teams, going winless for six years.

He found himself "lumped in a category with a hundred or more guys as having lots of talent and potential, but little luck and less success . . . his track record was liberally sprinkled with failures and disappointment."[48]

"Sure, there were times when I wondered if it was all worth it," he said. "But race drivers are a funny breed of men. You learn to live with disappointment and yes even pain and injury. I don't mean you accept it, but you live with it."[49]

Some, including Foyt on occasion, called him Johnny Wreckaford. All that changed when he joined Team McLaren for the 1973 season, and he won three times before arriving in Indianapolis for the 1974 race.

"My favorite race at the Speedway was obviously my first win," said Rutherford years later, after two more 500 victories. "The fact that I raced A.J. for a number of laps made it special.

"My car was very good. I mean it was excellent, and I knew I had a good chance. Then I came up to A.J., and he was running the Ford engine and it had just a little more grunt down the straightaways than I did. I could get up beside him, but I wouldn't challenge him into the turn, I would just back off and let him go. I just sat there and stayed in his rearview mirrors. It was fun for me, and it was fun for him, too. His car finally gave up, and I won the race. It was just one of those things, and of course just to race A.J. Foyt and to come out on top was a great honor."[50]

Rutherford, who'd settled in the Fort Worth area of Texas, was one of a handful of drivers Foyt would associate with away from racing.

"At the track A.J. pretty much did his own thing," Rutherford said. "He marches to his own drum. Some of us, [Jim] McElreath, myself, the Unsers, we'd go to the White Front and have a beer. A.J. didn't really drink. If he drank more than one beer, he was drunk. At least that's the way it appeared.

"I got to know him a little bit better as we went along. We'd go hunting together down at a place he had in southwest Texas. A.J. had a motorcoach and we'd meet in Houston and drive down. I remember one time there was a terrible ice storm. The Newell nearly got the wheel wells plugged up with ice, and we had to get out two or three times and clear the ice away. Still, it was a lot of fun. We'd hunt quail or turkey or whatever showed itself. Good times."[51]

For his part, Foyt had backhanded praise for Rutherford in his autobiography.

"My friend Johnny Rutherford can loop that race car of his and get right back in the race. He does it all the time. I used to kid him about being the best spinner at Indianapolis. But a driver like Rutherford is tough to beat when he's having a good day. Some days he's not."[52]

In a book foreword (something he rarely agreed to supply) for Rutherford's 2000 autobiography, *Lone Star J.R.*, Foyt acknowledged the other driver's strengths off the track, along with a few of his own weaknesses.

"Johnny has always been a great ambassador for racing. He is polished and knows the right thing to say in any situation. I think he did a lot for the sport in that way. And he still does a lot for the sport in the way he is guiding and advising young drivers coming into Indy car racing today. I have helped young drivers, but I think Johnny is better at getting his point across and leaving the drivers' egos intact.

"I admire his courage even more. He's been through some pretty tough accidents, but he always came back strong."[53]

At some point later in their careers, Foyt discovered Rutherford was actually born in Coffeyville, Kansas, moving to Dallas at a young age.

"You should have heard him when he found out I was from Kansas," J.R. said. "'Rutherford, you mean I'm still the only Texan ever to win the Indy 500?' I said, I guess so, A.J., I guess so."[54]

"I still think A.J. was the best driver to ever strap on a racing helmet. He was in every car he drove. An engine builder, chassis man, mechanic, and car owner, A.J. has done it all and he's done it well."[55]

HORSEPOWER AND HORSES

As the 1974 season went on, Foyt's disappointment and frustration grew, along with his fits of temper and anger. A week later at Milwaukee it was more of the same—Foyt on the pole and Rutherford in Victory Lane. He led eleven laps early before making a number of pit stops with tire problems. On one stop he got out of the car, took off his helmet, and berated the crew for the chassis alignment. He made a couple of adjustments, reentered the race, and was the fastest car on the track at the end, making up two laps and passing Rutherford and Dallenbach near the finish as they battled for the lead. He finished sixth and complained about the size of the Goodyear tires not matching up. It was a complaint made by several drivers, but again not what Foyt's major supporter wanted to hear.[56]

He desperately wanted to be the fastest qualifier for the June 30 race at Pocono, which would give him a pole position "hat trick" for the three five-hundred-mile races. He turned the fastest lap of the week at more than 185 mph on the first lap of his qualifying run, fast enough for the pole, but blew the engine the second time around. After leading his crew through a quick engine change, he was granted a shakedown run by officials, only to spin in oil on the track and damage his suspension. By the time it was repaired, pole qualifying was nearly over and there were four cars in line. Two agreed to let Foyt jump ahead, two others did not.

As the 6:00 p.m. deadline approached, Tom Bigelow took to the track in the car of longtime entrant Rolla Vollstedt. He was slow, reaching a top speed of just 168 mph before waving off after three of four laps. Carter was next and did a few slow laps before waving off as well. By then the session was over and with it Foyt's Triple Crown pole dream. As a second-day qualifier, the best he could start was twenty-ninth. He wasn't happy.

"That's really chicken shit," he said. "That's low life to go out there and use up that time, waste all those practice laps and then wave off after three qualifying laps. It means I'm going to have to start behind a bunch of idiots. I may not race."[57]

Not surprisingly, some of the other drivers didn't appreciate being called idiots, although few allowed themselves to be quoted by name.

"Give me Foyt's car and give him mine, we'll see who the idiot is," said one driver. "Johnny Rutherford had to start behind all of us idiots at Indianapolis and still won," said another.[58]

Vollstedt said he was "sorry that Foyt didn't get a chance to qualify. I think he'd have won the pole. But I had an obligation to my driver and my crew too. He had his chances to qualify just like we did. I have great admiration for him, and he's always been a help to me when I needed it. But he's wrong."[59]

Sammy Sessions, who'd driven for Foyt in the past, said, "I know how A.J. felt. He's a racer. I don't hold it against him. [Although] he could have worded it a little better."[60]

By race day Foyt had picked up on the "Johnny did it at Indy, I can do it here" theme, but the rematch never materialized. He'd just made it into the top ten when his suspension buckled, ending his day. He was scheduled to fly to Daytona with Rutherford for the Firecracker 400, so he was forced to wait while J.R. went on to win the race and handle his media interviews before the two of them were airlifted out of the track by helicopter. They arrived in Daytona in the early evening and were greeted by a memorable rainbow.

"We oughta go over there and pick up that pot of gold," said Rutherford, who'd just won his third straight Indy car race.[61]

"You son-of-a-gun, you've already found one pot of the stuff. I'm the one who should go over there looking," Foyt said.[62]

There would be no pot of gold on or off the track at Daytona. Rutherford's Indy 500 victory had earned him a special NASCAR appearance fee, although not in a competitive car. Foyt was driving for yet another NASCAR team, DiGard, as a teammate of Donnie Allison, who was having fun with the situation after out-qualifying his former boss.

"A few years ago I drove at Indianapolis in a team with A.J. and he gave me the slower car," Allison said. "Now A.J. is running one of my cars in this race and he qualified five miles per hour slower than I did. I don't have to say any more."[63]

Rutherford was out of the race before it was ten laps old, and although Foyt ran with the leaders early on, he was out before lap fifty.

The trip to Daytona wasn't a total loss, however, as Bill France made Foyt an offer he couldn't refuse. While Bill Jr. was officially running NASCAR, the founder was still very much involved, and he'd been bugging Foyt to come to the new Talladega track. Now he sweetened the deal, offering Foyt a chance at setting a closed-course speed record in his Coyote. The mark of 214.158 mph had been set by Andretti in Indy car qualifying at the Texas World Speedway and France knew a chance to top Mario always ranked high with A.J.

First up was a July 21 Indy car/stock car doubleheader at Michigan, where Foyt got back in Victory Lane. After qualifying second to Bobby Unser in both races, he led the opening Indy car race early before tire problems again surfaced. He pitted three times with punctured tires but still managed to finish thirteenth, three laps behind winner Unser.[64]

The stock car race was a different story. He was driving for yet another car owner, Hoss Ellington. It was an exciting race between two of the sport's best, with Foyt and Unser running side-by-side for much of the event, Foyt emerging victorious.

When it was over Unser raved about Foyt's car control and came away with a story he told often, including to William Nack of *Sports Illustrated*.

"I'm trying to pass Foyt for the lead and I started losing my car in his draft," Unser said. "I let my car get loose; my rear end started coming around. The air from his car is sucking mine up toward him. My car is going to spin. And I'm going to hit him because we're so dang close together. I made a mistake and I knew better. I'm going to have a wreck. I'm going to wreck him, too, and it's going to be my fault. Just as simple as A-B-C. At about, oh, 165 miles an hour.

"He saw it. Saw I'd lost it. You know what the guy does? This'll show you how smart he is. Most drivers would have shied away. Not A.J. Foyt. Instead of trying to run away, or pulling to the right to get away from me—and maybe he can get away and leave me to hit the wall, but maybe I hit him, too—no, no . . . he guaranteed the outcome. Guaranteed it. And he did it out of instinct. There wasn't time to think about it. He pulled down on me. On me! He backed off and came down and cut the draft between us. Let my car bump his. It was a very gentle thing. And he put my race car straight. We quivered a little bit but he got me straight."[65]

It may have been instinct, but Foyt knew what he'd done.

"Saved your ass, didn't I?" he said to Unser afterward.[66]

RECORD RUN

Foyt took the same Coyote he put on the pole at Ontario and Indianapolis to Talladega for the world record attempt. Not only was he making his first trip to the 2.66-mile tri-oval with thirty-three-degree banked turns, it would be the first Indy car to run at the speedway. The existing track record of 201.104 mph was held by Isaac in a stock car weighing about 2,500 pounds more than the Coyote.[67]

He was scheduled for a day of practice, to be followed by a record attempt on Saturday, August 3, that would be open to the public. The timing was designed to build interest in the Talladega 500 NASCAR race the following weekend.

A lap in the mid-220s was possible, Foyt said, with speeds topping 255 mph on the straight necessary to reach that mark. Foyt said his engine was putting out 1,100 horsepower and to cut drag, the Coyote was fitted with a much smaller rear wing than at Indianapolis. After a few practice laps under 210 mph, Foyt was back in the pits, saying the car was "awfully flighty" on the straight. It wasn't going to be as easy as he thought.

"Records are made to be broken," he said. "I've set a lot and I've seen a lot of mine broken. I hope we break it, but I've seen a lot of times before when something I thought was going to be a world beater wasn't. I felt like I was going to win at Indy this year. But I didn't."[68]

He took to the track shortly after 10:00 a.m. on Saturday, and after a warm-up lap of more than 210 mph, felt something wrong in the engine—"Halfway burned a piston," he'd say. He ran three more laps, setting a mark of 217.854 in the process, before pulling back into the pits.

"I got in trouble in turn two and almost got into the fence," he said of the record lap. "When you're running over 200 miles per hour the track is pretty narrow. When I found out I had the engine problem, I wasn't going to be foolish and lock it up and kill myself.

"My car would have passed inspection at Indianapolis. But if someone came here with an exotic car and plenty of time and just wanted to get the record as high as possible, he could possibly do 240 or 250. If somebody breaks the record, I'll come back better prepared."[69]

The previous overall record holder was not impressed.

"Everything was in Foyt's favor for his record run," Andretti said. "Texas World Speedway, where I made my run, is only two miles around. If I try to do the same thing at Talladega, it's a piece of cake. I'd easily best his record."[70]

Parnelli Jones, Andretti's car owner, offered to put up $100,000 for a winner-take-all, high-speed face-off at Talladega if Foyt did the same. A head-to-head race "was too dangerous," he said, but Jones wanted to see what the teams and drivers could do on solo runs under the same track and weather conditions.[71]

Foyt countered, saying he'd do it if they both put up "half a million." Jones said he thought Foyt was "only joking and kidding, but I think we can be serious about this. It would be a great promotion for racing. I don't know if he's willing."[72]

Andretti even seemed open to suggestions of a Talladega match race between himself and Foyt. "I don't know what it would prove, except that the public would see two good drivers compete with all stops pulled. I don't want to be shooting off my mouth about a match race with Foyt when I don't have the blessing of everyone concerned. Also, when you get right down to the nitty-gritty, it's more than pride involved. There must be a substantial amount of money to make the race worthwhile. I'm sure Foyt would have no qualms about the race."[73]

While negotiations continued for an Andretti/Foyt Talladega matchup, A.J. agreed to participate in the second running of the International Race of Champions (IROC) series. Several of his complaints from the previous year had been answered, with Chevrolet Camaros replacing the Porsches and half of the races scheduled for oval tracks. When Foyt and Bobby Unser said they wouldn't compete if there were any green cars in the race, one of the Camaros was repainted black.[74]

Others signing on included Bobby Allison, George Follmer, Johnny Rutherford, Emerson Fittipaldi, Graham Hill, Jody Schecter, Ronnie Peterson, Richard Petty, David Pearson, and Cale Yarborough. Although Firestone had already announced it would stop making tires for Indy car racing, drivers still under contract, including Mario Andretti and Al Unser, were again forced to sit out of the Goodyear event.

On his way from Talladega to Michigan for IROC and Indy car races, Foyt made his first visit to the Keeneland Fall Yearling Sales, an annual auction of young thoroughbred race horses. He paid $13,500 for one colt and $8,000 for another. He was far from the biggest spender, with one horse going for $56,000. He stopped at nearby Claiborne Farm, where he came face-to-face with 1973 Triple Crown winner Secretariat.

"I don't know what it is about him but he caught my eye when he was racing," he said of "Big Red," who ranks as one of the top racehorses of all time. "Since I wasn't involved in [horse] racing then, it must have been him that got my attention."[75]

Secretariat may have caught his eye, but it was his son Tony's interest in horses that took A.J. to Keeneland in the first place. When the eighteen-year-old graduated from high school earlier in the year, A.J. and Lucy had hoped he would be the first in the family to go to college, but Tony had other ideas.

"I wasn't that good of a student in high school," Tony said. "You look back on things and I wish I had tried a little harder. But I had already decided horses was the way I wanted to go, and I couldn't see where college was gonna do you any good. I think my mom and dad were a little disappointed, but then after I got out and proved to them I was going to work, and this was what I wanted to do, it was all good."[76]

His love of horses had started at a young age. Often during the month of May while A.J. was at the Speedway practicing, Tony and Lucy would spend time at the Hulman family farm in nearby Terre Haute, where they went riding. He had his own pony by the time he was ten, and the fascination increased during a family visit to the Georges' Circle S horse ranch in Wyoming. As a child he never talked of becoming a race car driver, which was fine with A.J., and especially Lucy.

"He never encouraged me or my brother [Jerry] to drive," Tony says. "He said it would be hard because everyone would expect me to be as good as he is."[77]

A.J. told variations of a story over the years about how Tony was frightened by a bad crash at a race when he was very young and was always afraid of race cars as a result. Details of when and where it happened varied, but the theme remained the same.

"Tony was a baby in my wife's arms in the grandstands," A.J. would say. "It was just real nasty. All the people in the stands were screaming. It was the shock, I guess. After that, every time I'd start up a motor, he would cry and scream."[78]

Not surprisingly Tony says he has no recollection of the incident. Regardless, his interest was always with the horses.

"I messed with horses almost my whole life," he says. "Growing up we always had a horse or two." Tony started working with show horses at the family ranch, including one purchased from driver Donnie Allison. At fourteen he rode the local halter-class champion mare and traveled to Kentucky, where he won his class at the state fair.

"Show horses really teach you a lot," Tony said, "but there's really no money in it. I decided that if I was going to make a living, I'd have to go with racehorses."[79]

"I asked my father when I was still in high school how I could get into racing. He was amazed since I had never showed any interest. Then I explained I meant horse racing. I'll never forget his reply. He said, 'Son, I can't help you there.' It was the best thing he ever said to me."[80]

Eventually, he did find a way to help, arranging for Tony to work at yet another of the Georges' ranches, this one in Ruidoso, New Mexico, where he learned to train quarter horses and also met his future wife, Nancy. Next stop was a move to Louisiana where he worked with thoroughbreds.

"I'm not disappointed he's not in auto racing," A.J. said. "I feel I'm doing what I really want to do and I'm successful. I want him to be the same way. Kids these days have too much free time, so I gave my boy something to do. I got interested because I wanted him to get involved in something. If not auto racing, then something he really wanted to do.

"It's just like the auto racing business, you can buy the best and put the best into it, but that isn't any kind of guarantee," Foyt said at Keeneland. "But I'd rather start with young stock. When dealing with older stock you might buy the best, but only accidentally. I certainly wouldn't sell you one of my best-proven cars if I were going to have to race against it.

"I've never had any other kind of sport to get involved in except cars, and I won't be able to drive cars forever. When I retire in four or five years I'll be able to watch my horses race all the time. It's amazing that as big as they are and as small as their legs are that they hold up when they run. I've always wanted to see the Derby, but normally I'm racing cars on weekends. When I retire, though, I'll be able to do a few more of these things I've wanted to."[81]

––––––––

The first race of the revamped IROC series was held on the oval track at Michigan in conjunction with an Indy car event. Foyt was the second-fastest qualifier, topped by Peterson, the defending Formula One champion. Running with the lead pack, he was clipped by a spinning Petty, putting him out of the race. Unser went on to win, ironically in the repainted black Camaro.

The fastest qualifier for the 250-mile Indy car race, Foyt jumped out at the start and was running two seconds a lap faster than the second-place car. It didn't last long; within five laps he was parked with a bad engine, finishing twenty-fourth and last.

A week later at Trenton for a pair of 150-mile races, he was on the pole again, the seventh time in nine races he'd accomplished the feat. He won the first, more the result of guessing correctly on fuel mileage than on speed. He lost the second to Bobby Unser for the same reason, running out of fuel six laps from the finish, Unser wrapping up the USAC championship.[82]

Having won Michigan's USAC stock car race earlier in the year in a car wrenched by Ellington, Foyt decided to try his luck with him at Charlotte, making it the third NASCAR team he'd race with since the start of the year. Ellington was also making changes, having tried nine different drivers in his cars since retiring himself three years earlier to become an owner.

Ellington had a reputation for celebrating "New Year's every night" and pushing the limits of regulation, a match for the legendary Smokey Yunick. Recently, he'd been trying to find a way around the carburetor restrictor plates mandated by NASCAR. Twice his pole-winning cars were disqualified, even though NASCAR's chief inspector called a manifold modification "one of the finest pieces of workmanship I've ever seen."[83]

There were no disqualifications at Charlotte as Foyt qualified sixth. He led twenty-five laps before dropping out with a blown engine, saying, "I had a heck of a good chance of winning."[84]

Noting the success Roger Penske was having with IROC, USAC decided to stage a similar event. Called the World Series of Auto Racing, the series pitted a dozen USAC drivers in four different races at Pocono Raceway for a $200,000 purse. The races for midgets and sprint cars were set for October 20 on a three-quarter-mile paved track. Stock and Indy car races on the big Pocono track would be held in the spring.

Many of the Indy car regulars had not raced a midget in years, and Rutherford and Bobby Unser each said they couldn't remember the last time they'd driven one. Carter won the opening midget race with Foyt sixth. In the second race for sprint cars, Foyt topped the series regulars, leading forty-eight of fifty laps, with Unser second. The series played into Foyt's strength of being able to set up a car, and although temperatures in the twenties held the crowd size down, he said afterward he thought the series was a truer test than IROC.

"I think this one is better," he said. "You can really classify the driver in all kinds of cars. I could put you in a Camaro and you could run it as well as it will run, but here each driver gets the chance to set up his own car to try to make it the best one."[85]

His comments didn't endear him to the IROC promoters, and a few days later he wired Les Richter that he was withdrawing from the series. The next day he changed his mind, although he'd already missed the first day of practice.[86]

"I got to thinking, sittin' around back home, that if they were going to have a race and call it the Race of Champions, it wouldn't be what they said without ol' A.J.," he said on the reversal. Others thought a sizable increase in his guaranteed purse might have also had something to do with it.[87]

Foyt led the first of the weekend's two races, eventually finishing third behind winner Fittipaldi. Bobby Allison won the second race, with Foyt fourth, putting him in the Daytona finale. It was also the third straight win for the green-now-black car, which officials announced afterward was being retired and would not run at Daytona.[88]

The last race of the year was November 24, a NASCAR event at Ontario. He'd won the two previous NASCAR races at the track, and it was billed as Foyt against the Southern series regulars. Driving a yellow No. 28 Chevrolet for Ellington, he qualified second to Petty, taking the lead on lap two. In a wild race featuring thirty-eight lead changes at the start/finish line and many more around the track, he battled Bobby Allison, Cale Yarborough, and David Pearson throughout. Going for the lead fourteen laps from the finish, he made a rare mistake, sliding high in Turn Three and into the wall, riding it for half a lap and dropping out of the fight for the lead. He eventually finished fourth as Allison went to Victory Lane.

The season over, the politics of racing moved to the forefront. Several of the top teams—including Penske, Jones, Gurney, and McLaren—were becoming increasingly disillusioned with USAC as costs continued to escalate. A race motor cost more than $30,000 and the teams wanted new regulations immediately that allowed for stock block engines, believing they would reduce costs by two-thirds.

Foyt opposed an immediate change saying, "The good stock block stuff won't be readily available and the major teams will get all the goodies, just like they did with Ford" back in the mid-1960s. He complained there should be more owners on USAC's board, and he was quickly added, although as a driver representative.[89]

USAC offered to further restrict the current engines while targeting 1976 as the first year for stock blocks. Jones and Bignotti said their teams might sit out the coming year if additional changes weren't made.

In the end USAC decided to do nothing, freezing its engine regulations for the coming year, while working to develop an engine equivalency formula allowing stock blocks to compete with existing powerplants—the Foyt and Offenhauser—beginning in 1976.

CHAPTER 36

———

LIFE BEGINS AT FORTY

1975

While much of the United States slipped deeper into a recession brought on by the energy crisis at the start of 1975, Houston was an "oasis of prosperity" according to the *New York Times*, the result of a booming oil industry struggling to keep up with demand. It was the fastest-growing city in the country, with "an explosion of new factories, shopping malls, sports stadiums, office towers, hotels and hospitals" and "the right city, in the right place, at the right time."[1]

Workers laid off in the Rust Belt were flocking to Houston, where unemployment was just 3.7 percent, about half the national average. The sixth-largest city in the 1970 national census, Houston already had moved past Detroit to take over the fifth spot and soon would bypass Philadelphia. The *Times* said even third-place Los Angeles was in danger of falling behind the Texas city.

Among those benefiting from the boom was A.J. Foyt, as his fortune grew to an estimated $10 million. He was also lucky to have a sponsor in Jim Gilmore, who was increasing his support, while others, including Firestone, STP, and Dan Gurney's benefactor, Ozzie Olsen, were cutting back or withdrawing completely. Gilmore announced plans to add sponsorship for twelve to fourteen NASCAR and USAC stock car races in the coming year.

"Being a businessman, I have to anticipate what the business climate will be a year from now," Gilmore said. "We've weighed the dollars and cents of racing and feel we can afford to continue in it."[2]

"I have a considerable amount of confidence in the economy and racing is my life. We've had our share of tough breaks and we expect them, it's part of racing. But this year we feel A.J. has an excellent chance to win in both the USAC and NASCAR divisions and we want to help him all we can."[3]

◄ "When you mellow too much, you start to lose your drive." *IMRRC, National Speed Sport News Collection*

485

"I hate to speak for him, but I know he just loves the stocks. I think he finds it more enthusiastic and that it appeals to his love of head-to-head competition. I think he finds it more of a personal test than the championship circuit."[4]

THE GILMORES

Gilmore and his wife Di, had become increasingly close to Foyt and his race team, and while the sponsorship increase in the midst of a recession surprised many, it was a natural extension of their relationship. As one reporter noted, "Gilmore and his wife . . . are probably the closest friends and confidants the burly, often-truculent Texan has."[5]

"I think the world of the guy," Gilmore said. "He's a man of integrity, one of the finest gentlemen I've ever known."[6]

A childhood car nut while growing up in Kalamazoo, Michigan, he'd taken over the family's popular downtown department store and launched Jim Gilmore Enterprises, adding an advertising agency, car dealerships, and radio and television broadcast stations to his company.

He made his first trip to the Indianapolis Motor Speedway in 1966 when Citibank took a number of its top customers to the opening weekend of qualifications. He was back the following year and saw Foyt win the 500. Soon after, he sponsored his first car, a one-race deal with Jack Brabham, and the following year sponsored Gordon Johncock, who'd been running his own team from nearby Hastings, Michigan.

The racing hook was set. Gilmore painted the chimney on his home black and white like a checkered flag, inlaid the words "Pit Stop" in the breakfast room floor, and hung one of Johncock's race cars from the ceiling of the family room. When Johncock received an offer from the stronger McLaren team, he'd been reluctant to leave his relationship with Gilmore until Jim encouraged him and said nothing could damage their friendship. In subsequent years Gilmore had sponsored Art Pollard, Mel Kenyon, and Wally Dallenbach. That's when Johncock's suggestion to Foyt that he contact Gilmore led to the start of their relationship. Gilmore's love of the sport was shaken when Pollard was killed in practice at Indy in 1973 and revived a few weeks later when Johncock won the 500, and he was among the first to congratulate his former driver.

Since their original one-page contract, Gilmore and Foyt renewed their deal each year by simply adding a signature page to the document. Through it all, Gilmore admitted the sponsorship didn't provide much in the way of a business benefit to his company.

"I don't really have anything to sell," Gilmore said. "There is the car agency in Kalamazoo, but that's local and the people who buy from us know us. I don't sell beer or cigarettes, and therefore what I spend in racing doesn't necessarily give us financial return in merchandising. I'm in racing because Di and I have a mutual interest in it. It provides a mutual respect and closeness that carries through to our daily lives. We are gung-ho about the sport. It's a big part of our lives now, and we're probably too deep in it to ever change."[7]

There may have been bigger sponsorship dollars available when Foyt and Gilmore signed their first contract at the start of the 1973 season, but A.J. had always preferred a personal relationship in his business dealings, and it was paying off.

"Some of these big sponsors who have come into Indy and auto racing in the last few years have had no feeling for those guys back in the garages, living in motel rooms for a month," Gilmore said. "All they care about is dollars and cents and it's easy to give up racing when that's all you're interested in."[8]

Foyt put it another way and took aim at those who'd helped drive up the cost of racing and were now complaining about it.

"With all that big sponsorship money we got a few years ago, we got spoiled. Now some of the sponsors have left. We spent money where we shouldn't have spent it. Instead of putting money into the cars for development and research, a lot of money would be funneled into other things, like motels and expenses. I've watched other drivers charter a jet to get to the track, send the race car in a big diesel truck and have a bunch of crewmen in the pits. Don't need all of that. At least I don't. We've inflated ourselves too much and it's hurting us right now. We've got to come back to earth."[9]

"Big money doesn't necessarily make you win races, I can assure you of that. Back when I was working on a budget of maybe $20,000 a year I won a helluva lot more races and almost as much money as we're winning now operating on a quarter-million dollars. Through the years without big money I've always had number one equipment. As long as I race, I'll have number-one equipment too. So I'm really not going to worry about money."[10]

DOWN UNDER

Foyt started the 1975 season about as far away from Houston as he could get, traveling to Australia and New Zealand for a series of midget races. He received a substantial appearance fee from a local promoter to run a week's worth of events and was driving the same midget—or speed car as they were called Down Under—that Mel Kenyon drove to an unprecedented fourth USAC midget title in 1974.

Kenyon had been an up-and-coming Indy car driver when he was badly burned at Langhorne in 1965, losing the fingers and thumb on his left hand. He'd made a special glove with a pin that fit into a socket on the steering wheel, allowing him to continue to race. After limited success on the Indy car circuit, he'd shifted his focus back to midgets in the late 1960s and began winning championships. Known as "Mr. Midget" in the US, he was "King of the Speed Cars" in Australia and New Zealand, where he'd become a fan favorite. This was his fourth trip Down Under, and he treated it like a vacation, bringing his family for more than a month.

With only a week to spare, Foyt had no interest in vacations. Kenyon, who considered A.J. the best active driver and perhaps the best ever, had repainted his car "Foyt Red," with a No. 1 superimposed on an American flag on its nose and flanks. There were five stars under the flag, one for each of A.J.'s national championships. The car was powered by a strong Volkswagen engine built by Autocraft, the series' top engine tuner.[11]

There was no sign of jet lag when Foyt arrived just in time for the January 12 Australian Grand Prix at Liverpool Raceway near Sydney. After winning two preliminary races, he was forced to start in the back of the twenty-car field alongside Kenyon, another heat race winner. He followed his car owner through the twenty-car field, and then passed him for the victory to the delight of the crowd, estimated at sixty thousand for the weekend, most of whom had come out to see Foyt in action.[12]

He finished second to Kenyon in the "world championship" speed car race in Auckland, New Zealand, and then won again in the final event of his trip, at Templeton Speedway in Christchurch, New Zealand, where he celebrated his fortieth birthday. Flying home overnight, he was able to celebrate a second time after crossing the international dateline. Despite the victories, Foyt didn't appreciate his first experience with the so-called "Australian Pursuit Race."

"They started me in the back of every goddamn race," he said years later. "They said it was because of my past experience, but I said, 'I ain't run midgets in fifteen years.' That was a bunch of crap as far as I was concerned. I had good race cars, but I wasn't running four or five times a week like most of them. It seemed like every race I had to start dead last.

"The people were great to me, don't get me wrong, and I enjoyed being down there. But as far as starting last, that was a bunch of crap."[13]

Returning to the states he paused long enough on his way to Daytona to set the fastest lap during Goodyear tire tests at Ontario but was surprised to see the second-fastest car. It was a new machine that looked a lot like his Coyote, and there was a good reason for it. George Bignotti had hired Bob Riley to design the car, telling him he wanted something like Foyt's. Even the name was similar, Bignotti calling it the Wildcat, although it was supposedly in recognition of team owner Pat Patrick, who'd made his money in wildcat oil wells.

There were more surprises when Foyt arrived in Daytona for the February 12 IROC finale and found Roger Penske and Mark Donohue on hand and ready to make an attempt on his closed-course speed record. Penske had convinced Donohue to come out of retirement after less than a year on the sidelines to drive for his new Formula One team. The original plan was for Peter Revson to drive the F1 car, but following Revson's death in South Africa, Donohue reluctantly agreed to the new challenge.

Penske brought his Porsche 917-30 Can-Am car to Daytona for the attempt. It was the same car Donohue drove to the 1973 championship in dominating style, taking six straight pole positions and races to close out the season and effectively putting an end to the first iteration of the series. Dubbed the "Panzerwagon," it was powered by a 1,000-horsepower, twelve-cylinder engine.

Donohue figured he should be able to do at least 225 miles per hour, "if the conditions are right." He said he wanted to set the record at Daytona "because Daytona is tradition," an apparent dig at Foyt's record being set at the new Talladega track, which was wider, smoother, and higher banked. He turned philosophical and a bit mystical when asked about the importance of a speed record.[14]

"Sometimes I even have trouble explaining that to myself," he admitted. "Having an honor no one else has, seeking that mystery quality. Going into the unknown. Some people go to the moon, some go to the bottom of the sea. To go faster than anyone else, that's an honor I'd really like to have."[15]

Like Foyt at Talladega, Penske and Donohue discovered that achieving speeds they "should" be able to hit according to a slide rule was more difficult in reality. Donohue noted the "turns are awfully narrow" and after two blown engines and a best lap of only 201 mph—a new Daytona best but well short of Foyt's record—they decided to pack up and try again at Talladega later in the year, sending the engines back to Germany for more work.

In the IROC race, Foyt and Bobby Unser used a tactic they'd learned earlier in the race at Michigan. In what at the time was called "the most spectacular race ever staged at Daytona," the two took turns pushing each other, locking bumpers at times. It allowed them to run faster than the other drivers employing a conventional draft and leaving space between the cars. It was perhaps the first example of what became known as "tandem racing" in later years. Foyt was where he wanted to be on the last lap, pushing Unser and going low to pass in the last turn, but coming up two feet short at the finish line.[16]

Foyt's preparations for the Daytona 500 weren't going nearly as well. Ellington had promised to "do everything possible to take the pole position" while saying he'd turned over a new leaf. "No tricks. Heck, with A.J. Foyt behind the wheel you don't need any other tricks."[17]

After damaging four engines in practice and qualifying, Foyt was ready for a few tricks and went looking for Smokey Yunick. The owner of the "Best Damned Garage in Town" said there was a basically "stock" engine Foyt could borrow, good for "third or fourth place" in the qualifying race. Yunick turned out to be a prophet as Foyt ran fourth. A.J. would return the favor later in the year, loaning Yunick a set of fuel injectors at Indianapolis.[18]

In the 500, Foyt ran with the leaders and was out front for eighteen laps in the early going, before losing time during pit stops. "I guarantee you we won't have this kind of [expletive deleted] happening from now on," he said of the pit work. "I come down here and work my [expletive deleted] off and then we look like a bunch of rank amateurs because of the pit crew."[19]

If there'd been any thoughts about Foyt mellowing at forty, they quickly disappeared. In fact, A.J. said he was guarding against it.

"When you mellow too much, you start to lose your drive and people start walking all over you. I still get hoppin' mad sometimes because I don't like it when people lie to me or try and jack me around. I think it stays with me a little longer now, because I just let it build up inside until I see the guy and tell him off. When I was younger, I'd blow up right on the spot, and that would be it."[20]

"When I have problems, I get mad. I admit it. People say A.J., you gotta do these things. I tell them I don't have to do a damn thing but die."[21]

––––––––––

The time between Daytona and the Indy car opener at Ontario was spent clearing land, plowing fields on one of his properties, and putting in a new road at his ranch, "stuff I've been trying to get done for four years," Foyt said. "I work out there from dawn to dusk, all by myself, and I love it. I don't much like crowds, they really make me feel too hemmed in. I really like it out there by myself."[22]

He missed the first couple of days of practice at Ontario, not all that unusual for a track where he'd run thousands of miles during tire tests. By midweek, however, Tony Foyt called wondering where he was, at which point he realized he'd confused Ontario's schedule with Daytona's, where the qualifying races were held on Thursday before the main event. At Ontario, qualifying and the qualifying races were scheduled for a week before the March 9 California 500.

He arrived in Ontario on Thursday afternoon, in time for a late practice session. After running several warm-up laps, he clocked one at more than 196 mph, four mph faster than Unser, who'd set the pace in practice up to that point. Midway through his second fast lap, however, his engine exploded in spectacular fashion, littering the track with parts and so much oil it had to close for the day for an extensive cleaning.

Speculation started regarding how much turbo boost he'd been using, most believing he'd been well above the eighty-inch limit that would be allowed in Saturday's official qualifying session. Among the doubters was Johnny Rutherford, who said, "I'm almost sure A.J. is running eighty-eight to ninety inches of boost."[23]

"That beauty really came apart," Foyt said after his short run, surprisingly upbeat for someone who'd just destroyed a $30,000 engine. "That was the first time since I've been building these engines that one actually exploded. It proved one thing, this car is really handling. I never got out of shape. I was never in trouble."[24]

While he was driving the same pole-winning Coyote from the year before, it had been reworked, with a narrower cowl the most obvious difference. Foyt was in his element, hinting there were numerous changes under the bodywork and noting he was running without a rear sway bar, the result of a new Goodyear tire he'd played a key role in developing. He said a new car was being built in Houston and if the changes worked out in Ontario, they'd be incorporated in the new Coyote. He was coy about the boost level he'd been running and disappointed "no one has protested me yet. Surely, *someone* will complain before the race."[25]

He missed Friday practice while replacing the engine and most of the Saturday morning warm-up while repairing a damaged clutch. It didn't seem to matter that he'd run only about ten laps in practice while most of the front-runners had spent a week at the track, as he qualified at better than 196 mph, two mph faster than Bobby Unser. Despite the speed advantage of the Foyt engine, Unser said he didn't want one.

"The only way you can purchase a Ford is from Foyt," he said, another of those who refused to call it a Foyt engine. "I can't see anyone in their right mind buying an engine from Foyt and then trying to race against him. There's no way on God's green earth he would sell what he'll run."[26]

As impressive as Foyt's pole run was, the next day's qualifying race was even more so. He led all forty circuits, lapping every car at least once. With a week between qualifying and the race, Foyt was in the spotlight, right where he wanted to be.

"George Bignotti has been staring at it all week," he said of his Coyote. "And I got to the track one day at nine o'clock and Bobby Unser was already in my garage. I never knew Bobby to get up that early before."[27]

Telling reporters "We have a new goodie, but I shouldn't talk about it," he proceeded to tell them, "I can change my fuel mixture during the race."[28]

The dial he'd used to change boost levels the previous year having been banned by USAC; the new one allowed him to choose from a dozen different air/fuel mixtures from the cockpit. Increasing the amount of fuel, a "rich" mixture, increased horsepower. Increasing the amount of air, a "lean" mixture, improved fuel economy. There was always the danger that adjusting too much in one direction could damage an engine, but it was a risk Foyt was willing to take.

"He has obviously done his homework over the winter," said Rutherford, no longer questioning Foyt's legality. "If he's there at the end, then the rest of us will be running for second place."[29]

Rutherford's "if" was a big one. In the five previous Indy car races at Ontario, Foyt had finished only once—nine laps behind the leaders. After tracing the problem with the first engine to new pistons, Foyt considered returning to Houston to rebuild his race engine. Although it had survived the pole run and the qualifying race, it was equipped with the same piston design and Foyt wanted to check them before the 500.

He eventually decided to disassemble the engine in the Ontario garage area and went to work with his father and Howard Gilbert, attracting a crowd. They had plenty of help, including Herb Porter, who'd designed the new piston, and George Salih, who'd helped manufacture it.

"We took a couple of wooden apple boxes, set the engine on it, and broke the block apart," Foyt said. "Then we replaced a piston. Added new rings. We worked in the dust and for the first time I had an engine that didn't leak any oil."[30]

Even with the rebuilt engine, Foyt hinted he might try and improve his chances of finishing by cruising around in the early going and "then try for a final surge."[31]

"My usual style is starting up front and giving everybody a good show until I break. You get a lot of publicity doing that, but it doesn't pay very much. Maybe dropping back and playin' possum is the way to do it."[32]

Few believed it.

"Foyt's no shrinking violet, it's simply not in his nature to watch someone else lead when he could be out there doing it," said Wally Dallenbach, the 1973 race winner. "The real A.J. Foyt wants to win and lead as much as he can. The only way we can beat him is to outlast him. I know Foyt's got four miles an hour over the rest of us, but I'm not worried about him."[33]

Dallenbach was right and wrong. Foyt wasn't about to lay back. When the race started Foyt disappeared, giving up the lead only during pit stops, leading 187 of 200 laps. He finished three-quarters of a lap ahead of Bobby Unser with the third-place car being three laps back. He became the first driver to win all three USAC five-hundred-mile races, adding to his previous Indianapolis and Pocono victories.

It was a stunning performance, one that impressed even *Los Angeles Times* columnist Jim Murray, who wasn't easily impressed. "A.J. Foyt won the California 500 by about a day," he wrote. "There was only one car on the same lap with him and only about three cars in the same week. At the age of forty, A.J. is blowing off the kids whose fathers he blew off nearly a generation ago."[34]

Foyt was late for his post-race press conference, having diverted his golf cart's chauffeur, Tony Hulman, to the garage area to check the spark plugs in his engine. He wanted to look at them before they cooled and his crew "mixed the plugs up. Number six cylinder was running lean before the race and I wanted to see how dry it run in the race."[35]

He took exception with reporter questions about the "easy" victory. He wanted to make sure everyone understood the dominating performance wasn't the result of tricks or illegal parts, but rather a lot of hard work. Mostly his.

"You take a twenty-four-hour day and make it a twenty-eight-hour day and that's how hard I work. While a lot of people are out in the bars having a ball, I'm usually in there with that race car trying to figure out something. That's the difference between A.J. Foyt and a lot of the guys."[36]

At the time he called the Ontario victory "the greatest race I ever drove. I caught the flags perfect. I made moves through traffic perfect. My crew was perfect. It was the most fascinating race I've been in. Just like a storybook."[37]

A week later at Phoenix, he qualified and finished third, missing out on any chance of victory when he made a late pit stop for tires. This time he credited winner Rutherford for his hard work.

"The way I beat everyone at Ontario, I thought I would win [Phoenix] easy," he said. "Get the pole and beat the bleep out of everyone. Couldn't do it because I wasn't prepared. It was all my fault. Then I watched Johnny Rutherford do all of the right things. He won because he was prepared and I wasn't."[38]

Missing from Phoenix were Mario Andretti and defending series champion Bobby Unser. Dan Gurney, Unser's car owner, said he'd been unable to secure sponsorship and wouldn't enter a car again until Indianapolis. Andretti was preparing to run his first full F1 season driving for Parnelli Jones and Vel Miletich. Still upset with USAC over the engine regulations, Jones decided to enter only the major Indy car events while fielding entries for Andretti and Al Unser in SCCA's rival Formula 5000 road racing series. With Donohue also set to run the full grand prix season for Penske, Foyt found himself answering questions about the allure of the European-based circuit.

"It's not different from any other type of racing," he said. "I've had two or three offers in the past to go over there and drive top-notch machines. But to do it right you damn near have to forget the United States and all the racing over here. I feel if it wasn't for the fans in the United States I wouldn't be who I am today. I feel as long as I'm racing, I'm going to race for the American people."[39]

"I've beaten them at Le Mans," he said when asked about the European drivers. "I beat them in the rain at Daytona. And I beat Jimmy Clark, Graham Hill, and Jackie Stewart at Indianapolis. But you have to spend a couple of years learning the circuits. Some of those drivers were born on them."[40]

He made it clear he was rooting for Andretti to succeed. "It's going to take him time, but I hope he does it because it would be a great honor for the United States. I really do wish him all the success in the world."[41]

Foyt rushed home after learning his mother had suffered a stroke, and he spent much of the week at her bedside, delaying his departure for an Atlanta stock car race until Saturday morning. He should have stayed home. Driving a car set up and qualified by another driver, he dropped out early, finishing thirty-fifth.

Phoenix having served as a wakeup call, Foyt arrived in Trenton for the April 6 Indy car race fully prepared. He started tenth after high winds and freezing temperatures canceled qualifying, the lineup being determined by random draw. It took him sixteen laps to move into first, and he gave up the front spot only on pit stops, including one for a pillow to be stuffed into the cockpit to support an aching neck. Despite the pillow stop, he lapped everyone except second-place Rutherford and shattered the track record for a two-hundred-mile race. It was his twelfth victory in thirty-six Indy car starts at Trenton and fiftieth overall Indy car victory, eighteen ahead of second-place Andretti.

Two weeks later he was back at the track for the finals of USAC's World Series of Auto Racing, which had been moved from Pocono to New Jersey in hopes of drawing a larger crowd. Attendance at both the Phoenix and Trenton races was down significantly, and only fifteen cars had started at Trenton. Advance ticket sales for the World Series were minuscule. The recession was largely to blame, but so was the lack of star power, and Foyt reversed course on his thoughts regarding Andretti racing in Europe.

"You people built up his name," he told a Philadelphia press luncheon designed to build interest in the Trenton event. "They wouldn't know him if it wasn't for you. He's cheating his own people to go over there and run. I like it here. I want to run for the people who made me what I am."[42]

Foyt was also upset with Andretti's sponsor, Viceroy, and car owners Jones and Miletich. Former series sponsor Marlboro had dropped out when Viceroy cars started winning races, and now Viceroy was shifting its focus to F1 and F5000 along with the team.

"Viceroy did that to the Marlboro people and now they [Viceroy] are not even supporting the [Indy car] circuit," Foyt said. He took a shot at Jones and Miletich. "Some people should stop playing Jet Set and start getting their hands dirty."[43]

Andretti was surprised by the comments. He'd been touched when Foyt was quoted wishing Mario "all the success in the world," but this was different. He spoke with Ray Marquette of the *Indianapolis Star* "in a tone as much of wonder as anger," according to the reporter.[44]

"I don't believe that guy," Andretti said. "Who does he think he is, anyway? I'm running just as many races in the States as he is—but what difference does it make. I have the right to race anywhere I want to. It's my choice. Right now, I want to do more road racing and that's what I'm doing. Personally, I'm glad Mark and I are representing America on the Grand Prix circuit. I've got a strong degree of patriotism and I'm sincere about this."[45]

Andretti said "it hurt" reading A.J.'s comments and that he had the "greatest respect" for Foyt. "I always will, but I sometimes wonder why he puts down other people."[46]

Foyt changed his tune again by the time the World Series rolled around, saying his comments weren't aimed at Andretti. "I wasn't taking any shots at Mario. Where he races is his business."[47]

Other drivers were amused by the exchange between the sport's two heavyweights.

"There's only one A.J. Foyt," said Gary Bettenhausen, who was earning a reputation for speaking his mind. "He's done things in racing no one else has come close to doing and he is number one. He deserves all the appearance money he gets because he'll make your race a big one by showing up and running.

"But I'll tell you this. If A.J. thought he could make more money running in Europe as he can make running the United States, he would be over there in a minute."[48]

Although looking to put the feud with Andretti behind him, Foyt received unwanted help from Bignotti as the teams gathered in Trenton. His former crew chief was harping about the legality of Foyt's engine and car, calling for more surprise field inspections at the races.

"It's well known that Foyt has been cheating all along, and some teams are upset because no action has ever been taken," Bignotti said. He claimed Foyt's car had been allowed to race at Ontario with an extra fuel tank.

"Something I've never done is cry about another man's race car," Foyt said, not exactly a denial. "[My engine] turns 9,000 rpm and his turns 2,200 more. That's why he uses a helluva lot more fuel."[49]

Bignotti claimed Foyt was injecting nitrous oxide directly into the engine during qualifying, using the line from a fire extinguisher. Nitrous bottles were small and provided only a few seconds of additional horsepower, but enough to make a difference during a pole run.

Commonly known as "laughing gas," it was originally used by doctors and dentists as an anesthetic and painkiller. German scientists discovered during World War II that it could improve the performance of fighter plane engines for short bursts, critical in dogfights. Nitrous was being widely and illegally used in NASCAR, where Bignotti suspected Foyt had picked up the trick.

That night Foyt confronted Bignotti in the hotel bar. "I just told him he was blowin' smoke out his exhaust," A.J. said later.[50]

The off-track controversies didn't bother Foyt on it, as he qualified on the pole for both the Indy and stock car events. He ran away with the stock car race and was leading the Indy car event when, ironically, he ran out of fuel, finishing fourth to Rutherford. It was still more than enough for Foyt to secure the championship and nearly $50,000 in prize money. Only 2,500 fans showed up on the cold day and organizers took a bath, although Foyt had nothing to say about it, leaving immediately and skipping the traditional press conference. Once again he upset reporters, including Bill Lyon, the *Philadelphia Inquirer* sports columnist, who'd been convinced to come out for the race and see what all the excitement was about.

"A.J. Foyt is perfectly willing to accept the money and the glory," he wrote. "But not much of the post-race responsibility.

"In the process he also managed to reinforce a widely held opinion that he may be a helluva driver but when it comes to getting along with people he should stick to carburetors and spark plugs.

"The A.J. initials, it has been suggested, stand for Arrogant Jerk."[51]

———

Foyt canceled his appearance in Talladega's Winston 500 stock car race and delayed his departure for the start of practice at Indianapolis when his now sixteen-year-old daughter, Terry, was hospitalized following a severe asthma attack. He picked Gordon Johncock to replace him at Talladega, an unusual choice given he was Bignotti's regular Indy car driver. When he finally arrived at Indianapolis, he discovered Bignotti had stepped up his verbal attacks, claiming A.J. should have been penalized for using an oversized fuel tank in the Ontario qualifying race.

"They [USAC] are not backing their rules," Bignotti charged. "If they think Foyt ran illegally then they should have fined him and removed his points so it would not happen again. Being my two cars fell out, I had no bitch. When we went to Trenton [USAC official] Dick King told me the tank was out, so he won that fair and square.

"I really admire him," Bignotti said of Foyt. "He won a lot of races for me and he doesn't have to cheat. I know he can set up his car to win and still run with the rest of us. I helped him win two 500s and I'd like to see him be a four-time winner and be legal. He has the possibility of doing it. But it would be a horrible thing for him to do it and then find he had an extra fuel bag in his car."[52]

When the cars were put through technical inspections prior to the start of practice at the Speedway, however, it was Bignotti's Wildcats that were flagged for having slightly oversized fuel tanks. He was asked to change them out—without penalty.

The new Riley-designed Wildcats were a mixture of Eagle, McLaren, and Coyote and, driven by Johncock and Dallenbach, topped the early speed charts. Then Foyt arrived. Although he was having trouble getting the new Coyote above 190 mph, Foyt took out the older car, now carrying the No. 10, and quickly ran a lap of 193 mph, more than two mph faster than the other two.

Foyt said he really wanted to drive the new No. 14 Coyote and considered it an all-new design rather than an extension of Riley's earlier car.

"It is quite a bit narrower for better aerodynamics, it has a narrower tread width, a smaller tub, and is two and a half inches lower. We run a lot less wing to give less drag."[53]

"I could have bought me an Eagle and raced it," Foyt said. "The Eagle's a fine car, the best you can buy. But what fun would that have been? I'm getting too old to just drive. When I was a kid that was okay, to get in a car and drive it for the satisfaction of winning. Today I get a bigger kick out of building it myself and beating the other guys with new ideas as much as I do beating them on the track."[54]

With the top two times for the month as qualifying approached, one for each of his cars, Foyt stayed behind his closed garage doors with "Keep Out" signs plastered everywhere and a more polite one that read "Please, Crew Members Only." It was in sharp contrast to the open-door policy of Team McLaren and its new sponsor, Gatorade. "Johnny Rutherford is the ideal man to drive a car sponsored by a consumer product," said a Gatorade spokesperson. "I've never heard anyone say a bad word about Johnny."[55]

It was Johncock and Bignotti who decided to play the mind games, Gordy turning a lap of 195 mph late Friday afternoon to set the unofficial fast time for the month. It was their turn to be coy, refusing to disclose what boost level they'd been using. In contrast, others were saying Foyt had been sandbagging, not running as fast as he could.

The Saturday qualifying-day action started early as the Foyt and Bignotti crews confronted each other on Pit Lane.

"I asked one of them [Foyt's crew] what they wanted," a Bignotti crew member told a reporter. "He said they were gonna kick our [bleeps]. I said, 'Let's have at it.'"[56]

Foyt was wearing a pair of fake eyeglasses, the kind with a big nose attached, made even bigger for the occasion, and he altered his nickname for his former crew chief to Big Nose Notti. Bignotti seemed to enjoy the extracurricular activity. "I really know how to get his dander up," he said of Foyt. "He came up to me and said, 'You know what you need? A punch in the nose.' I sure can get him riled up."[57]

The first of the really fast cars to make a qualifying attempt, Foyt pulled in after only a couple of laps at 189 mph, complaining about the front tires. Goodyear had five different types of front tires at the track, and when Foyt measured his, he said the wrong size had been mounted. The company later said Foyt got the tires he wanted and ignored the advice of their engineer.[58]

"Boy was he hot," crewman Steve Jordan said. "We pushed the car back to the garage and A.J. came in and screamed, 'Lock the doors. The first guy who tries and gets in, I'll deck.'"[59]

Johncock took the temporary pole but didn't sound overly confident about keeping it. "A.J. is mad and the madder he gets, the faster he runs."[60]

Displaying his flair for the dramatic, Foyt waited until 4:00 p.m.—and the start of live television coverage on *Wide World of Sports*—to make another qualifying attempt. He ran his first lap at more than 195 mph and four laps at an average of 193.976 mph, two mph faster than Johncock and good for his second consecutive pole position.

"I did everything I knew how to run fast," he said. During the cool-down lap he'd waved to Terry, who'd come to Indianapolis with Lucy for qualifying and was in the family's Turn Two suite. "I thrilled the hell out of myself a couple of times out there."[61]

"I really wasn't that concerned about the pole until you guys [the press] started writin' all those things that George was saying about me."[62]

Bignotti was no longer amused.

"He goes 189 mph in the morning, takes his car back to the garage, closes the door, covers the windows, and nobody goes in there for two hours but two of his men," he complained. "I know because I had someone watching it. Then he comes back out here and runs 195. There are a lot of things you can put in the fuel that they can't detect."[63]

Asked about the charges Foyt was doctoring his fuel, Frank DelRoy, USAC's technical supervisor and person in charge of the inspection process, said he'd heard enough complaining.

"We pull fuel samples immediately after the run. And we've got the best in the business to check them. I'm so tired of hearing that stuff. You can take my personal word, every car that qualifies out here is legal.

"By God, when I used to get beat, I just said I got beat fair and square," DelRoy added. "I just said the other guy beat me and I shut up!"[64]

As complaints about Foyt's car continued, however, DelRoy succumbed to the pressure and staged a surprise inspection of the top qualified cars, although everyone knew the Coyote was the target.

"We shook it every way but loose," DelRoy said. "We wanted to eliminate all this talk about nitro being injected into the intake manifold while the engine was running."[65]

What DelRoy and the competition didn't know was that Foyt and his team were stirring the pot. They'd somehow discovered that a little bit of black shoe polish inside the exhaust gave off the distinct smell of nitrous after a couple of laps and had started to use it just to upset the competition.

As always, Foyt took the challenges personally.

"I can't stand that picking, picking, picking, the crying. I've been a good winner and I've been a good loser. I never blame the other guy."[66]

"They were laughing at me three or four years ago but look at them now. They're wondering what makes me go so much faster. They're saying my engine's not legal. Well the only thing illegal about it is the hard work I put in on it. They just don't want to admit my car is that much superior."[67]

The pole secure, Foyt announced that his second car, which had won in dominating fashion at Ontario and Trenton earlier in the year and set the second-fastest unofficial time in practice, would stay in the garage. He wanted to focus on the No. 14.

Despite multiple requests for interviews with the pole winner, he stayed behind his locked garage doors for much of the next two weeks, emerging only to run a few practice laps and telling reporters he didn't have time for interviews.

It wasn't until Wednesday, the day before Carb Day, that reporters were surprised to see the door to Foyt's garage open. Several gathered outside, including Michael Knight of the *Philadelphia Daily News*, relatively new to the racing beat and one of those left standing in the cold without a winner's interview after Trenton's World Series race.

"The doors were open and A.J. knew we were out there," Knight recalled years later. "Finally, after about a half hour, he waved us in. Rumor had it that Foyt was cheating on horsepower. Those of us with some experience figured we'd ask him about that, but not until after we had gotten enough quotes to write a proper story. Unfortunately just a couple of minutes into our session, some guy—I think he was a Chicago columnist—blurted out a question on cheating. Sure enough A.J. blew up and told us all to 'Get the hell out of here.'"[68]

While the other journalists dispersed, Knight wandered a few garages away wondering what he was going to do. His editor wanted a column about Foyt, and the young journalist wasn't sure how he would provide it. That's when Tony Hulman walked up. In a bit of good fortune, Knight and Hulman had been seated next to each other at an industry dinner prior to the Daytona 500 and had an enjoyable conversation. Now the owner of the Speedway recognized the reporter. After an exchange of pleasantries, Hulman asked how things were going.

"I told him what had just happened," Knight said. "'Come with me' he said. When we got in front of [Foyt's] garage, Mr. H said to me, 'Wait here a minute.' He went inside and I watched as he had a few words with A.J. Just that quickly Tony came back out and said, 'Go on in!' Thanks to Mr. Hulman, I got an exclusive."

Foyt didn't give him much, but it was enough to build a column around and Knight didn't hold back.

"Foyt has withdrawn from this society of auto racers," he wrote in a story headlined "Foyt Becoming Too Much of a Big Wheel for Media."[69]

"I have too much work to do," he quoted Foyt as saying. "I'm sorry but that's the way it is." Knight wrote that the excuse was "like the seat in a frequently used pair of jeans. It becomes so worn, you can see through it."[70]

Some reporters asked other drivers about A.J. The talkative Bobby Unser was a favorite source.

"He's probably the most cantankerous person in the world, but he's a fantastic person," he said of Foyt. "And he's one of the cleanest drivers I've ever raced against. He may cheat you one hundred different ways, but when it comes to a race, he's probably the most honest man ever to get onto a track. He hardly ever makes a mistake and you seldom see him in wrecks."[71]

Emerging long enough on Carb Day for a final test run and turning in the fastest lap, Foyt said his lawyers were in contact with Bignotti regarding the cheating charges.

"My lawyers have written George a letter. He'll either retract everything he said or I'll see him in court."[72]

"I stand by everything I said," Bignotti shot back.

Eventually, Bignotti said he was misquoted and his words taken out of context, which was enough to satisfy Foyt, and an uneasy truce settled over the pair.

Foyt finally sat down with a reporter he'd opened up to in the past and trusted, Bill Verigan of the *New York Daily News*. It was Verigan who'd been haunted by the accidents of the 1973 Indianapolis 500 and admitted he "didn't get it" when Foyt tried to explain why he raced.

"Yeah, I get excited," Foyt admitted. "We're running for over a million dollars. I have to psych myself down for this race. I'll say if I'm going for the fourth victory, this is the time. But there are so many characteristics to this track that no one will ever be able to figure it out. You never know about oil problems or wrecks or what kind of debris will be out there. There are so many factors you can't count on, thousands of pieces that can break. I have no guarantee that I'll run one lap or 200 laps. I only hope for the best."[73]

The interview took a darker turn, and Foyt talked about why he avoided others on race morning. While he was often on the grid before a race, joking and bouncing from driver to driver, he'd tried to avoid everyone else, refusing to sign autographs or pose for pictures.

"I guess a lot want to look at you in case something happens during the race so they can say they were the last to talk to you or something like that. A lot of people want you to sign something just before you get in the car so they can say they got your last autograph. A lot of people on other teams are greedy too. They'd love to see me hit the wall on the first turn."[74]

For the second year in a row, Foyt brought the field down for a good start, and for the second year in a row, the driver in second jumped ahead by more than fifty yards at the starting line, as Johncock led into the first corner without retribution. Foyt took the lead on lap ten and began passing slower cars almost immediately. It was a closely packed group with Foyt and Johncock joined by Bobby Unser, Johnny Rutherford, and Wally Dallenbach, who'd quickly moved his Wildcat from the back to join the front-runners.

By lap twenty Johncock was out. Foyt still led after an exchange of pit stops, but Dallenbach soon passed him on the track, a rarity. In the pits, Gilmore didn't seem worried.

"Dallenbach won't be around at the end, mark my words," he said. "He's running too hard too soon. A.J. is driving with his head. The boost is down and he's saving fuel. He could care less about lap money. He's treating that car like it was a human being."[75]

That changed when another round of pit stops at the halfway mark dropped Foyt to third, thirty seconds behind Dallenbach. Moving to a richer fuel mixture, in eight laps he passed Rutherford for second and cut Dallenbach's lead in half. He was using more fuel, but it was a warm and humid day and thunderheads were building in the distance. The possibility of a rain-shortened race was growing, and he might not need all the fuel necessary to go the full five hundred miles.

The enriched fuel level threw off the team's calculations, however, and they let him run one lap too many before the next stop. While he was able to coast into the pits, he lost all the time he'd made up and a little more.

Back on the track and running hard, he closed on Dallenbach and Bobby Unser. The trio were gaining on an impressive rookie, Tom Sneva, who was turning laps nearly as fast as the leaders. But on lap 128, with the leaders looming in his mirrors, Sneva tangled with another rookie, Eldon Rasmussen, entering the second turn. Sneva's car hit the outside wall and started flipping, disintegrating in midair. What was left of the car landed right side up and in flames, although Sneva was already climbing out.

"I couldn't believe my eyes," Unser said. "The car was turning over and over, twisting in the air and parts were flying off in all directions."[76]

While Unser went high to avoid the crash, Foyt followed Dallenbach into the grass and was soon on the radio, telling the crew he'd cut a tire and to be ready to change the right side. When they noticed one of the left tires also needed replacing the stop dragged on. He came out a lap behind the leaders, Dallenbach, Unser, and now Rutherford.

With no need to save fuel, he started turning his fastest laps of the race. As predicted, Dallenbach dropped out with forty laps to go, having picked up some debris in the grass that damaged his engine. Ten laps later Foyt finally caught a break, pitting first when another caution came out and getting back on the same lap as the leaders. He was a long way behind, but the fastest car on the track. It soon became a moot point as the thunderheads opened up, drenching the track. The red and checkered flags were shown Bobby Unser, ending the race as Foyt, in third behind Rutherford, pulled alongside to acknowledge the winner.

In his garage Foyt was mad—mad at his crew and mad at officials who called the race official when he thought they should have waited and tried to dry the track. Most of all he was mad about the intangibles he'd talked about, the debris he'd picked up in the grass, the long caution flag, the rain, and his luck. He also made a quick trip to the infield care center, complaining he'd hurt his back bouncing through the infield trying to avoid Sneva's car.

"If I couldn't win it, I'm glad Bobby did," Foyt said, mimicking his comments about Rutherford the previous year. "It could have been a real race at the finish. Maybe the race of the century."[77]

When asked about the cheating charges that dominated the prerace coverage, Unser came up with an interesting idea. Put Foyt in charge. "He runs in NASCAR where they have the best cheaters in the world. They spend more time figuring out how to cheat than they do racing."[78]

His third-place finish at Indy left Foyt with a significant points lead heading into the second half of the season and he all but clinched the title as he won the next three races at Milwaukee, Pocono, and Michigan.

The Milwaukee victory was not without controversy. Following a caution period, Foyt was judged to have passed a car before the green flag and was black-flagged into the pits for a stop-and-go penalty. After first ignoring the flag, he made a quick stop, added a splash of fuel, and was back on the track, somehow losing only about five seconds. He quickly caught and passed leader Bobby Unser and drove away to the win.

Unser and Gurney huddled with second-place finisher Rutherford afterward, wondering why Foyt wasn't penalized a full lap and how he could have lost only five seconds while making a stop. They elected not to file an official protest, but saw it as another instance of USAC showing Foyt favoritism.

"We thought Foyt was unlapping himself," Gurney explained, having told Unser to let Foyt past. "We would have raced differently if we thought Foyt was on the same lap."[79]

Rutherford chimed in. "That's a lap penalty no matter how you look at it."[80]

Not surprisingly, Foyt disagreed.

"I thought it was a lousy call. If I had passed a guy in second place, it's a different story, but I didn't improve my position, so I didn't think I did anything wrong. I was losing ground because [Roger] McCluskey wouldn't get going, so I took off, but just got back to second."[81]

McCluskey admitted he was having car troubles and waved Foyt past, although nothing in the rule book recognized the move. USAC eventually gave Foyt the benefit of the doubt, although there were tense moments when Foyt at first wouldn't allow his car to be inspected.

––––––––

Practice and qualifying for the June 29 Pocono 500 stretched over two weeks, and Foyt spent as much time away from the track as on it. The newest member of the American Horse Council, he borrowed a plane for quick trips to Delaware Park to watch his pair of two-year-old colts and Kentucky Derby hopefuls run. Neither won, with Right On Mike finishing third in one race, Barbizon Drum second in another. Both would win races in the future, although not at the levels necessary to qualify for the Derby.

Little of the controversy from Indy and Milwaukee carried over to Pocono, as Johncock took the pole with Foyt second, allowing Bignotti to say, "I finally beat A.J."[82]

Foyt's biggest problem was just getting into the track, with a record crowd estimated at more than one hundred thousand jamming the limited access roads. Helicopters were called in to lift A.J. and other drivers and officials into the speedway, although the start was delayed by nearly two hours.

Once the race took the green flag, Foyt found himself battling with Johncock until the other driver spun and crashed. From there he kept a close eye on the clouds in the area and enhanced his fuel mixture as rain closed in, putting him well out in front of Dallenbach, the only other driver on the same lap when the rain stopped the race thirty laps from the finish. Afterward, he "was a man full of smiles and congeniality."[83]

"I wasn't gonna get caught with my britches down like I did at Indy," he said. "You know what they say about rain; it always evens itself out."[84]

He won the pole for both the Indy car and stock car races for the July 20 doubleheader at Michigan. He'd never won an Indy car event at the track but led more than half the race, passing Johncock for the final time with ten laps remaining, the victory wrapping up the national championship with four races left. He battled Bobby Allison in the stock car event until his transmission broke, driving into the garage area and immediately leaving the track.

He'd almost skipped both races. Lucy had called about 11:30 the night before with news Terry had collapsed and was in intensive care, apparently the result of another severe asthma attack. It was hard for A.J. to handle, his athletic, outdoor-loving tomboy daughter suffering while he was unable to help. Lucy told him to stay for the races, there was nothing more he could do at the moment. He called the hospital directly and talked to the doctors, who assured him she was resting comfortably.

While some reporters questioned Foyt's immediate departure, Joe Falls, the *Detroit Free Press* sports editor who'd ripped A.J. when he left abruptly at Indianapolis in 1974, was tipped off to Terry Foyt's illness—probably by Gilmore—and let everyone know.

"He wanted to go home the moment the call came," Falls wrote. "but he felt a responsibility here, too—to the promoters of the Speedway and the people who would come out on Sunday afternoon and pay big bucks to see him perform.

"Foyt is not so crass as to turn his back on his daughter. His emotions told him to return home. But he learned long ago in this uncompromising business of racing, that you have to set your emotions aside at times. The crowd didn't know of Foyt's personal plight. But they cheered him mightily, as they always do, and he didn't let them down . . .

"What we have here, I believe, is the greatest driver of all time, and we are rather fortunate to have the likes of Foyt . . . performing in our time.

"Something tells me Terry Foyt is lucky too."[85]

His daughter was much improved by the time A.J. made it home Sunday night, and she was released on Monday. By midweek, however, he was called back to the hospital, his mother having suffered another heart attack. In addition to a hereditary heart condition, Evelyn, fifty-seven, was a lifelong smoker and constant worrier at the racetrack. Doctors had tried to convince her to stop going to the races, and she'd grudgingly relented, except for Indianapolis. She'd also stopped sitting next to Lucy at the Speedway as they made each other too nervous. Again A.J. felt helpless. He was friends with the finest heart surgeons in the world, who told him there was little they could do.

With no major races scheduled for the weekend of July 27, Foyt decided to stay home. If he'd still been in Indianapolis, he might have gone to watch George Snider run the sprint car races at Winchester Speedway. Snider was having a career year and leading in series points. He'd won one of the Hoosier Sprints two nights before the Indy 500 and followed it up with an eighth place at the Speedway, his best finish ever in the race.

The half-mile paved Winchester oval featured thirty-seven-degree banked turns and billed itself as the "World's Fastest Half-Mile." Others called it the "Hills of Death." Foyt had never won a feature event at the track and stopped racing there in the fifties. Snider said it was "bad, real rough, you're airborne about half the time."[86]

"Winchester is a fast track and one of the hardest to learn how to run," he said before the race. "Your car has got to be running super good or you scare yourself to death."[87]

Running at the back of a heat race when the car in front of him suddenly slowed, Snider's car rolled up and over the slower machine and veered toward the outside wall. The impact put the car into a roll, and it jumped over the wall, tumbling out of sight down the other side.

It was a sixty-foot drop to where Snider's car came to a rest. It landed right side up, the protective roll cage ripped away. He was semiconscious, both his arms badly broken, one a compound fracture. His vision was blurry and there were numerous cuts on his face. Doctors at nearby Ball Hospital in Muncie put the arms in casts, warning surgery was necessary, and possibly even amputation. They were also concerned about his eyesight.

Snider's wife, Joy, wasn't waiting around. Asking a friend to call Foyt, she got her husband in their vehicle and set off for Indianapolis, about ninety miles away. They spent the night with Johncock, who took them to the airport in the morning and put them on a plane for Houston, where A.J. was waiting for them.

Foyt had gone into action after hearing of Snider's crash, arranging for the best orthopedic surgeons and eye specialists to be standing by at Memorial Hospital. Doctors put plates in both arms during a four-and-a-half-hour surgery. After a few days in the hospital, Snider was moved to the Foyt home to start his recovery.[88]

"It was just one of those things," Snider said of the crash. "If you run those sprinters, you're bound to take some knocks."[89]

He hadn't been surprised by Foyt's support. "He didn't waste any time," Snider would say. "It didn't surprise me none. He's a pretty soft touch about stuff like that."[90]

MARK DONOHUE

It wasn't until practice got underway for the August 10 Talladega 500 that Foyt returned to the track. Also there were Penske, Donohue, and the Porsche 917-30, now with 1,100 horsepower. They'd spent two weeks practicing for another attempt on Foyt's speed record.

It'd been a rough year for the pair on the F1 circuit. The uncompetitive Penske car had been parked and Donohue was driving a car purchased from March. He admitted to having second thoughts about coming out of retirement.

"Yes, I'm discouraged—very discouraged—about coming back to racing, our Formula One program, everything," he said. "A lot of people think I made a mistake by coming out of retirement. Maybe we should get another driver and see what happens. After a while I start to wonder about myself. Do I still have what it takes as a race driver? I don't feel like I've lost anything."[91]

The comments were brutally honest and surprising. Foyt had felt that way following his crashes in 1966 and other drivers questioned themselves at times, but few put the feelings into words.

There were no question marks when Donohue took to the track to make the record attempt, running a lap at 221.120 mph and edging past Foyt's mark. While Andretti had pooh-poohed Foyt's run, now it was A.J.'s turn to downgrade the Penske/Donohue record.

"I have no desire to drive one of those cars," he said, refusing to watch Donohue's effort. "They ain't nothing but a big old box with a lot of horsepower. I think we'll try for the record again, but I don't know exactly when we'll have time. But I like the challenge."[92]

"I believe I could back my Indy car off the trailer, make a couple of adjustments, and run 225 right now. I wouldn't need any two weeks to get ready for it."[93]

He resurrected the idea of a challenge run for the speed record with all comers putting up $100,000, winner take all, the previous talks with Andretti and Parnelli Jones having never come to fruition.

"It would have been more interesting if Mark had brought his Indy car down here and tried for my record in that fashion. I don't consider what he did a big deal. Mark didn't really break my record, he set one of his own."[94]

Donohue disagreed. "The record is the record, no matter what kind of car is used." He seemed open to the match race idea, "but we'll need to be talking about more money than that before we say yes."[95]

Rain moved into Talladega overnight, postponing the stock car event for a week and creating a conflict with Foyt, who was committed to run the Milwaukee Indy car race the following Sunday. He tabbed Donnie Allison to drive his stock car.

Foyt led the first four laps at Milwaukee before dropping out with a busted transmission. At Talladega, Allison led before finishing third, although there was bad news: driver Tiny Lund having been killed in a crash. There was more bad news from Europe, where Donohue crashed in a warm-up session for the Austrian Grand Prix. The car was destroyed, but early reports said he'd been able to walk away from the accident.

It didn't take long before reports from Europe took a turn. Donohue was hospitalized after complaining of a severe headache, and X-rays discovered a blood clot on his brain, requiring immediate surgery. He never regained consciousness. A course worker he hit also died.

Foyt ran the NASCAR race at Penske's Michigan International Speedway on August 24, dominating the early going before dropping out with a blown engine. He then joined Hulman to attend Donohue's funeral and told his team to stop preparing a car for an attempt on the closed-course speed record. He wouldn't challenge the record, at least "not as long as it belongs to Mark."[96]

He decided to drive in the upcoming Hoosier Hundred sprint car race, his first dirt track appearance in more than a year. After qualifying fourteenth, he raced through the field to finish second. When Billy Vukovich Jr. was badly injured in a crash, he agreed to sub for "Vuky" the next night in a midget race. He qualified fastest to the delight of the crowd and led early before dropping back with engine problems.

After the midget race Foyt decided to run in the International Race of Champions for the third consecutive year, although once again he had to be "encouraged" by Goodyear. Several new drivers were participating for the first time as a result of Firestone's withdrawal from racing, Andretti and Al Unser joining Foyt and Bobby Unser from the Indy car ranks. Others included stock car drivers Richard Petty, David Pearson, Bobby Allison, and Benny Parsons and F1 drivers Emerson Fittipaldi, Brian Redman, Jody Scheckter, and James Hunt.

He finished third behind Pearson and Allison in the IROC opener at Michigan International Speedway, then resumed his season-long battle with Johncock in the Indy car race. Both refused to slow their pace to conserve fuel as they swapped the lead seven times, each leading more than thirty of the seventy-five laps. They ran each other out of gas, however, and while Sneva led only seven laps, they were the last seven for his first Indy car victory and a much needed win for Penske Racing in the aftermath of Donohue's death.

Sidelined by the flu, Foyt arrived too late to practice for the next two IROC races at Riverside, October 25 and 26. He finished second in the first race and third in the second, taking the points lead with only the series finale at Daytona in February remaining.

Despite having long since wrapped up the Indy car title, he elected to run the last race of the year at Phoenix. Rutherford and Andretti dominated early, but in the end it was Foyt on top, the other two having dropped out.

"When it's your day, it's your day," he said. He could have been talking about the season as well as the race.[97]

He'd won seven of twelve Indy car races, no one else winning more than once. He won his sixth national championship, breaking his own record. He was the sport's top money winner at more than $400,000, the first to hold that title without winning the Indy 500. He became the first driver with career earnings topping $3 million and was voted Driver of the Year by a wide margin over Petty, NASCAR's champ.

By every measure it was an incredible year. Every measure except the one that meant everything to Foyt. The Indianapolis 500.

"Sure, it's nice winning the title, but I'd trade all my wins this year if I could have won Indy," he said. "I guess it's losing that gives me the desire to keep going." Making it worse, he blamed himself for the loss.[98]

"I should have won it. Everybody talks about how we got beat by the rain but that's not really the case. We beat ourselves by taking a chance on a pit stop and before I could get back into the lead, rain washed out the race."[99]

CHAPTER 37

BROKEN DREAMS

1976

Having failed in its efforts to find an equivalency formula to make turbo-charged and stock block engines compatible for 1976, USAC decided instead to limit turbo engines to seventy-five inches of boost and equip them with the "pop-off" valve at all times. It was hoped the valve would lower speeds and improve dependability, in turn lowering costs. The fuel allocation remained the same and cars still needed to average 1.8 miles per gallon. USAC also froze its regulations for five years.

Neither of the two main protagonists in the engine debate—A.J. Foyt and George Bignotti—were happy with the outcome. Foyt didn't see the need to limit boost and Bignotti wanted more fuel. The war of words between the two started up again.

"The only way we can beat A.J. is to have more fuel," Bignotti insisted. "He will continue to have a big edge in horsepower on us with the pop-off valve. He still has his advantage and we haven't gained a thing. I have several Ford engines in my shop, but I can't get the pieces from Foyt to make them competitive."[1]

"Why should I?" Foyt countered when asked if he would sell engine parts to Bignotti. "I've spent three years developing this engine and believe me, I've had a lot of problems. No one said anything about my having an unfair advantage during the two years when I was falling out of races all the time and never being able to compete."[2]

He argued the real strength of the Coyote was the chassis. It wasn't lost on him that Bob Riley was now working for Bignotti.

"My car is still aerodynamically better than his. It's something I've worked on for three years. I've had people working for me and other guys have hired them away, thinking they knew more than they really did about our chassis development. No one in our operation but me knows that much about it—and we have a damned good chassis.

◄ Too often A.J.'s day ended early in 1976. *The Henry Ford, David Friedman Collection*

"It's a funny thing to me, I've never cried or complained to the newspapers about someone having an advantage over me or my cars. I've never protested a car that beat me or said a word about it. If I thought someone had gotten around the rules and not been caught, then I've gone back to work and tried to do the same thing—only better."[3]

Bignotti was developing an Offenhauser-based engine of his own, called the Drake-Goossen-Sparks, or DGS, named for Offy pioneers Dale Drake, Leo Goossen, and Art Sparks. The new regulations also opened the door for another engine, a turbocharged version of the V8 Cosworth dominating the Formula One circuit.

The pop-off valve was tested extensively by Johnny Rutherford and Wally Dallenbach during tire tests at the Speedway, although Foyt refused to allow one to be fitted to his engine.

"You could tell it was there," Rutherford said of the valve. "The throttle felt soft when you started down the straightaways. But it never faltered or sputtered. I don't think using the valve is a bad deal, overall it's probably good. I want it to be tested for a lot of miles so we'll know it's reliable."[4]

During the offseason Foyt had put the recovering George Snider to work preparing a Speedcar for another trip to Australia and New Zealand. Although Snider wasn't ready to drive, he accompanied Foyt and maintained the car during their short visit. They arrived in time to celebrate New Year's Eve in Sydney.

Former world champions Jack Brabham and Denis Hulme, along with Bruce McLaren and Chris Amon, were among the drivers from Down Under who'd found success in F1, and Foyt didn't endear himself to the locals when he seemed to dismiss the series. "You have plenty of time to think [on a road course]. You can get through a corner on a dozen lines. But at the superspeedways you've got to get on that raggedy edge or there's some boy nipping at your butt."[5]

He won the Australian Speedcar Grand Prix on New Year's Day, overcoming an accident in a heat race. The locals seemed more willing to challenge Foyt than on the first trip, and he had a serious crash later in New Zealand, flipping his midget. Although complaining of a headache, he continued to race before eventually making a quick hospital visit.

"A.J. took a pretty nasty spill in his wreck and still has a bump on his head," reported Larry Rice, another of the American drivers on the tour. "One of the local guys ran into him and he was hot. But other than that, he's having a good time. The food's good, the girls are pretty, and the racing's been great."[6]

Back in the states, Foyt convinced his father to see a doctor. Tony Foyt had been complaining about not feeling well in general, but refused to get a checkup. When he finally agreed, the doctor was stunned by what he found.

The entire right side of Tony Foyt's heart was blocked, and the doctor said he was amazed he'd been able to walk into the office. He ordered Tony to go directly to the hospital and that he would require heart surgery in the very near future.

"I can't go," Tony protested. "I have to help my son get the car ready for Indianapolis."[7]

Finally convinced doing nothing wasn't an option, he went to the hospital, where he was watched around the clock until open heart surgery could be performed.

While a success, the surgery meant changes for the Foyts. There'd be no more changing tires on pit stops for Tony, and while he was still listed as the team's top engine man, most of those responsibilities had already shifted to Howard Gilbert. Tony would take on more of a comptroller role at A.J. Foyt Enterprises. Despite being a high-school dropout, he took to the role with the same attention to detail as he did when rebuilding an Indy car engine or transmission.

When A.J. made his way to Daytona, he soon found himself in the middle of another cheating scandal, once again centering around the use of nitrous oxide. It was widely used by many of the stock car teams to boost performance, especially during qualifying. Officials typically looked the other way.

When Foyt and Darrell Waltrip ran several miles an hour faster in qualifying than they had in practice to take the top two spots, however, the discrepancies were too great to ignore. Foyt, who was temporarily on the pole, tried to chalk it up to new tires and Hoss Ellington's loose car setup, saying, "I just went out and thrilled the hell out of myself."[8]

NASCAR officials weren't buying Foyt's explanation and announced they would take more than their normal cursory post-qualifying look at the cars. They were looking for the same thing USAC inspectors had been looking for at Indianapolis, evidence of nitrous oxide use.

Both teams at first denied using nitrous. They changed their tune only after NASCAR threatened to cut the cars apart until they found it, at which point they fessed up. Ellington had stashed a bottle in the car door, while Waltrip's was in the roll bar.

NASCAR said it found "fuel pressure assists" in the cars. The qualifying times of both drivers were disallowed and each fined $1,000. The third-fastest qualifier, Dave Marcis, also was disqualified and fined for having the aerodynamics on his car altered. That put a pair of USAC drivers, Ramo Stott and Terry Ryan, on the front row.[9]

"I don't feel bad about getting caught," Ellington said. "I just felt like the only way we could compete with them was to do what they were doing." He later claimed the bottle had been left over from a previous race and wasn't connected.[10]

Waltrip responded with what would become a classic line about cheating in NASCAR. "If you don't cheat you look like an idiot. If you do and don't get caught, you look like a hero. If you do it and get caught, you look like a dope."[11]

Foyt denied he knew Ellington was cheating, saying, "I didn't race clean for twenty-three years and then come down here and cheat just for this little NASCAR race.

"Let those people know that ol' A.J. doesn't cheat," he told reporters. "I'm sorry that we've had a problem here, but I don't build the race car. My job is to get in and drive as fast as I know how."[12]

Harry Hyde, Marcis's crew chief, found Foyt's comments laughable.

"Nitrous oxide is driver-operated," Hyde pointed out. "A.J. had to set the stuff off himself. He had to have a button hidden somewhere."[13]

Over the years a conspiracy theory developed. NASCAR and many of the top teams and drivers decided the nitrous usage was out of control and something needed to be done to curb its use. Foyt, the outsider, and Waltrip, who'd already developed his loudmouth reputation and wasn't much liked by the series regulars, were the fall guys. When everyone else laid off the nitrous in qualifying, the speeds of Foyt and Waltrip stood out and begged to be checked.

After NASCAR held the cars overnight, Foyt went out and set fast time again, running two mph faster than the official "pole" winner. It didn't matter, his starting position would still be decided in the qualifying race. While Waltrip won his qualifier and Marcis the other, Foyt suffered a blown engine and failed to finish, dropping him to thirty-first starting position for the 500.

"If I didn't think I would win, I'd go home now," he snapped when asked if he still had a chance. "My only worry is . . . when you're that far back you have some questionable cars and drivers you have to get around to get to the front of the field.

"I think some of those idiots get scared in the corners and just pull up and stop."[14]

The 1975–76 IROC finale was sandwiched between the qualifying race and the 500, and Foyt did more than enough to win the overall title. He finished second to Benny Parsons in the race and picked up the $50,000 series first-place prize, more money than it paid to win the Daytona 500. It was classic Foyt in Victory Circle.

"I'm really happy to win this. It's one of the few titles in racing that I had not won.

"My whole theory of racing has been that there is little difference in competitors. I don't figure one beats the other because he is that much better, but because he is sharper. And I have always figured myself to be the sharpest, or at least among the sharpest."[15]

He was certainly sharp from the start the next day as he passed eighteen cars during the first three laps and took the lead on lap forty-one. He was dominant thereafter, leading a race-high sixty-eight laps, and admitted he "started thinking about the checkered flag" when his engine let go a little more than one hundred miles from the finish. "If the damn thing was going to break," he said, "why didn't it do it early in the race?"[16]

The only thing people were talking about the next day, however, was the door-banging finish between David Pearson and Richard Petty, both cars spinning through the grass with Pearson managing to move his battered machine across the start/finish line first.

A few days after the race, Foyt's Daytona 500 check arrived at the Houston race shop. Instead of the $4,600 he expected, the $1,000 fine had been deducted, which set him off again. He didn't have the same relationship with Bill France Jr. as he did with the founder, and he sent the check back saying, "I didn't have my daddy's coattails to hold on to."[17]

"It could be doubtful that I'll ever race for those people again. I'd miss it, but I'm not going to lose sleep over it. Every year I get a lot older, but I get a little smarter, too. It's a hell of a note they don't trust you enough that they have to take the money before the next race. I sent every damn bit back. If they're that cheap I'd just as soon they keep it."[18]

He skipped the start of practice and qualifying for the February 29 Rockingham 500, eventually showing up and saying he was only there because he'd promised the promoter.

"There's no reason for this promoter to have to suffer," he said. "We made a deal with him, and it's very close to Hoss's home."[19]

"It's very possible I might not run Daytona again. Maybe they don't want us, but I ain't losing any sleep about it. I think they'd better change their techniques. It's run like a close family, which is good in one way and bad on the other hand. But when someone browbeats you that bad, what's the use. Get Ralph Nader on their ass and they'll change."[20]

He was just getting warmed up, taking aim at NASCAR's recent record profits.

"There is no corporation that needs to make $1.8 million. They should give more to the drivers, not the government. The fans are paying down good money but the hell of it is the drivers aren't getting enough.

"When they started and was in debt with everything, man, you couldn't find nicer people. But now they don't need you, the hell with you. I've seen a lot of empires built that way and I can tell you one thing—they can sure crumble fast in this day and time."[21]

Most shrugged off Foyt's threats—they'd heard it all before. But this was different. After running poorly at Rockingham, he pulled out of the Atlanta race and put his car up for sale.

With his NASCAR schedule on hold, Foyt entered the two early-season Indy car races at Phoenix and Trenton. He dropped out of both with car problems, but for once he wasn't the story. For the first time women drivers were competing in Indy cars, having competed successfully in Europe and sports car races. Foyt made his position known.

"They're just not physically strong enough," he said. Bobby Unser was more outspoken. "The good Lord built men and women differently. If I could talk to the women who are trying to be race drivers, I'd tell 'em they're shoveling sand against the tide."[22]

Arlene Hiss, an amateur sports car driver, high-school teacher, and ex-wife of driver Mike Hiss, became the first woman to qualify for an Indy car race at the Phoenix season opener. She was also the slowest qualifier and was lapped twenty-two times and black-flagged for driving dangerously slow. Afterward, drivers threatened to boycott upcoming events if she was allowed to compete.

"It's idiotic," said Pancho Carter, who'd finished second to Unser in a good race that was otherwise overlooked. "It's all the press's fault. She would have never been allowed to run, but the press made a big deal out of it so USAC let her go. A man wouldn't have been allowed to keep going that slow, driving that bad."[23]

At Trenton it was Janet Guthrie's turn. More experienced than Hiss, she'd been racing sports cars for thirteen years and competed at Daytona and Sebring in some of the same races as Foyt. She qualified fourteenth in a field of twenty-two, although ten mph slower than the pole sitter Foyt, who had introduced himself prior to the start.

"I was stunned to see A.J. Foyt walk up to me," she said after the race. "I don't remember exactly what he said, but he was basically supportive. That is a big guy!" she said, referring to his stature in the sport. She maintained an acceptable speed throughout and spun once before dropping out with engine problems. Her performance was enough to have her entry accepted for the Indianapolis 500.

Foyt entered two cars in the 500, deciding to stick with No. 14 for his primary entry, the 1975 car with minor modifications. The No. 1 he earned for winning the national championship went on the backup car, his updated 1973 Coyote, although he had no plans to add a teammate.

Turbocharged Offenhauser engines powered the majority of the field. The DGS engine was rebranded a "Bignotti," although most continued to use the original name. Parnelli Jones's team had the new turbocharged version of a Cosworth V8 for Al Unser.

After running some of the top speeds of the month, any hope Foyt had of becoming the first driver to win three consecutive pole positions vanished as his qualifying speeds dropped by more than five mph from the first lap to the last. He ended up fifth overall and laid into the unsuspecting track announcer who approached him for the post-qualifying interview.

"A.J., that was a pretty good run," the announcer said.[24]

"No it wasn't," Foyt snapped. "It was a disgrace to me, my car, my whole team. The damn thing just wasn't handling. If you had your eyes open, you could have seen that." Asked if he'd have it straightened out by the race Foyt warned if he didn't, "I'll park it."[25]

After a quick trip back to his ranch, Foyt returned to the Speedway. The crew had rebuilt the car and a couple of fast laps convinced him it was ready for race day.

His backup car had also been back on the track with an unexpected driver— Jackie Stewart. The now-retired Stewart was providing color commentary for ABC's race coverage. While he'd be in Monte Carlo on race day covering the Grand Prix, he was filming a taped piece for the 500 broadcast and convinced Jim Gilmore to let him do it from the seat of the No. 1 car. With the car's nose rigged with camera equipment, Stewart ran laps comparable to his 164 mph qualifying speed of 1967, the last year he'd run at the Speedway.

JANET GUTHRIE

The Stewart segment completed and the equipment removed, Foyt decided to run a few laps in the car to make sure all was right, turning the fastest "unofficial" lap of the month. No one was sure what boost level he was running, but the car was obviously fast and speculation started about who might attempt to qualify it. Tony Foyt, returning for the first time since his January heart surgery, didn't want to let anyone drive the machine, saying the team didn't have the engines nor manpower to run a second car. Lloyd Ruby was told no and arranged another ride, as did George Snider. Rumors persisted, however, and at the top of the list of would-be qualifiers was a surprise—Janet Guthrie.

"A.J. Foyt has been a great help because he came by and said I'm driving well," she said after passing her rookie test. "It's an incredible boost to have A.J. say that. It makes me glow all over."[26]

Since then she'd struggled to approach anything close to qualifying speed, her best lap of 173 mph well under the 180 mph threshold most thought would be necessary to make the field. The problem was with the car, a four-year-old Vollstedt powered by a tired turbo-Offy. More experienced drivers tried to go faster in the machine but couldn't. Operating on a shoestring budget, team owner Rolla Vollstedt asked Goodyear's racing chief Leo Mehl if there might be another car available for her to drive. Mehl went to talk with Tony Hulman.

On the eve of the final qualifying weekend, Foyt was asked again about his second car. He said he hadn't talked to anyone about driving it, but added, "I probably will put it in the qualifying line." Asked specifically about Guthrie, he said, "Right now I'd say no about Janet being in it."[27]

Guthrie was suddenly a hot commodity, and she'd reportedly been offered $100,000 to run the Charlotte NASCAR race the same day as the Indy 500, although all parties denied the dollar amount. "We're definitely interested in her running here, but we're not trying to take her away from Indianapolis," a spokesperson for Charlotte said. "We will just have to wait and see if she makes the field."[28]

The third day of qualifying passed without any sign of the No. 1 car. Tony Foyt had convinced his son not to let anyone drive it. The garage doors were opened only to allow the car of Sheldon Kinser to be rolled in, and again when it was rolled out.

Kinser, who'd made his name on dirt tracks and in sprint cars, was in his second year at the Speedway and having trouble getting a new car, built by Grant King and called a "Dragon," up to qualifying speed. After a five-year absence from the Speedway, J.C. Agajanian was back as co-owner of the car, and Foyt offered to help with the setup. Not one to give out his secrets, Foyt had the car brought to his garage, where he and the team made the changes and then told Kinser what to expect.

"He locked the doors and set it up just like his own car," King said. "He opened my eyes on some stuff. I didn't ask him. He came to me and offered help. He's a helluva competitor and champion. People think he's tough, but inside he's a real softy. He talked to Sheldon and helped us find five miles an hour in him and the car."[29]

It wasn't until late Saturday afternoon that Foyt heard from Hulman. The Speedway owner was loath to let NASCAR steal the media circus swirling around Guthrie and asked Foyt to allow her to test the No. 1 car. The decision on whether to qualify it would be strictly A.J.'s. Foyt had never turned down a request from Hulman, and he wasn't going to start now.

"Foyt is going to shake down the car at 10 a.m. Eastern Standard Time Sunday," Hulman told reporters, "and then give the car to Miss Guthrie."[30]

That touched off a flurry of activity as Guthrie went to Foyt's garage to be fitted for the test run. "Cinderella time," she called it in her autobiography. It was clear the crew wasn't in favor of the move. "We don't want him to run the backup car," one crewman told her. "We came to see A.J. win his fourth Indy and we don't want to do anything that would undercut the effort."[31]

Trying to manage expectations, Foyt said he agreed to the test drive "so she could tell if there is really a difference between cars. I'm going to let her try it out. I really don't want to run this car in the race, even though I know how good it is. There is nothing definite about giving Janet the car—only to let her take a ride and try it out."[32]

A large crowd turned out Sunday morning to see Guthrie. After a few warm-up laps by Foyt, he taped over the gauges, saying he didn't want Guthrie to be distracted. He also didn't want her, or any other prying eyes, to see what rpm levels and other specifications he was running. He told her to use only third gear and then "take it down to the corner and turn left."[33]

On her third lap she went faster than ever before at the Speedway and within ten laps hit nearly 181 mph, fast enough to qualify. She also set a closed-course speed record for women drivers.

"It had been like getting out of a Model T and into a Ferrari," she wrote. "What a car."[34]

The practice session over, Foyt pulled the tape away from the tachometer, the telltale needle indicating she'd been running at maximum rpms. "Next time use fourth gear," he said.

Would there be a next time? Guthrie recalls Foyt asking her if she could run faster and when she said yes, him telling the crew to refuel the car and push it into the qualifying line. But the car never came back and a little after 2:00 p.m. Foyt emerged from his garage to tell reporters there'd be no attempt. Tony, the crew, and Gilmore had talked him out of it.

"I just wanted to give her a chance to prove she's a race car driver," Foyt said. "And I think she is a pretty darned good driver."[35]

Guthrie stayed in her uniform, aware of Foyt's penchant for changing his mind and flair for the dramatic.

"I was still hoping until the final gun fired [ending qualifications] that A.J. would let me have the ride," she said, calling the test run "one of the biggest thrills of the month. It was not predetermined that I would attempt to qualify the car. I firmly believe that A.J. was considering letting me qualify it. But the final decision was determined by other factors.

"I'm very disappointed, but I understand why A.J. wouldn't want to run two cars in the race. He wants all of his crew's efforts directed toward his own car."[36]

Guthrie would still drive one of Foyt's cars come Memorial Day. Backers in Charlotte purchased the Chevrolet he'd turned the fastest lap with at Daytona and by Tuesday Guthrie was headed south, where she would finish fifteenth and still be running at the finish in the World 600.

"Mr. Hulman asked me to let her drive it, so I did," Foyt said years later. His appreciation for Guthrie grew over the years, and it was a trio of top-ten NASCAR finishes—at Charlotte, Bristol, and Rockingham—that really convinced Foyt of her capabilities. "Rockingham was a son of a bitch to get around. Say what you want about Danica [Patrick], to me Janet Guthrie was the best lady driver there ever was."[37]

For the second year in a row, rain was in the forecast for the Indianapolis 500, and this time Foyt planned to be ready for it. He would stay near the front at all times, keep one eye on the skies, and be ready to adjust his plan as seemed necessary.

Rutherford took the lead at the start, Foyt surging past on lap four. Along with Gordon Johncock, the trio took turns running out front. Foyt was in the lead on lap eighty when the handling on his car suddenly went away. Rutherford shot past as Foyt headed to the pits for two tires, hoping that would solve the problem. When it didn't, he changed his approach to the turns and started to slowly close on Rutherford.

Then the rain came. Rutherford was eleven seconds ahead of Foyt with Johncock in third, the only other driver on the lead lap.

With the field stopped on pit row, Foyt said, "We got cheated." He claimed Rutherford had closed the gap between the two leaders by eighteen seconds during an earlier caution period when cars were supposed to hold positions using a series of "pacer" lights. The lights had always been controversial, with yearly complaints about drivers improving their positions. If the gap had been maintained, Foyt now reasoned, he'd be in first place.[38]

While their driver was complaining to anyone who would listen, the team spotted a broken sway bar—the cause of the handling problem—and went to work fixing it. The track was drying nicely, and A.J. would be ready to pounce on the restart.

He never got his chance. After a lengthy two-hour-and-thirty-minute track-drying period, it was finally judged ready to race and drivers were called to their cars. The process continued to drag on, and when it started to rain again, harder this time, officials decided there wouldn't be enough time to dry it and run another 250 miles. Rutherford was declared the winner of the shortest Indy 500 in history at 103 laps or 255 miles.

"I wouldn't want to win like that," Foyt snapped as he retreated to the team garages in Gasoline Alley. Gilmore stood guard at the door and answered reporters' questions.

"We thought this one was ours all the way," Gilmore said. "He probably won't feel like saying much until tomorrow."[39]

"My personal view is that they could have started the race again. I regret that they did not make a decision sooner, and that there was a larger delay than necessary. I feel that as a team we have an obligation to the fans, and I am disappointed in the decision-making process of USAC. Even another half hour would have made a difference."[40]

Gilmore said the team wouldn't protest Rutherford gaining ground on the caution period, an official review seeming to answer his questions, if not Foyt's.

Having lost to Bobby Unser the previous year in similar fashion, Rutherford said he understood how Foyt felt. He'd spotted Foyt's handling problems earlier and said if they'd been fixed during the rain delay, the No. 14 would have been hard to beat if the race was restarted.

"I wanted to go back out there and test A.J.," Rutherford said. "At the same time, I had visions of Foyt whizzing past in about three of four laps and then more rain coming. I feel sad for A.J. He was loaded for bear and if there had been another green, he might have been gone.

"I just happened to be in the right place at the right time."[41]

DEATH OF ELMER GEORGE

It was late afternoon before the crowd in Gasoline Alley thinned to the point where Foyt could join his family and friends in the Turn Two suite. It was a subdued group until a loud argument broke out on the walkway behind the suites and Foyt went to investigate.

The Hulman family suite was next to Foyt's, and Elmer and Mari Hulman George were on the walkway arguing. Both had been drinking. They'd been married for eighteen years, but the last few years had been difficult, Mari filing for divorce on May 3. Elmer, well-known for his temper during his driving days, was yelling at Mari, who was crying.

Lucy Foyt and Mari had remained good friends over the years, sometimes vacationing together. A.J. and Elmer, while still friendly, weren't as close following the move of the George family out west.

Elmer believed Mari was having an affair with a man named Guy "Lum" Trolinger, who'd worked for them training quarter horses in Wyoming. When the ranch was sold, Trolinger moved to what was known as Hulman Farms, where he continued to train horses and serve as a general caretaker. Just east of Terre Haute, the farm covered more than one thousand acres and contained numerous buildings, including a large home, or lodge as it was called, along with other smaller houses, several occupied by employees. Trolinger lived in a small two-story home near the entrance to the property.

A.J. stepped between the arguing couple. He told Lucy to take Mari and two of the George daughters back to their rooms at the Speedway Motel, while he continued to talk with Elmer. Many years later Foyt said he didn't remember what they talked about. George, who had already fired Trolinger and told him to vacate the property, called him again, telling him to leave the house immediately. Shortly afterward George left the Speedway.

Foyt was asleep at the Speedway Motel, with Lucy, Mari, and the girls in the next room, when a call came "about three or four in the morning." Still groggy, Foyt says he doesn't know who called, but they were looking for Mari. "They said Elmer had been killed. I went and woke up Mr. Hulman and told him what happened."[42]

Foyt and Hulman decided to drive to the farm, and with A.J. driving it took less than an hour. They arrived to find a number of police cars and other official vehicles scattered around one of the houses. George's Buick pace car was parked nearby, as was a large truck partially filled with furniture. Trolinger apparently had been in the process of moving out.

Unsure what to expect, Foyt told Hulman to stay in the car. "I said if you see me get in a fight, just drive off. He said he couldn't let me go in by myself, but I said if you see something happening, you just leave."[43]

There was no need to worry, as Trolinger was already in police custody. He'd called police and admitted shooting and killing George, saying the other man broke into the house and fired first. Detectives described the scene as a "shoot-out," with bullet holes found both upstairs and downstairs in the house. Trolinger had been arrested and charged with assault and battery with intent to kill, with bail set at $100,000.[44]

Foyt identified the body and then returned to the car. He took Hulman to the main house where his grandson, Tony George, had gone after the race.

"I knew they were having marital issues," Tony George said forty-five years later. He was sixteen at the time. "I knew they were separated. The night before the race I was staying at our house near the third turn with my friend. We got in late and my dad was already in bed because he had to get up early to go over to the track. He said he wanted to talk to me in the morning. But he got up and went into the track too early. I was still asleep.

"I watched the race from the first-turn grandstands, I think it was the only time I watched the race from the grandstands. I never did see him that day. After the race my friend and I drove back to Terre Haute. I was at home, but I don't know what took place. The first thing I remember is my mom was sitting on my bed crying. I wondered why she would be crying, and then I said, 'Dad's dead, isn't he?' I don't know why I said that, but I did.

"That's all I remember, or really care to know. I don't know what happened over in Turn Two or what took place after that. I mean it doesn't matter now. Nothing changes. Doesn't make you feel worse, doesn't make you feel better. It really doesn't matter."[45]

In an indication of the Hulman family's status in the area, things began to happen quickly. Elmer George was buried two days later on Tuesday, June 1, in a private family funeral attended by A.J. and Lucy. A grand jury was empaneled by Vigo County the same day and taken to the scene of the shooting.

The grand jury began hearing testimony on Wednesday, and over two days heard from twenty-three witnesses, working late into the evening both days. Foyt, Hulman, and Mari Hulman George were subpoenaed and testified. The most riveting testimony reportedly came from Trolinger's aunt and uncle, who'd attended the 500 and were asleep in an upstairs bedroom when the gun battle erupted.

While grand jury proceedings are generally sealed and remain secret, news media reports pieced together much of what happened. Somewhere around 1:00 a.m., George arrived at the property and, armed with a .22 caliber semiautomatic handgun, forced open the rear door. Alerted by George's earlier call that there might be trouble, Trolinger was waiting for him with a .22 caliber rifle. Police said at least seventeen shots were fired, although perhaps only two by George, who was hit five times. An autopsy listed shots to his stomach and head as cause of death.

After a short deliberation, the grand jury announced midday Friday it would not indict Trolinger. They returned a "no bill" decision, amounting to justifiable homicide in the eyes of the Vigo County prosecutor. The charges were dropped, and the defendant's record cleared.

Trolinger's lawyer, public defender William G. Smock, said the grand jury's actions indicated they believed "everything [the defendant] said was true. He had no other course than to shoot this man when he busted into his house and started firing at him."[46]

Foyt had already returned to Texas, taking Tony George with him. Tony spent much of the summer on the ranch and attending races.

"A.J. put me to work painting fences," George said, "and there was a lot of fence. He was obviously trying to be supportive of a young guy who'd just lost his father. Just hanging around with him and some of the characters on the race team was helpful."[47]

Mari and the rest of the children also spent time in Houston and at the ranch. Mari would eventually go public with her relationship with Trolinger, sometimes introducing him as her boyfriend, although they would never marry.

––––––––

Distraught over the death of George, the way the 500 had ended, and his falling-out with NASCAR, Foyt initially considered shutting down his team for the year. For the first time he thought maybe fate was against him, maybe he wasn't meant to win a fourth Indy.

"The problems in qualifying, in practice, the Janet Guthrie thing, the pressure—all month seemed like a nightmare," he said.[48]

"All I wanted to do was get away from it all. I came pretty close to saying the heck with it and taking it easy the rest of the summer and getting started on next year's program."[49]

The feeling lasted only about a day. As he often did when faced with adversity, he turned to the one thing he could count on: racing. The USAC stock car series was running its first race of the year, a five hundred–miler at nearby Texas World Speedway, and Foyt had a new car built by Hutcherson-Pagan. He ordered it loaded onto a trailer and headed to the track.

Being back at a racetrack seemed to do the trick, one writer noting he was "humorous, feisty, talkative like he usually is away from Indianapolis."[50]

He embraced and joked with Rutherford, saying his mother "likes Johnny" and didn't want to see the race restarted, adding "she didn't want to see anyone hurt."[51]

It wasn't much of a race, the 140-degree track temperatures proving to be the biggest challenge. Foyt qualified on the pole, dominated throughout, and finished more than a lap ahead of the second-place car. There were no more thoughts of shutting down for the season.

"I still got some races to win and prove some points," he said afterward. "We are not giving up now."[52]

He entered a pair of Indy car races but dropped out early in each, before surprising everyone and saying he was going to Daytona for the Firecracker 400. Few had expected him to back down from NASCAR—and as it turned out he didn't. Bill France Jr. let it slip to a group of reporters that Foyt had been paid in full for the Daytona 500, and then immediately added, "I wish I hadn't said that."[53]

For his part, Foyt was on his best behavior. "I thought they slapped our hands pretty good and I didn't think the fine was fair. But I'm not going to say I came back because I was paid in full for February.

"I like the races here. I like to run them because I like to run against the best there is. I just want to go where I get treated the same as everybody else."[54]

Of course, he wasn't being treated like everybody else. None of the other fined drivers received rebates.

"It's the most mind-boggling thing I've heard this week," Waltrip said.[55]

Having sold his previous car to Guthrie, Foyt had a new Ellington-built Chevrolet and put it on the pole. He led a few laps early in the race before shredding a tire. After that he was forced to play catch-up and finished fourth, a lap back of winner Cale Yarborough.

Two weeks later at Michigan for an Indy car/stock car doubleheader, he dressed down his crew and threatened to withdraw after finding metal shavings in the oil of his Indy car engine and blamed it on sloppy workmanship. After changing the engine, he won the pole for both races.

He ran out of fuel early in the Indy car event—"I guess we didn't get the mileage we figured"—and fell two laps behind. He made them both up before running out again near the end and finishing third. In the stock car race he was stuck in third before a red flag allowed him to work on the car's handling, and when the race restarted, he drove to victory.[56]

On his way home from Michigan he stopped in Lexington, Kentucky, for the Keeneland Yearling auction. He was getting serious about the horse racing business and was part of a syndicate bidding on the first son of Secretariat. The yearling became the first horse sold for more than a million dollars and Foyt's group went to $1.45 million before dropping out of the bidding, the yearling going for $1.5 million. As it turned out, Foyt and his syndicate were the lucky ones. "Canadian Bound" failed to win in only four starts and, while he went on to sire 106 foals, failed to produce a single stakes winner.[57]

———

Two weeks later it was back to Texas World Speedway, where he became the first driver to pull off the doubleheader sweep, taking the pole and winning both events. When he qualified seven mph faster than the next fastest in the Indy car event, other drivers started to grumble that perhaps the pop-off valves provided by USAC weren't as equal as everyone thought. It became a common theme in the years to come.

He dominated the Indy car race, leading all but one lap. Between races the promoters played "The Ballad of A.J. Foyt" over the track public address system, a song written by daughter Terry and sung by her new husband, Larry Roberds, a country-western professional. "A.J. Foyt, we'll always know his name," went the chorus, "From the dusty dirt track of Houston, To the racin' Hall of Fame."[58]

The stock car race was more competitive, the outcome the same. Afterward, it sounded as if he'd just won his fourth Indy 500.

"This is one of the happiest days of my career," he said. "If I have to win somewhere, I'd just as soon it be here as any place in the world."[59]

A few days later he was in Talladega, attempting to make his first race start at the world's fastest speedway. He'd entered and even qualified in the past, but outside issues always kept him from taking the green flag.

He qualified third, but not without issue. An official crawled in his car on Pit Road searching for a bottle of nitrous oxide, even trying to get in Foyt's uniform.

"He jumped in the car and started feeling me up," Foyt recalled. "I didn't know what the hell they were doing. He said he was looking for a bottle on me. I told him to come see me that evening, I'm in room 286."[60]

Feeling ill, Foyt was also one of several drivers treated at the track hospital and sent back to their hotels. The NASCAR series had been at Pocono the week before and something being called Legionnaires' disease had killed twenty-nine people attending an American Legion convention in a nearby Philadelphia hotel. He started the race, but dropped out early.

Despite feeling the effects of the "Philadelphia flu," as he called it, and an encounter with bees on his ranch that left his arms reddened from stings, he was able to qualify on the pole for the Indy car event at Trenton. In one of the better races of the year, he battled with Johncock and Al Unser in the early going and was leading by three seconds when he tried to put another lap on Bill Simpson. He tried to pass on the outside into Turn Four but slid into the wall and out of the race.

"Simpson came right alongside me and forced me into the wall," a fired-up Foyt said. Despite television replays showing Simpson simply holding his line on the track, Foyt went to the pit wall, shaking his fist, then his finger at Simpson.[61]

"He was cooking all day," Simpson said. "If he had waited until we got onto the straight he could have passed me easily." Simpson would say Foyt apologized in private, but Foyt never acknowledged it publicly.[62]

After Trenton, racing took a back seat again as Foyt's mother suffered a stroke. He pulled out of Milwaukee and arrived late for the Ontario 500. He still qualified on the pole, but dropped out of the race early. He was late again to Indianapolis for the September 11 Hoosier Hundred dirt car race. Starting last, he drove through the field and took the lead after an accident claimed several of the other front-runners. Soon after, however, his fuel line started to leak, causing the engine to sputter and allowing Joe Saldana to repass him for his first USAC victory and by far his largest paycheck at $12,000.

"This is the biggest thing that has ever happened to me," said an emotional Saldana, who'd been struggling to make ends meet and failed to qualify at the fairgrounds just a week earlier. "I'm sure A.J. still can remember the first time he won this race. It's a great honor to run with him and beat him, but I've got to admit, if he had not been having troubles, he would have won."[63]

Foyt, who first won the race in 1960 and had captured it five times since, seemed embarrassed by it all. "You deserved to win," he told Saldana, adding words not often heard: "I'm happy with second."[64]

The following week he started the defense of his IROC championship at Michigan International Speedway against a field that included Richard Petty, Gordon Johncock, Al and Bobby Unser, Buddy Baker, Al Holbert, James Hunt, David Pearson, Johnny Rutherford, Jody Scheckter, and Cale Yarborough.

There was a 150-mile Indy car event as part of the day's racing, and Foyt qualified on the pole. He battled Johncock near the end, running race laps at more than 195 mph to win by three-tenths of a second, his second victory of the year.

The wild IROC race featured a series record twenty-five lead changes over fifty laps and three bad crashes, with Foyt out front more often than anyone else. Foyt and Bobby Unser were involved in one crash late in the race that knocked Unser out and dropped Foyt to fourth at the finish.

After the races Pat Patrick, owner of Johncock's car, protested the Indy car finish, saying Foyt had reentered the racing groove too soon after a pit stop and that he had passed three cars under a yellow flag. Patrick said he had a signed statement from Tom Sneva saying Foyt passed him under the yellow. He said he didn't want Foyt disqualified, but didn't feel like he should get away without a reprimand. "We can't have rules for A.J. and other rules for the rest," Patrick said. "It's got to stop sometime."[65]

Both protests were denied by USAC.

That led the *Indianapolis News* to run a column headlined, "Is A.J. above USAC Regulations?" Writer Dick Mittman, a regular on the racing beat and often a Foyt supporter, asked, "Is A.J. Foyt so big in championship auto racing he can get away with rules violations others can't?" He went on to answer his own question. "Foyt's crowd appeal is so great USAC is reluctant to chastise him publicly because he just might take his famed No. 14 Coyote race car and go home to Houston."[66]

It wasn't until Foyt went to Charlotte for the October 10 NASCAR race that he indirectly responded to Patrick's charges and the *Indianapolis News* column.

"I've always put my racing first," he said, "but it hasn't been as much fun recently. I'm probably tired of it more today than I was two years ago. It's the hassles, the politics. That gets old and that'll probably make me retire [someday]."[67]

If Foyt thought it would be fun getting back in a stock car he was mistaken. Ellington had built a new Monte Carlo and entered it for Donnie Allison. While Foyt qualified ahead of his teammate, he struggled early in the race and parked his car, finishing thirty-eighth of forty. The official reason for dropping out was listed simply as "quit."

"There wasn't any use in me staying out there in everybody's way, so I parked it," Foyt said. "I'll never sit in that car again, not unless they put it through a bandsaw and rebuild it.

"It's the same old story every time we come to a track, the car is never prepared. It handled so bad I couldn't keep it in a ten-acre briar patch. I'd rather build my own stock car than run a pile of hogwash like that."[68]

Asked if building his own car was a possibility, Foyt said, "I might, rather than run a piece of junk like that. Let's put it this way, I might run for Hoss again, but not in that car. If I race at Rockingham [in two weeks] it will not be in that car. I will be driving the Monte Carlo."[69]

Foyt had already left the track when Donnie Allison took the checkered flag for his first major NASCAR victory in five years, setting off a raucous victory celebration.

"I think I could get in that same car and win with it," Ellington said of Foyt's parked racer. It didn't sound like he had any intention of letting Foyt drive Allison's car in the upcoming Rockingham race.[70]

"The Monte Carlo? I couldn't let A.J. run that when a man has just won a race for me in it. I can't let Donnie down. Donnie's going to be in that car at Rockingham and Atlanta.

"I think A.J. is the world's greatest driver when it comes to driving different autos. I'm not taking anything away from A.J., but Donnie knows more about setting up cars here, because he does it more often."[71]

It would in fact be Foyt's last drive for Ellington, and his last NASCAR event of the year.

The next weekend there was a pair of IROC races at Riverside. Foyt skipped the first day of practice, and when he arrived he was clearly unhappy with what he considered the reckless driving in the series' first race that left several of the cars badly damaged and drivers feeling very lucky to have survived. Hunt, trailing Niki Lauda by three points for the F1 championship with the finale only a week away in Japan, pulled out rather than risk injury.

"If the junk keeps up like we had in the IROC opener at Michigan, then somebody is going to get hurt—bad," Foyt said. Added Petty, "Most of these cats are used to driving open cockpit cars. They get a roll bar and a sheet of metal over their heads and they think they're hurt-proof. I can vouch from experience, that is anything but the case."[72]

In the first of two races, Foyt ran near the front until Al Unser pointed toward the rear of his car under caution, a signal Foyt took that he had a tire going flat. He pulled into the pits and was told nothing was wrong with the tire, and that he was penalized a lap for pitting under the yellow.

Foyt felt Unser had done it on purpose and filed a protest, which was disallowed. He threatened to withdraw from the series until Unser spoke with him, assuring him he thought the tire was going flat. He lined up for the next race with better results, finishing second to Yarborough and moving into second place overall, one point behind Bobby Unser ahead of the February finals at Daytona.[73]

It was back to Texas for yet another USAC doubleheader and Foyt again claimed the pole for both races. It was seemingly all Foyt, all the time, as "The Ballad of A.J. Foyt" was played repeatedly over the loudspeakers. Rutherford, the Indy 500 winner and "the other Texan," who was battling for the series championship, seemed to understand.

"In my book, A.J. is the greatest driver who ever pulled on a helmet," he said. "I'm working for the same status for myself although I can't amass the kind of record A.J. has because of the time I have left to race. But I'll do the best I can and hope that someday I can be considered one of the best drivers who ever did it."[74]

Rutherford won the Indy car race, but only after Foyt, who dominated early, had a tire "let go," sending him into the Turn Four wall at more than 180 mph. The Coyote slid down the track and a "visibly stunned" Foyt remained in the car for several minutes before being helped out of the machine and taken to the track hospital.[75]

Despite admitting he was "woozy," he ignored a doctor's request not to drive in the second race and limped to his car for the start.[76]

"I even went to the car on the grid and asked him to please not run, but he wouldn't listen," said track doctor J.F. Cooper. "Most race drivers would have said okay. Not A.J. He's as tough as anybody I know. I think he would have been a contender even if he'd had a broken back."[77]

He led early and challenged late before finishing third to Bobby Allison. Returning home and complaining of chest and back pain, he went to see his doctors, who said he was lucky and foolish for running the second race. He agreed to take the rest of the season off, meaning the finale at Phoenix, where Johncock edged Rutherford for the championship.

His season over, Foyt retreated to his ranch and contemplated his future. Only he would consider the season something less than a success. He'd started twenty-eight races, qualified fastest in twelve, won five, and captured the IROC crown. But his dream of winning the Daytona 500 and Indianapolis 500 in the same year had been within his reach, only to have both elude him in the end.

His father wanted him to enter fewer races, allowing the team to focus on the big events.

"I think he drives too much," Tony Foyt said. "I wish he'd run the big 500s and forget all the rest of 'em. I'd like him to win a fourth time. It might change his attitude about how much he drives."[78]

The senior Foyt also knew it was pointless to pressure his son.

"I just let him go. Ain't nobody going to talk him out of it. He'll quit when he wants to."[79]

The family situation was not lost on Foyt. He was about to become a grandfather; his daughter Terry was expecting in February. His father was less than a year removed from open heart surgery, and his mother was still recovering from her stroke. Both were obviously slowing down.

"Mother's one wish is for me to quit while she's still living," he acknowledged. "She claims I told her I would quit if I ever won at Indy, but I don't remember saying that. Daddy worries. I know he does, although he tries not to let me know it. But I can't tell them when I'm quitting.

"I don't know myself."[80]

CHAPTER 38

FOUR'S A CHARM

1977

A.J. Foyt's Indy car program was at a tipping point. He'd been running the same basic engine/car package for four years and the competition was closing in.

After two years of development and victories by Al Unser at Pocono, Milwaukee, and Phoenix, the turbocharged version of the V8 Cosworth engine was clearly competitive and would power the cars of McLaren, Roger Penske, and Parnelli Jones. George Bignotti's DGS (he'd given up on rebranding it a "Bignotti") powerplant was more widely available, and even the standard turbocharged Offy remained competitive. As usual, A.J. was being secretive about his plans, although Chris Economaki wrote in his *National Speed Sports News* column that Foyt was talking with Ferrari about a new engine.[1]

Although the Ferrari talks went nowhere, Foyt was keeping a close eye on the technological advancements coming out of Formula One. He was intrigued by the six-wheel car being raced in F1 by Tyrrell, with four small tires in front. A six-wheel car had been raced at Indianapolis in the late 1940s, with four large wheels in the back, without much success. Four small tires on the front, however, could provide an aerodynamic advantage at places like the Indianapolis Motor Speed-way. He discussed the concept at an IROC event the previous year with Jody Scheckter, who'd won the Spanish Grand Prix in the car. The main stumbling block was a USAC regulation saying all tires must be fifteen inches in diameter. He approached the organization about the possibility of changing the rule passed back in 1963, but when it showed little inclination to do so, he dropped the idea.[2]

In the end he decided to stick with the tried and true, the Coyote built in 1975 he'd nearly driven to victory at Indianapolis the past two years. It had raced only one other time, winning the 1975 Pocono 500, and had been sitting

◀ Number Four. *Associated Press Photo Archive*

in the corner of the race shop for the past six months, the race engine still in the car. The two original 1974 cars would be used on other tracks and as backups at the Speedway.

Rebuffed by Ferrari, he decided to stick with the Foyt V8. Despite having previously "frozen" its engine regulations for five years, USAC reverted to allowing cars to run without a pop-off valve during races. Some thought the move would be a boon for Foyt. Others, including the recently crowned Indy car champion, weren't so sure.

"I think everybody else has caught up with Foyt," said Gordon Johncock, who was again driving for Bignotti. "But nobody is really sure what A.J. has come up with for this season. We'll have to wait and see.

"We'll be all right. I don't like the fuel restrictions, but I've got to admit it's made for close racing. We'll set up for a lot of yellow lights. If we get 'em and have enough fuel left near the finish, we'll turn up the boost and blow right past Foyt."[3]

The Indy car series also landed a much-needed sponsor for 1977, its first in four years. Citicorp, a mammoth financial services conglomerate, and its new line of First National City Travelers Checks was hoping to challenge American Express. It was spending freely in auto racing, including Indy cars, F1, and NASCAR, and putting up $300,000 in USAC for the Citicorp Cup championship. It was also sponsoring the cars driven by Johnny Rutherford, Roger McCluskey, and Al Unser.

After splitting with Hoss Ellington in NASCAR after three years, A.J. went against the wishes of his father and decided to bring his NASCAR program in-house. He'd have the support of car builders Dick Hutcherson and Eddie Pagan and a $200,000 check from Jim Gilmore. The engines would be built in his Houston shops.

"I just got tired of sitting on the pole, then running a few laps and blowing," Foyt said. "So I've decided to operate my own cars and team. Then if I don't do well, it'll be my fault.

"Running cars in NASCAR is a new experience for my operation and it may take us a couple of races to get going. I'll be strapped for more time and people, but I have more of both since I'm running only one car instead of preparing three or four for the Indianapolis 500."[4]

The season got off to a mixed start as Foyt qualified second for the February 20 Daytona 500—second to the car of Ellington and Donnie Allison.

"We just wanted to be the fastest," said Ellington, who'd declined Foyt's $1,000 bet on who would win the pole. "We didn't care who was second fastest. All that other stuff is behind us now." Allison was driving the same car Foyt raced at Daytona the year before.[5]

Foyt was among the first cars to qualify, and Allison said, "A.J. happened to be the fastest at the time I went on the track, so I definitely wanted to beat him. But I didn't come down here with the intention of outrunning A.J. I came down here with the intention of outrunning everybody. I don't let past things that happened between other people affect me."[6]

In the IROC race, Foyt lost his brakes early and dropped back before hooking up with Cale Yarborough. They perfected the art of bump drafting, Foyt repeatedly pounding away at the rear bumper of Yarborough's car and pushing the pair to the front. They finished one-two, second place being all Foyt needed to secure his second straight championship and another $50,000.

"I just had to draft," Foyt said. "I saw right away that my car wasn't competitive. The only way I could run fast was to hook onto Cale. That's just good racing. At the same time I'm drafting him, I was helping him because we're running faster and not letting the third car catch up."[7]

"I was giving him a pretty rough time, but I had to keep doing it to try and keep up. When I did bump him hard I tried to do it while we were going perfectly straight. I was helping us both accelerate more. That way, it made me a winner and him a winner. I think Cale understands what I was doing. I picked him as my good ol' buddy today."[8]

It hadn't taken Yarborough long to figure out Foyt's predicament and how he would benefit. "He bumped me just the right amount, but every now and then he kicked too hard and I had to shake my fist at him."[9]

Asked how he felt about taking his second IROC championship without actually winning a race, Foyt grinned. "I feel $100,000 richer, that's how."[10]

After leading early in the 500, Foyt saw Yarborough move in front on an exchange of pit stops. Tire problems, compounded by slow pit work by a mostly rookie crew, dropped Foyt further back and he finished sixth, three laps behind Yarborough.

Two weeks later at Ontario Speedway in California for a USAC stock car/Indy doubleheader, he qualified on the pole for the stock car race but was a disappointing sixth in the Indy car, complaining the pop-off valve didn't operate properly.

In the stock car race, he was well on his way to victory when a caution flag bunched the field with twenty laps to go and he lost the front spot during a series of pit stops. He worked his way back into the lead and was zigzagging down the straights in an attempt to break the draft of the second- and third-place cars when he cut a tire and was forced to make another pit stop, finishing third.

The Indy car event was billed as a preview to the Indianapolis 500, with Rutherford on the pole, followed by Tom Sneva and Al Unser, all with Cosworth engines, and Johncock in fourth with the DGS powerplant. With the pop-off valve removed for the race, Foyt took command midway through the event and stretched his lead to nearly two minutes ahead of Unser at the finish.

It was Foyt's 250th Indy car start and victory number fifty-seven, both adding to his records. He seemed not to notice. "It was just another race. I thought it was going to be a bad day after that stock car race, but I've lost a lot that way, and I've won a lot that way."[11]

Happy with the performance of his stock car team, he entered the March 20 Atlanta 500. Nothing seemed to go right after qualifying fourth, and he parked his car before the race was half over. About the only thing he was happy about afterward was the victory by Richard Petty.

"It seems whenever Richard has a good year, *I* have a good year," he said. Petty had won only three races in 1976, his lowest total in years. "When he has a bad one, I do too. As soon as I got here I saw Petty and asked him, 'Dammit, when are you going to start winning so we can start winning.' Richard asked me the same thing."[12]

———————

When the Indy car teams gathered in Phoenix a week later, everyone was talking about Johncock, who'd supposedly run the first lap of more than 200 miles per hour at Indianapolis during tire tests. Only Foyt seemed unimpressed. "So what," he said. "It didn't count."[13]

Johncock and Rutherford, who'd been feuding since the Michigan race the year before, qualified one-two. Johncock took the lead at the start with Foyt moving up from fifth to run third. Then the fun started.

Rutherford was black-flagged on lap twenty-one when officials spotted what they thought was an oil leak. It turned out to be a fuel overflow problem that was quickly corrected. He rejoined the race, coming on the track just behind Johncock and falling a lap down but ahead of second-place Foyt on the track. Although officials gave Rutherford the move-over flag, Foyt was unable to get past and blistered his tires trying, as Johncock pulled farther ahead.

"I saw the blue and orange flag and I moved over for three laps, but A.J. couldn't get by," Rutherford said years later. "I was running real good, and when I saw he couldn't make it, I forgot about the flag and took off. I didn't impede him one bit."[14]

A series of pit stops worked in Rutherford's favor, and he got back on the same lap as the two leaders, with Foyt now out front and Johncock second. When Rutherford pulled alongside Johncock the two cars touched several times, sending Johncock into a spin and then the pits for repairs, returning five laps behind. Rutherford passed Foyt on lap one hundred of 150 and went on to victory. Afterward Foyt was mad at the McLaren team, believing it had used the radio to tell Rutherford how to block Foyt's passing attempts, common practice in modern racing, but unheard of in 1977. He found Johncock and egged him on.

"After the race A.J. got out of his car and started barking to Gordie," Rutherford recalled. "He said, 'You know what they told that son of a bitch Rutherford to do? To stay in front of me! Hell they probably told him to spin you out!' A.J. was hot. I think he was frustrated that he burned up his tires."[15]

While Johncock headed toward Victory Lane, Foyt set off for the McLaren pits where, according to the *Los Angeles Times*, he "picked up Tyler Alexander, team manager of Rutherford's McLaren and not a small man, and shook him like a rag doll."[16]

"He grabbed my shirt and almost lifted me off the ground, yelling, 'Why don't you damn Limeys go back to England,'" Alexander wrote in his autobiography. "I said something to the effect of, 'Piss off! I'm from Boston!' With a somewhat puzzled look, A.J. let go of me and stormed off in the opposite direction. Guess he didn't like being beaten very much."[17]

Foyt went back to his car, where he ripped off the decal of the series sponsor, who also happened to sponsor Rutherford's car—First National City Travelers Checks—and the patch off his uniform. Meanwhile, Johncock, who'd been blocked from entering Victory Lane, waited in the press trailer, knowing Rutherford would eventually show up.

"You drove right into me and knocked me off the track," Johncock yelled at Rutherford when he walked in. "You know better than to drive like that. You didn't win that race."[18]

"That's racing, Gordie," Rutherford responded, "that's the way it is."

"Well if that's the way it is, the next time you're going over the wall. I'll do that."

Rutherford turned to the reporters. "You heard it." Then he turned back to Johncock. "You shouldn't say things like that. I'll have you thrown out of USAC for that, little man. If you can't stand the heat, you'd better stay out of the kitchen."[19]

That was too much for Johncock, who, despite giving up about five inches and thirty pounds, took a swing at Rutherford. They both got in a few blows before cops pulled them apart.

Calling it "absolutely disgraceful" and "a black eye for the sport we are not going to tolerate," USAC President Dick King fined Johncock $1,500 and gave both drivers "strong reprimands." Reporters, however, noted that nothing was said about Foyt's "rabble-rousing."[20]

Watching from home and reading the newspaper reports was Fred Stecher, the chairman of Citicorp Services, which included First National City Travelers Checks.

"They can't be in this business and talk like that," Stecher said. "They should walk it off, talk it off, and cool it off. Punching people out, or picking them up by the throat right off the ground is shortsighted to the point of being microscopic. I don't think the performance, right or wrong, was beneficial to the sport, and I'm sure it wasn't beneficial to the sponsorship. I didn't like what I saw and I liked less what I heard about what was not televised.

"If not for the assurances from Dick King, I would be gravely concerned about the future of the relationship."[21]

Rutherford and Johncock met with King the following Friday before a race in Texas. "We shook hands and even joked a little bit about it," Rutherford said. "There's no place in this business for carrying grudges and I'm sure we won't."[22]

There were no dramatics in the race as Foyt went from fifth to the lead on lap two and led most of the way until he dropped out on lap fifty-eight of one hundred with a busted radiator, Sneva going on for the victory.

Despite trailing Al Unser by just sixty points in the championship battle and being featured on the cover of the race program, Foyt decided to skip the upcoming Trenton event, saying he needed to focus on getting his car ready for Indianapolis. Some thought he held out for more appearance money that never came and others recalled his criticism of Mario Andretti for skipping Trenton the year before. Ironically, Andretti, now driving for Penske, entered this time around.

Things got complicated when Trenton was rained out and the race was pushed back a week, in conflict with the May 1 NASCAR race at Talladega where Foyt was entered and preferred to race. USAC eventually ruled that because Trenton was a rain date and not on the original schedule, it wasn't a violation of the rules, and Foyt headed for Alabama. He qualified on the pole and led before dropping out with a blown engine after just eighteen laps. He seemed happy with the outcome, saying, "I knew the engine was going to blow. But I didn't give a damn. I just wanted to show [them] I could run off and leave 'em. And I did."[23]

Practice for the sixty-first running of the Indianapolis 500 started on Saturday, May 7, but Foyt was in nearby Louisville for the 103rd running of the Kentucky Derby, where Seattle Slew posted an impressive victory.

At the Speedway the race to 200 mph was on. Andretti was the first in practice to unofficially hit the mark. The weather leading up to qualifying was near perfect, and the track, which had undergone its first complete repaving during the offseason, was receptive to high speeds. Foyt was next to hit 200, then Rutherford.

The new surface wasn't as porous as the old, however, and as the week of warm temperatures and no rain wore on, the buildup of tire rubber and oil combined to make for a slick track. "A light shower would really help," said Andretti, "but I don't think you'll see either that or a 200 lap." Sneva, Andretti's Penske team-mate, spun and did minor damage to his car trying to join the club on the Friday before qualifying. Foyt wasn't at the track, part of his new "low key" approach to the month of May.[24]

"This year I made up my mind I wasn't going to get all keyed up for this race," he said. "I wasn't going to get all tense the way I have for twenty years here. I went down to Churchill Downs where I had some horses running. I was determined I wasn't going to let this place upset me this year."[25]

He also didn't think a 200 mph lap was likely. "It could happen, but it would take a good draw [qualifying position] and perfect conditions."

Chief mechanic Jack Starne did his job, drawing the second qualifying position in the cool morning air. Rookie Danny Ongais was slated to go first; his chances went up in smoke along with his engine in early warm-ups. Foyt moved to the head of the line, setting the stage for a dramatic qualifying attempt.

With a crowd, estimated at more than three hundred thousand by Indiana State Police, in a frenzy, the excitement didn't last long, as he was well under 200 mph on his first lap, turning in a four-lap average of only 193.465 mph. Foyt said he considered waving off the run and trying again but remembered how that backfired on him in the past. "I guess it's all right, so long as we're in the first three or four rows," he told track announcer Jim Phillippe.[26]

With Andretti and Rutherford coming later in the order, the honor of being the first to 200 mph (and as it turned out the only one) went to Sneva, who hadn't been clocked at the mark all month. As he was still celebrating the run, however, he and everyone else was surprised to see the No. 14 being pushed back into the qualifying line.

Foyt was already back in his room at the Speedway Motel when word came that USAC technicians believed the pop-off valve on his car had malfunctioned during the qualifying run. Under the rules, he was allowed a second run—if he wanted. He did. Foyt said he wanted to make some chassis adjustments, but officials said no, it was now or never, and he hustled back to the track for a second run.

The announcement telling fans Foyt would be the first driver in history given a second run didn't sit well with the crowd, and he returned to the track to a chorus of boos. He was a little better than his first run but not much, running four laps at 194.563 mph. The booing continued as he pulled up for another post-qualifying interview with Phillippe.

"The Speedway people found that the valve had malfunctioned, my crew didn't find it," he said. "Some of those people who are booing over there don't know what the hell they're booing about."[27]

Initially he said the booing "didn't disturb" him, but that didn't last long.[28]

"They're a bunch of idiots running and jawing," he said of the boo-birds to the group of reporters who descended on him. In the scrum was Dick Mittman, who'd written the column asking if USAC favored Foyt, and Jon Barnes, a twenty-three-year-old stringer for UPI radio out of Fort Wayne. When they started to shout questions at Foyt, he said he'd talk with them back at his garage.[29]

"We all knew not to question him until we got there," Mittman recalled. "All but the rookie radio guy from out of town. We hadn't walked fifteen yards when the newcomer's mic was shoved in front of A.J.'s face. Foyt shouted at him, 'I told you I'd talk in front of the garage.' In another thirty yards or so the mic reappeared. This time A.J. told him exactly what he would do with that mic if it happened again. By now we had reached Foyt's garage and he turns around to talk to us. Guess what was in front of his face? A.J. exploded."[30]

Spotting what was about to happen, one of Foyt's crew members tried to move Barnes back, but A.J. was too quick. He grabbed the microphone and reporter's wrist and yanked them toward him, winding up with his right fist. Now Mittman stepped in.

"I grabbed Foyt around his stomach and jerked him backwards to prevent him from hitting this young reporter who didn't know what the word 'wait' meant," the *Indianapolis News* reporter said. "He would have had a big story if A.J.'s fist had reached its target. That is, once he got off the pavement."[31]

Photographers caught the scene and the next morning a picture of Foyt, Mittman, and Barnes was in newspapers across America. Mittman's mother called from California to say he was on the front page of the *San Francisco Chronicle*.

While insisting "I've got a right to an interview," Barnes later admitted to being a little afraid, "but more embarrassed, really. I didn't do anything to provoke him. There was no reason to assault somebody."[32]

Foyt wasn't the only disappointed driver at the end of the first day of qualifying as Andretti was even slower and Rutherford wasn't able to post a time at all, waving off one run and having his car quit on the second. The front row was filled out by Bobby and Al Unser, with Foyt, Johncock, and Andretti making up row two.

After working on his car's race setup during the week and pronouncing it ready after turning laps at 188 mph, Foyt got in his backup car on Friday before the final weekend of qualifying and ran a lap of more than 190 mph. He surprised his crew that night by offering it to Billy Vukovich Jr., who jumped at the opportunity. Vukovich's father had won the 500 in 1953 and 1954 and was leading in 1955 when he was killed in a crash. Billy had come close himself, with five top-ten finishes at Indy, including a second in 1973 and a third in 1974. But he was having trouble getting his car up to speed.

"A couple of days ago A.J. sort of asked me if I'd like to drive his other car. I wasn't sure he was serious or not, so I went over to the garage [Friday] night and told him I'd take it. The car is great, it's probably the best car I've ever had here."[33]

After about ten practice laps, Vukovich asked for the rear wing angle to be altered to create more rear downforce. Vuky knew Foyt was notorious for running less rear wing than anybody else and he wasn't comfortable in the car.

"I wanted more wing," Vukovich said. "A.J. said no, that the car would straighten out as it ran. I told him it was my butt that would get skinned because it would spin if it didn't have more wing. I won the argument and A.J. made the adjustment."[34]

"But A.J. was right. With more wing, the car got to the point where it was pushing more and more. If I had listened to him, I'm sure we would have been faster."[35]

———

Carb Day provided the final test session, and things didn't start well. Jim Murray of the *Los Angeles Times*, who was watching Foyt for a column he intended to do on the driver, noticed the difference.

"He left his garage Thursday with the angry stride of a man who had taken about all he could take. He looked mad enough to drive it off a cliff. His Gilmore crew all pretended to be looking the other way. They tiptoed around the pit wall.

"Fifteen minutes and ten hard laps later . . . the guy who stepped out [of his car] and took off his helmet looked like a guy who would feed birds and take thorns out a kitten's paws. A.J. had this beatific smile of a guy playing an angel in a school play. If you looked closely, you could see two checkered flags sticking out of his mouth like canary feathers."[36]

Speed was one thing that always seemed to cheer Foyt up, and he was fast, just a tick slower than Rutherford, who'd be starting well back. In a column under Foyt's byline in the *Indianapolis News*, he laid out his plan for the coming race.

"If I'm sitting there and can go for the lead early, then I will. If I can't, I'm not going to worry about it until 400 miles. I'm going to try to stay in contention all day instead of putting the push on early like I have the last several years. The last one hundred miles or so is when I'll make a run for it."[37]

He also noted he'd been asked by reporters about rumors he was considering taking over as Speedway president at year's end. "I know nothing about it and at the present time I'm not even interested in talking about it. I've never talked to Tony Hulman about it. Even if he wanted me to, I doubt if I'd have the time."[38]

He made one thing crystal clear: "Win or lose in Sunday's 500-mile race, I have no plans to retire."

After maintaining his mostly low-key approach to the month of May—with the one notable exception—Foyt carried it over to his prerace activities and was in bed by 10:00 p.m. the night before. With rain having cut short the race in three of the past four years, the first thing he did after getting up around 8:00 a.m. was check the weather. A hot and humid haze already hung in the air, and temperatures were expected to hover around ninety degrees. No rain was expected, although a late afternoon thunderstorm was always a possibility. He assigned a crew member to monitor a local radio channel for weather updates.

The "unquestionably biggest crowd ever, well over 300,000," according to the Speedway, was on its way to the track. ABC put it at closer to 400,000. The roads were clogged early and chief steward Tom Binford was among many who were forced to abandon his car and walk several miles to the track.

After a casual breakfast with family and friends—his regular prerace steak and eggs—Foyt had a much shorter commute from the Speedway Motel, arriving about 10:00 a.m. The Coyote was already on the track and he checked in with his crew before wandering back to the garage to put on his uniform, not returning to the track until about ten minutes before the start. There was none of the bantering and joking with other drivers as he'd often done in past years. He did a brief interview with a trackside reporter and, already hot, poured a cup of ice water down the front of his uniform.

Like most, he was curious about how Hulman would call for the engines to be started. Janet Guthrie had become the first woman to qualify for the race, and Foyt had discussed several possible replacements for "Gentlemen, start your engines" with the track owner but had no advance knowledge of what was to come. Hulman, who'd spent the night practicing, read from a piece of paper. He was simple and direct, recognizing the historic significance of the event.

"In company with the first woman ever to qualify at Indianapolis, gentlemen, start your engines."

Foyt dropped back at the start, running sixth going into Turn One as Bobby Unser took the lead from his second-place starting position. Johncock moved in front on lap eighteen and then Foyt led for four laps as the leaders made pit stops. Rutherford, the defending champion and winner of two of the last three races, was already out. He'd finish last.

A quick pit stop, the first in a day full of near-flawless stops, put Foyt out in front of Johncock. Only a car length or two typically separated the cars as Foyt led laps twenty-six through fifty-one. Following a caution period, Johncock got the jump on Foyt when the green came out on the backstretch, one of the few times anyone could remember Foyt being passed on the track.

They pitted together on lap sixty-seven, Johncock retaining the lead, and they again ran nose-to-tail while snaking through traffic. Andretti had joined Rutherford in the garage, and Sneva, Dallenbach, and the Unser brothers were falling back. No one else could run with Johncock or Foyt.

With another round of pit stops approaching, Foyt suddenly slowed on lap ninety-two, out of fuel. "We either miscalculated or had an air lock because of the temperature," he'd say, the team's one misstep of the day. Fortunately, it happened on the backstraight and he was able to coast into the pits. The crew did a good job of restarting the engine and getting him back on the track, but he was thirty-five seconds behind Johncock. Foyt's plan of waiting until the final fifty laps to run hard was out the window. He had no choice but to run as fast as his fuel levels allowed.

"When that happened," Foyt said. "I thought the bad luck was coming again. I figured it wasn't going to be my day."[39]

A few laps later Vukovich pulled into his adjacent pit stall. After starting twenty-third he'd been running hard, even leading a lap during pit stops. Now he was out with a broken piston. Among Foyt's crew a feeling of déjà vu set in, a fear the problems of the previous years were striking again.

"Son of a bitch," thought crew member Billy Woodruff, "here we go again."[40]

On the track, however, Foyt was cutting into Johncock's lead, occasionally running laps at 191 mph and picking up as much as a second a lap. He noticed the water temperature creeping up, chose to ignore it, and it eventually stabilized.

While Johncock led for the next eighty-three laps, even holding the lead while making pit stops, he was also starting to have problems. The Wildcat was beginning to understeer on the increasingly slick track, and he went high out of the groove at one point, nearly hitting the wall. ABC broadcasters Jackie Stewart and Jim McKay speculated the high temperatures were responsible for his "erratic" driving. He twice missed pit signals to stop under a yellow flag, which would have saved him precious seconds.

He may have been getting tired, but Johncock was also stretching his fuel as far as possible before the final stop and sprint to the finish. Foyt gained enough ground to briefly take the lead when Johncock next pitted, the stop stretching to more than sixteen seconds as he waited for more cold water to be poured on him. He then stalled the car leaving the pit and lost more time while the crew pushed it for a jump start. Foyt's stop was under thirteen seconds, his fastest of the day, and he came out trailing by seven seconds with seventeen laps remaining. He could see Johncock ahead on the long straights.

"I was savin' everything I had for one last banzai run," Foyt would say.[41]

"The crew got a little impatient with me at times. They keep showing me 'Fuel OK' on the pit board. I knew they wanted me to crank up the boost and go after him. I wanted to stay close enough so that in the final ten laps or so we could make a big banzai run at him. I kept saying, wait for later, wait for later."[42]

Back on the track, Johncock ran his two fastest laps of the day, both at about 190 mph. Then he felt a vibration, hoping it was a tire that could be changed if necessary. It was followed by a "rattling," and he glanced in his mirror on the front straightaway. Smoke. His engine was going, and he knew his day was over.

"I've been pushing that car hard all day," he told a group of reporters that met him when he returned to Pit Lane. He was still wet after jumping in the stream that ran along Turn One in an attempt to cool off. "I don't think I've ever been more tired than I am right now. It was the hottest 500 I've ever run." He also admitted it was the "biggest disappointment in my racing career. But what can you do about it? That's just something you have to get used to in racing."[43]

In the Foyt pit, engine man Howard Gilbert asked Jim Gilmore III, who'd been timing the interval between Johncock and Foyt, to see how far back now second-place Sneva was. Thirty-five seconds. Race queen Linda Vaughn arrived in the pit and photographers began to crowd into Vukovich's abandoned area, although one with a green shirt was asked to leave.

Foyt radioed Steve Jordan and asked how many more laps.

"Four, boss," he said. Sneva was the fastest car on the track, but still about thirty seconds back.[44]

"The Good Lord willing," Foyt responded, "we're coming home today."[45]

Despite having contemplated for ten years what it would mean to win a fourth Indianapolis 500, Foyt was at a loss for words when Bill Fleming, who was handling Victory Lane duties for *Wide World of Sports,* stuck a microphone next to the helmet and asked for the driver's first reaction.

"Oh I don't know, it's been so long," Foyt said. "I just can't really believe that it's true." His helmet off, it was replaced by a Goodyear ball cap. "We had our good breaks, we had our bad breaks. Still, I can't believe it. I knew Gordy was a tough competitor and Bignotti being one of my old mechanics, he's just a hard man to beat, and he made us work for it."[46]

As Foyt headed for the pace car and the traditional winner's drive around the track with Hulman and Lucy, he turned back and waved to the photographers, saying, "See you next year."[47]

With Foyt on his victory lap, Woodruff and other crew members pushed the race-winning car back to Gasoline Alley. *Indianapolis Star* reporter Robin Miller later noted the car was moved to the garage instead of the inspection area as rules required. Miller's implication was clear: if there'd been something illegal with the car, the crew had ample time to change it before the inspection took place.

Woodruff says there wasn't anything illicit going on, just in all the excitement and confusion of Victory Lane, and with rain in the area, they pushed the car into the garage and closed the door to keep the crowd out.

"The inspector couldn't have been more than two or three minutes behind us," Woodruff recalled. "We shut the door and then he came in a couple of minutes later. It wasn't like we were swapping out the engine or anything."[48]

Once No. 14 had passed inspection, Woodruff and other crew members commandeered the GMC pace truck that had been awarded to Starne as the race-winning crew chief. More than two dozen crew members jammed every square inch of the truck, "whooping and hollering," as they made a slow lap of the speedway. Woodruff clung to his position on the hood.[49]

While the victory laps were going on, the six-hundred-mile NASCAR race at Charlotte Motor Speedway was nearing its halfway point and Richard Petty was running a very uncharacteristic race. With the top lap leader in each fifty-lap segment of the four-hundred-lap event earning an extra $5,000, Petty had decided to abandon his normal moderate early-race pace aimed at being around for the finish, instead running flat out in pursuit of the bonus money.

"My crew chief, Dale Inman, radioed me and said, 'We got this race won,'" Petty recalled. He glanced in his mirror and saw David Pearson not far behind. "I said 'Man, it's only halfway through the race.' He said, 'Foyt just won Indy, so I know we're gonna win this one.'"[50]

Petty went on to win the 600 in dominating fashion, capturing seven out of eight bonus segments, leading 311 of 400 laps, and winning a stock car record $69,550.

The victory lap finally complete, Foyt had more reporters to talk to.

"God damn we did it," he said, then was immediately contrite. "No, I shouldn't use God's name in vain. He was very good to me today.

"I guess the Good Lord wanted a genuine four-time winner. We had a better shot at it last year and the year before that, but I guess he didn't want me to go 255 miles or 300 or 350. He wanted me to go all the way. I felt sorry for Gordon and for George Bignotti because I know how they felt. Just look at the hell that I've gone through out there the last two years. I really would have liked to race him to the end."[51]

He said he was giving the race-winning car to Hulman for the Speedway museum and then almost immediately reneged on the gift, saying he needed the car for the remainder of the season. It wouldn't make it to the Speedway museum until Tony George bought it at auction nearly twenty years later.

He repeatedly answered questions about his retirement plans. "Sure I'll be back next year to go for number five, if Mr. Tony Hulman doesn't bar me from the track.

"By the time they waved the checkered flag at me, I had completely changed my mind about retiring. I knew I wasn't anywhere near ready to walk away from that checkered flag. Or the cheering crowd. I wouldn't have quit for anything."[52]

He turned philosophical when asked if he'd ever given up hope of winning a fourth 500.

"When you give up hope, you just lay down and die. That's what's wrong with the world today. People just give up hope."[53]

It was a bitter loss for Bignotti and Johncock. "I thought we had it in the bag. If it hadn't broken, we would have won," Bignotti said. "We knew Foyt was going to be the one to beat. Whenever Foyt would try to catch up, we would turn the boost up. If Foyt would have turned the boost up too much, he would not have had enough fuel."[54]

There'd been eight lead changes between the two drivers, and Johncock wasn't quite as confident. "I thought we had it. We had a pretty good lead, but I'm sure it would have been close. You know A.J."[55]

That night Foyt returned to the track to do a live interview with Stewart and McKay at the conclusion of ABC's taped-delayed broadcast.

"Things looked bad about the middle part of the race when I had the problem and I ran out of fuel, but my crew was behind me. We never give up and we never quit," Foyt said.[56]

McKay asked if "never give up" was the theme for the race.

"This is quite true," he said. "You know, my children, they'll start a project and they want to give up and, like I said earlier, this is what's wrong with the world today, so many people will start a beautiful project and if things don't work out just right they want to give up. I've always said you can never be a winner if you wanna be a quitter. I think that's what made us successful at racing or whatever we've tried. We never give up."

Sports writers and columnists ran out of superlatives trying to describe Foyt's victory.

"After you say 'A.J.,' what is there left to say," wrote Shav Glick in the lede to his *Los Angeles Times* race story.

"Etch his name in lasting concrete beside such immortals as Ruth, Dempsey, Thorpe, Bobby Jones and Babe Zaharias," wrote Will Grimsley, columnist for the *Associated Press*, who'd been covering sports since before Foyt was born. "He is one of a kind."[57]

In a rarity, Murray did a second straight column on Foyt.

"The good ones win two Indianapolis 500s, the great ones win three. Only A.J. Foyt has won four," he wrote. "Winning one Indianapolis is one of the hardest things in sports. Winning four of them borders on supernatural. Everybody else is just another Sunday driver."[58]

It was an amazing column of tribute to a man who once told Murray he was too busy working on his car to do an interview. At various times Murray compared Foyt to Babe Ruth, Ty Cobb, Seattle Slew, Jack Dempsey, Ben Hogan, Jack Nicklaus, O.J. Simpson, Fred Astaire, Napoleon, George Patton, Shakespeare, Beethoven, Clark Gable, Gary Cooper, Liz Taylor, Robert Redford, and the FBI.

"This man is the greatest in the world at what he does," Murray wrote. "How many people ever get to say that in a lifetime?"[59]

CHAPTER 39

CROSSROADS

1977

For the man who just became the first person to win the Indianapolis 500 four times, the next day was anything but restful. A.J. Foyt was up early to pose with the team, most of whom having had only a couple hours of sleep, for the traditional winner photos at the Speedway along the historic yard of bricks. Then he headed for Louisville, where one of his horses was running at Churchill Downs.

It had been a good month for his horses. Mysto Hill, while falling short of a Derby bid, had finished second in a support race and would go on to win thirteen others. Foyt's stable was up to nine thoroughbreds, and he found it an increasingly enjoyable way to spend his time. When a promising two-year-old named Brown Coyote won its race, Foyt chided the jockey about only working "for a minute" while it took him four hours to win a race.[1]

He had to hustle back to Indianapolis for the victory dinner, where about two thousand people jammed the Expo Center. They saw him pick up a check for nearly $260,000, making him the first driver with career earnings of more than a million dollars at the Speedway. He tried to remain humble—and mostly succeeded.

"I'm really a man of few words," he said, "just the stooge" who does the driving. "We've had good days and we've had bad days. It's been a long, long wait. But myself and my crew, we were not going to quit. We never quit. We just kept coming back."[2]

Not quitting became the theme for the race.

"I don't care to have people put me on a pedestal. I don't say, 'Hey, I'm A.J. Foyt and I'm a race driver.' But I do like for people to know that I'm not a quitter. We're not quitters, me and my team."[3]

◄ "When I get ready to retire, I'll pull in the pits, jerk off my helmet, and tell you all to go to hell." *Steve H. Shunck Collection*

As he did after winning previous 500s, he recognized crew chief Clint Brawner and car owner Al Dean for giving him his first real chance at the Speedway. Notably, he left George Bignotti off his list of thank-yous. He then passed on the winner's ring to Jim Gilmore, saying, "You may lose everything else, but you won't lose this."[4]

"Records are made to be broken," he added, "and I'm sure there will be more four-time winners of this race before too many years."[5]

Asked about future plans, Foyt said he intended to win the stock car race at Texas World Speedway, less than a week away. He said he planned to maintain his new low-key approach, until somebody made him mad, which most thought that would happen sooner rather than later.

He arrived at the Texas track tired from a week of celebratory activities and with a touch of the flu. He "seemed somewhat different since winning his fourth Indy.

"A mature, wiser Foyt laughs more, gets mad less often and in general, seems more at peace with himself. His compulsion to win every race consumes the man. Winning seems to fulfill a need in Foyt, like eating and sleeping do for most folks."[6]

The Texas Legislature declared June 5 A.J. Foyt Day, and race officials decided the Texas 500 would start in eleven rows of three. President Jimmy Carter, whom Foyt first met as governor of Georgia, sent him a note of congratulations. Houston announced it would hold a parade in his honor and present him with keys to the city. The state of Indiana said it would start making vanity license plates, the first being FOYT-14.

It was all getting to be a bit much.

"It's embarrassing, really," Foyt said of the hoopla. "To be honest, I'd really like to get out of the limelight some and live more like I used to."[7]

During practice he gave a tip to Ron Hutcherson, the younger brother of his NASCAR car builder, who was driving for Foyt's friend Jack Housby. Hutcherson then went out and beat Foyt for the pole. "I didn't ever think I'd run that fast," said a surprised Hutcherson. "A.J. made some suggestions about our aerodynamics and we tried to make it as streamlined as possible."[8]

In the race Foyt jumped out front early, leading 116 of the first 123 laps before a broken stabilizer bar cut a tire, sending his car into the wall and out of the race.

He announced he was skipping the upcoming Indy car race at Milwaukee, even though the 500 victory moved him into the lead for the Citicorp Cup championship. The rumor was his appearance fee had gone from $5,000 before the 500 to $10,000 and even $15,000, a rumor he didn't exactly deny.

"I've always gone everywhere and raced during my career," he said. "I've never asked for more than expense money, often took a lot less. But when these people want you to spend $3,000 or $4,000 to bring a car and crew to their race and then guarantee you $500 appearance money, it's time for me to stay home some. I had planned to run the entire USAC circuit, but now I don't know."[9]

Instead he headed back to Churchill Downs where he watched the Milwaukee race on television and picked a number of winners on the track. He often bet on his own horses, typically $50 or $100. "I won more money than Rutherford [Johnny, the Milwaukee winner]," he bragged, "and had a lot more fun."[10]

He remained coy about his plans for the June 26 Pocono 500 Indy car race, entering the car Vukovich drove at the Speedway but listing the driver as "unassigned." Foyt was nowhere to be seen on the first day of practice and crew members said "Sam Houston" might drive as they put yellow "rookie stripes" on the back of the car. When he finally arrived, Foyt said he "doubted" he would drive in the race and indicated the recently retired Sammy Sessions would take the wheel.

The moves blindsided track owner Dr. Joseph Mattioli, who'd gotten along well with Foyt in the past. It made it difficult to promote the Indy winner's participation in the race, although Mattioli did his best to play nice and still boost lagging ticket sales.

"A.J. has never made a demand on me," he said. "He's never asked me for deal money and I've never discussed it with him. We want him here. He's a wonderful person and he's been very good to me. Foyt is a very intensive individual. Everybody who knows A.J. Foyt knows he's that kind of individual."[11]

"I'm sure nobody is going to drive A.J. Foyt's car but A.J. Foyt," he added.[12]

"Don't assume nutin'," Foyt told reporters.[13]

It soon emerged that someone had made him mad, and that someone was Fred Stecher, the executive in charge of Citicorp. Stecher was boasting he "verbally spanked" Gilmore for Foyt's antics at the Phoenix race. Foyt had responded at Indianapolis by refusing to wear a Citicorp uniform patch or put the company's stickers on his car, and, as a result, he was ineligible for the Citicorp Cup's bonus money. In picking a fight with Stecher, Foyt was going after one of the powerful people in racing, but that had never stopped him before.[14]

"That Stecher never bothered to call me," Foyt said at Pocono. "He called me a disgrace to racing after the run-in at Phoenix. He never apologized. Hadn't he ever seen two guys who were mad at each other? He insulted me. That's why I got out of their point fund. It was my private decision and other drivers should not be affected. They weren't giving me something for nothing like they tried to pretend. I don't need their money.[15]

"I'd like to make peace with that guy, but he won't look me in the eye and talk to me about what's bothering him. If he's blaming me for something, he owes me the courtesy to tell me what it's about."[16]

Caught in the middle was Rutherford, whose McLaren was sponsored by Citicorp.

"A.J. realizes this is a bad situation," he said. "I've talked to him about it. I can't blame him for standing up for what he believes in. The unfortunate thing is that this may indirectly or directly affect the little guy, the guy who counts on the money Citicorp puts in. It's a real ticklish situation. I don't know how it's going to be resolved."[17]

With Rutherford on the provisional Pocono pole, Foyt waited until thirty minutes remained before making a qualifying attempt. He said he was held in the pits while repairs were made to the track. Others thought it was more Foyt gamesmanship. Some fans, already upset by stories about the richest driver in auto racing quibbling over a couple thousand dollars in appearance fees, started to boo.

It didn't bother Foyt on the track, as he knocked Rutherford off the pole. But as the boos increased, he refused to do a post-race interview with the public address announcer and then skipped the press briefing. He also was a no-show for the front-row photo session, and a tricycle was rolled into the spot where the No. 14 should have been. Instead he signed autographs for a group of kids and then headed back to Churchill Downs, where three of his horses were running. As a result he missed the dinner honoring the pole winner, which more than 250 fans paid to attend.

"Bleep those people who booed," he said on the way out of the track. "Kids are beautiful but the adults sure as hell aren't."[18]

"I don't like the way the people acted. Those guys who boo don't know what they're talking about. I think that by going out and taking the pole position I answered any questions that needed to be answered."[19]

He denied making an obscene gesture to the crowd.

"I motioned for some big, fat, sloppy guy in the stands who was really on me to come down and say those things to my face. I've been booed before. I can take it. The reason I went back to the garage was that I didn't want to stay out there and be hassled. I knew if I stayed out I'd get mad." He said one of his crew members chased after someone who called the team "'a bunch of Texas bums.' It's a good thing I didn't hear that guy say that."[20]

Coming to Foyt's defense was the third-fastest qualifier, Mario Andretti.

"I don't condone what A.J. did, but I know how he feels," Mario said. "I might do the same thing in that situation. After you hang your guts out in qualifying, you sure deserve better appreciation than that from the fans."[21]

As Rutherford feared, Stecher announced Citicorp would not renew its sponsorship, calling Foyt's post-qualifying behavior "the straw that broke our back."[22]

"I don't think that it is in the best interest of Citicorp to be identified as a sponsor with a professional sports series where the conduct of the participants and the tolerance of that conduct isn't governed by rules within the sanctioning organization. I'm in no position to dictate to USAC, but on the other hand I don't have to sit down at a riot and pay the bills, either."[23]

Philadelphia Daily News reporter Michael Knight, who'd criticized Foyt at Indianapolis, did so again.

"There is something terribly sad in watching a great athlete take his wondrous talents and throw them to the ground, abuse them like an unwanted and unloved child," Knight wrote. "This week I have witnessed Anthony Joseph Foyt Jr. engage in the same sort of tomfoolery and it is no easier to swallow. [He] is playing games with the management of Pocono International Raceway, with the United States Auto Club and with his fellow competitors. But his victims are the thousands of people who have already shelled out up to $100 to see him do what he probably does better than anyone else in this universe—drive a race car. . . . By prolonging this comic farce until qualification day, he has done a grave injustice to the paying public, the same public who helped make A.J. Foyt what he is today."[24]

The mostly pro-Foyt *Indianapolis News* countered, noting A.J. was "sitting atop the tallest mountain ever scaled in auto racing and, like Caesar, should be acclaimed as the greatest. Instead, the fans, like Brutus did to Caesar, are stabbing him in the back with their fickleness." The paper observed how fans often pull for the underdog and now that Foyt had picked up his fourth 500 win, he was no longer an underdog in any sense of the word. The paper also said some fans thought it was time for Foyt to retire.[25]

With all the pre-event histrionics, the race was anticlimactic. Foyt was booed again at driver introductions and said, "For the first time in my life, I am going into a race that I don't care whether I win."[26] He relented to a plea from USAC head Dick King to add the First National City stickers to his car and the patch to his uniform.

He led the first thirteen laps and was running among the front-runners at the halfway point. When he turned up the turbocharger boost to make his move for the lead, however, he damaged the engine and he was out, the crowd cheering his demise. Fortunately, his horses did better than he did, winning an estimated $15,000, compared to his Pocono earnings of about $6,500.[27]

Having already entered the annual July 4 NASCAR race at Daytona, Foyt surprised many by showing up at Mosport, Canada, to practice for the July 3 Indy car road race. It meant he'd be putting some miles on his new De Havilland 125 jet, flying to Daytona on Friday after qualifying at Mosport, qualifying at Daytona on Saturday, returning to Mosport that night for the Sunday race, and then back to Daytona for Monday's Firecracker.

He got in only three laps before rain interrupted qualifying at Mosport. He still turned in the seventh-fastest time before leaving for Daytona, where he qualified sixth.

At Mosport he showed off his road-racing skills, running third to Al Unser and Danny Ongais. When those drivers dropped out with engine problems, Foyt took the lead and stretched it to more than a lap at the end, despite breaking off the transmission gearshift lever early in the race.

"I had about an inch to shift with," he said. "I didn't think I could win today. I started to park it, then I thought, 'Hell, I'll hang in there.'"[28]

At Daytona he hounded Richard Petty for the lead until a poor pit stop dropped him to fifth at the end as Petty continued his winning ways with his third victory in four tries since Charlotte. Afterward, Foyt admitted to being "tired and worn out" and that he was "going to take some time off."[29]

The vacation lasted less than two weeks, and he entered both races in the July 17 USAC Indy car/stock car doubleheader at Michigan International Speedway. The Coyote's suspension collapsed on his first practice lap and when officials refused to extend qualifying so he could repair his car (he said he needed fifteen minutes, Gilmore said it was more like an hour), Foyt ordered both cars loaded back on the trailer and headed home. Two weeks later at Texas World Speedway, he suffered another suspension failure and said he wouldn't race again until the September 4 Ontario 500.

This time he followed through, taking the entire month of August off, although it could hardly be called downtime. His typical day started before 6:00 a.m. at the race shop, where he worked for several hours before heading to the

Chevrolet dealership, which now boasted more than three hundred employees. He went to Keeneland to buy more horses and made several trips to the East Coast to watch them run, the series having moved to Delaware Park racetrack for a fifty-day meet.

While Foyt was away there was a growing chorus of those who thought he should make the break permanent. Rutherford expressed admiration for Foyt's business empire and other interests and was one of those implying his fellow Texan should consider hanging up his helmet.

"If anybody deserves to walk away it's A.J.," Rutherford said. "I'd like to see him retire, and it's not because I don't want to compete with him. I'd like to see him sit back and enjoy the rewards of what he has accomplished. But he's like the retired fire horse. Whenever he hears a bell ring, he's ready to go."[30]

When Foyt returned to the track at Ontario, he was met by a barrage of rumors and questions about retirement. With both his parents facing health challenges, was he ready to step away from the sport? Reporters saw him popping Maalox tablets and wondered if he had an ulcer. Even Tom Carnegie, handling the public address chores just as he did at Indianapolis, wondered aloud if fans were seeing Foyt on a racetrack for the last time.

He qualified sixth and finished second, although nearly a lap behind Al Unser. He called the retirement stories "bullshit" and said he'd race the following weekend in the Hoosier 100.

Rather than quash the retirement stories, they started anew. A six-time winner of the dirt track classic, he'd often said it was his favorite race after the Indianapolis 500. The new scenario had him retiring after it was over. He'd already picked his replacement driver, so the stories went, with Al Unser set to leave the Vel/Parnelli Jones team after nine years and replace Foyt.[31]

Fifty-two cars and twenty thousand spectators showed up at the Indianapolis Fairgrounds, but Foyt failed to be one of the twenty-four fastest qualifiers, as did Rutherford and a host of others. A consolation race was held with the top four finishers set to advance to the main event, and Foyt was running seventh when he purposely spun to avoid a crash involving Jim Hurtubise. It seemed almost to be a relief as he laughed and joked with Herk later. Not as funny were the ongoing questions about retirement.

"It gets kind of old," he said. "I went off and took a vacation. It was the first one I took in twenty-three years. I thought winning Indianapolis four times would be the greatest thing since popcorn. But a lot of people have tried to make me miserable as hell. People want me to do everything in the world. It's impossible."[32]

He brushed off concerns about his health. "I had a complete physical. The doctor said I've got to slow down. Instead of sleeping three hours a night he said I've got to sleep five." Foyt also said he'd turned down an invitation from President Carter to visit the White House. "I sent him a telegram and said I sure appreciated it and it was an honor but I couldn't come. I'm not a politician. I never have been a politician. That may be my downfall. I tell people the way I feel."[33]

At the end of the week, IROC organizers announced Foyt wouldn't try for a third consecutive title and he said he wouldn't run the Indy car race the same weekend at MIS. Reports said it was mainly about money, Foyt wanting more than the series was willing to pay. He wasn't the only one. F1 drivers James Hunt, Jody Scheckter, and Niki Lauda all backed out and Bobby Unser, Emerson Fittipaldi, and David Pearson weren't invited, amid speculation they all wanted more money.

"If some of those guys don't want to show up, that's okay because I've got lots of guys who want to be driving here—deserving guys, too," said IROC director Les Richter, whom Foyt had clashed with over money in the past. Richter was upset Foyt had waited until the morning of qualifying to confirm he wasn't coming and he had to scramble to get Johncock as a last-minute replacement. "The money is good enough in this series that we don't need to be giving any appearance money to Foyt or Hunt or anyone else. You start doing that for one guy, and what do you say to the other eleven?"[34]

"We've had the same problem with him every year. He wanted some 'Foyt-conditions' that we wouldn't give him. I told him we couldn't do things for him that we didn't do for the others and he said, 'Well, I don't think I want to race.'"[35]

Foyt fired back. "That IROC thing, that really burns me up. I told them last year that I wasn't going to run again. Then they keep stalling around letting the media and the fans think I was going to run. Well, I told them I wasn't, but who did they make bad in the press? Old A.J. Since IROC lost the Formula One drivers who meant anything it's a circus, a television show. It lost its credibility and I don't mean just because I wasn't in it. When we were racing against Europeans like Emerson Fittipaldi and James Hunt and the champions it meant something, but this year's group was a farce."[36]

Questions about retirement slowed after Foyt went to Indianapolis for Good-year tire tests, running nearly six hundred laps alongside Sneva, Dallenbach, and Johncock. He said he was building two new cars for the Indianapolis 500 and that Dick Hutcherson was building him a pair of new stock cars.

He went to Charlotte for the October 9 NASCAR race and, as was often the case, he seemed more relaxed with the Southern media, "gregarious, oozing charisma and graciousness," wrote one reporter.[37] He remained approachable even after qualifying a disappointing ninth, until he met with a representative of race sponsor NAPA Auto Parts. The company was paying $18,000 in bonuses for lap leaders, and the rep gave Foyt two NAPA decals to put on his car and a patch for his uniform, as called for in the race entry form. That didn't matter to Foyt, who refused to accept the materials.

"The bonus money is a good idea, but I've got a responsibility to a NAPA competitor and once I give somebody my word I'm not backing off. I have been badgered all year and I have a point to prove."[38]

He took off for Kentucky and another horse race and no one seemed sure if he would return. He now found himself in the crosshairs of the Southern media, whom he had praised just a few days earlier. An article headlined "Racing's 'Brat' Snubs Request by '500' Sponsor" noted, "In USAC circles he's known as Super Tex, but the NASCAR folks are working up to dubbing him Super Brat.

"He's right about one thing: he does have a point to prove. . . . It's fair to ask, 'what have you done lately?' and the only accurate answer is 'not much.' . . . In recent years on the NASCAR circuit he's been less than an also-ran. It would seem that the major point he's got to make is on the track during this 500-mile race."[39]

Former Foyt teammate Donnie Allison said, "You can't miss too many of these races and then show up for one and be competitive. You really have to work at it. NASCAR is more competitive. You can mess around, miss gears and spin out and all that stuff in a USAC race and still win. A.J. couldn't do that in NASCAR."[40]

Allison was having a good year, including a victory win at Talladega driving the Hoss Ellington car Foyt quit as uncompetitive. "A.J. is a good friend of mine, but I don't think he gave 100 percent when he drove Ellington's car."[41]

NAPA execs realized they were getting more publicity over the clash with Foyt than they ever would as simply the race sponsor and waved all requirements, saying he was still eligible for bonus money. They didn't have to worry, as Foyt failed to lead a lap and finished seventh, five laps behind the winner Benny Parsons.

Two weeks later he was home preparing for one of the honors that really mattered to him. He'd been named Houstonian of the Year and was to receive the award October 28 at a gala with over seven hundred attendees. Tony and Mary Hulman, John Mecom, and the Gilmores would be among those honoring Foyt, who designated the Foundation for Children, a local nonprofit focused on pediatric surgeries, as the recipient for all proceeds. Excitement about the event was dampened when Tony Hulman telephoned to say he wouldn't be able to attend.

"He said, 'I'm sorry, I've got to go to the hospital, I'm sick,'" Foyt recalled. "They were moving him from the hospital in Terre Haute to St. Vincent in Indianapolis, so I knew it must be serious. I told him not to worry about it, just go get better."[42]

The disappointment turned to shock the night before the gala when A.J. received word that Hulman had died while in surgery.

"The world probably lost one of the greatest sportsmen of all times," Foyt said in a statement. "He never forgot a name or a face, whether you were a rookie or the greatest driver in the world. I never heard him speak a bad word about anybody and it is a shame to see somebody like him move on."[43]

Foyt broke down at the gala while talking about Hulman, and he joined the family the next day in Terre Haute, the lone outsider allowed into the Hulman family circle. He filled in as a pallbearer when needed and was constantly at Mary Hulman's side throughout. He rode in the family car during the funeral procession and, when a light rain started, held an umbrella over her.

Speculation started even before the funeral about who would run the Speedway and Foyt's name was the one most often mentioned. One "bright, informed, neutral, forceful, open, reputable [and] dependable" source said Foyt was taking a year to clean up his business operations and then would assume the role.[44]

There was precedent for the move, three-time 500 winner Wilbur Shaw having served as track president when Hulman first bought it. Foyt admitted to having vague and cryptic discussions with Hulman earlier in the year about his possible future role in Speedway management, but said he told Hulman he wanted to keep racing and couldn't do both.

"Years down the road it could happen," Foyt said. "We've discussed it among ourselves. You know I was very close to the Hulman family and I would do anything to help them. If I feel I need to make some suggestions I am sure they would listen to me. As for it happening in the near future, I don't think so. Of course if I ran the Speedway I would have to get rid of all my cars. They know I don't want to quit racing and because of that they don't feel they could ask me to retire."[45]

Late in the year he agreed to several season-ending interviews where he made it clear he planned to continue racing.

"I've read and heard a lot of strange things, a lot of nasty digs at me since I won Indy," he said. "A lot of things have been happening the last couple of years to make you guys think I'm about to quit, but you're all wrong. I'll do the deciding when it's time for me to quit."[46]

"I've said it before and I'll say it again. When I get ready to retire, I'll just pull in the pits, jerk off my helmet, and tell you all to go to hell."[47]

He denied the rumors Al Unser would join the team as either his replacement or a teammate, and it was soon announced Unser was joining a team being formed by another Texan, Jim Hall of Chaparral fame.

"If I ever ran a second car—but I'm not—Al Unser is the driver I'd go after," Foyt said. "Al is a polished driver on any kind of a racetrack in any kind of a car. He's one of the finest race drivers in this country."[48]

––––––––

His stable of horses was now up to eighty-six, and A.J. said he'd invested more than a million dollars in them. Most were in training, but twenty-three were racing at several different tracks. Especially promising was a two-year-old named Foyt's Ack, son of Ack Ack, the 1971 horse of the year. Foyt's Ack would fall short of the Kentucky Derby but have career earnings of nearly $300,000.

Despite the growing stable, Foyt scoffed at the notion he was more interested in horse racing than car racing, although he did admit, "I've been cheatin' on my racing the last three years with all the other stuff. But next year I'm going to concentrate on it again.

"If I had to take my choice between auto racing and the horses, there's no question I'd stay with auto racing. I'm only into horses because my son is interested in them. He's the one that works with them all the time."[49]

––––––––

In a career of peaks and valleys, Foyt ascended to a new zenith in 1977 when he ended ten years of disappointment by winning his fourth Indianapolis 500 and became "the greatest in the world at what he does." But the highest peak is often followed by the lowest valley. Those who thought winning the 500 would lift years of frustration and knock the chip from his shoulder were badly mistaken. In fact, just the opposite happened.

The year had quickly descended into squabbles with promoters and sponsors over money. What some saw as petty, Foyt saw as a matter of principle. He was hounded about retirement, and it seemed everyone, including his parents, wanted him to quit. Cheered by fans and extolled in the press following his Indianapolis victory, he was being booed by crowds and condemned by the news media.

He'd also come face-to-face with mortality. Not his own, which he had shown in the past he could handle, but that of those closest to him. The health of his mother and father continued to deteriorate. Di Gilmore had been diagnosed with cancer. He'd already lost Tony Hulman, who he said "was like a second father to me."

A.J. Foyt's career was once again at a crossroads—a crossroads every bit as critical as the one he and Lucy had crossed twenty years earlier. Those urging him to retire and get on with the second half of life didn't remember what A.J. had said, that for good or bad, racing *was* his life, "the only thing I've ever really understood." He'd clawed his way to the top and he wasn't about to step aside just because he had accomplished all there was to accomplish. "Once you're in it," he'd said, "you love it so much you fight like to hell to stay in it."

The second half of his career was about to begin. There'd be more peaks to climb, more incredible days at the track, including victories, championships, and record speeds. There would also be valleys, including the loss of loved ones, terrible crashes, and serious injuries. And he'd also be dragged into a dark and bitter political battle that put the very future of the sport he loved so much at risk.

Through it all, Foyt would take on all comers the only way he knew how: straight on.

ACKNOWLEDGMENTS

———

There is one person without whom this book could not have been written, Anne Fornoro. She's been working for A.J. Foyt for most of the past forty years, most recently as director of marketing/PR for AJ Foyt Racing. She was instrumental in helping to arrange interviews with family, friends, and many in the racing world. Best of all, she paved the way and then got out of the way. She sometimes sat in on portions of interviews I did with A.J., but I don't recall a single instance where she broke in to "clarify" a response or change the direction of a conversation. A true public relations professional.

Anne is from a family of racers and married into a family of racers. Her husband Drew Fornoro was a nine-time Northeastern Midget Association champion. Drew passed away in May 2023, just a few weeks after the death of A.J.'s wife, Lucy. The deaths were a blow to all of those at AJ Foyt Racing, ones from which Anne and A.J. are still recovering.

I started the book in late 2019 and the COVID-19 pandemic and lockdown hit in early 2020. It turned out to be both a blessing and a curse. Trips to the Long Beach Grand Prix and the Indianapolis 500 to shadow A.J. were canceled. At the same time, people we had struggled to arrange interviews with were now trapped in their homes and suddenly available.

Writers will often tell you the most enjoyable part of any book is the research, finding a nugget in reporting from the day and interviewing the people who lived the stories. There's a list of those interviewed in the Sources section. Not everyone listed is quoted in the book, although in many cases they were helpful in providing important background and context.

Interviews with many of Foyt's racing peers were entertaining and informative, those with Mario Andretti, Darrell Waltrip, Donnie Allison, and Leonard Wood being a few of the most memorable. Donald Davidson set the record for a single interview, an enlightening five hours, not counting subsequent follow-ups.

Two interviews stand out, those with Al Unser and Rick Mears. Like Foyt, they are four-time winners of the Indianapolis 500. Unlike Foyt, they are generally considered on the quiet side. Each talked for about two hours, to the point I felt bad about hogging their time. They seemed not to care. Unser's story about Foyt getting down on his knees to draw Al a crude map of the Speedway and how to drive it was a classic. Oh, to have that map today.

Thank you to Mario Andretti for providing the foreword and to his assistant Patty Reid, who helped coordinate that effort.

From a research standpoint, Newspapers.com provides nearly all the news that's fit to print, from an era when news was still printed. During the process I was reunited with many of the writers I grew up reading. In addition to the listings in the Chapter Notes, some sort of special recognition needs to be given the reporters, columnists, and editors who covered motorsports on a daily basis during the 1960s and '70s, including: Bloys Britt, Jep Cadou Jr., Dick Denny, Chris Economaki, Shav Glick, Jack Kiser, Ron Lemasters, Ray Marquette, Robin Miller, Dick Mittman, George Moore, Bob Moore, Bob Myers, Dave Overpeck, Bob Renner, Joe Scalzo, Bill Simmons, Bob Thomas, Al Thomy, and Bill Verigan. Columnists who chimed in on Foyt from time to time included Bob Collins, Joe Falls, Wayne Fuson, Dave Kindred, and of course Jim Murray. Several of those writers are still alive and provided valuable sidebars to their experiences with A.J.

Special thanks to former *AutoWeek* editor Larry Edsall and former *Road & Track* editor Matt DeLorenzo for being early readers and making valuable edits and suggestions. And to the crew at Octane Press including project editor Faith Garcia, copyeditor Dana Henricks, book designer Tom Heffron, cover designer Krissy Haag, publicist Jo Snyder, publisher Lee Klancher, and the rest of the team.

Finally, it's probably odd to acknowledge the subject of a biography, but it's appropriate in this case. It was clear A.J. didn't really care if another biography was done on him or not. But he was always gracious and generous with his time. He never held back his thoughts or opinions, never said anything was "off the record." I told him I probably wasn't doing a very good job if I didn't piss him off at some point, and a couple of times I got the feeling I was overstaying my welcome. But I never felt the wrath of A.J., as long as you don't count the time I tried to pick up the check at lunch.

SOURCES

Author Interviews

Donnie Allison—Race car driver and Foyt teammate (July 7, 2020).

Mario Andretti—Race car driver (September 3, 2022).

Jack Arute—Reporter and Foyt friend (November 5, 2021).

Craig Baranouski—Longtime Foyt crewmember and friend (April 20, 2020).

Becky Baranouski—Associate at AJ Foyt Racing (April 23, 2021).

Bones Bourcier—Author (May 2022).

Donna Dale Burt—Foyt family friend, daughter of Dale Burt (January 2020).

Donald Davidson—Retired Indianapolis Motor Speedway historian (May 26, 2021).

Tim Delrose—Race car owner and family friend (November 17, 2020).

Bobby Dorn—Foyt crew member (May 2021).

Corinne Economaki—Former publisher of *National Speed Sport News*, daughter of Chris Economaki (December 28, 2023).

Anthony Joseph "A.J." Foyt Jr.—(2012*; 2016**; November 7, 2019; April 19–24, 2021; May 11, 2021; May 22, 2021; May 28, 2021. May 2022, 2023).

Anthony Joseph "Tony" Foyt III—A.J.'s son (April 26, 2021).

Jimmy Finger—Race car driver, family friend, and neighbor (October 4, 2022).

Jerry Foyt—A.J.'s son (January 30, 2021).

Larry Foyt—A.J.'s grandson and adopted son (November 10, 2020; February 11, 2021; April 28, 2021).

Lucy Foyt—A.J.'s wife (2016,** April 2, 2020).

Marlene Foyt—A.J.'s sister (June 23, 2021, January 8, 2024).

Nancy Foyt—A.J.'s daughter-in-law, married to Tony (April 21 and 23, 2021).

Terry Foyt—A.J.'s daughter (April 21, 2021).

Lewis Frank—Motorsports journalist (January 19, 2021).

Gary Friedman—Foyt family doctor (2020).

Edsel Ford—Retired Ford Motor Company executive (October 8, 2021).

Tony George—Grandson of Tony Hulman and Foyt family friend (May 2022).

Charlie Gray—Ford Racing executive (October 2022).

Jim Greer—Family friend, car sponsor, and entrant (2021).

Dan Gurney— Race car driver (2012*).

Evi Gurney—Wife of Dan Gurney (January 29, 2020).

Don Halliday—Motorsports engineer, former AJ Foyt Racing engineer (February 11, 2021).

Mike Harris—Associated Press motorsports reporter (April 2021).

Don Hayward—Engineer at Ford and numerous race teams (January 7, 2023).

Jonathan Ingram—Motorsports writer (February 8, 2021).

Bob Jenkins—Motorsports reporter and broadcaster (June 11, 2020).

Michael Knight—Motorsports reporter (May 28, 2021).

Steve Jordan—Foyt crew member (April 28, 2021).

Ed Justice Jr.—Racing sponsor (March 10, 2021).

Dave Kindred—General sports reporter and columnist (December 11, 2020).

Frank Lance—Foyt crew member (April 2022).

Peter Manso—Author (January 18, 2020).

John Mecom—1960s car owner and sponsor (November 18, 2020).
Robin Miller—Motorsports reporter and columnist (December 1, 2020; October 2, 2021).
Dick Mittman—*Indianapolis News* reporter (2015**).
Mose Nowland—Ford engineer (December 2019).
Paul Page—Radio and television announcer (September 28, 2020).
Richard Petty—Race car driver (March 11, 2021).
Tex Powell—NASCAR chief mechanic, car owner (August 8, 2020).
Bob Riley—Coyote designer (February 18, 2021).
Johnny Rutherford—Race car driver (June 17, 2020).
Carroll Shelby—Race car driver, team owner, and founder of Shelby American (2012*).
George Snider—Race car driver and friend (December 12, 2020).
Jack Starne—Longtime Foyt crewmember, crew chief, and friend (January 13, 2021).
Jackie Stewart—Formula One World Champion (April 28, 2022).
Tony Stewart—IndyCar and NASCAR champion (December 16, 2020).
Mike Teske—Automotive restorer (April 3, 2020).
Kevin Triplett—Racing historian (October 14, 2020).
Al Unser Sr.—Race car driver (December 16, 2020).
Bobby Unser—Race car driver (2012*).
Bobby Waltrip—Business associate and family friend (April 27, 2021).
Darrell Waltrip—NASCAR driver (November 6, 2020).
Leonard Wood—NASCAR team co-owner (April 15, 2020).
Billy Woodruff—Foyt crewmember and family friend (January 20, 2021; January 3, 2024).
Cale Yarborough—Race car driver (2021).

Others

Roger Penske provided a written response to a list of questions submitted to his public relations
representatives.
A.J. Foyt interview with David Goldstein, The Houston Oral History Project (2008).

*Author interviews originally conducted for *Black Noon: The Year They Stopped the Indy 500*, St.
Martin's Press, New York, 2014.
**Author interviews originally conducted for *Indy 500 Memories*, CreateSpace, 2016.

Books

Alexander, Tyler. *Tyler Alexander: A Life and Times with McLaren.* Phoenix: David Bull Publishing,
2015.
Andretti, Mario, with Bob Collins. *What's It Like Out There?* Chicago: NTC/Contemporary
Publishing, 1970.
Andretti, Mario, with Gordon Kirby. *A Driving Passion.* Phoenix: David Bull Publishing, 2001.
Argetsinger, Michael. *Mark Donohue: Technical Excellence at Speed.* Phoenix: David Bull Publishing,
2009.
Brawner, Clint, with Joe Scalzo. *Indy 500 Mechanic.* Philadelphia: Chilton Books, 1975.
Bechtel, Mark. *He Crashed Me So I Crashed Him Back.* Boston: Little, Brown and Company, 2010.
Bourcier, Bones. *Foyt, Andretti, Petty: America's Racing Trinity.* Newburyport, MA: Coastal, 2015.
Buss, Ted. *Lloyd Ruby.* Wichita Falls, TX: Midwestern State University Press, 2000.
Considine, Tim. *American Grand Prix Racing: A Century of Drivers and Cars.* Minneapolis, MN:
Motorbooks International, 1997.
Cotter, Tom, and Al Pearce. *Holman-Moody: The Legendary Race Team.* Beverly, MA: Motorbooks,
2003.
Daly, Derek. *Race to Win: How to Become a Complete Champion Driver.* Minneapolis: Motorbooks,
2008.
Daley, Robert. *This Cruel Sport: Grand Prix Racing 1959–1967.* Hoboken, NJ: Prentice-Hall, 1963.
Davidson, Donald, and Rick Shaffer. *AutoCourse Official History of the Indianapolis 500.* London:
Crash Media Group, 2006.
Dewitt, Norm. *Making It Faster II.* San Diego: Faster Publishing, 2018.
Dilamarter, Jimmy, and Ron Wicks Jr. *The Cars of Vel Miletich and Parnelli Jones,* Deerfield, IL: Dalton
Watson Books, 2013.

Dorson, Ron. *The Indy 500: An American Institution under Fire.* Newport Beach, CA: Bond/Parkhurst Books, 1974.

Economaki, Chris, with Dave Argabright. *Let 'Em All Go!* Fishers, IN: Books by Dave Argabright, 2006.

Engel, Lyle Kenyon. *The Incredible A.J. Foyt.* New York: Arco Publishing Company, 1977.

Ferguson, Andrew. *Team Lotus: The Indianapolis Years.* Sparkford, Somerset, England: Haynes Publishing, 1996.

Foyt, A.J., with William Neely. *A.J.: My Life as America's Greatest Race Car Driver.* New York: Times Books, 1983.

Granatelli, Anthony (Andy) Granatelli. *They Call Me Mister 500,* Washington D.C.: Henry Regnery Company, 969.

Neely, William. *The Jim Gilmore Story: Alone in the Crowd.* Tucson: Aztex Corporation, 1988.

Lerner, Preston and David Friedman. *Ford GT.* Minneapolis: Quarto Publishing Group, 2015.

Libby, Bill. *Parnelli: A Story of Auto Racing.* New York: Tower Publications, 1969.

Fox, Jack. *Mighty Midgets: The Illustrated History of Midget Auto Racing.* Madison, IN: Carl Hungness Publishing, 2004.

Garner, Art. *Black Noon: The Year They Stopped the Indy 500.* New York: St. Martin's Press, 2014.

Garner, Art, and Marc Spiegel. *Indy 500 Memories: An Oral History of the Greatest Spectacle in Racing.* CreateSpace Publishing, 2016.

Gates, Bob. *Hurtubise.* Marshall, IN: Witness Productions, 1995.

Gauld, Graham. *Jim Clark: A Racing Hero.* Germany: McKlein Media, 2014.

Gauld, Graham. *Jim Clark at the Wheel.* New York: Pocket Books, 1966.

Golenbock, Peter. *Miracle: Bobby Allison and the Saga of the Alabama Gang.* New York: St. Martin's Press, 2006.

Guthrie, Janet. *Janet Guthrie: A Life at Full Throttle.* Toronto: Sports Classic Books, 2005.

Henry, Charlie. *Kar-Kraft: Ford's Specialty Vehicle Activity Program.* Forest Lake, MN: CarTech Books, 2017.

Hill, Bill. *One Tough Circuit: Midget Racing in America's Heartland.* Bill Hill Productions, 1998.

Kenyon, Mel. *Burned to Life,* Minneapolis: Dimension Books, 1976.

Kirby, Gordon. *Jim McGee: Crew Chief of Champions.* Racemaker Press: Boston, 2014.

Kirby, Gordon. *Penske's Maestro: Karl Kainhofer and the History of Penske Racing.* Boston: Racemaker Press, 2016.

Kirk, Connie Ann. *Taken by Speed.* Lanham, MD: Rowman & Littlefield, 2017.

Levine, Leo. *Ford: The Dust and the Glory, A Racing History.* New York: Macmillan Company, 1968.

Levrier, Philip. *Texas Legacy: Tales from the Golden Days of Midget Auto Racing in Texas.* Siloam Springs, AR: Georgetown Lounge Productions, 1987.

Libby, Bill. *Foyt.* New York: Hawthorn Books, 1974.

Ludvigsen, Karl. *Indy Cars of the 1960s.* Hudson, WI: Iconografix, 2001.

Manos, Peter. *Vrooom!: Conversations with the Grand Prix Champions.* Funk & Wagnalls, 1969.

McGinnis, Joe. *They Call Him Cale: The Life and Career of NASCAR Legend Cale Yarborough.* Chicago: Triumph Books, 2008.

Moss, Stirling. *A Turn at the Wheel.* New York: Putnam Books, 1961.

Neely, Bill. *Tire Wars: Racing with Goodyear.* Tucson: AZTEC Corporation, 1993.

Nye, Doug. *The Story of Lotus, 61-71: Design Revolution.* United Kingdom: Motor Racing Publications, 1972.

O'Leary, Mike. *Rodger Ward: Superstar of American Racing's Golden Age.* Minneapolis, MN: Motorbooks, 2006.

Riley, Bob, with Jonathan Ingram. *The Art of Race Car Design.* United Kingdom: Icon Publishing: 2015.

Rutherford, Johnny, and David Craft. *Lone Star J.R.: The Autobiography of Racing Legend Johnny Rutherford.* Chicago: Triumph Books, 2000.

Scalzo, Joe. *Stand on the Gas!* Englewood Cliffs, NJ: Prentice-Hall, 1974.

Scalzo, Joe. *Indianapolis Roadsters, 1952–1964.* Osceola, WI: Motorbooks International, 1988.

Scalzo, Joe. *The American Dirt Track Racer.* Minneapolis, MN: Motorbooks International, 2001.

Scalzo, Joe. *City of Speed: Los Angeles and the Rise of American Racing.* Minneapolis, MN: Motorbooks International, 2007.

Sutton, Len. *My Road to Indy.* Marceline, MO: Walsworth Publishing, 2002.

Sutton, Stan. *The Curse of the Indy 500*. Bloomington, IN: Red Lightning Books, 2017.

Tremayne, David. *Jim Clark. The Best of the Best*. UK: Evro Publishing Limited, 2018.

Tulloch, Andrew. *Jim Clark: Grand Prix Legend*. United Kingdom: Weidenfeld &Nicolson, 2009.

Wallen, Dick. *The United States Auto Club: Fifty Years of Speed and Glory*. Glendale, AZ: Dick Wallen Productions, 2006.

Waltrip, Robert L., with James Chandler Harbour II. *A Boy from the Heights*. Dallas: LifeStories Company, 2020.

Whitaker, Sigur. *Tony Hulman: The Man Who Saved the Indianapolis Motor Speedway*. Jefferson, NC: McFarland & Company, 2014.

Young, Eoin S. *Bruce McLaren: The Man and His Racing Team*. United Kingdom: Haynes Publishing, 1995.

Additional Reference Sources

Benson Ford Research Center, The Henry Ford Museum

Indiana State Library

Indianapolis Motor Speedway Archives

Indy 500 and USAC Racing 1971–1978, www.OldRacingCars.com

International Motor Racing Research Center, Watkins Glen, New York

Racing Sports Cars, https://www.racingsportscars.com/driver/results/A.%20J._-Foyt-USA.html

The Dave Kindred Papers, Tate Archives and Special Collections, The Ames Library, Illinois Wesleyan University, Bloomington, Illinois, https://iwu.libraryhost.com/repositories/3/resources/11

Ultimate Racing History

ENDNOTES

INTRODUCTION. WHO IS A.J. FOYT?
1. Tony Stewart, 2021 interview with the author.
2. Bill Libby, *Parnelli: A Story of Auto Racing* (New York: Tower Publications, 1969).
3. "Benny Phillips," column, *High Point* (North Carolina) *Enterprise,* October 19, 1975.
4. Dan Gurney and Bobby Unser, 2012 interviews with the author conducted for *Black Noon: The Year They Stopped the Indy 500* (New York: St. Martin's Griffin, 2014).
5. Bloys Britt, "A.J. Foyt: Hard-Nosed Demon of the Ovals," Associated Press, *The Sports Immortals,* 1972.
6. Bill Verigan, "A.J. Foyt: 2d Best Not Good Enough," *New York Daily News,* May 25, 1974.
7. James Greer, 2020 interview with the author.
8. David Maraniss and Sarah Maraniss Vander Schaaff, "Making Lightning," in *Ink in Our Blood,* podcast, http://inkinourblood.davidmaraniss.com/episodes/making-lightning, August 6, 2022.
9. "Greatest Golf Quotes of All-Times," *Golf News,* January 17, 2014.

CHAPTER 1. YOU DONE FAIR
1. Robin Miller, "Super Tex '500' Winner 4th Time," *Indianapolis Star,* May 30, 1977.
2. Ray Holliman, "Foyt Quadruples His Indy Pleasure," *Tampa Bay* (Florida) *Times,* May 30, 1977.
3. Dave Overpeck, "God Wanted A 500-Mile Winner," *Indianapolis Star,* May 30, 1977.
4. "A.J.'s Day after 10 Frustrating Years," Associated Press, *South Bend* (Indiana) *Tribune,* May 30, 1977.
5. Lucy Foyt, 2017 interview with the author for *Indy 500 Memories: An Oral History of the Greatest Spectacle in Racing,* (CreateSpace Publishing, 2016).
6. A.J. Foyt, 2021 interview with the author.
7. Marlene Foyt, 2024 interview with the author.
8. Billy Woodruff, 2024 interview with the author.
9. A.J. Foyt, 2021 interview with the author.
10. Jim Murray, "As Night Follows Day . . ." *Los Angeles Times*, May 30, 1977.
11. Tom Tucker, "A.J. Foyt," *Atlanta Journal-Constitution,* May 28, 1978.
12. A.J. Foyt, 2021 interview with the author.

CHAPTER 2. MOMMA AND DADDY
1. Lucy Foyt, 2020 interview with the author.
2. In addition to interviews with family members, much of the story of the Foyt, Gloger, and Monk families was pieced together with the assistance of certified genealogists in Europe and the United States. Material from the Ancestry.com and Heritage.com websites including birth, wedding, and death certificates, federal census reports, and Houston city directories was also used.
3. "The Brazos River (Texas) Flood of June-July, 1899, and Its Effects upon the Agriculture of the Submerged Region," United States Department of Agriculture, Bureau of Statistics, 1899 (Government Printing Office, Washington, DC).
4. "Bohunk," Merriam-Webster, https://www.merriam-webster.com/dictionary/bohunk, July 23, 2020.
5. *Fort Worth Daily Gazette,* July 5, 1889.
6. Curtis Bishop, "Brazos Flood of 1899," Texas State Historical Association, *Handbook of Texas Online,* https://www.tshaonline.org/handbook/entries/brazos-flood-of-1899 May 7, 2021.
7. *Houston Post*, July 18, 1899.
8. Erik Larson, *Isaac's Storm* (New York: Random House, 2011).
9. United States census reporters, 1900, 1910, 1920, 1930.
10. Houston City Directory, 1911, 1919, 1923.

11. Marie Foyt, 2021 interview with the author.
12. Bill Libby, *Foyt* (New York: Hawthorn Books, 1974).
13. Ancestry.com.
14. Marlene Foyt, 2020 interview with the author.
15. A.J. Foyt, 2021 interview with the author.

CHAPTER 3. YOUNG A.J.
1. A.J. Foyt, 2021 interview with the author.
2. Marie Foyt, 2021 interview with the author.
3. William Nack, "Twilight of a Titan," *Sports Illustrated*, September 30, 1991.
4. A.J. Foyt, 2021 interview with the author.
5. Joseph Foyt III, 2021 interview with the author.
6. Bob Gaines, "The Screaming World of A.J. Foyt," *Family Weekly*, February 6, 1966.
7. A.J. Foyt with William Neely, *A.J.: My Life as America's Greatest Race Car Driver* (New York: Times Books, 1983).
8. Robert L. Waltrip with James Chandler Harbour II, *A Boy from the Heights* (Dallas: LifeStories Company, 2020).
9. Foyt with Neely, *A.J.*
10. AJ Foyt Racing website, "Indycar Racing Team, AJ Foyt Racing, United States," https://www. foytracing.com/.
11. Foyt with Neely, *A.J.*
12. Philip Levrier, *Texas Legacy: Tales from the Golden Days of Midget Auto Racing in Texas* (Siloam Springs, AR: Georgetown Lounge Productions, 1987).
13. Foyt with Neely, *A.J.*
14. Steve Wilstein, "Foyt Buckles Up for Final Run in the Indianapolis 500," Associated Press, *North County Times* (Oceanside, California), May 24, 1991.
15. Robert L. Waltrip with James Chandler Harbour II, *A Boy from the Heights.*
16. Donna Dale Burt, 2020 interview with the author,.
17. Foyt with Neely, *A.J.*
18. "Dale Burt Automotive . . . Even A.J. Isn't Safe!" *Southwest Imported Auto Parts News,* July, 1965.
19. Bob Ottum, "Champion of the Old Guard," *Sports Illustrated*, June 1, 1964.
20. Foyt with Neely, *A.J.*
21. William Nack, "Twilight of a Titan, *Sports Illustrated*, September 30, 1991.

CHAPTER 4. BASIC TRAINING
1. A.J. Foyt with William Neely, *A.J.: My Life as America's Greatest Race Car Driver* (New York: Times Books, 1983).
2. Donna Dale Burt, 2021 interview with the author.
3. The Greater Heights area where the Foyt family first settled in Houston would recover as urban sprawl, improved transportation options, and gentrification rebuilt the area. It is now considered one of the city's nicer neighborhoods. At one point Foyt was approached by developers who were putting in townhomes and condos along Twenty-Fifth Avenue, wondering if he wanted to buy his original family home. He initially expressed interest and considered moving it to one of his ranches to renovate and use as a guest house. When told it would cost about one million dollars, he had a different thought: "Tear the son of a bitch down."
4. Foyt with Neely, *A.J.*
5. Marlene Foyt, 2021 interview with the author.
6. A.J. Foyt, 2019 interview with the author.
7. Jimmy Greer, 2021 interview with the author.
8. John Mecom, 2022 interview with the author.

CHAPTER 5. PLAYLAND AND BEYOND
1. Marlene Foyt, 2020 interview with the author.
2. A.J. Foyt with William Neely, *A.J.: My Life as America's Greatest Race Car Driver* (New York: Times Books, 1983).
3. Philip Levrier, *Texas Legacy: Tales from the Golden Days of Midget Auto Racing in Texas* (Siloam Springs, AR: Georgetown Lounge Productions, 1984).
4. "Three Indianapolis Race Drivers Killed," *Reading* (Pennsylvania) *Eagle,* July 30, 1951.
5. Jim Kyle, "Foyt Captured First Race at 17," *Baytown* (Texas) *Sun,* April 18, 1971.
6. Foyt with Neely, *A.J.*
7. "Body of Young Drowning Victim Found, Rites Today," *Baytown* (Texas) *Sun,* January 12, 1953.
8. UPI, "Houston Boy Drowns When Boat Capsizes," *McAllen* (Texas) *Monitor,* January 9, 1953.
9. A.J. Foyt, 2022 interview with the author.
10. Levrier, *Texas Legacy.*
11. Jimmy Greer, 2020 interview with the author.
12. Levrier, *Texas Legacy.*
13. Gregory Curtis, "Pomp and Circumstance," *Texas Monthly*, March 1975.

14. A.J. Foyt, 2019 interview with the author.
15. Lucy Foyt, 2020 interview with the author.
16. Foyt with Neely, *A.J.*
17. "Ware Looks Back at Racing That Was," Ricci Ware, *San Antonio Express and News*, August 19, 1967.
18. Marie Foyt, 2020 interview with the author.
19. Paul Weisel, "AAA/USAC: The Real Story," *Classic Racing Times*, May 2015.
20. Calvin Mauldin, "Foyt's Wild Ride," *Vintage Motorsport Magazine*. September/October 1989.
21. "Feature Won by Rackley, *Corpus Christi Caller-Times*, August 21, 1955.
22. Steve Crowe, "Veteran Racer Drives Rookie Replacement," *Detroit Free Press*, May 29, 1993.

CHAPTER 6. FAIRGROUNDS

1. A.J. Foyt, 2008 interview with David Goldstein, the Houston Oral History Project, https://houstonlibrary.aviaryplatform.com/collections/2466/collection_resources/109545, July 22, 2008.
2. Marlene Foyt, 2020 interview with the author.
3. A.J. Foyt, 2019 interview with the author.
4. A.J. Foyt, 2015 interview with the author for *Indy 500 Memories: An Oral History of the Greatest Spectacle in Racing*, (CreateSpace Publishing, 2016).
5. A.J. Foyt with William Neely, *A.J.: My Life as America's Greatest Race Car Driver* (New York: Times Books, 1983).
6. Bones Bourcier, *Foyt, Andretti, Petty: America's Racing Trinity* (Newburyport, MA: Coastal) 181.
7. Roy Speer, "State Fair 'Bigger & Better than Ever,'" *Minneapolis Star*, August 24, 1956.
8. "Condition of Injured Auto Ace Critical," *Minneapolis Star*, August 25, 1956.
9. Foyt with Neely, *A.J.*
10. Dwayne Netland, "Pouelsen Wins Feature, Foyt Blanked," *Minneapolis Star Tribune*, September 3, 1956.
11. "Texan Involved in Race Mishap," *Corsicana* (Texas) *Daily Sun*, September 19, 1956.
12. A.J. Foyt, 2021 interview with the author.
13. "State Fair Auto Racer Killed in Kansas Crash," *Shreveport* (Louisiana) *Journal*, September 19, 1956.
14. Lucy Foyt, 2020 interview with the author.
15. Ted Buss, *Lloyd Ruby* (Wichita Falls, TX: Midwestern State University Press, 2000).
16. Hugh Harelson, "One Pilot In Critical Condition," *Arizona* (Phoenix) *Republic*, April 8, 1957.
17. Jay Simon, "Ruby Notches Win In Midget Feature," *Daily Oklahoman*, May 8, 1957.
18. "An Omaha Car Owner Named Les Vaughn and a Kid Named Foyt," Midwest Racing Archives, May 1, 2009, http://www.midwestracingarchives.com/2009/05/omaha-car-owner-named-les-vaughn-and.html.
19. Associated Press, "Sammy Says He's Done With '500,'" *Sioux Falls* (South Dakota) *Argus-Leader*, May 31, 1957.
20. Jeff Fraudo, "Doomed Racer," *East Bay* (Oakland, California) *Times,* January 10, 2007.
21. "Likes High Banks," *Columbus* (Indiana) *Republic*, April 25, 1958.
22. A.J. Foyt, 2021 interview with the author.
23. Bob Owns, "'Banks Rookie' A.J. Foyt Wins Feature at Salem," *Louisville* (Kentucky) *Courier-Journal*, June 17, 1957.
24. Russ Goodall, "Houstonian Foyt Feted at His 50th Indy 500," *Houston Chronicle*, May 27, 2007.
25. Betsy Harris, "Speedway's First Family," *Indianapolis Star*, May 10, 1992.
26. Robert Shaplen, "Hoosier Pied Piper," *Sports Illustrated*, May 1958.
27. Tony George, 2022 interview with the author.
28. A.J. Foyt, "I Go for Everything: Foyt," *Indianapolis News*, May 13, 1977.
29. Joe Scalzo, *The American Dirt Track Racer* (Minneapolis, MN: Motorbooks International, 2001).
30. Bourcier, *Foyt, Andretti, Petty*.
31. "Branson, Foyt among Latest Entries in Midget Race Here," *Terre Haute Tribune*, September 29, 1957.
32. "Farewell to Dean Not Final: Bryan," *Arizona* (Phoenix) *Republic*, December 8, 1957.
33. Associated Press, "Bryan-Dean Duo Split Up for Indy 500," *Arizona* (Tucson) *Daily Star*, December 7, 1957.
34. Clint Brawner with Joe Scalzo, *Indy 500 Mechanic* (Philadelphia: Chilton Books, 1975).
35. Dave Lewis, "Once Over Lightly," *Long Beach* (California) *Independent Press-Telegram*, March 21, 1958.
36. Robin Miller, "A.J. Rising," *Racer Magazine*, June 2021.
37. Ed Orman, "Linden is Critically Hurt in Clovis Race Crackup," *Fresno* (California) *Bee*, November 4, 1957.

CHAPTER 7. DEAN VAN LINES

1. A.J. Foyt with William Neely, *A.J.: My Life as America's Greatest Race Car Driver* (New York, Times Books, 1983).
2. Graham Justus, "Amick, Who'll Drive Here, Has Eyes on '500' Race," *Dayton* (Ohio) *Journal Herald*, March 19, 1958.
3. Steve Herman, "Foyt's Unmatched Feats Fulfill Prophecy of 1958," Associated Press, *Richmond* (Indiana) *Palladium-Item*, May 28, 1978.

4. Jimmy Bullock, "IMCA's A.J. Foyt Is Threat in 500-Miler," *Shreveport* (Louisiana) *Journal,* May 26, 1958.
5. Foyt with Neely, *A.J.*
6. Kenneth Rudeen, "Three for the 500," *Sports Illustrated*, May 26, 1958.
7. Foyt with Neely, *A.J.*
8. Associated Press, "Rathmann 147 Sets Lap Mark," *Fort Worth* (Texas) *Star-Telegram*, May 17, 1958.
9. Rudeen, "Three for the 500."
10. Bones Bourcier, *Foyt, Andretti, Petty: America's Racing Trinity* (Newburyport, MA: Coastal, 2015), 181.
11. Will Higgins, "Racers, Cheap Booze at White Front," *Indianapolis Star*, May 23, 2015.
12. A.J. Foyt, 2021 interview with the author.
13. Bill Libby, *Foyt* (New York: Hawthorn Books, 1974).
14. Wayne Fuson, "O'Connor Will Retire If He Can Win '500,'" *Indianapolis News*, May 29, 1958.
15. Jim Ayello, "A.J. Foyt: Scar Never Healed after Seeing Friend Die in Horrific Crash at 1958 Indy 500," *Indianapolis Star*, May 21, 2018.
16. W.F. Fox Jr., "The Annual Drivers Meeting," *Indianapolis News*, May 30, 1958.
17. A.J. Foyt, 2019 interview with the author.
18. Bob Collins, "Fatality Puts Chill on Bryan's Victory," *Indianapolis Star*, May 31, 1958.
19. Bill Libby, *Foyt* (New York: Hawthorn Books, 1974).
20. Wayne Fuson, "Ed Elisian Suspended by USAC," *Indianapolis News*, May 31, 1958.
21. Fuson, "Ed Elisian Suspended by USAC."
22. Fuson, "Ed Elisian Suspended by USAC."
23. Wayne Fuson, "'Esteemed' Was the Word for O'Connor," *Indianapolis News*, May 31, 1958.
24. A.J. Foyt, 2019 interview with the author.
25. Stirling Moss, *A Turn at the Wheel* (New York: Putnam Books, 1961).
26. Paul Carlson, "Sports Scene," *Moline* (Illinois) *Dispatch*, July 31, 1958.
27. Carlson, "Sports Scene."
28. Carlson, "Sports Scene."

CHAPTER 8. A DEADLY PROFESSION

1. Senator Richard L. Neuberger with Lester David, "Auto Racing Must Be Outlawed," *Mechanix Illustrated*, January 1959.
2. Associated Press, "Indy Track Not at Fault," *Arizona* (Tucson) *Daily Star*, May 21, 1959.
3. Jep Cadou Jr., "Death Takes '58 Rookie of Year in Fastest Race," *Indianapolis Star News*, April 5,1959.
4. Whitney Martin, "Amick Killed at Daytona," Associated Press, *Nashville Tennessean*, April 5, 1959.
5. Don O'Reilly, "Daytona Spin Another of Ward's Many Escapes," *Indianapolis News*, May 5, 1959.
6. Robin Miller, "That Was No Place for an Indycar," Amelia Island Concours d'Elegance program, 2009.
7. Angelo Angelopolous, "Bettenhausen Drives, Acts Like the Race Champ He Is," *Indianapolis News*, April 20, 1959.
8. A.J. Foyt with William Neely, *A.J.: My Life as America's Greatest Race Car Driver* (New York: Times Books, 1983).
9. Gordon Kirby, *Jim McGee: Crew Chief of Champions* (Boston: Racemaker Press, 2014).
10. Wayne Fuson, "'500' Pilot Shortage Bothers Speedway," *Indianapolis News*, May 7, 1959.
11. Jep Cadou Jr., "Parsons Retires," *Indianapolis Star*, May 18, 1959.
12. Bill Eggert, "Bettenhausen 'Miracle' Makes Everyone Happy—Including Tony," *Indianapolis Star*, May 17, 1959.
13. UPI, "Indy 500 Suffers Second Fatality," *Santa Rosa* (California) *Press Democrat*, May 20, 1959.
14. Jimmy Claus, "Sporting Around," *Terre Haute* (Indiana) *Tribune*, September 30, 1959.
15. "USAC Issues Fireproofing 'Must' Order," *Indianapolis News,* May 13, 1959.
16. John Morrison, "Texas Has 1 Driver Flying Flag in '500,'" *Fort Worth Star Telegram*, May 28, 1959.
17. "BEWARE! The Indianapolis 500 Again Proves Deadly and Case against It Grows with the Toll," *Life*, June 8, 1959.
18. Mrs. Pat O'Connor, "A Last Year's Widow Tells Her Story," *Life*, June 8, 1959.
19. Wayne Fuson, "Life Rough on '500,'" *Indianapolis News*, June 5, 1959.
20. Jep Cadou Jr., "George Blames Troubles on USAC Man's Grudge," *Indianapolis Star*, June 17, 1959.
21. Don O'Reilly, "George Faces 30-Day Suspension from USAC," *Indianapolis News*, June 15, 1959.
22. Clint Brawner with Joe Scalzo, *Indy 500 Mechanic* (Philadelphia: Chilton Books, 1975).
23. Associated Press, "Driver Killed in Milwaukee Race, Ed Elisian Burns to Death in Car," *Marshfield* (Wisconsin) *News-Herald*, August 31, 1959; Wayne Fuson, "Odds Too Great for Elisian in Milwaukee Race," *Indianapolis News*, August 31, 1959; Jep Cadou Jr., "Elisian Perishes in Crash; Fiery Death End to Controversial Driver's Career," *Indianapolis Star*, August 31, 1959.
24. Jimmy Brown, "Foyt Is Salem 100-Lap Victor," *Louisville* (Kentucky) *Courier-Journal*, September 14, 1959.
25. Rita Joerns, "Furious Rally by Jones Can't Overcome Foyt," *Fort Worth* (Texas) *Star-Telegram*, October 14, 1959.
26. Tom Kane, "Jim Hurtubise Wins 100 Mile Auto Race," *Sacramento* (California) *Bee,* October 29, 1959.
27. Foyt with Neely, *A.J.*

CHAPTER 9. BREAKTHROUGH

1. Ken Purdy, "At Ten Tenths of Capacity," *The Atlantic,* July 1965.
2. A.J. Foyt with William Neely, *A.J.: My Life as America's Greatest Race Car Driver* (New York: Times Books, 1983).
3. Bill Libby, *Foyt* (New York: Hawthorn Books, 1974).
4. Clint Brawner with Joe Scalzo, *Indy 500 Mechanic* (Philadelphia: Chilton Books, 1975).
5. A.J. Foyt, 2019 interview with the author.
6. Libby, *Foyt.*
7. Bob Barnet, "Drivers Near 'Ceiling'?," *Muncie* (Indiana) *Star Press,* May 16, 1960.
8. Wayne Fuson, "Steak for Breakfast, No Beer," *Indianapolis News,* May 28, 1960.
9. *Indianapolis News.* 500 Notes, May 31, 1960.
10. Libby, *Foyt.*
11. Foyt with Neely, *A.J.*
12. Lucy Foyt, 2020 interview with the author.
13. Foyt with Neely, *A.J.*
14. Libby, *Foyt.*
15. Mike Hembree, "The Killing Field: The Myth, the Legend of Langhorne Speedway," *AutoWeek,* January 2, 2018.
16. Bob Gates, *Hurtubise* (Marshall, IN: Witness Productions, 1995).
17. Moon Mullins, "Bryan Was Aggressive Auto Racing Champion," *Passaic* (New Jersey) *Herald-News,* June 21, 1960.
18. Gates, *Hurtubise.*
19. A.J. Foyt, 2023 interview with the author.
20. Jep Cadou Jr., "Foyt Cops First Big-Car Victory," *Indianapolis Star,* September 6, 1960.
21. Angelo Angelopolous, "Foyt Moves into Race Title Picture," *Indianapolis News,* September 6, 1960.
22. Corky Lamm, "Foyt Brings His Gusher in Well," *Indianapolis News,* September 19, 1960.
23. "3 Drivers Escape Serious Injurty in Spins, Flip," *Indianapolis Star,* September 19, 1960.
24. Wayne Fuson, "Foyt Stars in Rich, but Wild Hoosier 100 Drama," *Indianapolis News,* September 19, 1960.
25. Joe McCarron, "Indiana Drivers Win Features as 10,000 Fair Fans Watch," *Allentown* (Pennsylvania) *Morning Call,* September 25, 1960.
26. Wayne Fuson, "Johnny Thomson," *Indianapolis News,* September 26, 1960.
27. Bones Bourcier, *Foyt, Andretti, Petty: America's Racing Trinity,* (Newburyport, MA: Coastal 181), 2015.
28. Wilbur Adams, "Between the Lines," *Sacramento* (California) *Bee,* October 5, 1960.
29. A.J. Foyt, 2012 interview with the author.
30. A.J. Foyt, 2021 interview with the author.
31. "Drastic Final Changes In Car Gave Foyt Victory In 100 Miler," *Sacramento Bee,* October 31, 1960.
32. Foyt with Neely, *A.J.*
33. Dushman Lazovich, "Foyt Wins Ball Memorial," *Arizona* (Phoenix) *Republic,* November 21, 1960.
34. Staff Report, "Foyt: I Just Wanted to Win the Turkey," https://sprintcarandmidget.com/usac/foyt-i-just-wanted-to-win-the-turkey, November 28, 2019.
35. Jack Kiser, "Foyt: I know I've Been Lucky," *Philadelphia Daily News,* April 8, 1961.
36. Foyt with Neely, *A.J.*
37. Libby, *Foyt.*

CHAPTER 10. NUMBER ONE

1. Jack Kiser, "Foyt: 'I Know I've Been Lucky,'" *Philadelphia Daily News*, April 8, 1961.
2. Kiser, "Foyt: 'I Know I've Been Lucky.'"
3. Jack Kiser, "Sachs Figures He'll Win at Indy—and He Figured Right at Trenton," *Philadelphia Daily News*, April 10, 1961.
4. Jimmy Brown, "Foyt Is Winner; Jones Flagged," *Louisville* (Kentucky) *Courier-Journal*, May 1, 1961.
5. Wayne Fuson, "Jones's $670 Oil Leak Gives Foyt a Victory," *Indianapolis News*, May 1, 1961.
6. Jep Cadou Jr., "'Ride For Pal' Kills Tony," *Indianapolis Star*, May 13, 1961.
7. Wayne Fuson and Angelo Angelopolous, "29th Flip Ends Story of Old Indestructible," *Indianapolis News*, May 13, 1961.
8. A.J. Foyt, 2021 interview with the author.
9. A.J. Foyt with William Neely, *A.J.: My Life as America's Greatest Race Car Driver* (New York: Times Books, 1983).
10. 1961 Indianapolis 500 radio broadcast, IMS Radio Network, Indianapolis Motor Speedway.
11. Bones Bourcier, *Foyt, Andretti, Petty: America's Racing Trinity* (Newburyport, MA: Coastal 181), 2015.
12. Bob Collins, "Sachs' Pit Stop Hands Foyt 100 Gs," *Indianapolis Star*, May 31, 1961.
13. *Fort Worth Star-Telegram*, Notes, June 6, 1961.
14. Robert D. Lewis, "I'll Run All Races," Associated Press, *Winston-Salem* (Massachusetts) *Journal*, May 31, 1961.
15. Joe Jarvis, "Just Doing My Job' Says Relaxed '500' Champion," *Indianapolis News*, May 31, 1961.
16. UPI, "Top Thrill for Foyt," *Terre Haute* (Indiana) *Tribune*, May 31, 1961.
17. Bill Libby, *Foyt* (New York: Hawthorn Books, 1974).

18. Robert D. Lewis, "A.J. Foyt Victoriously Recalls Hulman Dare," Associated Press, *Terre Haute* (Indiana) *Star*, May 31, 1961.
19. Marlene Foyt, 2020 interview with the author.
20. Jep Cadou Jr., "Jep Cadou Jr. Calls 'Em," *Indianapolis Star*, May 31, 1961.
21. Bob Collins, "Sachs' Pit Stop Hands Foyt 100 Gs," *Indianapolis Star*, May 31, 1961.
22. Libby, *Foyt*.
23. Bill Eggert, "Two Big Decisions Settled Race," *Indianapolis Star*, May 31, 1961.
24. Cadou, "Jep Cadou Jr. Calls 'Em."
25. Kenneth Rudeen, "A New Era Opens at Indy's Golden Jubilee," *Sports Illustrated*, June 12, 1961.
26. Cadou, "Jep Cadou Jr. Calls 'Em."
27. Wayne Fuson, "Foyt Paid for 'Gold Race'; 500 Fund Hits $400,000," *Indianapolis News*, June 1, 1961.
28. Tom Kubat, "Foyt, Marmon Launch Co-sponsorship Effort," *Lafayette* (Indiana) *Journal and Courier*, May 28, 1993.
29. A.J. Foyt, 2021 interview with the author.
30. Joe Scalzo, *Stand on the Gas!* (Englewood Cliffs, NJ: Prentice-Hall, 1974).
31. Bourcier, *Foyt, Andretti, Petty*.
32. Cadou, "Jep Cadou Jr. Calls 'Em."
33. Wayne Fusion, "Foyt Finds Gold Crown Jewels Again in Hoosier Hundred Dirt," *Indianapolis News*, September 18, 1961.
34. Dave Overpeck, "Foyt, Hurtubise, Head Hut-100 Field," *Terre Haute* (Indiana) *Tribune*, October 1, 1961.
35. Dave Overpeck, "Foyt Talks Way into Race, Wins" *Terre Haute* (Indiana) *Tribune*, October 2, 1961.
36. Associated Press, "Foyt Buys Way into Terre Haute Race, Wins It," *Muncie* (Indiana) *Evening Press*, October 2, 1961.
37. Wayne Fuson, "Foyt 'Misses' Race and Still Wins It," *Indianapolis News*, October 2, 1961.
38. "Jones Out 'To Even Score,'" *Pomona* (California) *Progress-Bulletin*, November 2, 1961.
39. Richard Roberts, "Racing for a Future," *San Pedro* (California) *News-Pilot*, November 10, 1961.
40. Sid Ziff, "Foyt Not Resting on Indianapolis Laurels; He Just Loves to Race," *Los Angeles Mirror*, November 8, 1961.
41. A.J. Foyt, 2012 interview with the author.

CHAPTER 11. A RACING CHAMPION

1. Bill Gee, "'500' Winner Foyt Here for Rest Before Racing," *Honolulu Star-Bulletin*, January 11, 1962.
2. Lucy Foyt, 2020 interview with the author.
3. A.J. Foyt, 2023 interview with the author.
4 *Charlotte* (North Carolina) *News*, Notes, February 14, 1962.
5. Roger Penske written response to submitted questions.
6. Associated Press, "Auto Race Committee to Discuss Problems," *Rochester* (New York) *Democrat and Chronicle*, February 10, 1962.
7. Richard Roberts, "The Livest Stock," *San Pedro* (California) *News-Pilot*, February 26, 1962.
8. Rich Roberts, "Foyt Driving Himself Rich," *San Pedro* (California) *News-Pilot*, February 23, 1962.
9. Jep Cadou Jr., "Racing Bodies Let Down Bars on Crack Pilots," *Indianapolis Star*, February 27, 1962.
10. Al Thomy, "Fighting Champion Foyt Checks in for AIR 500," *Atlanta Constitution*, March 20, 1962.
11. Bob Talbert, "On the Hairy Edge of Death," *The State* (Columbia, SC) April 29, 1962.
12. Jack Kiser, "Foyt 'Never Really Opened Up' as He Beat the Trenton Jinx," *Philadelphia Daily News*, April 9, 1962.
13. Robert Irvin, "Sachs to Use 2-Way Radio in '500,'" UPI, *Terre Haute* (Indiana) *Tribune*, April 17, 1962.
14. Wayne Fusion, "Downpour in Dixie," *Indianapolis News*, March 3, 1962.
15. Wayne Fusion, "Foyt Calls Sachs Dumb, Cry Baby," *Indianapolis News*, April 18, 1962.
16. UPI, "Sachs Not Upset with Foyt's Blast," *Logansport* (Indiana) *Pharos-Tribune*, April 19, 1962.
17. Cadou, "Jep Cadou Jr. Calls 'Em."
18. Bob Talbert, "On the Hairy Edge of Death," *The State* (Columbia, SC), April 29, 1962.
19. UPI, "Fast-talker Sachs Predicts 150 Mph in 500 Qualifying," *Miami Herald*, May 4, 1962.
20. *Indianapolis Star*, Notes, April 28, 1962.
21. Thomy, "Fighting Champion Foyt Checks In."
22. Curley Grieve, "Hands of a Surgeon Create a Racing Car," *San Francisco Examiner*, April 7, 1962.
23. "He Nods and Smiles But His Mind Isn't on the Mob of Fans," *Indianapolis Times*, May 15, 1962.
24. Scotty Stirling, "Trio Eyes Indy Race," *Oakland* (California) *Tribune*, January 31. 1962.
25. "Clutching One Gold Ring, Foyt Comes Back For Another," Bill Pittman, *Indianapolis Times*, May 25, 1962.
26. "He Nods and Smiles but His Mind Isn't on the Mob of Fans," *Indianapolis Times*.
27. Thomy, "Fighting Champion Foyt Checks In."
28. Thomy, "Fighting Champion Foyt Checks In."
29. "Quarrel Ended, Foyt Aids Sachs," *Daytona Daily News*, May 14, 1962.
30. Angelo Angelopolous, "Foyt's Racer to Be Sold?" *Indianapolis News*, May 23, 1962.
31. Associated Press, "Foyt Catches Jones, Wins Indy Prelude," *Fort Worth* (Texas) *Star-Telegram*, May 28, 1962.

32. Wayne Fuson, "Foyt Sees Laps at 150, 500-Mile Mark Over 142," *Indianapolis News,* May 29, 1962.
33. Bob Ottum, "No Sport for Gentlemen," *Sports Illustrated*, May 31, 1965.
34. *Fort Worth* (Texas) *Star-Telegram*, Notes, June 6, 1962.
35. Associated Press, "Forced by Banks, Foyt Withdraws from Atlanta 500," *Charlotte* (North Carolina) *Observer,* June 5, 1962.
36. Jessie Outlar, "The 16th Street Crowd," *Atlanta Constitution*, May 29, 1962.
37. Jep Cadou Jr., "Foyt Booed in Milwaukee Triumph," *Indianapolis Star*, June 11, 1962.
38. Associated Press, "Foyt Wins Race, Then Wants to Fight Promoter," *Rushville* (Indiana) *Republican*, June 11, 1962.
39. Frank Wilson, "Victory at Milwaukee Shows Foyt Not a Popular Champion," *Indianapolis News*, June 11, 1962.
40. Associated Press, "Foyt Sorry He Blew Up," *Los Angeles Times*, June 12, 1962.
41. Frank Wilson, "Foyt Is Fined $1,000, Gets USAC Warning," *Indianapolis News,* June 15, 1962.
42. Bill Eggert, "$1,000 Finger Pointed at Foyt," *Indianapolis Star*, June 16, 1962.
43. Jack Kiser, "Hugh Randall Rides 'Jinx Car' to Death," *Philadelphia Daily News,* July 2, 1962.
44. Kiser, "Hugh Randall Rides 'Jinx Car' to Death."
45. Kiser, "Ward Puts Frosting on Trenton Promoter's Cake," *Philadelphia Daily News*, July 23, 1962.
46. Bob Renner, "Air of Peace Covers Foyt-Bowes Breakup," *Indianapolis News*, July 28, 1962.
47. A.J. Foyt with William Neely, *A.J.: My Life as America's Greatest Race Car Driver* (New York: Times Books, 1983).
48. Renner, "Air of Peace."
49. "Marshman, Bignotti to Join Ansted Team," *Indianapolis Star*, August 3, 1962.
50. Lee C. Bright, "Davis's Condition Serious after 'Slowdown Crash,'" *Daytona Daily News*, August 6, 1962.
51. Foyt with Neely, *A.J.*
52. Bill Libby, *Foyt* (New York: Hawthorn Books, 1974).
53. "Tireless Foyt Gamble Wins Salem Sprint," Dick Denny, *Indianapolis News*, October 1, 1962.
54. Jack Menges, "Foyt Cracks Track Record in 100-Mile Win at Sacramento," *Oakland* (California) *Tribune*, October 29, 1962.
55. UPI, "Auto Racers Fair Badly in Salton Sea Run," *Sacramento* (California) *Bee,* November 12, 1962.
56. Mike O'Leary, *Rodger Ward: Superstar of American Racing's Golden Age* (Minneapolis, MN: Motorbooks, 2006).

CHAPTER 12. FUNNY CARS AND FURRINERS

1. Ken Pivernetz, "USAC, NASCAR Participants Clash," *Long Beach* (California) *Independent Press-Telegram*, January 18, 1963.
2. Leo Levine, *Ford: The Dust and the Glory, A Racing History* (New York: Macmillan, 1968).
3. Bob Terrell, "Cause For Complain," *Asheville* (North Carolina) *Citizen-Times*, January 22, 1963.
4. Associated Press, "NASCAR Opens Door; Roberts Says USAC Didn't Return Favor," *Greenville* (South Carolina) *News*, January 9, 1963.
5. Bob Thomas, "Dan Gurney Cracks Jinx at Riverside," *Los Angeles Times*, January 21, 1963.
6. John Mecom, 2020 interview with the author.
7. Associated Press, "Goldsmith Wins Daytona 250-Mile Race," *Fort Myers* (Florida) *News-Press,* February 17, 1963.
8. Morry Meriam, "Tiny Lund Wins '500' at Daytona," *Orlando Sentinel*, February 25, 1963.
9. Al Thomy, "No Wheels, Foyt, Hurtubise, Jones Thumb Their Way to AIR Raceway," *Atlanta Constitution,* March 13, 1963.
10. Thomy, "No Wheels."
11. Al Thomy, "Foyt, Weatherly Duel to a Verbal Standoff at AIR," *Atlanta Constitution*, March 16, 1963.
12. Al Thomy, "Lorenzen Wins '500' before 55,000 Fans," *Atlanta Constitution*, March 18, 1963.
13. Richard Petty, 2021 interview with the author.
14. Jack Kiser, "Cowboy Hero of Langhorne," *Philadelphia Daily News*, April 12, 1963.
15. "Branson Wins Race; Foyt, Farmer Crash," *Indianapolis News*, April 1, 1963.
16. Ben Borowsky, "23-Year-Old Driver Killed at 'Horne," *Bristol* (Pennsylvania) *Daily Courier*, April 8, 1963.
17. Bill Fleishman, "Langhorne Site of Early NASCAR Deaths," *Philadelphia Daily News*, May 30, 2001.
18. John Lingle, *Hard Luck Lloyd* (Boston: Racemaker Press, 2013).
19. Associated Press, "Foyt Wins 100-Mile Trenton Race," *Asbury Park* (New Jersey) *Press*, April 22, 1963.
20. Jep Cadou Jr., "Jep Cadou Jr. Calls 'Em," *Indianapolis Star*, April 24, 1963.
21. Cadou, "Jep Cadou Jr. Calls 'Em."
22. Bill Libby, *Foyt* (New York: Hawthorn Books, 1974).
23. Jep Cadou Jr., "Foyt Wins Yankee 300 by 23 Seconds," *Indianapolis Star*, April 28, 1963.
24. Roger Penske's written response to submitted questions, 2023.
25. "Skill, Courage and Lady Luck Help Foyt Win Yankee 300," Bob Renner, *Indianapolis News*, April 29, 1963.
26. Jack Kiser, "A Word from the Wise," *Philadelphia Daily News*, May 2, 1963.
27. Bill Libby, *Foyt* (New York: Hawthorn Books, 1974).

28. Jep Cadou Jr., "Tire Issue Hot," *Indianapolis Star*, May 8, 1963.
29. "Foyt Breezes To Victory At Langhorne," Ben Borowsky, *Bristol* (Pennsylvania) *Daily Courier*, May 6, 1963.
30. Jack Kiser, "Foyt Wins 'Easiest Race Ever,'" *Philadelphia Daily News*, May 6, 1963.
31. Wayne Fuson, "Gasoline Alley," *Indianapolis News*, April 29, 1963.
32. Louise Durman, "Husband's Performances Draw Deep Concentration," *Indianapolis News*, May 18, 1963.
33. Foyt with Neely, *A.J.*
34. Wayne Fuson, "Goodyear Enters 500 Tire Pressure," *Indianapolis News*, May 8, 1963.
35. Jep Cadou Jr., "Foyt Goes 146 Testing Wider Speedway Tires," *Indianapolis Star*, May 9, 1963.
36. Wayne Fuson. Gasoline Alley. *Indianapolis News*, May 7, 1963.
37. Jim Hunter, "Junior Won't Drive at Indy," *Columbia* (South Carolina) *State*, May 24, 1963.
38. "Great Mechanics Make Great Drivers," *Indianapolis Star*, May 29, 1963.
39. Dave Nelson, "Sachs Gives Inside Story' on Fist Fight," *Quad-City* (Minnesota) *Times*, June 20, 1963.
40. Wayne Fuson, "Great Scott!" *Indianapolis News*, June 1, 1963.
41. Bob Renner, "Clark Learns Costly Lesson," *Indianapolis News*, May 31, 1963.
42. Foyt with Neely, *A.J.*

CHAPTER 13. A SUMMER ON THE RUN

1. Jack Kiser, "Can Jones Beat Odds, Long Left Turn Jinx?" *Philadelphia Daily News*, June 22, 1963.
2. Jack Kiser, "Little Bobby Faces Big Weekend," *Philadelphia Daily News*, July 20, 1963.
3. Ben Borowsky, "33,000 See A.J. Foyt Win at 'Horne," *Bristol* (Pennsylvania) *Daily Courier*, June 24, 1963.
4. UPI, "Yunick to Quit Racing Circuit," *Bristol* (Tennessee) *Herald Courier*, June 30, 1963.
5. DLBTV. "Best Smokey Yunick Quotes," YouTube. May 18, 2016.
6. Bob Renner, "A.J. Foyt Finds Time to Pause and Refresh," *Indianapolis News*, July 8, 1963.
7. Robert Daley, "Fast and Furious Foyt," *True Magazine*, June 1965.
8. "Foyt Sees Victory in Trenton Feature," *Hackensack* (New Jersey) *Record*, July 29, 1963.
9. Dick Denny, "'Time For Change' May Be New Offy Theme," *Indianapolis News*, August 20, 1963.
10. "Nelson, Foyt, Split; Goldsmith to Drive," *Racine* (Wisconsin) *Journal Times*, August 30, 1963.
11. Forrest R. Kyle, "Sports in Review," *Decatur* (Illinois) *Daily Review*, September 10, 1963.
12. Jack Kiser, "Ford in AJ's Future, but 'Goldie' Wows 'Horne," *Philadelphia Daily News*, September 9, 1963.
13. Jep Cadou Jr., "Ward Sweeps Hoosier Hundred Honors," *Indianapolis Star*, September 15, 1963.
14. Associated Press, "Jones Wins . . . Norm Nelson in Pileup," *Racine* (Wisconsin) *Journal Times*, September 16, 1963.
15. Associated Press, "Driving Team Does Better in Air than on Trenton Speedway Oval," *Red Bank* (New Jersey) *Daily Register*, September 25, 1963.
16. UPI, "New Tires May Go All the Way in Next 500," *Kingsport* (Tennessee) *Times-News*, November 17, 1963.
17. Jack Kiser, "Foyt's Offy a Money-Maker," *Philadelphia Daily News*, September 23, 1963.
18. John Frye, "Behind the Wheel," *Hagerstown* (Maryland) *Morning Herald*, November 5, 1963.
19. Leo Mehl, "Legends of a Legend," A.J. Foyt Media Guide, 1991.
20. A.J. Foyt with William Neely, *A.J.: My Life as America's Greatest Race Car Driver* (New York, Times Books, 1983).
21. Associated Press, "U.S. Auto Club Suspends National Driving Champ for Slugging Driver," *Anderson* (Indiana) *Herald*, October 9, 1963.
22. Lee Watson, "Foyt Snaps Mark Set 2 Weeks Ago," *San Angelo* (Texas) *Weekly Standard*, October 11, 1963.
23. Bill Neely, *Tire Wars: Racing with Goodyear* (Tucson: Aztec Corp, 1993).
24. UPI, "A.J. Foyt Plans to Appeal," *Terre Haute* (Indiana) *Tribune*, October 9, 1963.
25. "USAC Relents, Foyt Given Road Race Okay," *Indianapolis Star*, October 11, 1963.
26. John Mecom, 2020 interview with the author.
27. John Mecom, 2020 interview with the author.
28. "A.J. Foyt Enters Times Grand Prix," *Los Angeles Times*, October 8, 1963.
29. John Mecom, 2020 interview with the author.
30. "100-Miler Features Hot Duels," *Arizona* (Phoenix) *Republic*, November 10, 1963.
31. Glen Banner, "Gurney, Clark at Indianapolis to Test Revamped Lotus-Ford Creation," *Kokomo* (Indiana) *Tribune*, October 30, 1963.
32. Jack Lattimer, "Behind the Wheel," *San Mateo* (California) *Times*, October 3, 1963.
33. Wayne Fuson, "Foyt Cleared of Slugging Charges," *Indianapolis News*, October 31, 1963.
34. "Foyt Is Cleared," *Indianapolis Star*, November 1, 1963.
35. Associated Press, "USAC Clears Foyt on Fighting Charge," *Richmond* (Indiana) *Palladium-Item*, November 1, 1963.
36. UPI, "USAC Gives Foyt Clean Bill But Cautions Him to Wear Title with Dignity," *Anderson* (Indiana) *Herald*, November 1, 1963.
37. "Foyt Says He Can Do 155 Lap," *Indianapolis Star*, November 8, 1963.

38. Jerry Diamond, "Foyt Proves He Can Race on Road, Too," *San Francisco Examiner*, December 13, 1963.

39. Arthur Kelly, "Foyt Breaks Record in Nassau 250-Miler," *Boston Globe*, December 15, 1963.

40. Joe Scalzo, "Sumbitch on Wheels," *Circle Track*, May 1993.

41. Jim Giannell, "Foyt Snares Nassau Race," *Fort Lauderdale* (Florida) *News*, December 9, 1963.

42. Jim Giannell, "Midgets First Love Says Vet Race Winner," *Fort Lauderdale* (Florida) *News*, December 9, 1963.

CHAPTER 14. THE DINOSAURS

1. "Race Victim Spurned Use of Harness Belt," *Los Angeles Times*, January 20, 1964.

2. Associated Press, "Death Comes to the Clown Prince," *Oakland* (California) *Tribune*, January 20, 1964.

3. A.J. Foyt, 2021 interview with the author.

4. Frank Gianelli, "Foyt Captures Twin-50 Sprint Car Honors," *Arizona* (Phoenix) *Republic,* January 27, 1964.

5. "Foyt Sets Mark Here" *Arizona* (Phoenix) *Republic*, January 9, 1964.

6. "160 Mph Possible in New Car: Foyt," *Indianapolis News*, January 30, 1964.

7. Jerry Diamond, "S.F.-Built Offy Sets World Mark," *San Francisco Examiner*, January 31, 1964.

8. Andrew Ferguson, *Team Lotus, the Indianapolis Years* (United Kingdom: Haynes Publishing, 1996).

9. Leo Levine, *Ford: The Dust and the Glory, A Racing History* (New York: Macmillan, 1968).

10. Bernie Kennedy, "Win Came Almost as 'Planned,'" Associated Press, *High Point* (North Carolina) *Enterprise*, February 16, 1964.

11. Kennedy, "Win Came Almost as 'Planned.'"

12. Robert Daley, "Fast and Furious Foyt," *True Magazine,* June 1965.

13. Mario Andretti, 2022 interview with the author.

14. Pete Bratager, "Richard Wins It Fair and Square," *Miami Herald*, February 24, 1964.

15. Nat Kleinfield, "Speaking of Speed," *Illustrated Speedway News,* February 25, 1964.

16. Bob Smith, "Men, Machines Tackle Sebring," *Tampa* (Florida) *Tribune*, March 21, 1964.

17. Daley, "Fast and Furious Foyt."

18. Dick Denny, "Marshman Has New Love—Lotus," *Indianapolis News,* March 28, 1964.

19. Jep Cadou Jr., "Unser Covers Straightaway at Hot 194.38," *Indianapolis Star,* March 28, 1964.

20. Johnny Rutherford and David Craft, *Lone Star J.R.: The Autobiography of Racing Legend Johnny Rutherford* (Chicago: Triumph Books, 2000).

21. UPI, "Foyt Wins Indy-Marred Sprint," *Evansville* (Indiana) *Press,* March 30, 1964.

22. Daley, "Fast and Furious Foyt."

23. "A. J. Foyt—Is He Greatest Race Driver Ever?" *Greenville* (South Carolina) *News*, March 10, 1964.

24. Jack Kiser, "Foyt Drives to 'Perfection,'" *Philadelphia Daily News,* April 20, 1964.

25. John Albers, "Larson Winner at New Bremen in Wreck-Marred Sprint Show," *Dayton* (Ohio) *Journal Herald,* May 4, 1964.

26. "Foyt Wins Fourth Straight 100-Mile Race at Trenton," *Dayton* (Ohio) *Journal Herald*, April 20, 1964.

27. Bob Renner, "Foyt Has a Ford in His 500 Future," *Indianapolis New,* April 20, 1964.

CHAPTER 15. THE MAGNIFICENT AND THE MACABRE

1. Associated Press, "Front-Rear-Engine Battle to Resume at '500' Track," *South Bend* (Indiana) *Tribune,* April 29, 1964.

2. Bob Renner, "Parnelli Has High Hopes to Top 156," *Indianapolis News*, May 8, 1964.

3. A.J. Foyt, 2012 interview with the author conducted for *Black Noon: The Year They Stopped the Indy 500* (New York: St. Martin's Press, 2014).

4. Bob Renner, "Parnelli Definitely Will Race Roadster," *Indianapolis News,* May 11, 1964.

5. "Foyt Is Planning to Test Lotus-Ford," *Indianapolis News,* May 15, 1964.

6. Dan Gurney and Bobby Unser, 2012 interviews with the author conducted for *Black Noon: The Year They Stopped the Indy 500.*

7. Robert Daley, "Fast and Furious Foyt," *True Magazine,* June 1965.

8. Leo Levine, *Ford: The Dust and the Glory: A Racing History* (New York: Macmillan, 1968).

9. A.J. Foyt, 2008 interview with David Goldstein, the Houston Oral History Project, https://houstonlibrary. aviaryplatform.com/collections/2466/collection_resources/109545, July 22, 2008.

10. Bob Ottum, "Champion of the Old Guard," *Sports Illustrated*, June 1, 1964.

11. A.J. Foyt, 2012 interview with the author.

12. Bill Van Fleet. Quotes from Sports World. *Fort Worth* (Texas) *Star-Telegram*, May 20, 1964.

13. A.J. Foyt, 2021 interview with the author.

14. Humpy Wheeler, 2012 interview with the author conducted for *Black Noon: The Year They Stopped the Indy 500.*

15. Ron Lemasters, "Erupting Gasoline Doesn't Hide Horror," *Muncie* (Indiana) *Star Press,* May 31, 1964.

16. A.J. Foyt, 2012 interview with the author conducted for *Black Noon: The Year They Stopped the Indy 500.*

17. Donald Davidson, 2012 interview with the author conducted for *Black Noon: The Year They Stopped the Indy 500.*

18. Bob Ottum, "The Magnificent and the Macabre," *Sports Illustrated,* June 8, 1964.

19. Robert Daley, "Fast and Furious Foyt," *True Magazine*, June 1965.
20. Bill Blodgett, "They Wanted to Live," *Atlanta Constitution*, December 19, 1964.
21. Tony Chamblin, "What Makes A.J. Run?" *Evansville* (Indiana) *Press*, May 30,1965
22. Steve Van Cleve, "We Planned It Just Like It Went—Foyt," Associated Press, *Richmond* (Indiana) *Palladium-Item,* May 31, 1964.
23. A.J. Foyt, 2023 interview with the author.
24. Max Muhleman, "A.J. Foyt: King of Racing's World," *Charlotte* (North Carolina) *News,* June 1, 1964.
25. Ottum, "The Magnificent and the Macabre."
26. Bob Gaines, "The Screaming World of A.J. Foyt," *Family Weekly,* February 6, 1966.
27. Wayne Fuson, "A.J.'s Victory Dinner Is 15c Dinner," *Indianapolis News,* June 1, 1964.
28. "Lone Star Speed Zone," website, http://www.lonestarspeedzone.com/topic/25422-playland-park/?page=7.
29. Robert Daley, "Fast and Furious Foyt," *True Magazine*, June 1965.
30. Bill Libby, *Parnelli: A Story of Auto Racing* (New York: Tower Publications, 1969).
31. Dan Gurney, 2012 interview with the author.
32. Daley, "Fast and Furious Foyt."
33. Ottum, "The Magnificent and the Macabre."

CHAPTER 16. EUROPEAN VACATION

1. Wire Services, "Controversy Still Racing Over Gasoline's Use as Fuel," *Muncie* (Indiana) *Star Press*, June 1, 1964
2. Leo Levine, *Ford: The Dust and the Glory: A Racing History* (New York: Macmillan, 1968).
3. George Moore, "Champ Mulls Quitting after 'Hairy' Victory," *Indianapolis Star*, June 8, 1964.
4. Lee C. Bright, "Fireproof Suits Irritate Drivers," *Dayton* (Ohio) *Daily News*, June 12, 1964.
5. Bob Renner, "A.J. Foyt Proving You CAN Win 'Em All," *Indianapolis News*, June 8, 1964.
6. Associated Press, "Engine Formulas Change Voted by USAC Group," *The* (Nashville) *Tennessean*, June 10, 1964.
7. Kenneth Carr, "Foyt May Shift to Rear-Engine Race Car Next Year," UPI, *Lansing* (Michigan) *State Journal.*
8. Glen Banner, "Foyt Wins Terre Haute Feature," *Kokomo* (Indiana) *Tribune*, June 15, 1964.
9. Bob Renner, "Foyt Flashes 2 Different Sides during Sprint Card," *Indianapolis News*, June 15, 1964.
10. Jack Kiser, "Foyt Stretches String to 5, Eyes New World to Conquer," *Philadelphia Daily News,* June 22, 1964.
11. Bob Gates, *Hurtubise* (Marshall, IN: Witness Productions, 1995).
12. Bob Renner, "Hurtubise Vows He'll Race Again," *Indianapolis News*, June 25, 1964.
13. A.J. Foyt, November 7, 2019, interview with the author.
14. UPI, "Foyt Visits Jim Hurtubise," *Terre Haute* (Indiana) *Tribune*, June 25, 1964.
15. Johnny Rutherford, June 17, 2020, interview with the author.
16. Joe Whitlock, "Inches Make Difference as Isaac Edged for First," *The State* (Columbia, SC), July 5, 1964.
17. Joe Whitlock, "Foyt: 'Thought I Could get Around,'" *The State* (Columbia, SC), July 5, 1964.
18. Bob Hoffman, "Foyt Took the High Road," *High Point* (North Carolina) *Enterprise*, July 5, 1965.
19. Bob Renner, "A.J. Foyt's 'Antique' Machine Carries a Big Money Load," *Indianapolis News*, July 20, 1964.
20. Bill Simmons, "A.J. Foyt Solves Recent Problems with New Machine of Own Design," *Philadelphia Inquirer*, April 7, 1974.
21. Dave Overpeck, "Foyt to Race in Europe, May Look for '500' Car," *Indianapolis Star*, July 26, 1964.
22. Robert Daley, "Fast and Furious Foyt," *True Magazine*, June 1965.
23. Robert Daley, *This Cruel Sport: Grand Prix Racing 1959–1967* (Hoboken, NJ: Prentice-Hall, 1963).
24. Daley, "Fast and Furious Foyt."
25. John Mecom, interview with the author #2.
26. John Mecom, interview with the author #2.
27. UPI, "A.J. Foyt Says He'll Drive Ferraris in Europe," *Evansville* (Indiana) *Press*, August 6, 1964.
28. A.J. Foyt, November 7, 2019, interview with the author.

CHAPTER 17. THE YEAR OF FOYT

1. "Parnelli to Race at Salem," *Louisville* (Kentucky) *Courier-Journal,* July 29, 1964.
2. A.J. Foyt, 2021 interview with the author.
3. Bob Renner, "Foyt Cusses Himself, but Don Smiles," *Indianapolis News,* August 10, 1964.
4. Dave DeLong, "Larson Wins Allentown Fair Feature," *Allentown* (Pennsylvania) *Morning Call,* August 16, 1964.
5. Mario Andretti, 2021 interview with the author.
6. George Moore, "Foyt Wins Seventh Straight," *Indianapolis Star,* August 23, 1964.
7. Associated Press, "A.J. May Race Lotus," *Tacoma* (Washington) *News Tribune,* August 22, 1964.
8. Wayne Fuson, "Jones Joins 'Em," *Indianapolis News,* August 24, 1964.
9. Ed Staats, "A.J. Foyt to Drive Lotus-Ford in '500,'" Associated Press, *South Bend* (Indiana) *Tribune,* August 26, 1964.

10. Dave Overpeck, "Foyt Wins Horn 100 in Record Time," *Indianapolis Star,* September 8, 1964.
11. "A. J. Winner in Sulky, Too," *Indianapolis News,* September 10, 1964.
12. George Cunningham, "Fabulous Foyt," *Charlotte* (North Carolina) *Observer,* September 13, 1964.
13. Gary Galloway, "A Race to Remember," *Hammond* (Indiana) *Times,* September 10, 1964.
14. Jack Kiser, "No Doubt about It: Foyt No. 1," *Philadelphia Daily News,* September 14, 1964.
15. Dave Overpeck, "Foyt Sets Records in 100-Miler," *Indianapolis Star,* September 27, 1964.
16. Wayne Fuson, "Foyt the Winner," *Indianapolis News,* August 22, 1964.
17. "USAC's Pole Car Is Worth Riding In—Ask A.J., P.J.," *Indianapolis News,* September 28, 1964.
18. Robert Daley, "Fast and Furious Foyt," *True Magazine,* June 1965.
19. Bill Libby, *Parnelli: A Story of Auto Racing* (New York: Tower Publications, 1969).
20. Shave Glick, "Jones Tough in Clutch, Wins without One," *Los Angeles Times,* October 12, 1964.
21. Joe Whitlock, "Angry Racing Champ Blasts Inspectors," *Columbia* (South Carolina) *State,* October 15, 1964.
22. Ton Kane, "Foyt Races to Golden State Win," *Sacramento* (California) *Bee,* October 26, 1964.
23. "Ward to Quit Bouncing around on Dirt," *Illustrated Speedway News,* November 17, 1964.
24. Dave Overpeck, "Foyt, 2-Time 500 Champ, Will Have Choice in May," *Indianapolis Star,* November 15, 1964.
25. Prescott Sullivan, "Some Driving Tips From Parnelli Jones," *San Francisco Examiner,* October 22, 1964.
26. Gerry Pierson, "Foyt Crashes Wall in Bobby Ball Practice," *Arizona* (Phoenix) *Republic,* November 21, 1964.
27. Bob Crawford, "Ruby Outlasts Favorites," *Tucson Daily Citizen,* November 23, 1964.
28. Joe Buchanan, "Foyt Beats Jones in Hanford 200-Mile Race," *Hanford* (California) *Sentinel,* November 30, 1964.
29. Associated Press, "Marshman Dies of Crash Burns," *Allentown* (Pennsylvania) *Morning Call,* December 4, 1964.
30. Warren Howard, "Marshman Is Listed Very Critical; Dad Is Certain 'Professionals' Can Save Son's Life," *Pottstown* (Pennsylvania) *Mercury,* November 30, 1964.
31. A.J. Foyt, interview with the author.
32. John Kunda, "Sports Call," *Allentown* (Pennsylvania) *Morning Call,* December 4, 1964.
33. Pat Putnam, "Penske Favored over Foyt in Nassau Classic," *Miami Herald,* December 6, 1964.
34. Jim Anderson, "Man of the Year—Foyt," *Greenville* (South Carolina) *News,* December 20, 1964.
35. John Wilson, "Penske the Favorite over A.J. Foyt for Nassau Trophy," *Miami News,* December 5, 1964.
36. Pat Putnam, "$40,000 Sports Car a White Elephant on Circuit; Even Foyt Can't Make It Go," *Miami Herald,* December 8, 1964.
37. Robert Daley, "Fast and Furious Foyt," *True Magazine,* June 1965.
38. Pat Putnam, "Penske Holds off Foyt, Wins Nassau Trophy Race," *Miami Herald,* December 5, 1964.
39. Foyt column in AutoWeek following the death of Gurney.
40. Leo Mehl, "Legends of a Legend," A.J. Foyt Media Guide, 1991.
41. Bob Gaines, "The Screaming World of A.J. Foyt," *Family Weekly,* February 6, 1966.
42. Daley, "Fast and Furious Foyt."
43. Jack Kofoed, "We're Pretty Rugged, But We May Crack Yet," *Miami Herald,* August 4, 1964.
44. Bill McCormick, "A Day in the Life of Best Race Driver in the Nation," *Newspaper Enterprise Association,* October 4, 1964.
45. Bob Gaines, "The Screaming World of A.J. Foyt," *Family Weekly,* February 6, 1966.
46. Bob Myers, "Lucy Foyt: A Converted Football Fan," *Charlotte* (North Carolina) *News,* August 5, 1964.
47. Wayne Fuson, "Foyt the Winner," *Indianapolis News,* August 22, 1964.
48. Mark Kiegel, *Namath: A Biography* (New York: The Penguin Group, 2004).
49. Wilbur Adams, "Between the Sport Lines," *Sacramento* (California) *Bee,* January 19, 1965.
50. A.J. Foyt, 2008 interview with David Goldstein, the Houston Oral History Project, https://houstonlibrary.aviaryplatform.com/collections/2466/collection_resources/109545, July 22, 2008.
51. Tom Kane, "Foyt Would Quit If He Thought Racing Dangerous," *Sacramento* (California) *Bee,* October 26, 1964.

CHAPTER 18. SHEET TIME

1. The Hickok Manufacturing Company was purchased by Tandy Corporation in 1970, and the last award was presented in 1976. It was reestablished in 2012. No auto-racing driver has ever won the award.
2. Dave Overpeck, "Foyt Logical Choice for Hickok Award," *Indianapolis Star,* December 29, 1964.
3. George Vecsey, "Sports of the Times, Dick Young in His Time," *New York Times,* September 2, 1987.
4. Dick Young, "His Toast to the Indy 500: Here's Blood in Your Eye!," *New York Daily News,* May 30, 1966.
5. Gene Ward, "Ward to the Wise," *New York Daily News,* January 11, 1965.
6. Hank Hollingworth, "Athlete of Year: Foyt," *Long Beach* (California) *Independent Press-Telegram,* January 14, 1965.
7. Hollingworth, "Athlete of Year: Foyt."

8. UPI, "Jim Brown Awarded Hickok Belt," *Casper* (Wyoming) *Star Tribune,* January 25, 1965.
9. Shav Glick, "Tell a Driver He's No Athlete; You'll Drive Him up the Wall," *Los Angeles Times,* November 6, 1974.
10. Ray Sons, "More than Speed in Decision to Abandon the Offy for Ford," *Chicago Daily News,* May 19, 1965.
11. Joe Heiling, "Wade Best Driver on Austin Asphalt," *Austin American,* January 6, 1965.
12. Bernard Kahn, "Wade Killed in Test Run," *Daytona News-Journal,* January 6, 1965.
13. A.J. Foyt, 2019 interview with the author.
14. Tom Cotter and Al Pearce, *Holman-Moody: The Legendary Race Team* (Beverly, MA: Motorbooks, 2003).
15. Bob Thomas, "Foyt Doing Well, Asks for Papers," *Los Angeles Times,* January 19, 1965.
16. Bill Blodgett, "Junior Thanks a Friend for Cassius-like Action," *Atlanta Constitution,* April 1, 1965.
17. Leonard Wood, interview with the author.
18. "500 Champ Put in Intensive Care Ward," Press Association reports, *Indianapolis News,* January 19, 1965.
19. Bones Bourcier, *Foyt, Andretti, Petty: America's Racing Trinity* (Newburyport, MA: Coastal, 2015), 181.
20. Bill Libby, *Foyt* (New York: Hawthorn Books, 1974).
21. Richard Petty, 2021 interview with the author.
22. A.J. Foyt, 2019 interview with the author.
23. Associated Press, "Foyt May Leave Hospital Soon," *Indianapolis News,* January 21, 1965.
24. "Foyt Races Six Weeks 'in Bed,'" Star Special Report, *Indianapolis Star,* January 24, 1965.
25. Lucy Foyt, interview with the author.
26. Ron Lemasters, "A.J. Changes Gears with New Sponsor," *Muncie* (Indiana) *Star Press,* May 6, 1983.
27. The Henry Ford Research Collection video.
28. Jack Lattimer, "Bignotti Makes Lotus Bloom for Indy 500," *San Mateo* (California) *Times,* April 16, 1965.
29. Jerry Diamond, "Foyt Will Race at Phoenix," *San Francisco Examiner,* March 17, 1965.
30. Dave Overpeck, "Phoenix to Preview 500 Field," *Indianapolis Star,* March 24, 1965.
31. Overpeck, "Phoenix to Preview 500 Field."
32. Bob Thomas, "Branson Win Clouds Indy Issue," *Los Angeles Times,* March 29, 1965.
33. Jack Lattimer, "Bignotti Makes Lotus Bloom for Indy 500," *San Mateo* (California) *Times,* April 16, 1965.
34. "Holman and Moody Build Foyt Car," *Charlotte* (North Carolina) *News,* March 4, 1965.
35. Leonard Laye, "Lorenzen May Team with Foyt in Indianapolis 500," *Greenville* (South Carolina) *News,* April 5, 1965.
36. Bill Blodgett, "Junior Thanks a friend for 'Cassius'-like Action," *Atlanta Constitution,* April 1, 1965.
37. Bill Blodgett, "Foyt to Sit Back before 'Tromping,'" *Atlanta Constitution,* April 3, 1965.
38. Bill Libby, *Parnelli: A Story of Auto Racing* (New York: Tower Publications, 1969).
39. Blodgett, "Foyt to Sit Back before 'Tromping.'"
40. Bill Blodgett, "Panch, Foyt Share 'Wheels' in Speeding to '500' Victory," *Atlanta Constitution,* April 12, 1965.
41. Associated Press, "Non-Cooperative Label Doesn't Concern Foyt," *Greenville* (South Carolina) *News,* May 14, 1965.
42. AP, "Non-Cooperative Label Doesn't Concern Foyt."
43. Dave Overpeck, "Foyt Slams Wall Twice in 987-Ft. Slide," *Indianapolis Star,* May 6, 1965.
44. Overpeck, "Foyt Slams Wall Twice in 987-Ft. Slide."
45. Wayne Fuson, "A.J. Foyt's Car Owner Watches Scary Spin," *Indianapolis News,* May 6, 1965.
46. Bob Renner, "Private Changes May Cause the Weaknesses: Lotus Official," *Indianapolis News,* May 7, 1965.
47. Bob Renner, "2 Drivers Brighten Dark Garage 53," *Indianapolis News,* May 11, 1965.
48. Rob Renner, "Foyt Misses Lap of 162.5," *Indianapolis News,* May 17, 1965.
49. Charlie Gray, 2022 interview with the author.
50. Ray Marquette, "Pole Sitter A.J. One Texan Who Has Everything," *Indianapolis Star,* May 16, 1965.
51. Dick Mittman, "Foyt Putting in More Effort," *Indianapolis News,* May 19, 1965.
52. Lyle Mannweiler, "There's Saturday, Sunday A.J. Foyts," *Indianapolis News,* May 17, 1965.
53. Rich Roberts, "Cotton in the Wind," *Long Beach* (California) *Independent Press-Telegram,* May 30, 1965.
54. Wire Services, "Controversy Still Raging Over Gasoline's Use as Fuel," Munice (Indiana) Star, June 1, 1964.
55. Dave Overpeck, "Foyt, Al Unser to Use Gasoline In Race," *Indianapolis Star,* May 27, 1965.
56. Leonard Laye, "Lorenzen May Team with Foyt in Indianapolis 500," *Greenville* (South Carolina) *News,* April 5, 1965.
57. Al Unser, 2020 interview with the author.
58. Kurt Freudenthal, "Unser Brother Act Is Triple Threat in 1965 500-Mile Race," UPI, *Logansport* (Indiana) *Tribune,* May 28, 1965.
59. Bill Pittman, "Lola about Ready and So Is Foyt," *Indianapolis News,* May 11, 1965.
60. Bill Pittman, "Foyt Formula for Driving 500 Given," *Indianapolis News,* May 29, 1965.

61. Al Unser, 2020 interview with the author.
62. "Behind the Scenes with IndyCar Legends," Motorsports on NBC, April 28, 2022, https://www.youtube.com/watch?v=f5a38wHoXzM.
63. Dave Cabrillo, "4-time Indy 500 Winner Al Unser Sr. Remembered," *WTHR*, Indianapolis, December 10, 2021.
64. Wayne Fuson, "It's Wide-Open Race, but Smart Bet Is Foyt, Clark," *Indianapolis News*, May 29, 1965.
65. Leonard Wood, 2021 interview with the author.
66. Dale Burgess "Head-On Clash Seen for A.J. Foyt, Jimmy Clark," Associated Press, *Orlando Evening Star,* May 28, 1965.
67. Dave Overpeck, "Clark Wins 500," *Indianapolis Star*, June 1, 1965.
68. Bob Renner, "Everything Went Right for Jimmy," *Indianapolis News*, June 1, 1965.
69. "Lotus Owner Chapman Praises Johns, Pit Crew," *Charlotte* (North Carolina) *Observer*, June 1, 1965.
70. Ray Marquette, "Clark May Not Try 500 Again," *Indianapolis Star,* June 1, 1965.
71. "Gear Box Ends Foyt's Chase on 116th Lap," *Indianapolis Star*, June 1, 1965.

CHAPTER 19. THE BREAKUP

1. "Maybe I'll Quit Says A.J. Foyt," *Indianapolis News,* June 1, 1965.
2. Tony Chamblin, "What Makes A.J. Run?" *Evansville* (Indiana) *Press,* May 30, 1965.
3. Chamblin, "What Makes A.J. Run?"
4. Kurt Freudenthal "Clark Lauds Chapman," UPI, *Tipton* (Indiana) *Daily Tribune,* June 2, 1965.
5. Bill Libby, *Foyt* (New York: Hawthorn Books, 1974).
6. Cooper Rollow, "In the Wake of the News," *Chicago Tribune,* May 12,1965.
7. John Mecom, interview with the author.
8. HTNS, "A.J. Foyt to Enter Le Mans," *Montreal Gazette,* May 29, 1965.
9. Jim Anderson, "Man of the Year—Foyt," *Greenville* (South Carolina) *News,* December 20, 1964.
10. Tim Cline, "Anthony Joseph Foyt—Why Does He Keep on Racing?" *South Bend* (Indiana) *Tribune*, September 29, 1964.
11. Dick Ralstan, "Speaking of Cars," *Kokomo* (Indiana) *Morning News,* June 21, 1965.
12. "Bignotti Split with Foyt (Again) over Car Setup," *Indianapolis News,* June 21, 1965.
13. George Moore, "Ansted Doesn't Blame Bignotti for Quitting," *Indianapolis Star,* June 22, 1965.
14. UPI, "Chief Mechanic, Foyt Parting after 5 Years," *Muncie* (Indiana) *Star Press,* June 21, 1965.
15. Dick Ralstin, "Foyt's 'Man with Wrench,' Quits," *Kokomo* (Indiana) *Morning Times,* June 15, 1965.
16. Rodger Ward, "Foyt Abuses His Equipment: Ward," *Indianapolis News,* June 7, 1965.
17. Jack Lattimer, "'I've Had It with Foyt,' Says Bignotti," *San Mateo* (California) *Times,* June 25, 1965.
18. A.J. Foyt with William Neely, *A.J.: My Life as America's Greatest Race Car Driver* (New York: Times Books, 1983).
19. Dave Overpeck, "Moves of Foyt, Bignotti, Ward Seem Best for All," *Indianapolis Star*, June 27, 1965.
20. John Oreovicz, "Indy Mechanic George Bignotti Dies," ESPN, September 30, 2013.
21. John Mecom, 2021 interview with the author.
22. "Pouelsen Joins Foyt; Jones Now Looking," *Indianapolis News*, July 8, 1965.
23. Joe Scalzo, *The American Dirt Track Racer* (St. Paul, MN: MBI Publishing, 2001).
24. Benny Phillips, "Track, Mounts—They're All Same," *High Point* (North Carolina) *Enterprise,* July 5, 1965.
25. Jimmy Mann, "'Hurts' Place Winner Foyt in Driver's Seat," *St. Petersburg* (Florida) *Times,* July 5, 1965.
26. "Foyt Wins Firecracker," Bob Smith, *Tampa* (Florida) *Tribune,* July 5, 1965.
27. "Stars Say Foyt's Famine to End Soon," Jack Kiser, *Philadelphia Daily News,* July 10, 1965.
28. Bill Simmons, "New Combos Get 1st Tests," *Philadelphia Inquirer*, July 11, 1965.
29. Associated Press, "Foyt Wins Trenton 150," *Central New Jersey Home News*, July 19, 1965.
30. Jack Kiser, "Like Old Times, Foyt Wins Trenton 150," *Philadelphia Daily News*, July 19, 1965.
31. Kiser, "Like Old Times, Foyt Wins Trenton 150."
32. Lyle Mannweiler, "Mario Gives Race a European Twist," *Indianapolis News*, July 26, 1965.
33. Wayne Fuson, "IRP Race for 500 Cars an 'Artistic' Success," *Indianapolis News,* July 26, 1965.
34. Bill Blodgett, "A New Perspective On Johnny's Reward," *Atlanta Constitution*, August 2, 1965.
35. Johnny Rutherford, 2021 interview with the author.
36. Jack Kiser, "Horne '100' Field Complete—Foyt Has Entered," *Philadelphia Daily News*, Tuesday, June 15, 1965.
37. Dick Ralstin, "Springfield-Milwaukee Race Weekend Tops in Year's Championship Circuit," *Kokomo* (Indiana) *Morning News*, August 24, 1965.
38. Robin Miller, "Remembering A.J. Foyt's Greatest Moment," *Racer*, July 10, 2015.
39. The Henry Ford Research Collection video.
40. Tim Delrose, 2020 interview with the author.
41. Benny Phillips, "Foyt Likes to Race Autos at Charlotte—Or Anywhere," *High Point* (North Carolina) *Enterprise*, October 17, 1965.
42. Benny Phillips, "Freddie Added His 10th in Record Fashion," *High Point* (North Carolina) *Enterprise*, October 18, 1965.

43. Bob Myers, "Lorenzen Tops Foyt in Late-Race Duel," *Charlotte* (North Carolina) *News*, October 18, 1965.
44. Phillips, "Freddie Added His 10th in Record Fashion."
45. Bloys Britt, "Fred Lorenzen: At Home in a Dinner Jacket or Dirty Coveralls," Associated Press, *Burlington* (North Carolina) *Times-News*, December 15, 1965.
46. Libby, *Foyt*.
47. Scalzo, *The American Dirt Track Racer*.
48. Mario Andretti, 2021 interview with the author.

CHAPTER 20. WILY COYOTE

1. A.J. Foyt, 2019 interview with the author.
2. George Snider, 2020 interview with the author.
3. Tom Meehan, "Snider Is Not Just Puffing Away at Pipe Dreams, Will Race in East," *Fresno* (California) *Bee*, April 11, 1966.
4. Bob Thomas, "Foyt Returns to Scene of 'Crime,'" *Los Angeles Times,* January 19, 1966.
5. Jerry Diamond, "Foyt Enjoys Little Luck at Riverside," *San Francisco Examiner,* January 22, 1966.
6. Mario Andretti, 2022 interview with the author.
7. Hal Hayes, "Hurtubise Hurries to 500 Win," *Atlanta Constitution*, March 28, 1966.
8. "Twilight of a Titan," *Sports Illustrated,* September 30, 1991.
9. "Foyt Wins Ascot Midget Feature," *Los Angeles Times,* April 10, 1966.
10. George Moore, "Speaking of Speed," *Indianapolis Star,* May 4, 1966.
11. Leo Levine, "Mario Faces Twin Jinx at Trenton," *New York Times News Service,* April 17.
12. Bill Clark, "'Pick and Choose Not for Andretti," *Daytona Daily News*, April 15, 1966.
13. Jack Kiser, "Foyt vs. Andretti Means War," *Philadelphia Daily News*, April 23, 1966.
14. Joe McGinnis, *They Call Him Cale: The Life and Career of NASCAR Legend Cale Yarborough* (Chicago: Triumph Books, 2008).
15. Cale Yarborough, 2021 interview with the author.
16. "Wind or What? Crash Cause Puzzles Foyt," *Indianapolis Star*, May 16, 1966.
17. Ray Marquette, "Foyt Backup 9 Hour Marvel," *Indianapolis Star*, May 16, 1966.
18. Mario Andretti, "With Trails Over, Word Begins," *Charlotte* (North Carolina) *Observer*, May 21, 1966.
19. Bob Renner, "A.J. Idling Now—But Wait till Race Day, Fans," *Indianapolis News*, May 20, 1966.
20. Bob Moore, "Yarborough's Newest Love," *Charlotte* (North Carolina) *Observer,* May 29, 1966.
21. "33 Fastest Test Cars and Nobody Is Happy," *Indianapolis News*, May 27, 1966.
22. "Andretti vs. Foyt: No Love Lost," Joe Falls, *Detroit Free Press*, May 30, 1966.
23. Bob Renner, "A.J. Idling Now—But Wait till Race Day, Fans," *Indianapolis News*, May 20, 1966.
24. Ed Orman, Fresno's Snider Draws Praise for Indy Qualifying Run," *Fresno* (California) *Bee*, May 22, 1966.
25. "Pinched Clark Didn't Know Race Started," *Indianapolis Star*, May 31, 1966.
26. Cy McBride, "Pileup Began after I Was Hit," *Indianapolis Star*, May 31, 1966.
27. A.J. Foyt, April 19–24, 2021, interviews with the author.
28. ABC's *Wide World of Sports*, June 4, 1966.
29. Mike Kupper, "Hill Wins 500 in Demolition Derby," *Milwaukee Journal*, May 31, 1966.
30. *Indianapolis Star.* Notes. May 31, 1966.
31. Bob Ottum, "A Crazy Mixed Up 500," *Sports Illustrated*, June 6, 1966.
32. *Indianapolis Star.* Notes.
33. Pat Truly, "Foyt's Radiator Still Boiling," *Fort Worth* (Texas) *Star-Telegram*, May 31, 1966.
34. A.J. Foyt, April 19-24, 2021, interviews with the author.
35. Star Speedway Staff, "Pit Pass," *Indianapolis Star*, May 31, 1966.
36. Joe Scalzo, "Smart Rookie," *Motor Sport Magazine*, March 2002.
37. Pat Truly, "Foyt's Radiator Still Boiling," *Fort Worth* (Texas) *Star-Telegram*, May 31, 1966.
38. Ray Marquette, "Stewart Top Rookie, Total Purse $691,304," *Indianapolis Star*, June 1, 1966.
39. Robert Daley, *This Cruel Sport: Grand Prix Racing 1959–1967* (Hoboken, NJ: Prentice-Hall, 1963).
40. Bob Colllins, "Sports over Lightly," *Indianapolis Star*, September 19, 1966.
41. Marquette, "Stewart Top Rookie, Total Purse $691,304."
42. "The 50th Indianapolis 500 Mile Race," *Motor Sport Magazine,* July 1966.

CHAPTER 21. BAD BREAKS

1. Andrew Ferguson, *Team Lotus: The Indianapolis Years* (United Kingdom: Haynes Publishing, 1996).
2. "The 50th Indianapolis 500 Mile Race," *Motor Sport Magazine,* July 1966.
3. Ray Marquette, "Foyt Hurt in Crash," *Indianapolis Star*, June 5, 1966.
4. Associated Press, "Foyt Burned in Crack-Up," *Wausau* (Wisconsin) *Daily Herald*, June 6, 1966.
5. *Charlotte* (North Carolina) *News*. Motorsport Notes. June 23, 1966.
6. Ray Marquette, "Foyt Hurt in Crash," *Indianapolis Star*, June 5, 1966.
7. A.J. Foyt, 2008 interview with David Goldstein, the Houston Oral History Project, https:// houstonlibrary. aviaryplatform.com/collections/2466/collection_resources/109545, July 22, 2008.
8. A.J. Foyt, April 19–24, 2021, interviews with the author.

9. Tony Foyt, April 26, 2021, interview with the author.

10. Terry Foyt, April 21, 2021, interview with the author.

11. A.J. Foyt, November 17, 2019, interview with the author.

12. Bobby Unser, 2012 interview with the author conducted for *Black Noon: The Year They Stopped the Indy 500* (New York: St. Martin's Press, 2014).

13. A.J. Baime, "10 Reasons Why A.J. Foyt Is Still America's Toughest SOB," *The Drive,* December 16, 2015.

14. Associated Press, "Foyt Recalls How His Hands Hurt," *La Crosse* (Wisconsin) *Tribune,* June 6, 1966.

15. Dave Overpeck, "Foyt Is Peppy as Ever and Ready to Go Racing," *Indianapolis Star,* July 22, 1966.

16. Bob Renner, "Foyt Planning to Run in Sunday's Atlanta 300," *Indianapolis News,* June 21, 1966.

17. A.J. Foyt, 2008 interview with David Goldstein.

18. Joe McGinnis, "Bignotti Opponent Is Age, Not Foyt," *Philadelphia Inquirer,* August 5, 1966.

19. Dave Overpeck, "There's Room at Top for Rog," *Indianapolis Star,* August 8, 1966.

20. Omer Crane, "Sports Thinks," *Fresno* (California) *Bee,* August 30, 1966.

21. Associated Press, "A.J. Foyt and Chief Mechanic Break up Following Argument," *Terre Haute* (Indiana) *Star,* August 20, 1966.

22. Mario Andretti with Bob Collins, *What's It Like Out There?* (Chicago: NTC/Contemporary Publishing, 1970).

23. Mario Andretti, "My Race against Hate," *Lenten Guideposts/Burlington* (North Carolina) *Daily Times-News,* February 24, 1972.

24. Dick Ralstin, "Foyt Can't Stop, Mario Goes to Victory," *Kokomo* (Indiana) *Morning Times,* September 11, 1966.

25. Mario Andretti, 2022 interview with the author.

26. "'My Greatest Rival,' Mario Andretti on A.J. Foyt," *Motor Sport Magazine,* December 28, 2020.

27. Mario Andretti, September 3, 2022, interview with the author.

28. Chris Economaki with Dave Argabright, *Let 'Em All Go!* (Fishers, IN: Books by Dave Argabright, 2006).

29. A.J. Foyt, 2019 interview with the author.

30. Bob Renner, "Foyt Quits for '66, Vows Comeback Next Year," *Indianapolis News,* September 13, 1966.

31. Associated Press, "Foyt Mulls Entering 200 at Trenton," *Asbury Park* (New Jersey) *Press,* September 21, 1966.

32. Bob Thomas, "A.J. Foyt Latest Star to Join Field for Times Grand Prix Race," *Los Angeles Times,* October 9, 1966.

33. Bob Renner, "Mario Is Fuel for Thought," *Indianapolis News,* September 26, 1966.

34. Bob Terrell, "Cassius Rides Again," *Asheville* (North Carolina) *Citizen-Times,* October 9, 1966.

35. Bob Moore, "Foyt, Friel Feud over Inspections," *Charlotte* (North Carolina) *Observer,* October 13, 1966.

36. Bill Libby, *Parnelli: A Story of Auto Racing* (New York: Tower Publications, 1969).

37. Libby, *Parnelli.*

38. Bob Garner, "Foyt Wins First Race of Season," *Redwood* (California) *City Tribune,* November 14, 1966.

39. A.J. Foyt, November 7, 2019, interview with the author.

40. Mario Andretti, 2022 interview with the author.

41. Leon Mandel, "Mario Staves off Parnelli," *AutoWeek,* December 10, 1966.

42. Dave Heerrn, "Foyt under His Car More than in It," *Fort Lauderdale* (Florida) *News,* December 4, 1966.

43. Bob Thomas, "Ford Moves to Streamline Unwieldy Racing Operation," *Los Angeles Times,* March 2, 1967.

44. Bob Myers, "The Ford Award," *Charlotte* (North Carolina) *News,* December 20, 1966.

45. Bob Collins, "Sports over Lightly," *Indianapolis Star,* July 23, 1967.

46. Jeff Scott, "There Is Only One A.J. Foyt," *Auto Racing Magazine,* December 1966.

47. Collins, "Sports over Lightly."

48. Bill Simmons, "Foyt Mellows Despite 'Barren' Trail," *Philadelphia Inquirer,* July 30, 1967.

CHAPTER 22. SCARED SHITLESS

1. A.J. Foyt, 2019 interview with the author.

2. Robin Miller, "Joe Leonard, 1932–2017," *Racer,* April 29, 2017.

3. Shav Glick, "Leonard Traveled Hard Road to Riches," *Los Angeles Times,* October 26, 1971.

4. A.J. Foyt with William Neely, *A.J.: My Life as America's Greatest Race Car Driver* (New York: Times Books, 1983).

5. Louis Galanos, "1967 24 Hours of Daytona—Race Profile," *Sports Car Digest,* January 20, 2012.

6. Preston Lerner, "Mr. Fix It," *All American Racers Archive,* 1990.

7. "Le Mans 50th Anniversary Video Interview," Long Beach, California, 2017.

8. Bill Clark, "Foyt Blows His Cool at Daytona," *Dayton* (Ohio) *Daily News,* February 25, 1967.

9. Mario Andretti, 2019 interview with the author.

10. Bob Collins, "Sports over Lightly," *Indianapolis Star,* February 26, 1967.

11. "Andretti's the Name, Mister," Bob Myers, *Charlotte* (North Carolina) *News,* February 28, 1967.
12. Preston Lerner, "Mr. Fix It," *All American Racers Archive,* 1990.
13. Foyt with Neely, *A.J.*
14. A.J. Foyt, 2021 interview with the author.
15. "Mario Andretti Will Run Atlanta 500 April 2," *Anniston* (Alabama) *Star,* March 5, 1967.
16. Ray Marquette, "Andretti Back on Top in Trenton 150," *Indianapolis Star,* April 24, 1967.

CHAPTER 23. THE TROUBLE WITH TURBINES

1. A.J. Foyt, 2019 interview with the author.
2. Richard Nisley, "Wild Coyotes," *Vintage Racecar,* May 2005.
3. "Speaking of Speed," George Moore, *Indianapolis Star,* March 19, 1967.
4. Nisley, "Wild Coyotes."
5. Bob Riley with Jonathan Ingram, *The Art of Race Car Design* (United Kingdom: Icon Publishing, 2015).
6. Star Speedway Staff, "Pit Pass," *Indianapolis Star,* May 9, 1967.
7. Bill Clark, "Foyt No Believer in Invading Aces," *Dayton* (Ohio) *Daily News,* April 30, 1967.
8. Bill Wildhack, "Texans Worked Hard on Coyotes, Foyt Says," *Indianapolis News,* June 1, 1967.
9. Ray Marquette, "Wreck Molds Foyt's Philosophy," *Indianapolis Star,* May 26, 1967.
10. Doug Nye, *The Story of Lotus, 61-71: Design Revolution* (United Kingdom: Motor Racing Publications, 1972).
11. Murray Olderman, "Gentlemen, Start Your Engines," NEA, *Wilmington* (Delaware) *Daily News,* May 26, 1967.
12. Jessie Outlar, "Jimmy Clark, Indy Roulette," *Atlanta Constitution,* May 30, 1967.
13. UPI, "Granatelli Takes Stand for Turbines," *Linton* (Indiana) *Daily Citizen,* March 13, 1968.
14. A.J. Foyt, 2019 interview with the author.
15. George Bolinger, "Bolinger on Sports," *Lafayette* (Indiana) *Journal and Courier,* May 15, 1967.
16. Ray Marquette, "Wreck Molds Foyt's Philosophy," *Indianapolis Star,* May 26, 1967.
17. Don Compton, "Jones Turbine Crowd Pleaser," *Richmond* (Indiana) *Palladium-Item,* May 14, 1967.
18. A.J. Foyt, 2019 interview with the author.
19. Murray Hurt, "Foyt Just a Spectator," *Rock Island* (Illinois) *Argus,* May 23, 1967.
20. Jack Martin, "Yankee Doodle Dandy Role Is Taken by Foyt," *Lafayette* (Indiana) *Journal,* May 23, 1967.
21. Bob Latshaw, "Turbine Could Win Indy by 5 Laps," *Detroit Free Press,* May 30, 1967.
22. Associated Press, "Jones' Turbine Seen Unbeatable," *Orlando Evening Star,* May 23, 1967.
23. Jim Flynn, "Out for English Blood," *Moline* (Illinois) *Dispatch,* May 25, 1967.
24. Associated Press, "Gurney Comes up with Idea," *Terre Haute* (Indiana) *Tribune,* May 31, 1967.
25. Johnny McDonald, "Viewpoint," Copley News Service, *San Pedro* (California) *News-Pilot,* May 27, 1967.
26. John Lake, "The Speed Game," *Newsweek*, May 29, 1967.
27. Mario Andretti, 2019 interview with the author.
28. Jessie Outlar, "Indy Roulette," *Atlanta Constitution,* May 30, 1967.
29. Ray Marquette, "Foyt a Study in Racing Action," *Indianapolis Star,* May 25, 1967.
30. Marquette, "Wreck Molds Foyt's Philosophy."
31. Dick Mittman, "Pappy Foyt Gives Vote for A.J.," *Indianapolis News*, May 25, 1967.

CHAPTER 24. THERE HE IS!

1. Ray Marquette, "Foyt Is Most Relaxed," *Indianapolis Star*, May 31, 1967.
2. "Dan's Plan Could Even the Race," *Indianapolis News*, May 31, 1967.
3. Dave Overpeck, "32 to Resume '500' Today," *Indianapolis Star,* May 31, 1967.
4. Dave Overpeck, "Foyt Grabs 3D '500' Win," *Indianapolis Star,* June 1, 1967.
5. ABC's *Wide World of Sports,* taped delayed broadcast of the 1967 Indianapolis 500 [ESPN Classic Rebroadcast Version], May 31, 1967.
6. ABC's *Wide World of Sports,* tape delayed broadcast.
7. Dick Mittman, "Voice Has No Car Know-How," *Indianapolis News,* May 22, 1975.
8. Mittman, "Voice Has No Car Know-How."
9. ABC's *Wide World of Sports,* taped delayed broadcast.
10. Ray Marquette, "'I Thought I Was Out of It.'" *Indianapolis Star,* June 1, 1967.
11. Overpeck, "Foyt Grabs 3D '500' Win."
12. A.J. Foyt, November 7, 2019, interview with the author.
13. Cy McBride, "$6 Ball Bearing Takes Ball from Parnelli," *Indianapolis Star,* June 1, 1967.
14. Art Garner and Marc B. Spiegel, *Indy 500 Memories: An Oral History of the Greatest Spectacle in Racing* (CreateSpace Publishing, 2016).
15. Marquette, "'I Thought I Was Out of It.'"
16. A.J. Foyt, November 7, 2019, interview with the author.
17. UPI, "Granatelli Takes Stand for Turbines," *Linton* (Indiana) *Daily Citizen*, March 13, 1968.
18. Wayne Fuson, "Hulman, Hill Win 500 Laughs; Foyt Money," *Indianapolis News,* June 1, 1967.
19. Richard K. Shull, "The Cars Had Stopped, but TV Went On and On," *Indianapolis News,* June 1, 1967.

20. Bob Ottum, "Gentlemen, Junk Your Engines," *Sports Illustrated*, June 12, 1967.
21. Corky Lamm, "Foyt Was a Driver with Plan," *Indianapolis News*, June 1, 1967.
22. Dick Mittman, "Foyt Enjoys 3-Win Idea," *Indianapolis News*, June 1, 1967.
23. Paul Dean, "Instinct Pays Off for Champ Foyt," *Arizona* (Phoenix) *Republic*, June 1, 1967.
24. A.J. Foyt, November 7, 2019, interview with the author.
25. Frank Lance, October 26, 2022, interview with the author.
26. Will Higgins, "When 2 Mercury Astronauts Tried to Keep Their Indy 500 Entry under Wraps," *Indianapolis Star*, May 16, 2017.
27. Jack Starne, interview with the author.
28. Jack Starne, interview with the author.

CHAPTER 25. LE MANS

1. Mario Andretti, 2019 interview with the author.
2. A.J. Foyt, 2019 interview with the author.
3. Frank Litsky, "Gurney, Foyt Win Grueling Le Mans," *New York Times*, June 12, 1967.
4. Earl Scudday, "Some Notes Slipped through the Bars," *Lubbock* (Texas) *Avalanche-Journal*, June 19, 1967.
5. A.J. Foyt, 2019 interview with the author.
6. A.J. Foyt, 2019 interview with the author.
7. A.J. Foyt, 2019 interview with the author.
8. A.J. Foyt, 2019 interview with the author.
9. A.J. Foyt, 2019 interview with the author.
10. Leo Levine, *Ford: The Dust and the Glory, A Racing History* (New York: MacMillan Company, 1968).
11. A.J. Foyt with William Neely, *My Life as America's Greatest Race Car Driver* (New York: Times Books, 1983).
12. Robert Markus, "In the Wake of the News," *Chicago Tribune*, November 29, 1967.
13. Mario Andretti, 2019 interview with the author.
14. More than fifty years later, neither Foyt nor Andretti recalled a meeting of Indy car drivers. "I don't remember us having a meeting, I really don't," Foyt said. "It's possible. I just remember the Shelby team and the other team was always separate. Like I said, it might have been the Indy car drivers, but a lot of times I didn't do things with the other drivers. Maybe I'm an asshole or whatever. I was kinda always with my team or by myself."
15. Marshall Pruett, *Road & Track*, June 6, 2017.
16. Foyt with Neely, *A.J.*
17. Mario Andretti, September 3, 2022, interview with the author.
18. Foyt with Neely, *A.J.*
19. Levine, *Ford: The Dust and the Glory.*
20. Bob Ottum, "The Glorious Double," *Sports Illustrated*, June 19, 1967.
21. Pruett, *Road & Track*, June 6, 2017.
22. Carroll Shelby, 2011 interview with the author.
23. Mark Cole, "Sports Car 365," January 15, 2018.
24. Denis Sargent Jenkinson, "Ford Wins Great Battle," *MotorSport*, July 1967.
25. A.J. Foyt, 2019 interview with the author.
26. Ottum, "The Glorious Double."
27. Mario Andretti with Gordon Kirby, *A Driving Passion* (Phoenix: David Bull Publishing, 2001).
28. Andretti with Kirby, *A Driving Passion.*
29. Ray Marquette, "Andretti Crashes, but Not Hurt Seriously," *Indianapolis Star*, June 11, 1967.
30. A.J. Foyt, 2019 interview with the author.
31. A.J. Foyt, 2019 interview with the author.
32. Dan Gurney, Edison-Ford Medal video, the Henry Ford Museum, 2014.
33. Gurney, Edison-Ford Medal video.
34. Ray Marquette, "Foyt, Gurney Capture Le Mans Grind," *Indianapolis Star*, June 12, 1967.
35. A.J. Foyt, 2019 interview with the author.
36. Michael Argetsinger, *Mark Donohue: Technical Excellence at Speed* (Phoenix: David Bull Publishing, 2009).
37. A.J. Foyt, 2019 interview with the author.
38. Marquette, "Foyt, Gurney Capture Le Mans Grind."
39. Marquette, "Foyt, Gurney Capture Le Mans Grind."
40. John Hall, "The Big Initials," *Los Angeles Times*, November 22, 1974.
41. Tim Considine, *American Grand Prix Racing: A Century of Drivers and Cars* (Minneapolis, MN: Motorbooks International, 1997).
42. Denis Sargent Jenkinson, "Le Mans 24-Hours: Ford Wins a Great Battle," *MotorWeek*, July 1967.
43. "Dan Gurney on 1967's Golden Week," Marshall Pruett podcast, June 16, 2017.
44. Carroll Shelby, 2011 interview with the author.
45. Gurney, Edison-Ford Medal video.
46. Dan Gurney, 2012 interview with the author.
47. Letter from Dan Gurney supplied by All-American Racers, 2021.

48. Dan Gurney and A.J. Foyt, April 7, 2017, video interview with Robin Miller, *Racer Magazine*.
49. Marquette, "Foyt, Gurney Capture Le Mans Grind."
50. A.J. Foyt with William Neely, *My Life as America's Greatest Race Car Driver* (New York: Times Books, 1983).
51. A.J. Foyt, April 19–24, 2021, interviews with the author.
52. A.J. Foyt, 2019 interview with the author.
53. Dan Gurney and A.J. Foyt, April 7, 2017, video interview with Robin Miller, *Racer Magazine*.

CHAPTER 26. RETURN OF THE KING

1. Bob Collins, "Sports over Lightly," *Indianapolis Star*, July 23, 1967.
2. Bob Myers, "The Good Sleep," *Charlotte* (North Carolina) *News*, June 13, 1967.
3. Bob Myers, "The Moods of Foyt," *Charlotte* (North Carolina) *News*, July 3, 1967.
4. Myers, "The Moods of Foyt."
5. Myers, "The Moods of Foyt."
6. Lyle Mannweiler, "USAC Set for Double Race Dose," *Indianapolis News*, June 16, 1967.
7. George Hanson, "Race Organizers Hit Snags," *Montreal Star*, June 17, 1967.
8. A.J. Foyt, 2019 interview with the author.
9. "Leonard Quits Foyt's Team," *Indianapolis Star*, July 20, 1967.
10. A.J. Foyt, 2019 interview with the author.
11. Ed Schuyler, "Foyt Wants to Join Grand Prix Circuit," Associated Press, *Des Moines* (Iowa) *Tribune*, June 22, 1967.
12. Jack Starne, January 13, 2021, interview with the author.
13. Jack Starne, January 13, 2021, interview with the author.
14. Bill Simmons, "Foyt Mellows Despite 'Barren' Trail," *Philadelphia Inquirer*, July 30, 1967.
15. Dick Mittman, "2 Toughs' Move onto USAC Block," *Indianapolis News*, September 11, 1967.
16. Ray Marquette, "Whipping Foyt Gives Mario 'Special Glow,'" *Indianapolis Star*, September 10, 1967.
17. Skip Hess, "Wingfoot's in Mouth," *Kokomo* (Indiana) *Morning Times*, September 22, 1967.
18. "Foyt Switching," *Dayton* (Ohio) *Daily News*, October 8, 1967.
19. Lyle Mannweiler, "Goodyear Cancels Foyt's Contract," *Indianapolis News*, September 20, 1967.
20. Ray Marquette, "Early Crash Sends Mario to Sidelines," *Indianapolis Star*, September 25, 1967.
21. Bill Simmons, "Foyt Roars from Last, Wins Wreck-Marred Trenton 200," *Philadelphia Inquirer*, September 25, 1967.
22. Associated Press, "Foyt Tacks Trenton Victory to Skein of Auto Race Laurels," *Shamokin* (Pennsylvania) *News-Dispatch*, September 25, 1967.
23. Associated Press, "Foyt Tacks Trenton Victory to Skein of Auto Race Laurels."
24. Don Bloom, "Foyt Sets Mark with 4th Capital Win," *Sacramento* (California) *Bee*, October 2, 1967.
25. Bob Moore, "Foyt Says He'll Outrun Them All," *Charlotte* (North Carolina) *Observer*, October 12, 1967.
26. Jim Ayello, "Why 1967 Produced the Greatest Starting Field in Indianapolis 500 History," *USA Today*, May 27, 2017.
27. A.J. Foyt, November 7, 2019, interview with the author.
28. "Foyt Is Fourth; Andretti Spins," *Indianapolis Star*, October 23, 1967.
29. Bob Thomas, "Foyt Plans No 'Caution' for Payoff Race," *Los Angeles Times*, November 23, 1967.
30. Bob Thomas, "Gurney Has Flat, but Wins Weird '300,'" *Los Angeles Times*, November 27, 1967.
31. "Press Notes," Riverside International Raceway, November 26, 1967.
32. Thomas, "Gurney Has Flat, but Wins Weird '300.'"
33. Bruce Grant, "A.J. Foyt 'King of Road' after Fifth-Place Finish," *San Bernadino* (California) *Sun-Telegram*, November 27, 1967.
34. Bill Libby, *Foyt* (New York: Hawthorn Books, 1974).
35. Associated Press, "Foyt Wins Title; Gurney, the Race," *Santa Cruz* (California) *Sentinel*, November 27, 1967.
36. Dennis Wood, "McCluskey Defends Car Loan to Foyt," *Arizona* (Phoenix) *Republic*, December 1, 1967.
37. "Sporting Gesture," *Indianapolis News*, January 12, 1968.
38. Wood, "McCluskey Defends Car Loan to Foyt."
39. "Press Notes," Riverside International Raceway, November 26, 1967.
40. Wood, "McCluskey Defends Car Loan to Foyt."
41. Bob Myers, "Profile of a Champion," *Charlotte* (North Carolina) *News*, January 6, 1968.
42. Myers, "Profile of a Champion."
43. Myers, "Profile of a Champion."
44. "Ford Honors Foyt," *Indianapolis News*, January 5, 1968.
45. A.J. Foyt, May 22, 2021, interview.

CHAPTER 27. TAXICABS AND TURBOS

1. UPI, "Clark Called Greatest," *Columbus* (Indiana) *Republic*, April 8, 1968.
2. David Tremayne, *Jim Clark. The Best of the Best*. (United Kingdom: Evro Publishing Limited, 2018).

3. Jim Ayello, "Why 1967 Produced the Greatest Starting Field in Indianapolis 500 History," *USA Today*, May 27, 2017.

4. Dennis Wood, "Rutherford Injured in 3-Car Mishap," *Arizona* (Phoenix) *Republic*, April 8, 1968.

5. William Nack, "Twilight of a Titan" *Sports Illustrated*, September 30, 1991.

6. Johnny Rutherford and David Craft, *Lone Star J.R.* (Chicago: Triumph Books, 2000).

7. Rutherford and Craft, *Lone Star J.R.*

8. Bob Garner, "Why Speed Increase?" *Redwood City* (California) *Tribune*, February 23, 1968.

9. Lyle Mannweiler, "A.J. Foyt Yankee 250 Winner, but Real Action Came Later," *Indianapolis News*, May 6, 1968.

10. Dave Overpeck, "Foyt Starts Last, Wins Yankee the Hard Way," *Indianapolis Star*, May 6, 1968.

11. Mark Morrow, "Urge to Win, A.J.'s Main 'Driving Force,'" *Kokomo* (Indiana) *Tribune*, May 28, 1968.

12. Wayne Fuson, "A.J. Predicts 171 for Pole," *Indianapolis News*, May 15, 1968.

13. Ray Marquette, "Foyt 'Sure' of Going Full 500," *Indianapolis Star*, May 20, 1968.

14. "Brawl Suit Charges Foyt and McCluskey," *Indianapolis Star*, May 25, 1968.

15. "Brawl Suit Charges Foyt and McCluskey," *Indianapolis Star*.

16. "$200,000 Suit against Foyt, 2 Others Dismissed," *Indianapolis Star*, September 13, 1968.

17. Cy McBride, "Foyt Phasing Out but Still Wants Fourth 500 Victory," *Indianapolis Star*, May 31, 1968.

18. McBride, "Foyt Phasing Out but Still Wants Fourth 500 Victory."

19. Ray Marquette, "A.J. Foyt Easily Captures Road Race," *Indianapolis Star*, July 8, 1968.

20. Associated Press, "A.J. Foyt Wins Miller 200 Race," *La Crosse* (Wisconsin) *Tribune*, July 15, 1968.

21. Al Dunning, "The Weekend That Was," *Evansville* (Indiana) *Press*, July 22, 1968.

22. Barry Cobb, "Sleepy Foyt Wins at Tri-County," *Cincinnati Post*, September 14, 1968.

23. Art Glattke, "Pit Stop," *Modesto* (California) *Bee*, November 8, 1968.

24. Pete Erickson, "Bettenhausen Survives Demolition Race," *Tucson* (Arizona) *Daily Citizen*, November 18, 1968.

CHAPTER 28. DRIVER OF THE DECADE

1. Ryan Bees, "Petty Debuts with Ford by Winning Rain-Delayed Riverside 500," *San Bernardino* (California) *County Sun*, February 2, 1969.

2. "Foyt Offers 'Good' Words," *AutoWeek & Competition Press*, March 15, 1969.

3. John Lyst, "Participating Companies Find 500 Race Big Asset," *Indianapolis Star*, March 5, 1969.

4. Dick Mittman, "McCluskey Out to Beat His Boss A.J. Foyt," *Indianapolis News*, May 9, 1969.

5. Pete Erickson, "McCluskey Has New Wheels for Bryan," *Tucson* (Arizona) *Daily Citizen*, March 29, 1969.

6. "Foyt to Qualify at IRP; USAC May Face Law Suit," *Indianapolis Star*, April 27, 1969.

7. "Trenton Yields to Indianapolis Race," *Terre Haute* (Indiana) *Tribune*, May 1, 1969.

8. Mittman, "McCluskey Out to Beat His Boss A.J. Foyt."

9. George Moore, "Aerodynamics Not Just for the Birds," *Indianapolis Star*, May 16, 1969.

10. Ray Marquette, "Foyt Came to Win—A Logical Thought," *Indianapolis Star*, May 11, 1969.

11. Mario Andretti with Bob Collins, *What's It Like Out There?* (New York: Bantam Books, 1970).

12. Joe Hamelin, "Foyt, Stablemate McCluskey Unwind . . . Like Two Coyotes," *Indianapolis Star*, May 25, 1969.

13. Dale Burgess, "Unhappy Foyt on Pole," Associated Press, *Muncie* (Indiana) *Star Press*, May 25, 1969.

14. Ray Marquette, "Engine Goes Thunk, Foyt Grumbles," *Indianapolis Star*, May 25, 1969.

15. Dick Mittman, "Pole Was Yesterday; Racing Is Today for A.J.," *Indianapolis News*, May 26, 1969.

16. Star Speedway Staff, "Pit Pass," *Indianapolis Star*, May 25, 1969.

17. Wayne Fuson, "A.J. Steps Aside to Honor Top Mechanic, His Father," *Indianapolis News*, May 28, 1969.

18. Fuson, "A.J. Steps Aside To Honor Top Mechanic, His Father."

19. Richard K. Shull, "One Thing and Another and He Had a Big Deal," *Indianapolis News*, June 14, 1968.

20. Jack Martin, "A.J. Foyt Takes His 500s 'One at a Time,'" *Lafayette* (Indiana) *Journal and Courier*, May 27, 1969.

21. Martin, "A.J. Foyt Takes His 500s 'One at a Time.'"

22. Shav Glick, "Andretti's New Air Cooler Outlawed at Indy," *Los Angeles Times*, May 29, 1969.

23. Dave Overpeck, "Fengler Changes Mind; Foyt Gets Culprit Role," *Indianapolis Star*, May 29, 1969.

24. Shav Glick, "Andretti's New Air Cooler Outlawed at Indy," *Los Angeles Times*, May 29, 1969.

25. Glick, "Andretti's New Air Cooler Outlawed at Indy."

26. Glick, "Andretti's New Air Cooler Outlawed at Indy."

27. Shav Glick, "Foyt Confident He Can Triumph . . . Pole to Flag at Indy Today," *Los Angeles Times*, May 30, 1969.

28. Shav Glick, "Andretti, Granatelli Shatter Indy Jinx," *Los Angeles Times*, May 31, 1969.

29. Dave Overpeck, "24-Minute Stop Foils Foyt in Bid for 4th," *Indianapolis Star*, May 31, 1969.

30. Dave Overpeck, "Mario Exception to Track Serenity," *Indianapolis Star*, June 1, 1969.

31. Ray Marquette, "Desire Rates High with Parnelli," *Indianapolis Star*, June 17, 1969

32. A.J. Foyt, November 7, 2019, interview with the author.

33. UPI, "Racing Still Fun for A.J., Despite Father's Wishes," *Indianapolis Star*, June 4, 1969.
34. Lyle Mannweiler, "Fairgrounds Winner A.J. Is a Mellow Fellow Now," *Indianapolis News*, June 23, 1969.
35. Larry Rea, "McCluskey Wins the 200; Calls Course the Toughest," *Memphis Commercial Appeal*, June 30, 1969.
36. Ray Marquette, "Unser, Ford Triumph at DuQuoin; Fuelless Car Foils Foyt," *Indianapolis Star*, September 2, 1969.
37. Ray Marquette, "Du Quoin Plans Same Program," *Indianapolis Star*, September 3, 1969.
38. Johnny Rutherford, 2020 interview with the author.
39. Ray Marquette, "'This One, 500,' Are Races A.J. Wants to Win," *Indianapolis Star*, September 7, 1969.
40. Kyle Griffin, "USAC Fills Memphis' October Book," *Memphis Commercial Appeal*, September 9, 1969.
41. Tommy Horton, "Road Racing Title on the Line," *Memphis Press-Scimitar*, October 24, 1969.
42. Tommy Horton, "Foyt Is Amazingly Calm," *Memphis Press-Scimitar*, October 21, 1969.
43. Pete Erickson, "Roger Trades Foyt for Brawner—And Away He Goes," *Tucson* (Arizona) *Daily Citizen*, November 4, 1969.
44. Ron Lemasters, "Racing Around," *Muncie* (Indiana) *Star Press*, December 7, 1969.
45. Dave Overpeck, "The 'Dirt' On Racing Game," *Indianapolis Star*, December 14, 1969.
46. George Moore, "Foyt Gets Ford 500 Offer," *Indianapolis Star*, November 26, 1969.

CHAPTER 29. TURNING POINTS

1. Jack Lattimer, "Big Year for NASCAR," *San Mateo* (California) *Times*, January 22, 1970.
2. Bloys Britt, "A.J. Foyt Claims Travel Is Getting to Be a Chore," *High Point* (North Carolina) *Enterprise*, October 11, 1969.
3. Tommy Horton, "Foyt Is Amazingly Calm," *Memphis* (Tennessee) *Press-Scimitar*, October 21, 1969.
4. Mike Murphy, "Foyt Outlives Riverside 500 Jinx," *San Bernardino* (California) *County Sun*, January 19, 1970.
5. Shav Glick, "Parnelli's Clutch Fails; Foyt Wins at Riverside," *Los Angeles Times*, January 19, 1970.
6. Glick, "Parnelli's Clutch Fails; Foyt Wins at Riverside."
7. Glick, "Parnelli's Clutch Fails; Foyt Wins at Riverside."
8. Associated Press, "'Fat' Foyt Can't Find Vee Formula, *Tampa Bay* (Florida) *Times*, February 7, 1970.
9. Bloys Britt, "Stott Takes ARCA 300 at Daytona," Associated Press, *Fort Pierce* (Florida) *News Tribune*, February 16, 1970.
10. Donnie Allison, July 7, 2020, interview with the author.
11. Dale Burgess, "Foyt after Fourth Indy 500 Victory," Associated Press, *Seymour* (Indiana) *Tribune*, May 13, 1970.
12. Donnie Allison, July 7, 2020, interview with the author.
13. Peter Golenbock, *Miracle: Bobby Allison and the Saga of the Alabama Gang* (New York: St. Martin's Press, 2006).
14. Joe Hamnelin, "Vuky No Longer Whipping a Dead Horse," *Indianapolis Star*, May 3, 1970.
15. Ray Marquette, "USAC Scans Shrinkage after Foyt's Triumph," *Indianapolis Star*, March 16, 1970.
16. Ray Marquette, "Ford's Racing Population Flays Away at A.J.," *Indianapolis Star*, March 17, 1970.
17. Marquette, "Ford's Racing Population Flays Away at A.J."
18. "People," *Sports Illustrated*, April 20, 1970.
19. "People," *Sports Illustrated*, April 20, 1970.
20. Richard K. Shull, "About Those Two Cubs Orphaned on an Ice Cap," *Indianapolis News*, January 29, 1971.
21. A.J. Foyt, April 19–24, 2021, interviews with the author.
22. Don White, "The Foyts of Texas," *Evansville* (Indiana) *Courier and Press*, May 10, 1970.
23. Bob Moore, "Lure of Indy Has Allison Ready to Go," *Charlotte* (North Carolina) *Observer*, March 22, 1970.
24. Terry Foyt, April 21, 2021, interview with the author.
25. Ron Lemasters, "Racing Around," *Muncie* (Indiana) *Star Press*, May 10, 1970.
26. Terry Foyt, April 21, 2021, interview with the author.
27. Lemasters, "Racing Around."
28. A.J. Foyt, April 19–24, 2021, interviews with the author.
29. Dick Mittman, "A.J.'s 3rd Yank 250 Starts 500 Thoughts," *Indianapolis News*, May 4, 1970.
30. Terry Foyt, April 21, 2021, interview with the author.
31. Terry Foyt, April 21, 2021, interview with the author.
32. Mittman, "A.J.'s 3rd Yank 250 Starts 500 Thoughts."
33. Ray Marquette, "A.J. Foyt Wins Yankee 250 3rd Time," *Indianapolis Star*, May 4, 1970.
34. Ron Lemasters, "Numerologists Say 1970 Is Year for A.J. to Win Again," *Muncie* (Indiana) *Star Press*, May 27, 1970.
35. Donald Davidson, "NASCAR's Allison Brothers Shed Fenders, Showed Skill at Indy during 1970s," IMS (website), June 11, 2020.
36. "Veteran NASCAR Driver Discovers He's Only a Rookie at the Speedway," *Lafayette* (Indiana) *Journal and Courier*, May 26, 1970.

37. Star Speedway Staff, "Pit Notes," *Indianapolis Star*, May 17, 1970.
38. Associated Press, "Chevy Salesman Hopes to Win 500 Mile Race with Ford Engine," *Rushville* (Indiana) *Republican*, May 8, 1970.
39. Donnie Allison, July 7, 2020, interview with the author.
40. John Bansch, "Some Mechs Stand Taller than Others," *Indianapolis News*, May 29, 1970.
41. Dick Mittman, "It's Four for A.J. Foyt, Who's Going for 4 Too," *Indianapolis News*, May 25, 1970.
42. Don Compton, "McElreath Puts 4th Foyt Car In," Richmond (Indiana) Palladium-Item, May 25, 1970.
43. Bruce Ramey, "Minute Details Keys to Victory," *Lafayette* (Indiana) *Journal and Courier*, May 28, 1970.
44. John Bansch, "Record 500 Title Eludes Foyt Again," *Indianapolis Star*, May 31, 1970.
45. Bansch, "Record 500 Title Eludes Foyt Again."
46. Bansch, "Record 500 Title Eludes Foyt Again."
47. Donnie Allison, July 7, 2020, interview with the author.
48. Al Unser, December 16, 2020, interview with the author.
49. John Jopes, "A.J. Wreck Gave Jimmy Shot at Win," *Upland* (California) *Daily Report*, September 7, 1970.
50. Ontario Race Notes Column, *Indianapolis News*, September 7, 1970.
51. Shav Glick, "180,223 See McElreath Win 500 by 2 Seconds," *Los Angeles Times*, September 7, 1970.
52. Allen Wolfe, "No Tears as Gurney Puts Brakes to Driving Career," *Long Beach* (California) *Independent Press-Telegram*, October 6, 1970.
53. Dick Mittman, "Ward Says Foyt Should Quit," *Indianapolis News*, October 8, 1970.
54. Ron Lemasters, "A.J. Plans to Retire?" *Muncie* (Indiana) *Star Press*, September 27, 1970.
55. Woody Holm, "Foyt Accepts Challenge of Lonely Tunnel," *Ontario Daily Report*, September 1, 1970.
56. Allen Wolfe, "David Pearson: He's Pinching Pennies Now," *Long Beach* (California) *Independent Press-Telegram*, January 21, 1971.
57. Bob Latshaw, "Auto Racing Shock Wave . . . Ford Pulls Out of Sport!" *Detroit Free Press*, November 21, 1970.
58. Tom Cotter and Al Pearce, *Holman-Moody, the Legendary Race Team*, 2nd ed. (Austin: Octane Press, 2013).
59. Charlie Henry, *Kar-Kraft: Ford's Specialty Vehicle Activity Program* (Forest Lake, MN: CarTech Books, 2017).

CHAPTER 30. FORD OUT, FOYT IN

1. Jim Kyle, "Wedges May Give Foyt Inside Track at Indy," *Baytown* (Texas) *Sun*, April 20, 1971.
2. Charlie Gray, October 2022 interview with the author.
3. Charlie Gray, October 2022 interview with the author.
4. Bloys Britt, "What Do the Drivers Say?" Associated Press *Durham* (North Carolina) *Sun*, November 21, 1970.
5. Cale Yarborough, 2021 interview with the author.
6. Bloys Britt, "Plumpish A.J. Foyt Already Laying Plans for Indy 500," Associated Press, *Paducah Sun*, December 25, 1970.
7. Britt, "Plumpish A.J. Foyt Already Laying Plans for Indy 500."
8. Blake Z. Rong, "Jim Hall and the Chaparral 2J: The Story of America's Most Extreme Race Car," *Road & Track*, January 23, 2017.
9. "Donohue's 'Vacuum Cleaner' Ready (if Needed) for Indy," *Star-Gazette* (Elmira, New York), January 17, 1971.
10. Bob Riley with Jonathan Ingram. *The Art Of Race Car Design*. (United Kingdom: Icon Publishing, 2015).
11. Bob Riley, February 18, 2021, interview with the author.
12. Bob Riley, February 18, 2021, interview with the author.
13. Ray Marquette, "USAC Turns Down Foyt Car Proposal," *Indianapolis Star*, January 24, 1971.
14. Bob Riley, February 18, 2021, interview with the author.
15. Bob Moore, "Foyt, Wood Brothers Team," *Charlotte* (North Carolina) *Observer*, January 16, 1971.
16. Bob Moore, "Foyt's Advantage—Wood Brothers' Work," *Charlotte* (North Carolina) *Observer*, April 6, 1971.
17. Leonard Wood, April 15, 2020, interview with the author.
18. Leonard Wood, April 15, 2020, interview with the author.
19. Leonard Wood, April 15, 2020, interview with the author.
20. Leonard Wood, April 15, 2020, interview with the author.
21. Bloys Britt, "Restrictor Plates Trouble Designer," Associated Press, *Del Rio* (Texas) *News Herald*, February 4, 1971.
22. Bucky Albers, "Cale's Car Displaying Foyt Look," *Dayton* (Ohio) *Journal Herald*, February 11, 1971.
23. Benny Phillips, "Benny Phillips Talks about Racing," *High Point* (North Carolina) *Enterprise*, February 12, 1971.
24. Phillips, "Benny Phillips Talks about Racing."
25. Phillips, "Benny Phillips Talks about Racing."

26. Allen Wolfe, "A.J. Foyt's Philosophy: 'First Place or Nothing,'" *Long Beach* (California) *Independent Press-Telegram*, February 26, 1971.
27. Jack Flowers, "Richard Petty Gets Checkered Flag at Daytona," *Palm Beach* (Florida) *Post*, February 15, 1971.
28. Bucky Albers, "Foyt Error Helps Petty," *Dayton* (Ohio) *Journal Herald*.
29. Phillips, "Benny Phillips Talks about Racing."
30. Phillips, "Benny Phillips Talks about Racing."
31. Bob Myers, "To Lose—and Win," *Charlotte* (North Carolina) *News*, February 1971.
32. "Foyt Cashes in Again at Ontario," March 1, 1971.
33. Associated Press, "Foyt, with Ace Pit Crew, Wins Miller," *Monroe* (Louisiana) *News-Star*. March 1, 1971.
34. Wayne Biessert, "What Price Glory?" *Bridgewater* (New Jersey) *Courier-News*, March 5, 1971.
35. Pat Ray, "Al Unser Phoenix Victor; Bobby 2nd," *Los Angeles Times*, March 28, 1971.
36. Shav Glick, "Questor Race 'Most Important'—Stewart," *Los Angeles Times*, March 14, 1971.
37. Glick, "Questor Race 'Most Important'—Stewart."
38. Allen Wolfe, "Stewart: He's a Travelin' Man," *Long Beach* (California) *Independent Press-Telegram*, March 12, 1971.
39. Ryan Rees, "Stewart on Pole, but Ickx Should Win Race," *San Bernardino* (California) *County Sun*, March 28, 1971.
40. Racing Sports Cars, home page, https://www.racingsportscars.com.
41. "Andretti Wins Questor Prix," *Long Beach* (California) *Independent Press-Telegram*, March 29, 1971.

CHAPTER 31. A.J. FOYT VS. TIME INC.

1. Bob Moore, "Foyt's Advantage—Wood Brothers' Work," *Charlotte* (North Carolina) *Observer*, April 6, 1971.
2. A.J. Foyt, April 19–24, 2021, interviews with the author.
3. Al Thomy, "A.J. Quietly Makes Mark," *Atlanta Constitution*, April 2, 1971.
4. Thomy, "A.J. Quietly Makes Mark."
5. "Drivers Enjoy Fete at Governor's Mansion," *Atlanta Constitution*, April 2, 1971.
6. Gwilym S. Brown, "It's Not How Long You Wear Your Hair But . . . ," *Sports Illustrated*, April 5, 1971.
7. Jim Hunter, "Foyt Angered by Magazine," *Atlanta Constitution*, April 4, 1971.
8. Hunter, "Foyt Angered by Magazine."
9. Hunter, "Foyt Angered by Magazine."
10. Benny Phillips, "Foyt Apologizes, but Wins at Atlanta," *High Point* (North Carolina) *Enterprise*, April 5, 1971.
11. Phillips, "Foyt Apologizes, but Wins at Atlanta,"
12. Phillips, "Foyt Apologizes, but Wins at Atlanta."
13. Tom Powell, "Magazine Quotes Draw Foyt's Fire," *Nashville Tennessean*, April 5, 1971.
14. Jackie Stewart, April 28, 2022, interview with the author.
15. Associated Press, "Foyt Sues Time," *Brownwood* (Texas) *Bulletin*, August 20, 1971.
16. A.J. Foyt, April 19–24, 2021, interviews with the author.
17. UPI, "Foyt Charges Misquote in Libel Suit for Million," *Camden* (New Jersey) *Courier-Post*, June 19, 1973.
18. UPI, "Foyt Libel Quote Traced," *Argus* (Fremont, California), June 21, 1973.
19. Associated Press, "Libel Suit Continues," *Terre Haute* (Indiana) *Tribune*, June 20, 1973.
20. A.J. Foyt with William Neely, *A.J.: My Life as America's Greatest Race Car Driver* (New York: Times Books, 1983).
21. A.J. Foyt, April 19–24, 2021, interviews with the author.
22. Jim Kyle, "Foyt Captured First Race at 17," *Baytown* (Texas) *Sun*, April 18, 1971.
23. Dick Mittman, "Foyt Wishes No. 4 a Winged Victory," *Indianapolis News*, May 14, 1971.
24. Wayne Fuson, "Gentlemen, Start Your Pocketbooks," *Indianapolis News*, May 11, 1971.
25. Bob Riley, February 18, 2021, interview with the author.
26. Bob Riley, February 18, 2021, interview with the author.
27. Jim Kyle, "Wedges May Give Foyt Inside Track at Indy," *Baytown* (Texas) *Sun*, April 20, 1971.
28. Associated Press, "Foyt Unveils New '500' Car," *Munster* (Indiana) *Times*, April 29, 1971.
29. Darrell Mack, "Foyt Confident," UPI, *Franklin* (Indiana) *Daily Journal*, April 30, 1971.
30. Bob Riley, February 18, 2021, interview with the author.
31. Bob Riley, February 18, 2021, interview with the author.
32. Gordon Kirby, *Penske's Maestro: Karl Kainhofer and the History of Penske Racing* (Boston: Racemaker Press, 2016).
33. George Moore, "Foyt Doesn't Fear Mark's Wolf," *Indianapolis Star*, May 8, 1971.
34. Ray Marquette, "Mark Tops 172.5 Mph on 18 Laps at Track," *Indianapolis Star*, May 6, 1971.
35. Bob Riley, February 18, 2021, interview with the author.
36. Bob Riley, February 18, 2021, interview with the author.
37. Donnie Allison, July 7, 2020, interview with the author.
38. Bob Moore, "D. Allison Selected to Drive for Woods," *Charlotte* (North Carolina) *Observer*, April 9, 1971.

39. Bob Riley, February 18, 2021, interview with the author.
40. Donnie Allison, July 7, 2020, interview with the author.
41. Donnie Allison, July 7, 2020, interview with the author.
42. Donnie Allison, July 7, 2020, interview with the author.
43. Donnie Allison, July 7, 2020, interview with the author.
44. Bloys Britt, "A.J. Foyt Makes Masterful Move," Associated Press, *Terre Haute* (Indiana) *Tribune-Star*, May 23, 1971.
45. Jim Hunter, "Woods Join Foyt at Indy," *Atlanta Journal and Constitution*, April 11, 1971.
46. Bloys Britt "Foyt Adds Mechanic to Speedway Crew," Associated Press, *Salem* (Oregon) *Statesman*, May 26, 1971.
47. Mike Tarpey, "Manifold Problem Slows Foyt," *Indianapolis Star*, May 30, 1971.
48. Donnie Allison, July 7, 2020, interview with the author.
49. Don White, "Super Tex Rides Again," *Evansville* (Indiana) *Courier and Press*, May 30, 1971.
50. Shav Glick, "Unser Switches to Offy," *Los Angeles Times*, September 3, 1971.
51. Dick Mittman, "A.J. (and Only A.J.) and Ford (and Only Ford) in '71," *Indianapolis News*, September 9, 1971.
52. Mittman, "A.J. (and Only A.J.) and Ford (and Only Ford) in '71."
53. Tom Powell, "Magazine Quotes Draw Foyt's Fire," *Nashville Tennessean*, April 5, 1971.
54. Donnie Allison, July 7, 2020, interview with the author.
55. Peter Golenbock, *Miracle: Bobby Allison and the Saga of the Alabama Gang* (New York: St. Martin's Press, 2006).
56. Donnie Allison, July 7, 2020, interview with the author.
57. Ed Hinton, "Forgotten Man from Hueytown," *Atlanta Constitution*, March 13, 1988; A.J. Foyt, 2021 interview with the author.
58. Dick Mittman, "A.J. (and Only A.J.) and Ford (and Only Ford) in '71," *Indianapolis News*, September 9, 1971.
59. Mike Garrett, "A.J. Grabs First Win since 1969," *Arizona Republic*, October 24, 1971.
60. Bob Myers, "Foyt Bad News for Stockers," *Charlotte* (North Carolina) *News*, October 22, 1971.
61. Myers, "Foyt Bad News for Stockers."
62. Myers, "Foyt Bad News for Stockers."

CHAPTER 32. DAYTONA TO DU QUOIN

1. Phil Flinck, "Versatile Foyt in Pole Lead," *San Francisco Examiner*, January 21, 1972.
2. Shav Glick, "Petty Wins Foggy Race at Riverside," *Los Angeles Times*, January 24, 1972.
3. Bill Verigan, "Spinnin' Wheels," *New York Daily News*, February 13, 1972.
4. Verigan, "Spinnin' Wheels."
5. Bloys Britt, "Beating A.J. Foyt for Pole Big Thrill," Associated Press, *Rocky Mount* (North Carolina) *Telegram*, February 14, 1972.
6. Bloys Britt "Isaac Wins Daytona Pole as Predicted by Foyt's Dream," Associated Press, *Rocky Mount* (North Carolina) *Telegram*, February 13, 1972.
7. Britt, "Isaac Wins Daytona Pole as Predicted by Foyt's Dream."
8. Bloys Britt, "Mark Donohue Knows Chances Loom Slim in Daytona 500," Associated Press, *Miami Herald*, February 16, 1972.
9. Allen Wolfe, "Foyt Wears Stocker Hat Today in '500,'" *Long Beach* (California) *Independent Press-Telegram*, January 23, 1972.
10. Associated Press, "Friday Hassler Killed in Daytona Smashup," *Atlanta Constitution*, February 18, 1972.
11. "Thoughts of Death Hang Heavy on Racers' Minds," *Charlotte* (North Carolina) *News and Observer*, February 20, 1972.
12. Leonard Laye, "Living with Death," *Gastonia* (North Carolina) *Gazette*, February 20, 1972.
13. Donnie Allison, July 7, 2020, interview with the author.
14. Leonard Wood, April 15, 2020, interview with the author.
15. Leonard Laye, "Foyt Never Had to Eat Words," *Gastonia* (North Carolina) *Gazette*, February 21, 1972.
16. Bob Moore, "A.J. Foyt Captures 'Dull' Daytona 500," *Charlotte* (North Carolina) *Observer*, February 21, 1972.
17. A.J. Foyt, 2019 interview with the author.
18. F.T. MacFeely, "Foyt Gets 'Another Dream' in Biggest Stock Car Race," Associated Press, *Fort Myers* (Florida) *News Pilot*, February 21, 1972.
19. MacFeely, "Foyt Gets 'Another Dream' in Biggest Stock Car Race."
20. Bob Di Pietre, "Foyt's Goal: To Win Record Fourth Indy 500," UPI, *Harlingen* (Texas) *Valley Morning Star*, February 27, 1972.
21. Shav Glick, "Foyt Fast, Then Faster to Win Pole for Miller 500 at 153.217," *Los Angeles Times*, March 3, 1972.
22. Leonard Wood, April 15, 2020, interview with the author.
23. Glick, "Foyt Fast, Then Faster to Win Pole for Miller 500 at 153,217."
24. Shav Glick, "Foyt Does It Again in Miller 500 at Ontario," *Los Angeles Times*, March 6, 1972.

25. Dave Daniel, "Just Call Miller 500 Foyt's Show," *Pomona* (California) *Progress-Bulletin*, March 6, 1972.
26. Jim Fulton, "Wood Brothers Get Credit," *Pomona* (California) *Progress-Bulletin*, March 6, 1972.
27. "ABC's Chris Economaki Is the 'Foyt' of Announcing," *Baytown* (Texas) *Sun*, March 12, 1972.
28. Joe Buckles, "Gary Bettenhausen Survives Rough Dome to Win Houston," *Terre Haute* (Indiana) *Star*, March 17, 1972.
29. Allen Wolfe, "A.J. Wins by 'Nose' in Miller 500," *Long Beach* (California) *Independent Press-Telegram*, March 6, 1972.
30. Ray Holliman, "Wood Brothers Still Fastest," *Florida Today*, February 22, 1972.
31. Gerald Martin, "Atlanta Chase Set for Today," *Charlotte* (North Carolina) *News and Observer*, March 26, 1972.
32. Martin, "Atlanta Chase Set for Today."
33. Phil Finch, "Allison's Futile Chase," *San Francisco Examiner*, March 6, 1972.
34. Sig Splichal, "Allison Breaks Chevy Jinx at Atlanta," March 27, 1972.
35. Bob Riley, 2020 interview with the author.
36. Don White, "Super Tex Rides Again," *Evansville* (Indiana) *Courier and Press*, May 30, 1971.
37. UPI, "New Jones Team Looks Awesome on Racing Trail," *Ogden* (Utah) *Standard-Examiner*, November 5, 1971.
38. Shav Glick, "Racing's Super Revolution: Viceroy Packs Men, Machine," *Los Angeles Times*, March 10, 1972.
39. Bob Riley, February 18, 2021, interview with the author.
40. Bob Riley, February 18, 2021, interview with the author.
41. UPI, "There's a Foyt in A.J.'s Future," *Santa Rosa* (California) *Press Democrat*, April 28, 1972.
42. Glick, "Racing's Super Revolution: Viceroy Packs Men, Machine."
43. Ray Marquette, "Jigger Alone in Speedway Rain," *Indianapolis Star*, May 9, 1972.
44. Bob Riley, February 18, 2021, interview with the author.
45. Jack Martin, "A.J. Competitor All the Way," *Lafayette* (Indiana) *Journal and Courier*, May 23, 1972.
46. "A Happy Day for Foyt," *Franklin* (Indiana) *Daily Journal*, May 20, 1972.
47. Dick Mittman, "Ford: Going, Going . . ." *Indianapolis News*, May 19, 1972.
48. Dick Mittman, "500 Needs Younger, Stronger Officials: A.J.," *Indianapolis News*, June 13, 1972.
49. Associated Press, "Some Speedway Officials Old, Quick on the Draw: A.J. Foyt," *Kokomo* (Indiana) *Tribune*, June 14, 1972.
50. Associated Press, "Some Speedway Officials Old, Quick on the Draw: A.J. Foyt."
51. William Nack, "Twilight of Titans," *Sports Illustrated*, September 30, 1991.
52. Foyt Racing, "Q&A with Jack Starne," March 13, 2020. https://www.foytracing.com/single-post/2020/04/13/QA-with-Jack-Starne/.
53. UPI, "A.J. Foyt Out for Two Months," *Jasper* (Indiana) *Herald*, May 30, 1972.
54. Mittman, "500 Needs Younger, Stronger Officials: A.J."

CHAPTER 33. TAKING CARE OF BUSINESS

1. Larry Bortstein, "The Rich Men of American Sports," *Family Weekly*, June 3, 1973.
2. Dan Jedlicka, "Foyt Prefers Talking Business to His Chances at Indianapolis," *Chicago Sun Times*, April 25, 1973.
3. Bob Ottum, "Champion of the Old Guard," *Sports Illustrated*, June 1, 1964.
4. Paul Burga, "Power," *Texas Monthly*, December 1987.
5. Bob Moore, "First or Nothing Is Foyt's Game," *Charlotte* (North Carolina) *Observer*, April 1, 1973.
6. A.J. Foyt, April 19–24, 2021, interviews with the author.
7. Paul Burga, "Power," *Texas Monthly*, December 1987.
8. John Maddrey, "Chuck Barnes," *Fort Lauderdale* (Florida) *News*, March 17, 1969.
9. Bob Gaines, "The Screaming World of A.J. Foyt," *Family Weekly*, February 6, 1966.
10. *Fort Worth Star Telegram*, June 2, 1965.
11. Jim Greer, 2020 interview with the author.
12. Jim Greer, 2020 interview with the author.
13. Tim Delrose, 2020 interview with the author.
14. Benny Phillips, "A.J. Foyt All Smiles over New Indy Car," *High Point* (North Carolina) *Enterprise*, March 31, 1973.
15. Lucy Foyt, April 2, 2020, interview with the author.
16. A.J. Foyt, April 19–24, 2021, interviews with the author.
17. Dick Mittman, "Leonard Has 'Winning' Ideas," *Indianapolis News*, May 2, 1969.
18. A.J. Foyt, April 19–24, 2021, interviews with the author.
19. Bill Verigan, "A Prerace Appraisal on the Crashes," *New York Daily News*, May 28, 1973.
20. Bob Renner, "Money Talks Fast in Auto Racing; Little Fella Hurtin,'" *Indianapolis News*, April 7, 1972.
21. "Sammy Sessions Seeking His First Victory Here," *Terre Haute* (Indiana) *Tribune*, August 2, 1973.
22. Ron Roach, "Crutches Make A.J. Cranky," *San Bernardino County* (California) *Sun*, August 29, 1972.
23. UPI, "Al Unser Takes Lead Early, Holds It to Edge A.J. Foyt," *Muncie* (Indiana) *Star Press*, August 21, 1972.

24. Glen Banner, "A.J. Foyt: The Driver, the Legend," *Kokomo* (Indiana) *Tribune*, January 28, 1973.
25. Bob Moore, "Wood Stable Poses Threat to Dominate," *Charlotte* (North Carolina) *Observer*, October 5, 1972.
26. Moore, "Wood Stable Poses Threat to Dominate."
27. "Script Changes for A.J., David," *Gastonia* (North Carolina) *Gazette*, October 9, 1972.
28. Bob Moore, "Only One Car," December 3, 1972.
29. Leonard Wood, April 15, 2020, interview with the author.
30. Bloys Britt, "Foyt Gets the Bull, Baker the Horns," Associated Press, *Charlotte* (North Carolina) *News*, November 11, 1972.
31. "Baker Noses Out Foyt at Finish," *Charlotte* (North Carolina) *Observer*, November 13, 1972.
32. Bloys Britt, "Baker Wins over Foyt," Associated Press, *Fort Worth* (Texas) *Star-Telegram*, November 13, 1972.
33. Bob Moore, "Only One Car," *Charlotte* (North Carolina) *Observer*, December 3, 1972.
34. "Foyt, Pearson Share Sponsor," *Indianapolis Star*, January 17, 1973.
35. Leonard Wood, April 15, 2020, interview with the author.
36. Leonard Wood, April 15, 2020, interview with the author.
37. Bloys Britt, "A.J. Foyt Hard-Nosed Demon of the Ovals," Associated Press, *The Sports Immortals*, 1972.
38. Dave Anderson, "'500' Nothing Like New York Traffic," *New York Times*, November 4, 1972.
39. William Neely, *The Jim Gilmore Story, Alone in the Crowd* (Tucson: Aztex Corporation, 1988).
40. Neely, *The Jim Gilmore Story, Alone in the Crowd.*
41. "Foyt Will Have Gilmore Backing," *Indianapolis Star*, January 21, 1973.
42. Associated Press, "A.J. Foyt Signs," *Lumberton* (North Carolina) *Robesonian*, January 21, 1973.

CHAPTER 34. FIRE AND RAIN

1. Bob Riley, 2020 interview with the author.
2. Gerald Martin, "A.J., Banjo: They Click," *Charlotte* (North Carolina) *News and Observer*, December 24, 1972.
3. Bob Myers, "Banjo Mathews—The Henry Ford of Race Cars," *Hot Rod Magazine*, February 1, 1997.
4. Gerald Martin, "A.J., Banjo: They Click," *Charlotte* (North Carolina) *News and Observer*, December 24, 1972.
5. Dick Mittman, "A.J. Foyt Is Seeking 'Double' at Daytona," *Indianapolis News*, February 17, 1973.
6. Darrell Waltrip, November 6, 2020, interview with the author.
7. Darrell Waltrip, November 6, 2020, interview with the author.
8. Darrell Waltrip, November 6, 2020, interview with the author.
9. Associated Press, "Waltrip Expected to Be Next Challenger to Racing Stalwarts," *Fort Worth* (Texas) *Star-Telegram*, April 11, 1973.
10. Associated Press, "Waltrip Expected to Be Next Challenger to Racing Stalwarts."
11. Dick Denny, "A.J. and Mario Find Silver Lining," *Indianapolis News*, April 16, 1973.
12. Associated Press, "New Car For Foyt," *Terre Haute* (Indiana) *Tribune*, March 19, 1973.
13. Benny Phillips, "A.J. Foyt All Smiles over New Indy Car," *High Point* (North Carolina) *Enterprise*, March 31, 1973.
14. Randy Laney, "A.J. Foyt: He lives and Drives by the 'First-or-Nothing" Creed," April 4, 1971.
15. Michael Lutz, "Foyt Raps High Speeds," Associated Press, *Valley Morning Star* (Texas), April 4, 1973.
16. Lutz, "Foyt Raps High Speeds."
17. Dick Denny, "Trenton Richer—A.J.'s in Field," *Indianapolis News*, April 14, 1973.
18. "Foyt, Bobby U. Qualify 2-3," *Indianapolis Star*, April 15, 1973.
19. Ray Marquette, "Mario 1st overall; Vukovich Is Second," *Indianapolis Star*, April 16, 1973.
20. Bill Simmons, "Foyt, Andretti Halt Losing Streaks," *Philadelphia Inquirer*, April 16, 1973.
21. Harvey Duck, "Race Cars Dangerous with Wings," *Chicago Daily News*, April 19, 1973.
22. Johnny Rutherford, June 17, 2020, interview with the author.
23. Duck, "Race Cars Dangerous with Wings."
24. Ed Sainsbury, "Foyt Eyes 4th '500,'" UPI, *Daily Greenfield* (Indiana) *Reporter*, April 21, 1973.
25. UPI, "Unser Steeped in Race History," *Galveston Daily News*, May 5, 1973.
26. Mark Twain, *The Tragedy of Pudd'nhead Wilson* (New York: Charles L Webster Company, 1893).
27. Jack Flowers, "Fear: Constant Companion of Race Drivers," *Tampa Bay* (Florida) *Times*, February 15, 1974.
28. A.J. Foyt, 2008 interview with the Houston Project.
29. Dick Mittman, "A.J. Foyt: Mr. Tradition," *Indianapolis News*, May 27, 1983.
30. Ray Marquette, "Foyt Not Happy with Trials Run," *Indianapolis Star*, May 13, 1973.
31. Don Compton, "How Fast Is Too Fast at Indy? Rutherford Would Favor a Cut," *Richmond* (Indiana) *Palladium-Item*, May 13, 1973.
32. Ray Marquette, "Stay on Pole Short but Sweet," *Indianapolis Star*, May 13, 1973.
33. UPI, "Three-Time Winner Talks about Forfeiting Position," *Terre Haute* (Indiana) *Tribune*, May 15, 1973.
34. Dick Denny, "Texas Trip Has Both A.J. and Engine Feeling Much Better," *Indianapolis News*, May 19, 1973.

35. Dick Mittman, "A.J. to Test It Tomorrow," *Indianapolis News*, May 17, 1973.
36. Mittman, "A.J. to Test It Tomorrow."
37. Mittman, "A.J. to Test It Tomorrow."
38. Bob Renner, "Speedway Goes 1ˢᵗ Class," *Indianapolis News*, April 25, 1973.
39. Don White, "Waltrip Remembers the Alamo," *Evansville* (Indiana) *Courier and Press*, June 17, 1973.
40. Will Grimsley, "Foyt Picks Foyt," Associated Press, *Lakeland* (Florida) *Ledger*, May 30, 1973.
41. Bill Verigan, "A Prerace Appraisal on the Crashes," *New York Daily News,* May 28, 1973.
42. Dave Overpeck, "Foyt, A Good Poker Player, Gets Two on the Last Hand," *Indianapolis Star*, May 21, 1973.
43. Bloys Britt, "Indy 500—This Year's Front Row Is Meanest," *Mexica* (Texas) *Daily News*, May 25, 1973.
44. Bloys Britt, "Bobby Unser Gives '500' Rundown," Associated Press, *Terre Haute* (Indiana) *Tribune*, May 25, 1973.
45. Will Grimsley, "Both A.J. Foyt's Determined to Win 4th Indianapolis 500," *Rocky Mount* (North Carolina) *Telegram,* May 30, 1973.
46. Don Compton, "Fiery First-Lap Crash, Rain Delay 500 until Today," *Richmond* (Indiana) *Palladium-Item*, May 29, 1973.
47. "Calls Drivers Yahoos," *New York Daily News*, May 31, 1973.
48. Associated Press, "Start of '500' Delayed Again," *South Bend* (Indiana) *Tribune*, May 29, 1973.
49. Associated Press, "Start of '500' Delayed Again."
50. "Foyt, Krisiloff, Revson Fined," *Indianapolis News*, May 29, 1973.
51. Fred Girard, "Memories of Miracles," *Tampa Bay* (Florida) *Times*, July 8, 1973.
52. "Indy 500 Notes," *Indianapolis Star*, May 29, 1973.
53. Joe Falls, "They Must Slow up or Rebuild Indy," *Detroit Free Press*, May 31, 1973.
54. Ray Marquette, "Salt Returns to Add Spice to USAC," *Indianapolis Star*, January 20, 1974.
55. Milton Richman "Walther Back on Track, Goes Quickly," UPI, *Anderson* (Indiana) *Daily Bulletin*, January 16, 1974.
56. Will Grimsley, "Foyt Picks Foyt," Associated Press, *The Lakeland* (Florida) *Ledger*, May 30, 1973.
57. Dave Overpeck, "Johncock's Victory Lane a Bittersweet Path," *Indianapolis Star*, May 31, 1973.
58. George Snider, December 12, 2020, interview with the author.
59. Will Grimsley, "Wished for Full 500" Associated Press, *South Bend* (Indiana) *Tribune*, May 31, 1973.
60. Milton Richman, "It Was Good, Bad and Horrible for Gordon Johncock and His Mates," UPI, *Martinsville* (Indiana) *Reporter-Times*, May 31, 1973.
61. Jim Murray, "End of No-Name 500," *Los Angeles Times*, May 31, 1973.
62. Bill Verigan, "An Auto Racing Writer Is Haunted by Ghosts of Those Who Died at Indy," *Sports Illustrated*, May 10, 1976.
63. "Revisions at Indy," Wire Services, *Evansville* (Indiana) *Courier and Press*, June 3, 1973.
64. John DePrez Jr., "USAC Action Disappoints Indy Winner Johncock," UPI, *Columbus* (Indiana) *Republic*, June 9, 1973.
65. "Bill France Gets Bums Rush Out of Speedway Track," *Tampa* (Florida) *Tribune*, May 14, 1954.
66. Bob Riley, February 18, 2020, interview with the author.
67. Bob Riley, February 18, 2020, interview with the author.
68. Gordon Kirby, *Penske's Maestro: Karl Kainhofer and the History of Penske Racing* (Boston: Racemaker Press, 2016).
69. Joe Miegoc, "Foyt Doubted Chances for Victory," *Pocono* (Pennsylvania) *Record*, July 2, 1973.
70. Associated Press, "Racing Notes," *Lawton* (Oklahoma) *Constitution*, July 2, 1973.
71. "Auto World Mourning Swede Savage's Death," *Asbury Park* (New Jersey) *Press*, July 3, 1973.
72. "Auto World Mourning Swede Savage's Death," *Asbury Park* (New Jersey) *Press*.
73. Bill Simmons, "Foyt Loses Cool, Wins Pocono Pole," *Philadelphia Inquirer*, July 29, 1973.
74. Joe Miegoc, "Petty Outduels Hartman, Wins Acme 500," *Pocono* (Pennsylvania) *Record*, July 30, 1973.
75. "Names In Sports" *Indianapolis News*, October 3, 1973.
76. Michael Lutz, "A.J. Foyt Puts on Show; Both in Pit and Track," Associated Press, *Terre Haute* (Indiana) *Tribune,* October 6, 1973.
77. Lutz, "A.J. Foyt Puts on Show; Both in Pit and Track."
78. Bloys Britt, "Series of Match Races Schedule," Associated Press, *Indianapolis News*, July 31, 1973.
79. Britt, "Series of Match Races Schedule."
80. Shav Glick, "A.J. Foyt Enters Race of Champions," *Los Angeles Times*, October 18, 1973.
81. Glick, "A.J. Foyt Enters Race of Champions."
82. Shav Glick, "Gurney: Road Racers' Edge Is Slight." *Los Angeles Times*, October 21, 1973.
83. Glick, "Gurney: Road Racers' Edge Is Slight."
84. Glick, "Gurney: Road Racers' Edge Is Slight."
85. Michael Argetsinger, *Mark Donohue: Technical Excellence at Speed* (Phoenix: David Bull Publishing, 2009).
86. Gary Friedman, 2020 interview with the author.
87. Associated Press, "Houston Hepatitis Epidemic Growths," *Victoria* (Texas) *Advocate,* November 8, 1973.

CHAPTER 35. DANCING WITH A BUZZSAW

1. Associated Press, "A.J. Foyt Is Preparing to Race Again In 1974," *Indianapolis Star*, December 12, 1973.
2. Jim Cour, "Foyt Taking Aim at Big Last Year," UPI, *Miami Herald*, January 25, 1973.
3. Cour, "Foyt Taking Aim at Big Last Year."
4. Allen Wolfe, "Auto Race Sanction Bodies Cooperate in Energy Crisis," *Long Beach* (California) *Independent Press-Telegram,* February 8, 1974.
5. Ray Marquette, "Foyt High on New Low-Gravity Chassis," *Indianapolis Star*, March 6, 1974.
6. "Benny Phillips," column, *High Point* (North Carolina) *Enterprise*, February 14, 1974.
7. Associated Press, "Foyt Fastest at Ontario," *Modesto* (California) *Bee*, February 27, 1974.
8. Shav Glick, "USAC's Operation Slowdown' Debuts Today at Ontario," *Los Angeles Times,* March 2, 1974.
9. Ryan Rees, "Foyt Captures Cal 500 Pole," *San Bernardino* (California) *County Sun*, March 3, 1974.
10. Shav Glick, "Foyt Pulls a Fast One and Wins Cal 500 Pole," *Los Angeles Times,* March 3, 1974.
11. Shav Glick, "Foyt Runs Away from Field," *Los Angeles Times,* March 4, 1974.
12. UPI, "A.J. Foyt Takes Back-to-Back Wins," *Hartford* (California) *Sentinel*, March 4, 1974.
13. Bloys Britt, "Foyt Has His Foes All 'Psyched' Up," Associated Press, *Terre Haute* (Indiana) *Tribune*, March 7, 1974.
14. Associated Press, "Walther Return 'Sinks' Foyt," *Indianapolis Star,* March 11, 1974.
15. Associated Press, "Walther Return 'Sinks' Foyt."
16. Bob Cox, "Foyt Given Best Chances for Victory," *Torrance* (California) *Daily Breeze,* March 3, 1974.
17. George Moore, "Foyt Team's 'No Secrets, Hard Work' Act Pays Off," *Indianapolis Star,* May 10, 1974.
18. Bob Riley, February 18, 2021, interview with the author.
19. "Foyt Receives Design Award," *Columbus* (Indiana) *Republic,* June 1, 1974.
20. Dave Anderson, "A.J. Foyt Hasn't Mellowed," *New York Times,* April 7, 1975.
21. Paul Reinhard, "Trenton 200-Miler Heads Schedule," *Allentown* (Pennsylvania) *Morning Call,* April 5, 1974.
22. George Moore, "Foyt Team's 'No Secrets, Hard Work' Act Pays Off," *Indianapolis Star,* May 10, 1974.
23. Dick Denny, "1974: Year of the Coyote," *Indianapolis News*, May 10, 1974.
24. Associated Press, "A.J. Foyt Seems to Have Found Key," *Lafayette* (Indiana) *Journal and Courier,* May 19, 1974.
25. Wayne Fuson, "Foyt Qualifies 1ˢᵗ at 191.632," *Indianapolis News,* May 11, 1974.
26. Fuson, "Foyt Qualifies 1ˢᵗ at 191.632."
27. Ray Marquette, "Great Blower Battle Gets Hotter," *Indianapolis Star,* May 14, 1974.
28. Associated Press, "A.J. Foyt Seems to Have Found Key," *Lafayette* (Indiana) *Journal and Courier,* May 19, 1974.
29. Shav Glick, "Foyt Seeks Record 4th Indy Victory Today," *Los Angeles Times,* May 26, 1974.
30. Glick, "Foyt Seeks Record 4th Indy Victory Today."
31. Glick, "Foyt Seeks Record 4th Indy Victory Today."
32. Glick, "Foyt Seeks Record 4th Indy Victory Today."
33. A.J. Foyt, April 19–24, 2021, interviews with the author.
34. Dick Mittman, "Foyt Shows 'Kids' How in Sprint Races," *Indianapolis News,* May 25, 1974.
35. A.J. Foyt, April 19–24, 2021, interviews with the author.
36. Bloys Britt, "A.J. Foyt in 'Nothing Race,' to Cut Tension," Associated Press, *Muncie* (Indiana) *Star Press,* May 25, 1974.
37. George Moore, "Hoosier Sprinters Follow A.J. Around," *Indianapolis Star,* May 25, 1974.
38. Associated Press, "Foyt Grabs 2 Main Events," *Muncie* (Indiana) *Evening Press,* May 25, 1974.
39. A.J. Foyt, April 19–24, 2021, interviews with the author.
40. Dave Overpeck, "Broken Pump Kayos Foyt," *Indianapolis Star,* May 27, 1974.
41. Falls, "A.J. Foyt Can Run but He Can't Hide."
42. Associated Press, "Foyt Never Got to Duel," *South Bend* (Indiana) *Tribune,* May 27, 1974.
43. Dave Overpeck, "Route to Victory Lane 'Bumpy,'" *Indianapolis Star,* May 27, 1974.
44. Dick Mittman, "Near Tears, Admits A.J.," *Indianapolis News,* May 27, 1974.
45. Associated Press, "Reflection: Victory at Indy," *Victoria* (Texas) *Advocate,* May 28, 1974.
46. "He Was the Second Choice . . ." *Indianapolis Star,* May 28, 1974.
47. Associated Press, "Reflection: Victory at Indy," *Victoria* (Texas) *Advocate,* May 28, 1974.
48. Bill Simmons, "Indy 500 Winner Rutherford Starts 2nd Career at Pocono," *Philadelphia Inquirer,* June 16, 1974.
49. Associated Press, "Reflection: Victory at Indy."
50. Johnny Rutherford, June 17, 2020, interview with the author.
51. Johnny Rutherford, June 17, 2020, interview with the author.
52. A.J. Foyt with William Neely, *A.J.: My Life as America's Greatest Race Car Driver* (New York: Times Books, 1983).
53. Johnny Rutherford and David Craft, *Lone Star J.R.: The Autobiography of Racing Legend Johnny Rutherford* (Chicago: Triumph Books, 2000).
54. Johnny Rutherford, June 17, 2020, interview with the author.
55. Johnny Rutherford, June 17, 2020, interview with the author.

56. Dick Mittman, "Winning Appears in Johnny's New Rules," *Indianapolis News,* June 10, 1974.
57. Bill Verigan, "Foyt Blows His Engine, Then Top; Loses Pole," *New York Daily News,* June 23, 1974.
58. Bill Verigan, "Foyt's Storm Brews during Schaefer Rain," *New York Daily News,* June 24, 1974.
59. Paul Reinhard, "Rain Erases Schaefer Trials," *Allentown* (Pennsylvania) *Morning Call,* June 24, 1974.
60. Bill Verigan, "Foyt's Storm Brews during Schaefer Rain," *New York Daily News,* June 24, 1974.
61. Associated Press, "Rutherford, Foyt at Firecracker 400," *Richmond* (Indiana) *Palladium-Item,* July 2, 1974.
62. Associated Press, "Rutherford, Foyt at Firecracker 400."
63. "Daytona Qualifying," *High Point* (North Carolina) *Enterprise,* July 4, 1974.
64. Ray Marquette, "Gurney Solves Personal Fuel Crisis," *Indianapolis Star,* July 23, 1974.
65. Nack, "Twilight of a Titan."
66. Nack, "Twilight of a Titan."
67. Associated Press, "Foyt Will Attempt Closed Course Mark," July 24, 1974.
68. Phillip Marshall, "A.J. Foyt: Speed Record Should Be His Today," *Birmingham* (Alabama) *Post-Herald,* August 3, 1974.
69. Associated Press, "Foyt Runs 217.854 MPH in Coyote for World Mark," *Indianapolis Star,* August 4, 1974.
70. "Mario Knocks Foyt's Record," *New York Daily News,* August 11, 1974.
71. Associated Press, "Andretti-Foyt 'Runoff' Offer Made by Parnelli," *Indianapolis Star,* August 15, 1974.
72. Associated Press, "Andretti-Foyt 'Runoff' Offer Made by Parnelli."
73. "Mario Knocks Foyt's Record," *New York Daily News,* August 11, 1974.
74. Ryan Bees, "Donohue-Prepared Camaros Help Improve IROC Series," *San Bernardino* (California) *County Sun,* October 23, 1974.
75. Maryjean Wall, "Another Kind of Racing; A.J. Purchases Yearlings," *Lexington* (Kentucky) *Herald-Leader,* September 11, 1974.
76. Tony Foyt, April 21, 2021, interview with the author.
77. Eddie Donnally, "This Foyt Fools Around with Horses," *Dallas Morning News,* March 13, 1983.
78. Donnally, "This Foyt Fools Around with Horses."
79. Demmie Stathoplos, "A Rebel without a Pause," *Sports Illustrated,* April 7, 1986.
80. Jim Lassiter, "This Foyt Prefers Whinnies," *Daily Oklahoman,* February 9, 1985.
81. Gary Kale, "'I've Done Everything I Wanted to Do'–Foyt," UPI, *Muncie* (Indiana) *Star,* June 25, 1978.
82. Ed Albin, "Foyt, Unser Triumph in Trenton 150-Milers," *Central New Jersey Home News,* September 23, 1974.
83. Bob Myers, "How a Hoss, Top Cop Play Hide and Seek," *Charlotte* (North Carolina) *News,* October 2, 1974.
84. Charlotte race notes, *Charlotte* (North Carolina) *News,* October 8, 1974.
85. Paul Reinhard, "Carter, Foyt Win as Series Promoter Takes Bath," *Allentown* (Pennsylvania) *Morning Call,* October 21, 1974.
86. Associated Press, "A.J. Drops Out, Then in IROC Show," *Indianapolis Star,* October 25, 1974.
87. Shav Glick, "A.J.: The Designing Driver," *Los Angeles Times,* March 5, 1975.
88. Shav Glick, "Allison Gets Last Ride in No. 7 and It Turns Out a Winner," *Los Angeles Times,* October 28, 1974.
89. Ron Lemasters, "USAC Champ Owners Locked in Death Struggle," *Muncie* (Indiana) *Star Press,* November 10, 1974.

CHAPTER 36. LIFE BEGINS AT FORTY

1. Peter Michelmore, "Energy Makes Houston Oasis of Prosperity," *New York Times,* January 2, 1975.
2. Associated Press, "Kalamazoo's Gilmore Helps Indy Promotion," *South Bend* (Indiana) *Tribune,* May 20, 1975.
3. Bob Latshaw, "Car Racing Gilmores Branch Out," *Detroit Free Press,* November 30, 1975.
4. Ross Newman, "Foyt to Step Up NASCAR Campaign with New Team," *Atlanta,* November 25, 1974.
5. Bloys Britt, "Foyt Part of Gilmore Family," Associated Press, *South Bend* (Indiana) *Tribune,* May 16, 1974.
6. Britt, "Foyt Part of Gilmore Family."
7. Britt, "Foyt Part of Gilmore Family."
8. Associated Press, "Kalamazoo's Gilmore Helps Indy Promotion," *South Bend* (Indiana) *Tribune,* May 20, 1975.
9. Leroy Samuels, "A.J. Never Got Spoiled, He Just Worked Harder," *Camden* (New Jersey) *Courier-Post,* April 5, 1975.
10. UPI, "Winning in U.S. Still Good Enough for A.J.," *Indianapolis Star,* March 12, 1975.
11. Mel Kenyon, *Burned to Life* (Minneapolis, MN: Dimension Books, 1976).
12. "Foyt Shows Why He Is the Best," *Sydney* (Australia) *Morning Herald,* January 13, 1975.
13. A.J. Foyt, April 19–24, 2021, interviews with the author.
14. Associated Press, "Donohue to Seek Auto Racing Mark," *Baltimore Evening Sun,* February 4, 1975.
15. Associated Press, "Donohue to Seek Auto Racing Mark."
16. Ray Holliman, "Unser Triumphs in IROC," *Florida Today,* February 15, 1975.

17. Gerald Martin, "Woods Set for Riverside," *Raleigh News and Observer*, January 12, 1975.
18. UPI, "Stock Car Drivers Qualify at Daytona," *Naples* (Florida) *Daily News*, February 14, 1975.
19. "Benny Phillips," column, *High Point* (North Carolina) *Enterprise*, February 17, 1975.
20. Paul Reinhard, "A.J. Foyt Hopes He's Not Mellowing with Age," *Allentown* (Pennsylvania) *Morning Call*, April 6, 1975.
21. Associated Press, "Outside Distractions Bother A.J. Foyt," *Richmond* (Indiana) *Palladium-Item*, April 4, 1975.
22. Reinhard, "A.J. Foyt Hopes He's Not Mellowing."
23. Allen Wolfe, "Foyt Outfoxes 'Em, Captures Cal 500 Pole," *Long Beach* (California) *Independent Press-Telegram*, March 2, 1975.
24. Wolfe, "Foyt Outfoxes 'Em."
25. Wolfe, "Foyt Outfoxes 'Em."
26. Shav Glick, "Andretti's Time Threatened," *Los Angeles Times*, February 27, 1975.
27. Bob Cox, "Foyt Blisters Field at 177," *San Pedro* (California) *News-Pilot*, March 3, 1975.
28. Cox, "Foyt Blisters Field at 177."
29. Cox, "Foyt Blisters Field at 177."
30. Leroy Samuels, "A.J. Never Got Spoiled, He Just Worked Harder," *Camden* (New Jersey) *Courier-Post*, April 5, 1975.
31. Associated Press, "Critical Day for A.J., Ontario," *Bakersfield Californian*, March 9, 1975.
32. Allen Wolfe, "Foyt Man to Beat in Today's Cal 500," *Long Beach* (California) *Independent Press-Telegram*, March 9, 1975.
33. Wolfe, "Foyt Man to Beat in Today's Cal 500."
34. Jim Murray, "It Had All the Excitement of an America's Cup," *Los Angeles Times*, March 10, 1975.
35. Rich Roberts, "28-Hour Days Key to Foyt's Racing Success," *Long Beach* (California) *Independent Press-Telegram*, March 10, 1975.
36. Roberts, "28-Hour Days Key to Foyt's Racing Success."
37. Bill Verigan, "Indy 500 Favorite A.J. Foyt: No Guarantees—Just Hope," *New York Daily News*, May 24, 1974.
38. Samuels, "A.J. Never Got Spoiled."
39. UPI, "Winning in U.S. Still Good Enough for A.J.," *Indianapolis Star*, March 12, 1975.
40. Owen Kearns Jr., "The Enigmatic A.J. Foyt," *Bakersfield Californian*, March 16, 1975.
41. UPI, "Winning in U.S. Still Good Enough for A.J."
42. Paul Reinhard, "Andretti's Schedule Reads Like a Travel Brochure," *Allentown* (Pennsylvania) *Morning Call*, April 20, 1975.
43. Dick Mittman, "A.J. Puts Needle into Mario's Back," *Indianapolis News,* April 18, 1975.
44. Ray Marquette, "Mario Speaks Piece on Foyt, Formula 1," *Indianapolis Star*, April 23, 1975.
45. Marquette, "Mario Speaks Piece on Foyt, Formula 1."
46. Mittman, "A.J. Puts Needle into Mario's Back."
47. "For Foyt, Trenton Pole Is Only Eye of Storm," *Philadelphia Inquirer*, April 27, 1975.
48. Don White, "Bettenhausen Comes Back," *Evansville* (Indiana) *Courier and Press*, April 20, 1975.
49. Associated Press, "Bignotti Accuses Foyt of Fuel Cheating," *Indianapolis Star*, April 26, 1975.
50. Bill Lyon, "The Foyt Story: Go, Go, and No Show," *Philadelphia Inquirer*, April 28, 1975.
51. Lyon, "The Foyt Story: Go, Go, and No Show."
52. Dick Mittman, "Bignotti Charges USAC 'Indecisive,'" *Indianapolis News*, May 3, 1975.
53. Bill Pittman, "500 Word: Beat Foyt," *Indianapolis News*, May 12, 1975.
54. Shav Glick, "A.J.: The Designing Driver," *Los Angeles Times*, March 5, 1975.
55. J.D. Lewis, "No Question about It—I've Got Indy on the Brain," *Columbus* (Indiana) *Republic*, May 7, 1975.
56. John Sonderegger, "Needle Bignotti's Best Tool," *St. Louis* (Missouri) *Post-Dispatch*, May 12, 1975.
57. Sonderegger, "Needle Bignotti's Best Tool."
58. Dick Mittman, "This the Year Foyt Wins 4th 500?," *Indianapolis News*, May 23, 1975.
59. Robin Miller, "Racing with A.J. Beats Rice Farming," *Indianapolis Star*, May 15, 1975.
60. Dick Mittman, "Wrong Tires Foil Foyt, J.C. Gets Right with A.J." *Indianapolis News*, May 12, 1975.
61. Bob Barnet, "Man from Texas—The Best There Is!" *Muncie* (Indiana) *Star Press*, May 12, 1975.
62. Dave Overpeck, "A.J. Leaves 'Em Laughing with Fourth Pole-ish Joke," *Indianapolis Star*, May 11, 1975.
63. John Sonderegger, "Needle Bignotti's Best Tool," *St. Louis Post-Dispatch*, May 12, 1975.
64. Sonderegger, "Needle Bignotti's Best Tool."
65. "A.J.'s New Coyote Passes Super-Strict Inspection by USAC," *National Speed Sport News*, May 14, 1975.
66. Bill Verigan, "Indy 500 Favorite A.J. Foyt: No Guarantees—Just Hope," *NY Daily News*, May 24.
67. Shav Glick, "A.J.: The Designing Driver," *Los Angeles Times*, March 5, 1975.
68. Michael Knight, May 28, 2021, interview with the author.
69. Michael Knight, "Foyt Becoming Too Much of a Big Wheel for Media?" *Philadelphia Daily News*, May 23, 1975.
70. Knight, "Foyt Becoming Too Much of a Big Wheel for Media?"

71. Bob Latshaw, "The Terrible Texan: Indy Favorite at 40," *Detroit Free Press*, May 23, 1975.
72. Associated Press, "Foyt Asks Bignotti For Retraction," *Evansville* (Indiana) *Courier and Press*, May 25, 1975.
73. Bill Verigan, "Indy 500 Favorite A.J. Foyt: No Guarantees—Just Hope," *NY Daily News*, May 24, 1975.
74. Verigan, "Indy 500 Favorite A.J. Foyt: No Guarantees—Just Hope."
75. Thomas R. Keating, "Foyt Drove with His Head," *Indianapolis Star*, May 26, 1975.
76. Associated Press, "Lady Luck Costs Foyt," *South Bend* (Indiana) *Tribune*, May 26, 1975.
77. J.D. Lewis, "Calm Race Day Helped by 'Wild' Night Before," *Columbus* (Indiana) *Republic*, May 28, 1975.
78. Associated Press, "Let Foyt Stop Indy Cheaters," *Indianapolis Star*, May 31,1975
79. Associated Press, "Confusion Clouds Foyt's Win," *Fond du Lac* (Wisconsin) *Reporter*, June 9, 1975.
80. Associated Press, "Confusion Clouds Foyt's Win."
81. Associated Press, "Confusion Clouds Foyt's Win."
82. Jerry Garrett, "Finally George Beats A.J.," *Indianapolis News*, June 23, 1975.
83. Jack Jordan, "Foyt Finding Right Combination," *Scranton* (Ohio) *Times-Tribune*, June 20, 1975.
84. Paul Reinhard, "Foyt Didn't Get Caught Short This Time," *Allentown* (Pennsylvania) *Morning Call*, June 30, 1975.
85. Joe Falls, "Foyt Had to Make a Tough Decision," *Detroit Free Press,* July 21, 1975.
86. Owen Kearns Jr., "Snider Lucky to Survive Spectacular Crash," July 31, 1975.
87. Dick Mittman, "Ziggy More than No. 1 500-mile Backup Driver," *Indianapolis News,* July 25, 1975.
88. Dick Mittman, "Foyt Gets Specialist for Snider after Spectacular Sprint Crash," *Indianapolis News*, July 29, 1975.
89. Owen Kearns Jr., "Snider Lucky to Survive Spectacular Crash."
90. George Snider, December 12, 2020, interview with the author.
91. Jerry Garrett, "Do I Still Have What It Takes?—Donohue," Associated Press, *Detroit Free Press*, July 24, 1975.
92. Associated Press, "Donohue Zips to Record 221.120 at Talladega," *Indianapolis Star*, August 10, 1975.
93. Associated Press, "Foyt Offers Challenge after Donohue's Run," *Muncie* (Indiana) *Evening Press*, August 11, 1975.
94. Associated Press, "Foyt Offers Challenge after Donohue's Run."
95. Associated Press, "Foyt Offers Challenge after Donohue's Run."
96. Bill Simmons, "Foyt Is Also Fast to Give Opinions," *Philadelphia Inquirer*, December 21, 1975.
97. Associated Press, "Foyt's Coyote Speeds to FasTrack Victory," *Yuma Daily Sun*, November 10, 1975.
98. Paul Bailey, "Desire, Three Indy wins not enough for Foyt," *Akron Beacon Journal*, September 24, 1975.
99. Simmons, "Foyt Is Also Fast to Give Opinions."

CHAPTER 37. BROKEN DREAMS

1. Ray Marquette, "USAC Unit Nixes Stock Blocks," *Indianapolis Star*, July 22, 1975.
2. Ray Marquette, "Does A.J. Have 'Unfair Advantage'?" *Indianapolis Star*, August 31, 1975.
3. Marquette, "Does A.J. Have 'Unfair Advantage'?"
4. Ray Marquette, "Pop-Off Valve Cuts Speed in Speedway Tests," *Indianapolis Star*, October 9, 1975.
5. Phillip Christensen, "Tough Texan Still Winning," *Sydney Morning Herald*, January 1, 1976.
6. Robin Miller, "Larry Rice Making Thunder in Midget Tour Down Under," *Indianapolis Star*, January 12, 1976.
7. Ray Holliman, "The Winningest Racer," *Tampa Bay* (Florida) *Times*, July 3, 1977.
8. Dave Kindred, "Foyt Leaves Them Giggling about His Laughing Gas," *Louisville* (Kentucky) *Courier-Journal*, February 13, 1976.
9. Associated Press, "Foyt, Marcis and Waltrip Disqualified," *Danville* (Virginia) *Register*, February 9, 1976.
10. Ed Hinton, "Not Cheating Pays Off, Reed on Daytona Pole," *Orlando Sentinel*, February 10, 1976.
11. Tom Shafter, "Let's Just Say They Cheated," *Florida Today*, February 10, 1976.
12. Associated Press, "A.J. Foyt Says: 'We Don't Have to Cheat to Win, and We Didn't,'" *Vincennes* (Indiana) *Sun-Commercial*, February 11, 1976.
13. Dave Kindred, "Foyt Leaves Them Giggling about His Laughing Gas," *Louisville* (Kentucky) *Courier-Journal*, February 13, 1976.
14. Frank Vehorn, "Mellow Foyt Ready for Daytona Today," *Greenville* (South Carolina) *News*, February 15, 1976.
15. "Benny Phillips," column, *High Point* (North Carolina) *Enterprise*, February 14, 1976.
16. Wayne Fuson, "Bunching up for Classic End," *Indianapolis News*, February 16, 1976.
17. Gerald Martin, "What's Good for the Goose Is Good for the Gander?," *Raleigh* (North Carolina) *News and Observer*, July 4, 1976.
18. Gerald Martin, "Foyt Blasts NASCAR; May Reduce Schedule," *Raleigh* (North Carolina) *News and Observer*, February 28, 1976.
19. Associated Press, "A.J. Foyt Left in Pits," *Asheville* (North Carolina) *Citizen*, February 28, 1976.

20. Richard Waters, "Daytona Has Foyt Fuming," Associated Press, *Durham Herald-Sun*, February 28, 1976.
21. Waters, "Daytona Has Foyt Fuming," Associated Press, *Durham Herald-Sun*, February 28, 1976.
22. Associated Press, "Drivers Rap Gals' Intervention" *Munster* (Indiana) *Times*, October 24, 1976.
23. Associated Press, "Driver Arlene Hiss Makes More enemies," *Lafayette* (Indiana) *Journal and Courier*, March 15, 1976.
24. Ron Lemasters, "Poor Run Leaves Foyt Boiling Mad," *Muncie* (Indiana) *Star*, May 16, 1976.
25. Lemasters, "Poor Run Leaves Foyt Boiling Mad."
26. Jerry Garrett, "Only Goal Now Is to Qualify," Associated Press, *Terre Haute* (Indiana) *Tribune*, May 18, 1976.
27. "Is Janet Guthrie Prepared to 'Jump' from Bryant Car?" *Indianapolis Star*, May 22, 1976.
28. Jerry Garrett, "A.J. Foyt Offers No. 1 Car to Guthrie for 500 Try," Associated Press, *Terre Haute* (Indiana) *Tribune*, May 23, 1976.
29. Leal Beattie, "Foyt's Goal Elusive," *Dayton* (Ohio) *Journal Herald*, June 1, 1976.
30. Garrett, "A.J. Foyt Offers No. 1 Car to Guthrie for 500 Try."
31. Janet Guthrie, *Janet Guthrie: A Life at Full Throttle.* (Toronto: Sports Classic Books, 2005).
32. Ray Marquette, "Janet Ready to Switch?" *Indianapolis Star*, May 23, 1976.
33. Harold Lowe, "Janet's 500 Bid Fails," *South Bend* (Indiana) *Tribune*, May 42, 1976.
34. Guthrie, *Janet Guthrie.*
35. Marquette, "Janet Ready to Switch?"
36. Al Stilley, "'Twas a Class Weekend at Indy," *Franklin* (Indiana) *Daily Journal*, May 24, 1976.
37. A.J. Foyt, April 19–24, 2021, interviews with the author.
38. Paul Bailey, "Rutherford Reigns in Indy 500," *Akron* (Ohio) *Beacon Journal*, May 31, 1976.
39. Bailey, "Rutherford Reigns in Indy 500."
40. Bill Pittman, "A.J. Came So Close to No. 4 . . . Again," *Indianapolis News*, May 31, 1976.
41. Paul Bailey, "Rutherford Reigns in Indy 500."
42. A.J. Foyt, April 19–24, 2021, interviews with the author.
43. A.J. Foyt, April 19–24, 2021, interviews with the author.
44. Associated Press, "Grand Jury Will Investigate Shootout That Killed George," *Lafayette* (Indiana) *Journal and Courier*, June 1, 1976.
45. Tony George, May 2021 interview with the author.
46. Bill Pittman, "No Indictment in Elmer George Death," *Indianapolis News*, June 4, 1976.
47. Tony George, May 2021 interview with the author.
48. Jerry Garrett, "Foyt Glad 500 May Over," Associated Press, *Bedford* (Indiana) *Times-Mail*, June 5, 1976.
49. Ray Marquette, "After Indy, Foyt Gave Thought to Passing Rest of Year," *Goodyear Motorsports Club Newsletter*, July 1976.
50. Jerry Garrett, "Glad It's Over!" Associated Press, *South Bend* (Indiana) *Tribune*, June 6, 1976.
51. Garrett, "Glad It's Over!"
52. UPI, "Foyt Captures Texas 500," *Denton* (Texas) *Record-Chronicle*, June 7, 1976.
53. Gerald Martin, "What's Good for the Goose Is Good for the Gander?," *Raleigh* (North Carolina) *News and Observer*, July 4, 1976.
54. Associated Press, "Foyt Back to Daytona," *Indianapolis News*, June 17, 1976.
55. Gerald Martin, "What's Good for the Goose Is Good for the Gander?," *Raleigh* (North Carolina) *News and Observer*, July 4, 1976.
56. Associated Press, "Johncock, Foyt Win at Michigan," *Indianapolis News*, July 19, 1976.
57. "A Memorable Date: First Seven-Figure Yearling Sold," *BloodHorse*, July 20, 2006.
58. Skip Hess, "Record about Daddy Is off to Fast Start," *Indianapolis News*, May 18, 1976.
59. Joe Kammlah, "Foyt Plan Pays Off," *Bryan* (Texas) *Eagle*, August 2, 1976.
60. A.J. Foyt, April 19–24, 2021, interviews with the author.
61. UPI, "Got His Help," *Franklin* (Indiana) *Daily Journal*, August 16, 1976.
62. Bob Barnet, "Trackside Tantrum—the Magic Tarnished," *Muncie* (Indiana) *Star Press*, August 16, 1976.
63. Dick Mittman, "Beating Foyt Rich Reward for Joe," September 13, 1976.
64. Ray Marquette, "Saldana Wins Hoosier Hundred," *Indianapolis Star*, September 12, 1976.
65. Dick Mittman, "Is A.J. above USAC Regulations?" *Indianapolis News*, September 20, 1976.
66. Mittman, "Is A.J. above USAC Regulations?"
67. Leonard Laye, "Fun Fades for Foyt," *Charlotte* (North Carolina) News, October 9, 1976.
68. Associated Press, "Foyt Won't Drive 'Pile of Hogwash,'" *Anderson* (Indiana) *Herald*, October 13, 1976.
69. Benny Phillips, "Ellington, Foyt Headed for Split??" *High Point* (North Carolina) *Enterprise*, October 11, 1976.
70. Jonathan Ingram, "Worn Tires Aid Allison," *Durham* (North Carolina) *Herald-Sun*, October 11, 1976.
71. Ingram, "Worn Tires Aid Allison."
72. Tom Higgins, "Champs Race Needs Control," *Charlotte* (North Carolina) *Observer*, October 16, 1976.
73. Associated Press, "Cale Takes IROC," *Indianapolis Star*, October 18, 1976.

74. Associated Press, "Johnny Rutherford Can Clinch Crown," *Modesto* (California) *Bee*, October 31, 1976.
75. "Johnny and Bobby Score in Texas as A.J. Crashes," *National Speed Sport News*, November 3, 1976.
76. Ray Marquette, "Rutherford Takes Texas 200-Miler," *Indianapolis Star*, November 1, 1976.
77. Jerry Waggoner, "Foyt Displays Iron-Man Driving Nerve," *Bryan* (Texas) *Eagle*, November 3, 1976.
78. Dick Mittman, "A.J. Wants A.J. to Slow Down," *Indianapolis News*, May 28, 1976.
79. Mittman, "A.J. Wants A.J. to Slow Down."
80. Gerald Martin, "Outspoken Foyt Seeks Liberalization of NASCAR Rules," *Raleigh* (North Carolina) *News and Observer*, February 15, 1976.

CHAPTER 38. FOUR'S A CHARM

1. "A.J. Foyt Has Confided in Friends . . ." *Indianapolis News*, December 14, 1976.
2. Dick Mittman, "Foyt Considering 6-Wheeler for 500," *Indianapolis News*, June 14, 1976.
3. Jerry Garrett, "Is Rule Change Boon for Foyt?" Associated Press, *Durham* (North Carolina) *Herald-Sun*, January 27, 1977.
4. Bob Myers, "Foyt Back in NASCAR," *Charlotte* (North Carolina) *News*, January 7, 1977.
5. "Donnie Allison Wins Daytona 500 Pole," *Orlando* (Florida) *Sentinel*, February 14, 1977.
6. "Donnie Allison Wins Daytona 500 Pole," *Orlando* (Florida) *Sentinel*.
7. Tom Brettingen, "Cash Goes to Foyt," Associated Press, *Terre Haute* (Indiana) *Tribune*, February 19, 1977.
8. Ed Hinton, "Cale Pulls, Foyt Pushes; Both in Winner's Circle," *Orlando Sentinel*, February 19, 1977.
9. Hinton, "Cale Pulls, Foyt Pushes; Both in Winner's Circle."
10. "Foyt Shaded by Cale but Wins $50,000 in IROC," *Indianapolis Star*, February 19, 1977.
11. Shav Glick, "Foyt, Insolo Win before Only 26,093," *Los Angeles Times*, March 7, 1977.
12. Gerald Martin, "Pole Sitter Foyt Hopes Petty Gets Act Together," *Raleigh* (North Carolina) *News and Observer*, July 4, 1976.
13. Dick Mittman, "Johncock's 200 Unlikely in May," *Indianapolis News*, March 22, 1977.
14. Johnny Rutherford, June 17, 2020, interview with the author.
15. Johnny Rutherford, June 17, 2020, interview with the author.
16. Shav Glick, "The Winnah—Rutherford," *Los Angeles Times*, March 28, 1977.
17. Tyler Alexander, *Tyler Alexander: A Life and Times with McLaren* (Phoenix: David Bull Publishing, 2015).
18. Glick, "The Winnah—Rutherford."
19. Glick, "The Winnah—Rutherford."
20. Dick Mittman, "Absolutely Disgraceful," *Indianapolis News*, March 29, 1977.
21. Ron Lemasters, "Has Success Spoiled John Rutherford?" *Muncie* (Indiana) *Star News*, April 3, 1977.
22. Robin Miller, "Gordie, J.R. Make Up in Texas Rain," *Indianapolis Star*, April 2, 1977.
23. Charles Hollis, "Cross Up," *Anniston* (Alabama) *Star*, May 2, 1977.
24. Robin Miller, "Rutherford Hopes for 200 Mph," *Indianapolis Star*, May 14, 1977.
25. Miller, "Rutherford Hopes for 200 Mph."
26. Bob Barnet, "What Goes on Here!—And Tom Was Best," *Muncie* (Indiana) *Star Press*, May 14, 1977.
27. Barnet, "What Goes on Here!—And Tom Was Best."
28. David Mannweiler, "A.J. Just Trying to Be 'Nice Guy,'" *Indianapolis News*, May 16, 1977.
29. Mannweiler, "A.J. Just Trying to Be 'Nice Guy.'"
30. Art Garner and Marc B. Spiegel, *Indy 500 Memories: An Oral History of the Greatest Spectacle in Racing* (CreateSpace Publishing, 2016).
31. Garner and Spiegel, *Indy 500 Memories*.
32. Robert Markus "Boos Burn Foyt," UPI, *Chicago Tribune*, May 17, 1977.
33. Ron Lemasters, "Vukovich Switches Cars, Then Qualifies for '500,'" *Muncie* (Indiana) *Star Press*, May 22, 1977.
34. Lemasters, "Vukovich Switches Cars, Then Qualifies for '500.'"
35. Dave Overpeck, "Vuky Knows Now Foyt's Tip Right," *Indianapolis Star*, May 22, 1977.
36. Jim Murray, "The Lion Is Smiling," *Los Angeles Times*, May 27, 1977.
37. A.J. Foyt, "Foyt to Keep on Racing," *Indianapolis News*, May 27, 1977.
38. Foyt, "Foyt to Keep on Racing."
39. Ray Holliman, "Foyt Quadruples His Indy Pleasure," *Tampa Bay* (Florida) *Times*, May 30, 1977.
40. Billy Woodruff, 2020 interview with the author.
41. Robin Miller, "Super Tex '500' Winner 4th Time," *Indianapolis Star*, May 30, 1977.
42. Miller, "Super Tex '500' Winner 4th Time."
43. Ray Compton, "Johncock: We Had It," *Indianapolis News*, May 30, 1977.
44. Art Harris, "Foyt Beats Rain," *Indianapolis News*, May 30, 1977.
45. Associated Press, "A.J.'s Day after 10 Frustrating Years," *South Bend* (Indiana) *Tribune*, May 30, 1977.
46. ABC Sports, 1977 tape-delayed race broadcast.
47. Garner and Spiegel, *Indy 500 Memories*.
48. Billy Woodruff, January 3, 2024, interview with the author.
49. Billy Woodruff, January 3, 2024, interview with the author.
50. Richard Petty, March 11, 2021, interview with the author.

51. Ron Lemasters, "Humble and Happy, Foyt Discusses Divine Guidance," *Muncie* (Indiana) *Star Press*, May 30, 1977.

52. Wayne Fuson, "It Was Super for Foyt, Fans," *Indianapolis News*, May 30, 1977.

53. Lemasters, "Humble and Happy, Foyt Discusses Divine Guidance."

54. Lemasters, "Humble and Happy, Foyt Discusses Divine Guidance."

55. Ray Compton, "Johncock: We Had It," *Indianapolis News,* May 30, 1977.

56. Jim McKay and Jackie Stewart, ABC's *Wide World of Sports,* 1977 Indianapolis 500 broadcast, May 29, 1977.

57. Will Grimsley, "Time to Take off Our Hats to the Ol' Grandpappy, A.J. Foyt," Associated Press, *Eureka* (California) *Times Standard,* May 31, 1977.

58. Jim Murray, "As Night Follows Day . . ." *Los Angeles Times,* May 30, 1977.

59. Murray, "As Night Follows Day . . ."

CHAPTER 39. CROSSROADS

1. Bill Verigan, "Back in the Driver's Seat He's the Same Old Foyt," *New York Daily News*, May 31, 1977.

2. Steve Herman, "Humble A.J. Calls Himself 'Stooge,'" Associated Press, *Bakersfield Californian,* May 31, 1977.

3. Ed Hinton, "Nineteen Years Later, A.J. Could Buy the Gate," *Orlando* (Florida) *Sentinel*, May 30, 1977.

4. Lisa Perlman, "From Racing to Business, Gilmore Wins," Associated Press, *Los Angeles Times,* April 14, 1988.

5. Wayne Fuson, "A.J. Gets $259,791," *Indianapolis News*, May 31, 1977.

6. Kirk Bohls, "Foyt: Just One of the Guys," *Austin-American*, June 6, 1977.

7. Associated Press, "Hutcherson on Texas Pole," *Evansville* (Indiana) *Press*, June 5, 1977.

8. Bohls, "Foyt: Just One of the Guys."

9. Thomas Keating, "A.J. Still Running All Out," *Indianapolis News*, June 15, 1977.

10. Keating, "A.J. Still Running All Out."

11. Sam Moses, "Running Fast and Furious," *Sports Illustrated*, July 4, 1977.

12. Michael Knight, "Foyt's Car Is at Pocono, but Will He Drive?" *Philadelphia Daily News*, June 21, 1977.

13. Associated Press, "Foyt Files Entry for Schaefer 500 Race," *Lancaster* (Pennsylvania) *Intelligencer Journal*, June 21, 1977.

14. Moses, "Running Fast and Furious."

15. "A.J. Foyt a Crusader On and Off Racetrack," Bill Verigan, *New York Daily News,* June 25, 1977.

16. Associated Press, "Foyt Talks of Retiring, *Terre Haute* (Indiana) *Tribune,* June 25, 1977.

17. Moses, "Running Fast and Furious."

18. Michael Knight, "Fans Boo Foyt," *Philadelphia Daily News*, June 24, 1977.

19. Moses, "Running Fast and Furious."

20. Associated Press, "Foyt Talks of Retiring, *Terre Haute* (Indiana) *Tribune,* June 25, 1977.

21. Associated Press, "Boos Bring Angry Response from A.J.," *Charlotte News*, June 24, 1967.

22. Dick Mittman, "Controversy Shadows Pocono 500," *Indianapolis News*, June 25, 1977.

23. Moses, "Running Fast and Furious."

24. Michael Knight, "Is Foyt Shafting Pocono Race Fans?" *Philadelphia Daily News*, June 23, 1977.

25. Dick Mittman, "Foyt Finds Out about Fickle Fate," *Indianapolis News*, June 29, 1977.

26. Pat Singer, "A.J. Foyt Would Rather 'Load It up and Go Home,'" *Wilmington* (New Jersey) *Daily News,* June 26, 1977.

27. Bill Simmons, "Crowd Boos Foyt, Then Burned Piston Completes His Day," *Philadelphia Inquirer*, June 27, 1977.

28. Dick Mittman, "Foyt Ready to Take a Rest after Busy Race Weekend," *Indianapolis News,* July 4, 1977.

29. Mittman, "Foyt Ready to Take a Rest after Busy Race Weekend."

30. Bob Clayton, "Promotions, Sponsorship Important to Rutherford," *Fort Worth* (Texas) *Star-Telegram,* July 30, 1977.

31. J.D. Lewis, "Rumors Circulate Foyt Will Retire after Hoosier 100," *Columbus* (Indiana) *Republic,* September 9, 1977.

32. Dick Mittman, "Foyt to Drive in Hoosier 100," *Indianapolis News*, September 7, 1977.

33. Mittman, "Foyt to Drive in Hoosier 100."

34. Associated Press, "Unser Nips Yarborough," *White Plains* (New York) *Journal News,* September 19, 1977.

35. Charlie Vincent, "Foyt Squabbles with MIS, Skips Race of Champs," *Detroit Free Press*, September 17, 1977.

36. Shav Glick, "Foyt Bristles over Reports of Retirement," *Los Angeles Times*, November 18, 1977.

37. Bob Myers, "A.J. Foyt: Is He Really A Good Ol' Boy?" *Charlotte News,* October 5, 1977.

38. Bob Brown, "Racing's Brat Snubs Request by '500' Sponsor," *Richmond* (Virginia) *Times-Dispatch,* October 9, 1977.

39. Brown, "Racing's Brat Snubs Request by '500' Sponsor."

40. Associated Press, "Donnie Allison Is Winning with 'Slow' A.J. Foyt Car," *Greenwood* (South Carolina) *Index-Journal*, October 24, 1977.

41. Associated Press, "Donnie Allison Is Winning with 'Slow' A.J. Foyt Car."
42. A.J. Foyt, interview with the author.
43. "Public Figures Hail Hulman," *Indianapolis Star*, October 29, 1977.
44. David Mannweiler, "Gents, Start Your Rumors," *Indianapolis News*, November 11, 1977.
45. Shav Glick, "Foyt Bristles over Reports of Retirement," *Los Angeles Times,* November 18, 1977.
46. Glick, "Foyt Bristles over Reports of Retirement," *Los Angeles Times,* November 18, 1977.
47. Michael Knight, "Foyt Calls Retirement Rumors So Much Bull," *Philadelphia Daily News*, September 26, 1977.
48. Glick, "Foyt Bristles over Reports of Retirement."
49. Glick, "Foyt Bristles over Reports of Retirement."

INDEX

Photo section pages are indicated with a "*P–*" before the page number. Photo section one contains pages *P–1* through *P–16*; photo section two contains pages *P–17* through *P–32*.